Shame

Dedications

LOVERN KINDZIERSKI

To Wally Wood - for introducing me to Zorg, Zara, Arachne and the Curse he brought into my world.

JOHN BOLTON

To Liliana for keeping me on this planet!

Shame

Conception

Pursuit

Redemption

Written by
Lovern Kindzierski

Art by
John Bolton

Letters by
Todd Klein

Edited by
Alexander Finbow

RENEGADE
Arts Entertainment

2016

SHAME

WRITER
LOVERN KINDZIERSKI

ART
JOHN BOLTON

LETTERS AND LOGO DESIGN
TODD KLEIN

EDITOR AND PUBLISHER
ALEXANDER FINBOW

TALES OF HOPE LETTERS BY
ANNIE PARKHOUSE

Shame: the series, conceived and written by Lovern Kindzierski.
Published by Renegade Arts Canmore Ltd trading as Renegade Arts Entertainment Ltd.

ISBN: 9781987825046
Office of Publication 25 Prospect Heights, Canmore, Alberta T1W 2S2
Renegade Arts Entertainment Ltd and logos are TM and copyright Renegade Arts Canmore Ltd

Renegade Arts Entertainment is
Alexander Finbow Doug Bradley Alan Grant John Finbow Luisa Harkins
Nick Wilson Emily Pomeroy.

Printed September 2016 in Canada by Friesens.

Check out more titles from Renegade Arts Entertainment at our website.

RenegadeArtsEntertainment.com

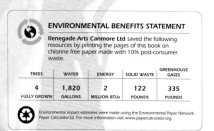

ENVIRONMENTAL BENEFITS STATEMENT
Renegade Arts Canmore Ltd saved the following resources by printing the pages of this book on chlorine free paper made with 10% post-consumer waste.

TREES	WATER	ENERGY	SOLID WASTE	GREENHOUSE GASES
4 FULLY GROWN	1,820 GALLONS	2 MILLION BTUs	122 POUNDS	335 POUNDS

Environmental impact estimates were made using the Environmental Paper Network Paper Calculator 3.2. For more information visit www.papercalculator.org.

MIX
Paper from responsible sources
FSC® C016245
www.fsc.org

Contents

Foreword

SHAME is a fairy tale, and like all fairy tales, can be read on many levels.

This fairy tale just happens to be for grown ups.

The village crone, wise and good Virtue, cares for the children of a beautiful enchanted land. She makes a wish: a "selfish" wish, for a baby all her own.

The wishes of good women, "virtuous" women, are selfless wishes. Even the simple, human desire for a child, the natural desire of eons of women before her, is too much for "true" virtue.

And so, Virtue is poisoned by a dark magic that waits in the shadows, waits to pounce and destroy.

The demon Slur, Shadow of Ignorance, grants Virtue her wish and implants his tainted seed.
Virtue brings forth Shame, beautiful, magical, twisted Shame.

All of Virtue's planning and enchanted protections cannot save her daughter from the shame of her conception, as sullied things are victims of the recesses of a world that demands perfection of women from the very idea of the moment they are conceived. In revenge, Shame embarks on a journey to destroy her mother and her mother's creations, ironically implanting in her and her mother the seed of their redemption.

There is a chance you might not even read the actual story at first sitting, because the gorgeous John Bolton art will dazzle you, and your eyes will dance across the page, soaking up the stunning images, leaving you in a watercolour induced trance.

This fairy tale for grown ups, of high fashion magical nymphets with smoky eyes and magnificent hair, twisted forests, and demons with inky attenuated limbs, is glamorous and clever, as if Anna Wintour had hired Grace Coddington to get the most beautiful girls in the world to act out a kinky photoshoot for Vogue. The imagery is decadent and delicate, sensitive and coolly chic.

Author Lovern Kindzierski, also known as one of the comic art industry's top colorists, brings a European sensibility, a Bande Desinée feel, to this tale, its anachronistic touches still very much of their own time and place, the kind of thing that only works in comics. Or in movies by Luc Besson.

Enjoy your taste of Shame.

Colleen Doran
June 23rd 2016

Preface

My father started all of this. I blame him. He would carry me along, like Tiny Tim, on his shoulders to the drug store to buy his weekly supply of comic books. Then we would head back to the apartment above the family store. He would sit down on the floor with me propped up in his lap. As he read his comics he would hold them up so I could see the pictures and hopefully follow along.

Later when I was old enough and motivated enough to collect drink bottles, I returned to the drug store on my own. Classics Illustrated introduced me to the Devil and colourfully dressed characters I came to know as super heroes.

Later in my teens I discovered the wonders of Creepy and Eerie magazines. I found my self more satisfied with the dark tales I found in these short stories. They addressed the back stories I felt lay behind the lighter fare of my younger years.

So it is really no surprise that, decades later, when called on to provide a story as a preventative from the boredom of a long road trip, I thought of Wally Wood's "The Curse". As I started to relate Woody's tale my nasty vixen of vice, Shame, made herself known to me. She sprung into life full blown languorously revealing more of her repellent beauty as I stumbled for the words to expose her crimes and punishments.

Some time later I made what then was an expensive cross Atlantic call to one of my all-time favourite artists in the hope of interesting him in illustrating the saga of Shame. John Bolton not only took my cold call, he loved my little minx of malevolence. In short order the adoption papers were drawn and Shame had her parents and I had a dream come true.

After many ups and downs, steps forward and back, fits and starts, we came to know Alexander Finbow and his wonderful publishing company Renegade Arts Entertainment. Alexander was taken in by Shame, the demoiselle of destruction, and now you are about to be woven into this torturous tale and become part of Shame's world, as hopelessly ensnared in her clutches as the rest of us.

And now you hold in your hands the collected work of three years. You can dive into the whole story right now, but please take a moment to thank all the readers that supported each of the three books that came out before this collection. I know I do. Meeting with each of them at different conventions and listening to their compliments on John's wonderful paintings and the rhymes I wrote for the Shadows buoyed us up while we toiled away in solitude producing this little gem. Now I will expect to hear from you and delight at your observations of Shame's passage through the first book of our fantasy. Yes. I did say first. The second story is underway! John is working away, in Italy at the moment, on the fourth chapter of this adventure and I am working on the sixth chapter in a lovely apartment here in Winnipeg. So get comfortable and settle in for the adventure.

Lovern Kindzierski
June 2016

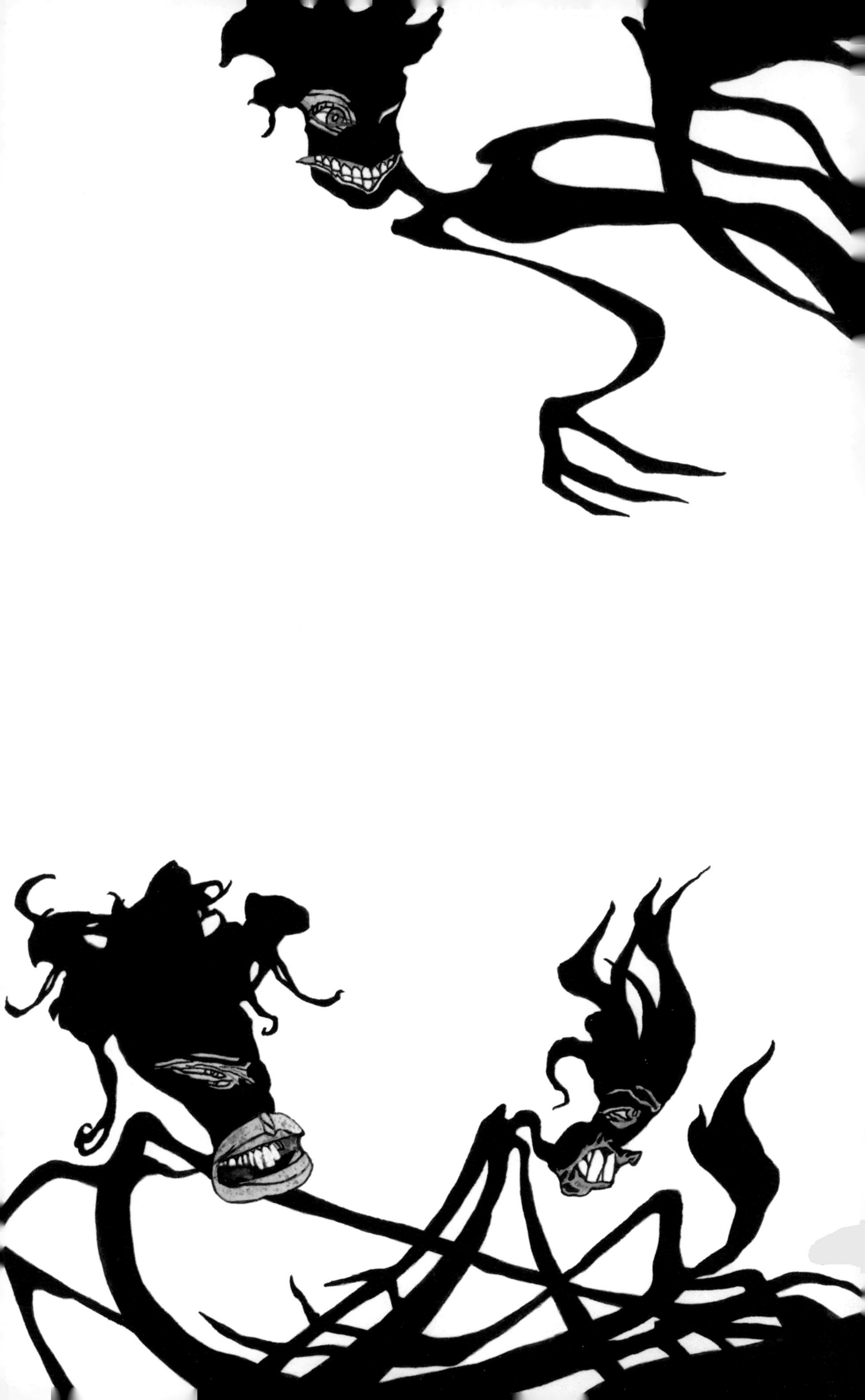

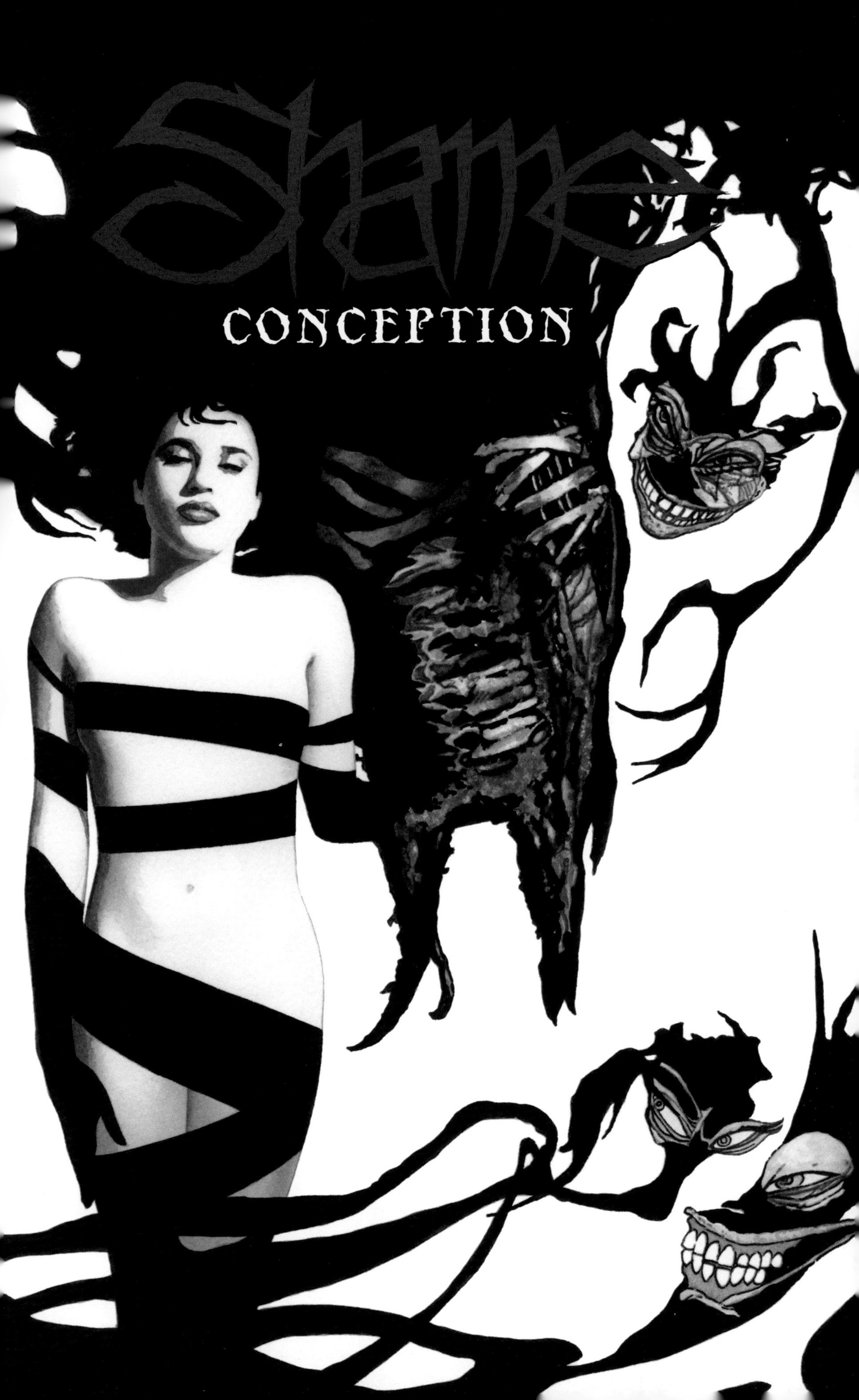
Shame
CONCEPTION

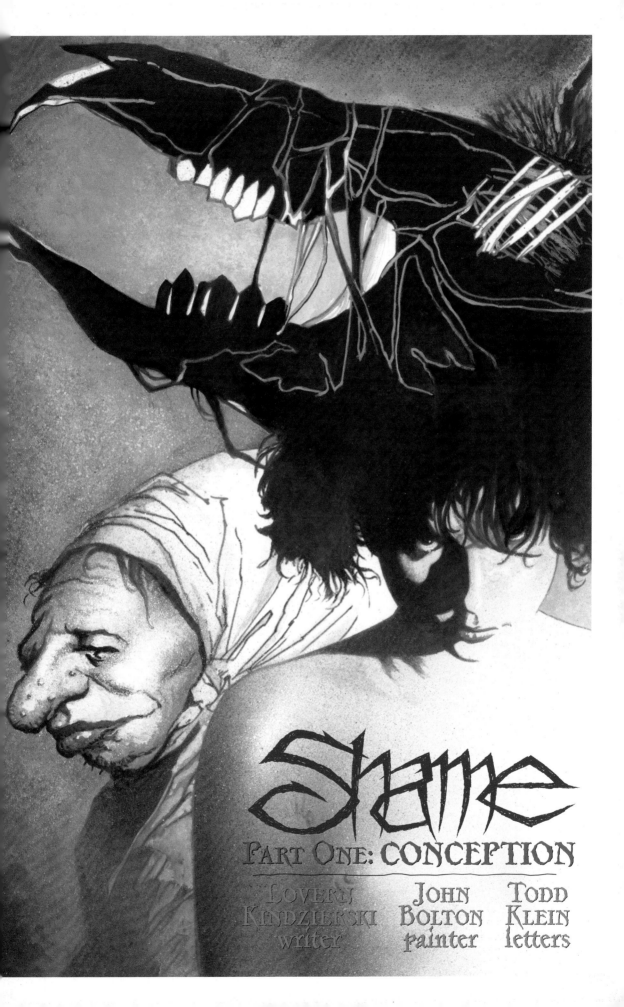

Shame

PART ONE: CONCEPTION

LOVERN KINDZIERSKI	JOHN BOLTON	TODD KLEIN
writer	painter	letters

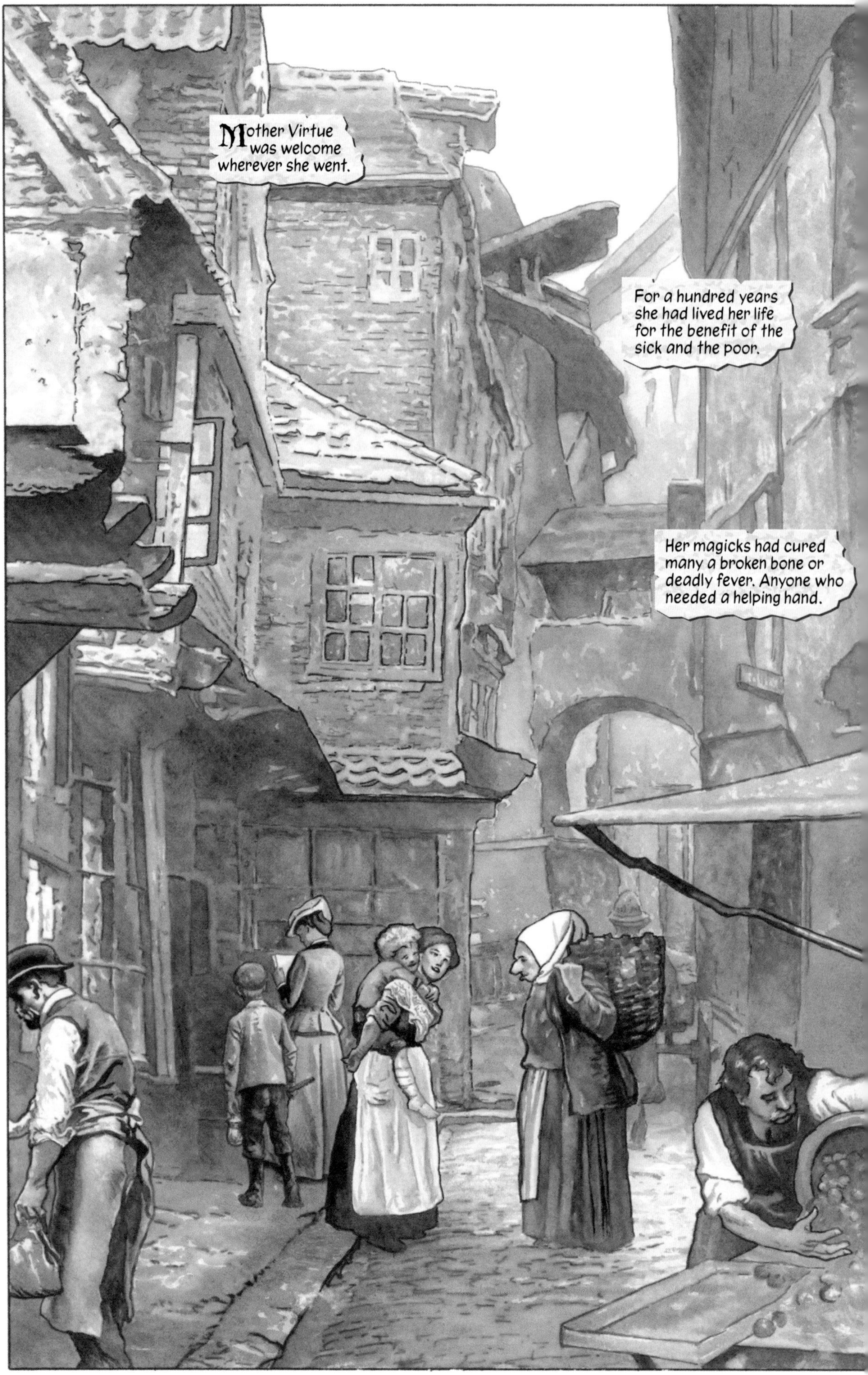
Mother Virtue was welcome wherever she went.
For a hundred years she had lived her life for the benefit of the sick and the poor.
Her magicks had cured many a broken bone or deadly fever. Anyone who needed a helping hand.

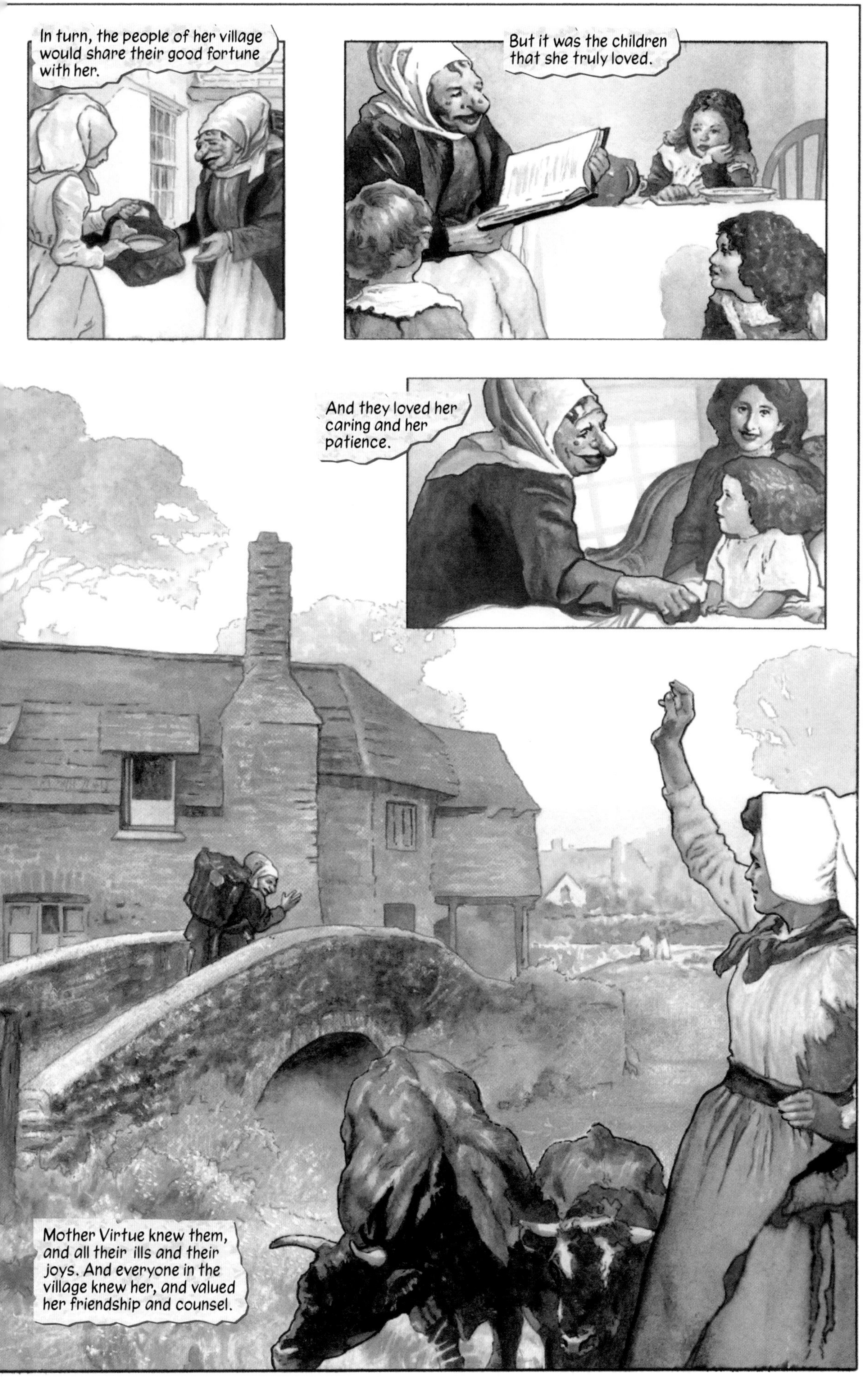
In turn, the people of her village would share their good fortune with her.
But it was the children that she truly loved.
And they loved her caring and her patience.
Mother Virtue knew them, and all their ills and their joys. And everyone in the village knew her, and valued her friendship and counsel.

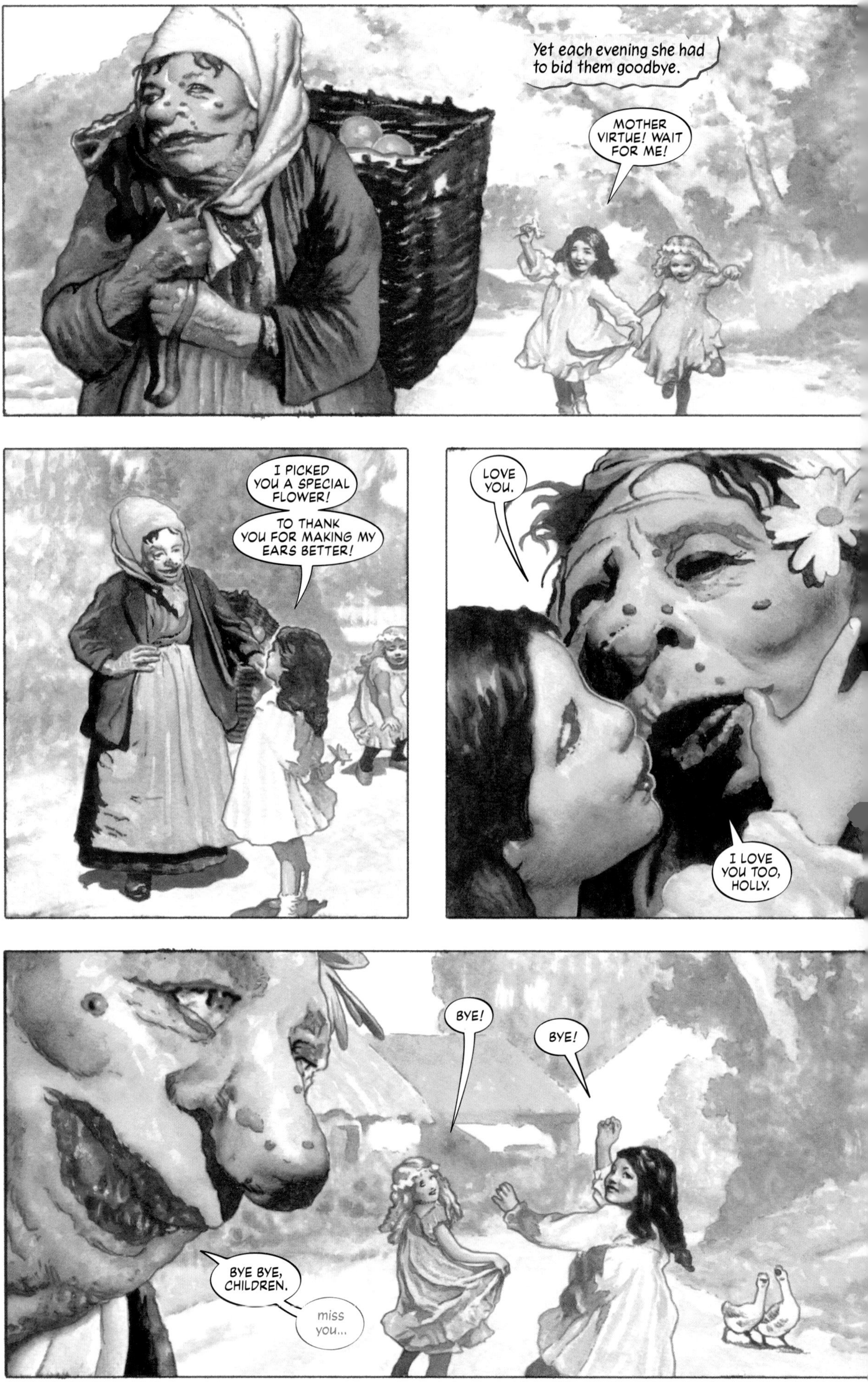
Yet each evening she had to bid them goodbye.
MOTHER VIRTUE! WAIT FOR ME!
I PICKED YOU A SPECIAL FLOWER!
TO THANK YOU FOR MAKING MY EARS BETTER!
LOVE YOU.
I LOVE YOU TOO, HOLLY.
BYE!
BYE!
BYE BYE, CHILDREN.
miss you...

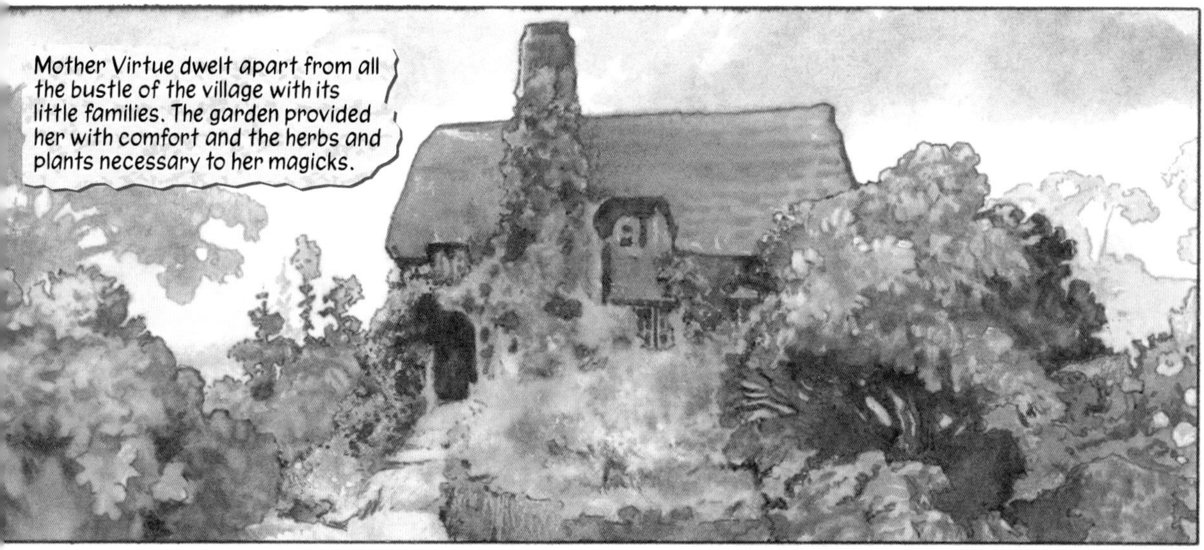
Mother Virtue dwelt apart from all the bustle of the village with its little families. The garden provided her with comfort and the herbs and plants necessary to her magicks.

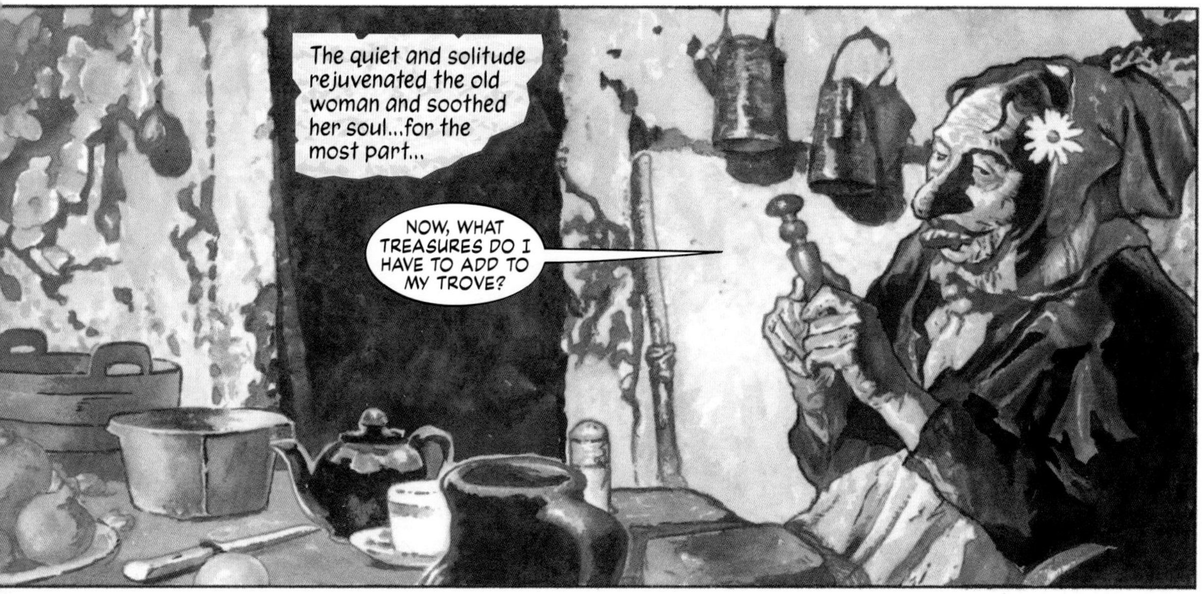
The quiet and solitude rejuvenated the old woman and soothed her soul...for the most part...
NOW, WHAT TREASURES DO I HAVE TO ADD TO MY TROVE?

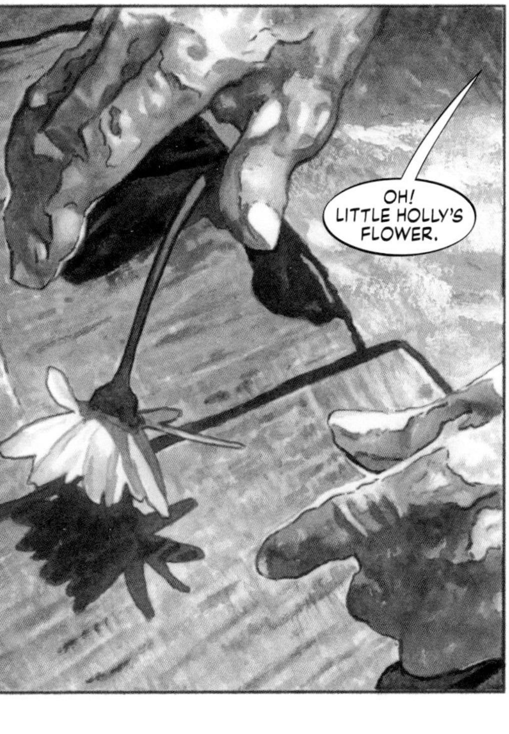
OH! LITTLE HOLLY'S FLOWER.

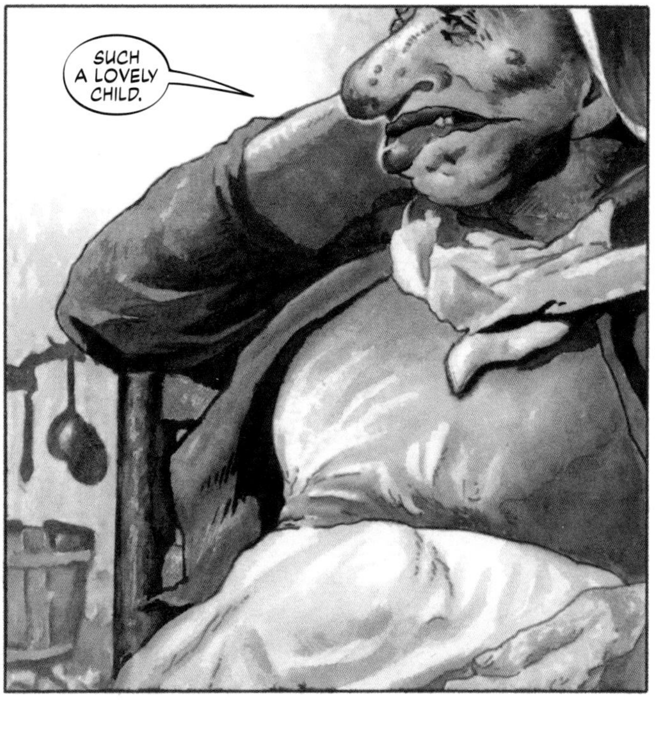
SUCH A LOVELY CHILD.

I'VE CARED FOR SO MANY CHILDREN, BUT NEVER ONE OF MY OWN. NEVER MET THE RIGHT MAN AND NOW THAT TIME HAS PASSED. OH, BUT IF I HAD ONE WISH IT WOULD SURELY BE FOR A CHILD.

MY *DAUGHTER!* NOT ONE THAT I SHARE.

SURELY I DESERVE THAT MUCH.

AH, ME! WISHING AND DAYDREAMING WON'T GET SUPPER ON THE FIRE.

Sadly, as often is the case, Mother Virtue's selfish wish echoed like a dinner bell in the Heart of Darkness...

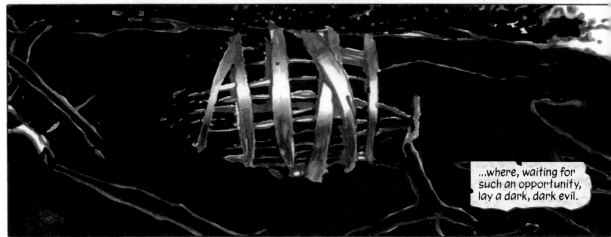

...where, waiting for such an opportunity, lay a dark, dark evil.

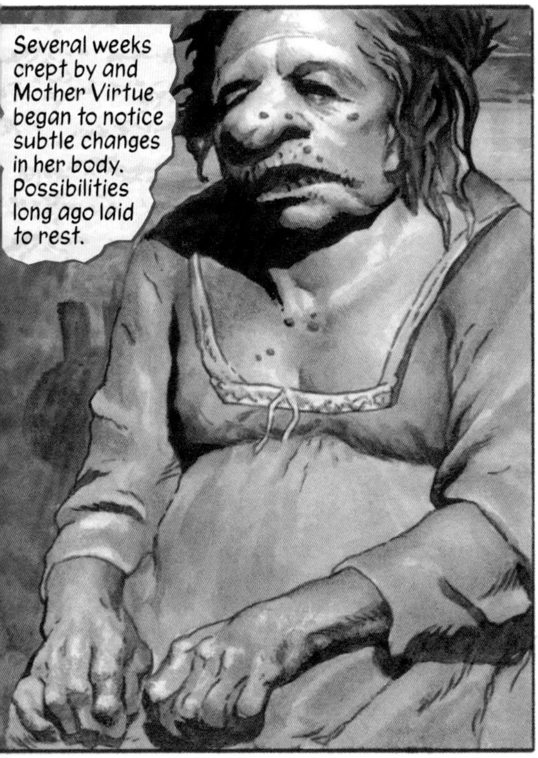
Several weeks crept by and Mother Virtue began to notice subtle changes in her body. Possibilities long ago laid to rest.

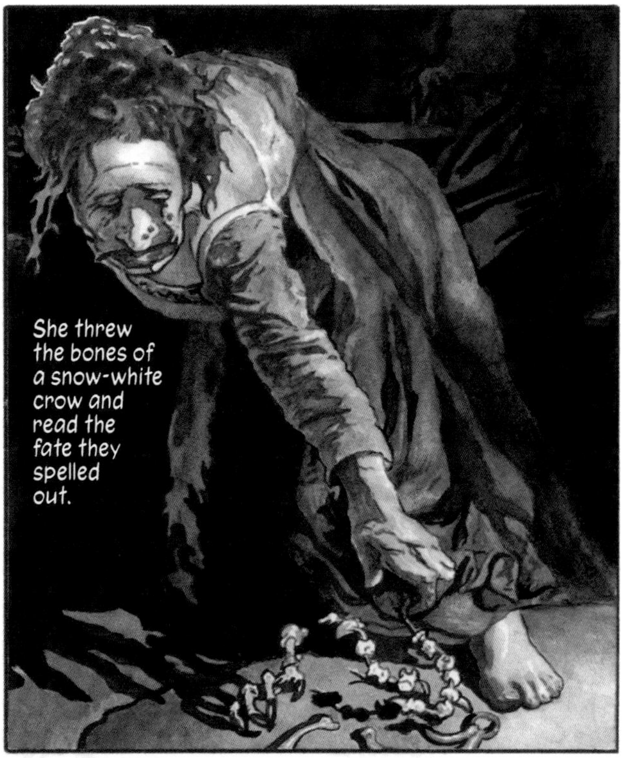
She threw the bones of a snow-white crow and read the fate they spelled out.

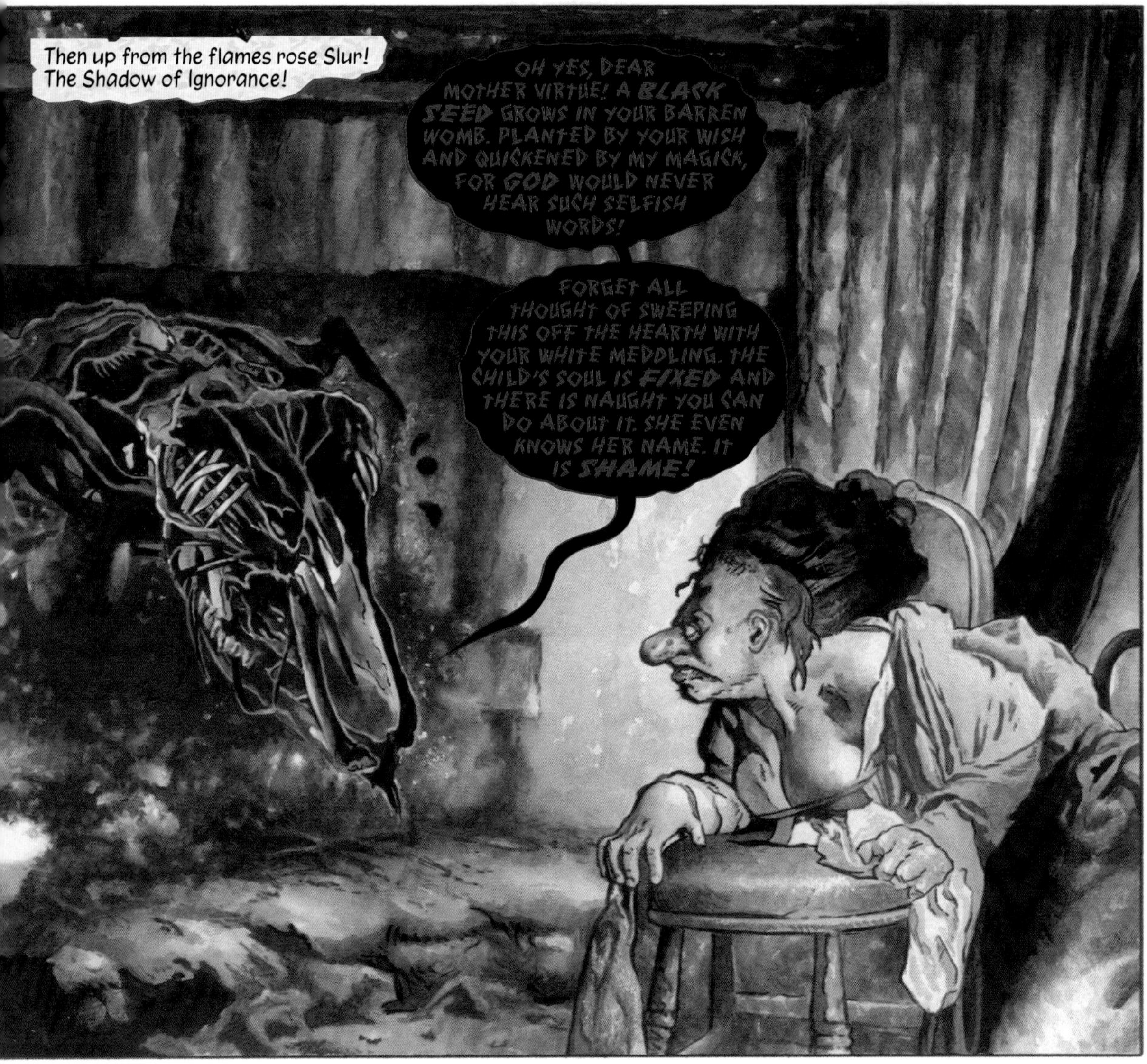
Then up from the flames rose Slur! The Shadow of Ignorance!
OH YES, DEAR MOTHER VIRTUE! A BLACK SEED GROWS IN YOUR BARREN WOMB. PLANTED BY YOUR WISH AND QUICKENED BY MY MAGICK, FOR GOD WOULD NEVER HEAR SUCH SELFISH WORDS!
FORGET ALL THOUGHT OF SWEEPING THIS OFF THE HEARTH WITH YOUR WHITE MEDDLING. THE CHILD'S SOUL IS FIXED AND THERE IS NAUGHT YOU CAN DO ABOUT IT. SHE EVEN KNOWS HER NAME. IT IS SHAME!

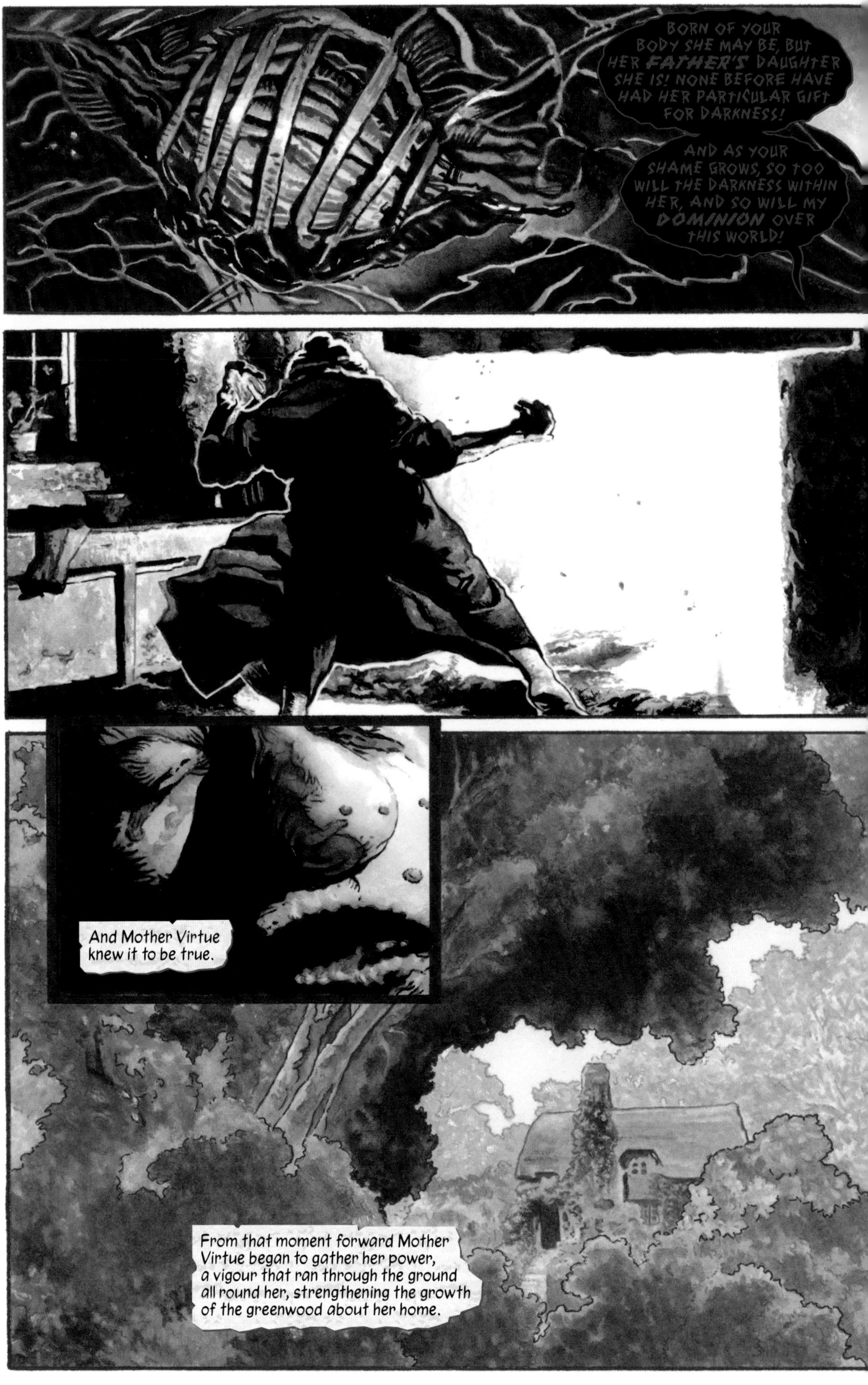
BORN OF YOUR BODY SHE MAY BE, BUT HER FATHER'S DAUGHTER SHE IS! NONE BEFORE HAVE HAD HER PARTICULAR GIFT FOR DARKNESS!
AND AS YOUR SHAME GROWS, SO TOO WILL THE DARKNESS WITHIN HER, AND SO WILL MY DOMINION OVER THIS WORLD!
And Mother Virtue knew it to be true.
From that moment forward Mother Virtue began to gather her power, a vigour that ran through the ground all round her, strengthening the growth of the greenwood about her home.

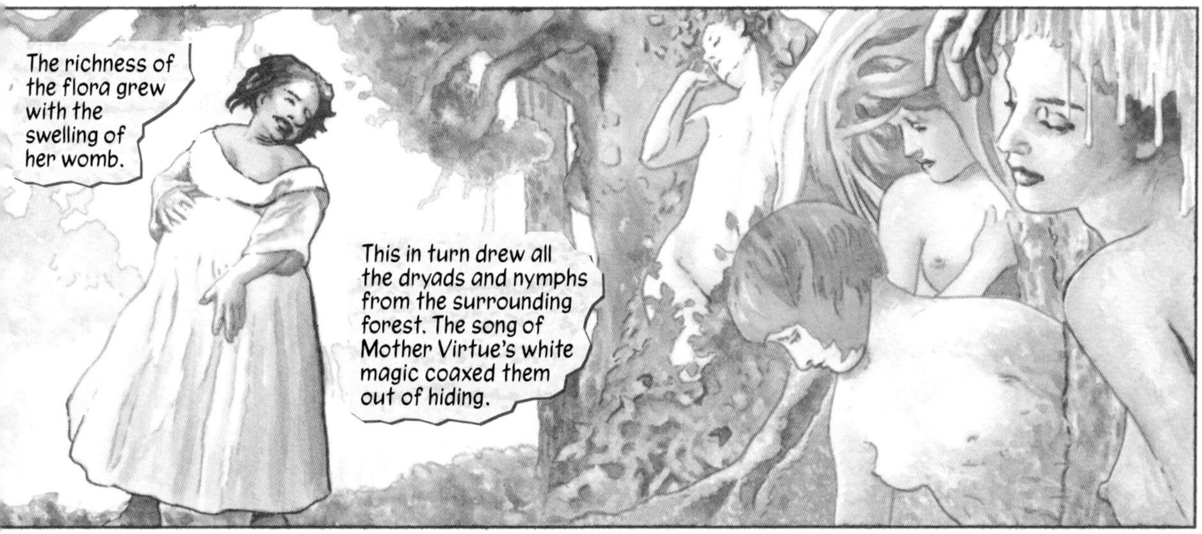
The richness of the flora grew with the swelling of her womb.
This in turn drew all the dryads and nymphs from the surrounding forest. The song of Mother Virtue's white magic coaxed them out of hiding.

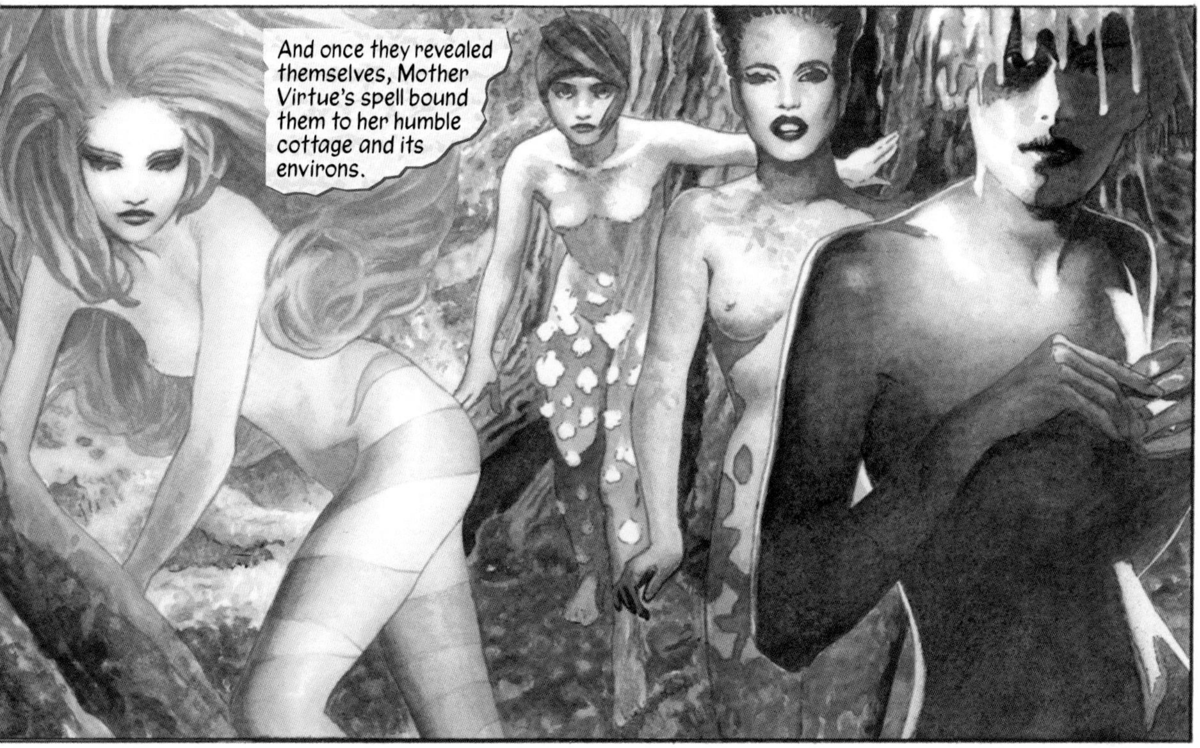
And once they revealed themselves, Mother Virtue's spell bound them to her humble cottage and its environs.

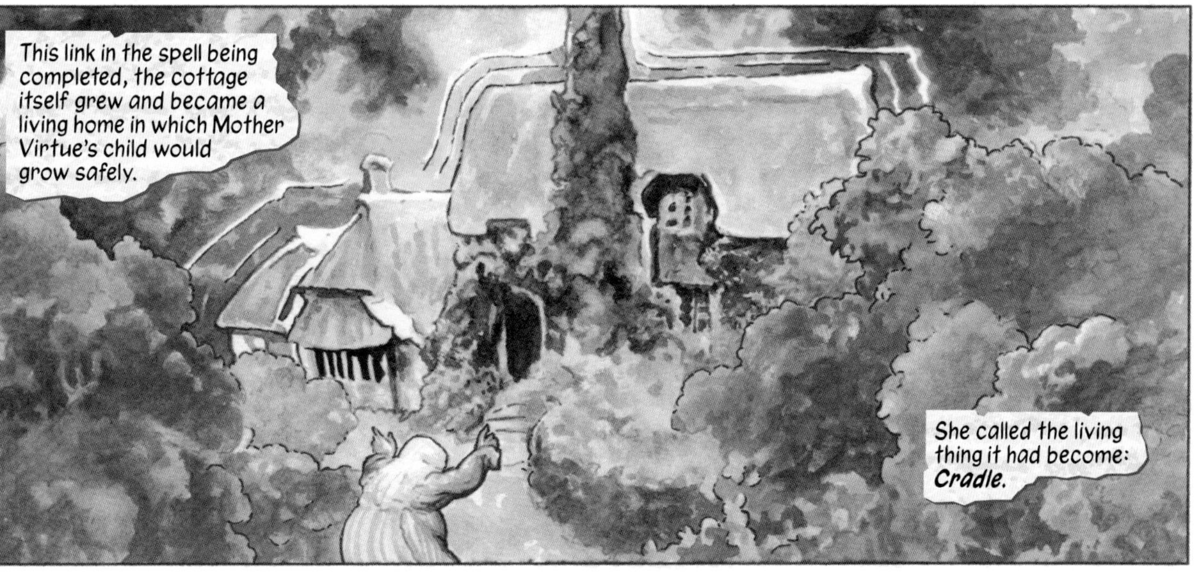
This link in the spell being completed, the cottage itself grew and became a living home in which Mother Virtue's child would grow safely.
She called the living thing it had become: ***Cradle.***

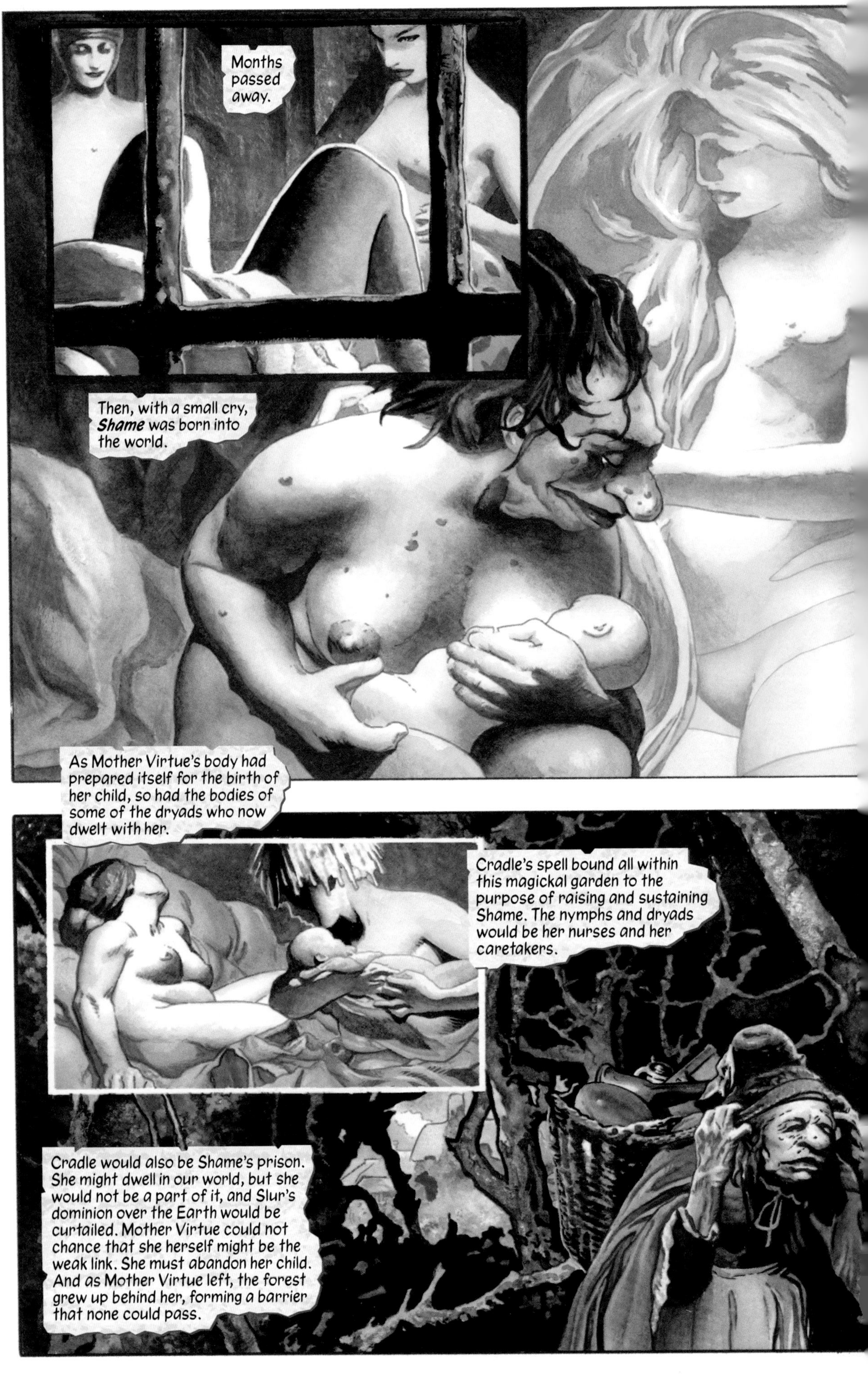
Months passed away.
Then, with a small cry, **Shame** was born into the world.
As Mother Virtue's body had prepared itself for the birth of her child, so had the bodies of some of the dryads who now dwelt with her.
Cradle's spell bound all within this magickal garden to the purpose of raising and sustaining Shame. The nymphs and dryads would be her nurses and her caretakers.
Cradle would also be Shame's prison. She might dwell in our world, but she would not be a part of it, and Slur's dominion over the Earth would be curtailed. Mother Virtue could not chance that she herself might be the weak link. She must abandon her child. And as Mother Virtue left, the forest grew up behind her, forming a barrier that none could pass.

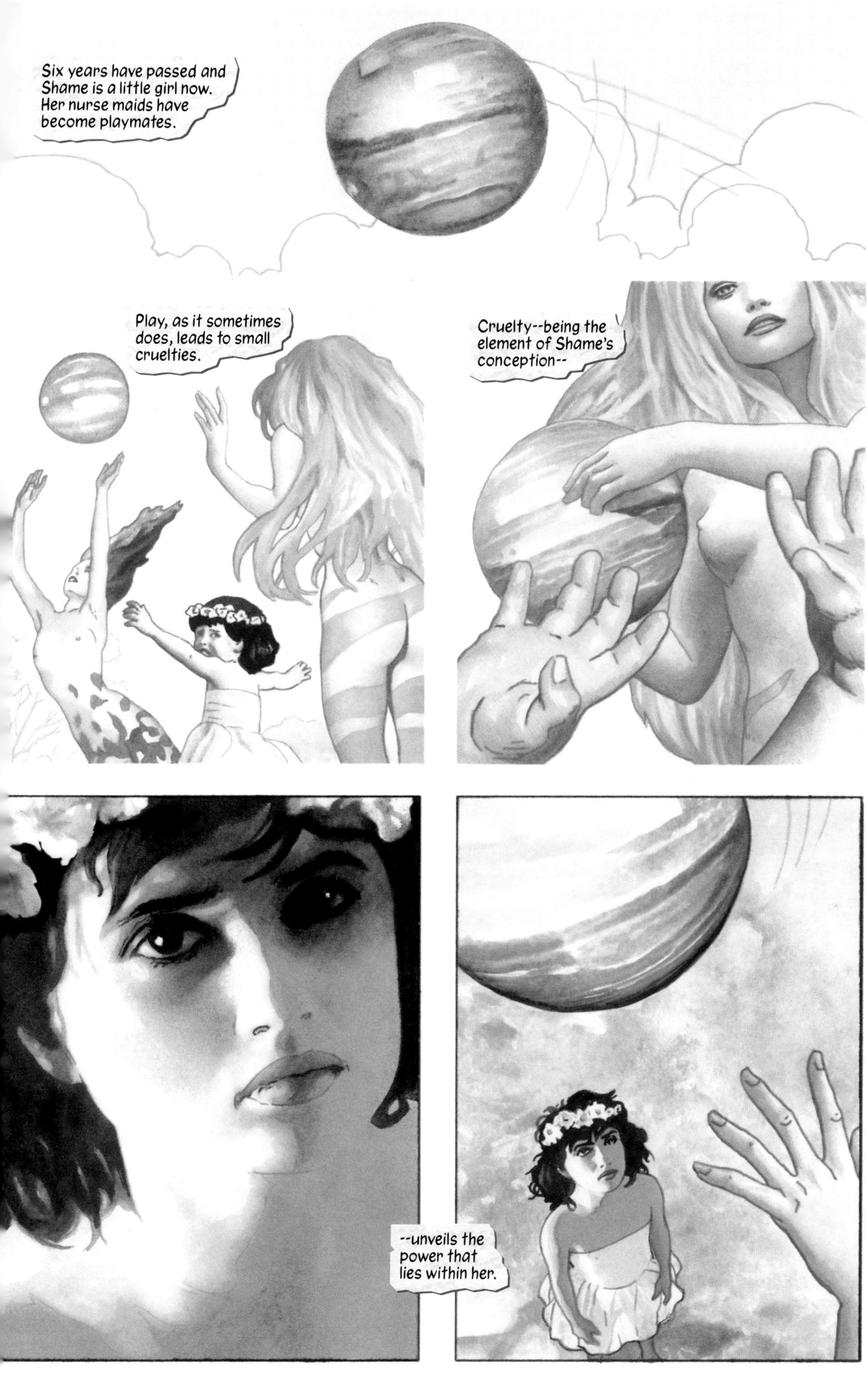
Six years have passed and Shame is a little girl now. Her nurse maids have become playmates.
Play, as it sometimes does, leads to small cruelties.
Cruelty--being the element of Shame's conception--
--unveils the power that lies within her.

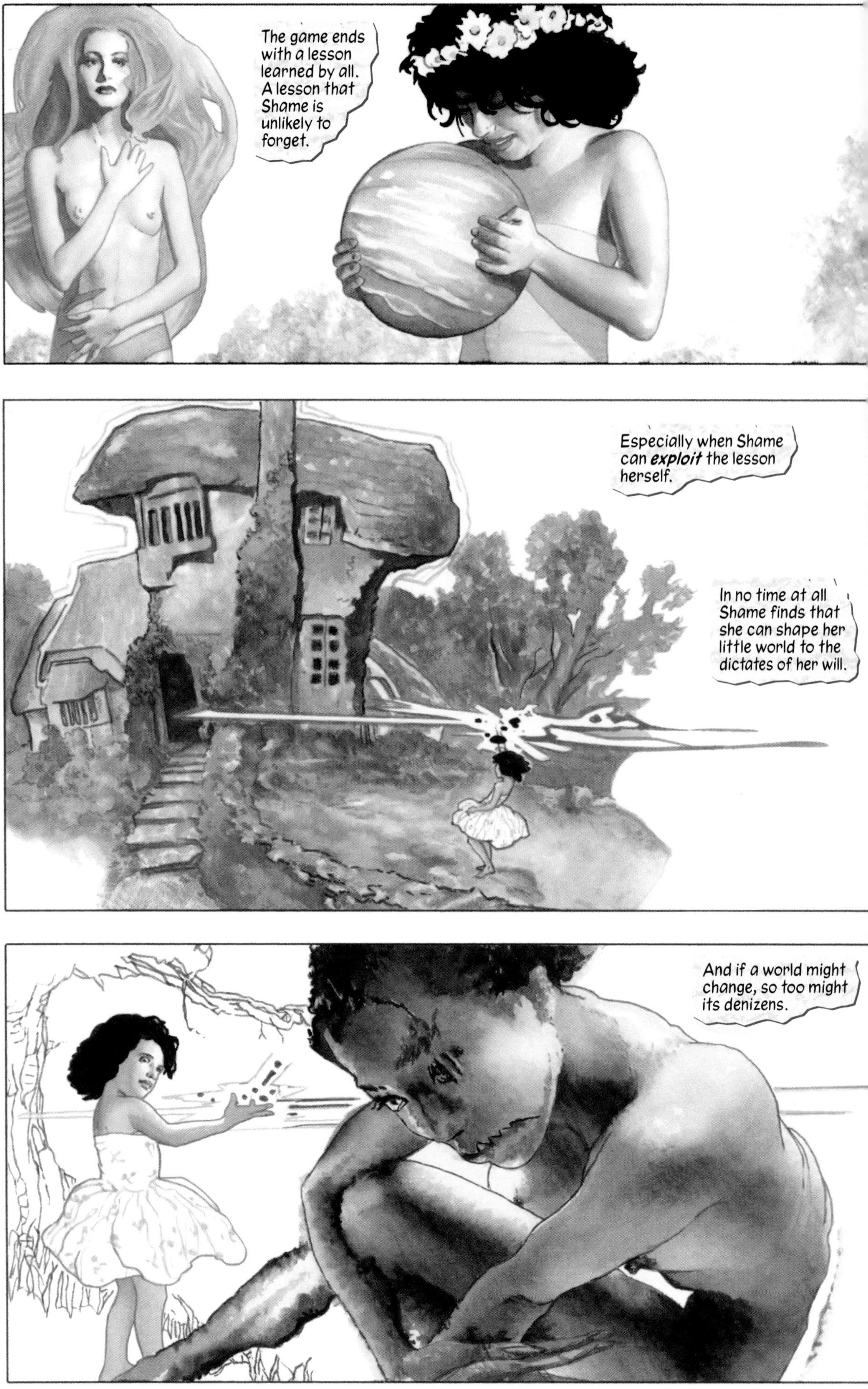

The game ends with a lesson learned by all. A lesson that Shame is unlikely to forget.
Especially when Shame can ***exploit*** the lesson herself.
In no time at all Shame finds that she can shape her little world to the dictates of her will.
And if a world might change, so too might its denizens.

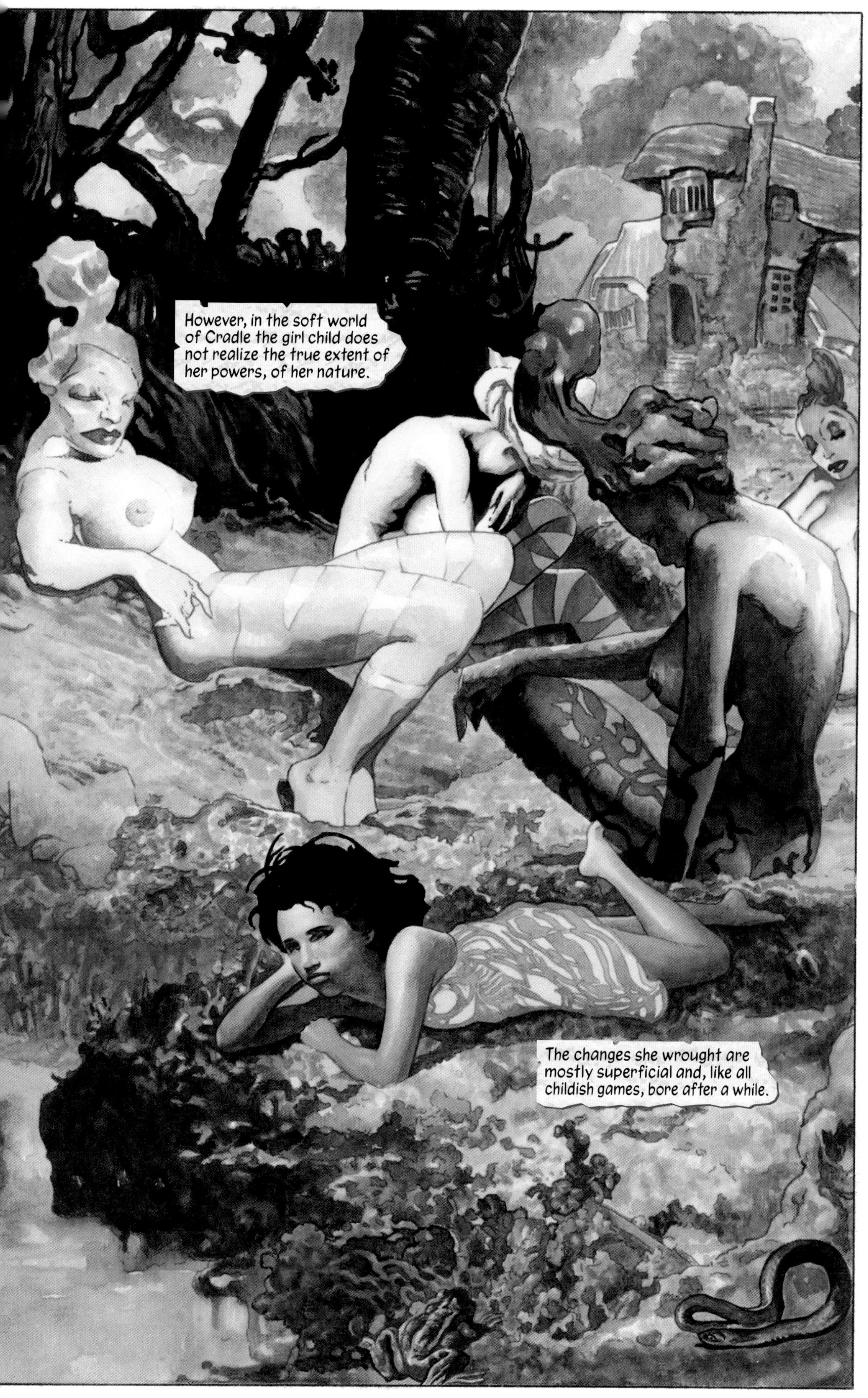
However, in the soft world of Cradle the girl child does not realize the true extent of her powers, of her nature.
The changes she wrought are mostly superficial and, like all childish games, bore after a while.

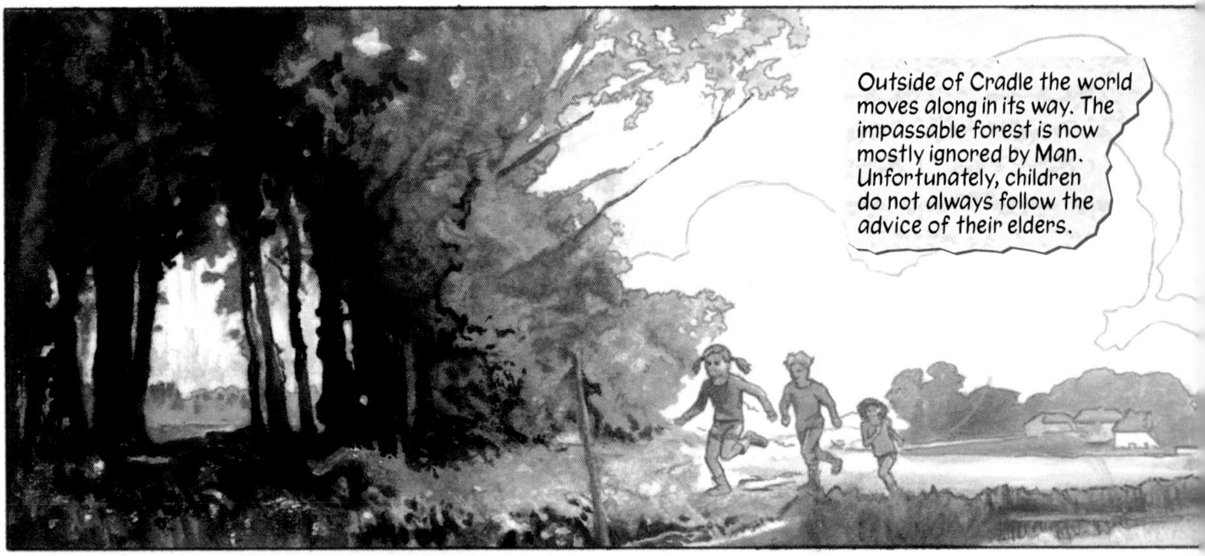
Outside of Cradle the world moves along in its way. The impassable forest is now mostly ignored by Man. Unfortunately, children do not always follow the advice of their elders.

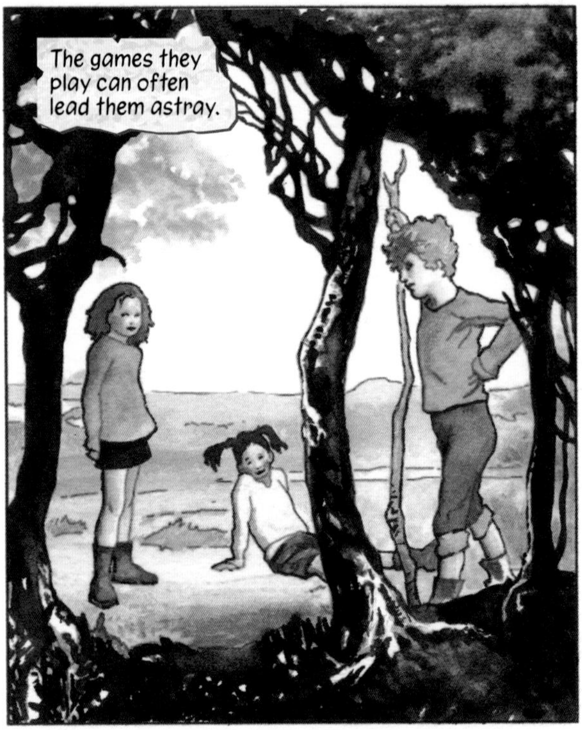
The games they play can often lead them astray.

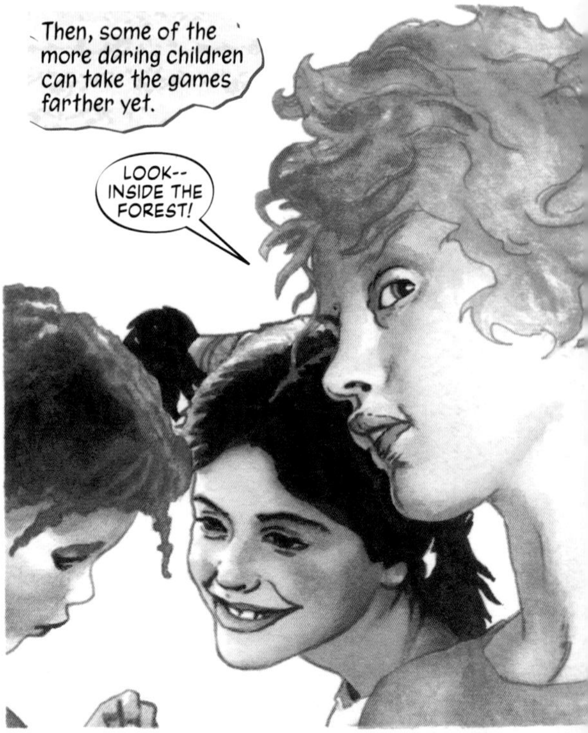
Then, some of the more daring children can take the games farther yet.
LOOK-- INSIDE THE FOREST!

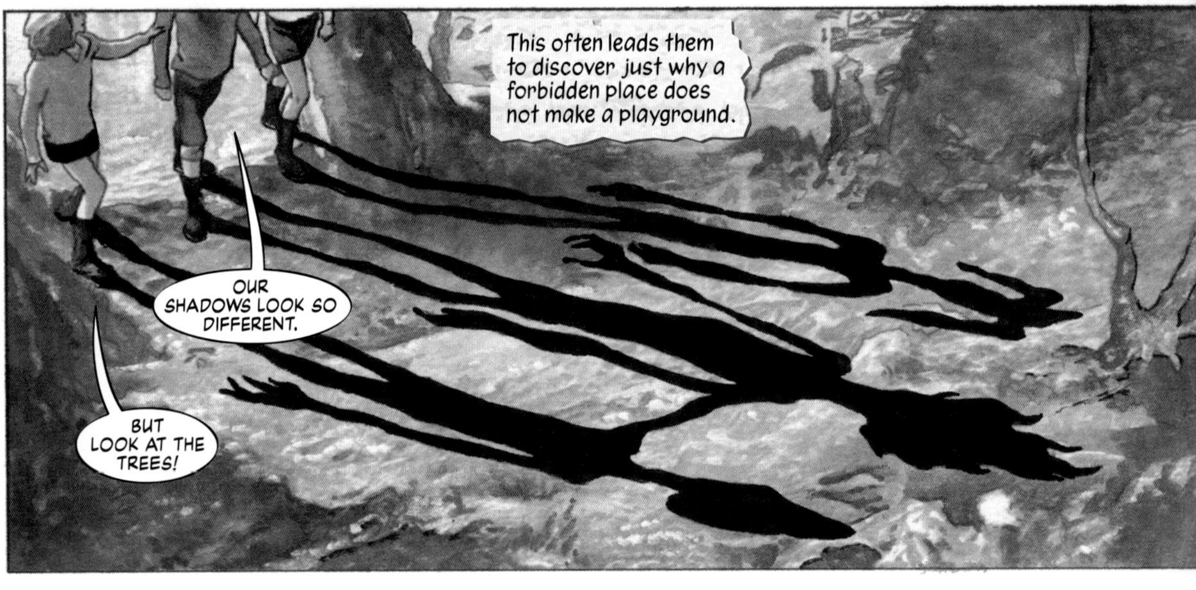
This often leads them to discover just why a forbidden place does not make a playground.
OUR SHADOWS LOOK SO DIFFERENT.
BUT LOOK AT THE TREES!

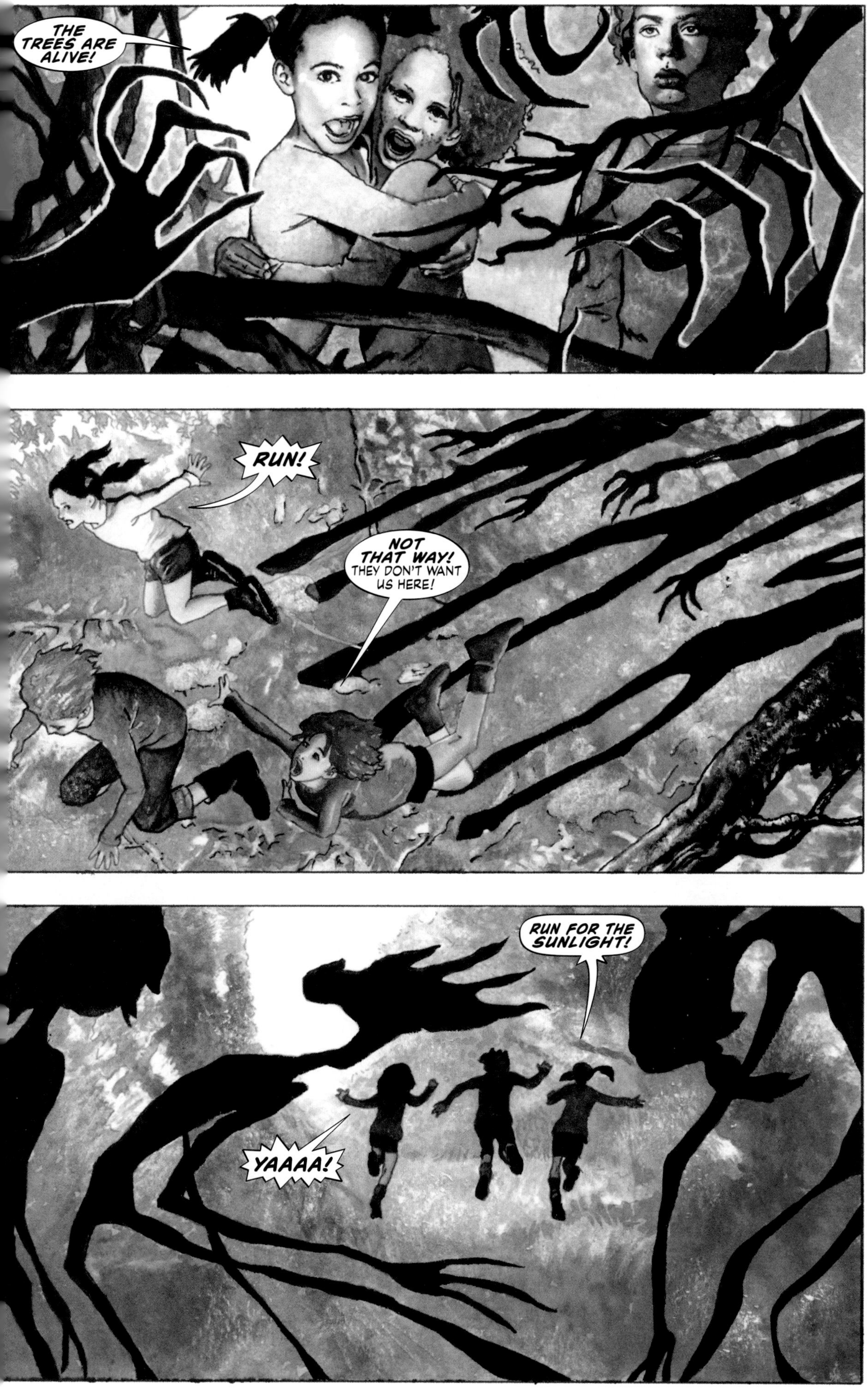
THE TREES ARE ALIVE!
RUN!
NOT THAT WAY! THEY DON'T WANT US HERE!
RUN FOR THE SUNLIGHT!
YAAAA!

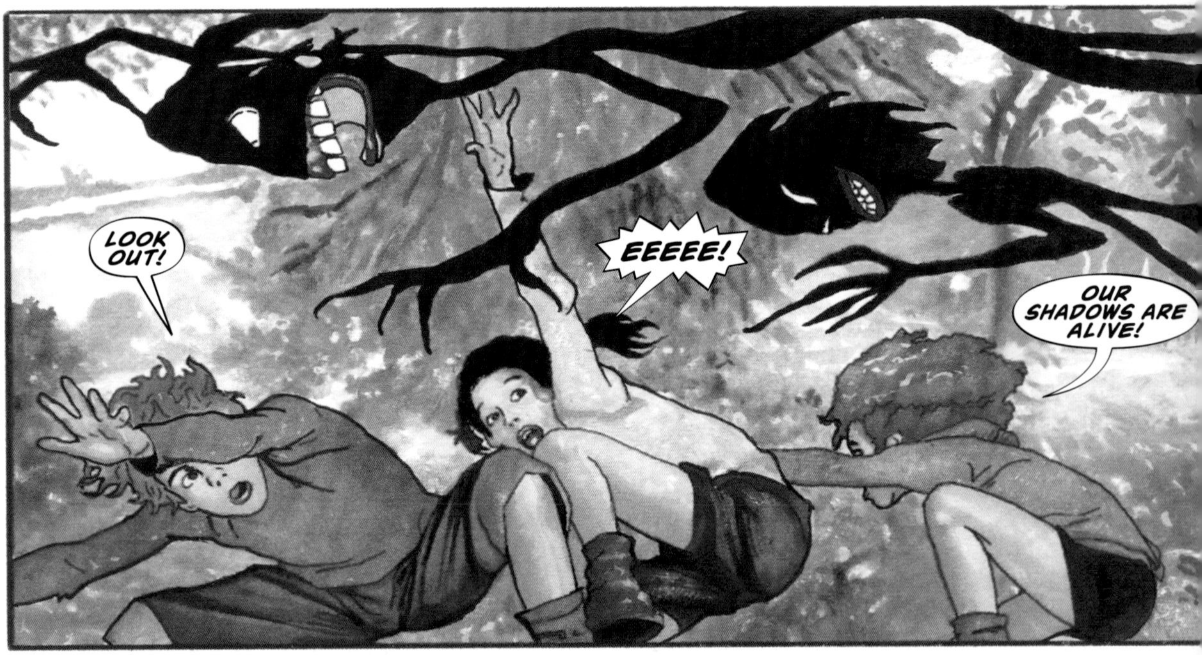
LOOK OUT!
EEEEE!
OUR SHADOWS ARE ALIVE!

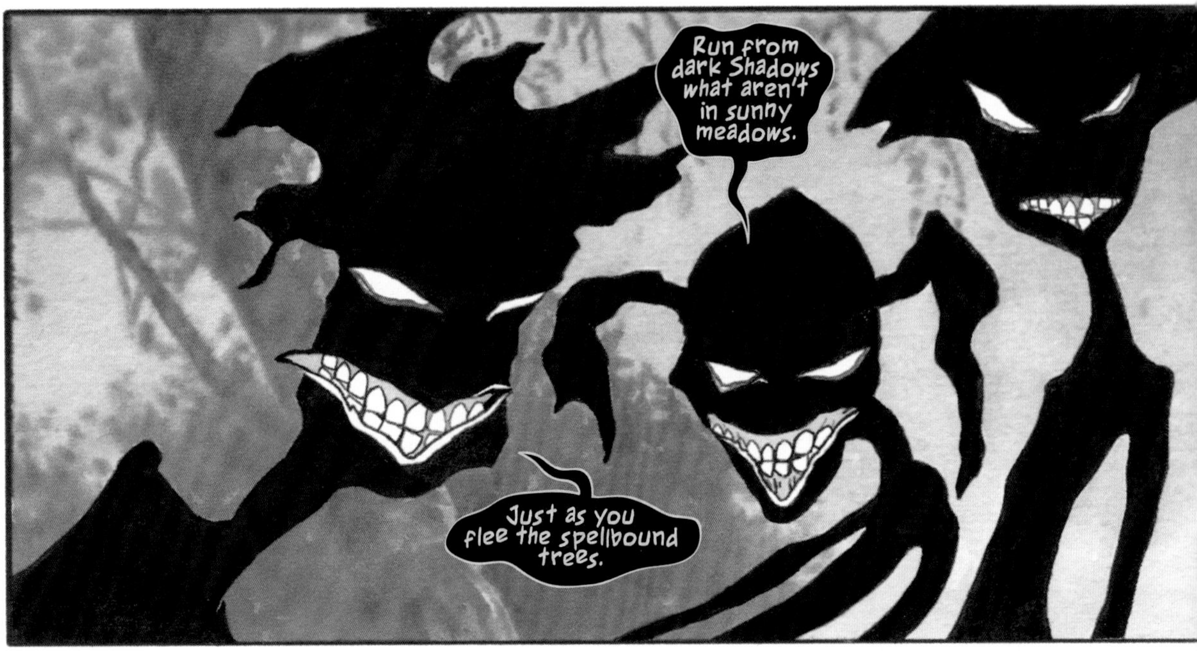
Run from dark Shadows what aren't in sunny meadows.
Just as you flee the spellbound trees.

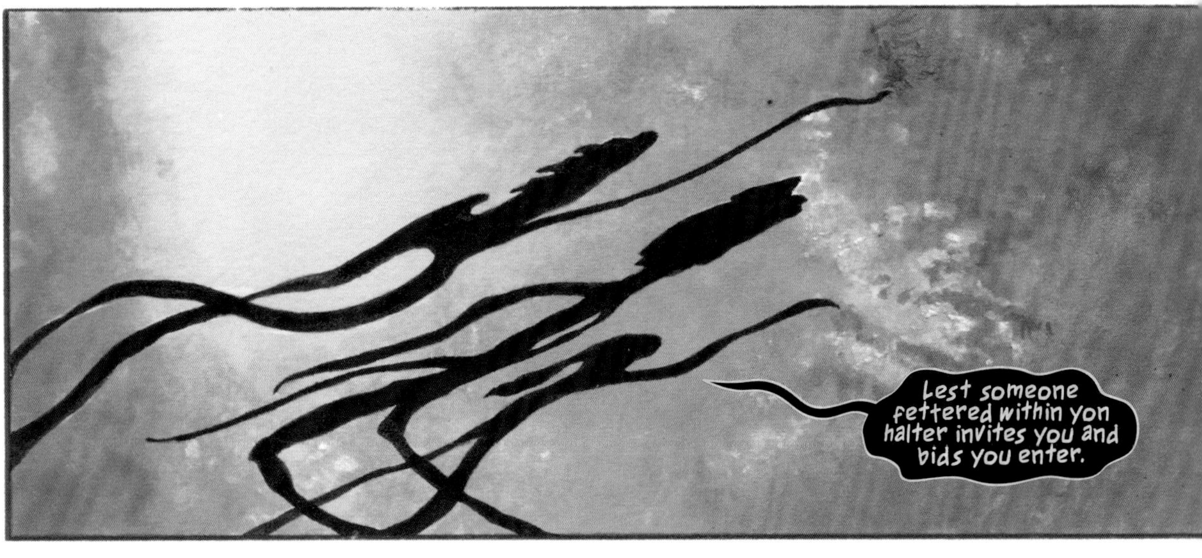
Lest someone fettered within yon halter invites you and bids you enter.

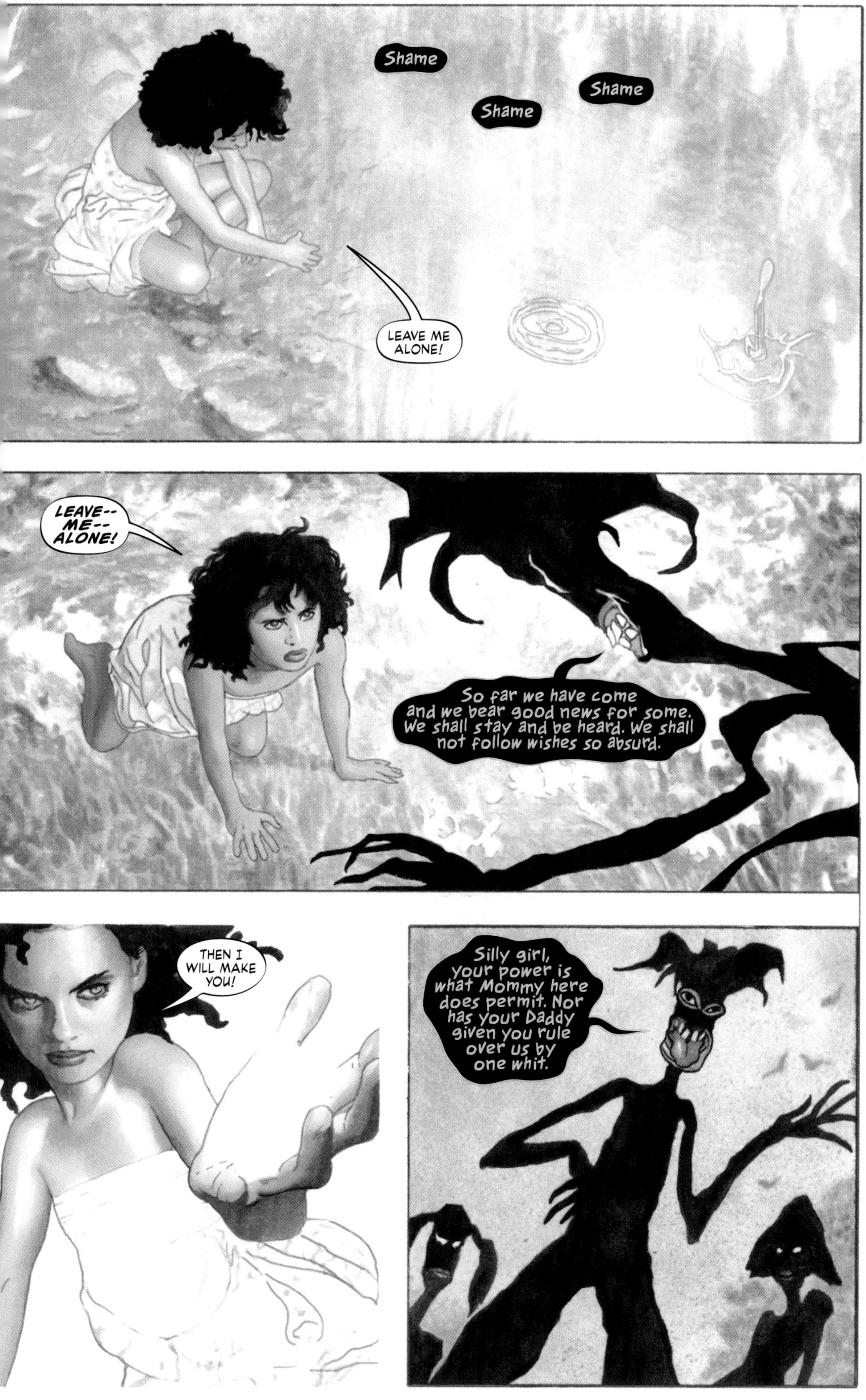
Shame
Shame
Shame
LEAVE ME ALONE!
LEAVE-- ME-- ALONE!
So far we have come and we bear good news for some. We shall stay and be heard. We shall not follow wishes so absurd.
THEN I WILL MAKE YOU!
Silly girl, your power is what Mommy here does permit. Nor has your Daddy given you rule over us by one whit.

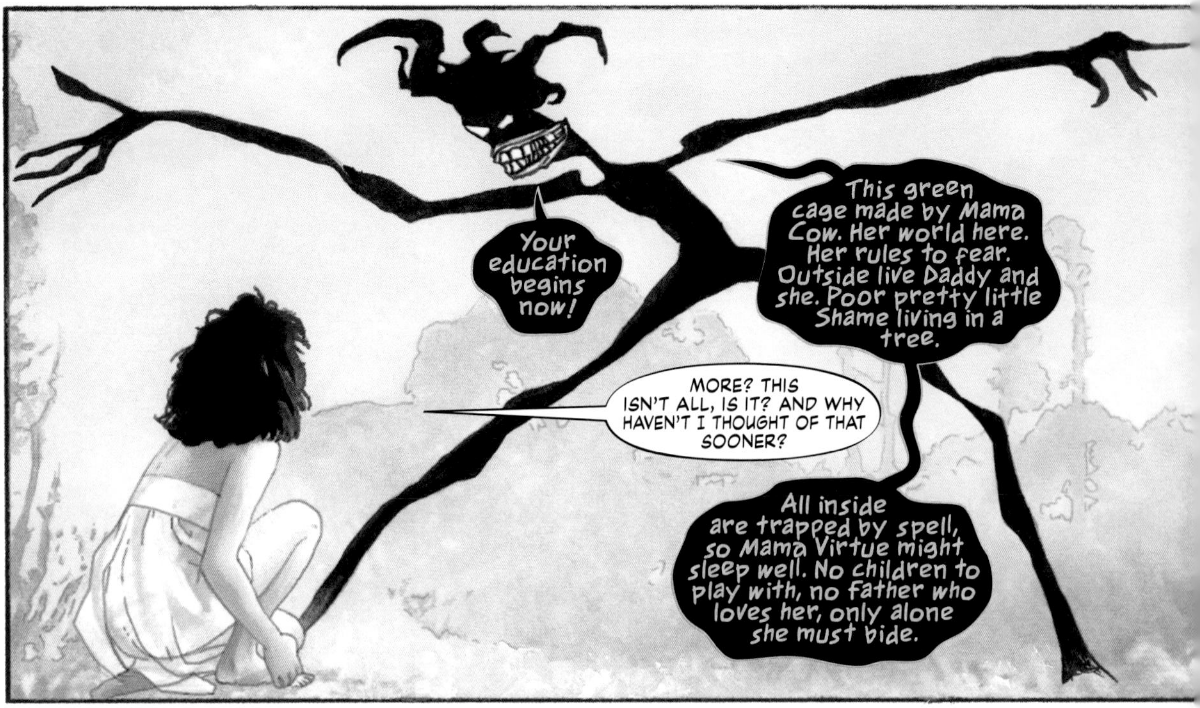
Your education begins now!
This green cage made by Mama Cow. Her world here. Her rules to fear. Outside live Daddy and she. Poor pretty little Shame living in a tree.
MORE? THIS ISN'T ALL, IS IT? AND WHY HAVEN'T I THOUGHT OF THAT SOONER?
All inside are trapped by spell, so Mama Virtue might sleep well. No children to play with, no father who loves her, only alone she must bide.

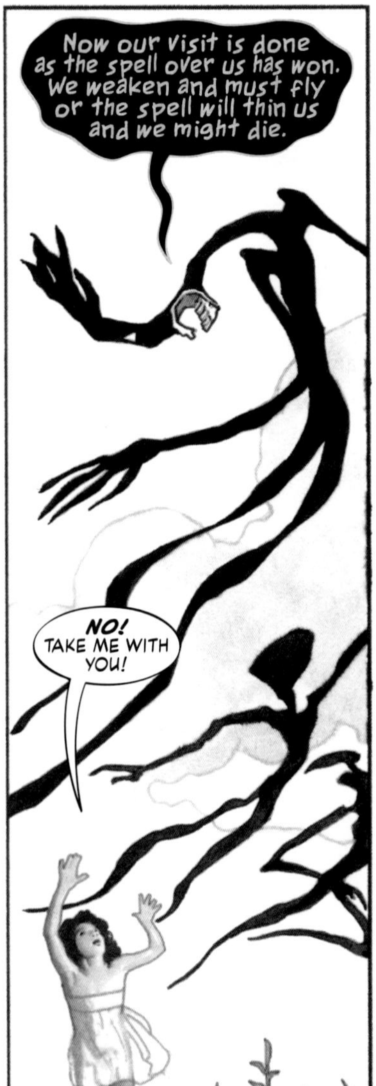
Now our visit is done as the spell over us has won. We weaken and must fly or the spell will thin us and we might die.
NO! TAKE ME WITH YOU!

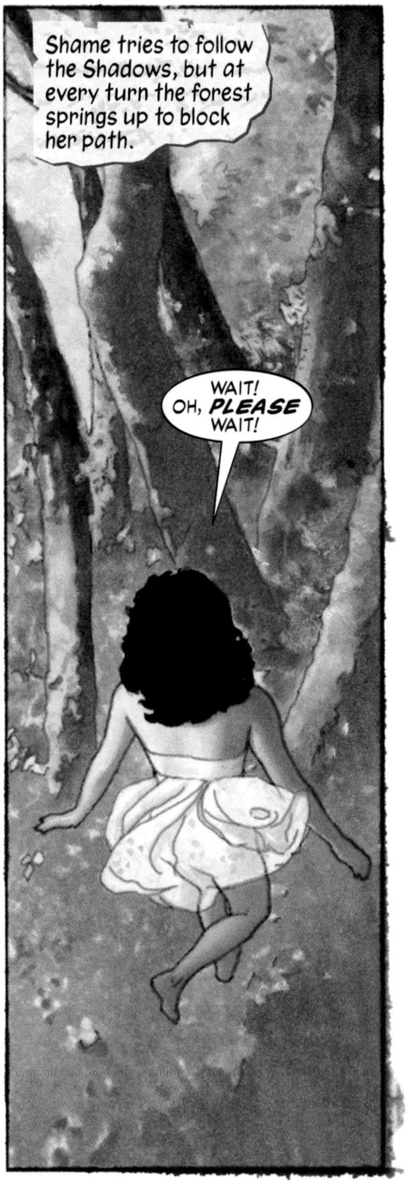
Shame tries to follow the Shadows, but at every turn the forest springs up to block her path.
WAIT! OH, PLEASE WAIT!

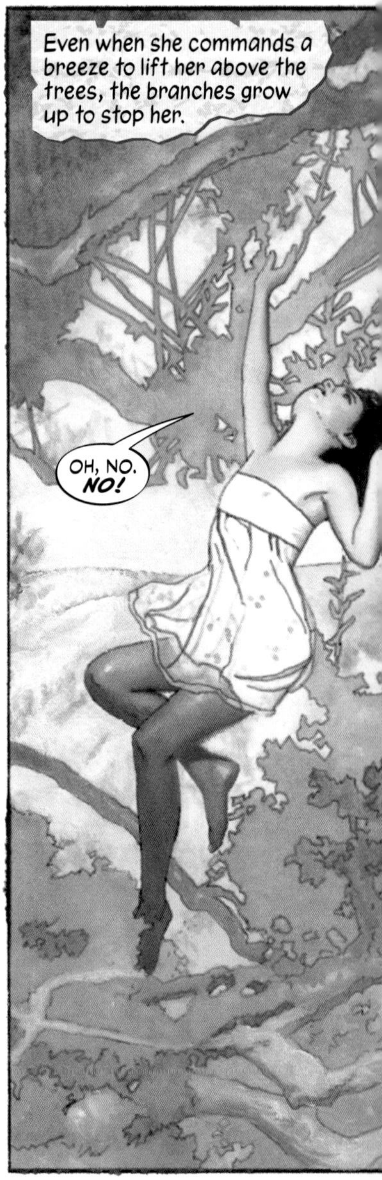
Even when she commands a breeze to lift her above the trees, the branches grow up to stop her.
OH, NO. NO!

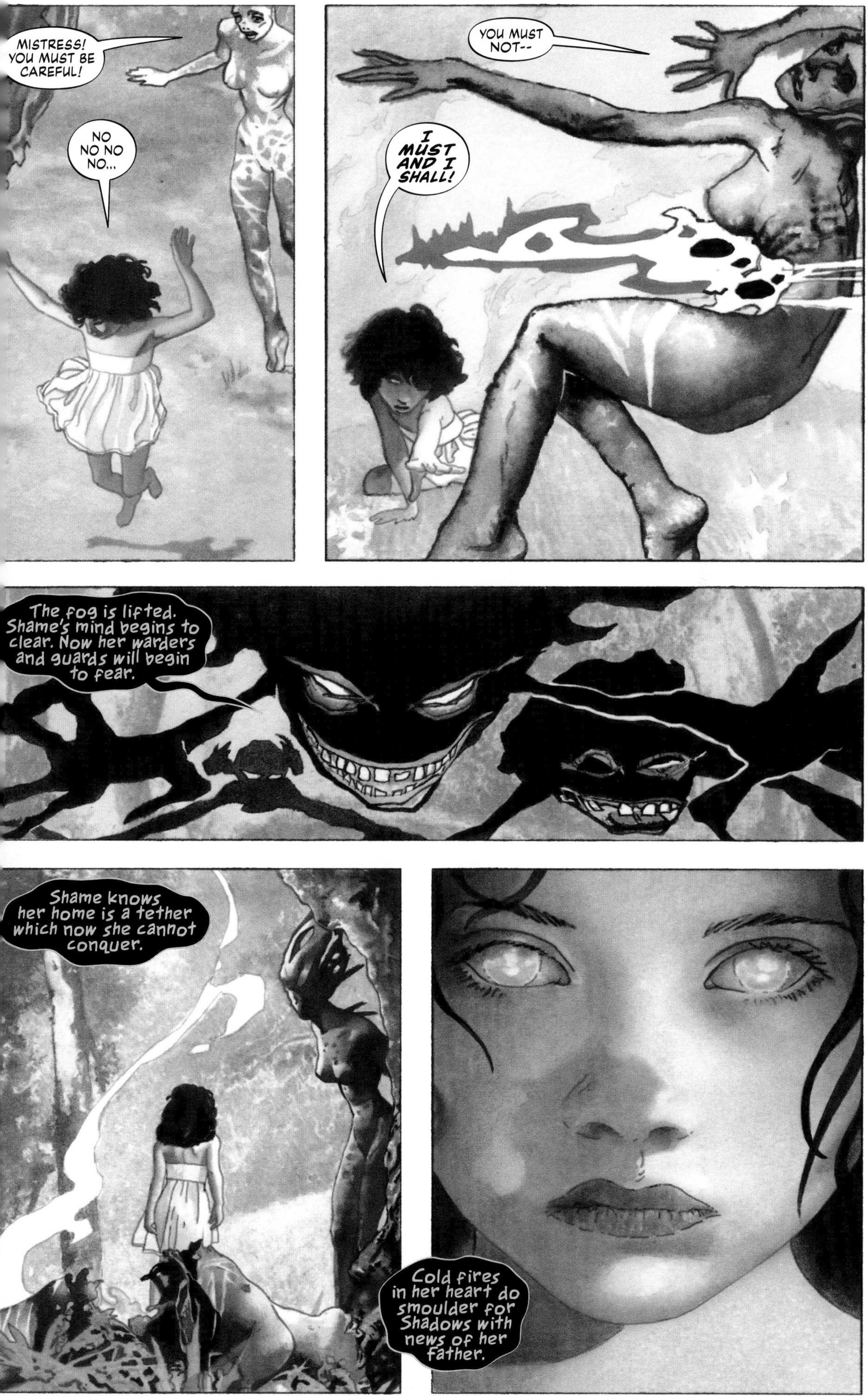
MISTRESS! YOU MUST BE CAREFUL!
NO NO NO NO...
YOU MUST NOT--
I MUST AND I SHALL!
The fog is lifted. Shame's mind begins to clear. Now her warders and guards will begin to fear.
Shame knows her home is a tether which now she cannot conquer.
Cold fires in her heart do smoulder for Shadows with news of her father.

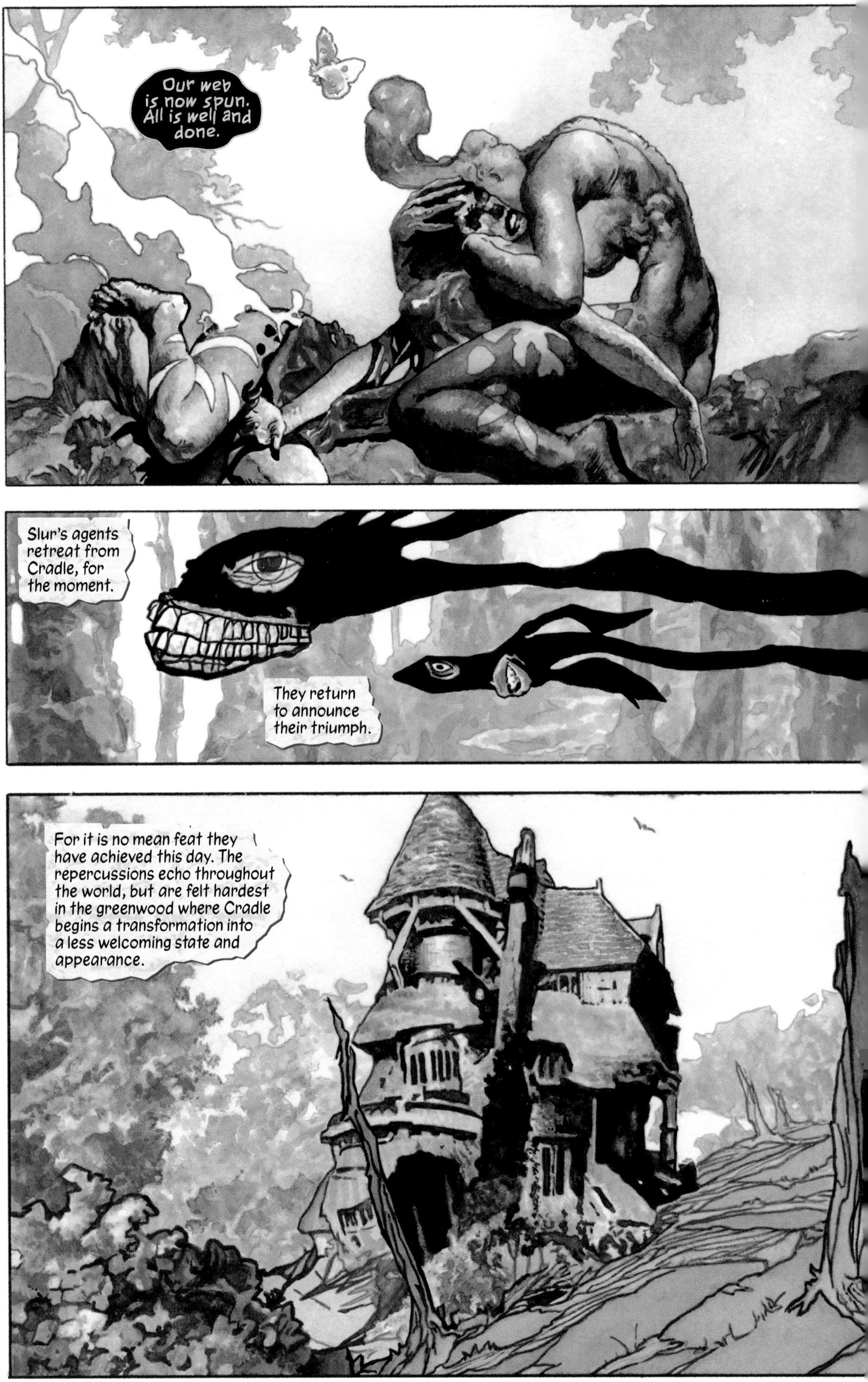
Our web is now spun. All is well and done.
Slur's agents retreat from Cradle, for the moment.
They return to announce their triumph.
For it is no mean feat they have achieved this day. The repercussions echo throughout the world, but are felt hardest in the greenwood where Cradle begins a transformation into a less welcoming state and appearance.

The Shadows make many more visits and warp the fabric of Virtue's spell by teaching Shame more and more of her Father's ways.

With your power you fold water into a ball.

Then push it up so tall.

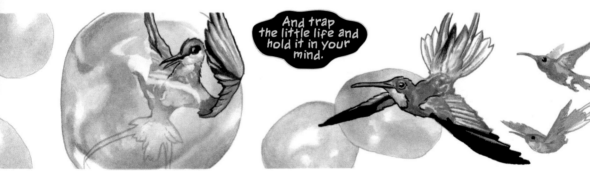

And trap the little life and hold it in your mind.

As the bird's life flees it is trapped in the ball, and now the globe can be so much more.

It can be a third eye to see what your others cannot. And all you need is a thought.

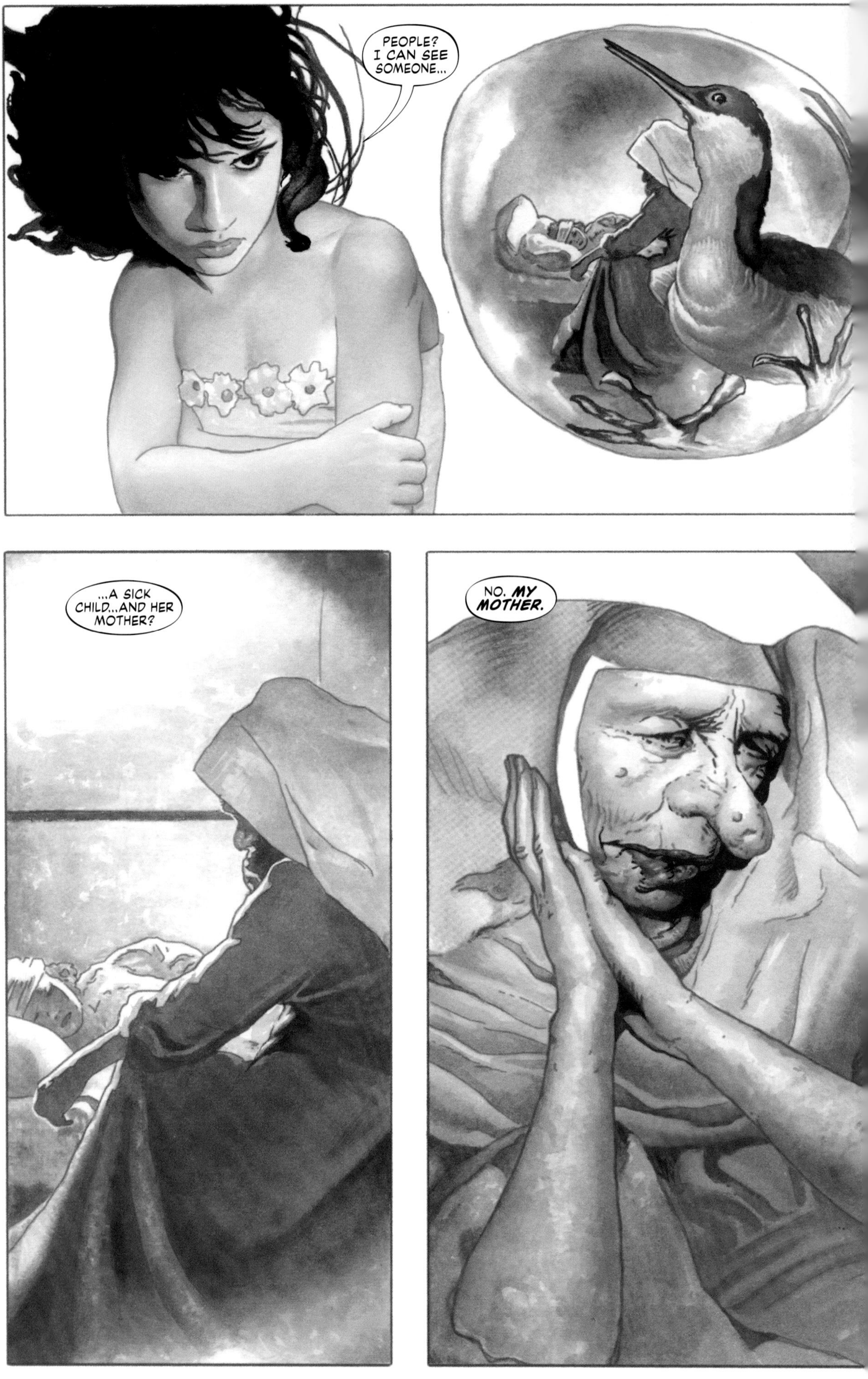
PEOPLE? I CAN SEE SOMEONE...
...A SICK CHILD...AND HER MOTHER?
NO. **MY MOTHER.**

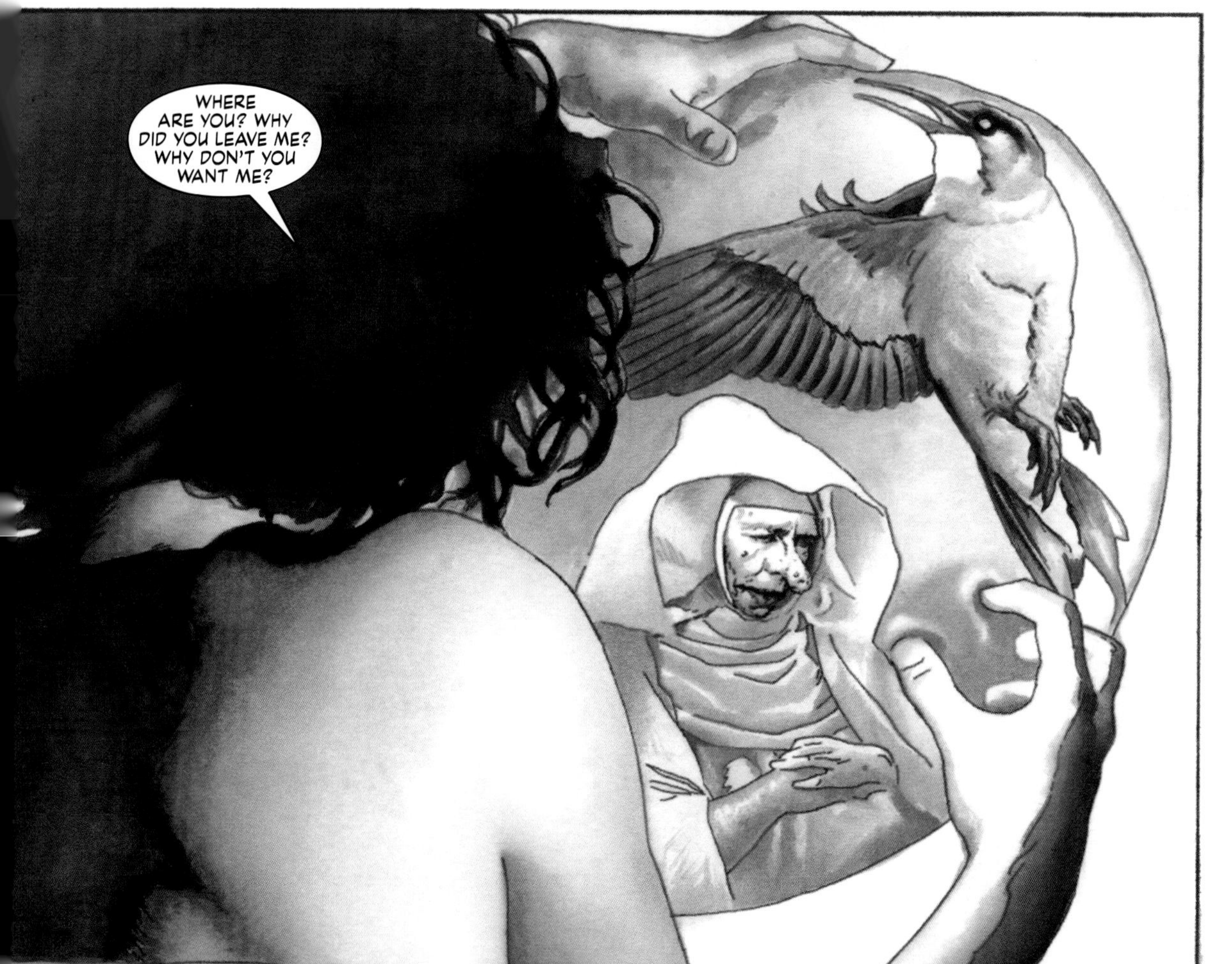
WHERE ARE YOU? WHY DID YOU LEAVE ME? WHY DON'T YOU WANT ME?

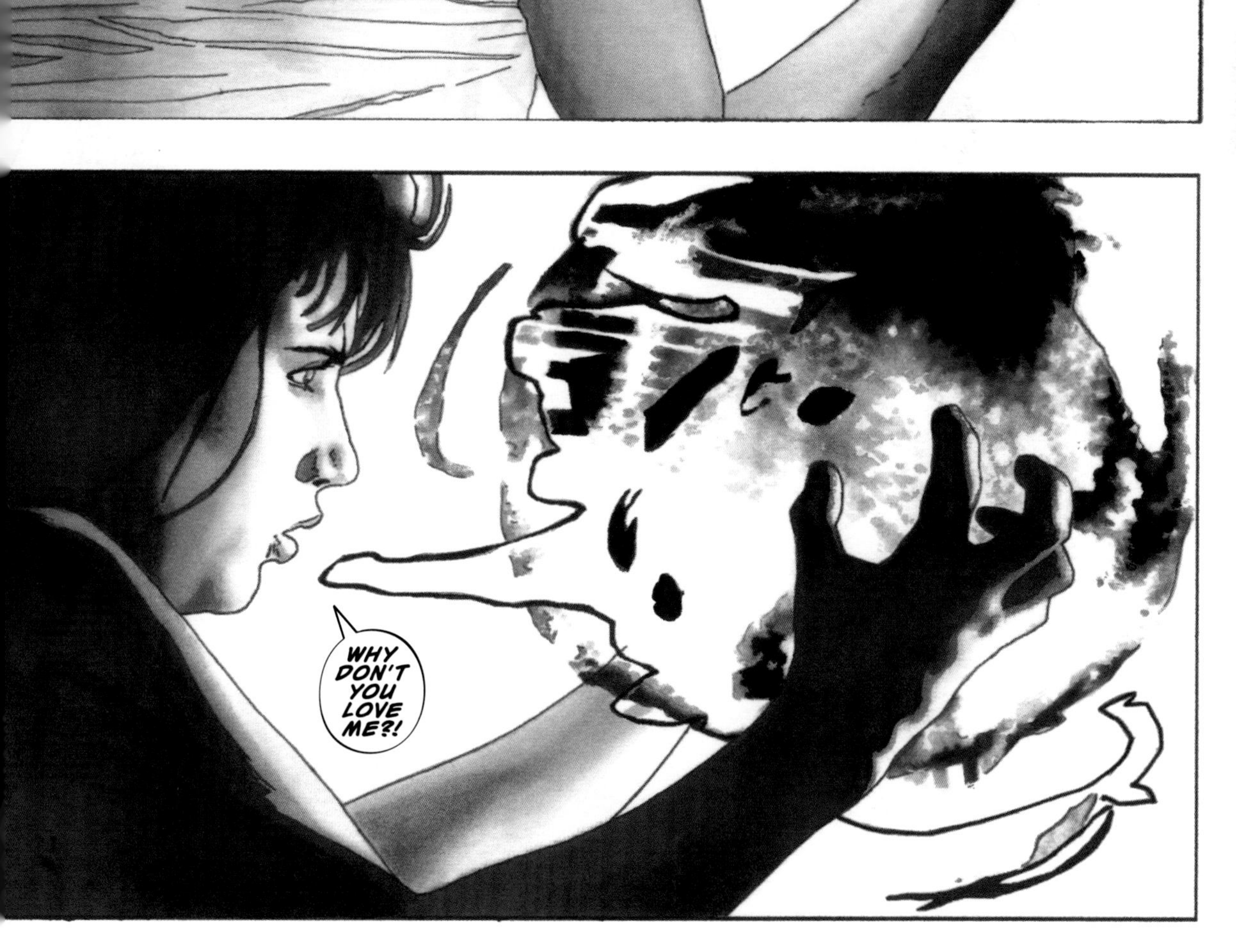
WHY DON'T YOU LOVE ME?!

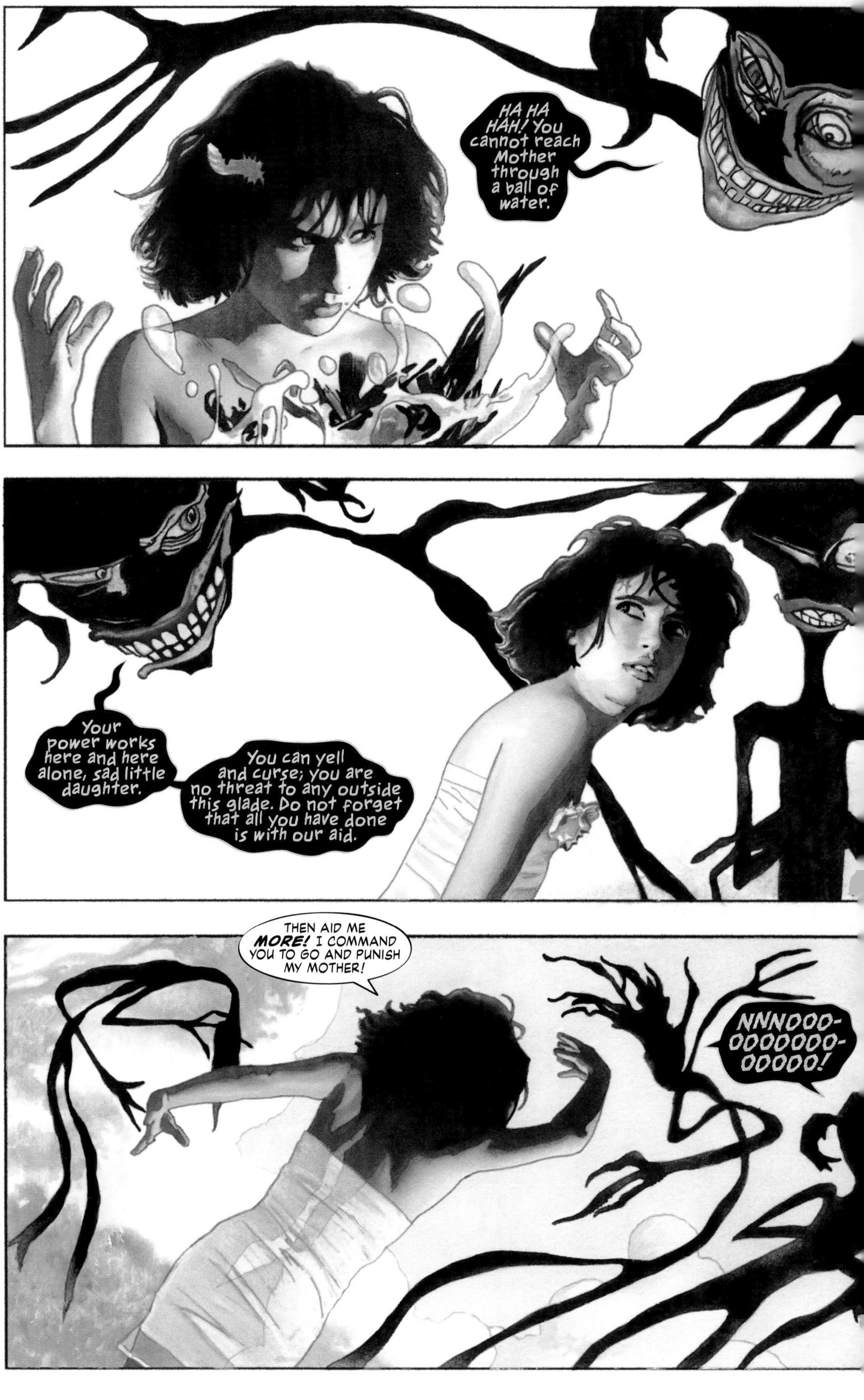
HA HA HAH! You cannot reach Mother through a ball of water.
Your power works here and here alone, sad little daughter.
You can yell and curse; you are no threat to any outside this glade. Do not forget that all you have done is with our aid.
THEN AID ME ***MORE!*** I COMMAND YOU TO GO AND PUNISH MY MOTHER!
NNNOOO-OOOOOOO-OOOOO!

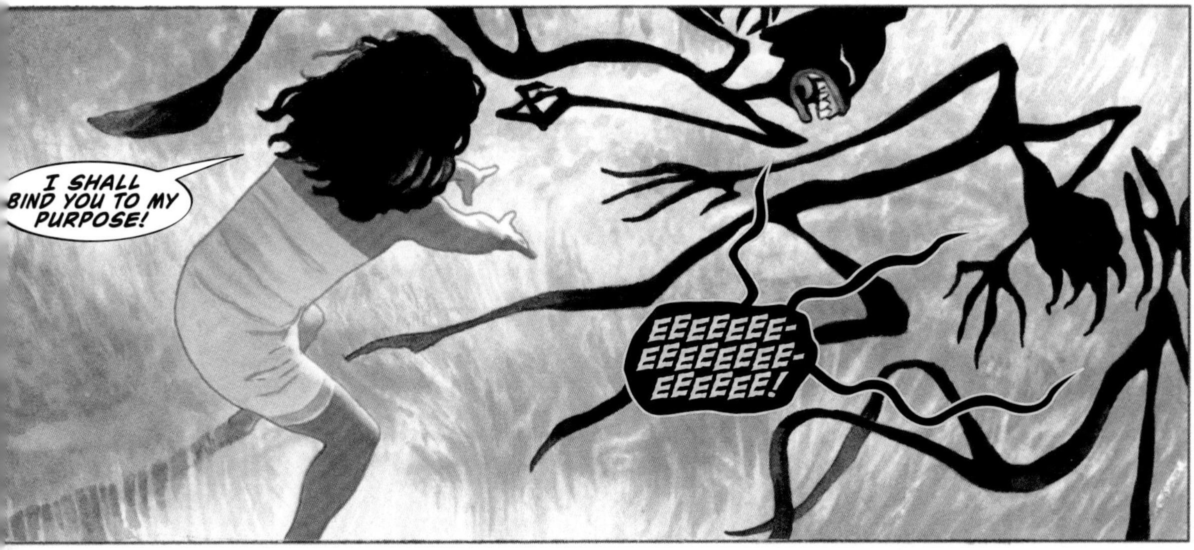
I SHALL BIND YOU TO MY PURPOSE!
EEEEEEE-EEEEEEEE-EEEEEE!

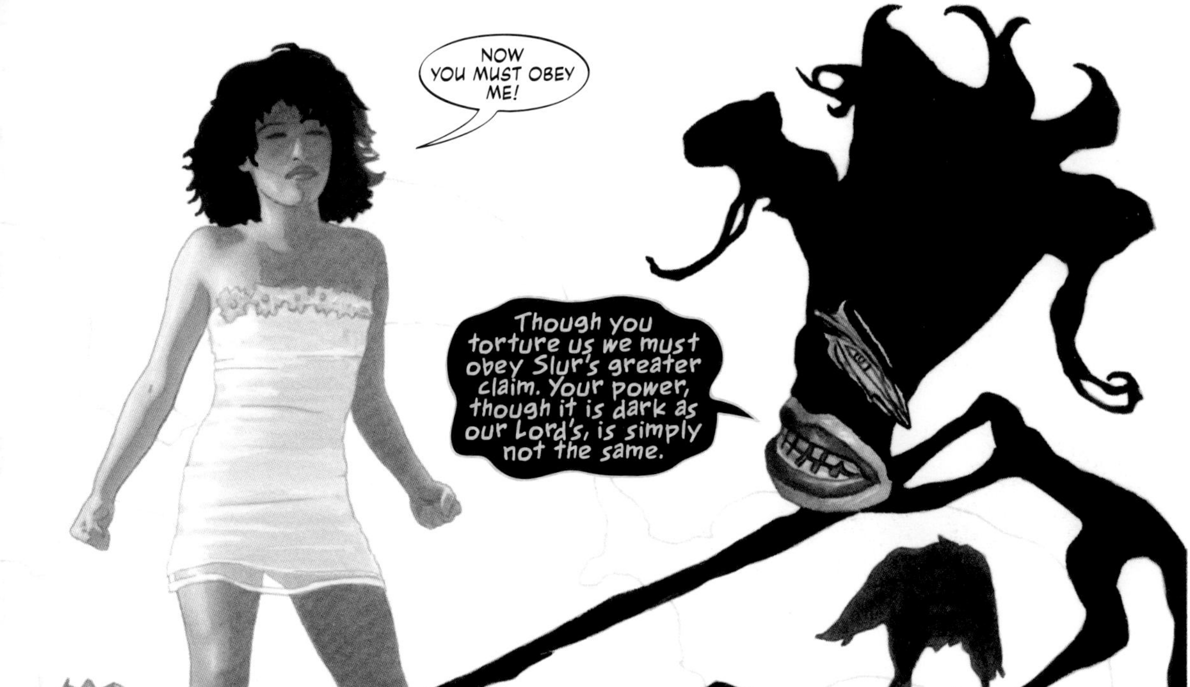
NOW YOU MUST OBEY ME!
Though you torture us we must obey Slur's greater claim. Your power, though it is dark as our Lord's, is simply not the same.

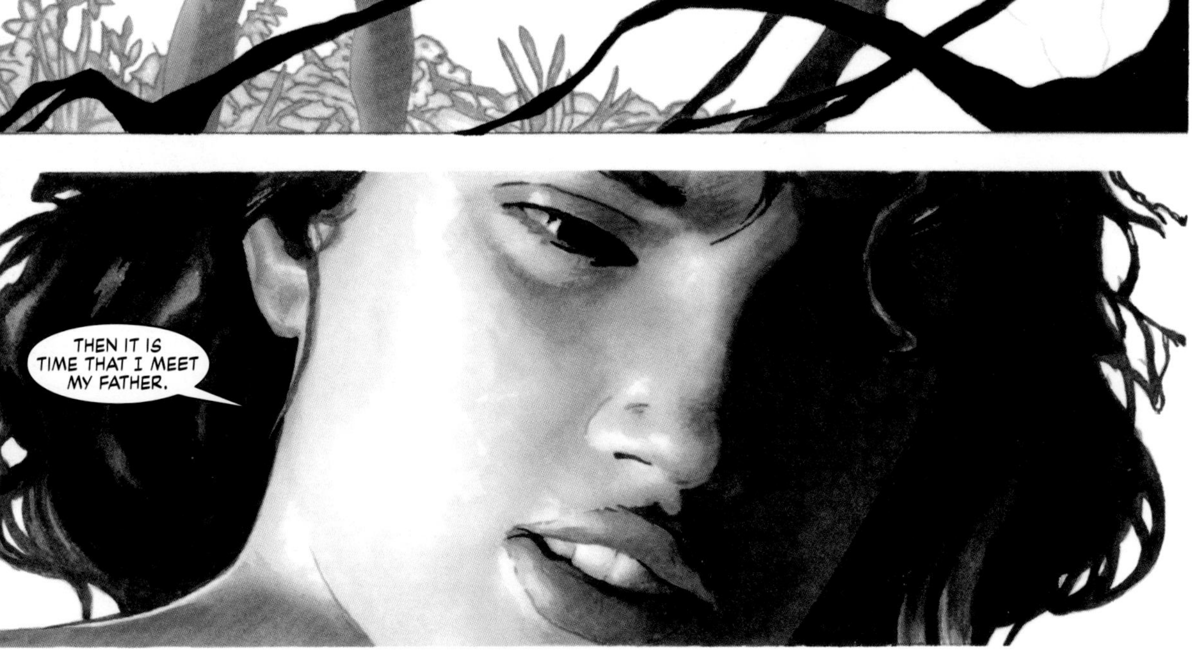
THEN IT IS TIME THAT I MEET MY FATHER.

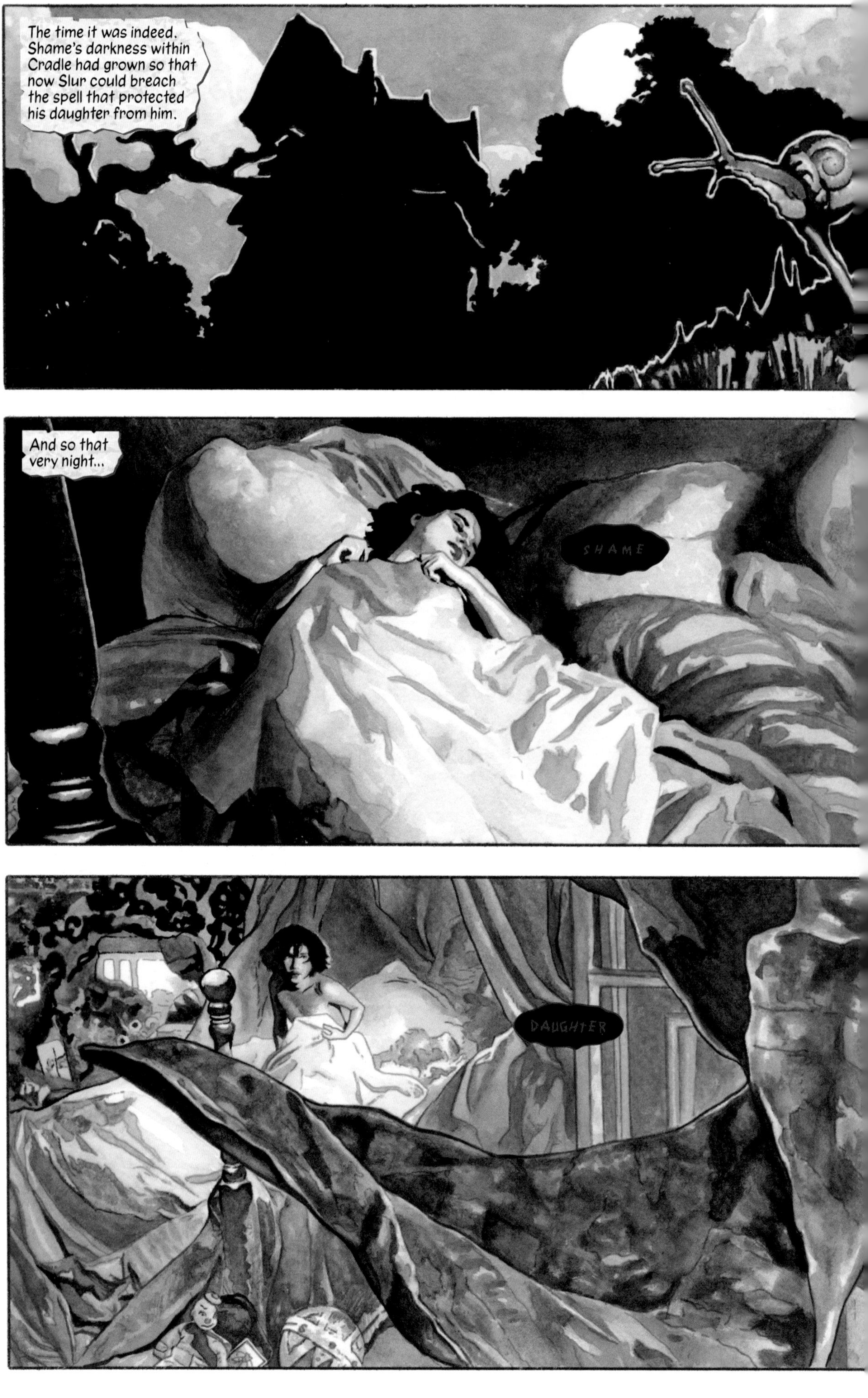
The time it was indeed. Shame's darkness within Cradle had grown so that now Slur could breach the spell that protected his daughter from him.
And so that very night...
SHAME
DAUGHTER

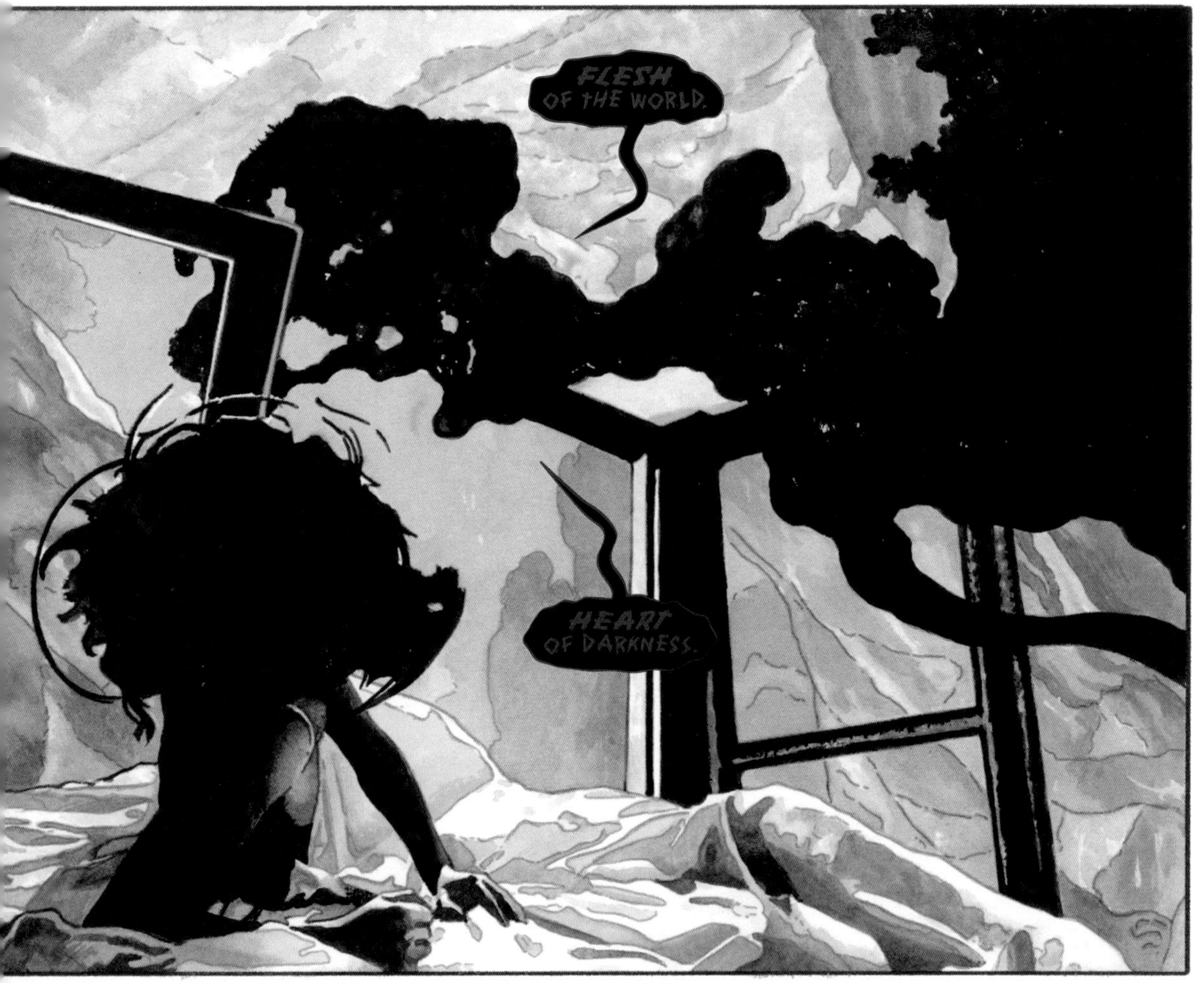
FLESH OF THE WORLD.
HEART OF DARKNESS.

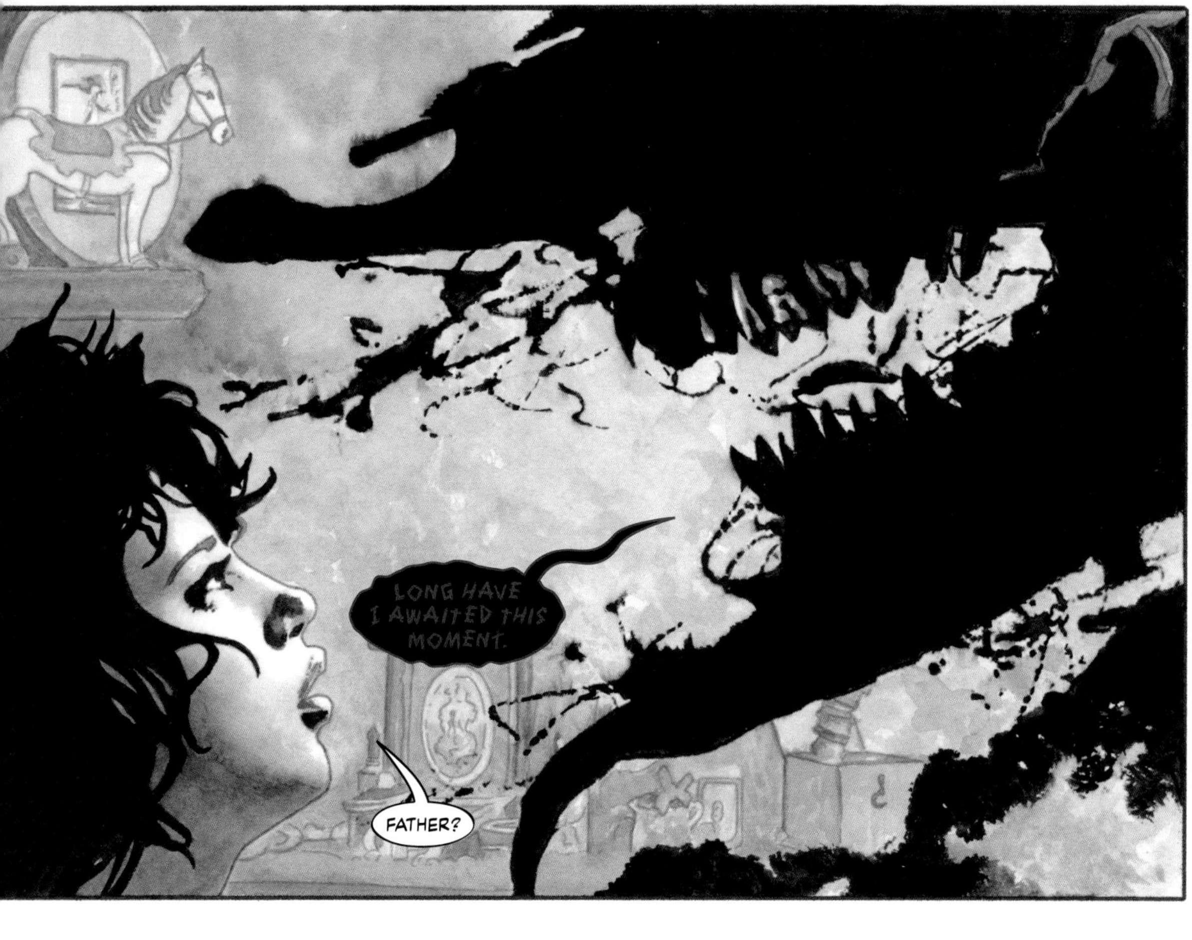
LONG HAVE I AWAITED THIS MOMENT.
FATHER?

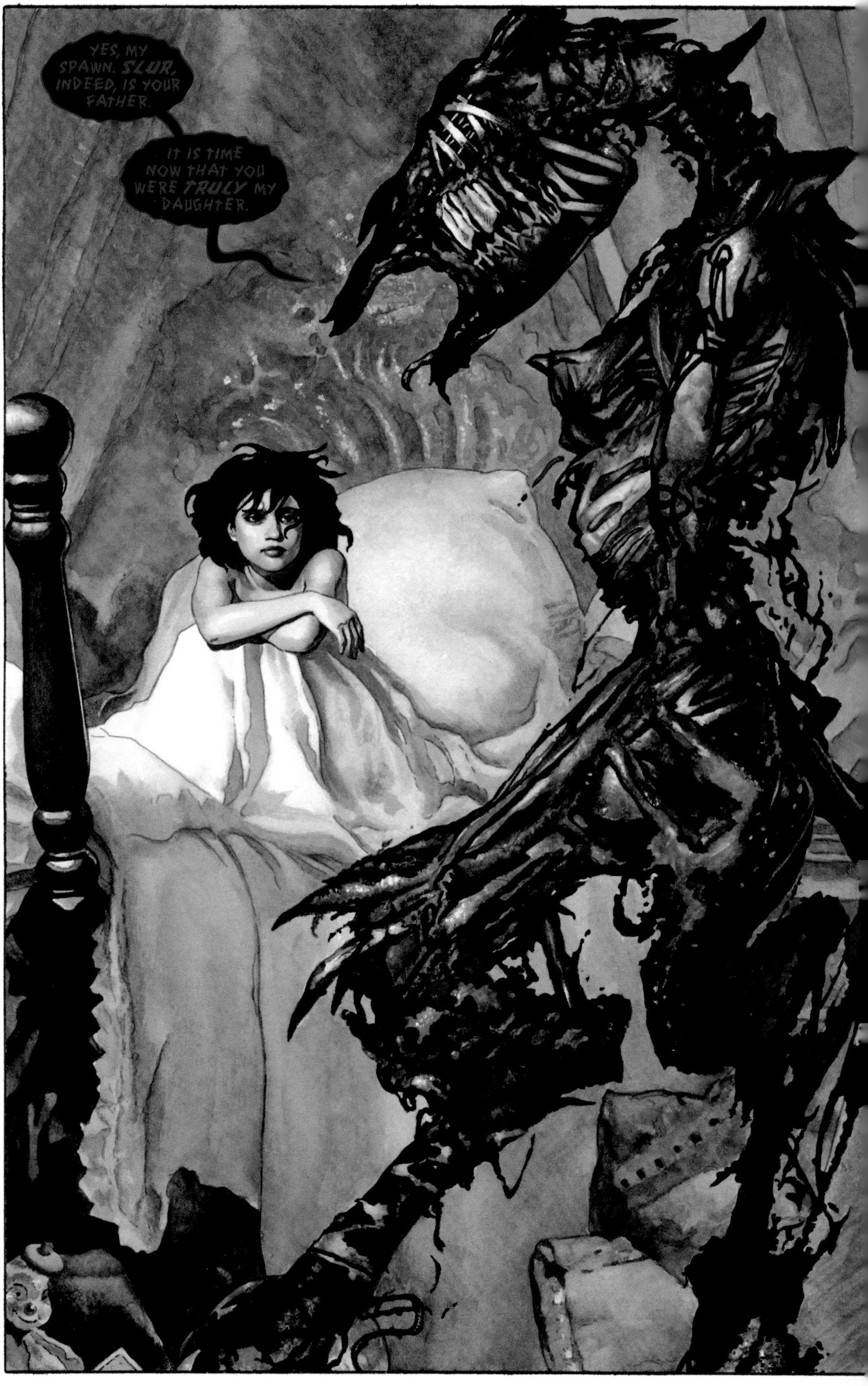
YES, MY SPAWN. SLUR, INDEED, IS YOUR FATHER.
IT IS TIME NOW THAT YOU WERE TRULY MY DAUGHTER.

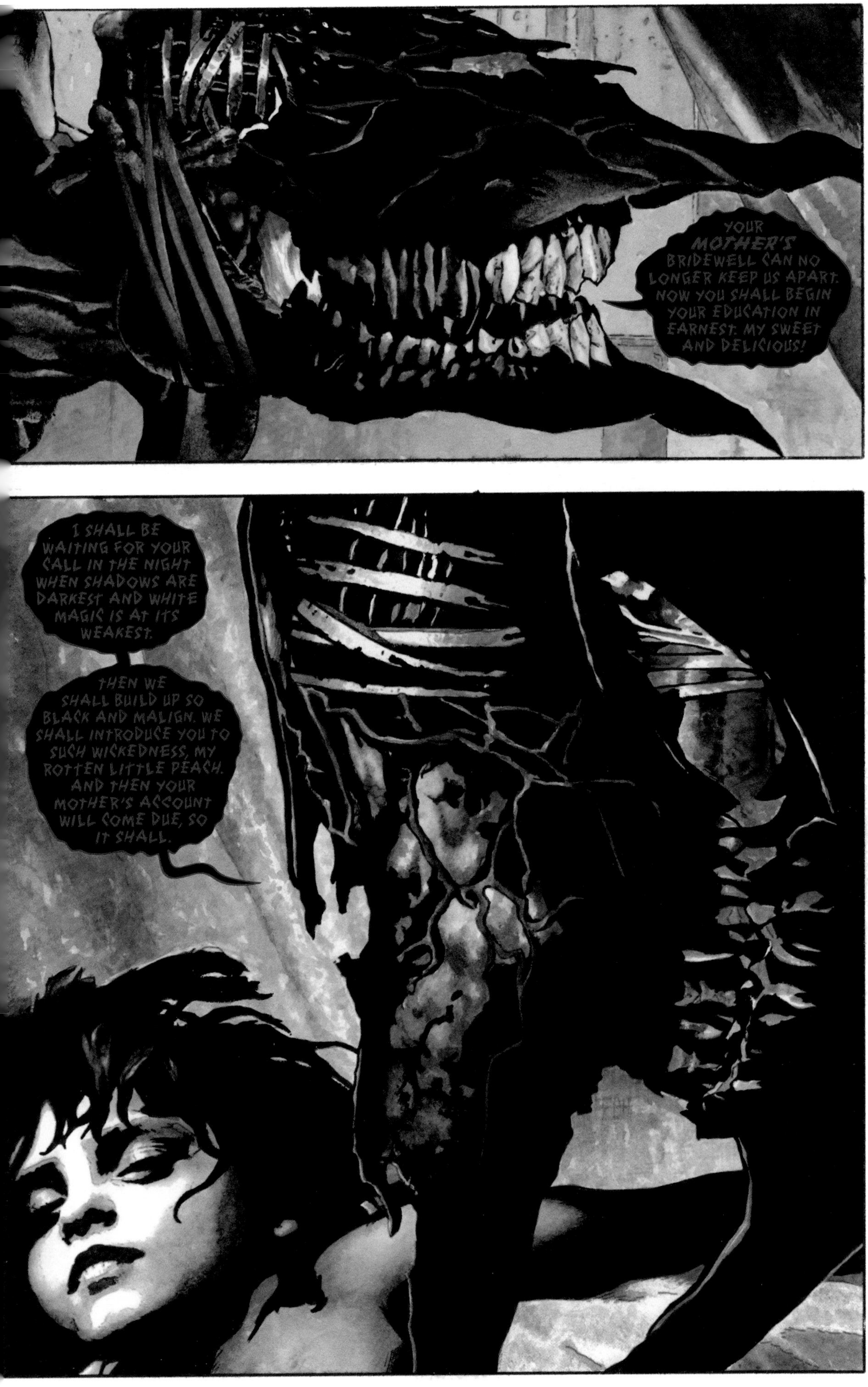
YOUR MOTHER'S BRIDEWELL CAN NO LONGER KEEP US APART. NOW YOU SHALL BEGIN YOUR EDUCATION IN EARNEST, MY SWEET AND DELICIOUS!
I SHALL BE WAITING FOR YOUR CALL IN THE NIGHT WHEN SHADOWS ARE DARKEST AND WHITE MAGIC IS AT ITS WEAKEST.
THEN WE SHALL BUILD UP SO BLACK AND MALIGN. WE SHALL INTRODUCE YOU TO SUCH WICKEDNESS, MY ROTTEN LITTLE PEACH. AND THEN YOUR MOTHER'S ACCOUNT WILL COME DUE, SO IT SHALL.

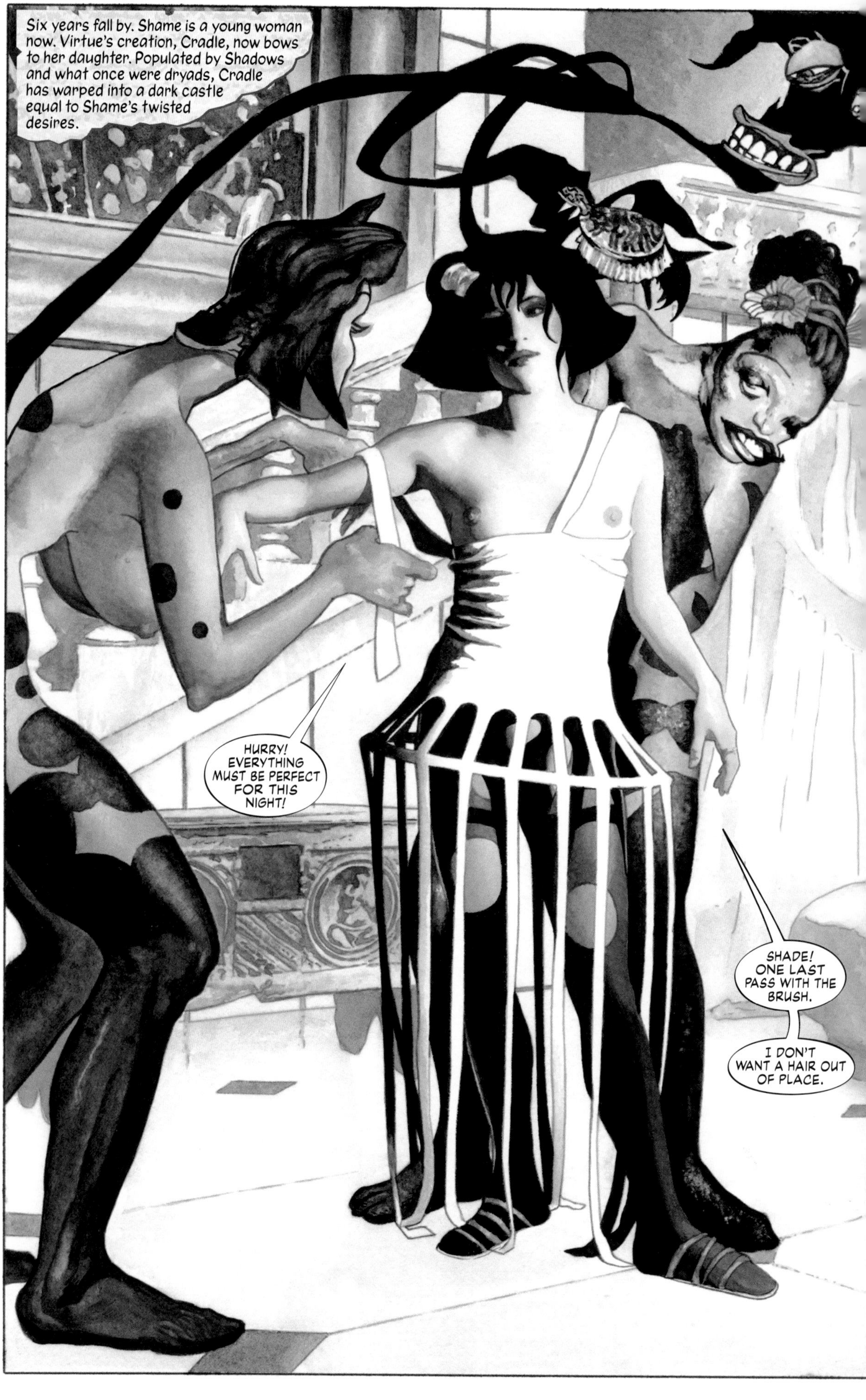
Six years fall by. Shame is a young woman now. Virtue's creation, Cradle, now bows to her daughter. Populated by Shadows and what once were dryads, Cradle has warped into a dark castle equal to Shame's twisted desires.
HURRY! EVERYTHING MUST BE PERFECT FOR THIS NIGHT!
SHADE! ONE LAST PASS WITH THE BRUSH.
I DON'T WANT A HAIR OUT OF PLACE.

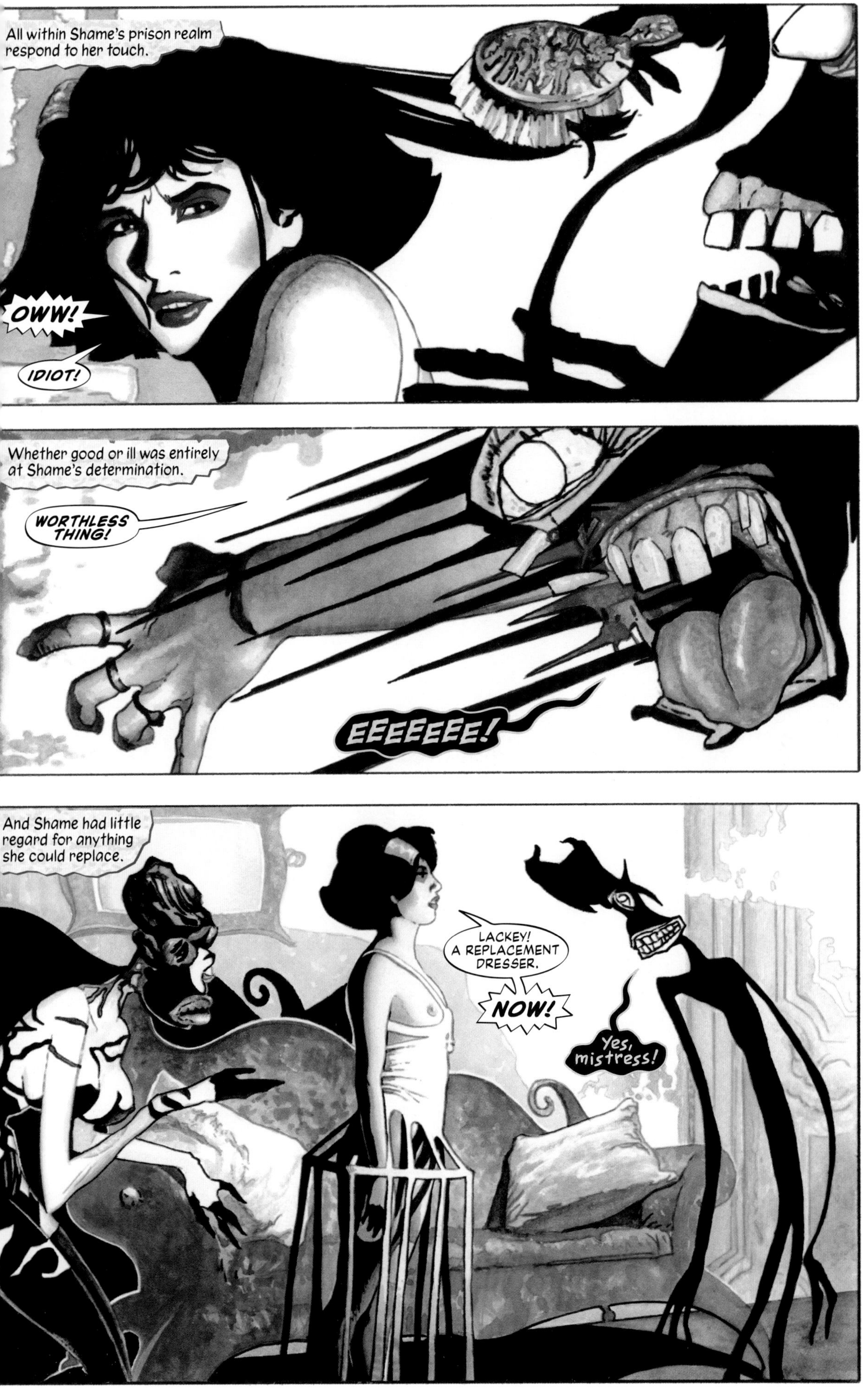
All within Shame's prison realm respond to her touch.
OWW!
IDIOT!
Whether good or ill was entirely at Shame's determination.
WORTHLESS THING!
EEEEEEE!
And Shame had little regard for anything she could replace.
LACKEY! A REPLACEMENT DRESSER.
NOW!
Yes, mistress!

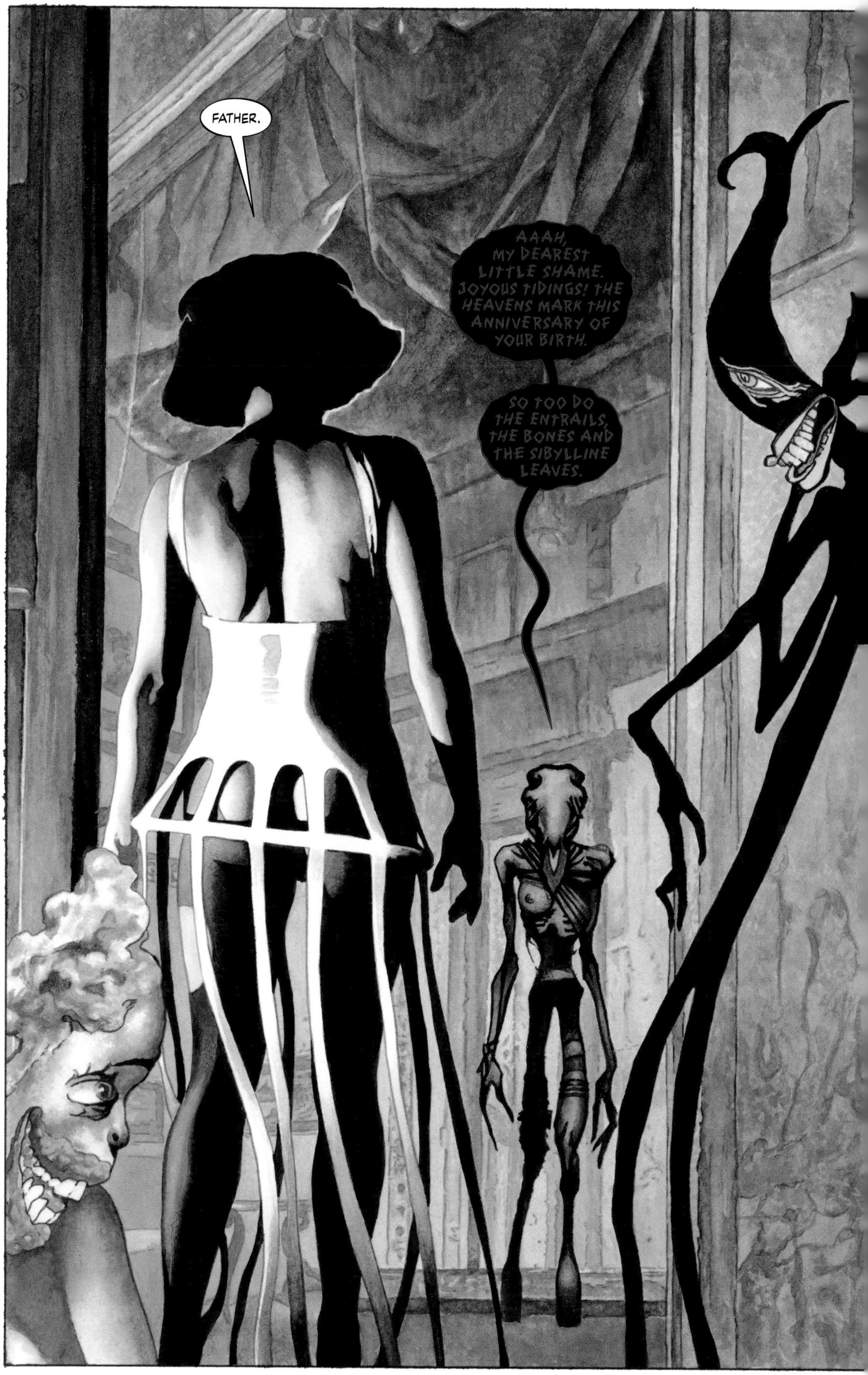
FATHER.
AAAH, MY DEAREST LITTLE SHAME. JOYOUS TIDINGS! THE HEAVENS MARK THIS ANNIVERSARY OF YOUR BIRTH.
SO TOO DO THE ENTRAILS, THE BONES AND THE SIBYLLINE LEAVES.

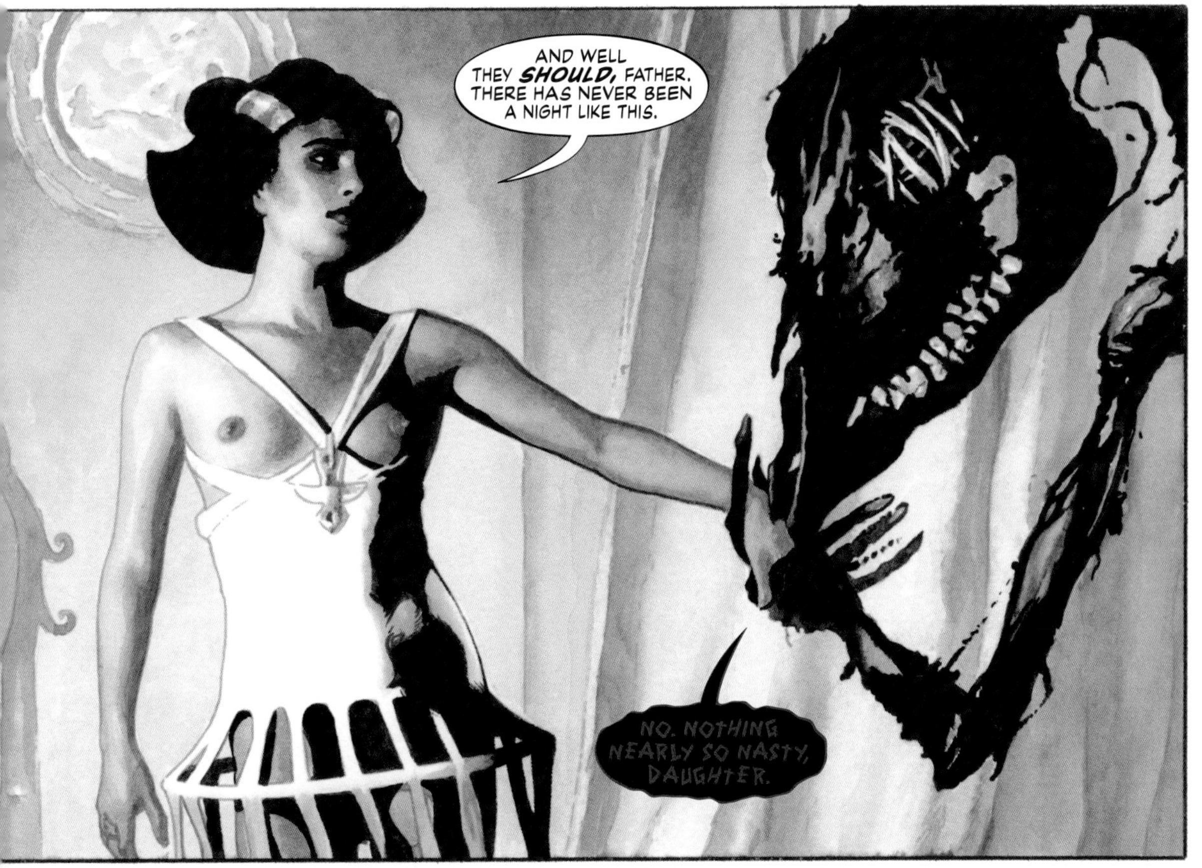
AND WELL THEY SHOULD, FATHER. THERE HAS NEVER BEEN A NIGHT LIKE THIS.
NO. NOTHING NEARLY SO NASTY, DAUGHTER.

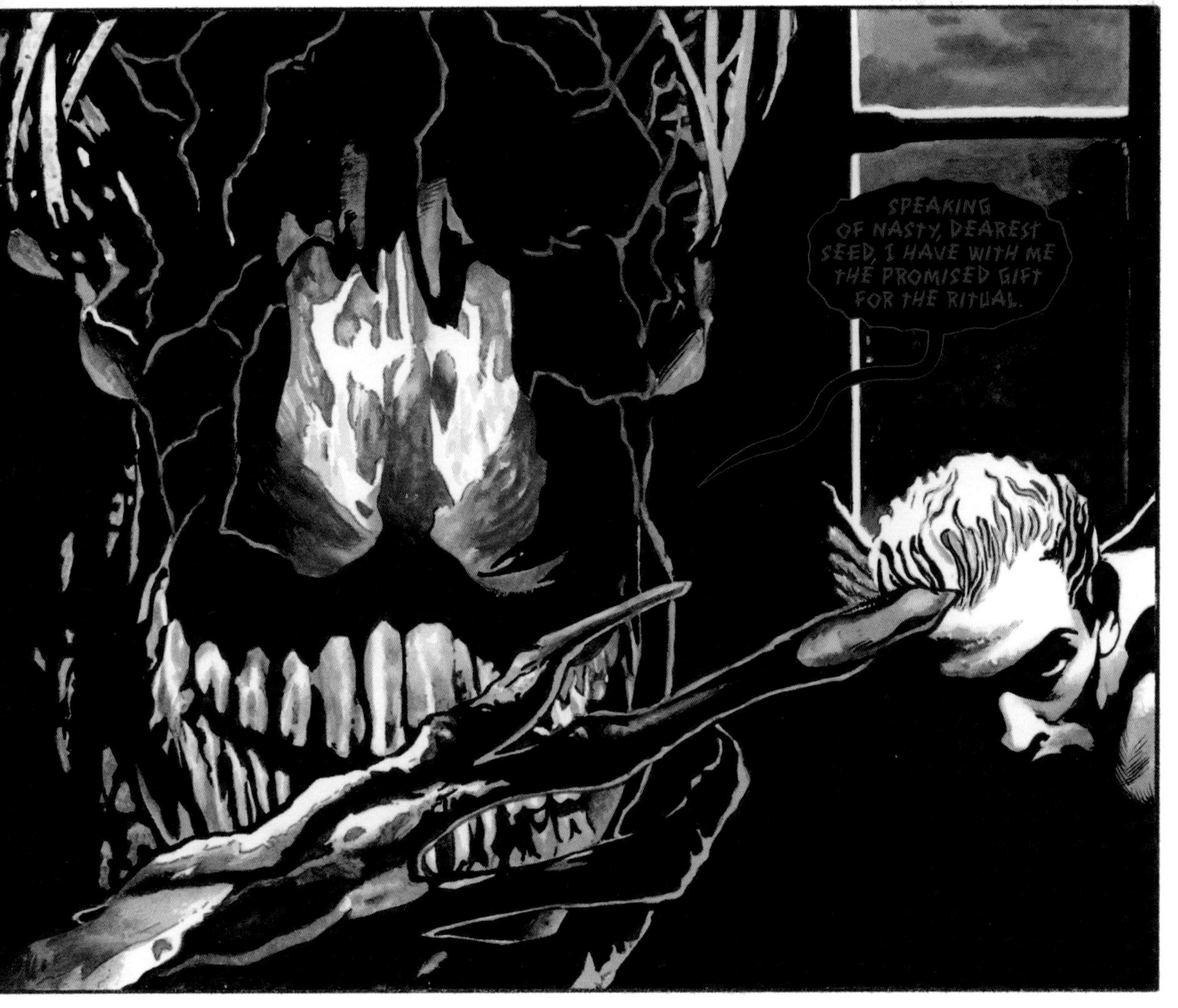
SPEAKING OF NASTY, DEAREST SEED, I HAVE WITH ME THE PROMISED GIFT FOR THE RITUAL.

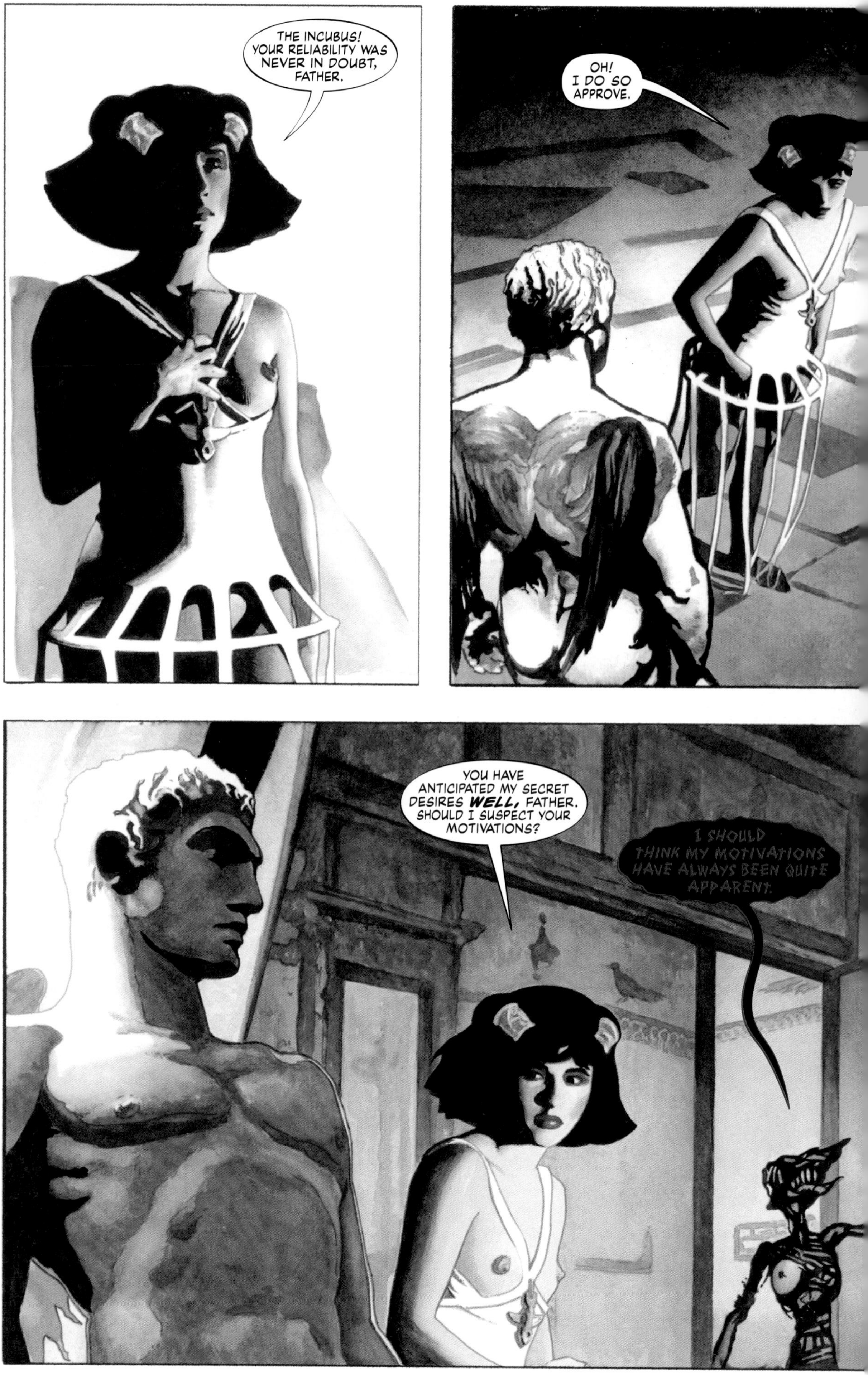
THE INCUBUS! YOUR RELIABILITY WAS NEVER IN DOUBT, FATHER.
OH! I DO SO APPROVE.
YOU HAVE ANTICIPATED MY SECRET DESIRES WELL, FATHER. SHOULD I SUSPECT YOUR MOTIVATIONS?
I SHOULD THINK MY MOTIVATIONS HAVE ALWAYS BEEN QUITE APPARENT.

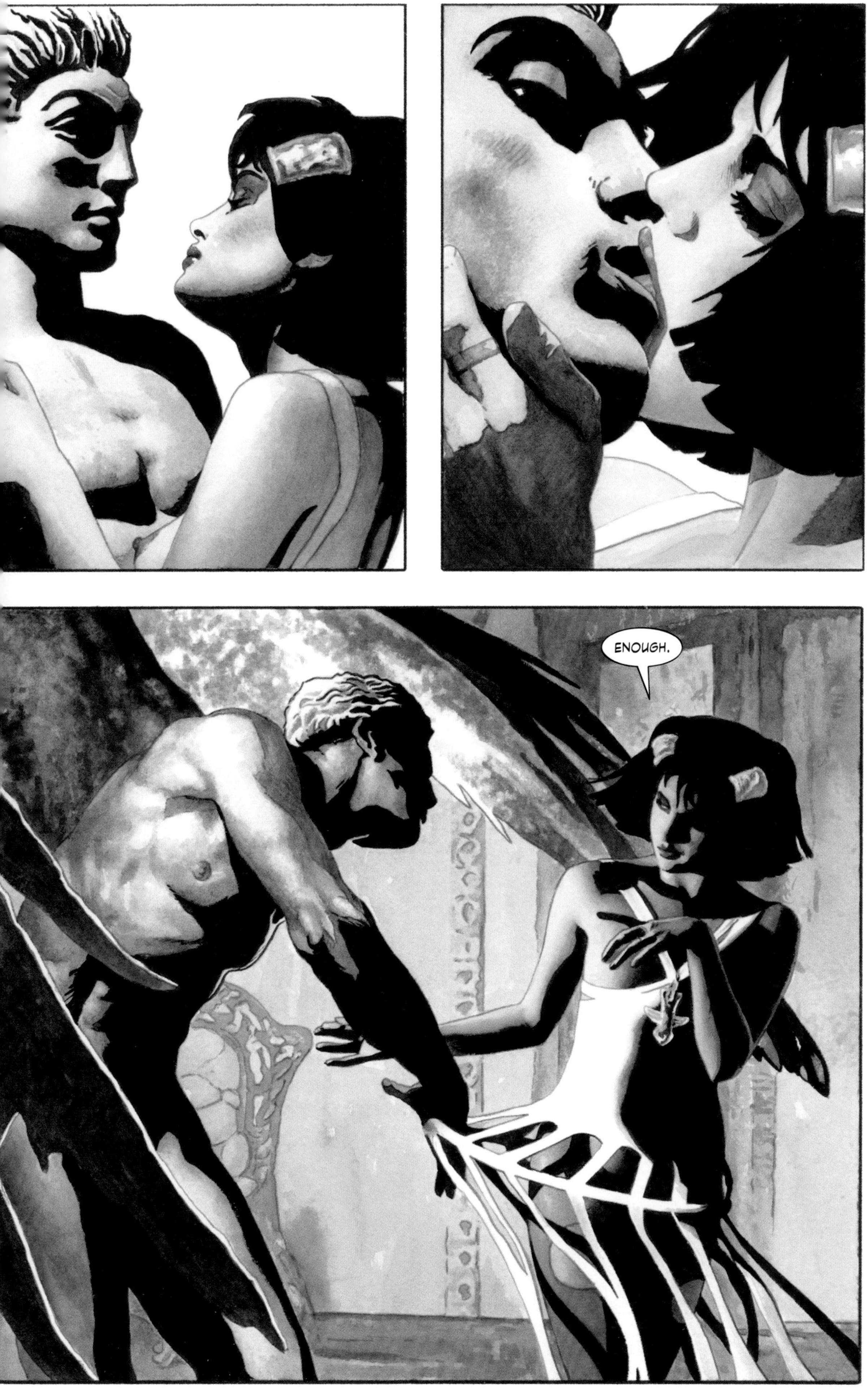
ENOUGH.

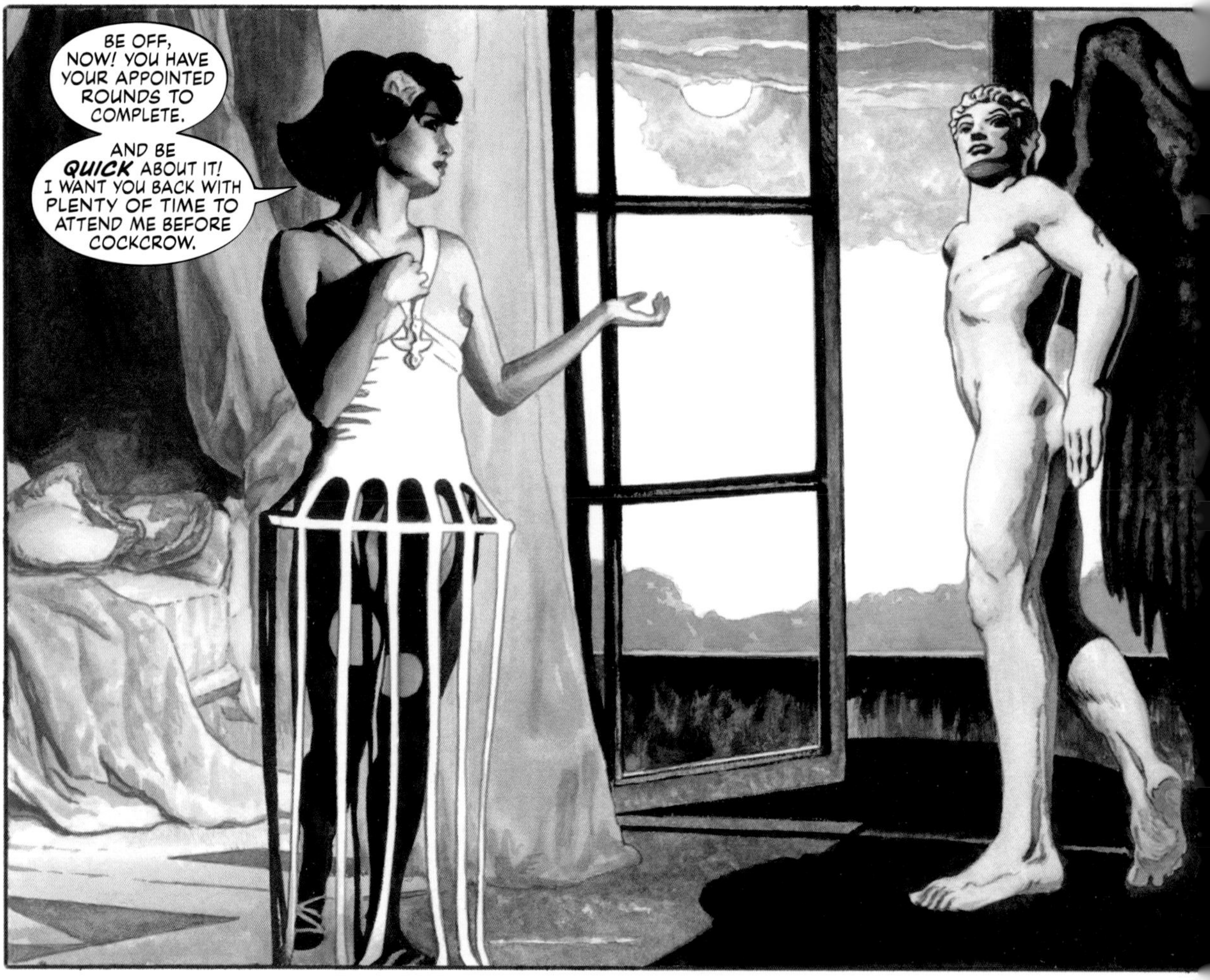
BE OFF, NOW! YOU HAVE YOUR APPOINTED ROUNDS TO COMPLETE.
AND BE **QUICK** ABOUT IT! I WANT YOU BACK WITH PLENTY OF TIME TO ATTEND ME BEFORE COCKCROW.

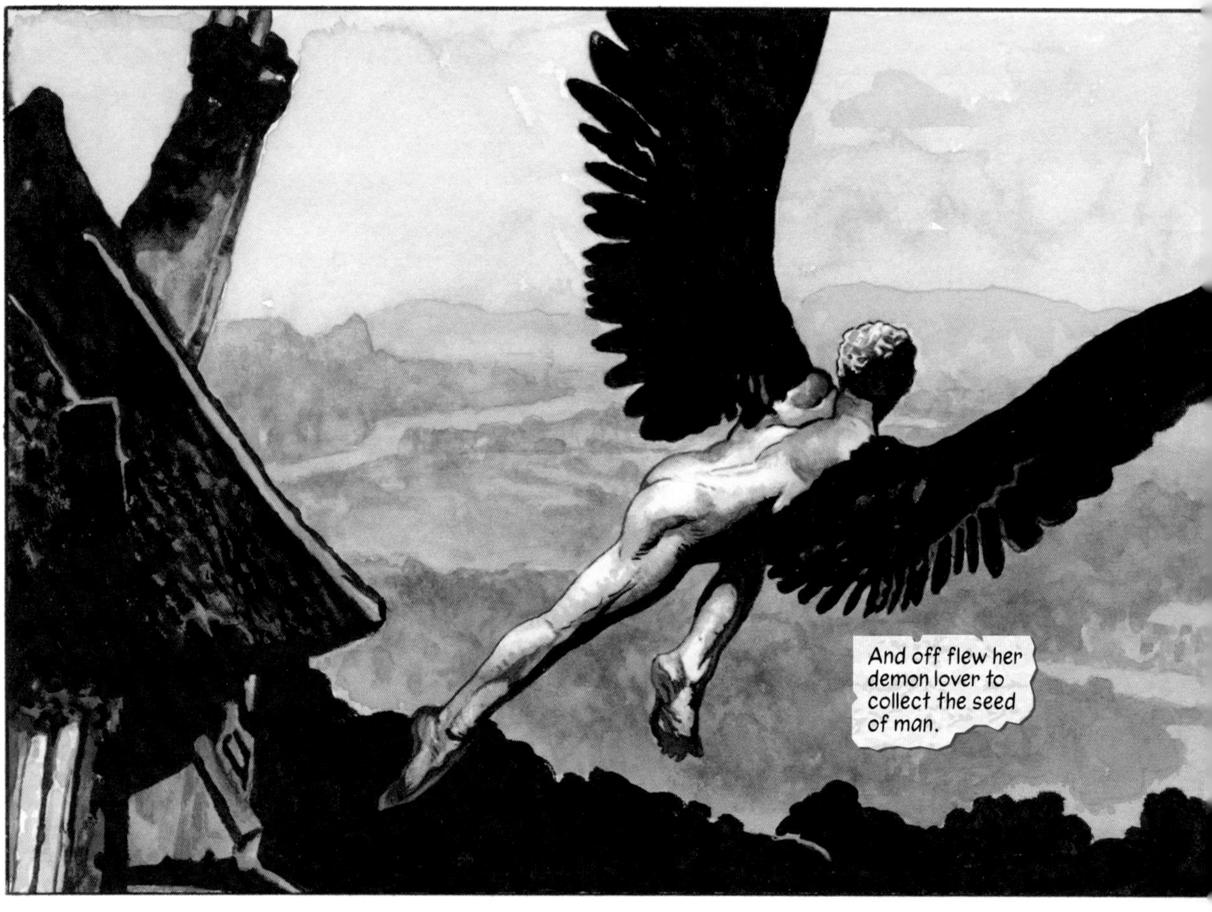
And off flew her demon lover to collect the seed of man.

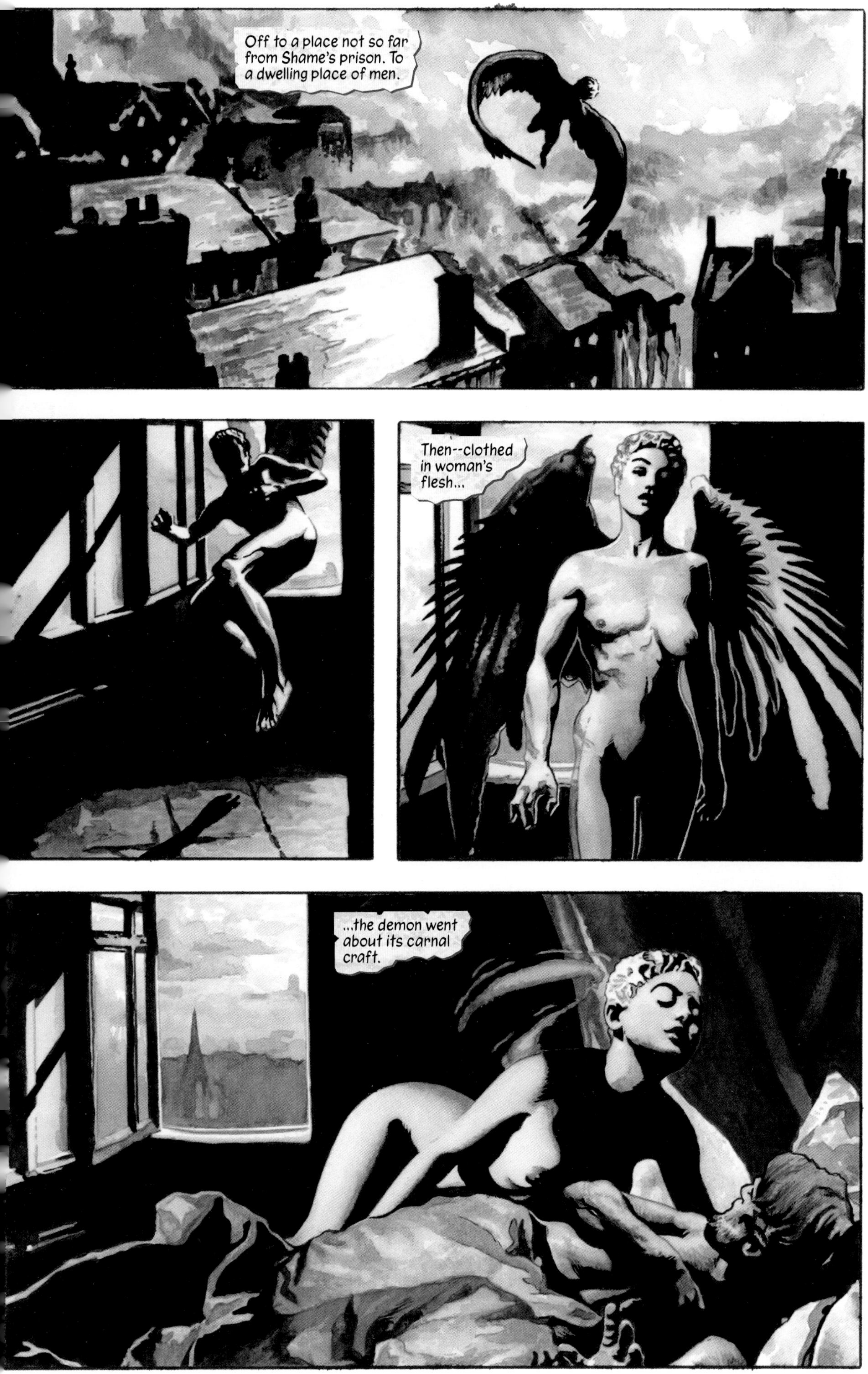
Off to a place not so far from Shame's prison. To a dwelling place of men.
Then--clothed in woman's flesh...
...the demon went about its carnal craft.

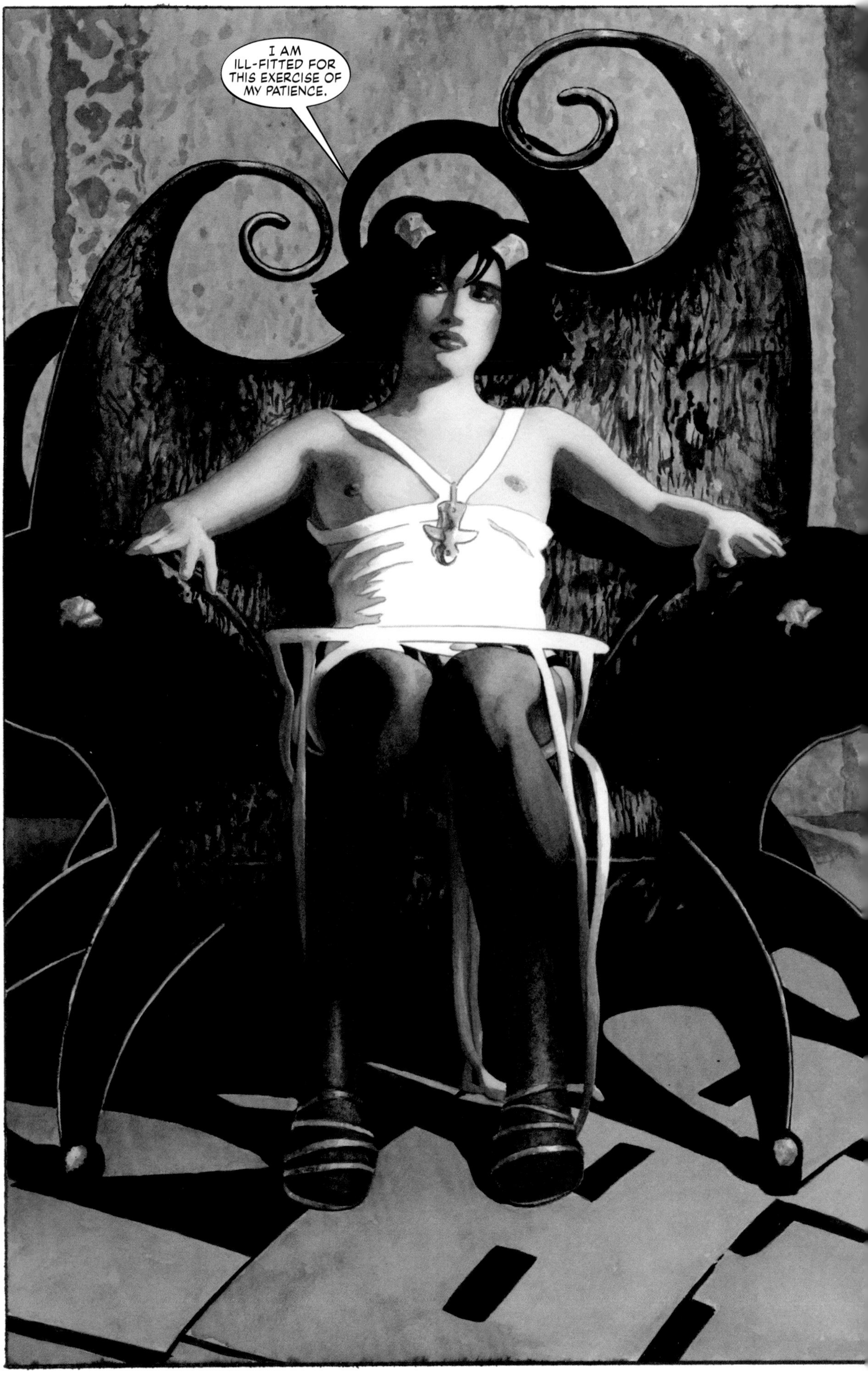
I AM ILL-FITTED FOR THIS EXERCISE OF MY PATIENCE.

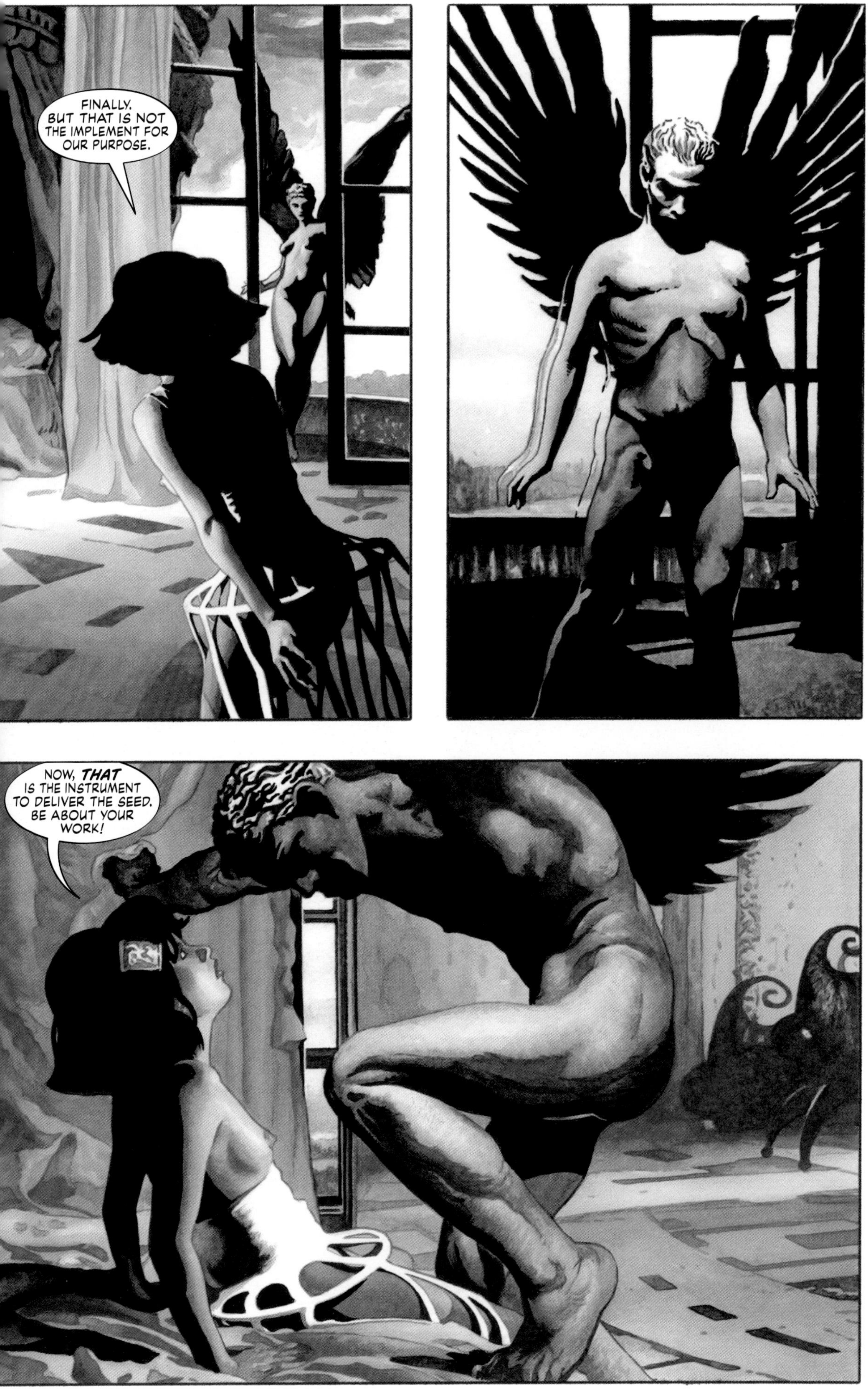
FINALLY. BUT THAT IS NOT THE IMPLEMENT FOR OUR PURPOSE.
NOW, ***THAT*** IS THE INSTRUMENT TO DELIVER THE SEED. BE ABOUT YOUR WORK!

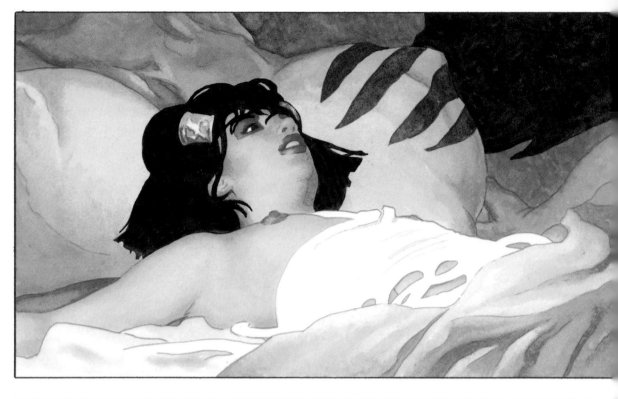

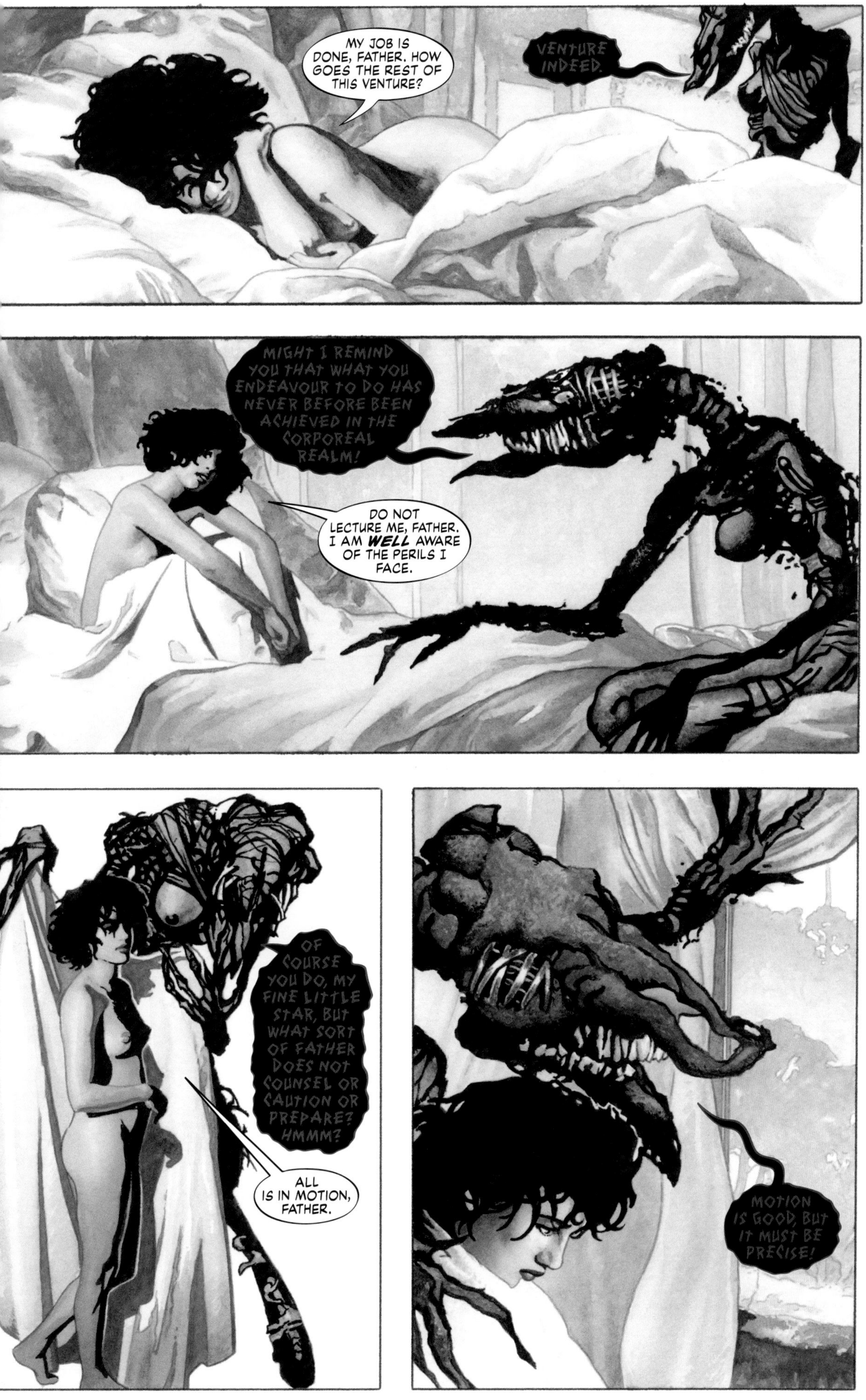
MY JOB IS DONE, FATHER. HOW GOES THE REST OF THIS VENTURE?
VENTURE INDEED.
MIGHT I REMIND YOU THAT WHAT YOU ENDEAVOUR TO DO HAS NEVER BEFORE BEEN ACHIEVED IN THE CORPOREAL REALM!
DO NOT LECTURE ME, FATHER. I AM WELL AWARE OF THE PERILS I FACE.
OF COURSE YOU DO, MY FINE LITTLE STAR, BUT WHAT SORT OF FATHER DOES NOT COUNSEL OR CAUTION OR PREPARE? HMMM?
ALL IS IN MOTION, FATHER.
MOTION IS GOOD, BUT IT MUST BE PRECISE!

Nine long months have passed.

Cradle and its grounds reek with the smell of oils torn from the living plants and creatures of the darkling glade.

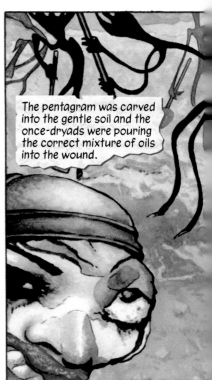

The pentagram was carved into the gentle soil and the once-dryads were pouring the correct mixture of oils into the wound.

CAREFUL WITH THAT MIXTURE OR YOU'LL BE IN THE *PRESS* FOR THE NEXT BATCH!

And so proceeded the plans for the night of revenge!

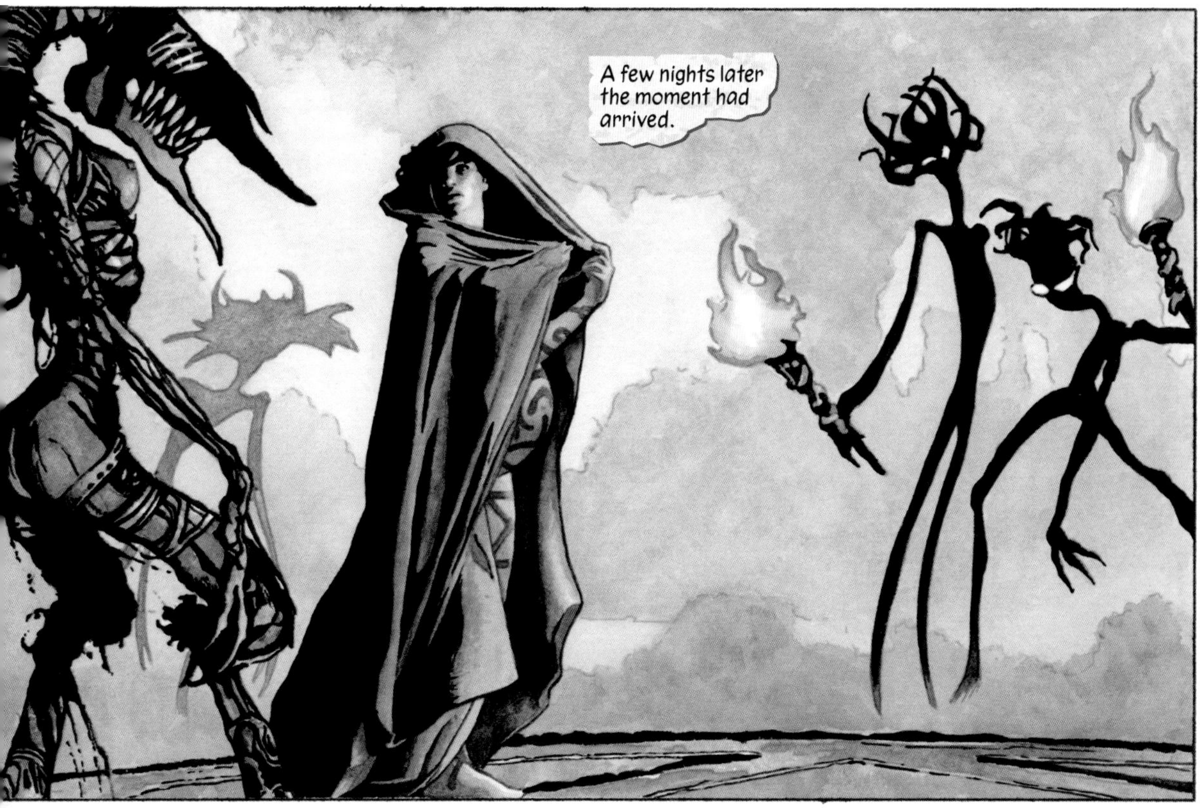
A few nights later the moment had arrived.

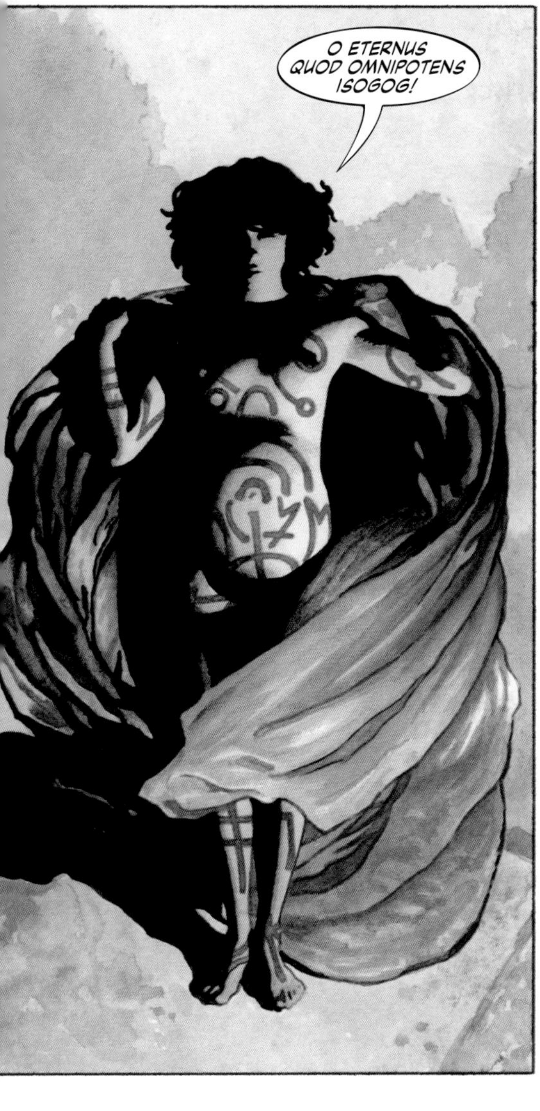
O ETERNUS QUOD OMNIPOTENS ISOGOG!

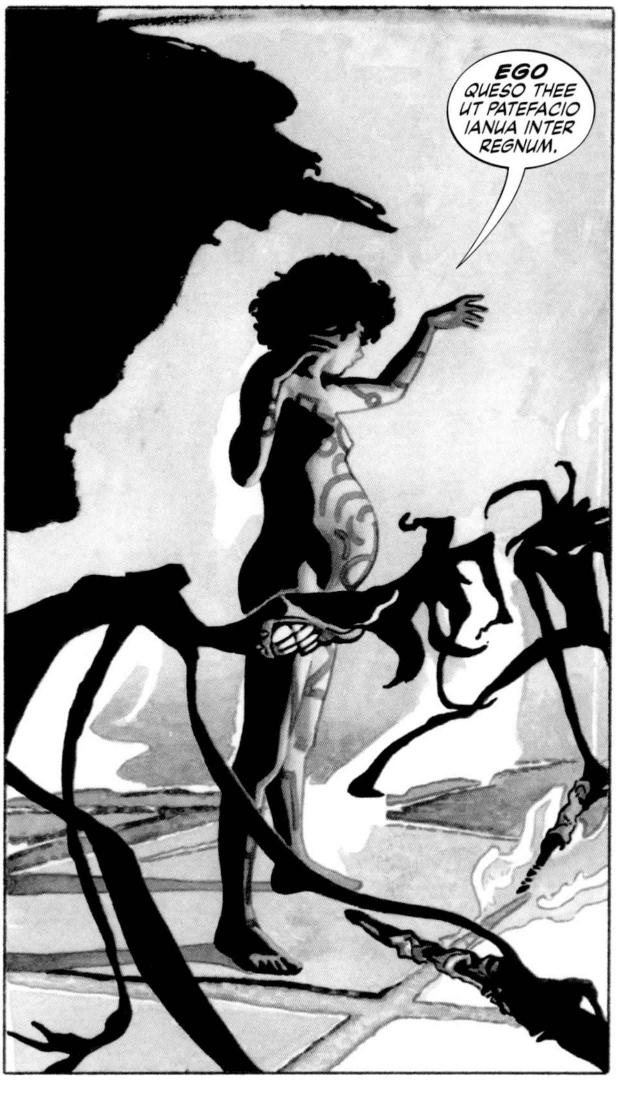
EGO QUESO THEE UT PATEFACIO IANUA INTER REGNUM.

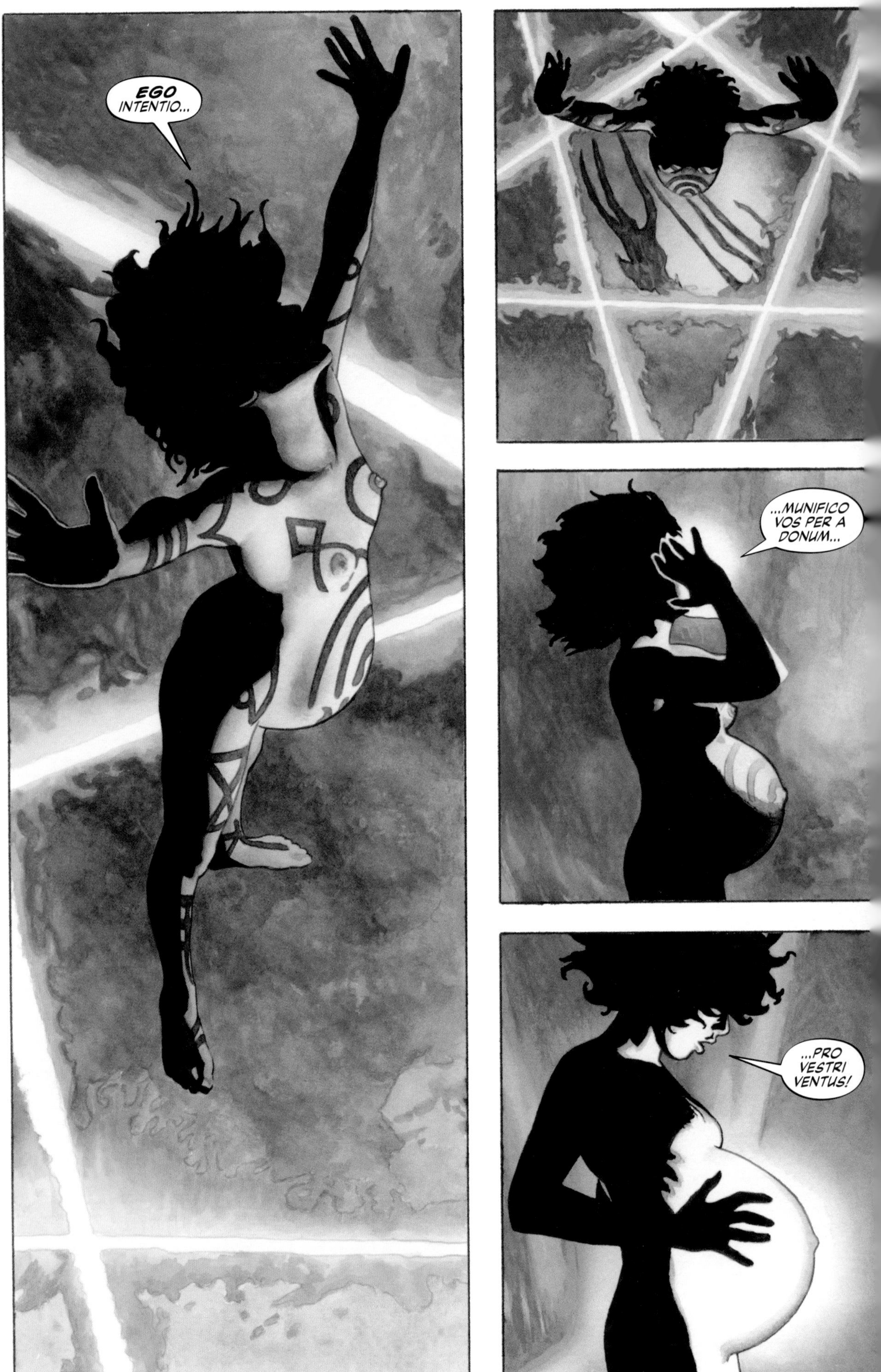
EGO INTENTIO...
...MUNIFICO VOS PER A DONUM...
...PRO VESTRI VENTUS!

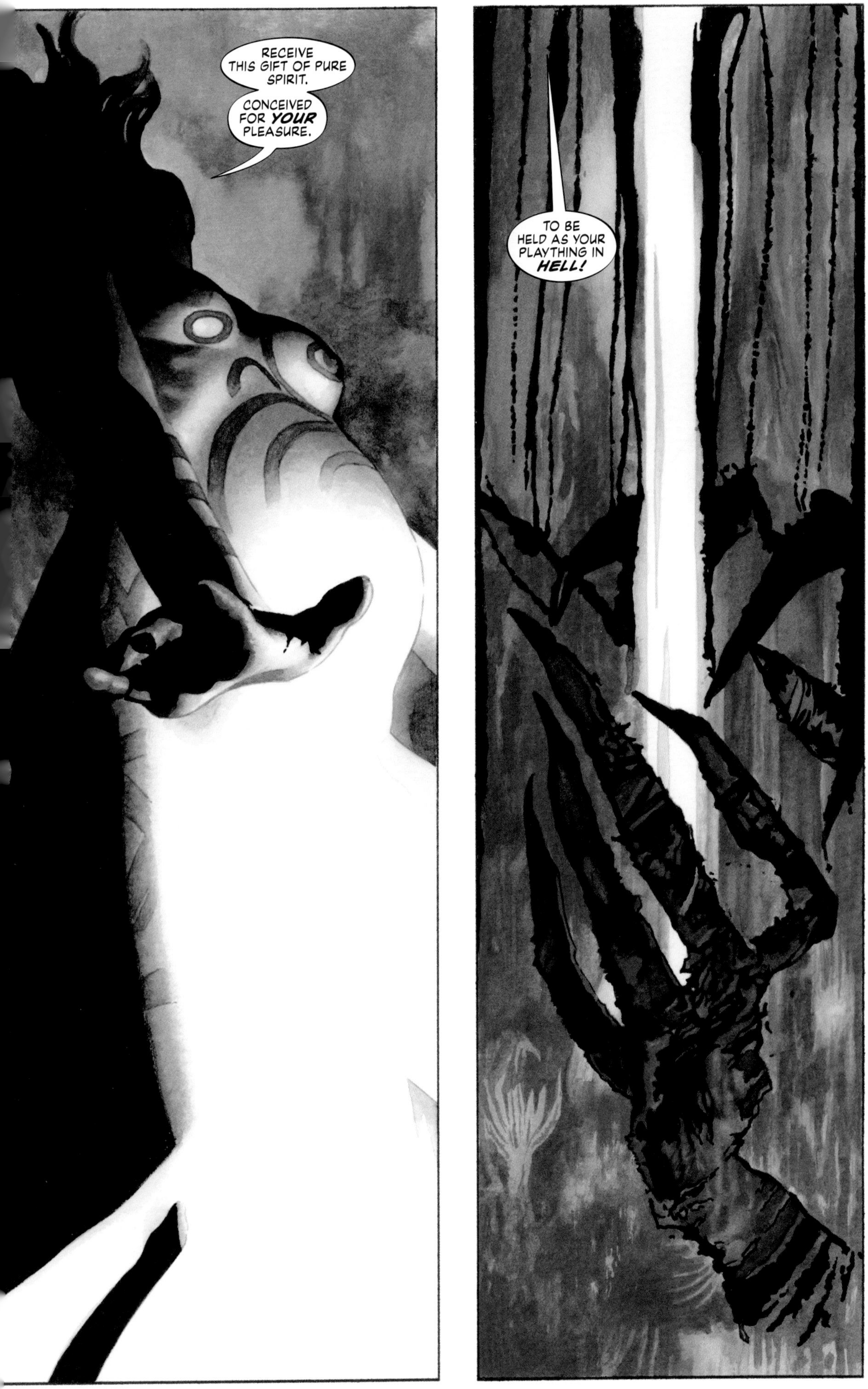
RECEIVE THIS GIFT OF PURE SPIRIT.
CONCEIVED FOR YOUR PLEASURE.
TO BE HELD AS YOUR PLAYTHING IN HELL!

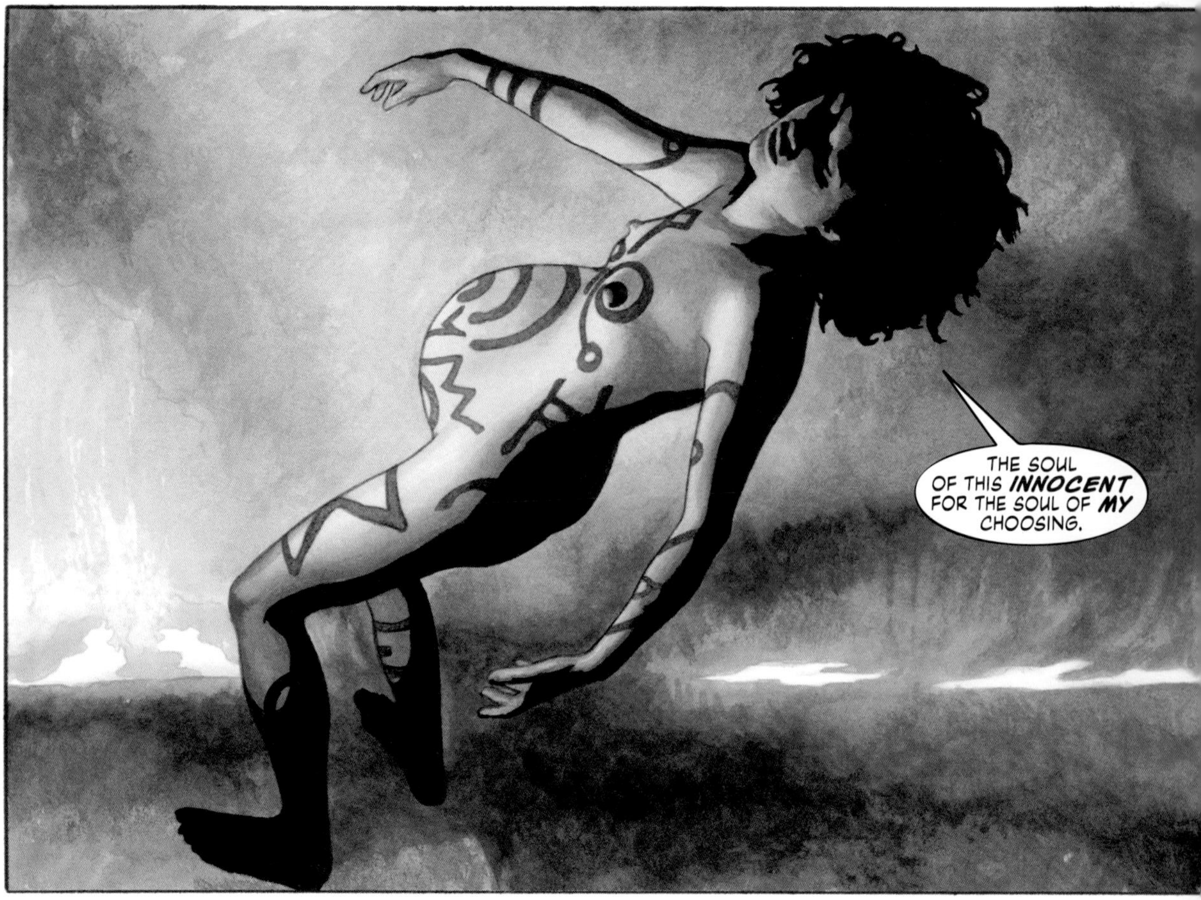
THE SOUL OF THIS **INNOCENT** FOR THE SOUL OF **MY** CHOOSING.

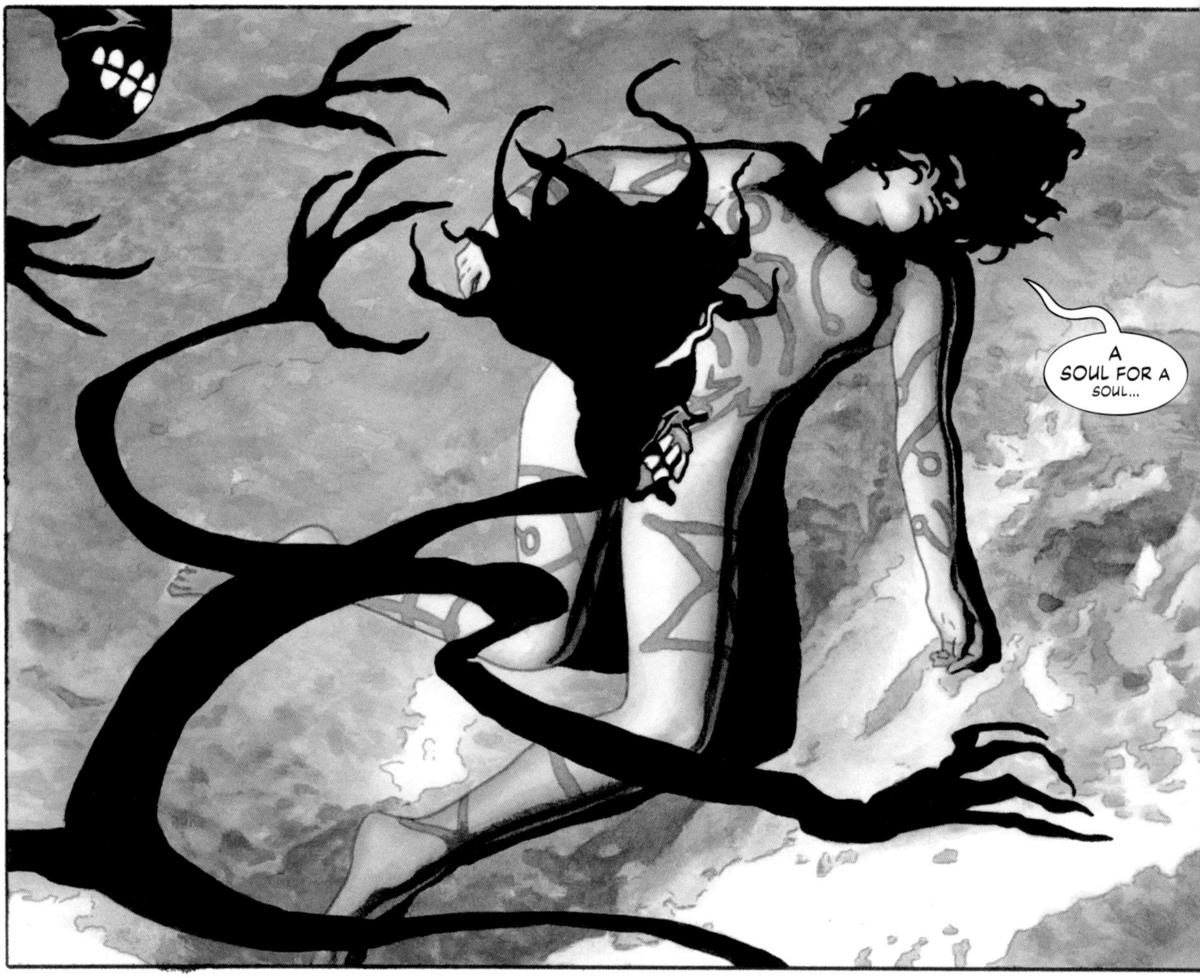
A SOUL FOR A SOUL...

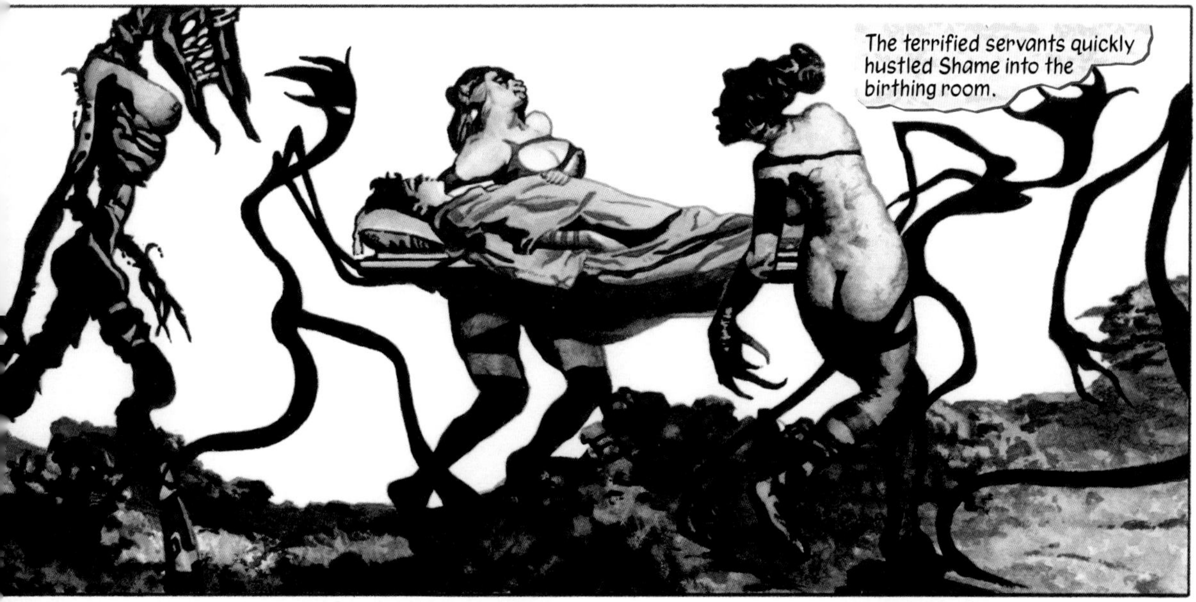
The terrified servants quickly hustled Shame into the birthing room.

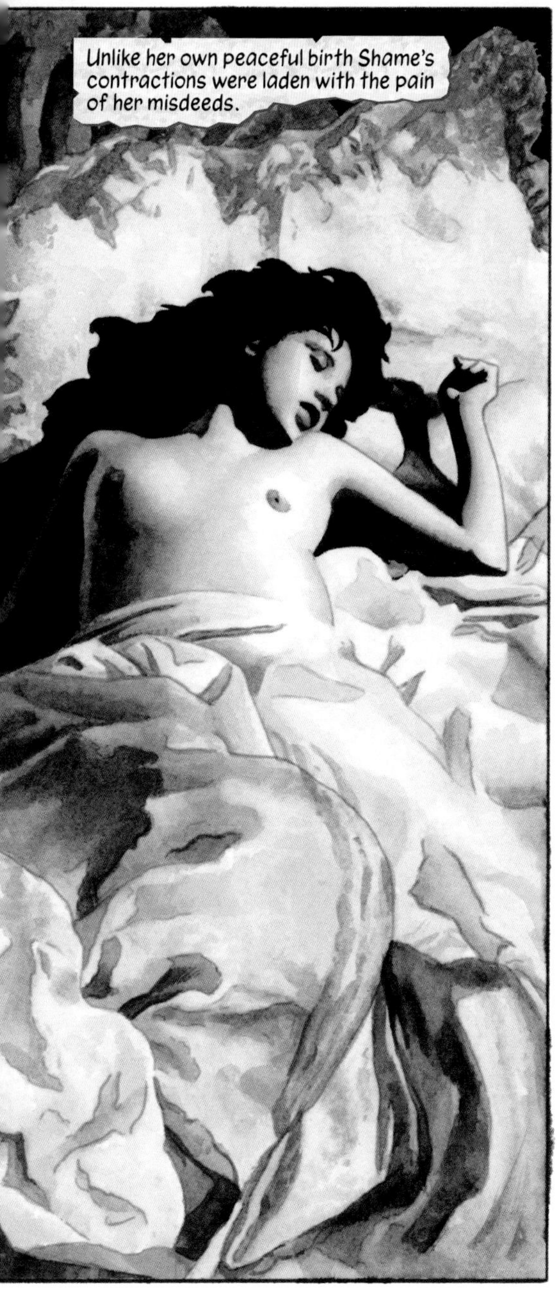
Unlike her own peaceful birth Shame's contractions were laden with the pain of her misdeeds.

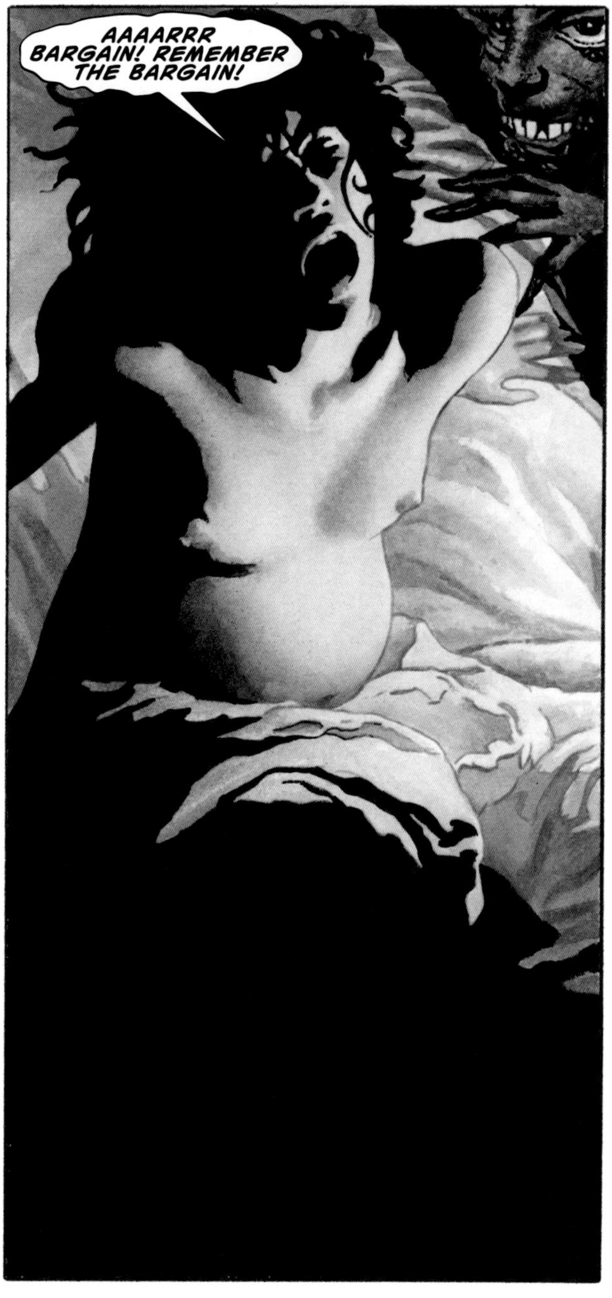
AAAAARRR BARGAIN! REMEMBER THE BARGAIN!

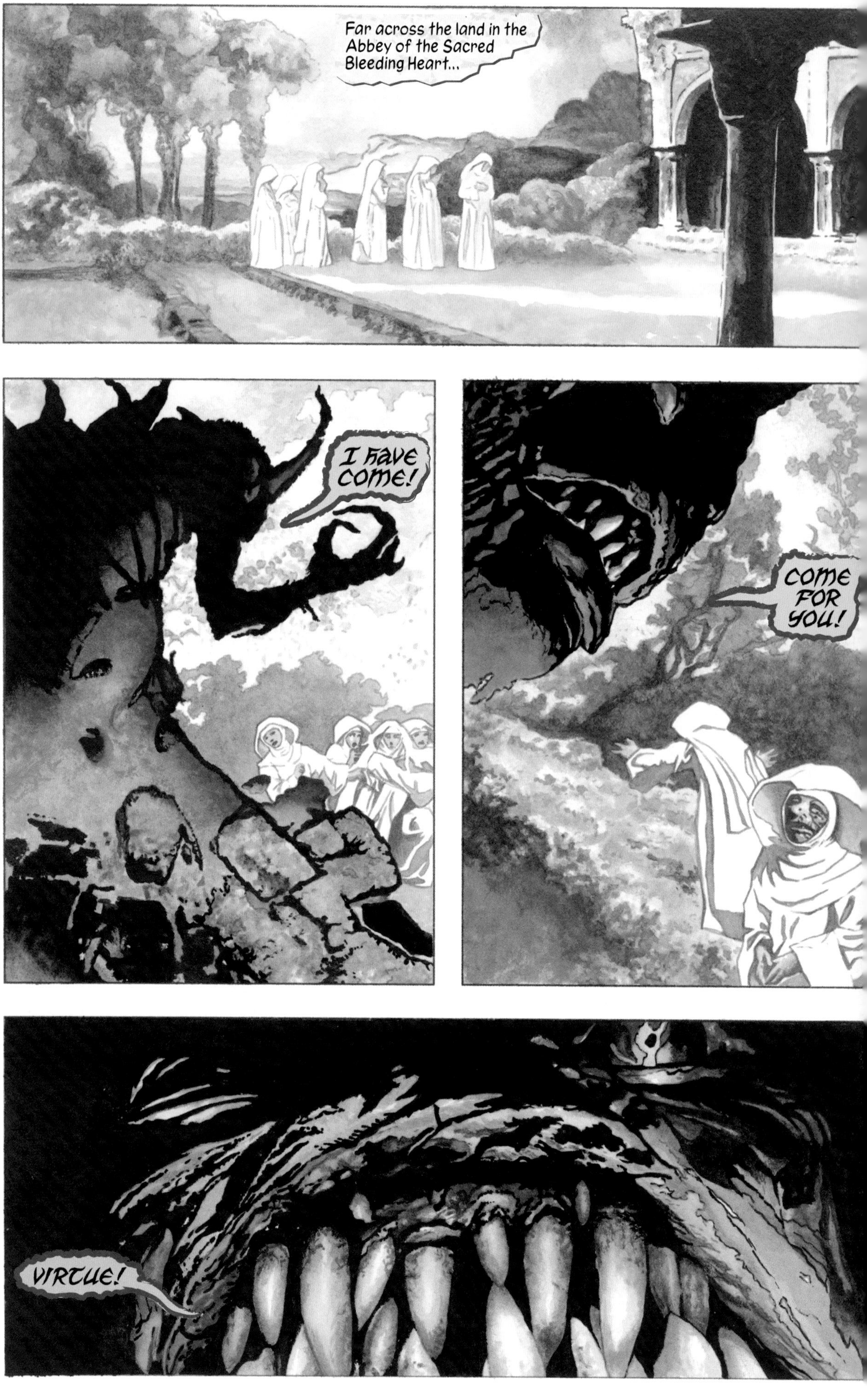
Far across the land in the Abbey of the Sacred Bleeding Heart...
I have come!
Come for you!
Virtue!

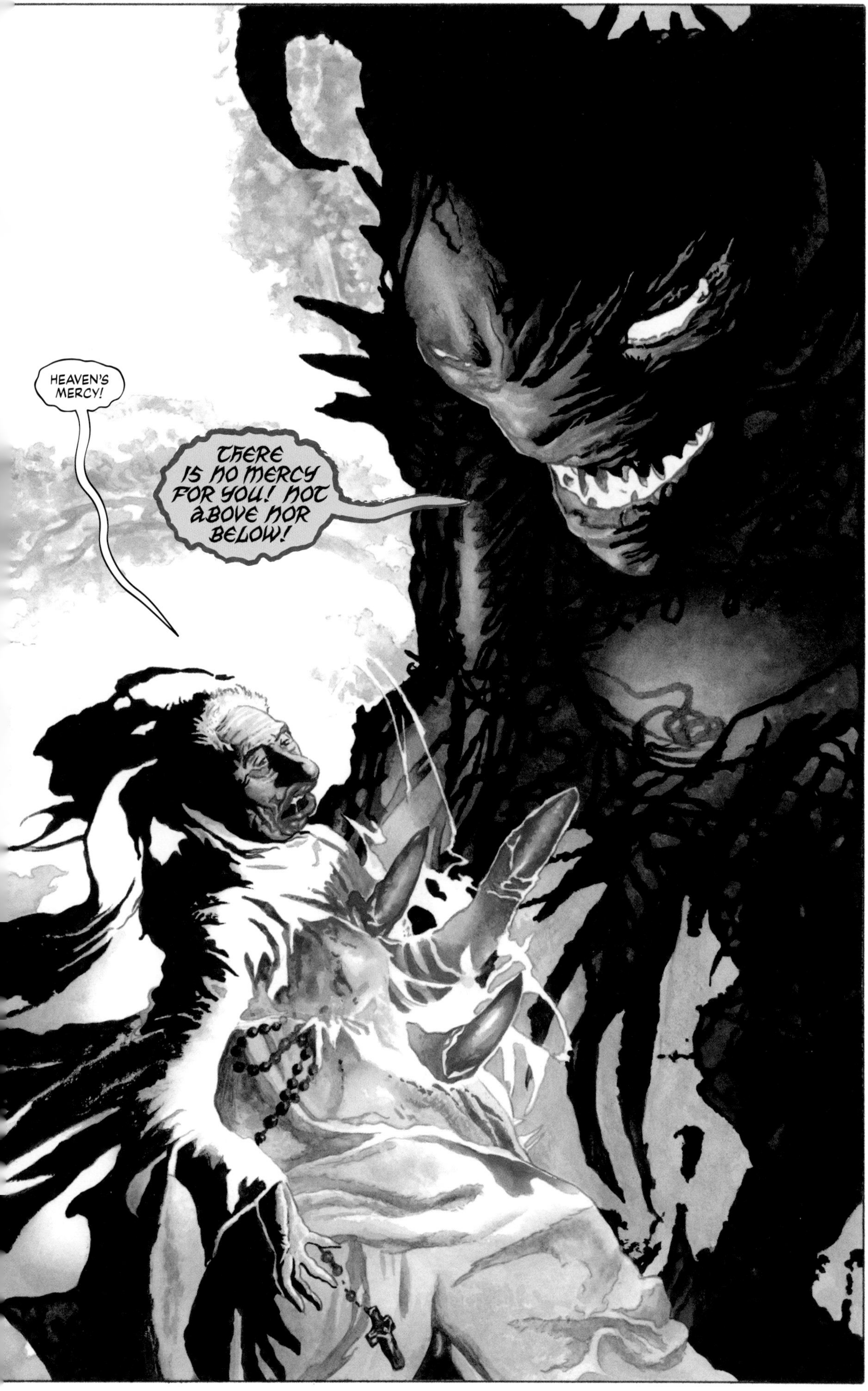
HEAVEN'S MERCY!
THERE IS NO MERCY FOR YOU! NOT ABOVE NOR BELOW!

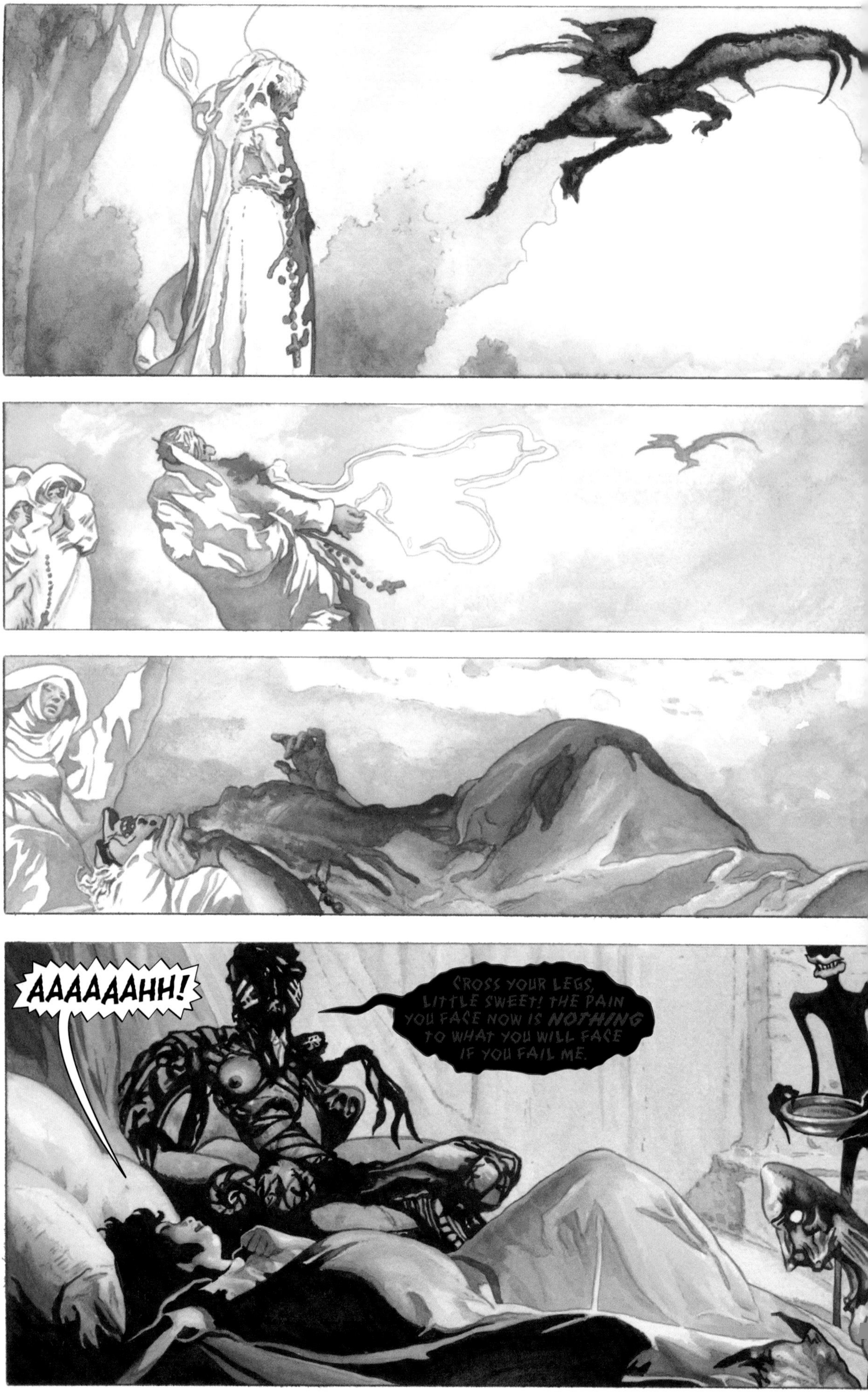
AAAAAAHH!
CROSS YOUR LEGS, LITTLE SWEET! THE PAIN YOU FACE NOW IS NOTHING TO WHAT YOU WILL FACE IF YOU FAIL ME.

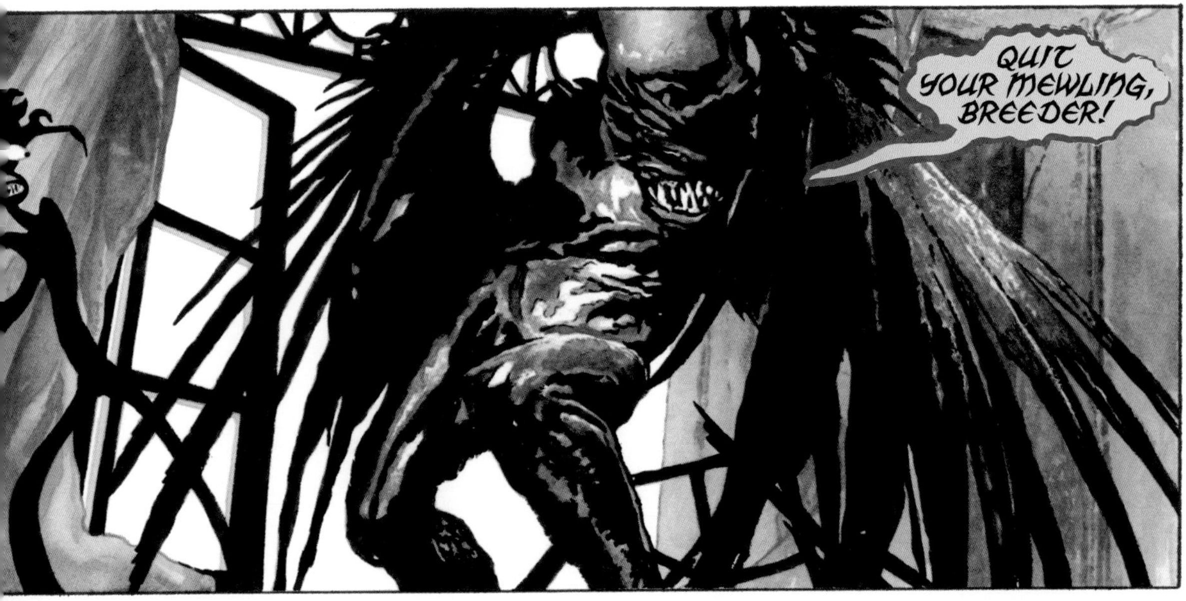
QUIT YOUR MEWLING, BREEDER!

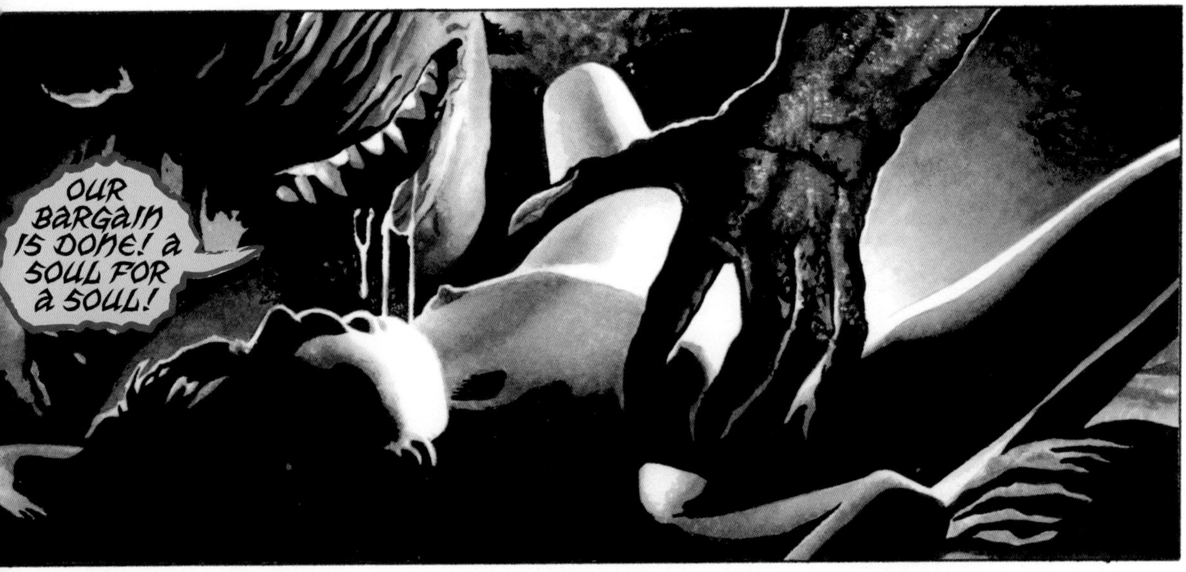
OUR BARGAIN IS DONE! A SOUL FOR A SOUL!

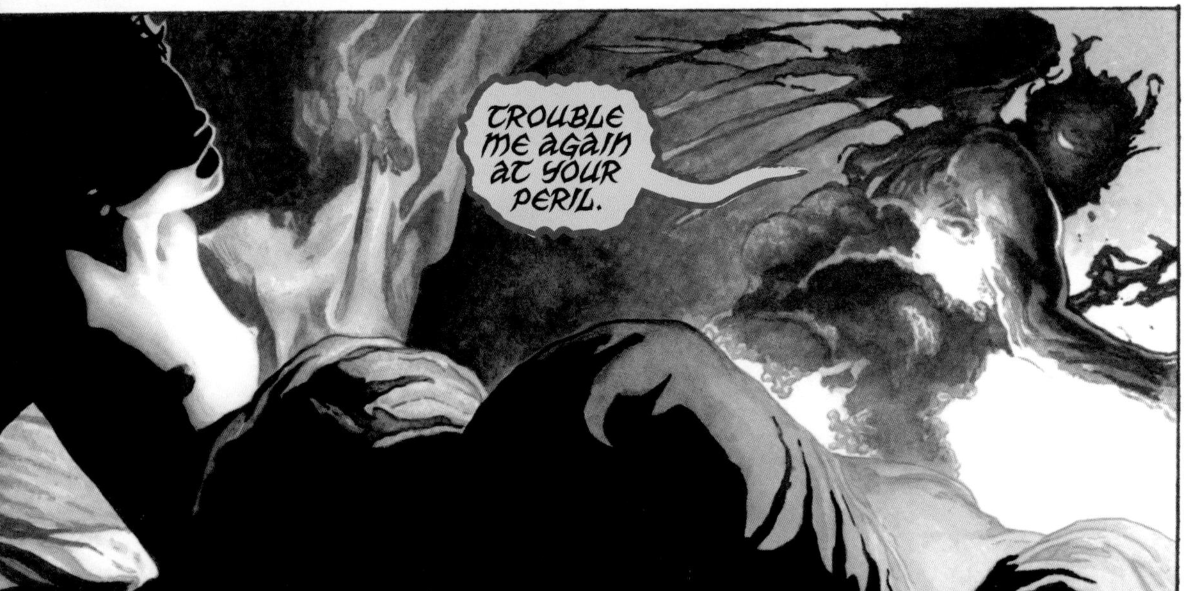
TROUBLE ME AGAIN AT YOUR PERIL.

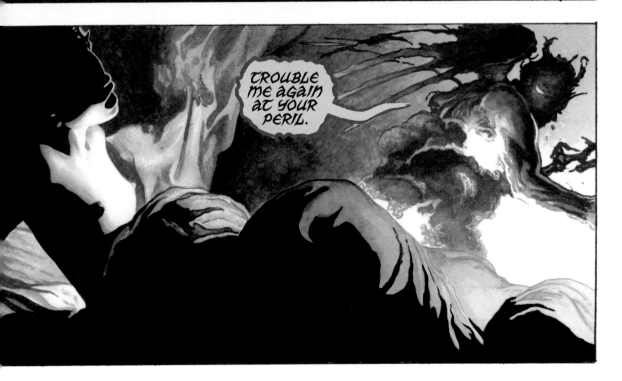

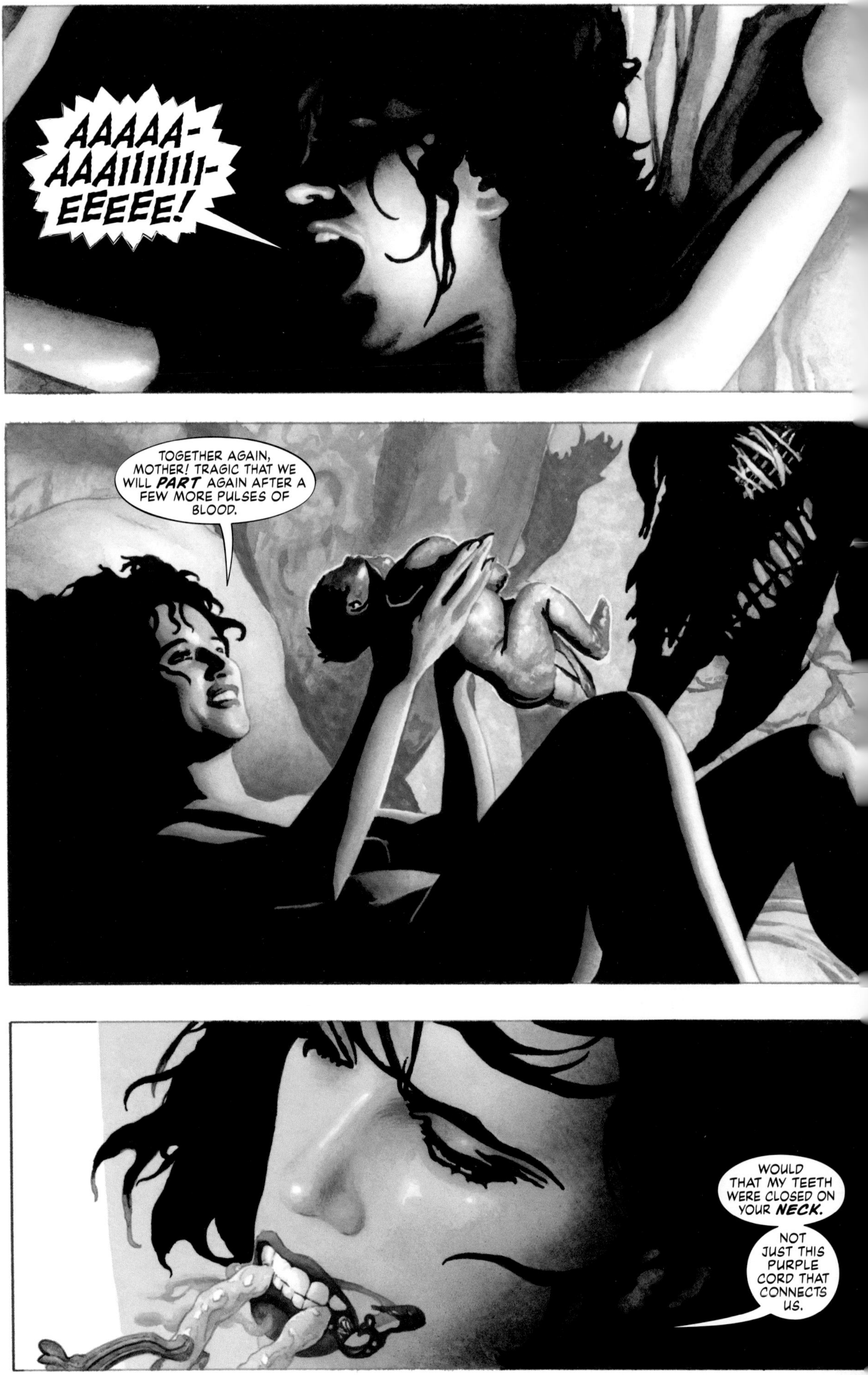
AAAAA-AAAIIIIIII-EEEEE!
TOGETHER AGAIN, MOTHER! TRAGIC THAT WE WILL **PART** AGAIN AFTER A FEW MORE PULSES OF BLOOD.
WOULD THAT MY TEETH WERE CLOSED ON YOUR **NECK.**
NOT JUST THIS PURPLE CORD THAT CONNECTS US.

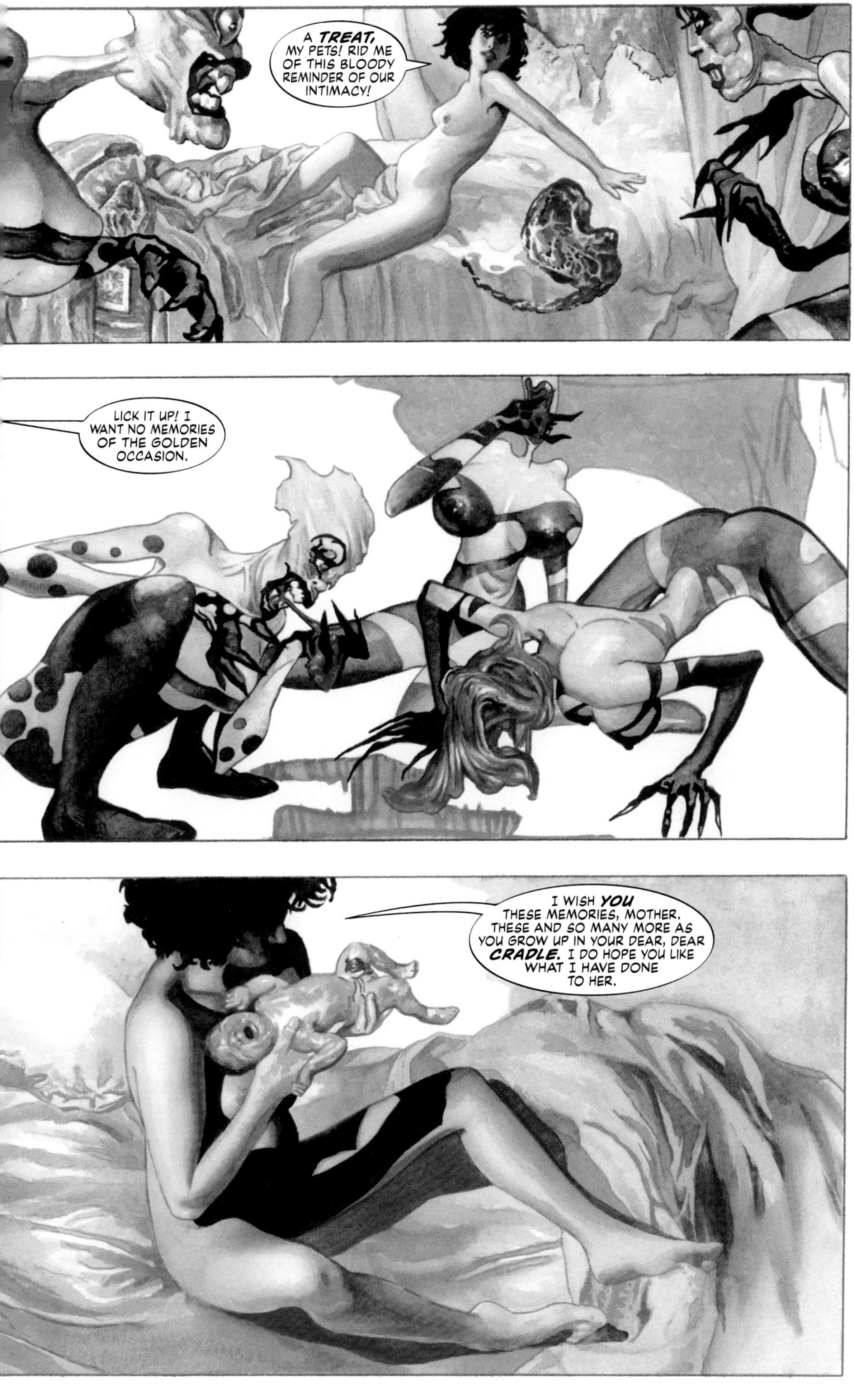
A *TREAT,* MY PETS! RID ME OF THIS BLOODY REMINDER OF OUR INTIMACY!
LICK IT UP! I WANT NO MEMORIES OF THE GOLDEN OCCASION.
I WISH *YOU* THESE MEMORIES, MOTHER. THESE AND SO MANY MORE AS YOU GROW UP IN YOUR DEAR, DEAR *CRADLE.* I DO HOPE YOU LIKE WHAT I HAVE DONE TO HER.

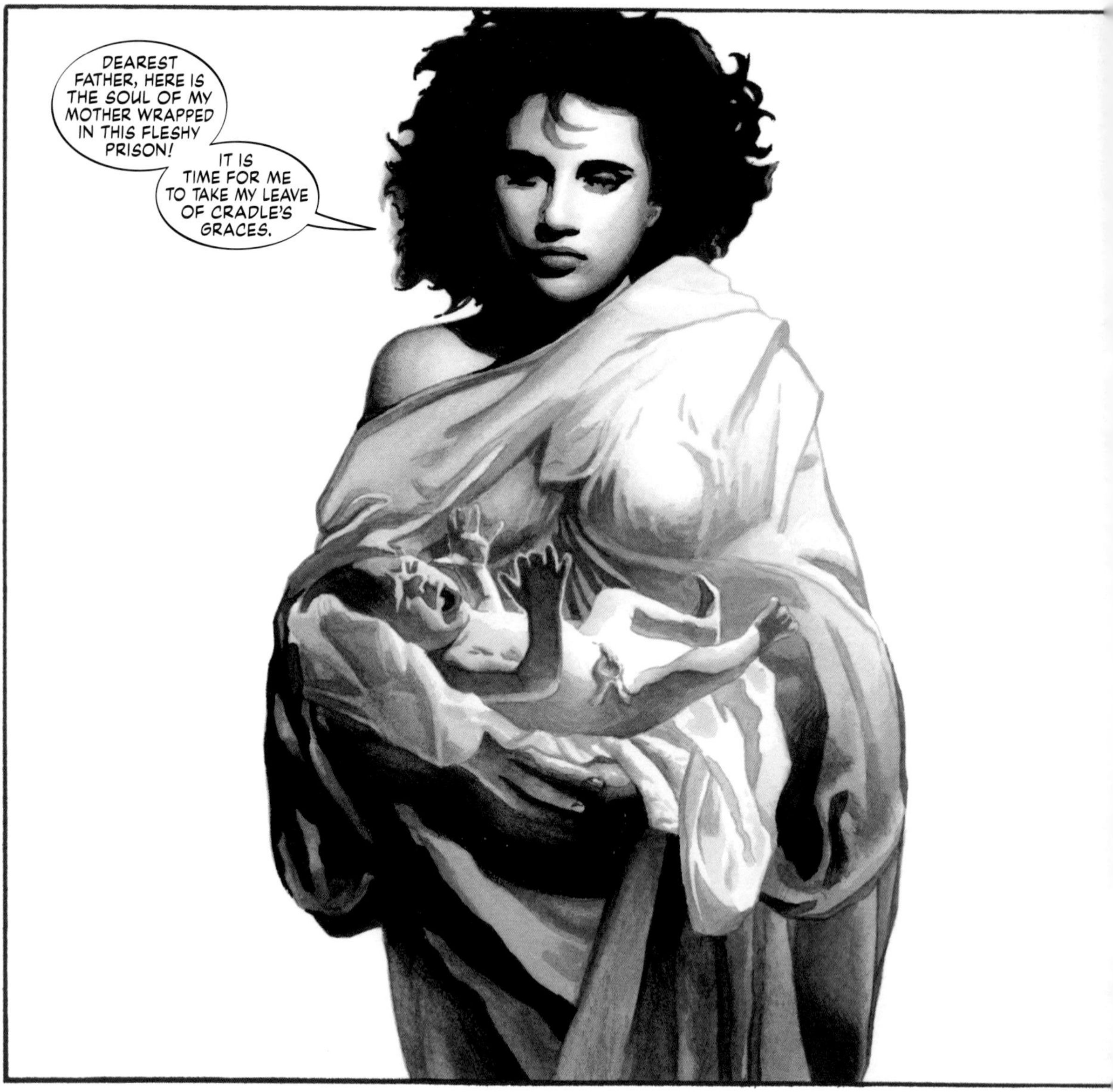
DEAREST FATHER, HERE IS THE SOUL OF MY MOTHER WRAPPED IN THIS FLESHY PRISON!
IT IS TIME FOR ME TO TAKE MY LEAVE OF CRADLE'S GRACES.

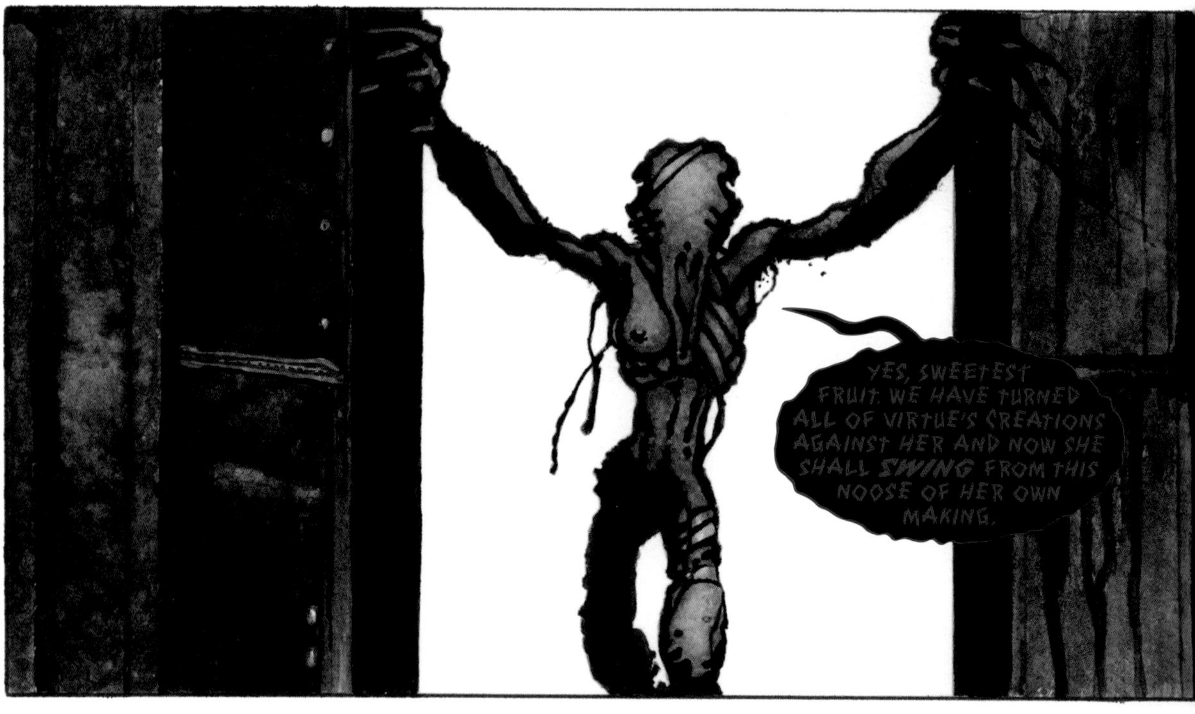
YES, SWEETEST FRUIT. WE HAVE TURNED ALL OF VIRTUE'S CREATIONS AGAINST HER AND NOW SHE SHALL SWING FROM THIS NOOSE OF HER OWN MAKING.

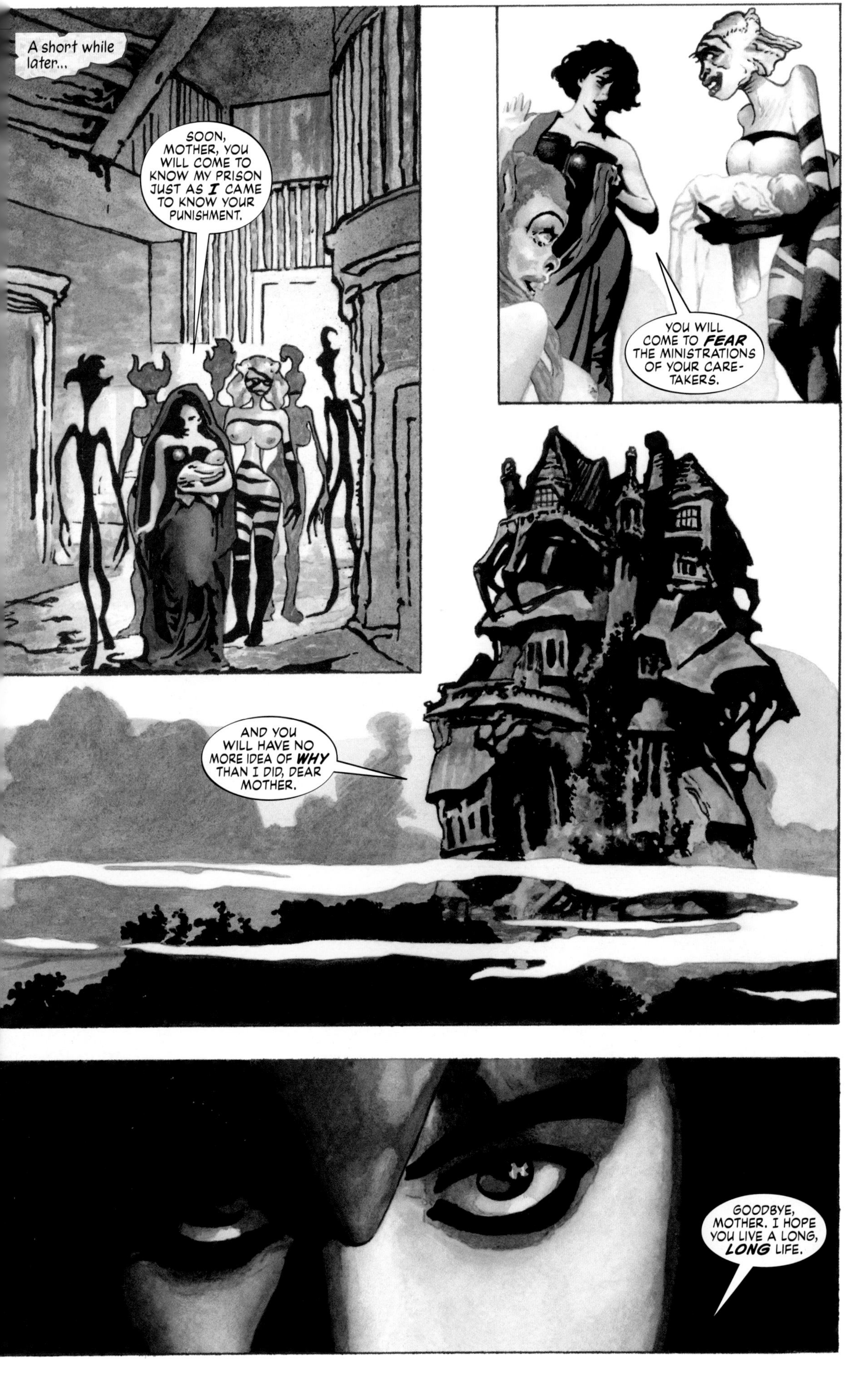
A short while later...
SOON, MOTHER, YOU WILL COME TO KNOW MY PRISON JUST AS I CAME TO KNOW YOUR PUNISHMENT.
YOU WILL COME TO FEAR THE MINISTRATIONS OF YOUR CARE-TAKERS.
AND YOU WILL HAVE NO MORE IDEA OF WHY THAN I DID, DEAR MOTHER.
GOODBYE, MOTHER. I HOPE YOU LIVE A LONG, LONG LIFE.

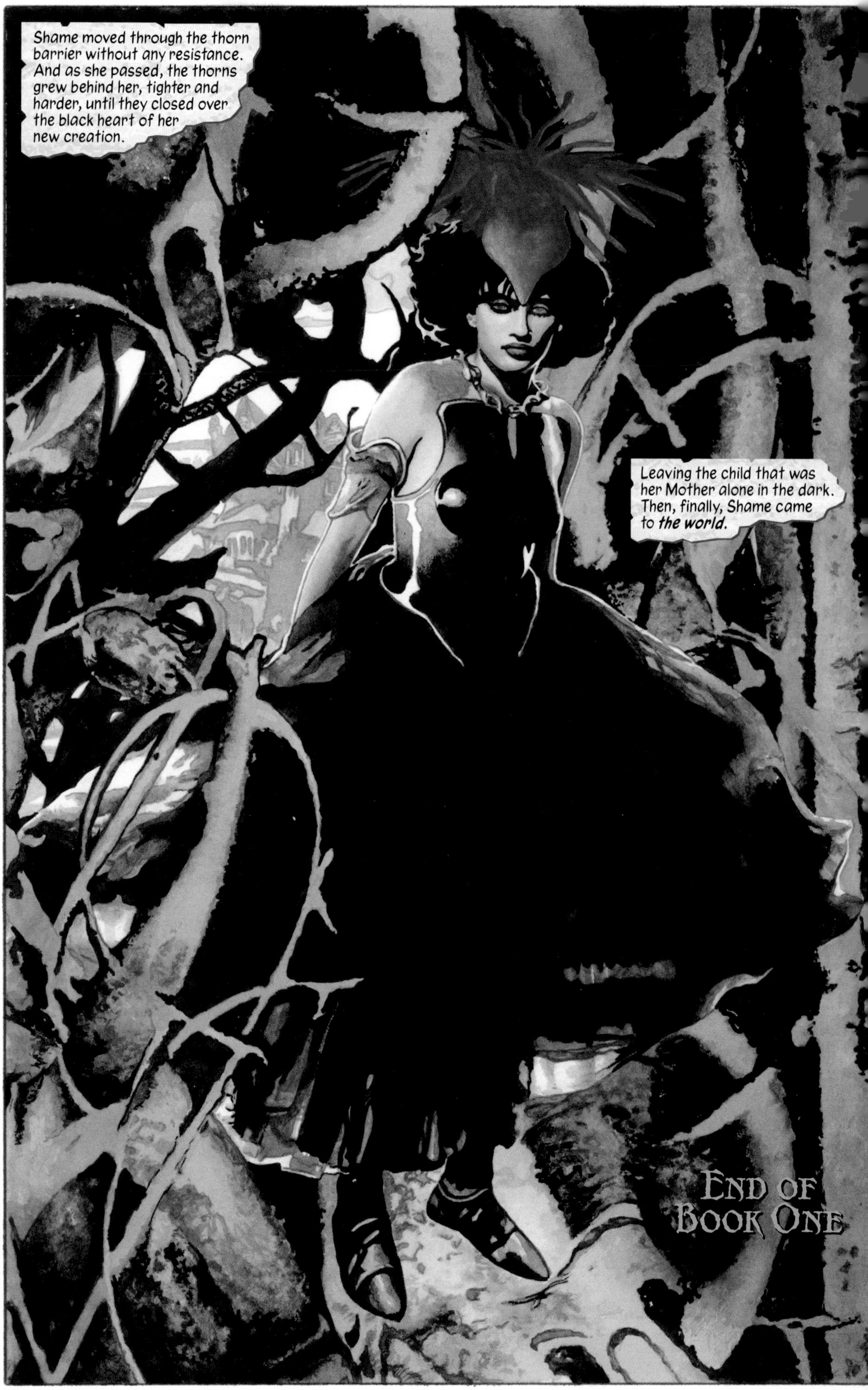
Shame moved through the thorn barrier without any resistance. And as she passed, the thorns grew behind her, tighter and harder, until they closed over the black heart of her new creation.
Leaving the child that was her Mother alone in the dark. Then, finally, Shame came to *the world*.
END OF BOOK ONE

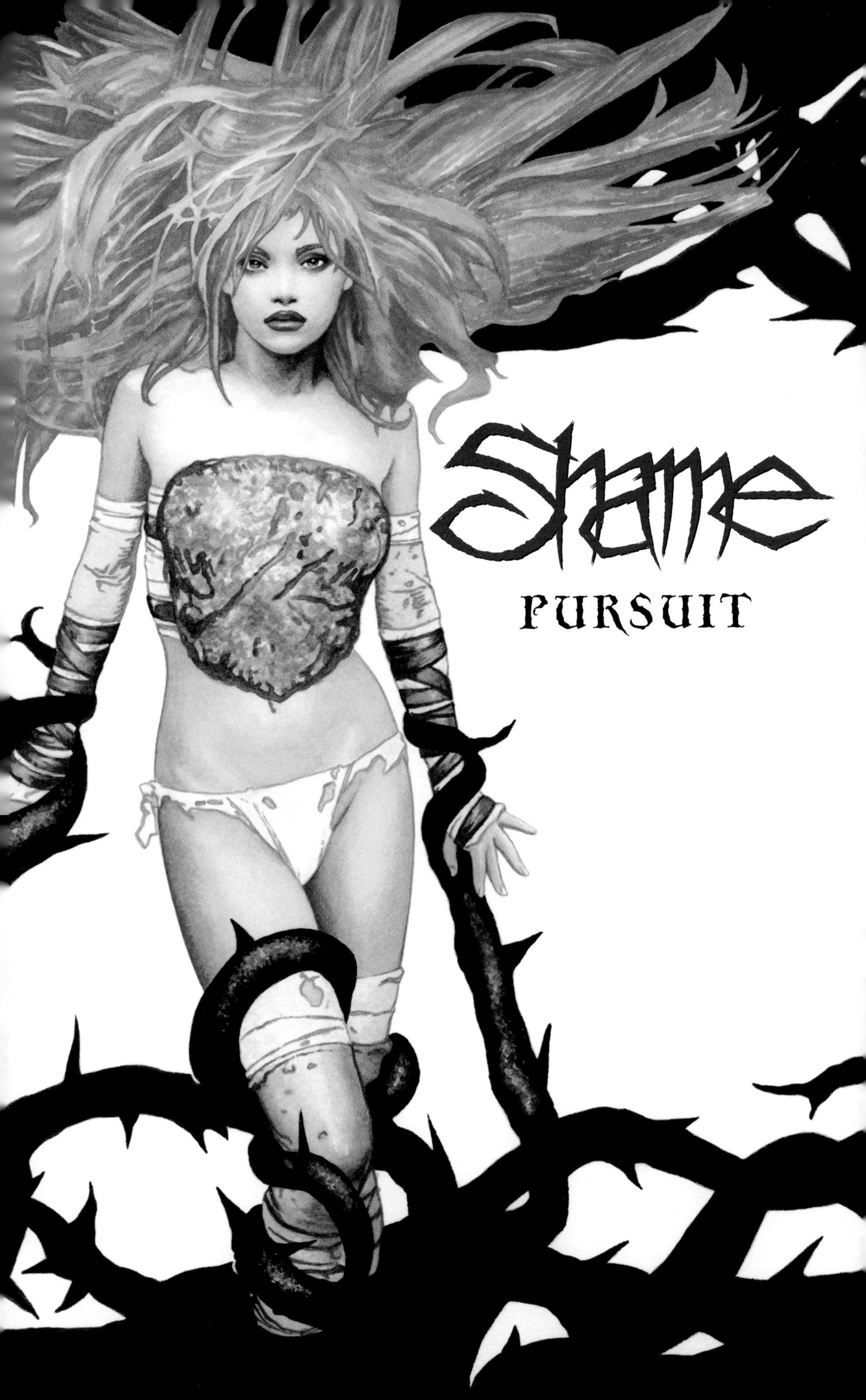
Shame
PURSUIT

SHAME
PART TWO: PURSUIT

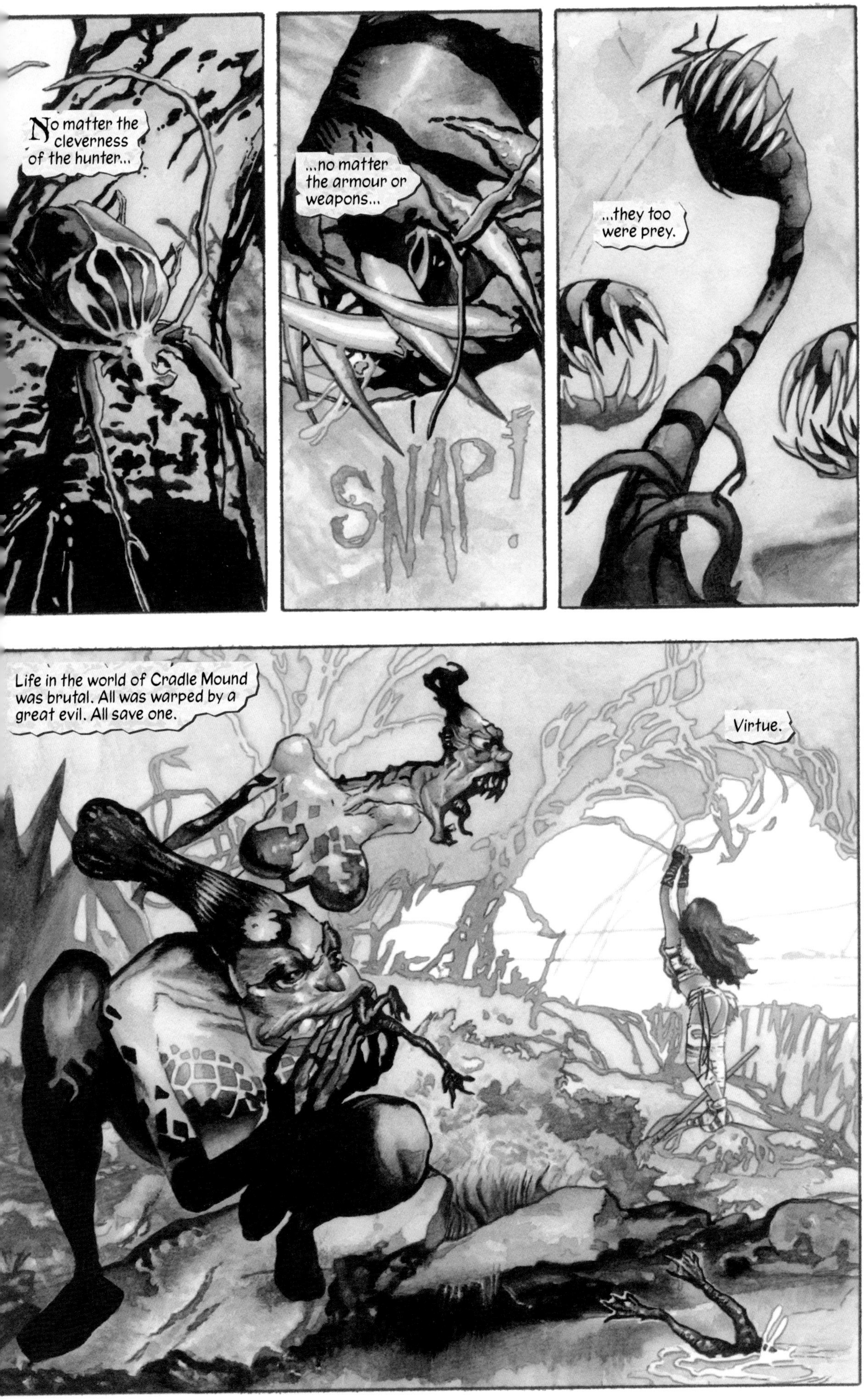
No matter the cleverness of the hunter...
...no matter the armour or weapons...
SNAP!
...they too were prey.
Life in the world of Cradle Mound was brutal. All was warped by a great evil. All save one.
Virtue.

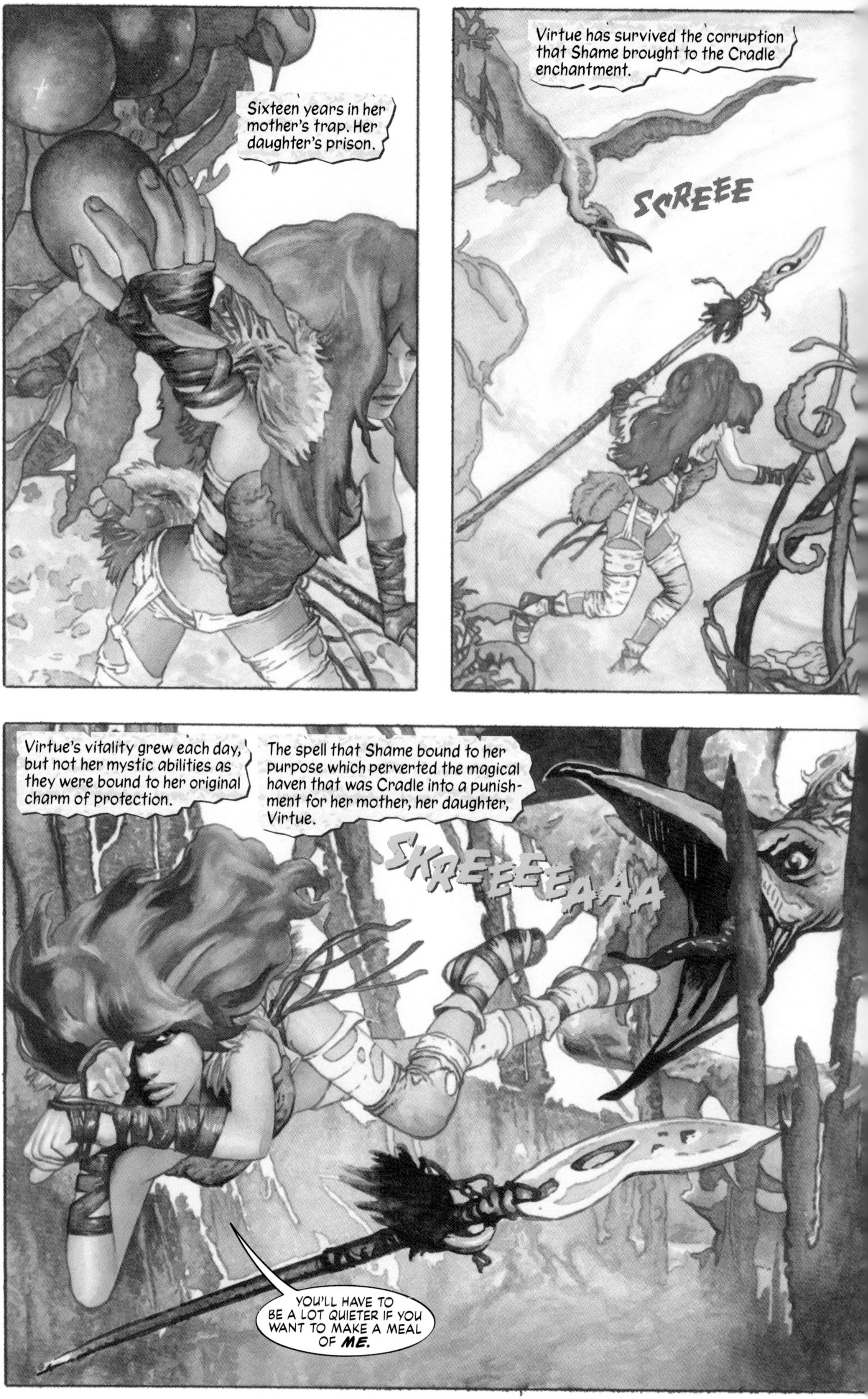
Sixteen years in her mother's trap. Her daughter's prison.
Virtue has survived the corruption that Shame brought to the Cradle enchantment.
SCREEE
Virtue's vitality grew each day, but not her mystic abilities as they were bound to her original charm of protection.
The spell that Shame bound to her purpose which perverted the magical haven that was Cradle into a punishment for her mother, her daughter, Virtue.
SKREEEEAAA
YOU'LL HAVE TO BE A LOT QUIETER IF YOU WANT TO MAKE A MEAL OF ME.

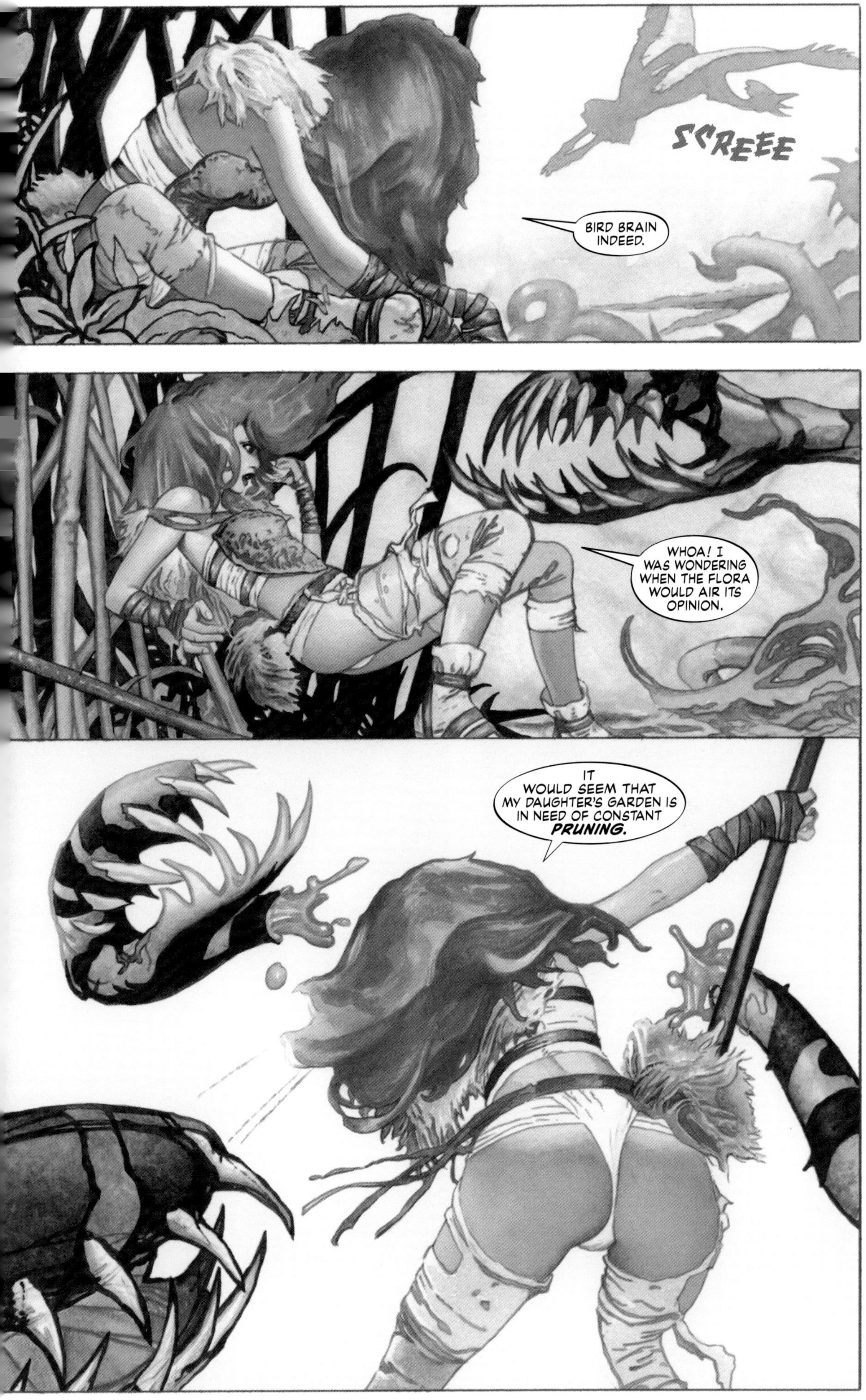
SCREEE
BIRD BRAIN INDEED.
WHOA! I WAS WONDERING WHEN THE FLORA WOULD AIR ITS OPINION.
IT WOULD SEEM THAT MY DAUGHTER'S GARDEN IS IN NEED OF CONSTANT PRUNING.

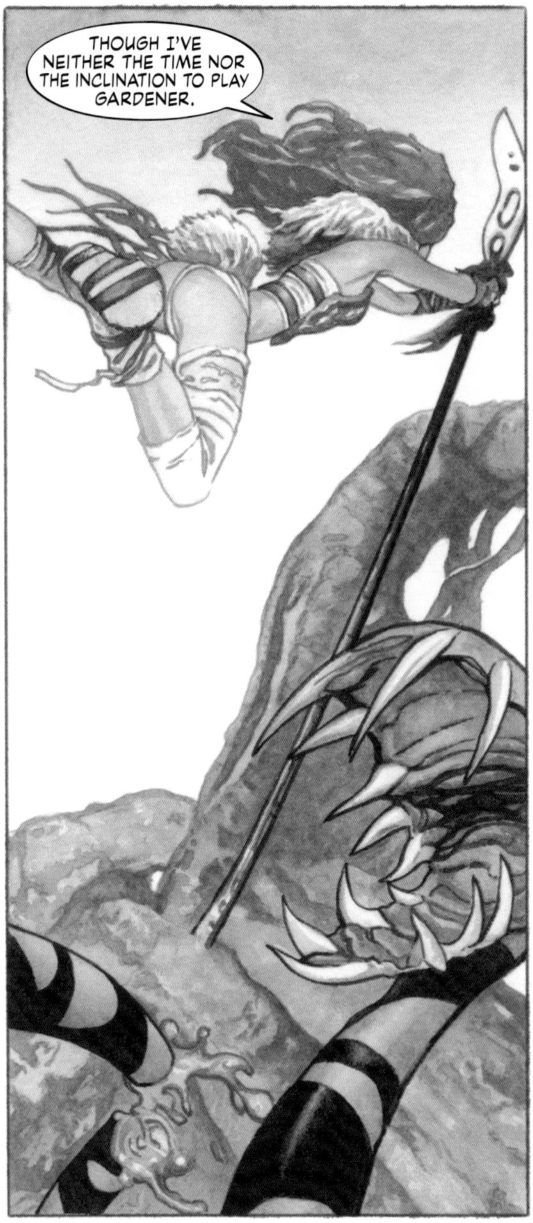
THOUGH I'VE NEITHER THE TIME NOR THE INCLINATION TO PLAY GARDENER.

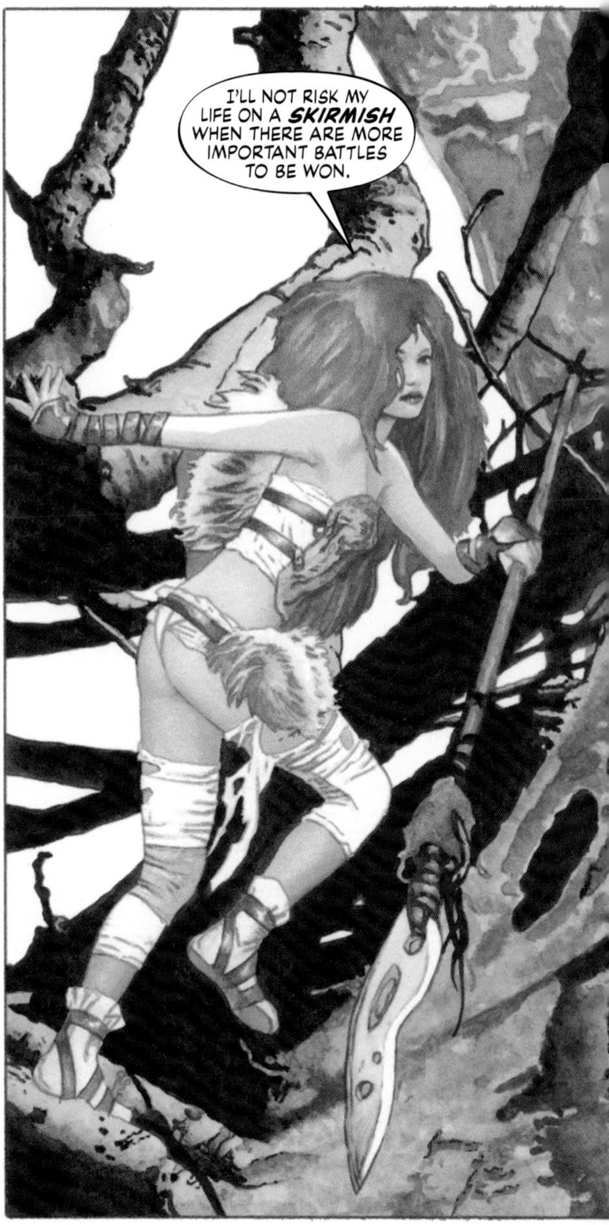
I'LL NOT RISK MY LIFE ON A SKIRMISH WHEN THERE ARE MORE IMPORTANT BATTLES TO BE WON.

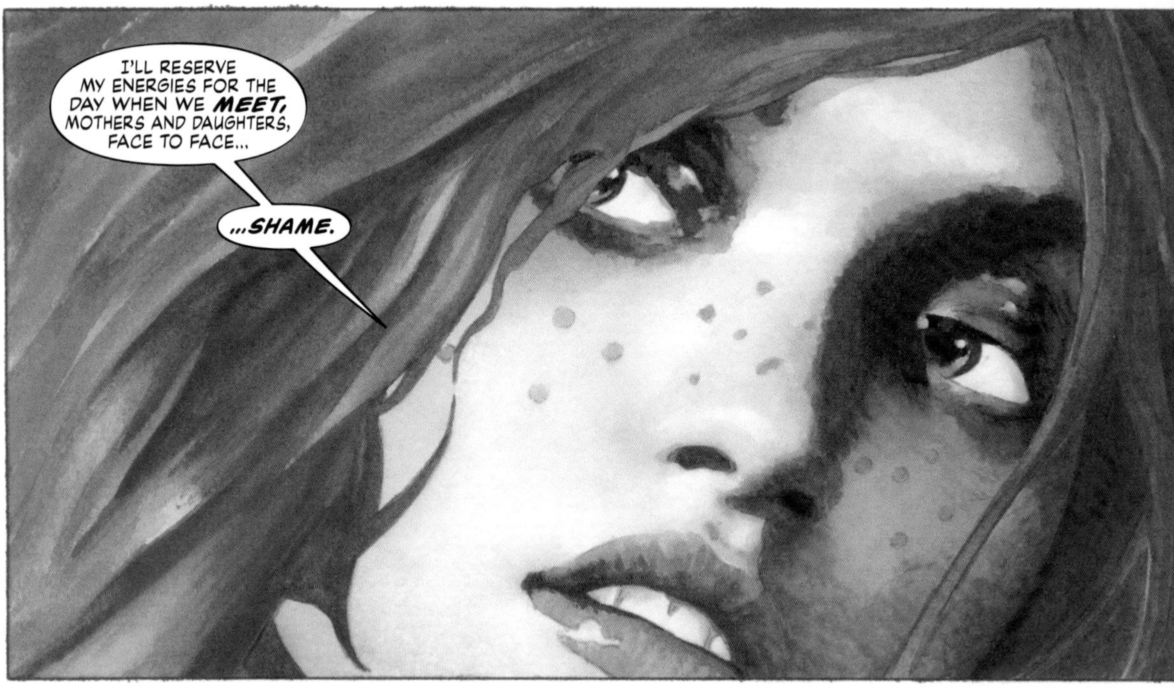
I'LL RESERVE MY ENERGIES FOR THE DAY WHEN WE MEET, MOTHERS AND DAUGHTERS, FACE TO FACE...
...SHAME.

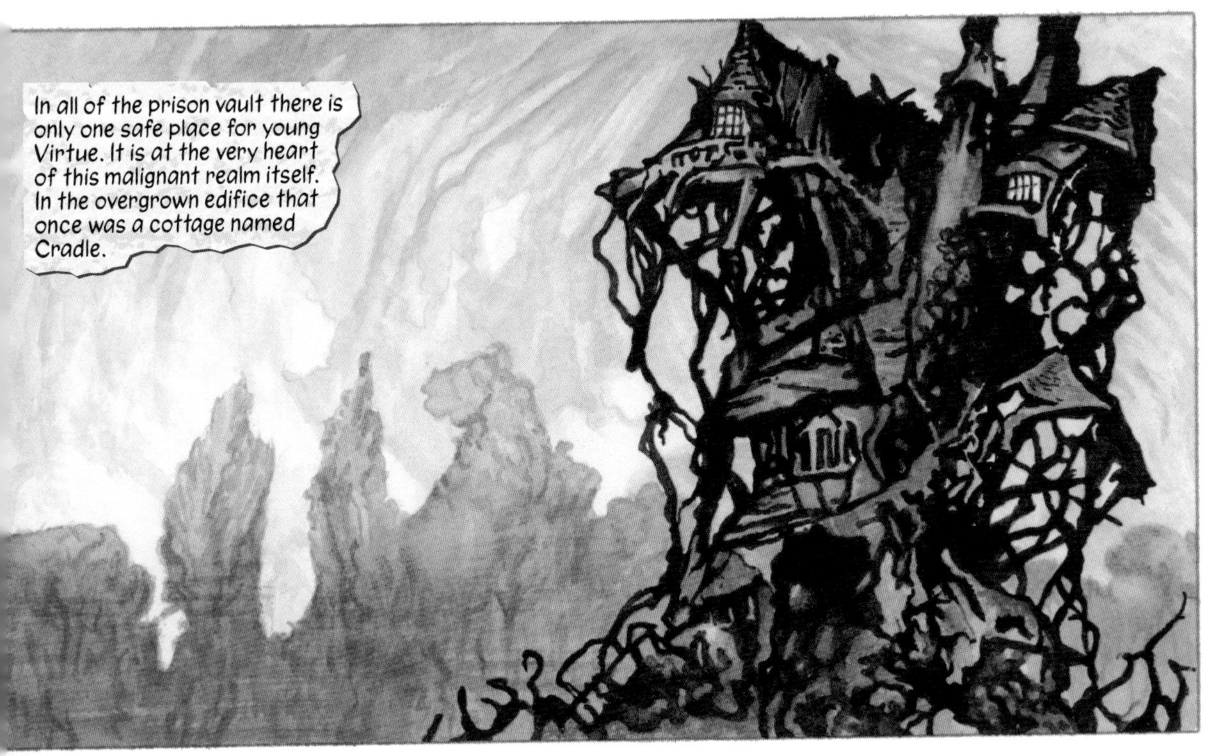
In all of the prison vault there is only one safe place for young Virtue. It is at the very heart of this malignant realm itself. In the overgrown edifice that once was a cottage named Cradle.

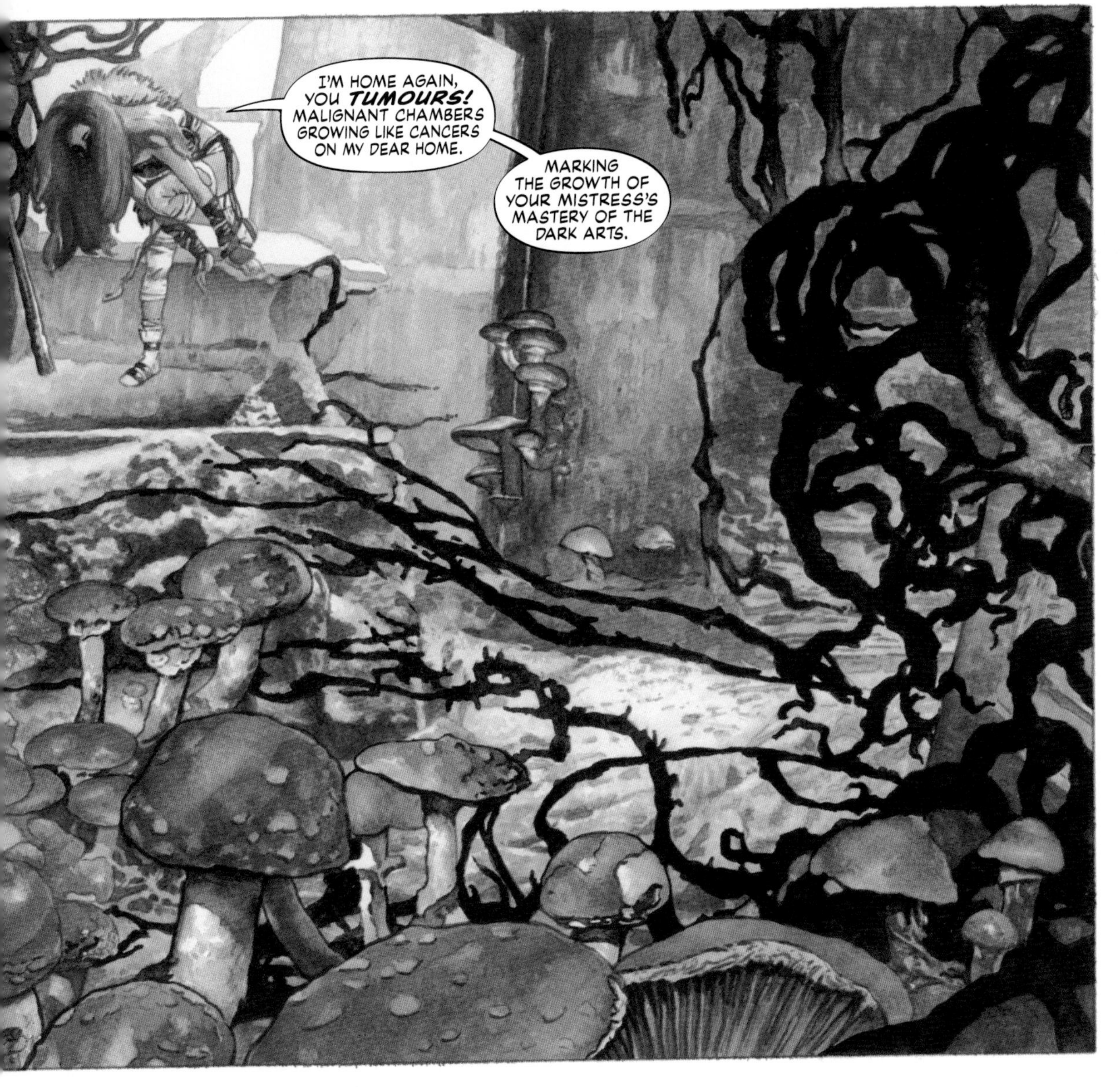
I'M HOME AGAIN, YOU TUMOURS! MALIGNANT CHAMBERS GROWING LIKE CANCERS ON MY DEAR HOME.
MARKING THE GROWTH OF YOUR MISTRESS'S MASTERY OF THE DARK ARTS.

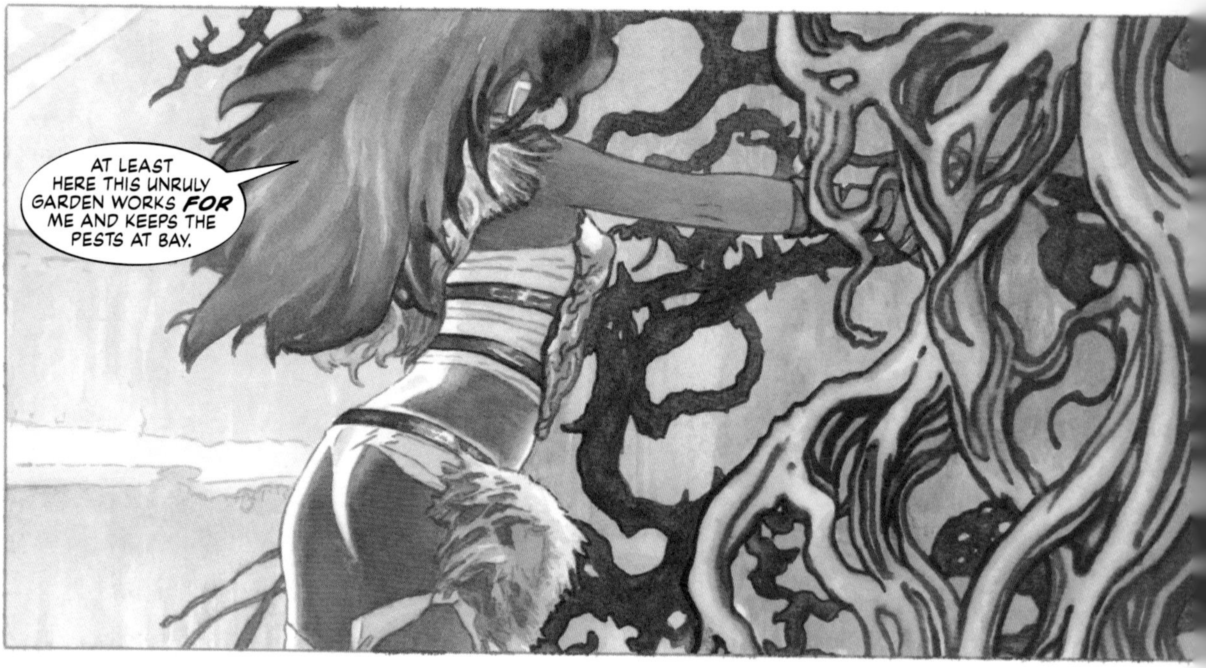
AT LEAST HERE THIS UNRULY GARDEN WORKS **FOR** ME AND KEEPS THE PESTS AT BAY.

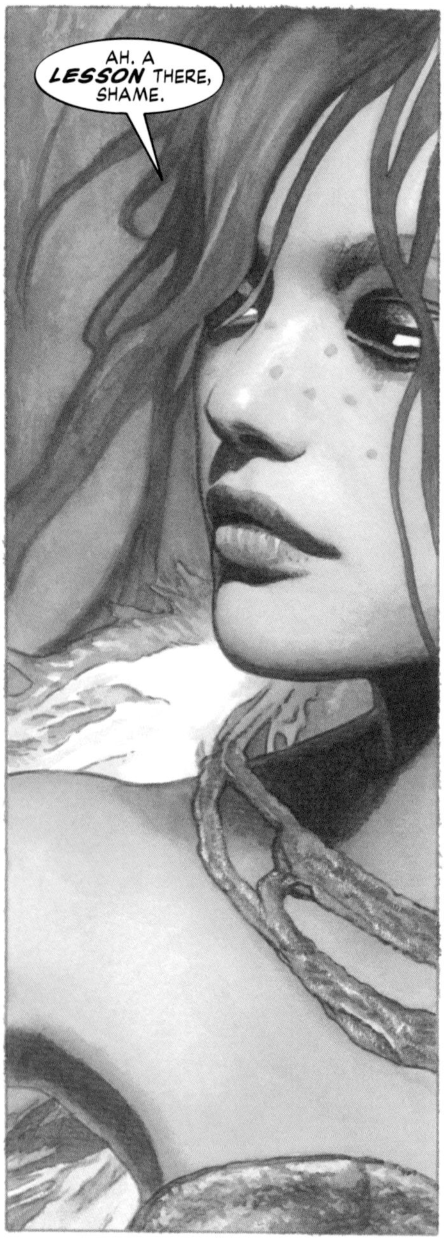
AH. A **LESSON** THERE, SHAME.

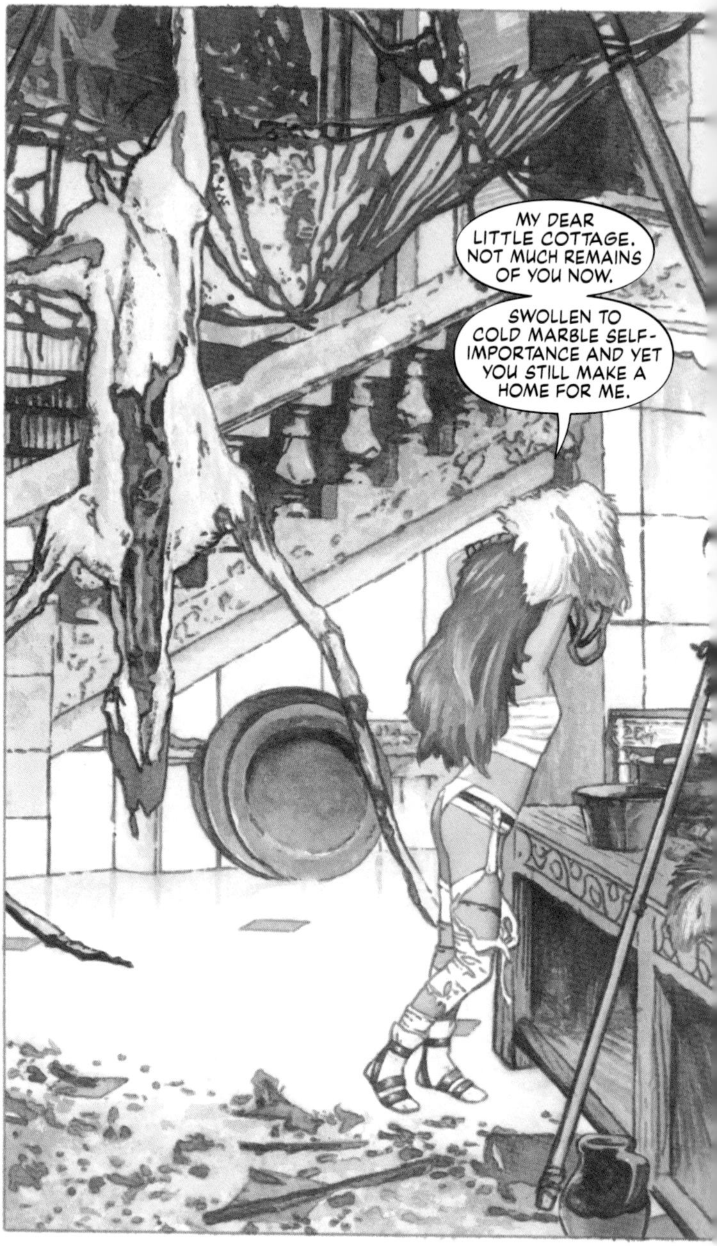
MY DEAR LITTLE COTTAGE. NOT MUCH REMAINS OF YOU NOW.
SWOLLEN TO COLD MARBLE SELF-IMPORTANCE AND YET YOU STILL MAKE A HOME FOR ME.

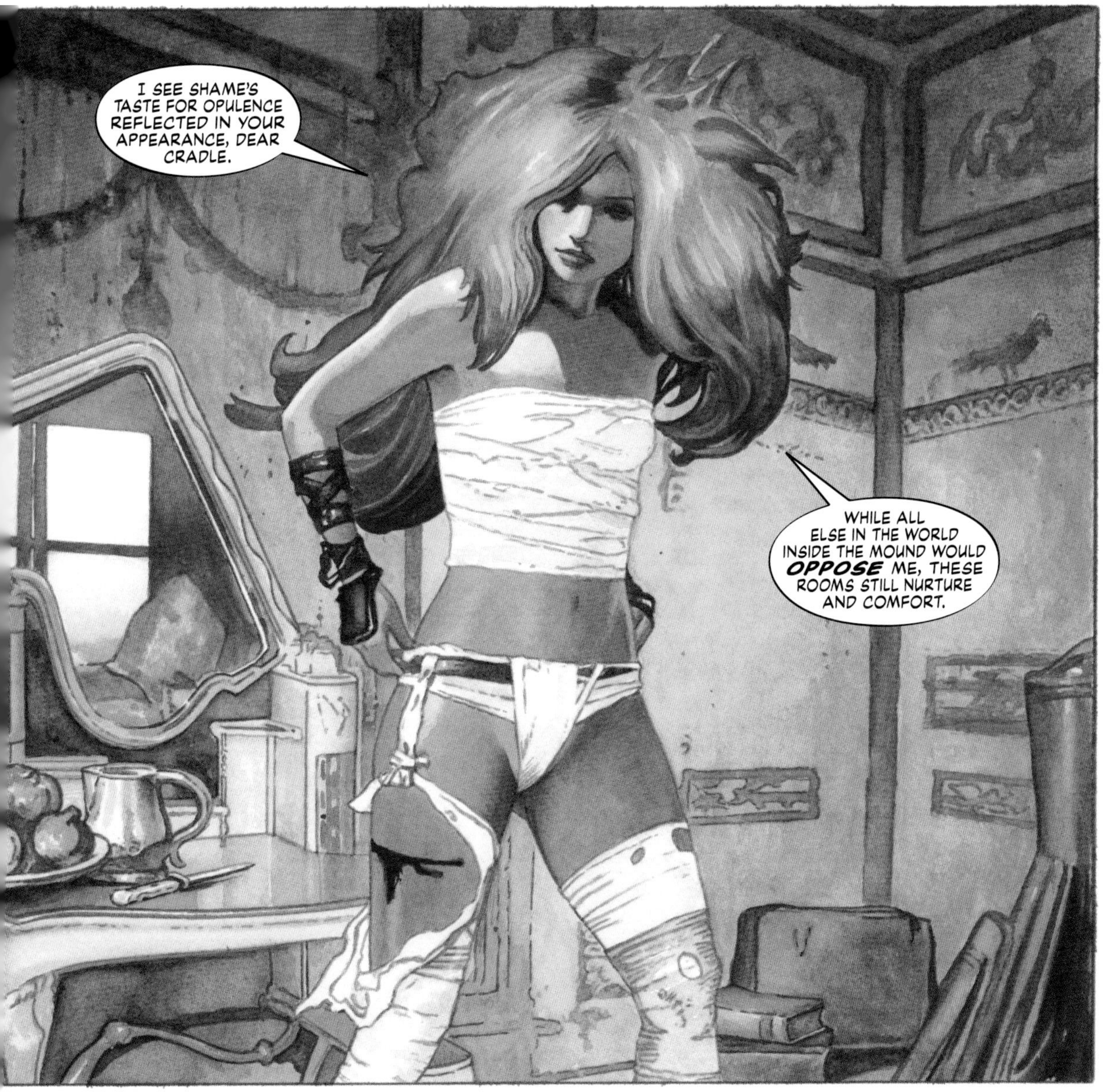
I SEE SHAME'S TASTE FOR OPULENCE REFLECTED IN YOUR APPEARANCE, DEAR CRADLE.
WHILE ALL ELSE IN THE WORLD INSIDE THE MOUND WOULD **OPPOSE** ME, THESE ROOMS STILL NURTURE AND COMFORT.

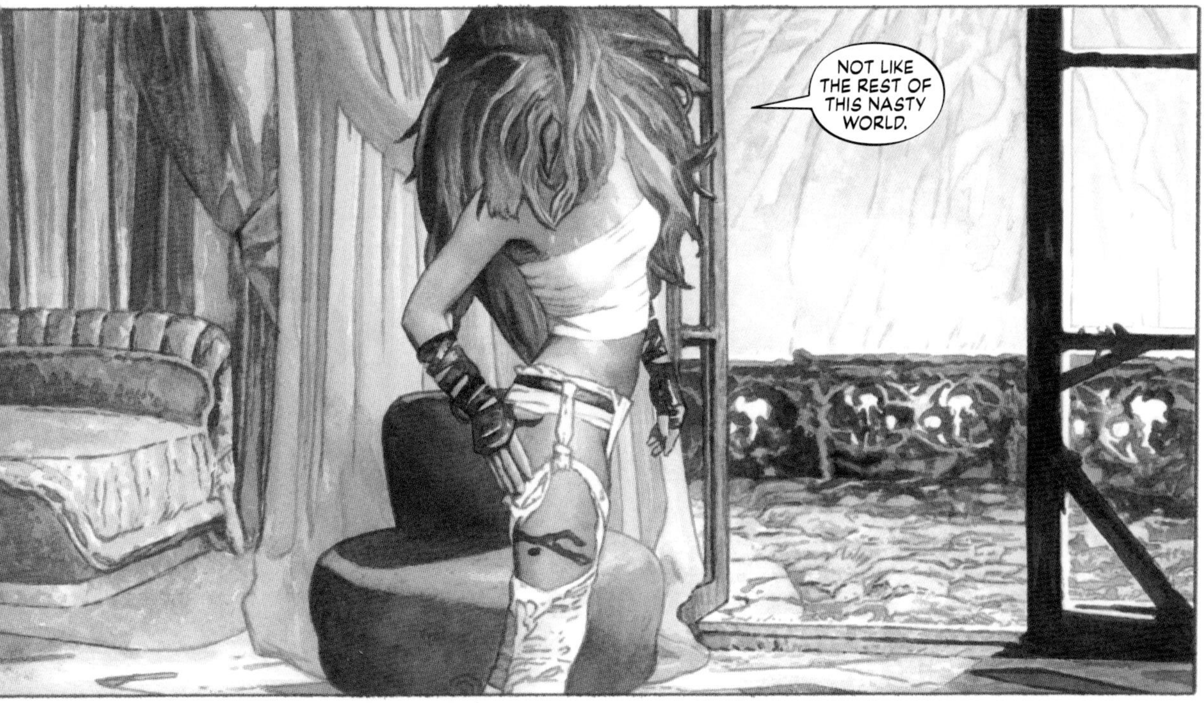
NOT LIKE THE REST OF THIS NASTY WORLD.

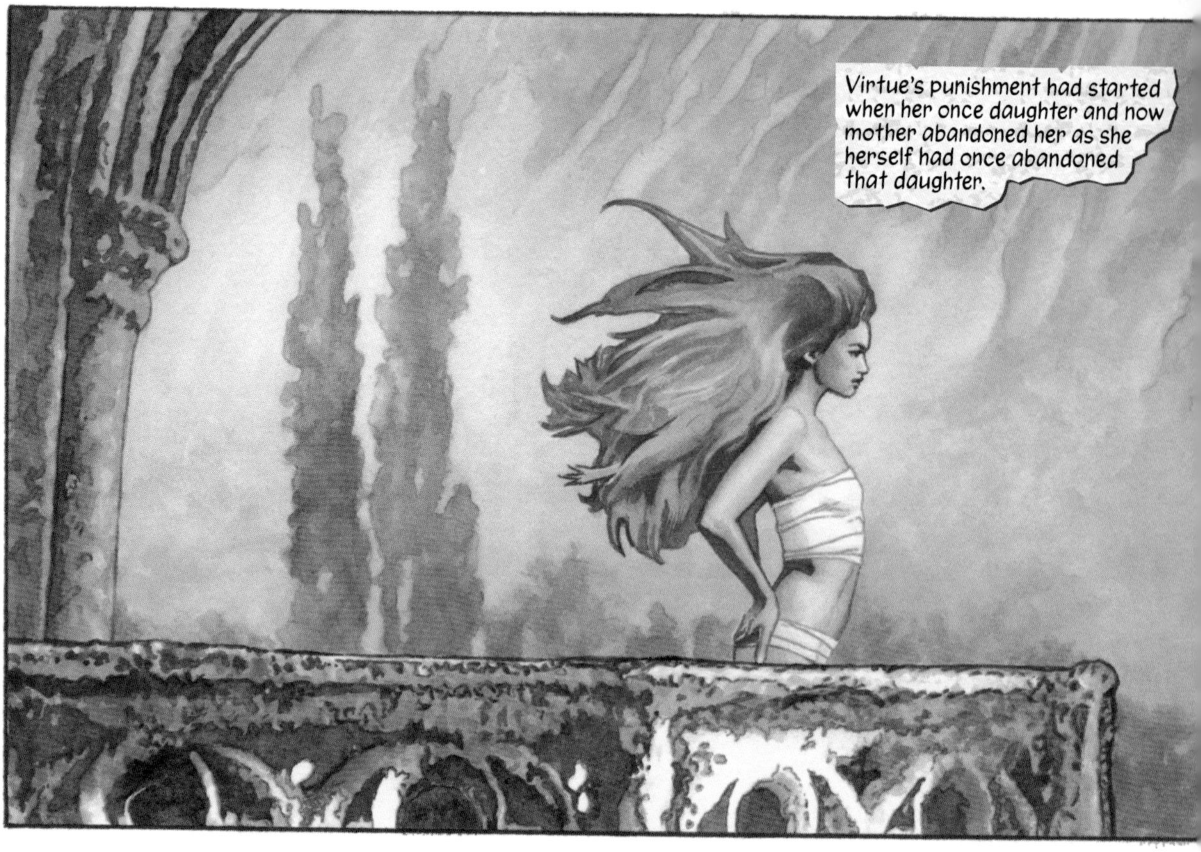
Virtue's punishment had started when her once daughter and now mother abandoned her as she herself had once abandoned that daughter.

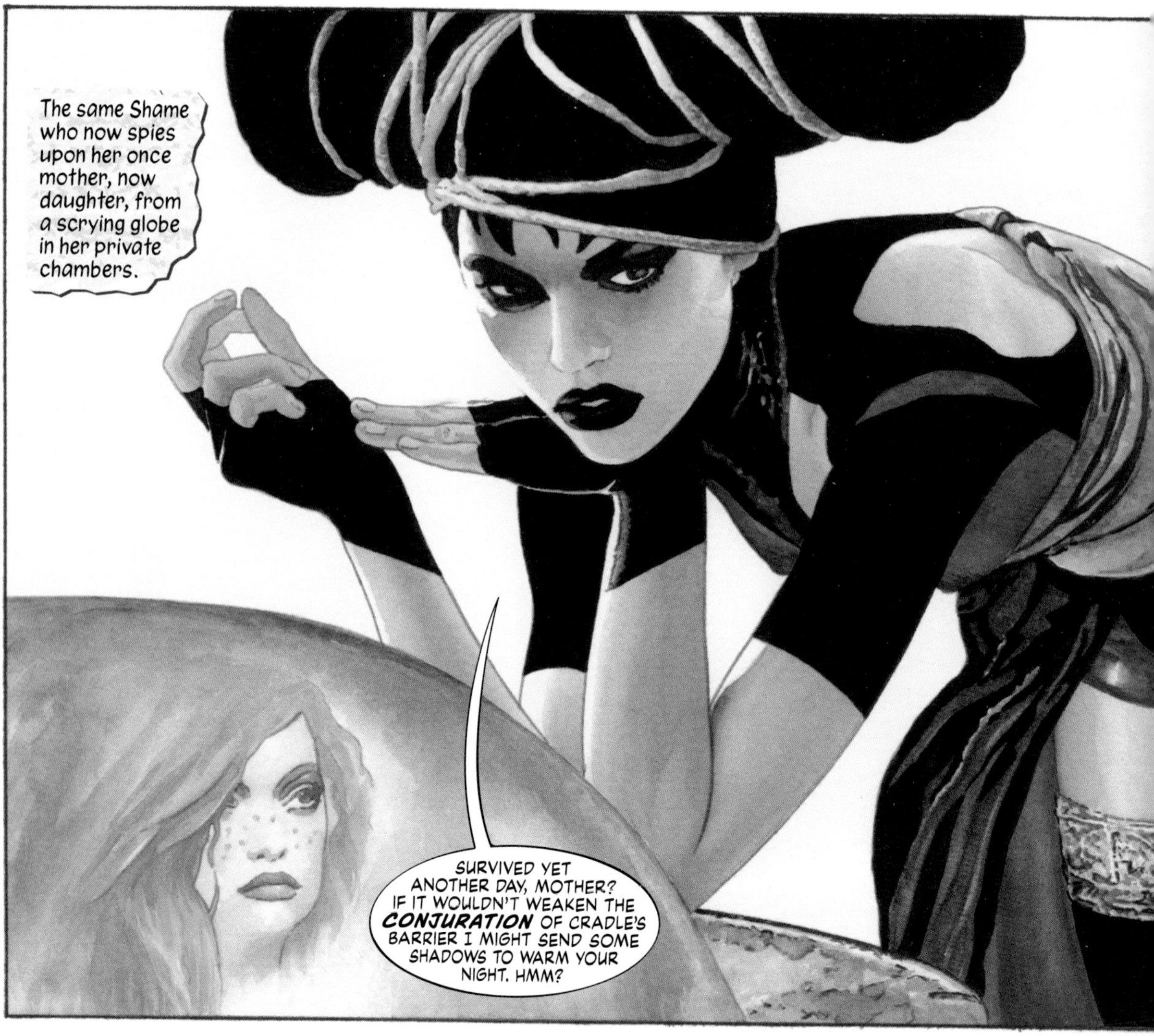
The same Shame who now spies upon her once mother, now daughter, from a scrying globe in her private chambers.
SURVIVED YET ANOTHER DAY, MOTHER? IF IT WOULDN'T WEAKEN THE CONJURATION OF CRADLE'S BARRIER I MIGHT SEND SOME SHADOWS TO WARM YOUR NIGHT. HMM?

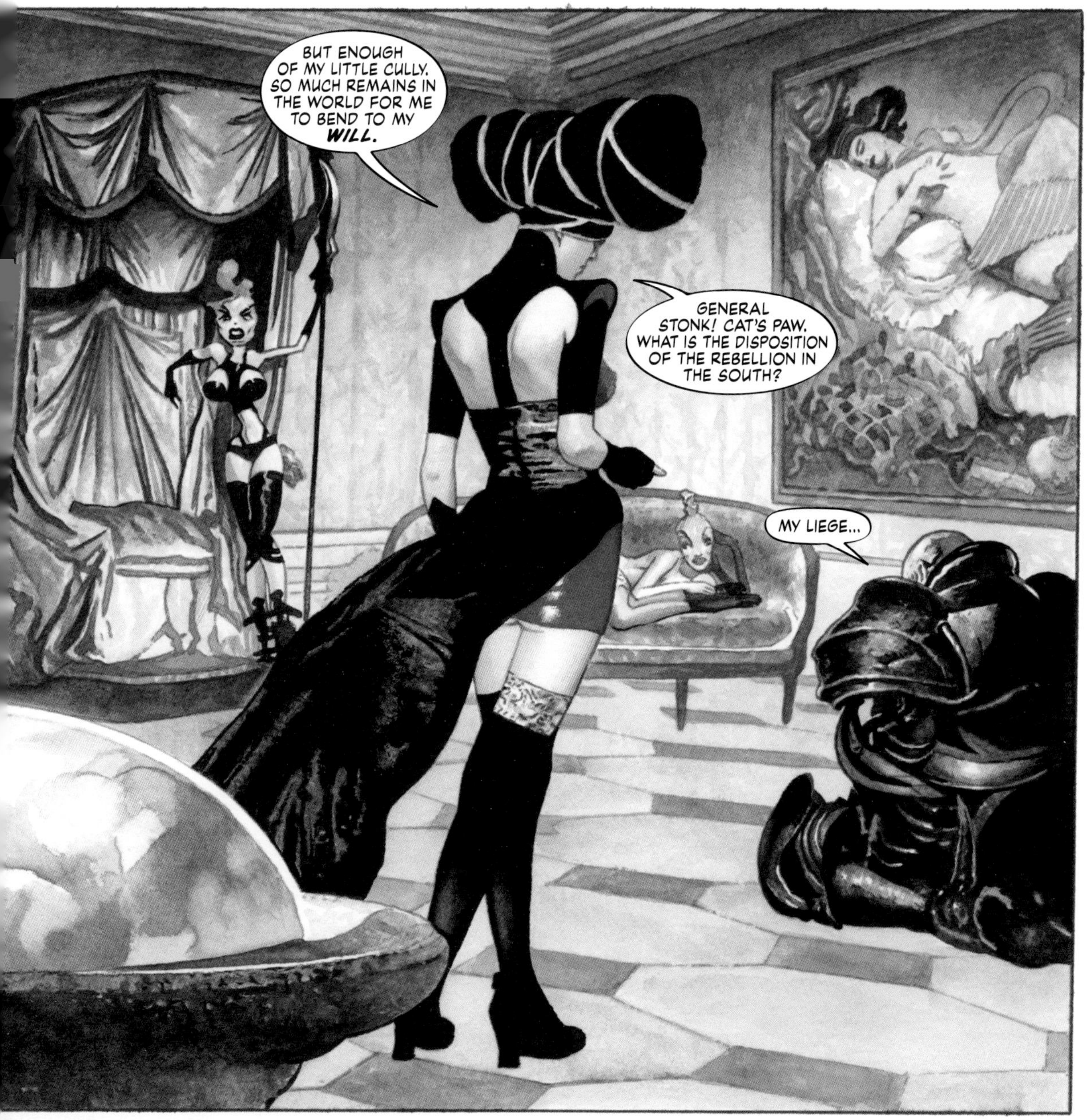
BUT ENOUGH OF MY LITTLE CULLY. SO MUCH REMAINS IN THE WORLD FOR ME TO BEND TO MY *WILL.*
GENERAL STONK! CAT'S PAW. WHAT IS THE DISPOSITION OF THE REBELLION IN THE SOUTH?
MY LIEGE...

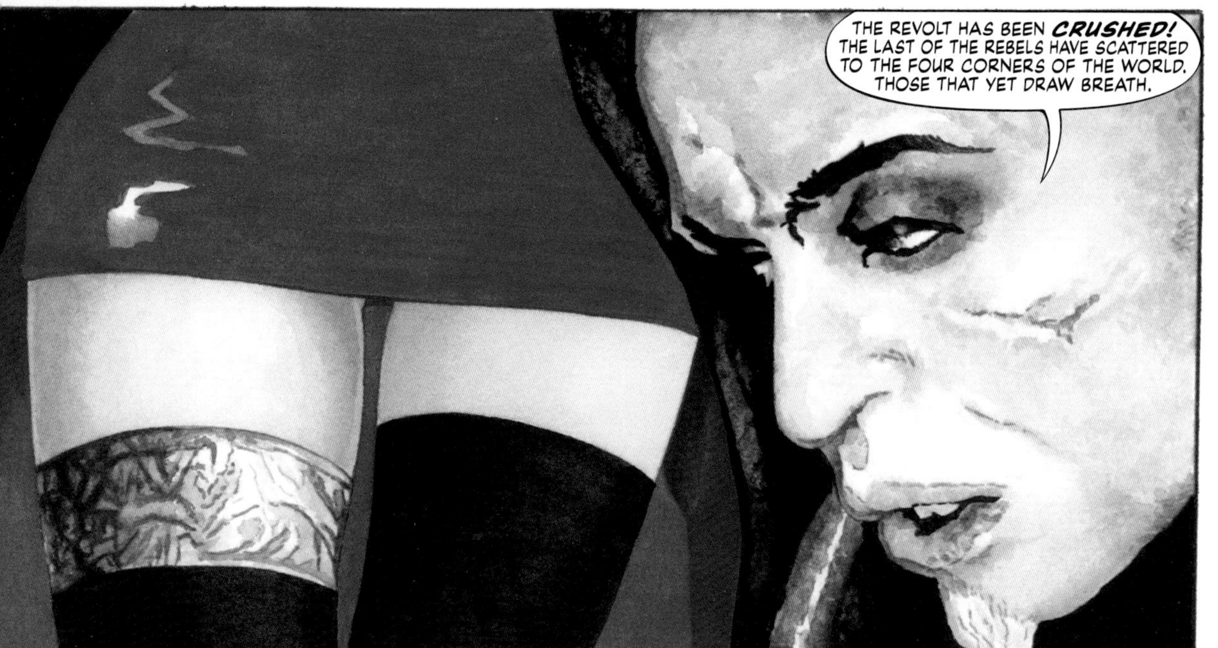
THE REVOLT HAS BEEN *CRUSHED!* THE LAST OF THE REBELS HAVE SCATTERED TO THE FOUR CORNERS OF THE WORLD. THOSE THAT YET DRAW BREATH.

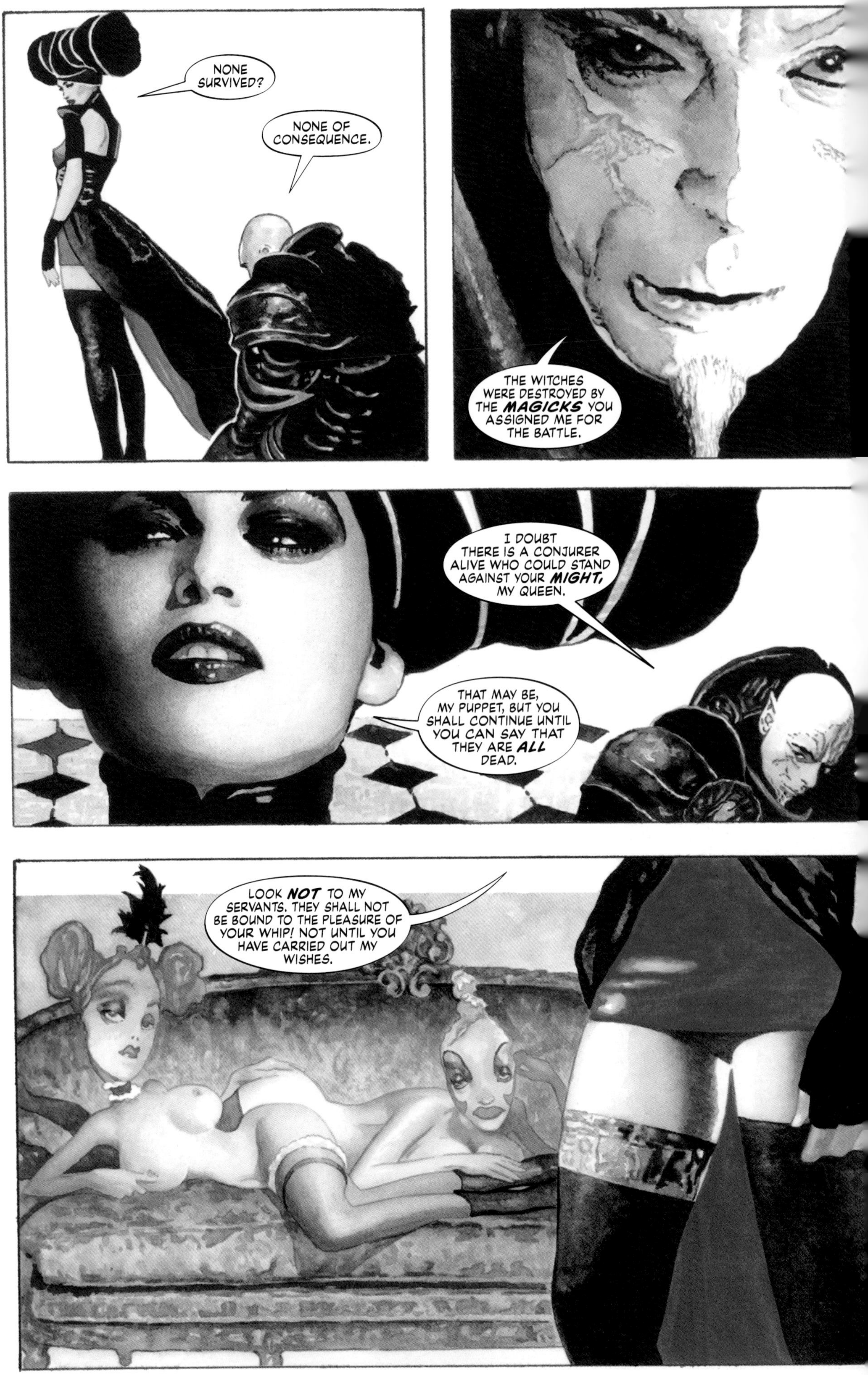
NONE SURVIVED?
NONE OF CONSEQUENCE.
THE WITCHES WERE DESTROYED BY THE MAGICKS YOU ASSIGNED ME FOR THE BATTLE.
I DOUBT THERE IS A CONJURER ALIVE WHO COULD STAND AGAINST YOUR MIGHT, MY QUEEN.
THAT MAY BE, MY PUPPET, BUT YOU SHALL CONTINUE UNTIL YOU CAN SAY THAT THEY ARE ALL DEAD.
LOOK NOT TO MY SERVANTS. THEY SHALL NOT BE BOUND TO THE PLEASURE OF YOUR WHIP! NOT UNTIL YOU HAVE CARRIED OUT MY WISHES.

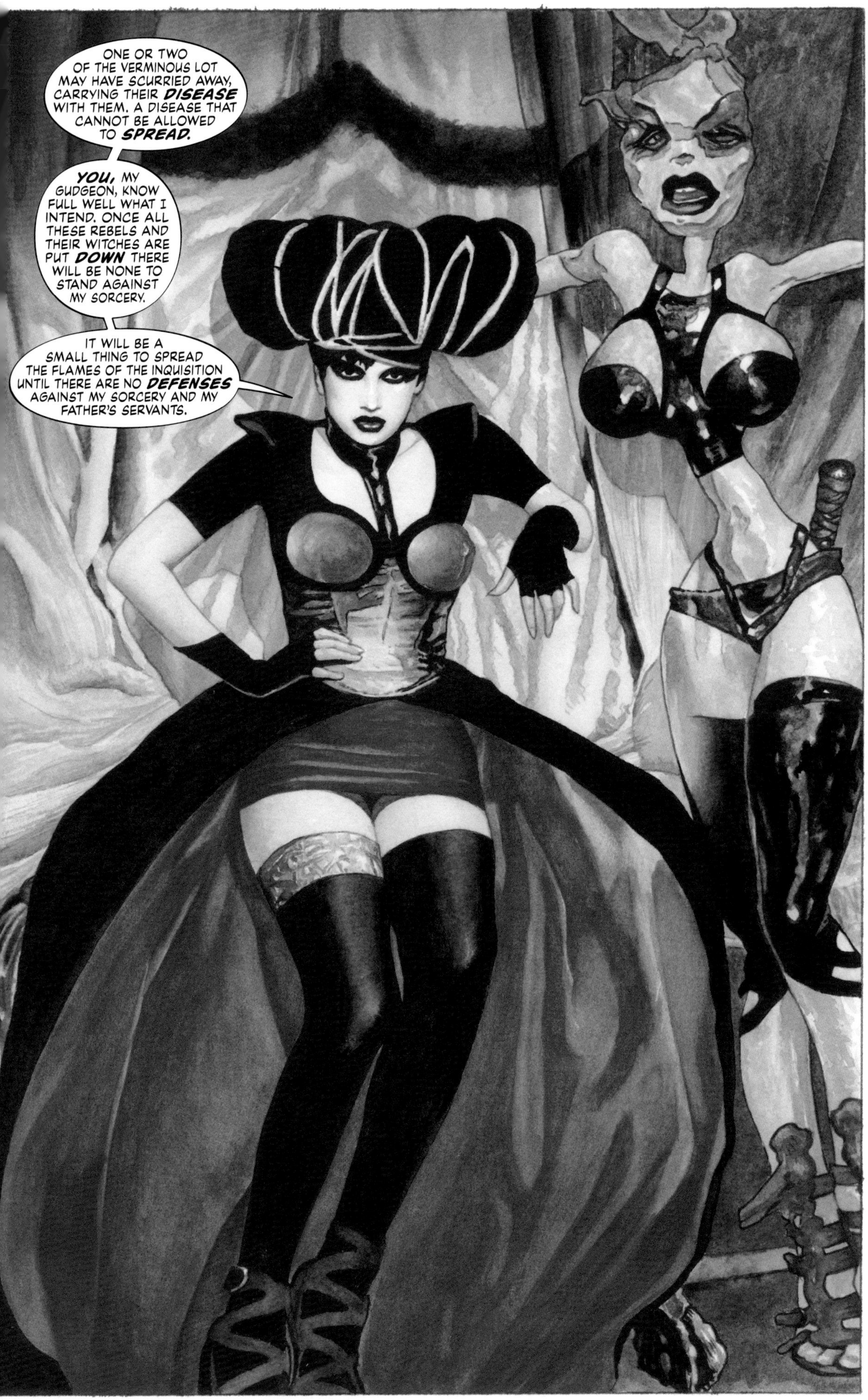
ONE OR TWO OF THE VERMINOUS LOT MAY HAVE SCURRIED AWAY, CARRYING THEIR DISEASE WITH THEM. A DISEASE THAT CANNOT BE ALLOWED TO SPREAD.
YOU, MY GUDGEON, KNOW FULL WELL WHAT I INTEND. ONCE ALL THESE REBELS AND THEIR WITCHES ARE PUT DOWN THERE WILL BE NONE TO STAND AGAINST MY SORCERY.
IT WILL BE A SMALL THING TO SPREAD THE FLAMES OF THE INQUISITION UNTIL THERE ARE NO DEFENSES AGAINST MY SORCERY AND MY FATHER'S SERVANTS.

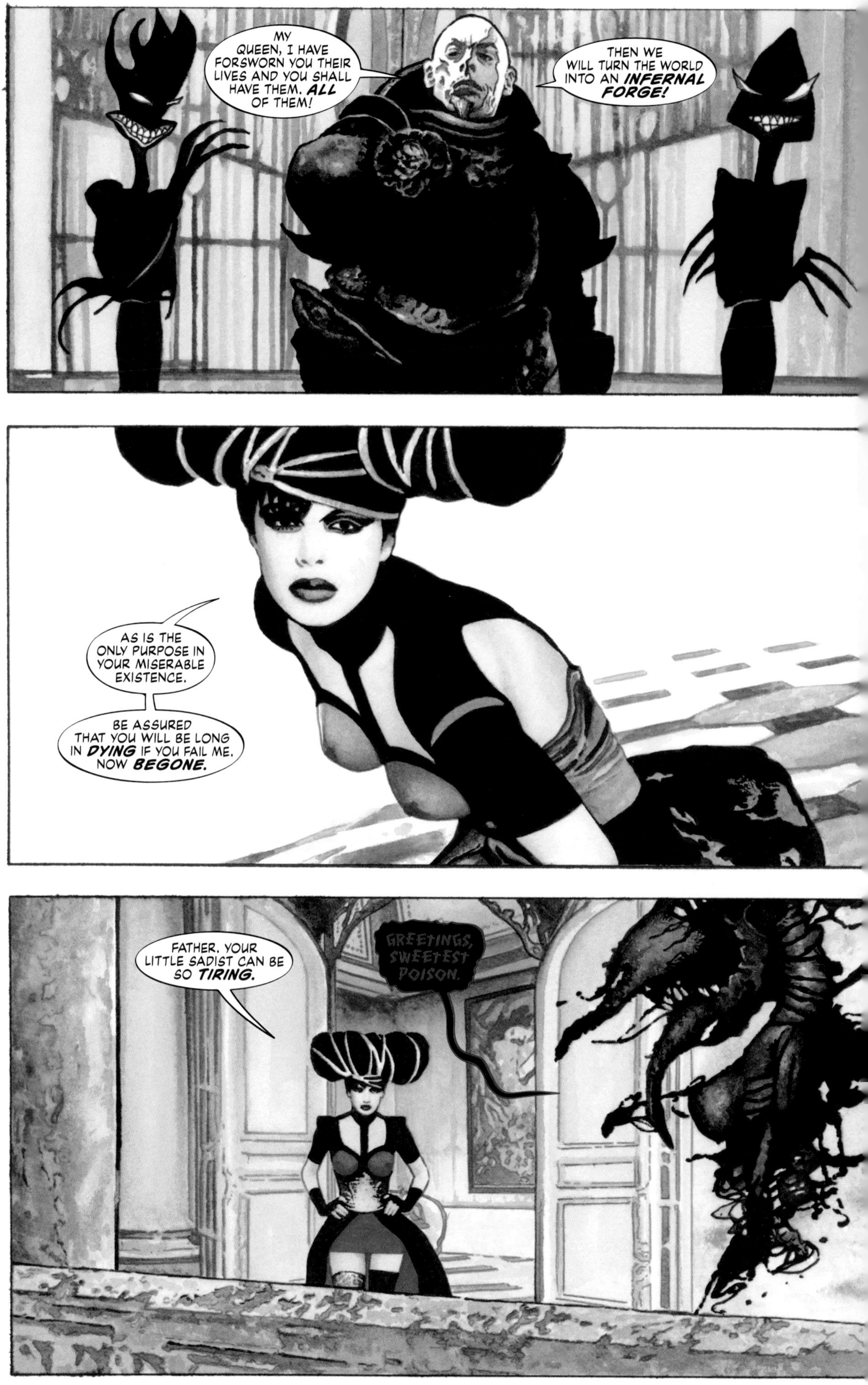

MY QUEEN, I HAVE FORSWORN YOU THEIR LIVES AND YOU SHALL HAVE THEM. ALL OF THEM!
THEN WE WILL TURN THE WORLD INTO AN INFERNAL FORGE!
AS IS THE ONLY PURPOSE IN YOUR MISERABLE EXISTENCE.
BE ASSURED THAT YOU WILL BE LONG IN DYING IF YOU FAIL ME. NOW BEGONE.
FATHER. YOUR LITTLE SADIST CAN BE SO TIRING.
GREETINGS, SWEETEST POISON.

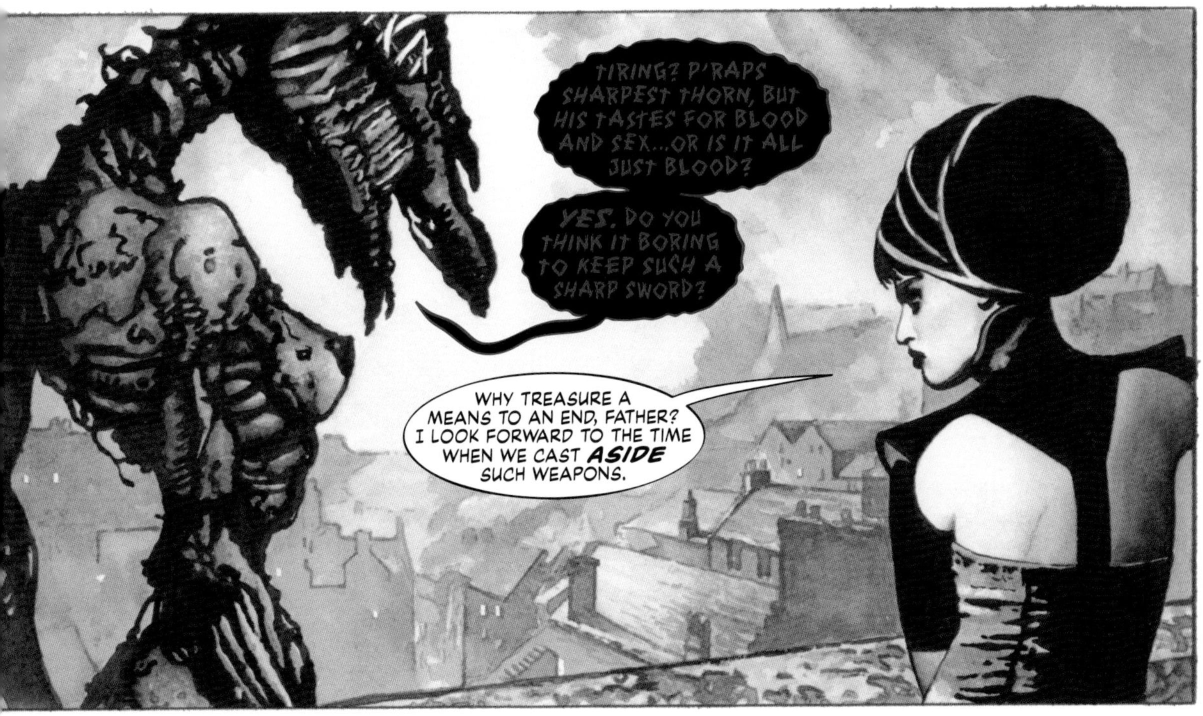
TIRING? P'RAPS SHARPEST THORN, BUT HIS TASTES FOR BLOOD AND SEX...OR IS IT ALL JUST BLOOD?
YES. DO YOU THINK IT BORING TO KEEP SUCH A SHARP SWORD?
WHY TREASURE A MEANS TO AN END, FATHER? I LOOK FORWARD TO THE TIME WHEN WE CAST ASIDE SUCH WEAPONS.

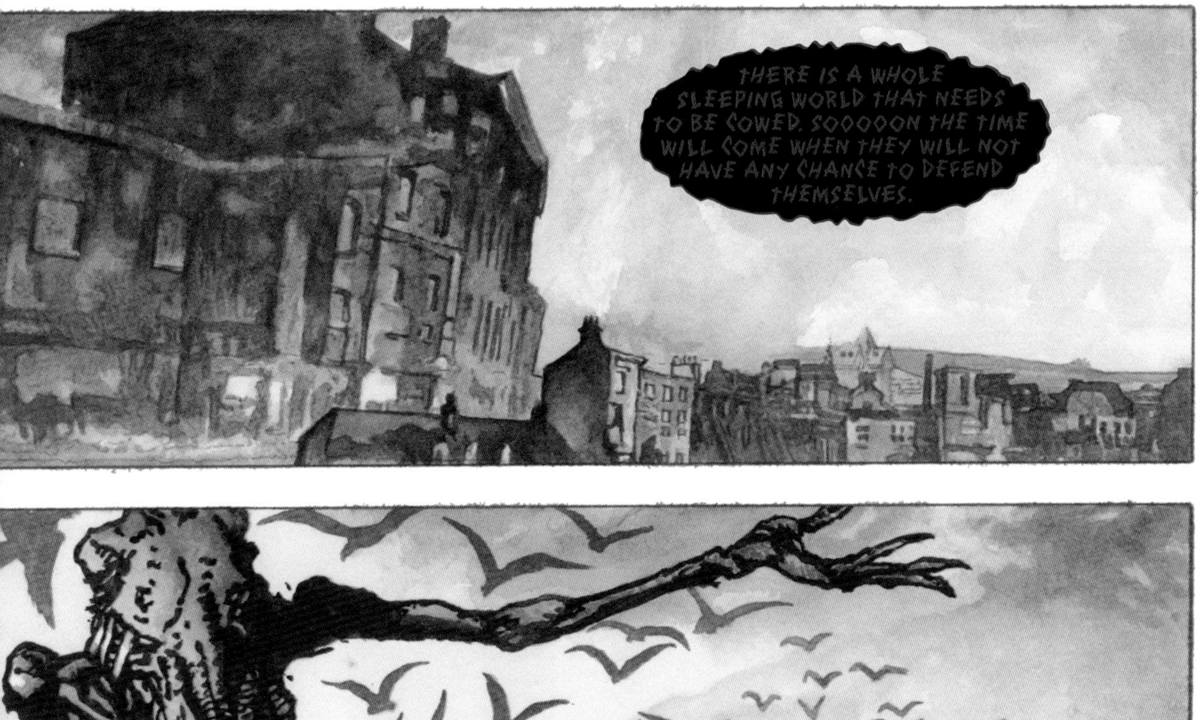
THERE IS A WHOLE SLEEPING WORLD THAT NEEDS TO BE COWED. SOOOOON THE TIME WILL COME WHEN THEY WILL NOT HAVE ANY CHANCE TO DEFEND THEMSELVES.

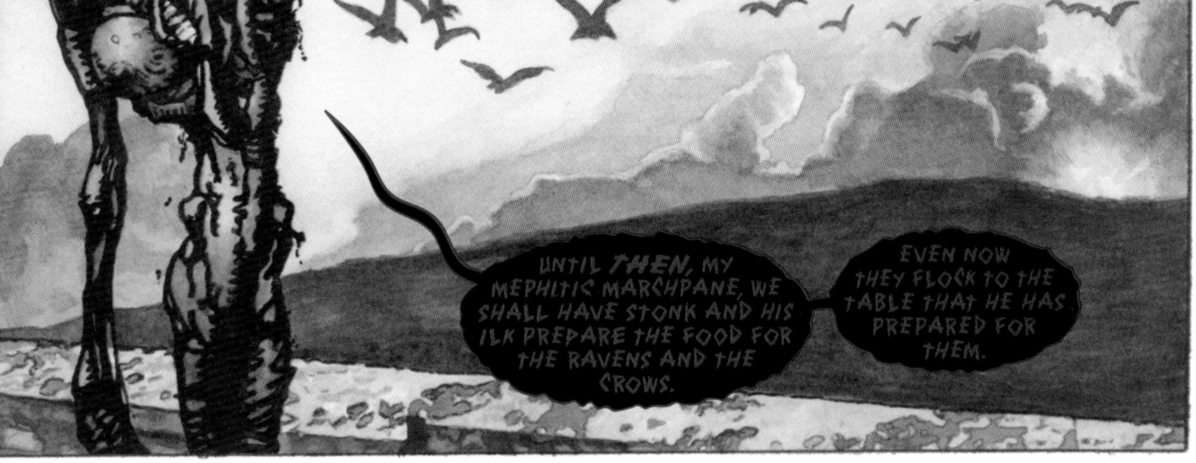
UNTIL THEN, MY MEPHITIC MARCHPANE, WE SHALL HAVE STONK AND HIS ILK PREPARE THE FOOD FOR THE RAVENS AND THE CROWS.
EVEN NOW THEY FLOCK TO THE TABLE THAT HE HAS PREPARED FOR THEM.

"YOUR MOTHER FILLED YOUR HEAD WITH TOO MANY *FOOLISH* STORIES, MY SON.

"LISTEN, MERRITT. YOU HAVE TO REMEMBER WHAT I TOLD YOU. DON'T TRUST NOBODY, JUST TRUST *YOURSELF*. REMEMBER WHAT I TOLD YOU IS *RIGHT*."

SORRY, BOY. I DIDN'T MEAN TO LEAVE YOU SO SOON. I...I...✳

PAPA?

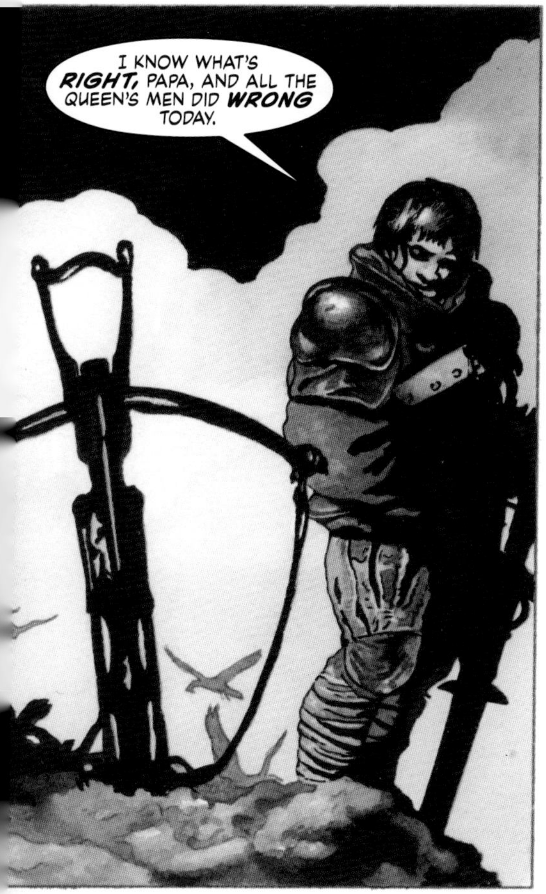
I KNOW WHAT'S **RIGHT,** PAPA, AND ALL THE QUEEN'S MEN DID **WRONG** TODAY.

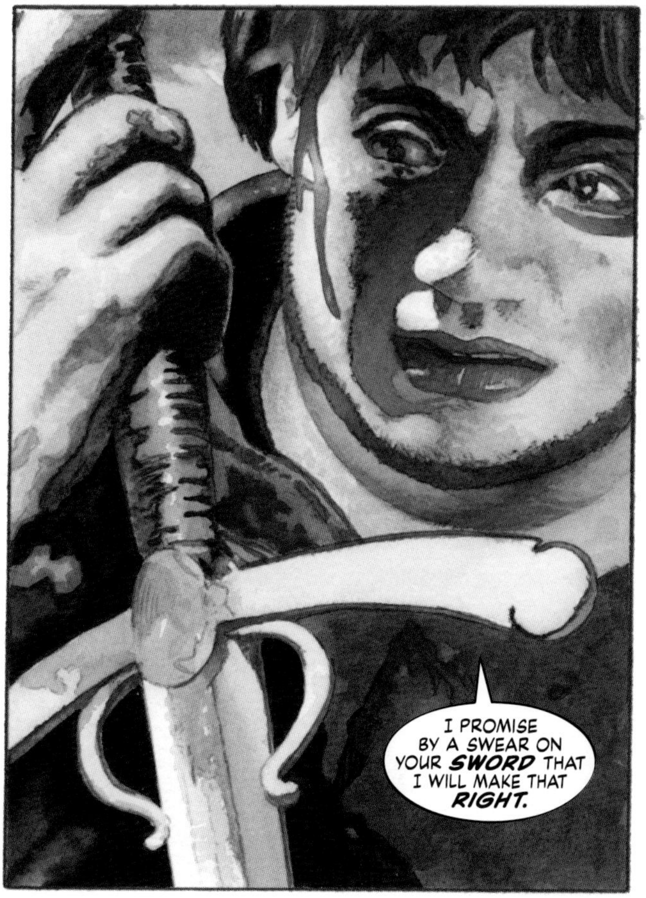
I PROMISE BY A SWEAR ON YOUR **SWORD** THAT I WILL MAKE THAT **RIGHT.**

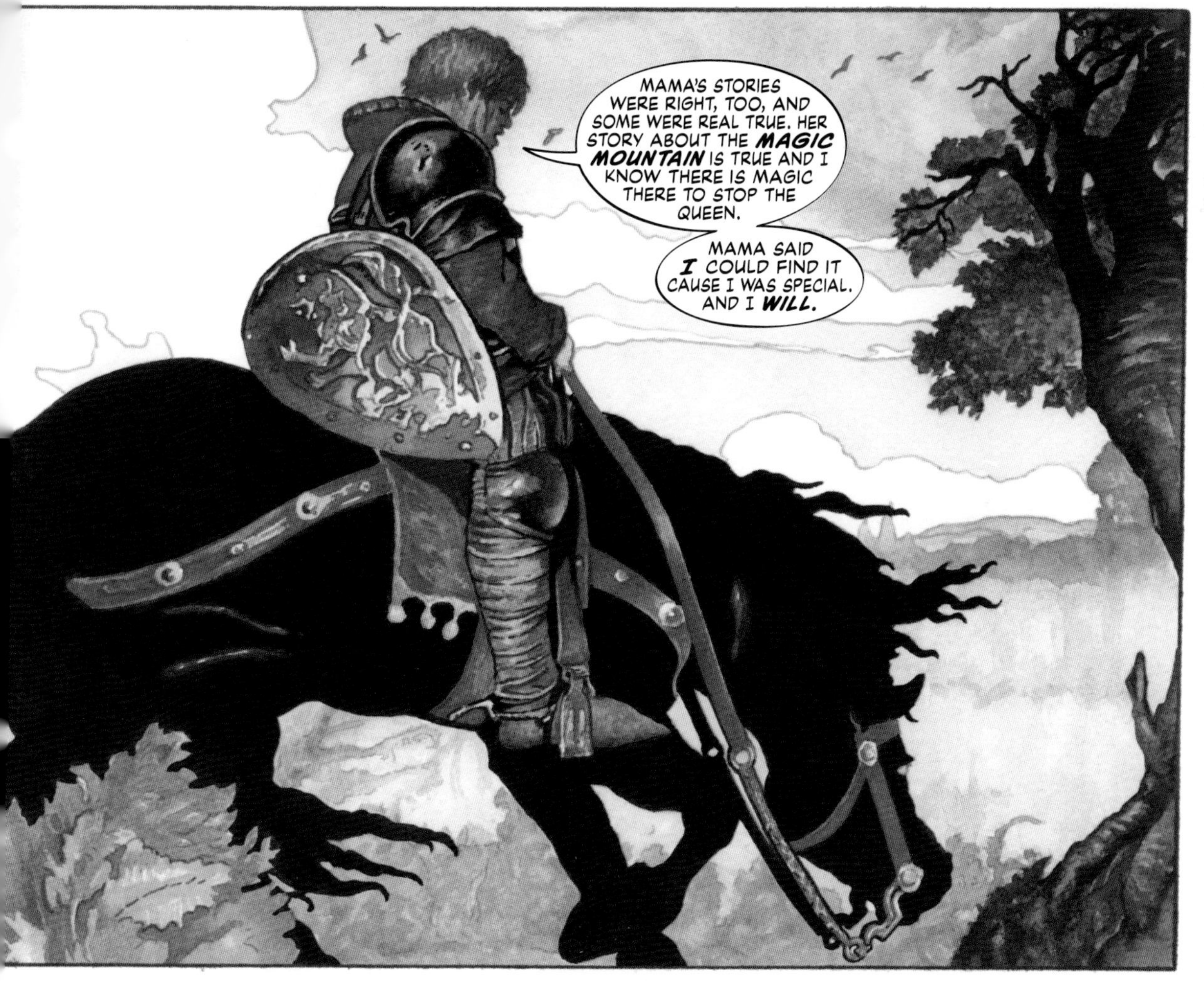
MAMA'S STORIES WERE RIGHT, TOO, AND SOME WERE REAL TRUE. HER STORY ABOUT THE **MAGIC MOUNTAIN** IS TRUE AND I KNOW THERE IS MAGIC THERE TO STOP THE QUEEN.
MAMA SAID **I** COULD FIND IT CAUSE I WAS SPECIAL. AND I **WILL.**

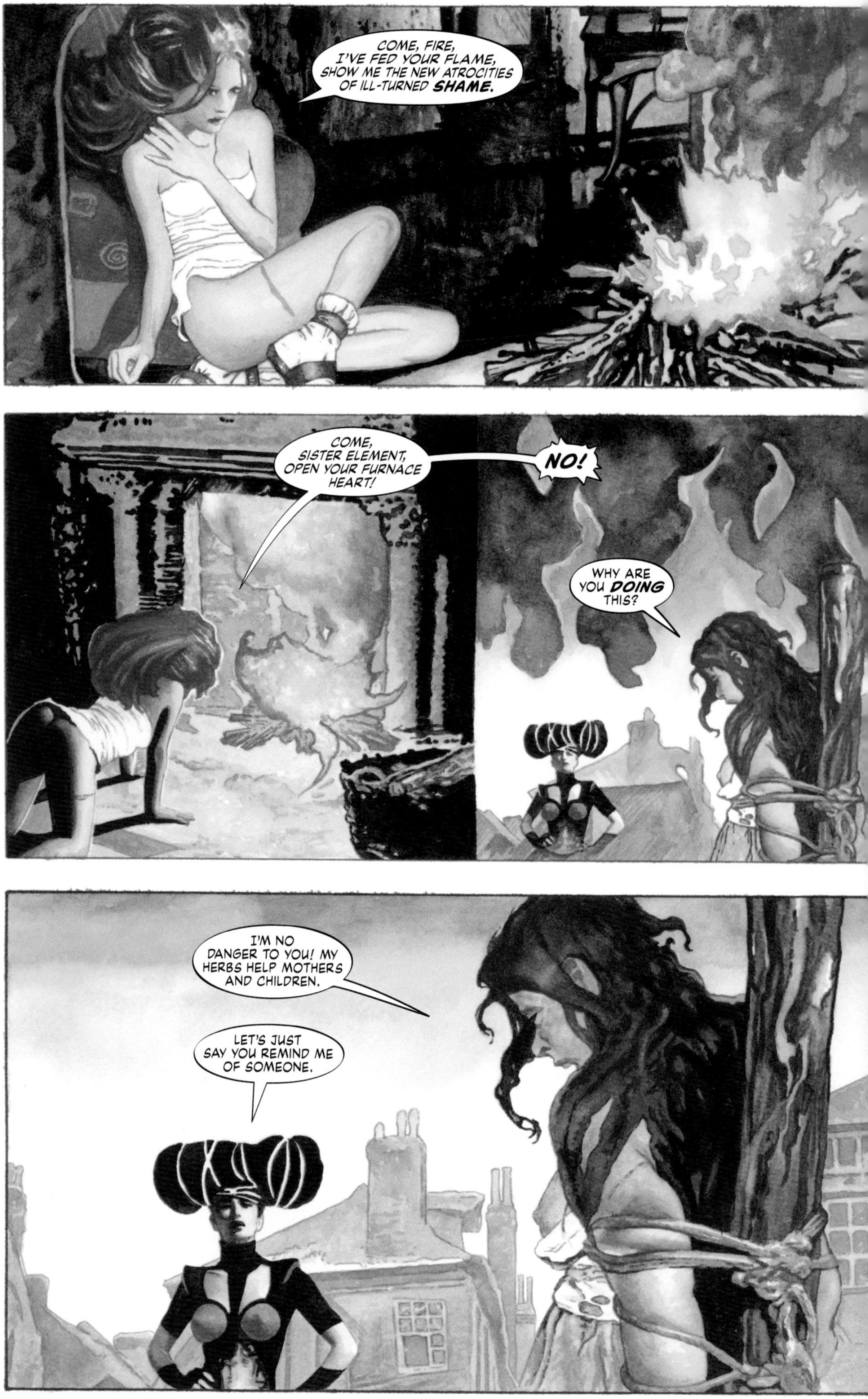
COME, FIRE, I'VE FED YOUR FLAME, SHOW ME THE NEW ATROCITIES OF ILL-TURNED **SHAME.**
COME, SISTER ELEMENT, OPEN YOUR FURNACE HEART!
NO!
WHY ARE YOU **DOING** THIS?
I'M NO DANGER TO YOU! MY HERBS HELP MOTHERS AND CHILDREN.
LET'S JUST SAY YOU REMIND ME OF SOMEONE.

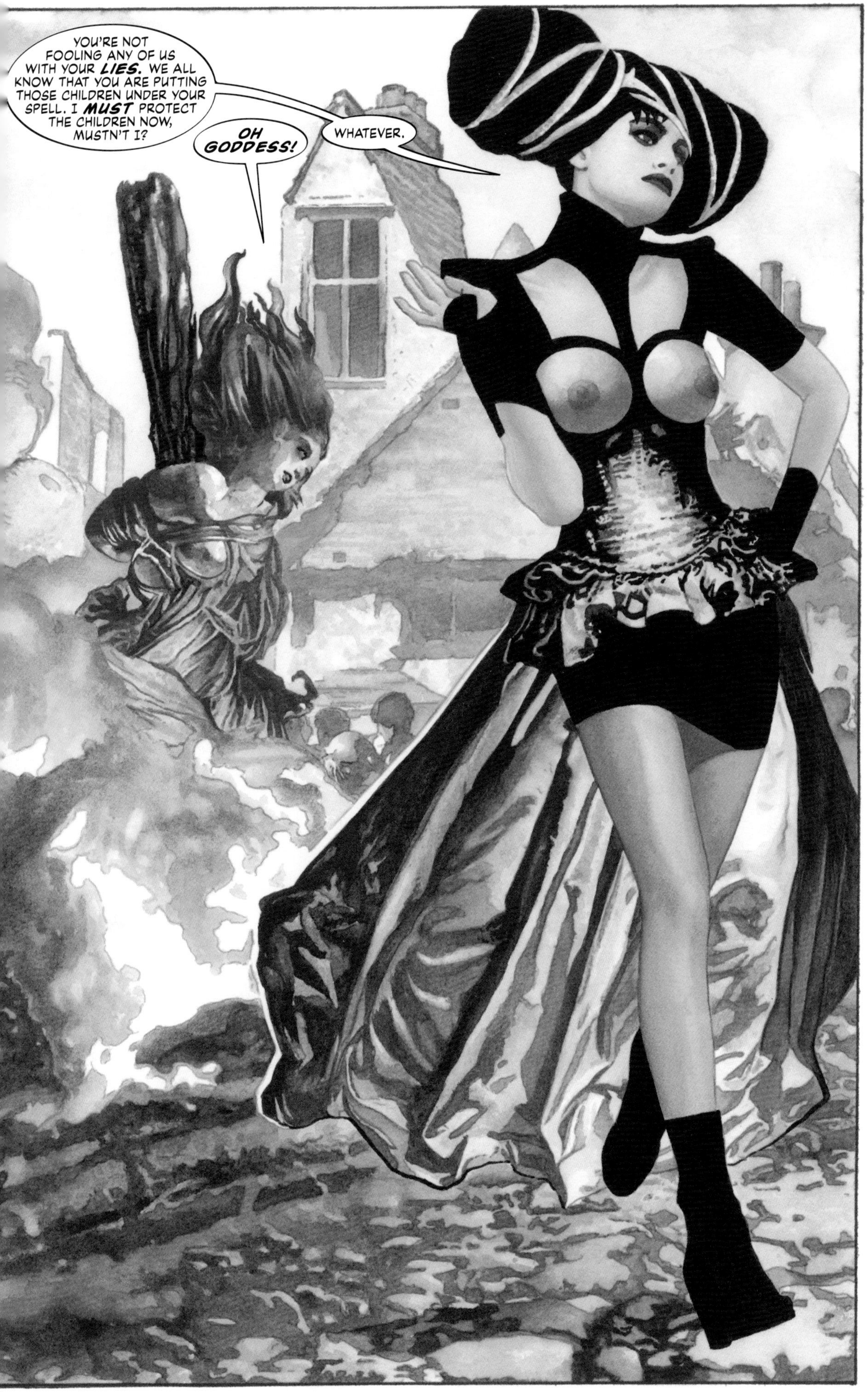
YOU'RE NOT FOOLING ANY OF US WITH YOUR LIES. WE ALL KNOW THAT YOU ARE PUTTING THOSE CHILDREN UNDER YOUR SPELL. I MUST PROTECT THE CHILDREN NOW, MUSTN'T I?
WHATEVER.
OH GODDESS!

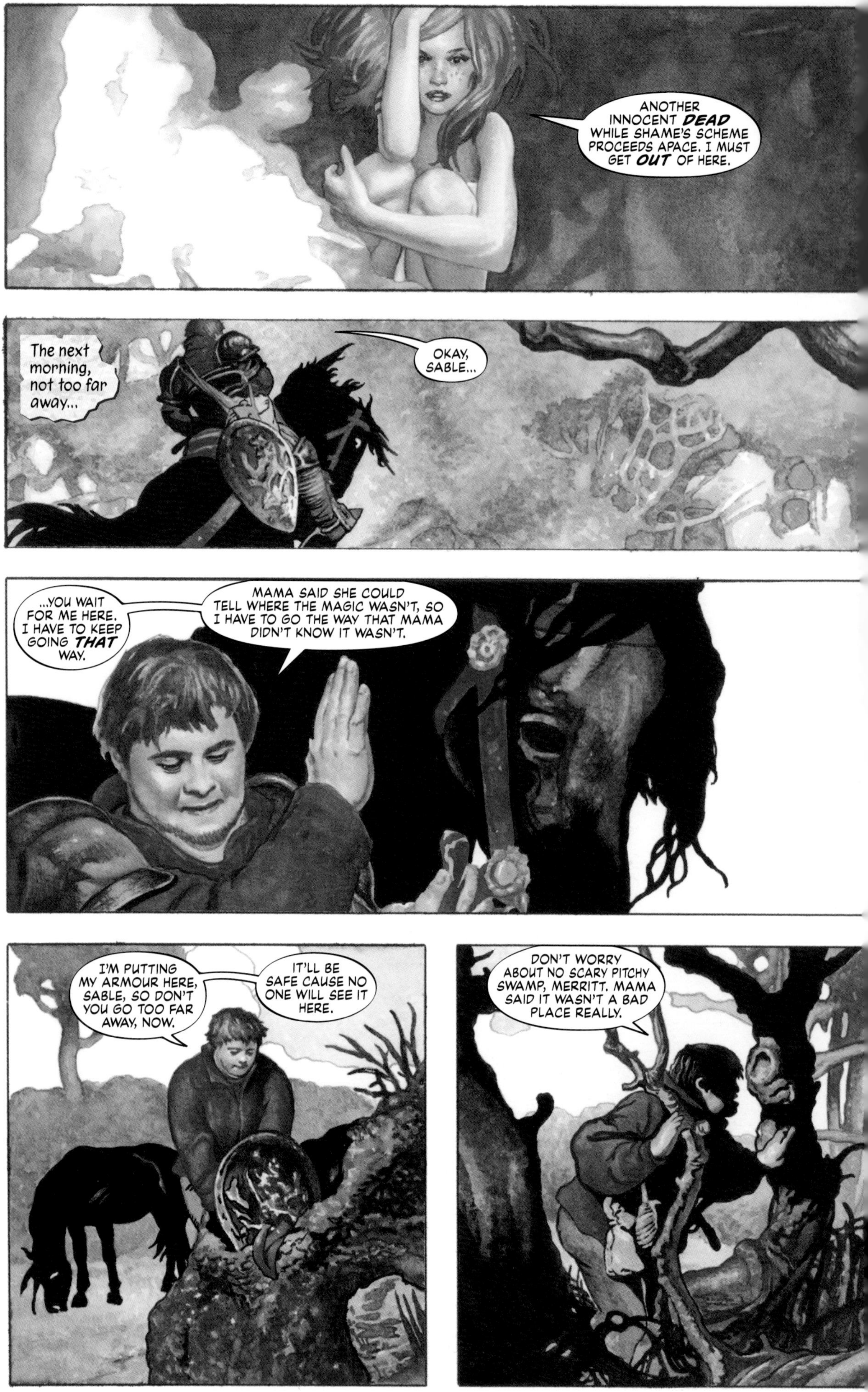
ANOTHER INNOCENT DEAD WHILE SHAME'S SCHEME PROCEEDS APACE. I MUST GET OUT OF HERE.
The next morning, not too far away...
OKAY, SABLE...
...YOU WAIT FOR ME HERE. I HAVE TO KEEP GOING THAT WAY.
MAMA SAID SHE COULD TELL WHERE THE MAGIC WASN'T, SO I HAVE TO GO THE WAY THAT MAMA DIDN'T KNOW IT WASN'T.
I'M PUTTING MY ARMOUR HERE, SABLE, SO DON'T YOU GO TOO FAR AWAY, NOW.
IT'LL BE SAFE CAUSE NO ONE WILL SEE IT HERE.
DON'T WORRY ABOUT NO SCARY PITCHY SWAMP, MERRITT. MAMA SAID IT WASN'T A BAD PLACE REALLY.

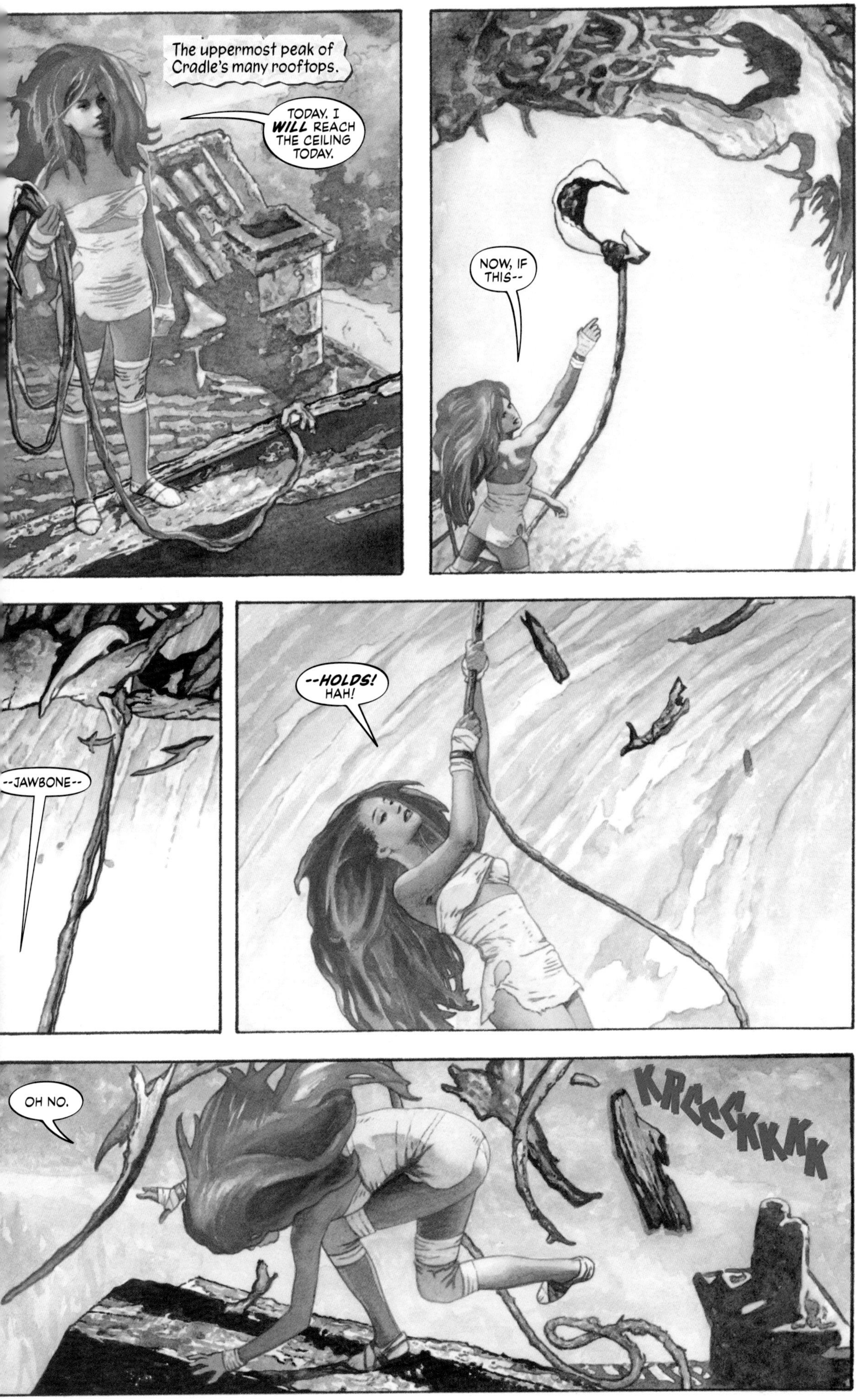

The uppermost peak of Cradle's many rooftops.
TODAY. I WILL REACH THE CEILING TODAY.
NOW, IF THIS--
--JAWBONE--
--HOLDS! HAH!
OH NO.
KRCCCKKKK

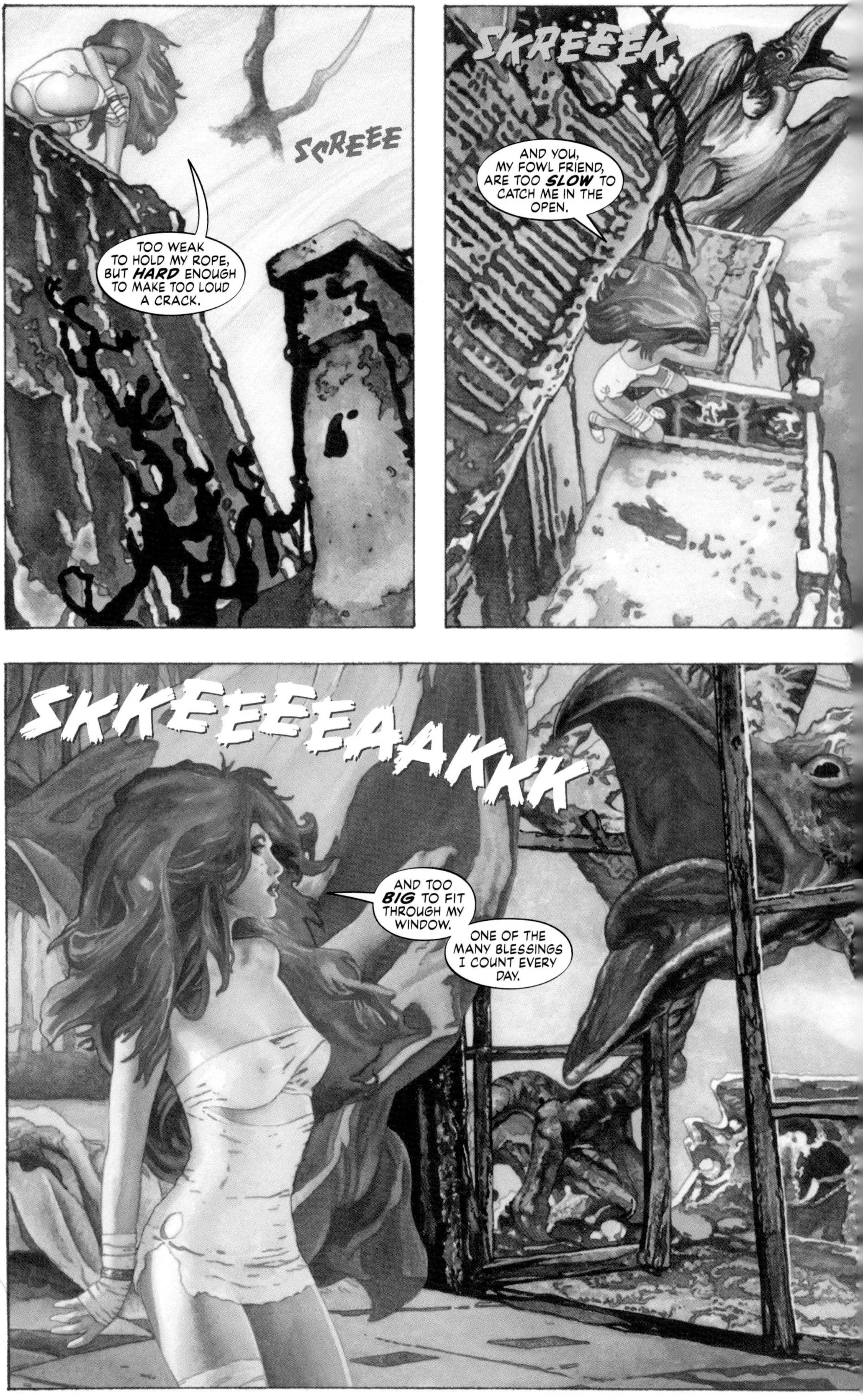
SCREEE
TOO WEAK TO HOLD MY ROPE, BUT HARD ENOUGH TO MAKE TOO LOUD A CRACK.
SKREEEK
AND YOU, MY FOWL FRIEND, ARE TOO SLOW TO CATCH ME IN THE OPEN.
SKKEEEEEAAKKK
AND TOO BIG TO FIT THROUGH MY WINDOW.
ONE OF THE MANY BLESSINGS I COUNT EVERY DAY.

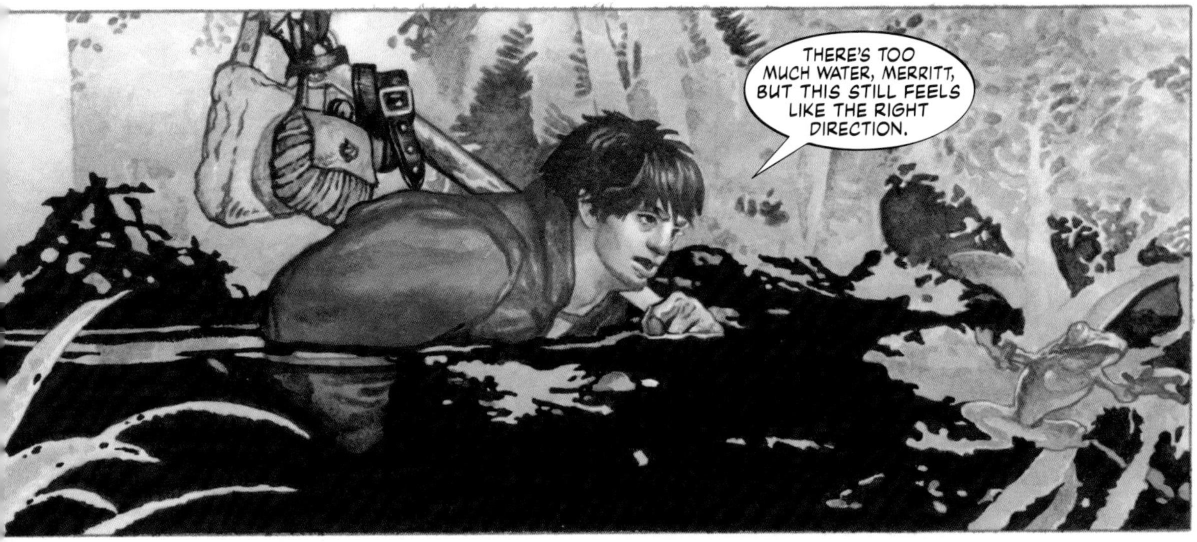
THERE'S TOO MUCH WATER, MERRITT, BUT THIS STILL FEELS LIKE THE RIGHT DIRECTION.

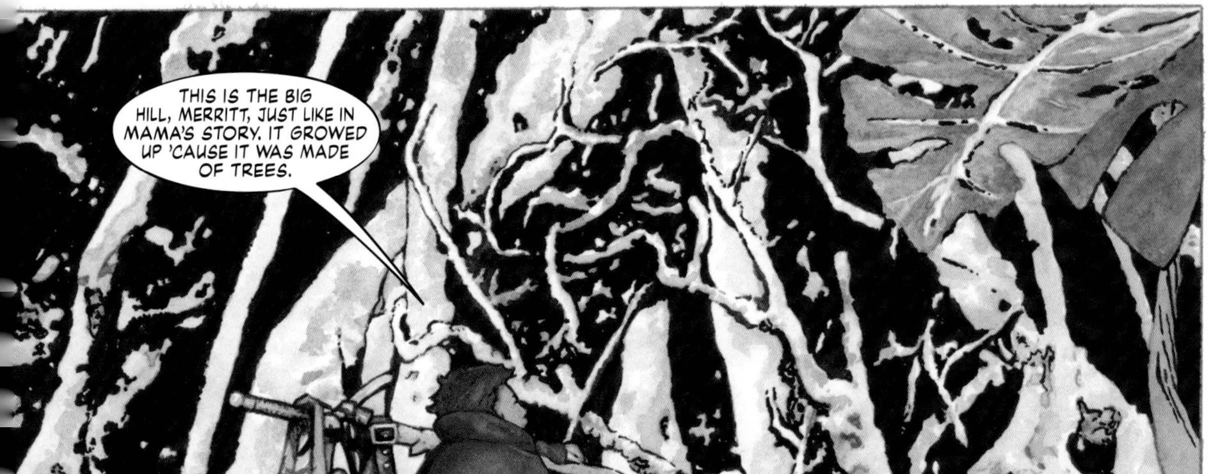
THIS IS THE BIG HILL, MERRITT, JUST LIKE IN MAMA'S STORY. IT GROWED UP 'CAUSE IT WAS MADE OF TREES.

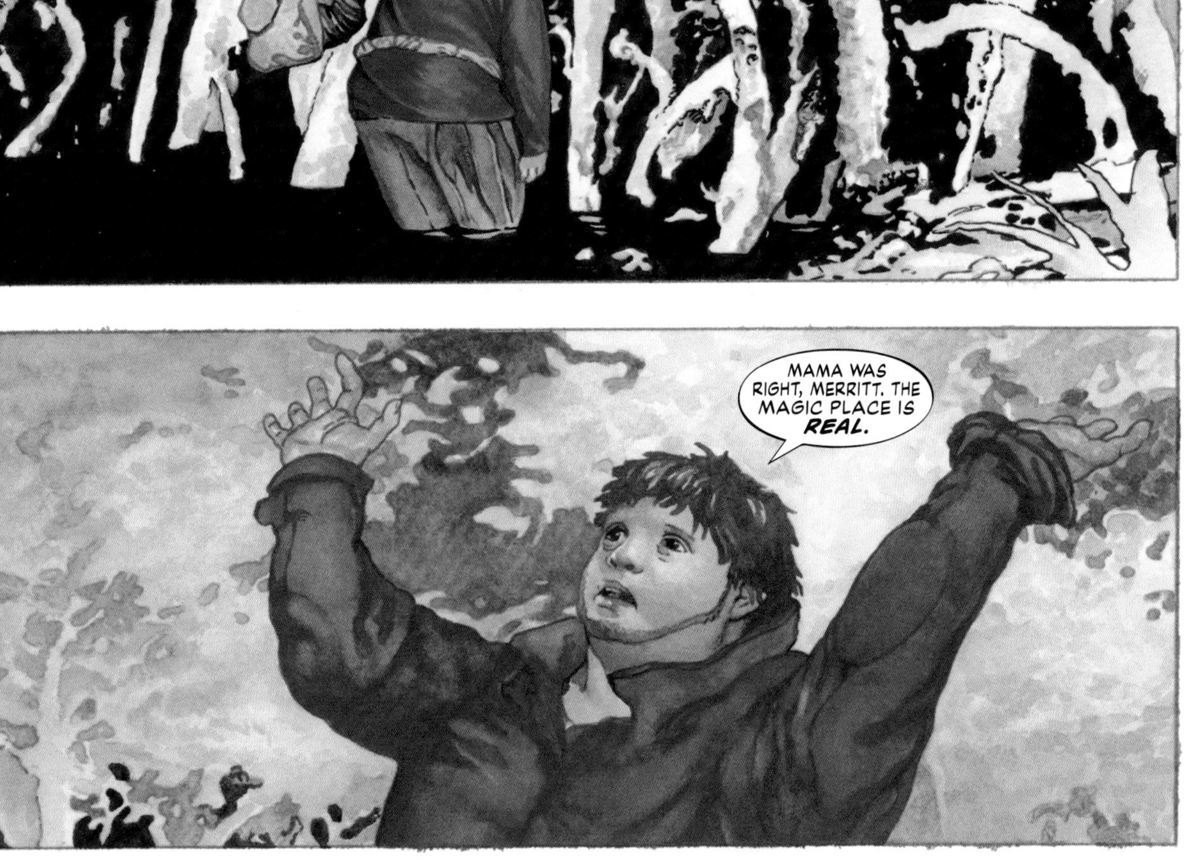
MAMA WAS RIGHT, MERRITT. THE MAGIC PLACE IS ***REAL.***

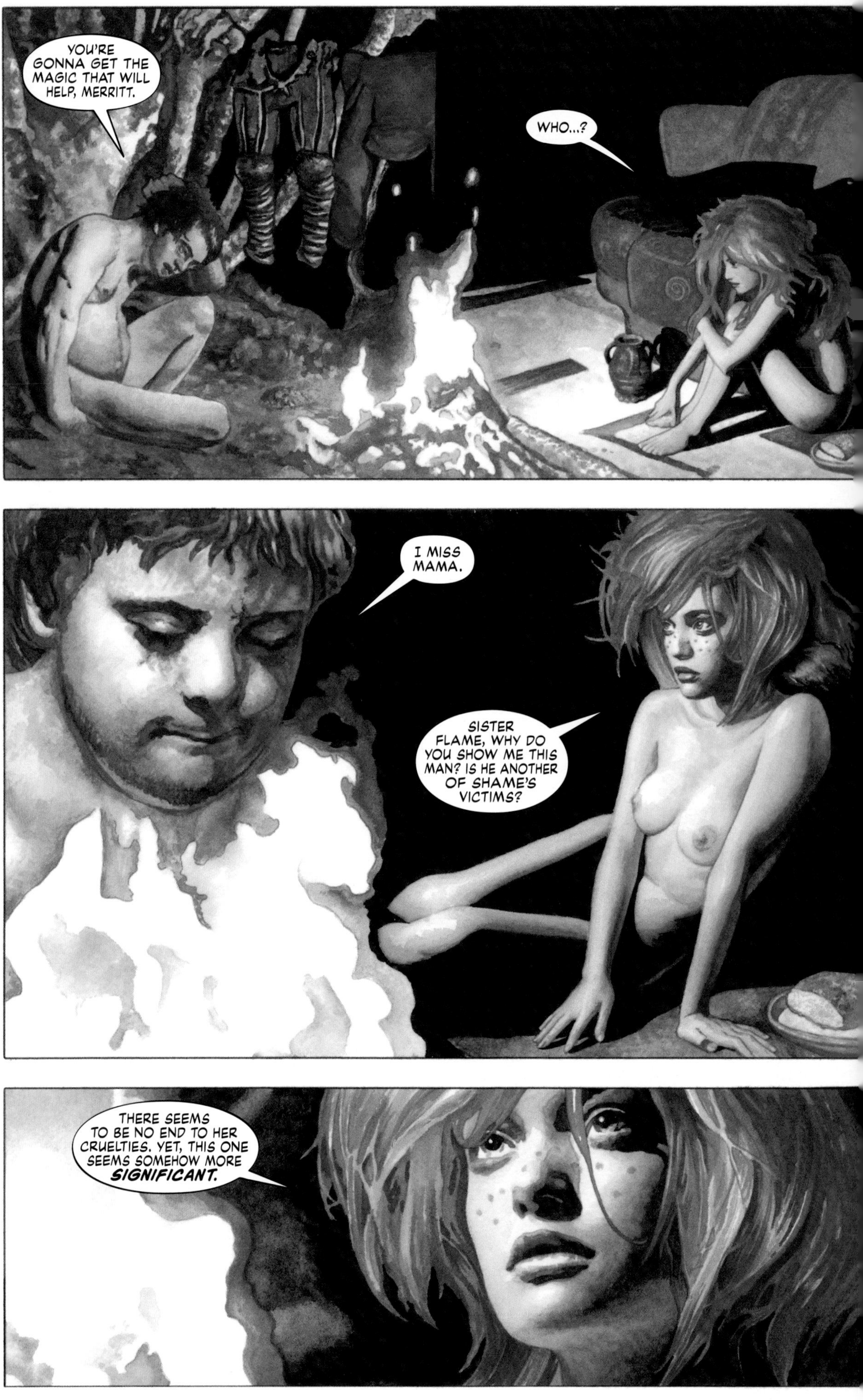
YOU'RE GONNA GET THE MAGIC THAT WILL HELP, MERRITT.
WHO...?
I MISS MAMA.
SISTER FLAME, WHY DO YOU SHOW ME THIS MAN? IS HE ANOTHER OF SHAME'S VICTIMS?
THERE SEEMS TO BE NO END TO HER CRUELTIES. YET, THIS ONE SEEMS SOMEHOW MORE ***SIGNIFICANT.***

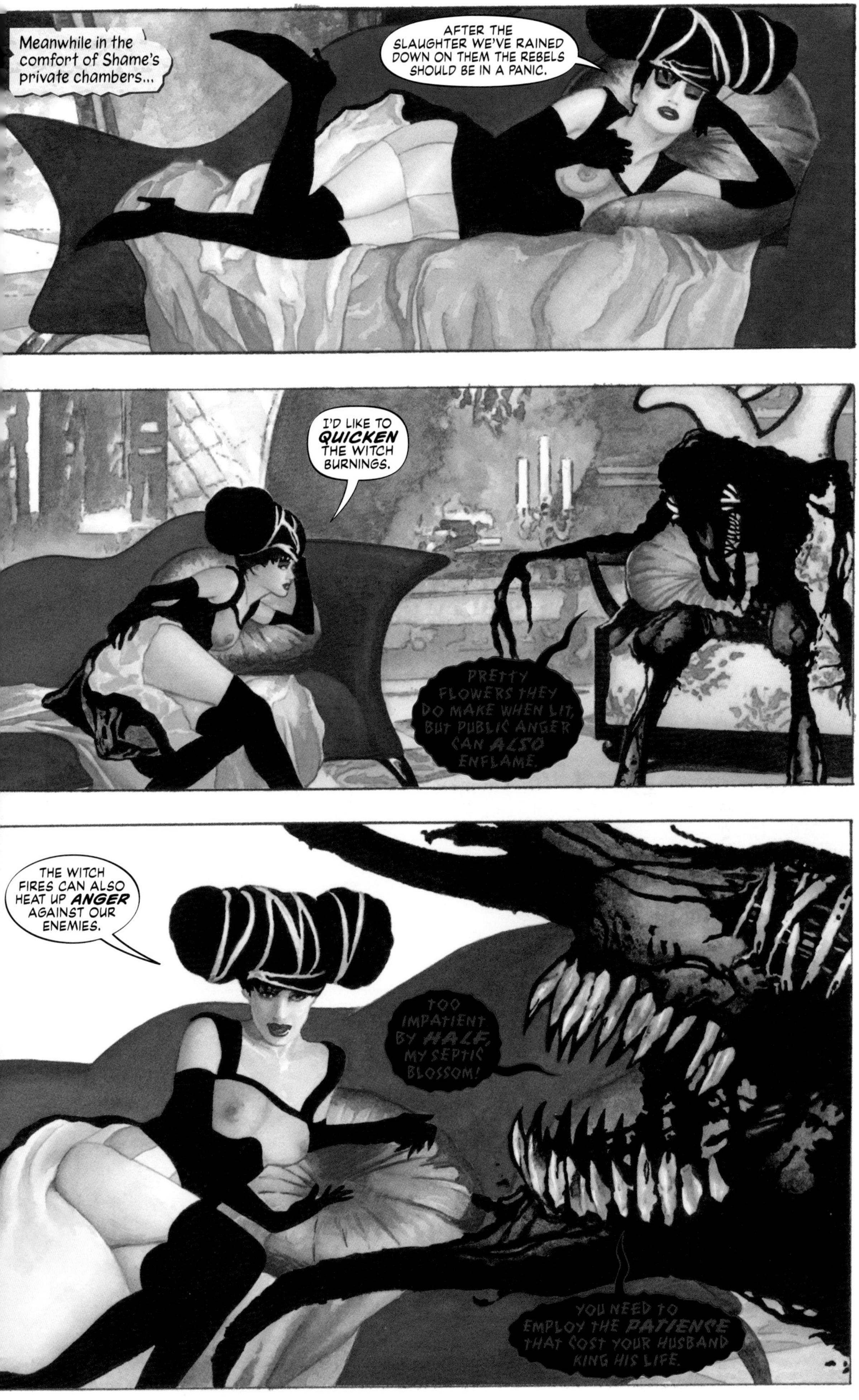
Meanwhile in the comfort of Shame's private chambers...
AFTER THE SLAUGHTER WE'VE RAINED DOWN ON THEM THE REBELS SHOULD BE IN A PANIC.
I'D LIKE TO QUICKEN THE WITCH BURNINGS.
PRETTY FLOWERS THEY DO MAKE WHEN LIT, BUT PUBLIC ANGER CAN ALSO ENFLAME.
THE WITCH FIRES CAN ALSO HEAT UP ANGER AGAINST OUR ENEMIES.
TOO IMPATIENT BY HALF, MY SEPTIC BLOSSOM!
YOU NEED TO EMPLOY THE PATIENCE THAT COST YOUR HUSBAND KING HIS LIFE.

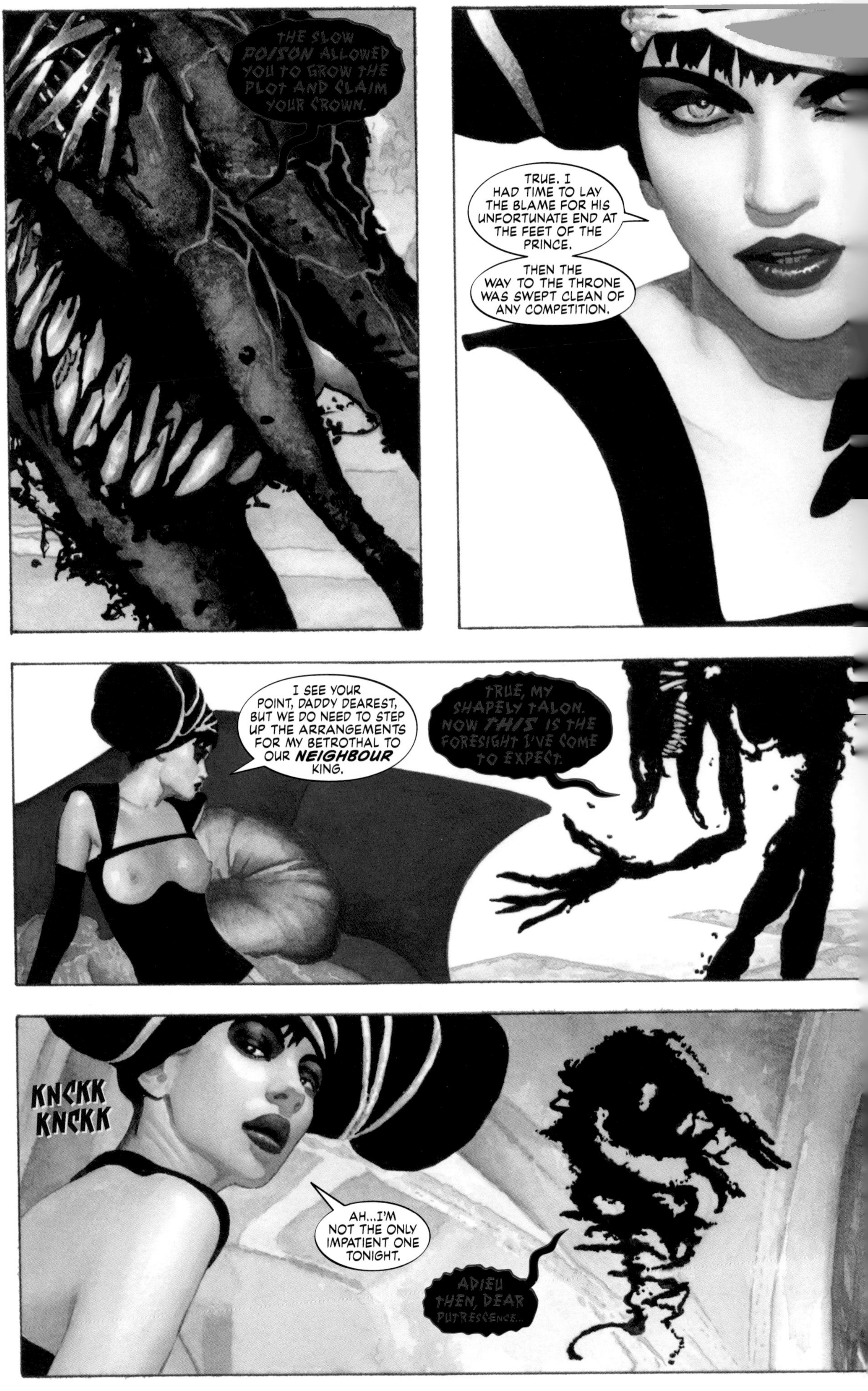
THE SLOW POISON ALLOWED YOU TO GROW THE PLOT AND CLAIM YOUR CROWN.
TRUE. I HAD TIME TO LAY THE BLAME FOR HIS UNFORTUNATE END AT THE FEET OF THE PRINCE.
THEN THE WAY TO THE THRONE WAS SWEPT CLEAN OF ANY COMPETITION.
I SEE YOUR POINT, DADDY DEAREST, BUT WE DO NEED TO STEP UP THE ARRANGEMENTS FOR MY BETROTHAL TO OUR NEIGHBOUR KING.
TRUE, MY SHAPELY TALON. NOW THIS IS THE FORESIGHT I'VE COME TO EXPECT.
KNCKK KNCKK
AH...I'M NOT THE ONLY IMPATIENT ONE TONIGHT.
ADIEU THEN, DEAR PUTRESCENCE...

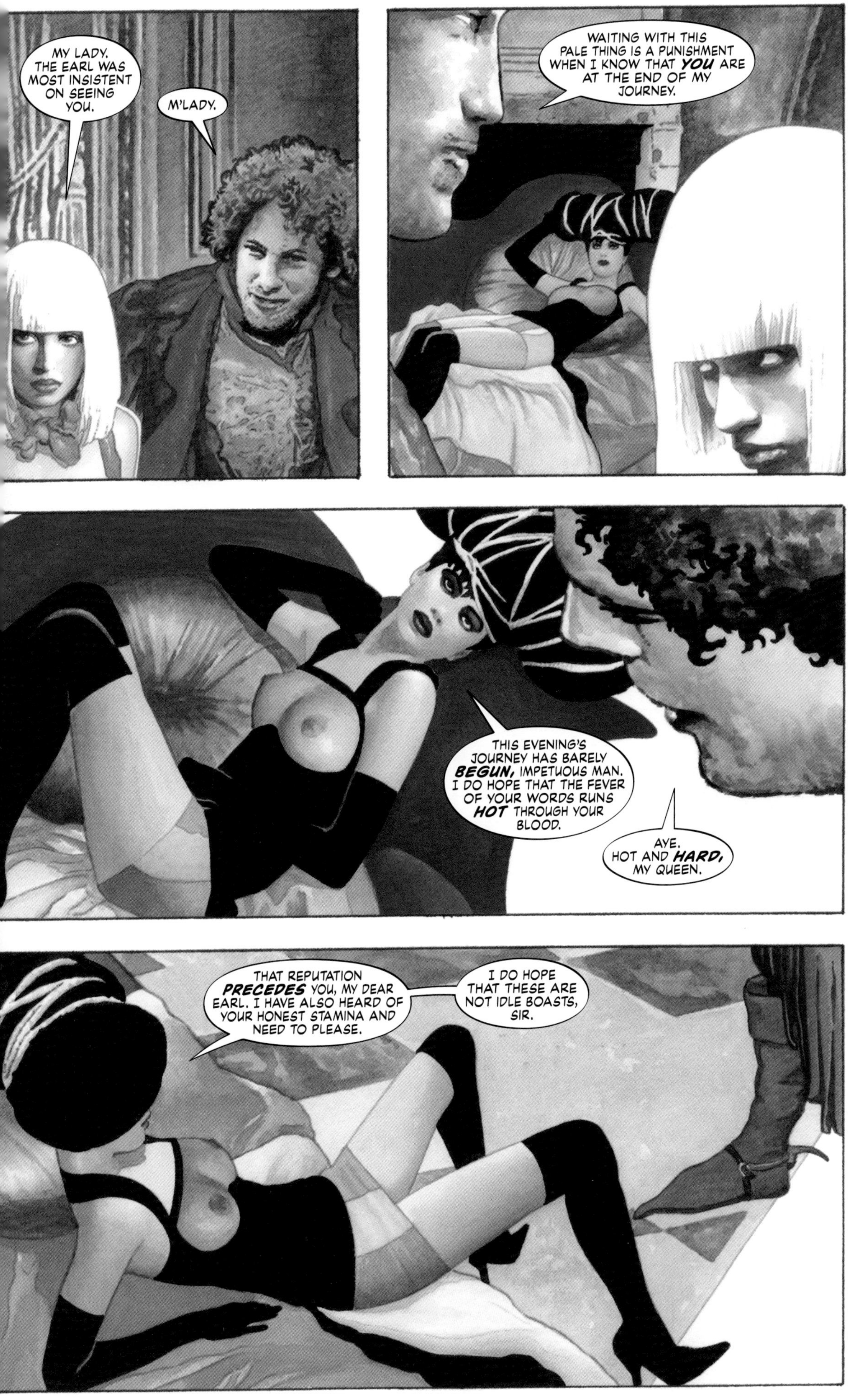
MY LADY. THE EARL WAS MOST INSISTENT ON SEEING YOU.
M'LADY.
WAITING WITH THIS PALE THING IS A PUNISHMENT WHEN I KNOW THAT *YOU* ARE AT THE END OF MY JOURNEY.
THIS EVENING'S JOURNEY HAS BARELY *BEGUN,* IMPETUOUS MAN. I DO HOPE THAT THE FEVER OF YOUR WORDS RUNS *HOT* THROUGH YOUR BLOOD.
AYE. HOT AND *HARD,* MY QUEEN.
THAT REPUTATION *PRECEDES* YOU, MY DEAR EARL. I HAVE ALSO HEARD OF YOUR HONEST STAMINA AND NEED TO PLEASE.
I DO HOPE THAT THESE ARE NOT IDLE BOASTS, SIR.

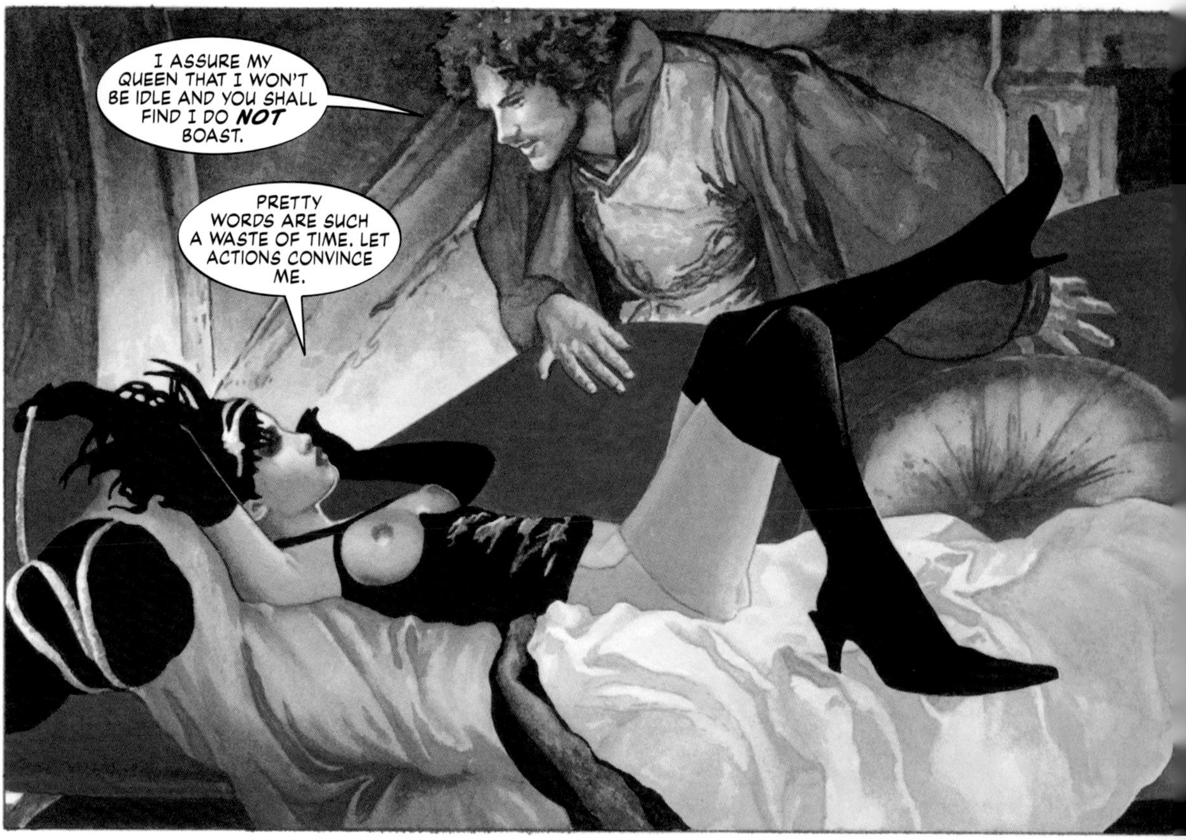
I ASSURE MY QUEEN THAT I WON'T BE IDLE AND YOU SHALL FIND I DO **NOT** BOAST.
PRETTY WORDS ARE SUCH A WASTE OF TIME. LET ACTIONS CONVINCE ME.

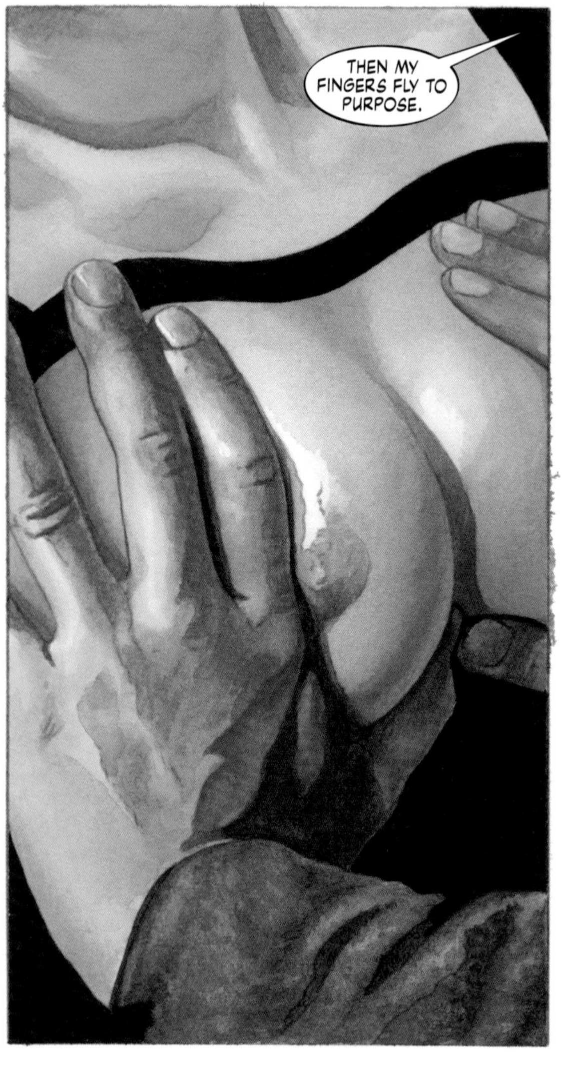
THEN MY FINGERS FLY TO PURPOSE.

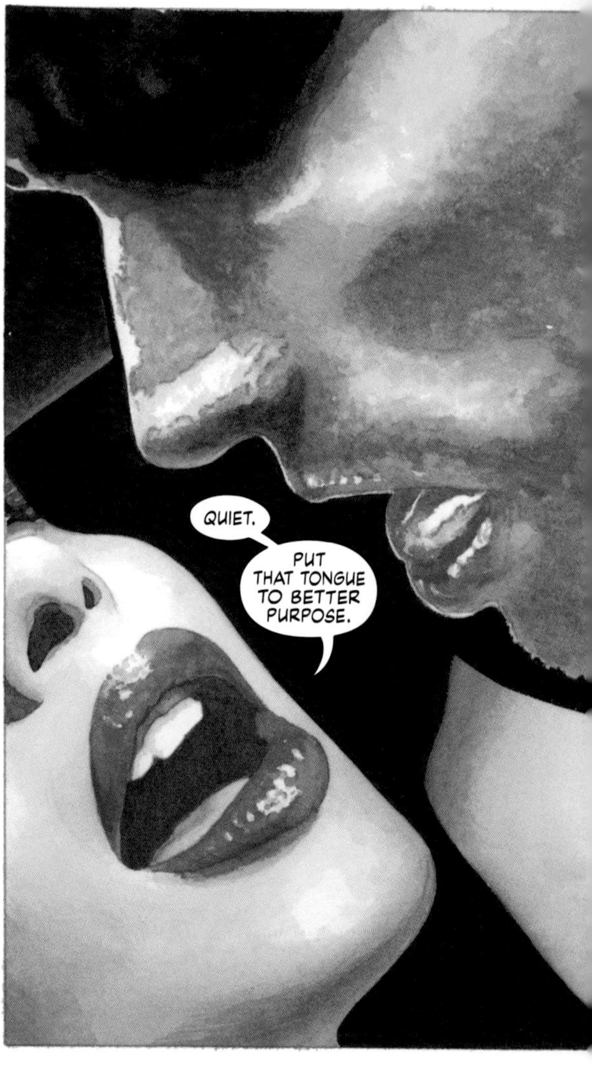
QUIET.
PUT THAT TONGUE TO BETTER PURPOSE.

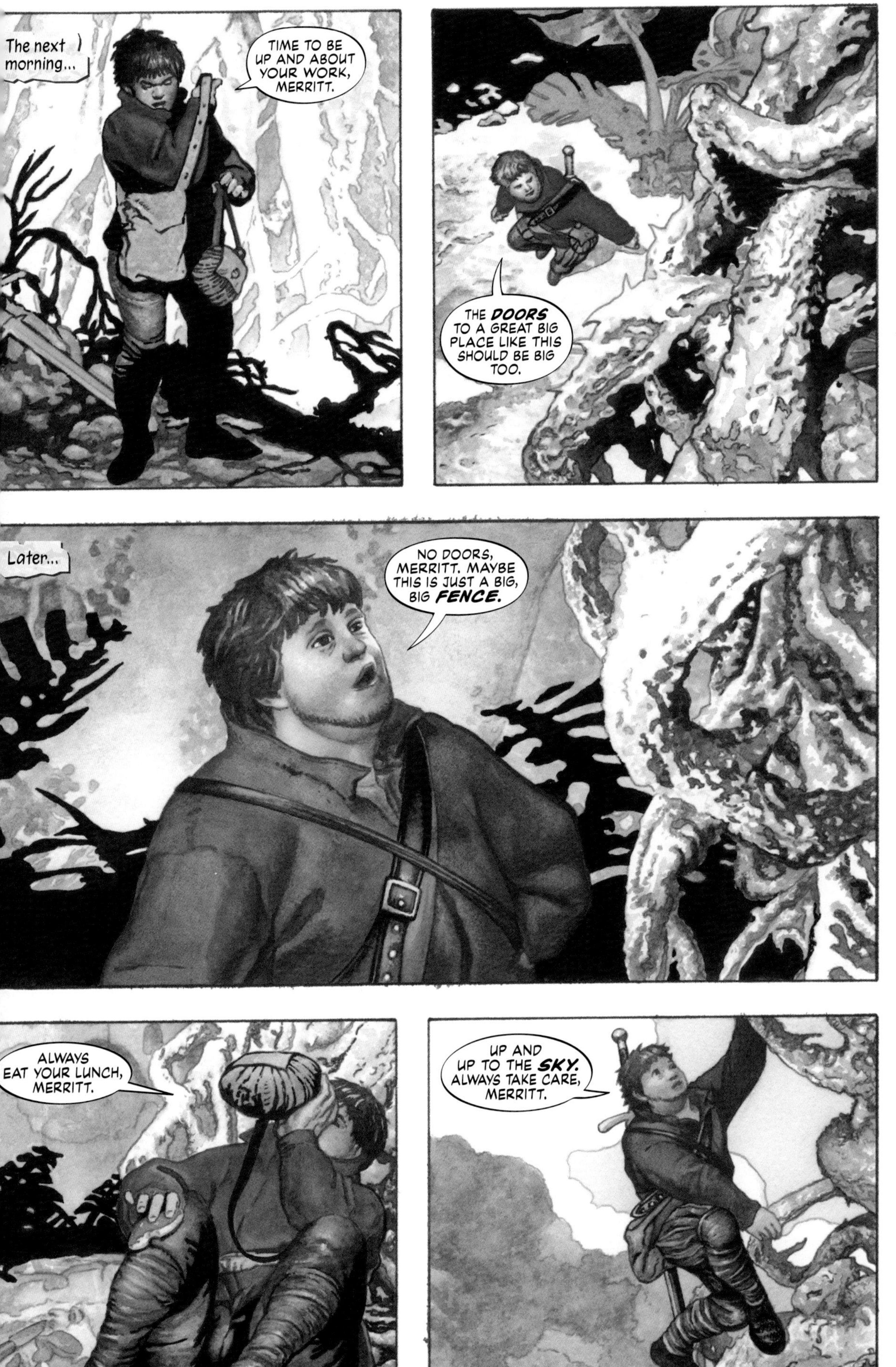
The next morning...
TIME TO BE UP AND ABOUT YOUR WORK, MERRITT.
THE **DOORS** TO A GREAT BIG PLACE LIKE THIS SHOULD BE BIG TOO.
Later...
NO DOORS, MERRITT. MAYBE THIS IS JUST A BIG, BIG **FENCE.**
ALWAYS EAT YOUR LUNCH, MERRITT.
UP AND UP TO THE **SKY.** ALWAYS TAKE CARE, MERRITT.

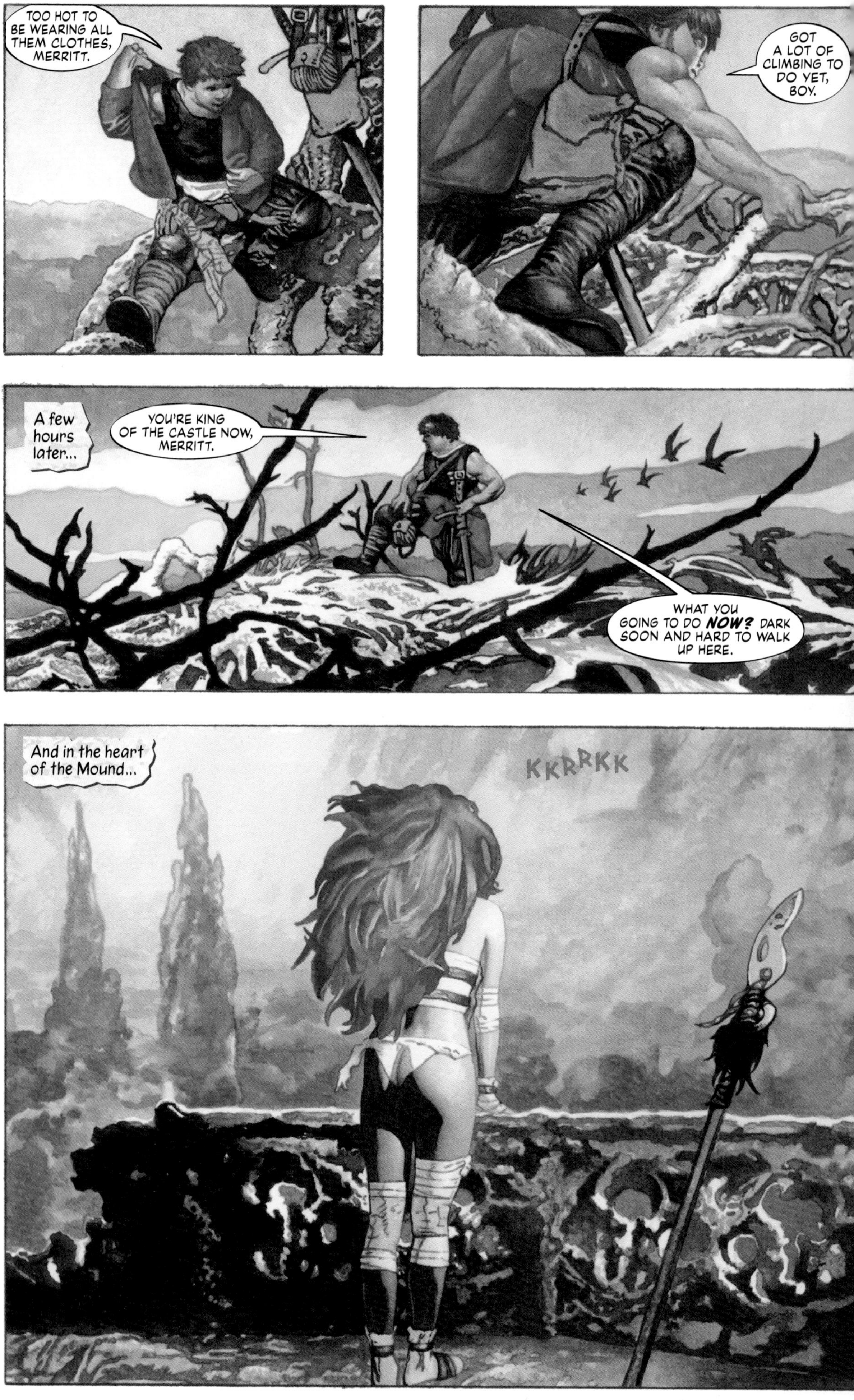

TOO HOT TO BE WEARING ALL THEM CLOTHES, MERRITT.
GOT A LOT OF CLIMBING TO DO YET, BOY.
A few hours later...
YOU'RE KING OF THE CASTLE NOW, MERRITT.
WHAT YOU GOING TO DO **NOW?** DARK SOON AND HARD TO WALK UP HERE.
And in the heart of the Mound...
KKRRKK

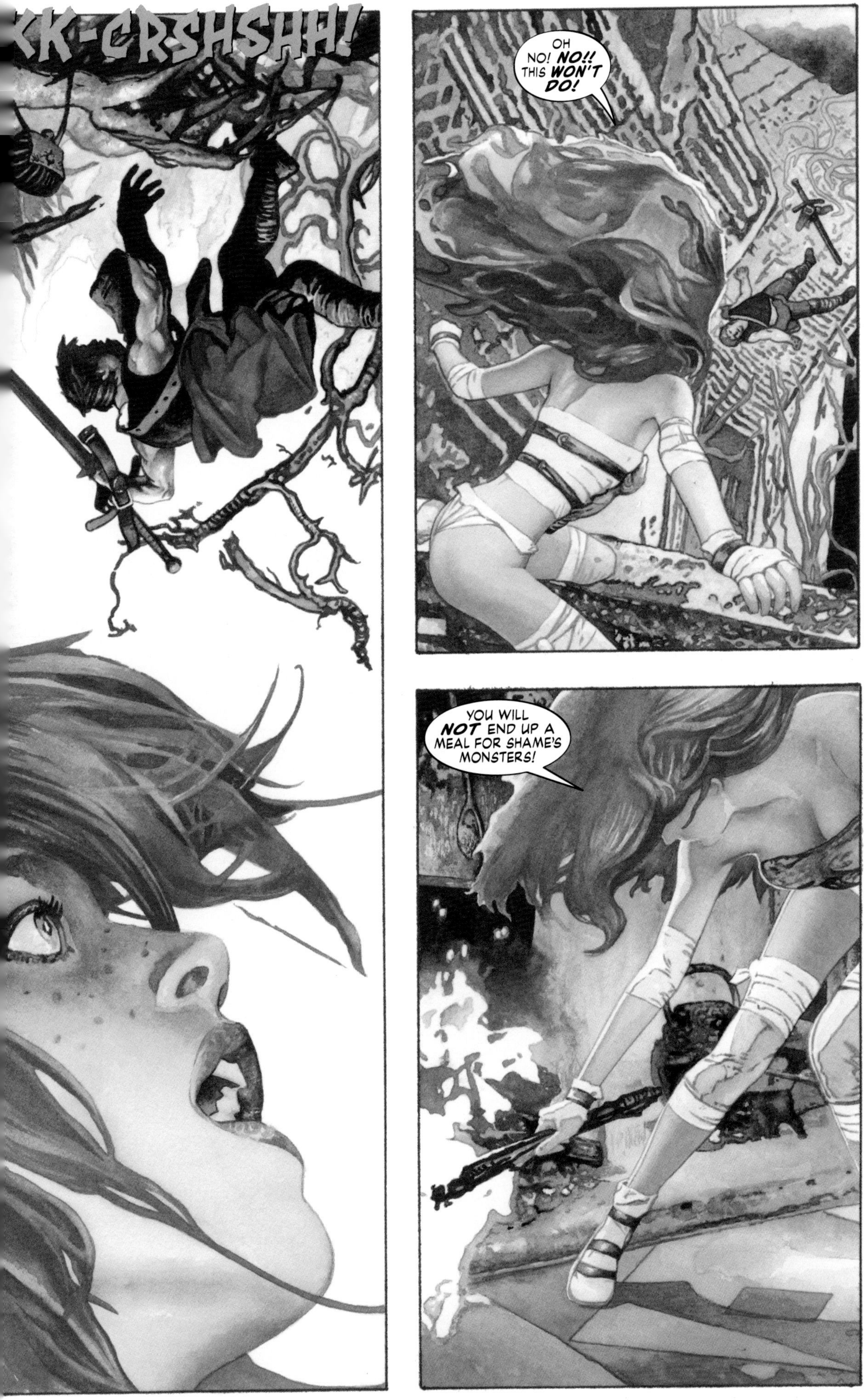
KK-CRSHSHH!
OH NO! NO!! THIS WON'T DO!
YOU WILL NOT END UP A MEAL FOR SHAME'S MONSTERS!

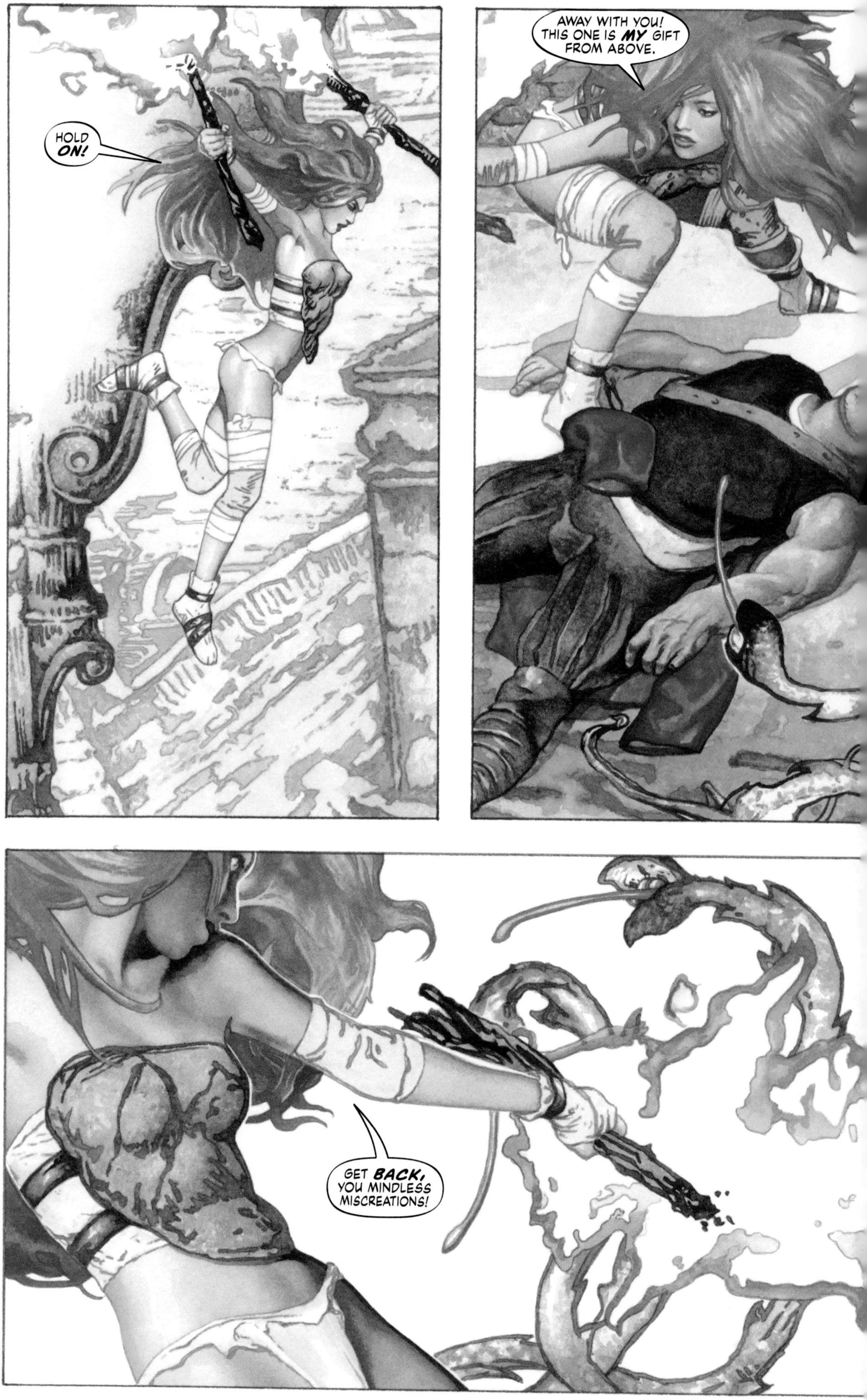
HOLD ON!
AWAY WITH YOU! THIS ONE IS MY GIFT FROM ABOVE.
GET BACK, YOU MINDLESS MISCREATIONS!

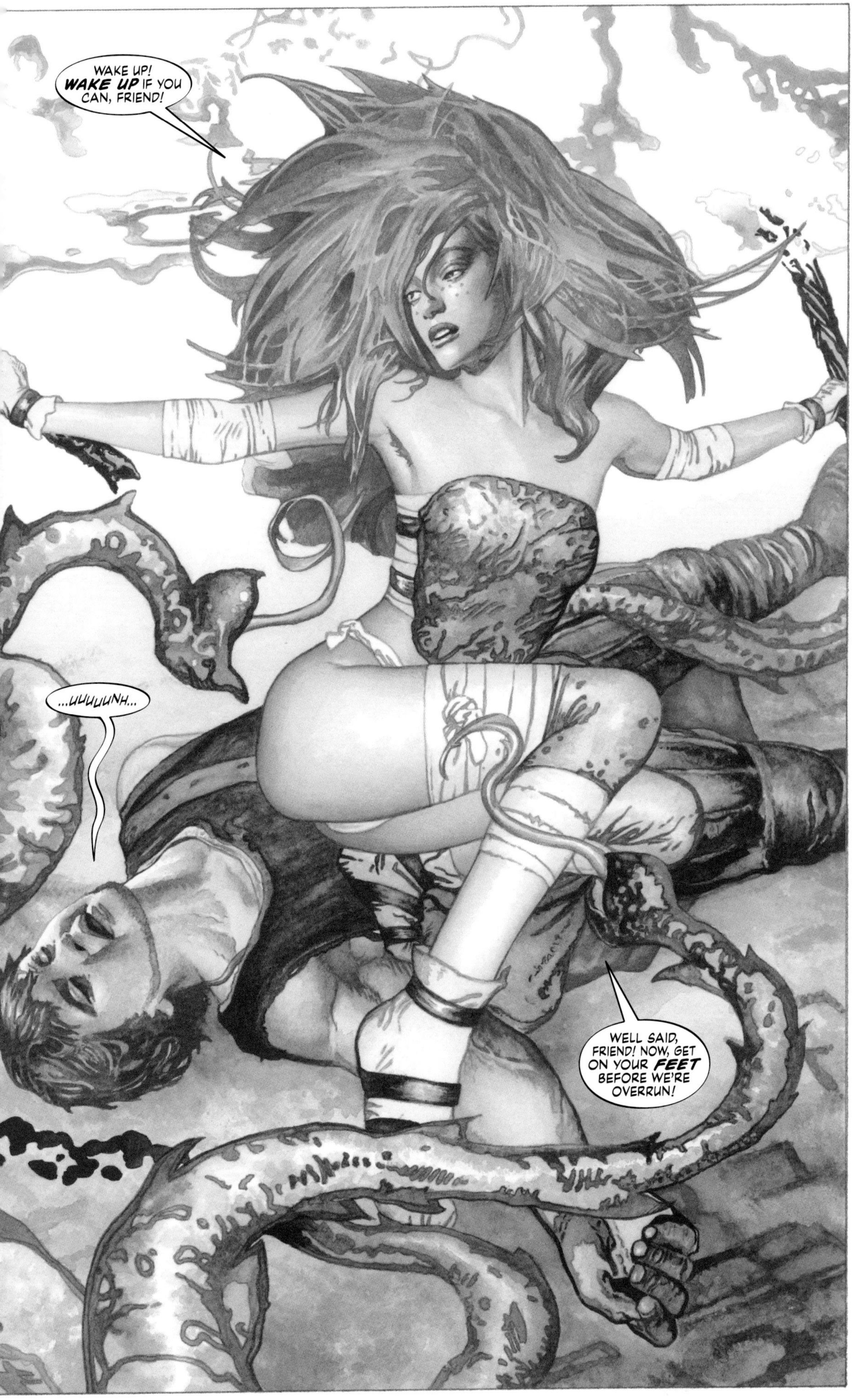
WAKE UP! WAKE UP IF YOU CAN, FRIEND!
...UUUUUNH...
WELL SAID, FRIEND! NOW, GET ON YOUR FEET BEFORE WE'RE OVERRUN!

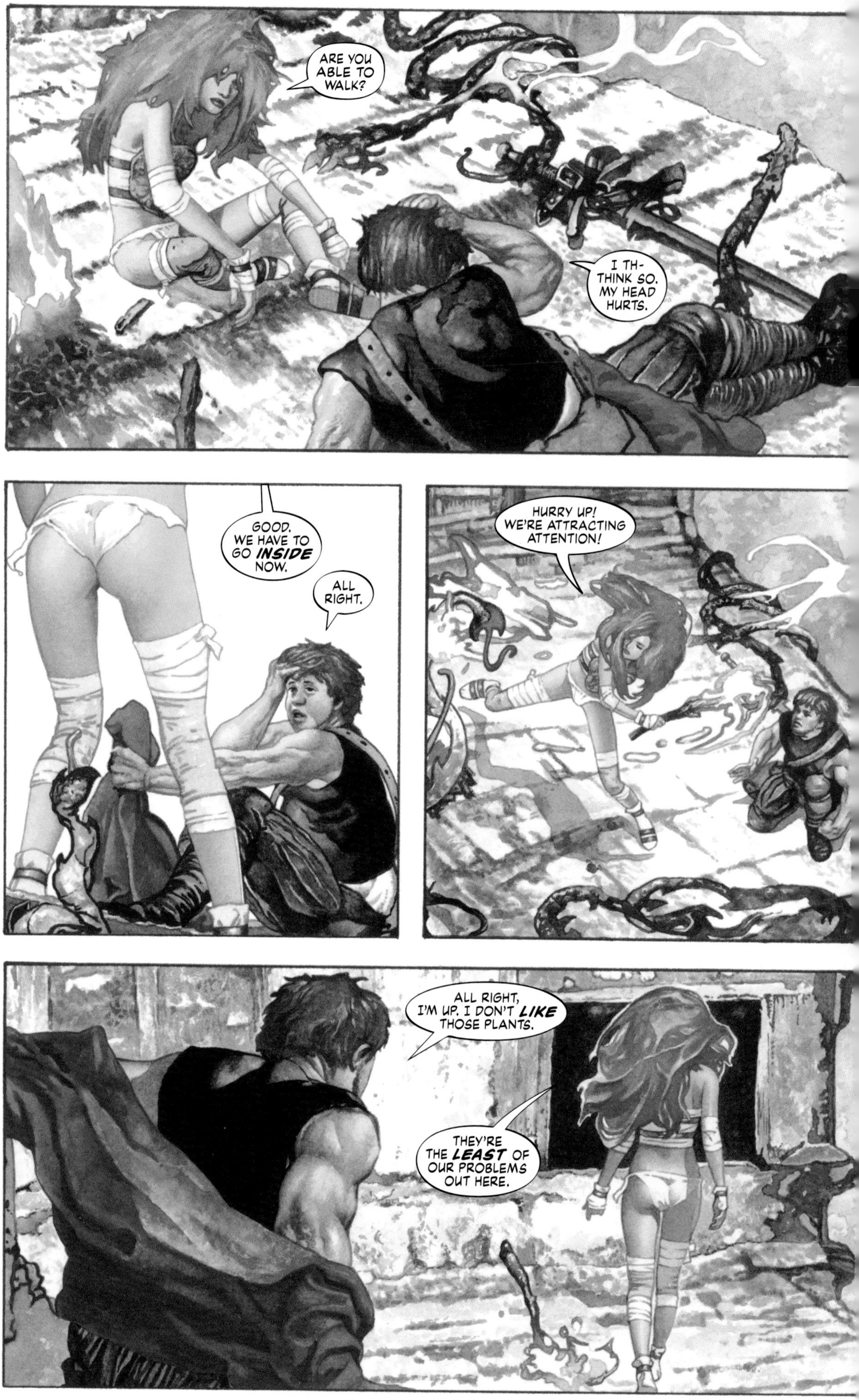

ARE YOU ABLE TO WALK?
I TH- THINK SO. MY HEAD HURTS.
GOOD. WE HAVE TO GO INSIDE NOW.
ALL RIGHT.
HURRY UP! WE'RE ATTRACTING ATTENTION!
ALL RIGHT, I'M UP. I DON'T LIKE THOSE PLANTS.
THEY'RE THE LEAST OF OUR PROBLEMS OUT HERE.

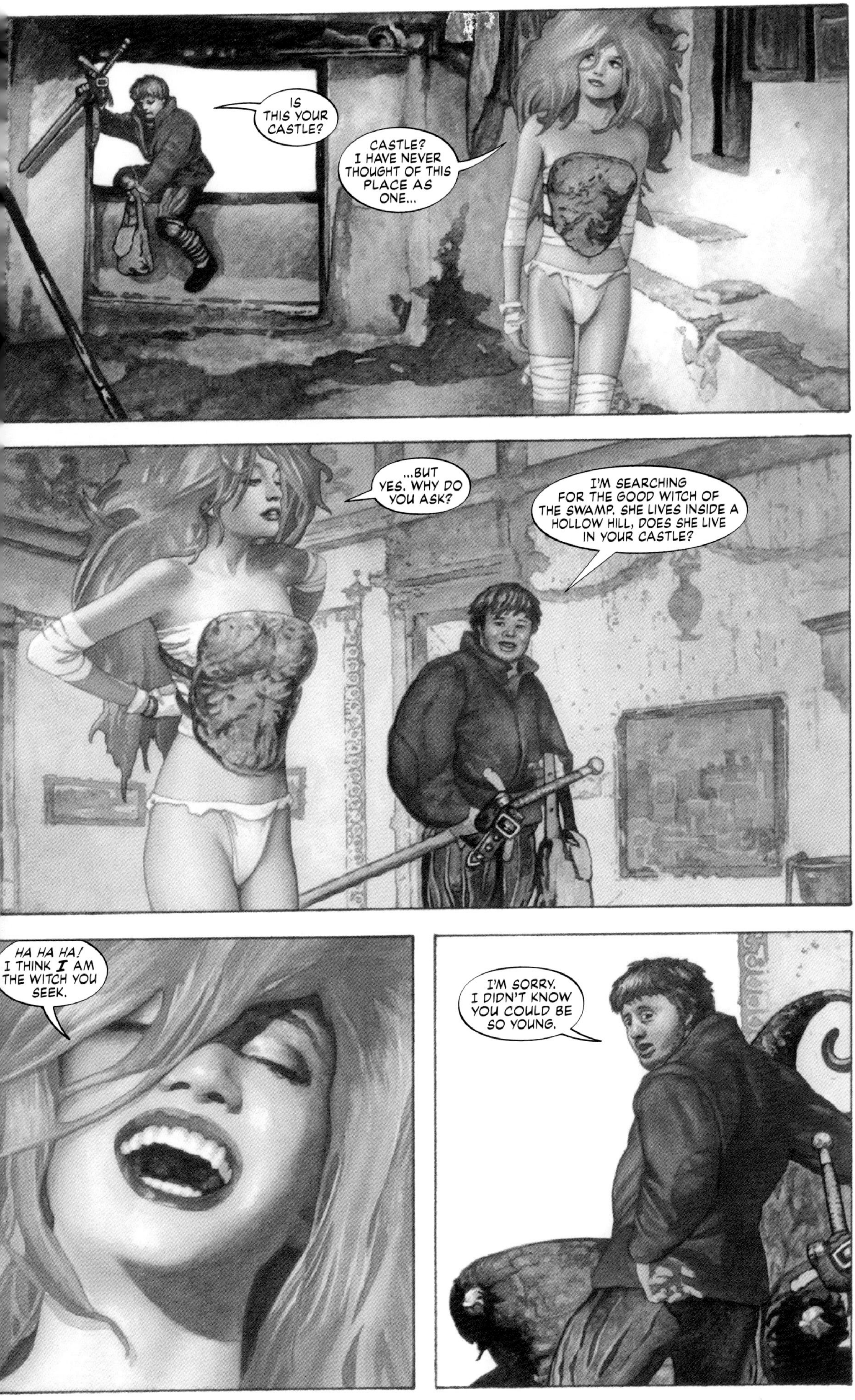
IS THIS YOUR CASTLE?
CASTLE? I HAVE NEVER THOUGHT OF THIS PLACE AS ONE...
...BUT YES. WHY DO YOU ASK?
I'M SEARCHING FOR THE GOOD WITCH OF THE SWAMP. SHE LIVES INSIDE A HOLLOW HILL, DOES SHE LIVE IN YOUR CASTLE?
HA HA HA! I THINK I AM THE WITCH YOU SEEK.
I'M SORRY. I DIDN'T KNOW YOU COULD BE SO YOUNG.

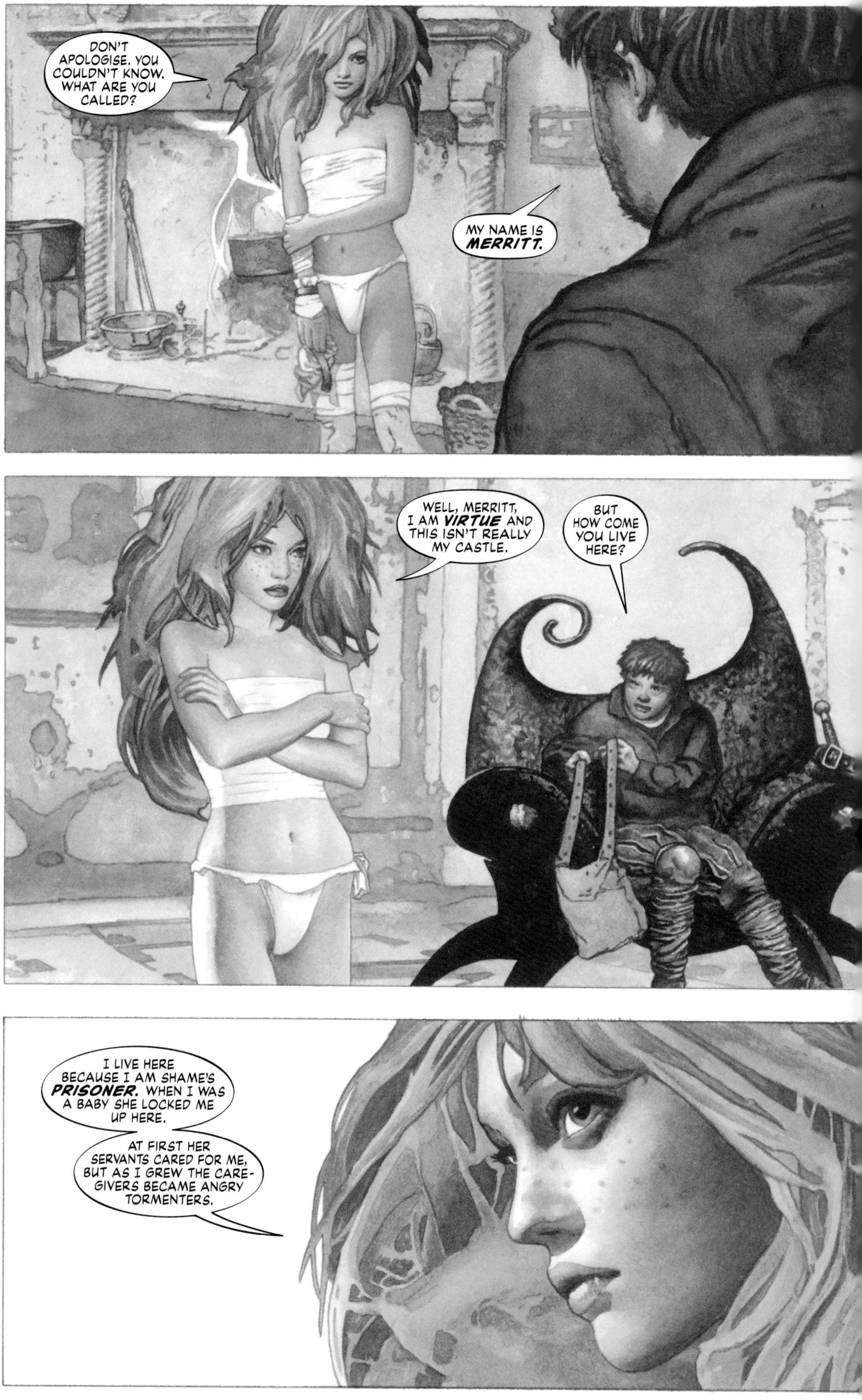
DON'T APOLOGISE. YOU COULDN'T KNOW. WHAT ARE YOU CALLED?
MY NAME IS MERRITT.
WELL, MERRITT, I AM VIRTUE AND THIS ISN'T REALLY MY CASTLE.
BUT HOW COME YOU LIVE HERE?
I LIVE HERE BECAUSE I AM SHAME'S PRISONER. WHEN I WAS A BABY SHE LOCKED ME UP HERE.
AT FIRST HER SERVANTS CARED FOR ME, BUT AS I GREW THE CARE-GIVERS BECAME ANGRY TORMENTERS.

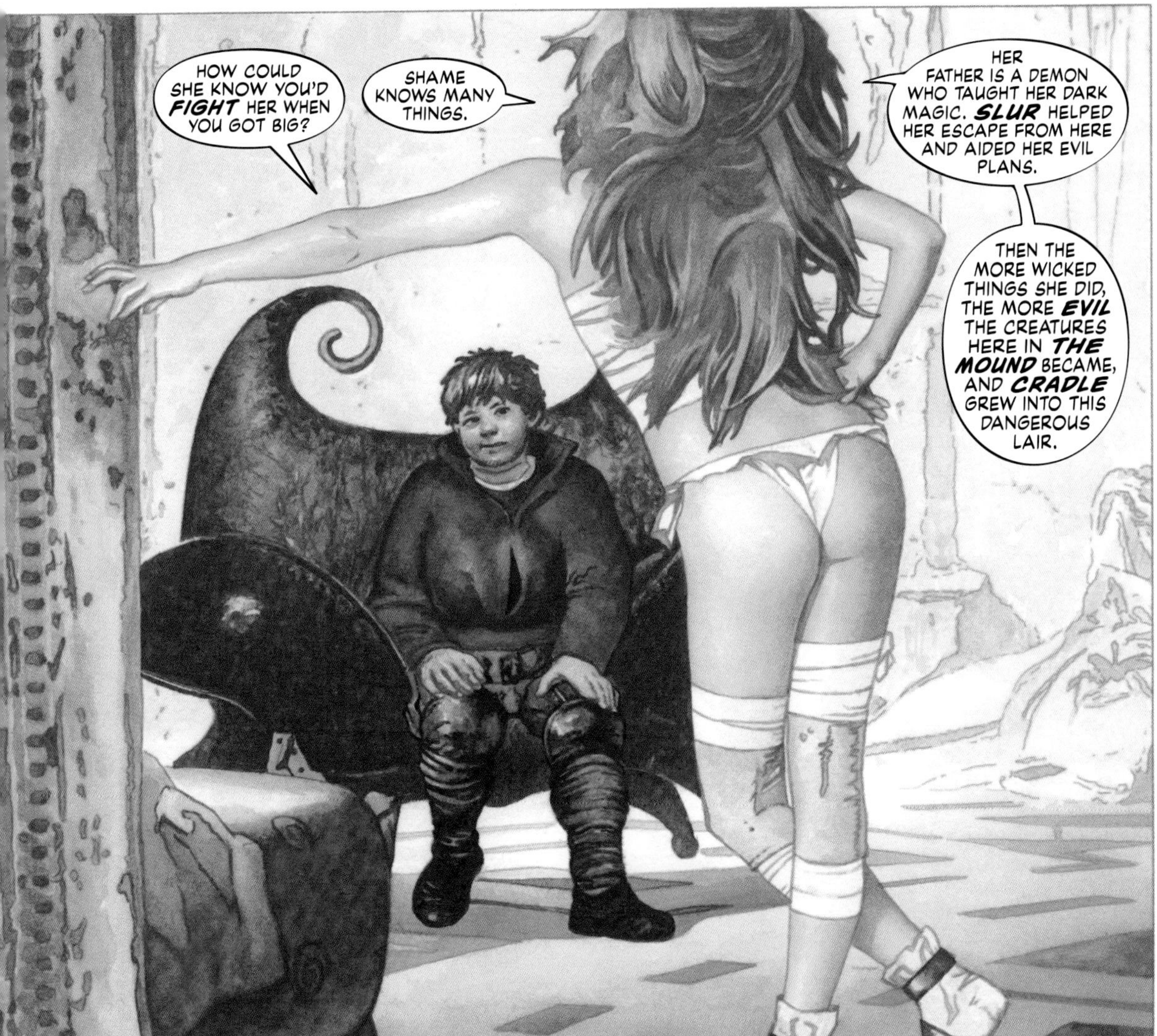
HOW COULD SHE KNOW YOU'D FIGHT HER WHEN YOU GOT BIG?
SHAME KNOWS MANY THINGS.
HER FATHER IS A DEMON WHO TAUGHT HER DARK MAGIC. SLUR HELPED HER ESCAPE FROM HERE AND AIDED HER EVIL PLANS.
THEN THE MORE WICKED THINGS SHE DID, THE MORE EVIL THE CREATURES HERE IN THE MOUND BECAME, AND CRADLE GREW INTO THIS DANGEROUS LAIR.

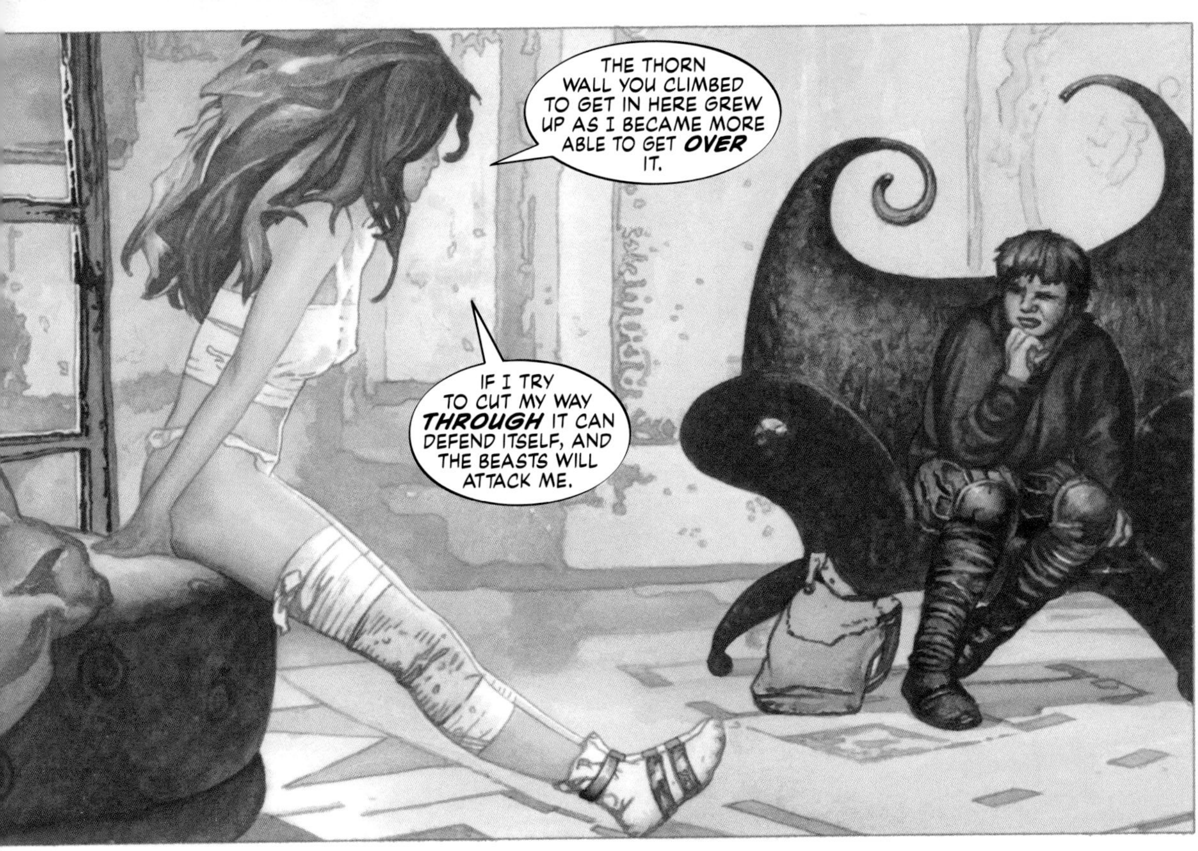
THE THORN WALL YOU CLIMBED TO GET IN HERE GREW UP AS I BECAME MORE ABLE TO GET OVER IT.
IF I TRY TO CUT MY WAY THROUGH IT CAN DEFEND ITSELF, AND THE BEASTS WILL ATTACK ME.

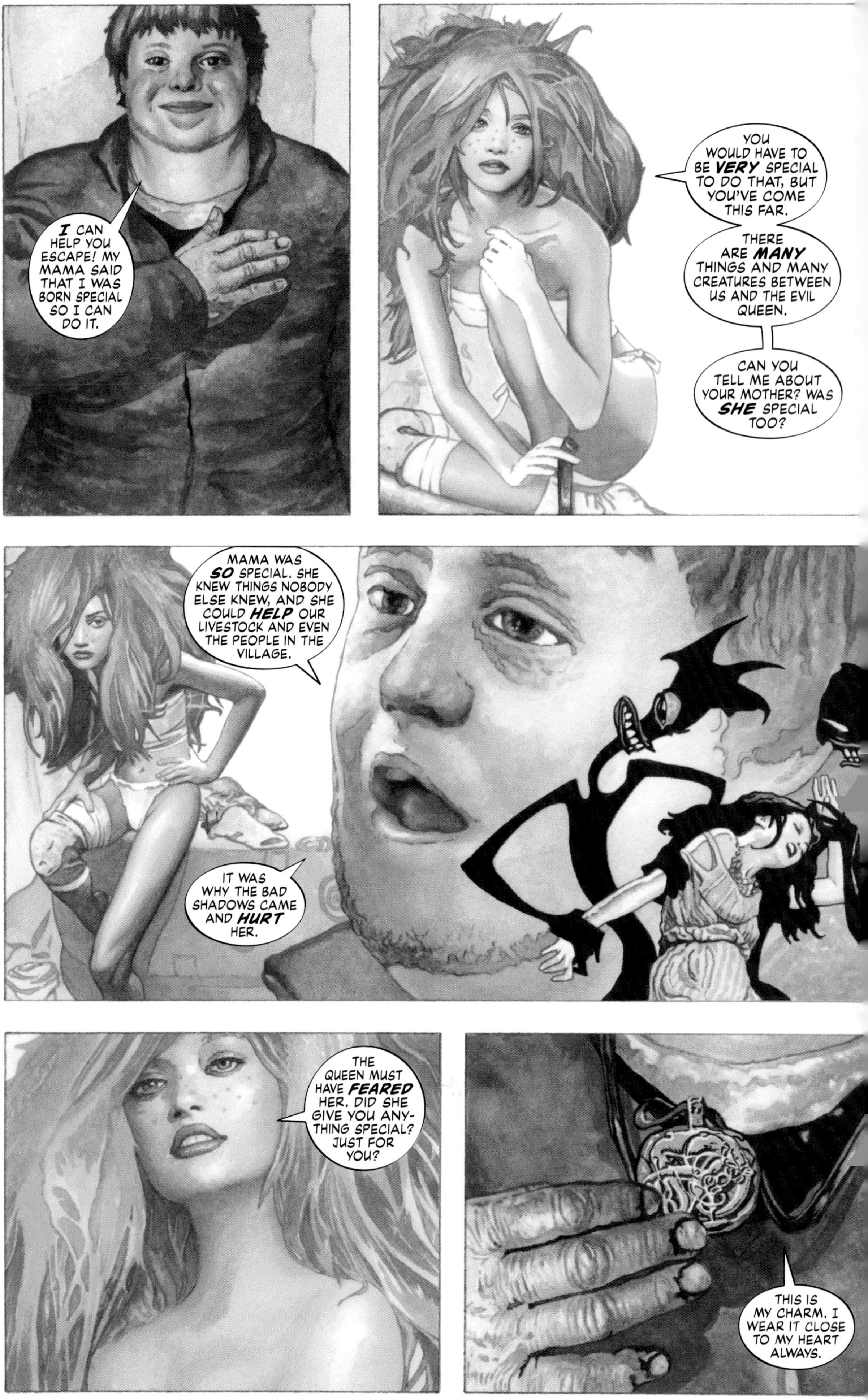
I CAN HELP YOU ESCAPE! MY MAMA SAID THAT I WAS BORN SPECIAL SO I CAN DO IT.
YOU WOULD HAVE TO BE VERY SPECIAL TO DO THAT, BUT YOU'VE COME THIS FAR.
THERE ARE MANY THINGS AND MANY CREATURES BETWEEN US AND THE EVIL QUEEN.
CAN YOU TELL ME ABOUT YOUR MOTHER? WAS SHE SPECIAL TOO?
MAMA WAS SO SPECIAL. SHE KNEW THINGS NOBODY ELSE KNEW, AND SHE COULD HELP OUR LIVESTOCK AND EVEN THE PEOPLE IN THE VILLAGE.
IT WAS WHY THE BAD SHADOWS CAME AND HURT HER.
THE QUEEN MUST HAVE FEARED HER. DID SHE GIVE YOU ANY-THING SPECIAL? JUST FOR YOU?
THIS IS MY CHARM. I WEAR IT CLOSE TO MY HEART ALWAYS.

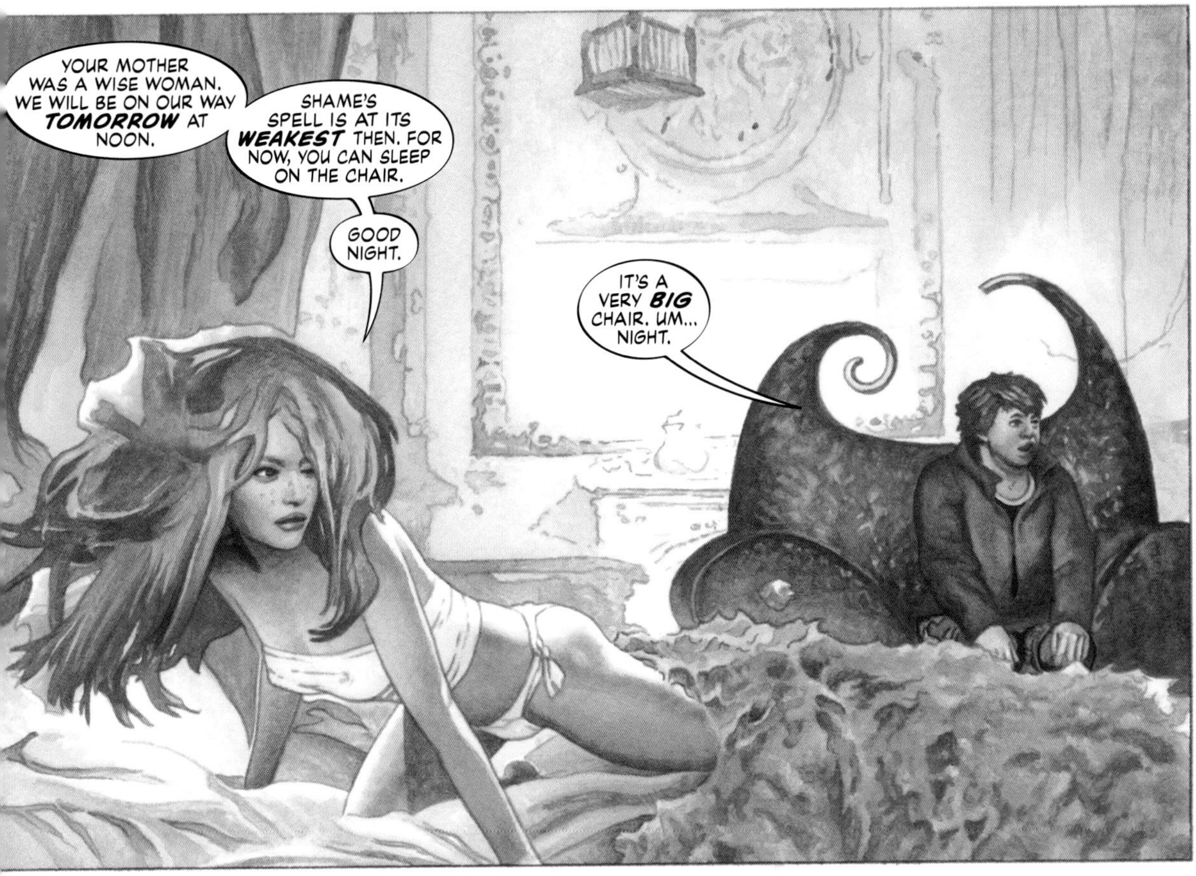
YOUR MOTHER WAS A WISE WOMAN. WE WILL BE ON OUR WAY TOMORROW AT NOON.
SHAME'S SPELL IS AT ITS WEAKEST THEN. FOR NOW, YOU CAN SLEEP ON THE CHAIR.
GOOD NIGHT.
IT'S A VERY BIG CHAIR. UM... NIGHT.

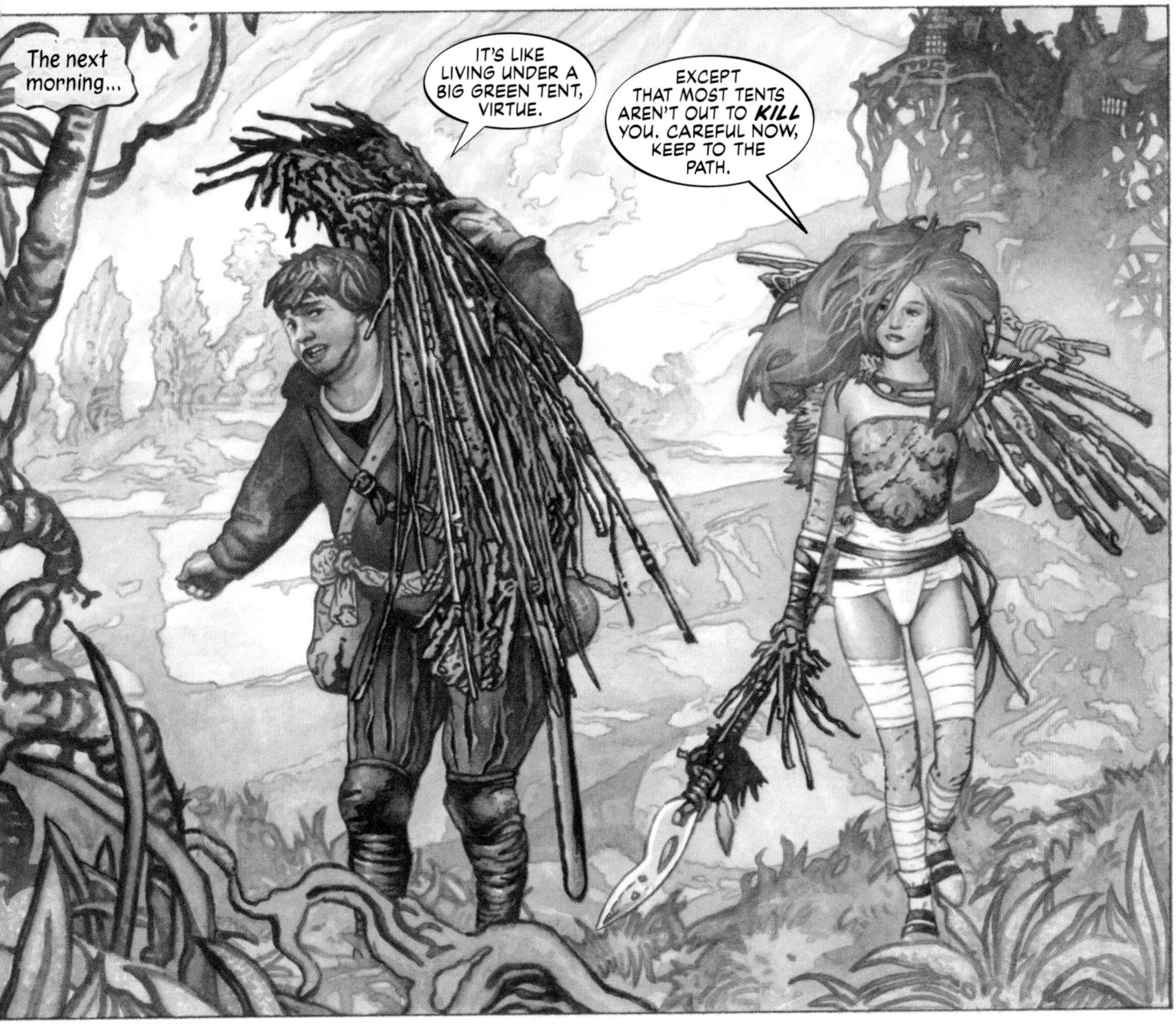
The next morning...
IT'S LIKE LIVING UNDER A BIG GREEN TENT, VIRTUE.
EXCEPT THAT MOST TENTS AREN'T OUT TO KILL YOU. CAREFUL NOW, KEEP TO THE PATH.

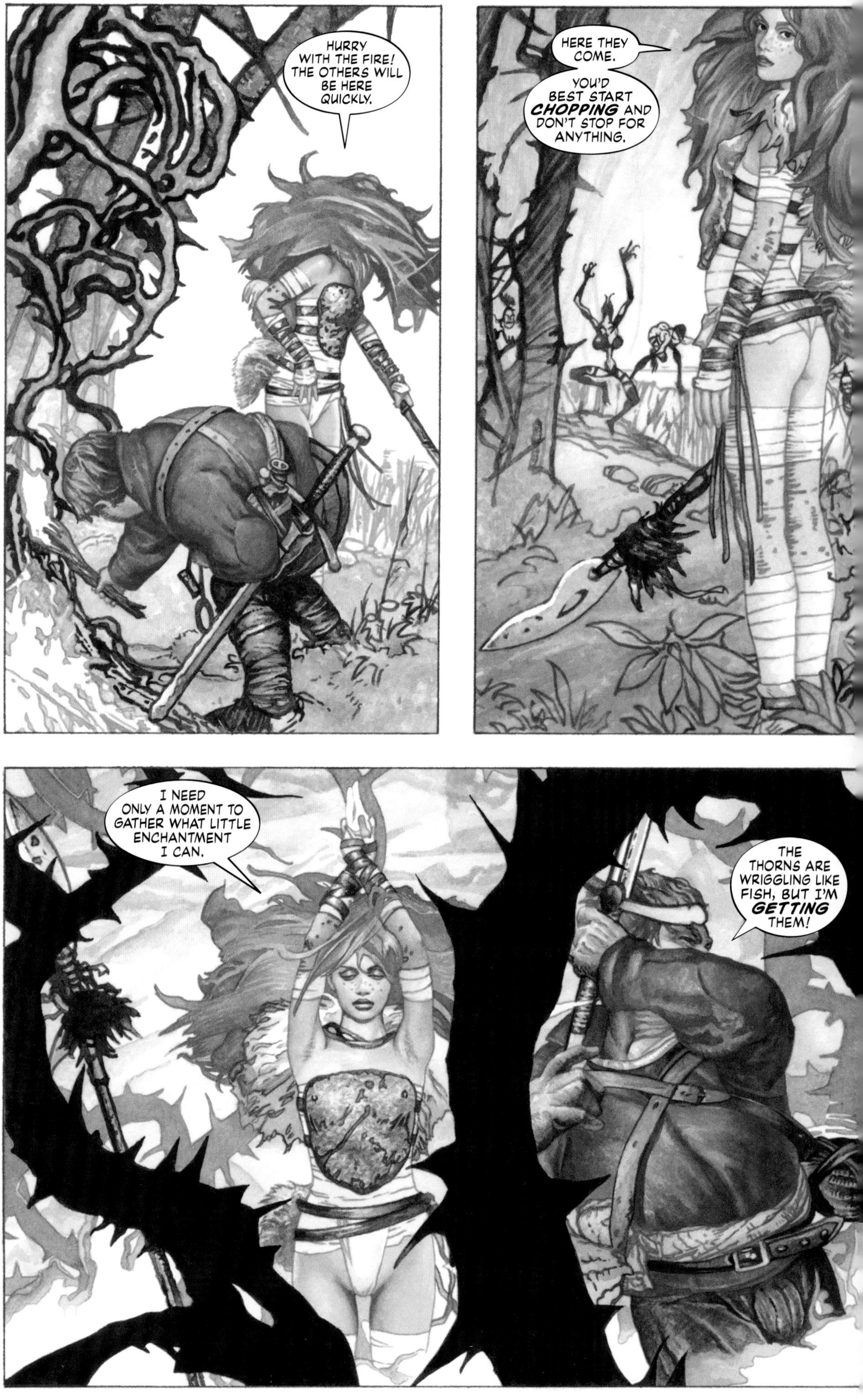
HURRY WITH THE FIRE! THE OTHERS WILL BE HERE QUICKLY.
HERE THEY COME.
YOU'D BEST START **CHOPPING** AND DON'T STOP FOR ANYTHING.
I NEED ONLY A MOMENT TO GATHER WHAT LITTLE ENCHANTMENT I CAN.
THE THORNS ARE WRIGGLING LIKE FISH, BUT I'M **GETTING** THEM!

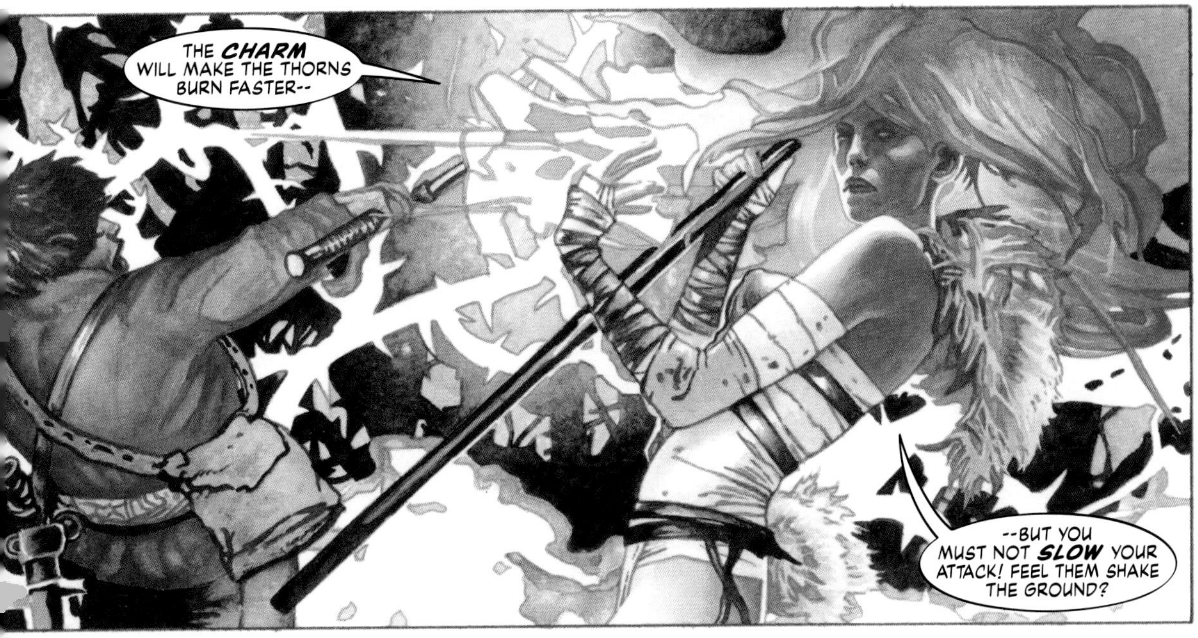
THE CHARM WILL MAKE THE THORNS BURN FASTER--
--BUT YOU MUST NOT SLOW YOUR ATTACK! FEEL THEM SHAKE THE GROUND?

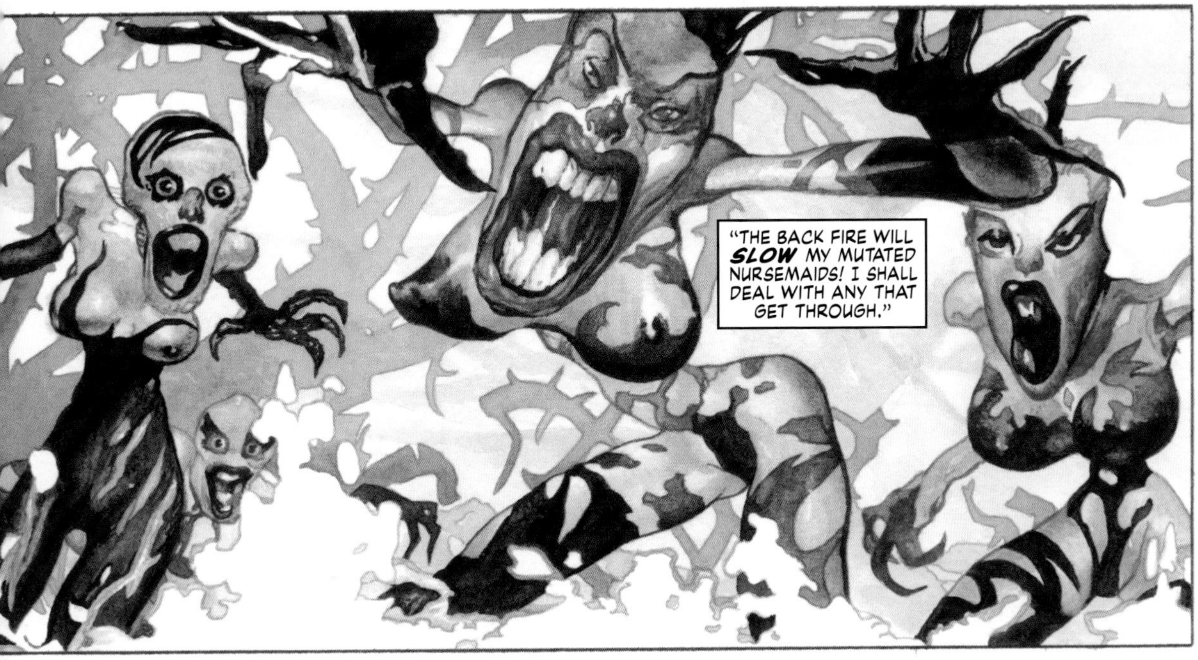
"THE BACK FIRE WILL SLOW MY MUTATED NURSEMAIDS! I SHALL DEAL WITH ANY THAT GET THROUGH."

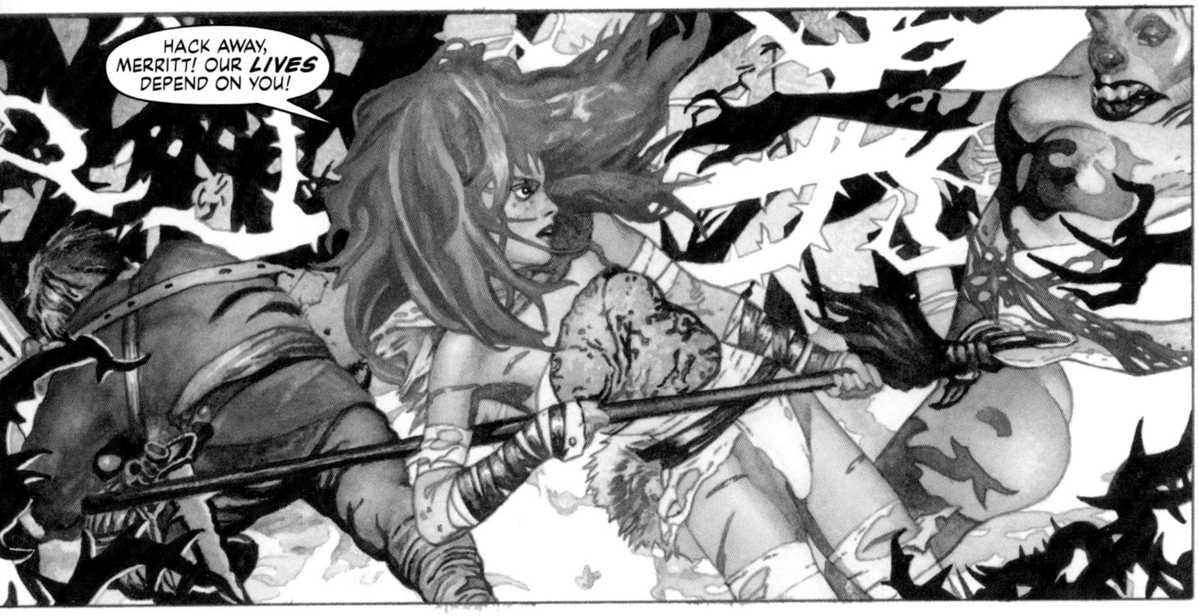
HACK AWAY, MERRITT! OUR LIVES DEPEND ON YOU!

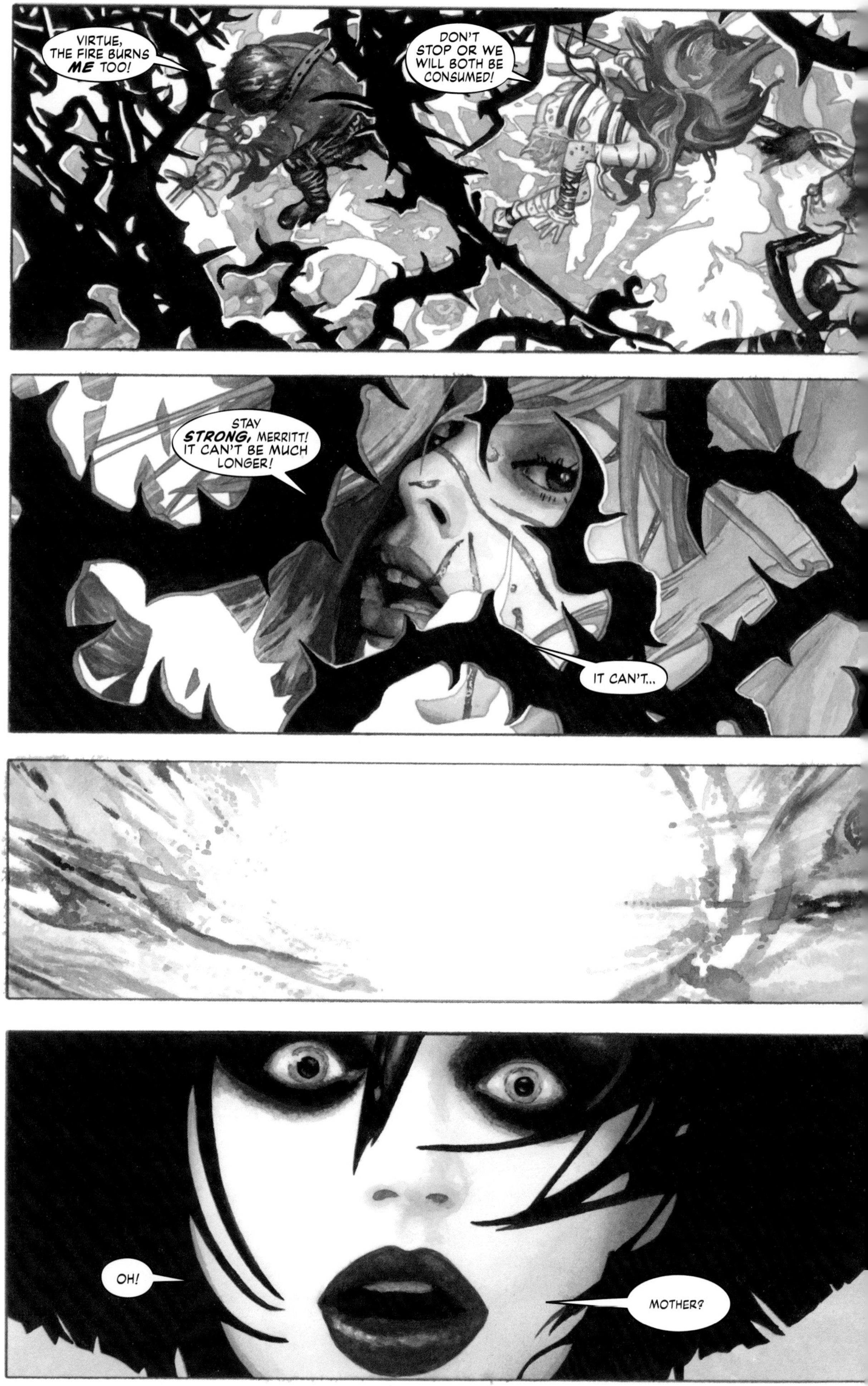
VIRTUE, THE FIRE BURNS ME TOO!
DON'T STOP OR WE WILL BOTH BE CONSUMED!
STAY STRONG, MERRITT! IT CAN'T BE MUCH LONGER!
IT CAN'T...
OH!
MOTHER?

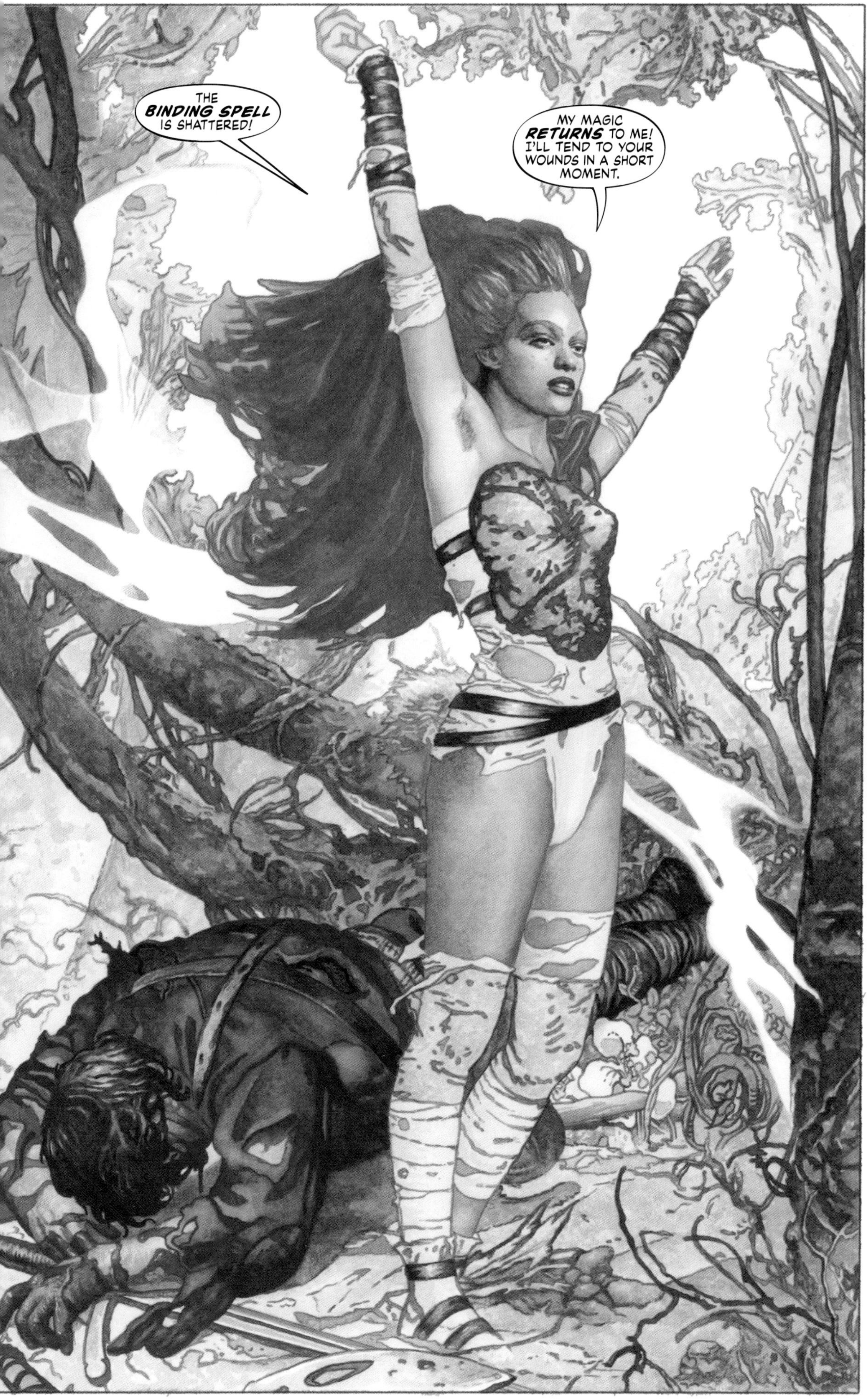
THE BINDING SPELL IS SHATTERED!
MY MAGIC RETURNS TO ME! I'LL TEND TO YOUR WOUNDS IN A SHORT MOMENT.

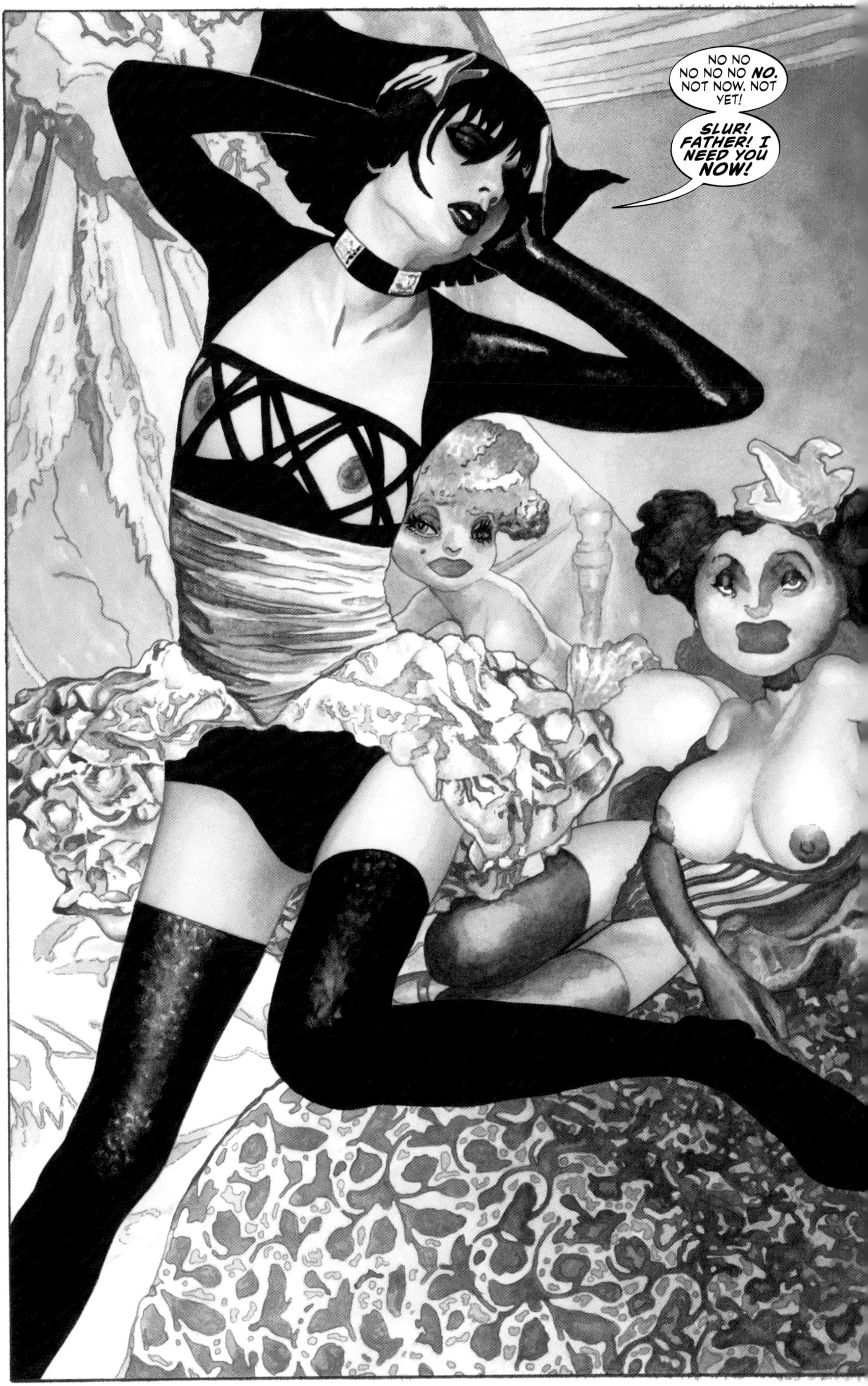
NO NO NO NO NO ***NO.*** NOT NOW. NOT YET!
SLUR! FATHER! I NEED YOU NOW!

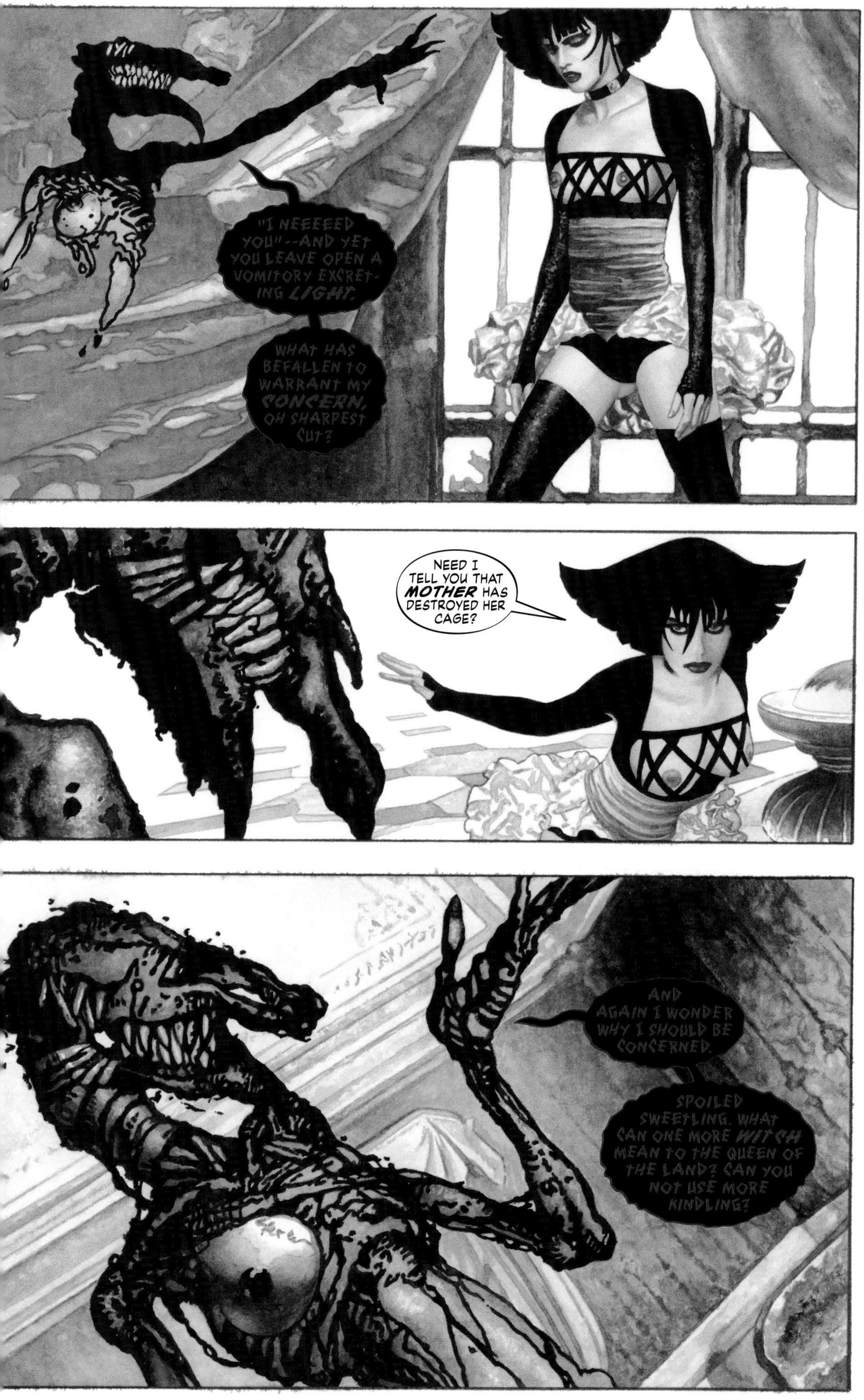
"I NEEEEED YOU"--AND YET YOU LEAVE OPEN A VOMITORY EXCRETING *LIGHT*.
WHAT HAS BEFALLEN TO WARRANT MY *CONCERN*, OH SHARPEST CUT?
NEED I TELL YOU THAT **MOTHER** HAS DESTROYED HER CAGE?
AND AGAIN I WONDER WHY I SHOULD BE CONCERNED.
SPOILED SWEETLING. WHAT CAN ONE MORE *WITCH* MEAN TO THE QUEEN OF THE LAND? CAN YOU NOT USE MORE KINDLING?

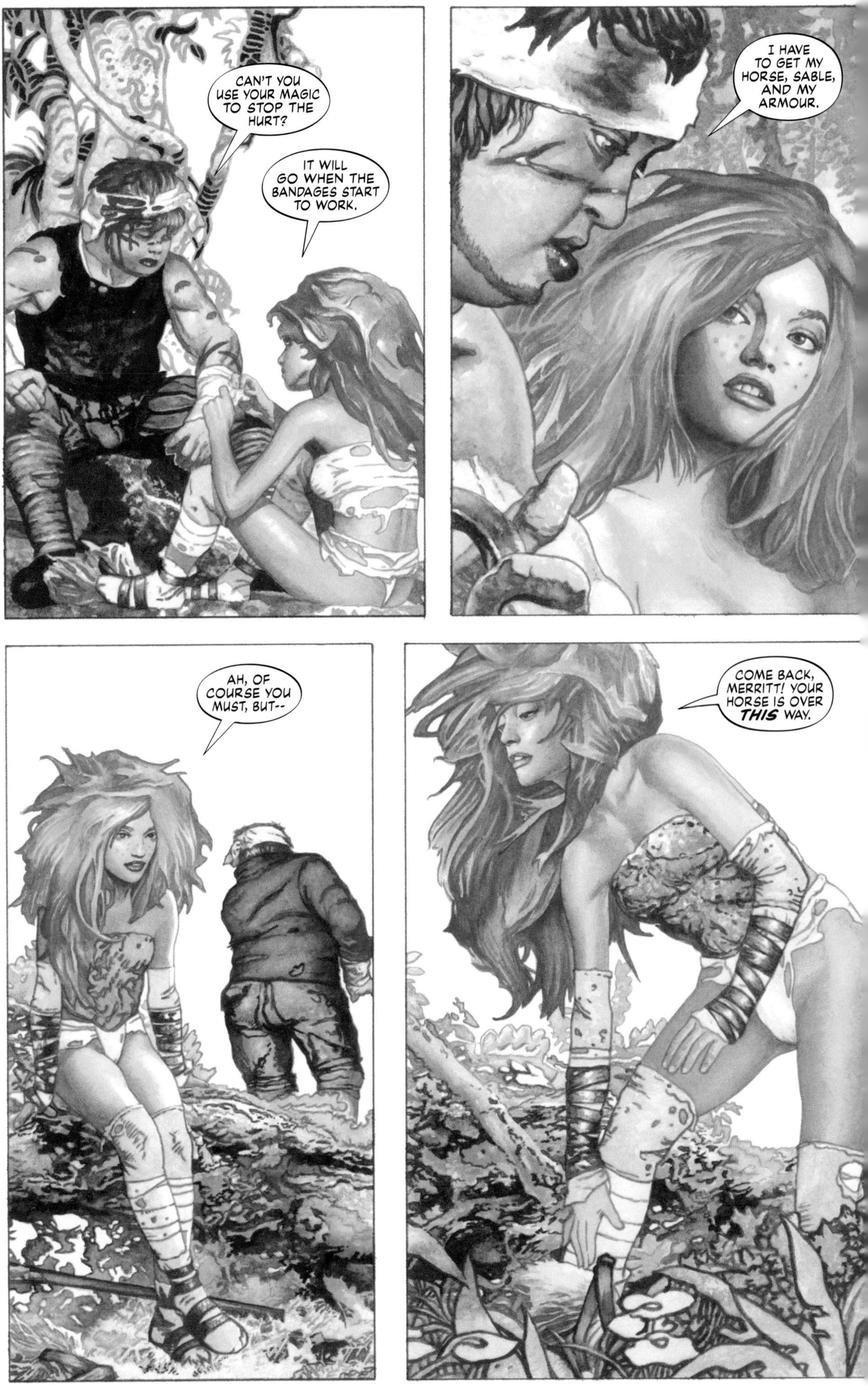
CAN'T YOU USE YOUR MAGIC TO STOP THE HURT?
IT WILL GO WHEN THE BANDAGES START TO WORK.
I HAVE TO GET MY HORSE, SABLE, AND MY ARMOUR.
AH, OF COURSE YOU MUST, BUT--
COME BACK, MERRITT! YOUR HORSE IS OVER THIS WAY.

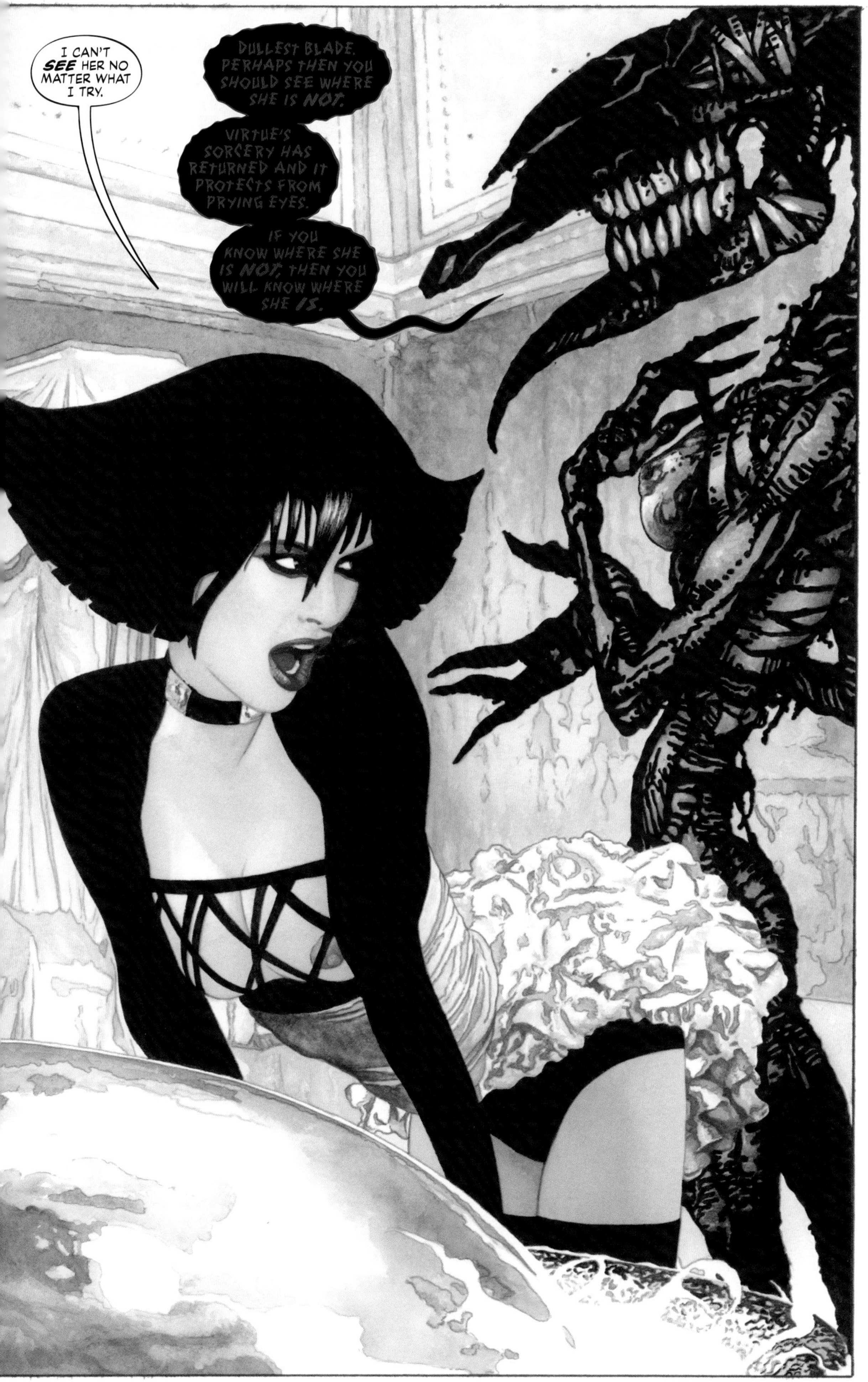
I CAN'T **SEE** HER NO MATTER WHAT I TRY.
DULLEST BLADE. PERHAPS THEN YOU SHOULD SEE WHERE SHE IS **NOT.**
VIRTUE'S SORCERY HAS RETURNED AND IT PROTECTS FROM PRYING EYES.
IF YOU KNOW WHERE SHE IS **NOT,** THEN YOU WILL KNOW WHERE SHE **IS.**

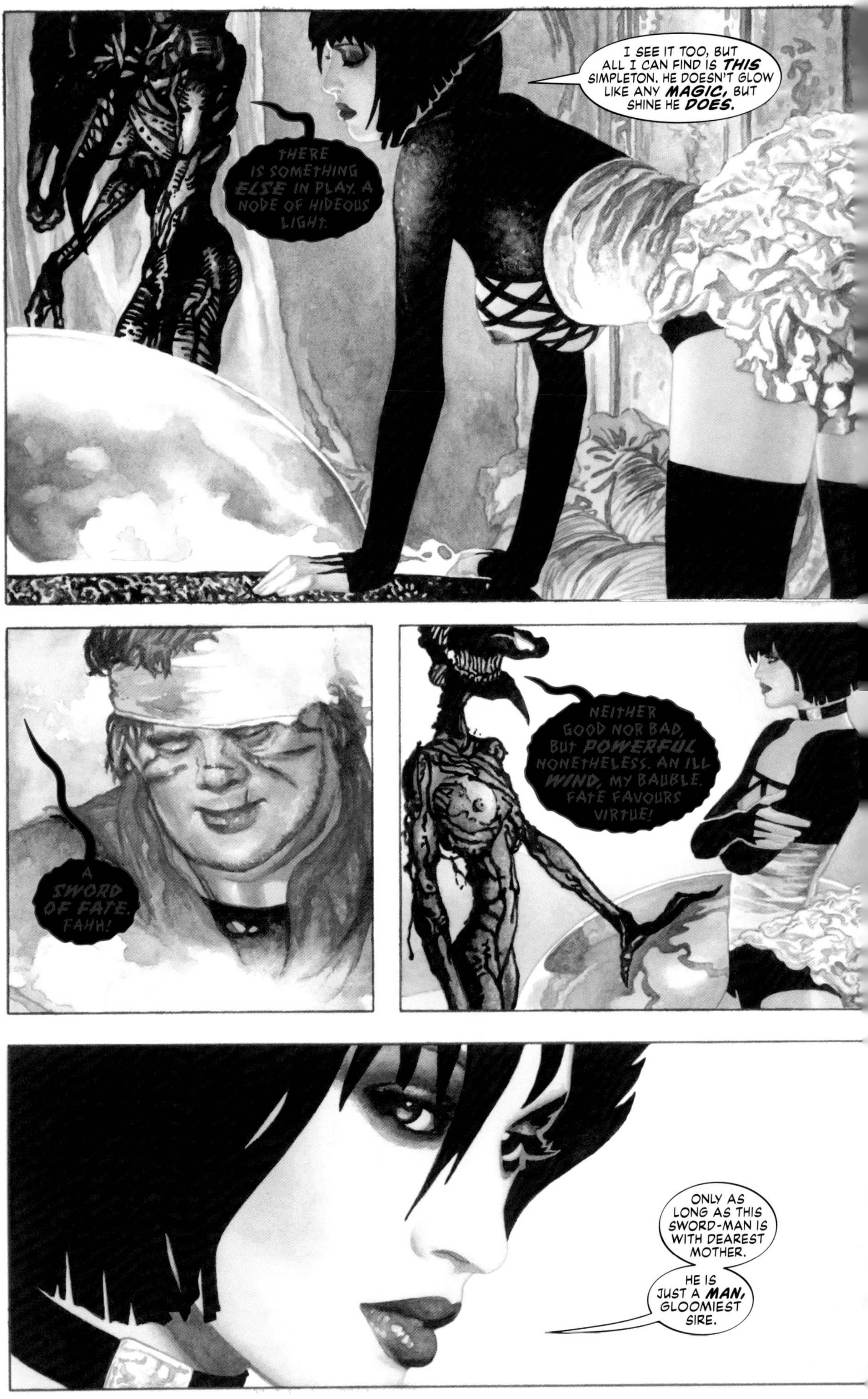

I SEE IT TOO, BUT ALL I CAN FIND IS THIS SIMPLETON. HE DOESN'T GLOW LIKE ANY MAGIC, BUT SHINE HE DOES.
THERE IS SOMETHING ELSE IN PLAY. A NODE OF HIDEOUS LIGHT.
A SWORD OF FATE. FAHH!
NEITHER GOOD NOR BAD, BUT POWERFUL NONETHELESS. AN ILL WIND, MY BAUBLE. FATE FAVOURS VIRTUE!
ONLY AS LONG AS THIS SWORD-MAN IS WITH DEAREST MOTHER.
HE IS JUST A MAN, GLOOMIEST SIRE.

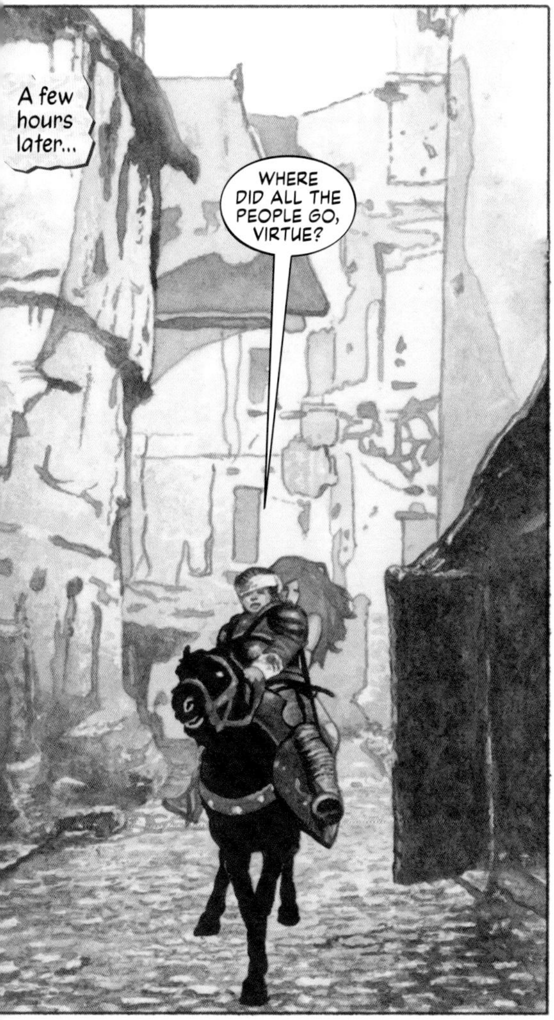
A few hours later...
WHERE DID ALL THE PEOPLE GO, VIRTUE?

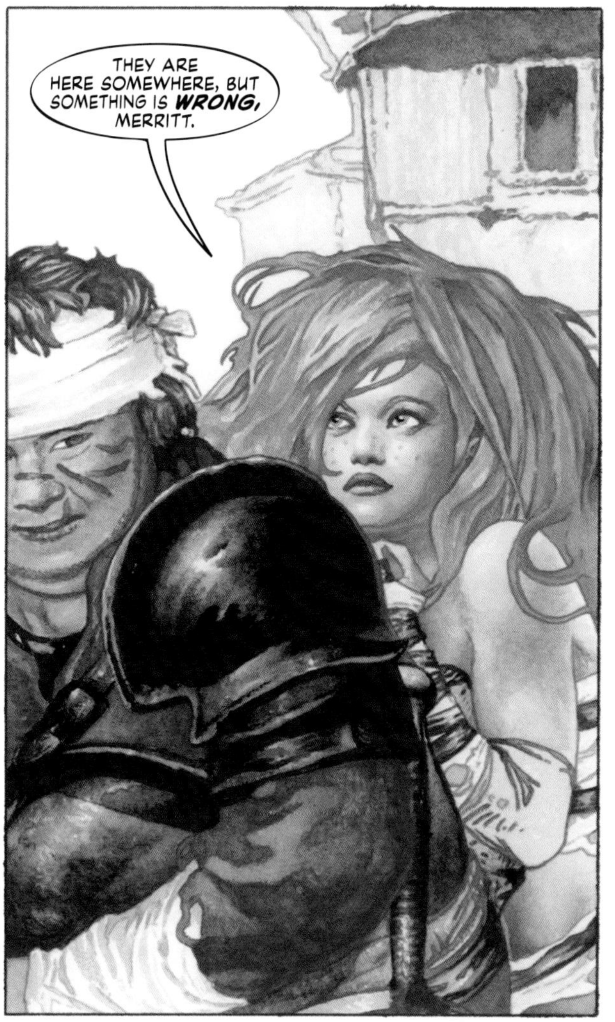
THEY ARE HERE SOMEWHERE, BUT SOMETHING IS **WRONG,** MERRITT.

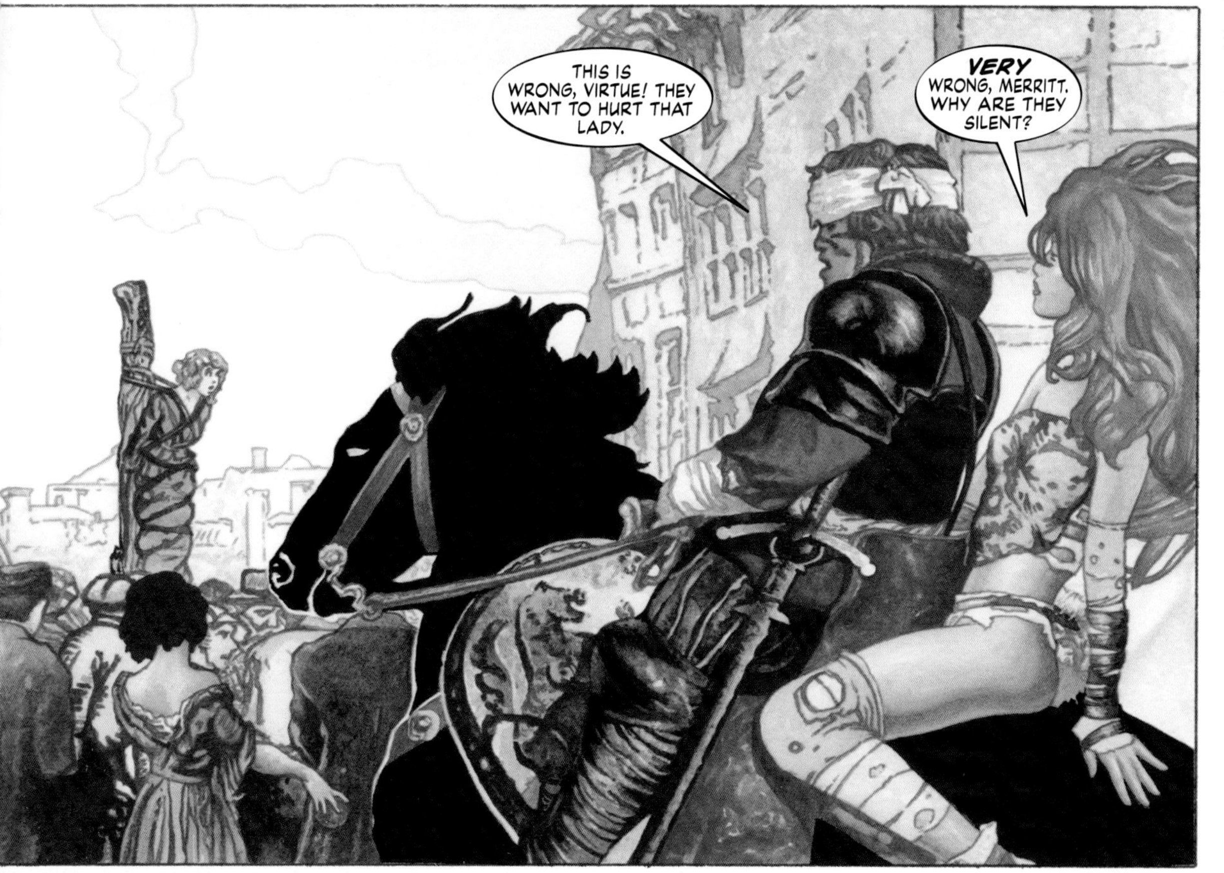
THIS IS WRONG, VIRTUE! THEY WANT TO HURT THAT LADY.
VERY WRONG, MERRITT. WHY ARE THEY SILENT?

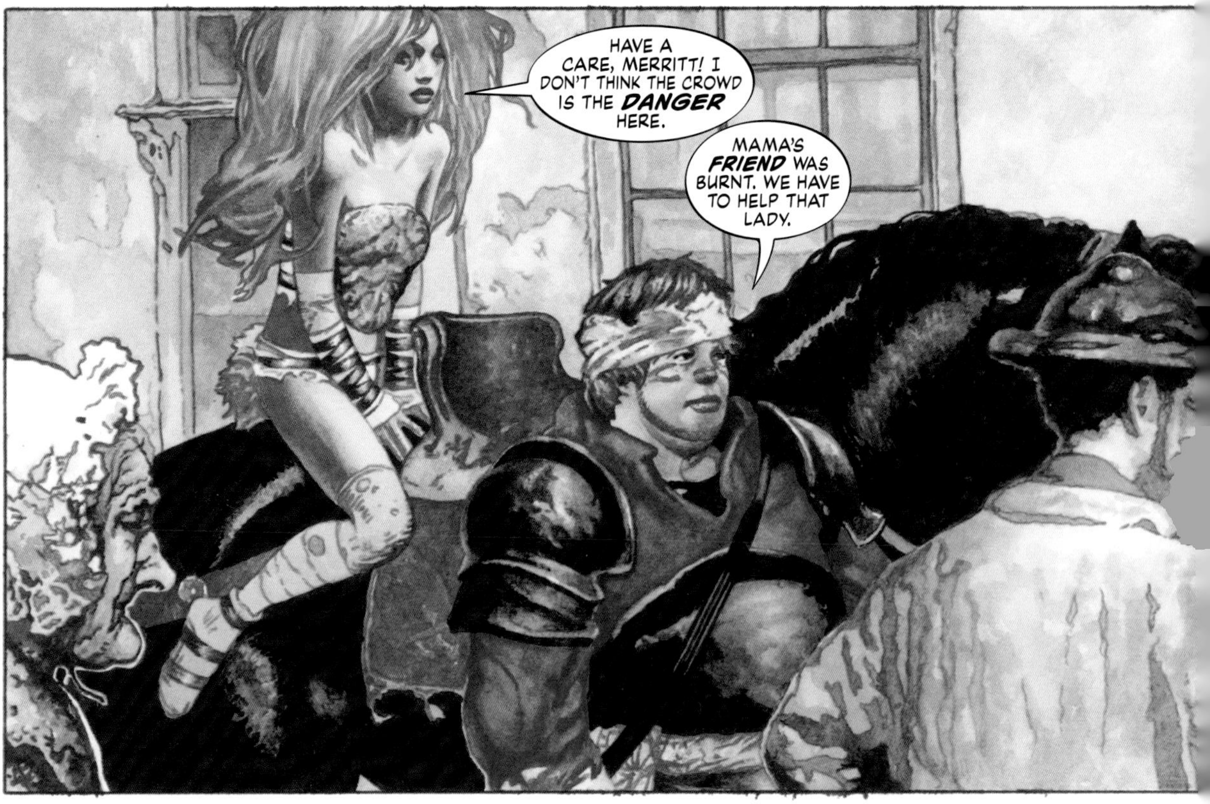
HAVE A CARE, MERRITT! I DON'T THINK THE CROWD IS THE DANGER HERE.
MAMA'S FRIEND WAS BURNT. WE HAVE TO HELP THAT LADY.

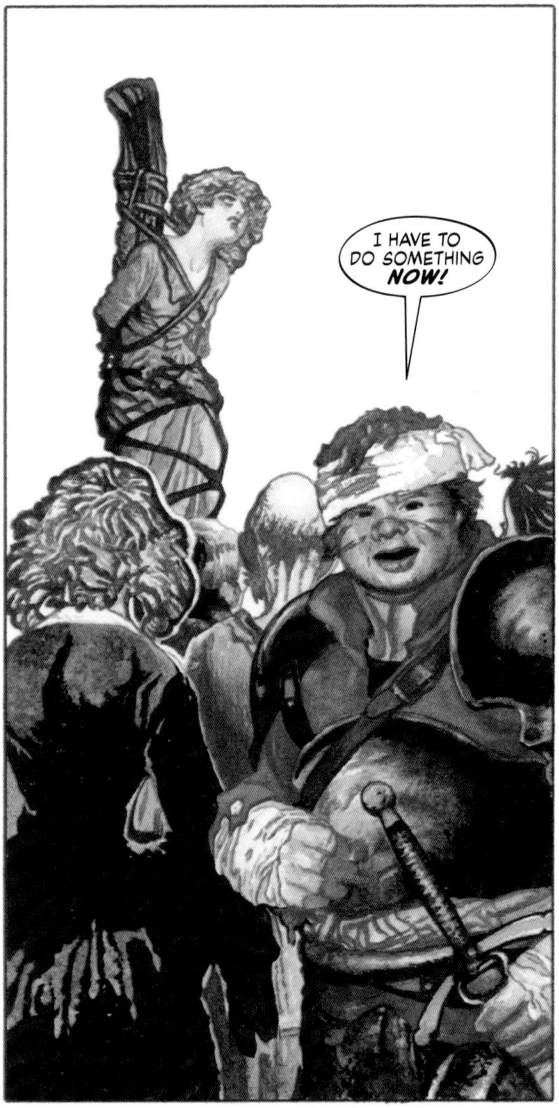
I HAVE TO DO SOMETHING NOW!

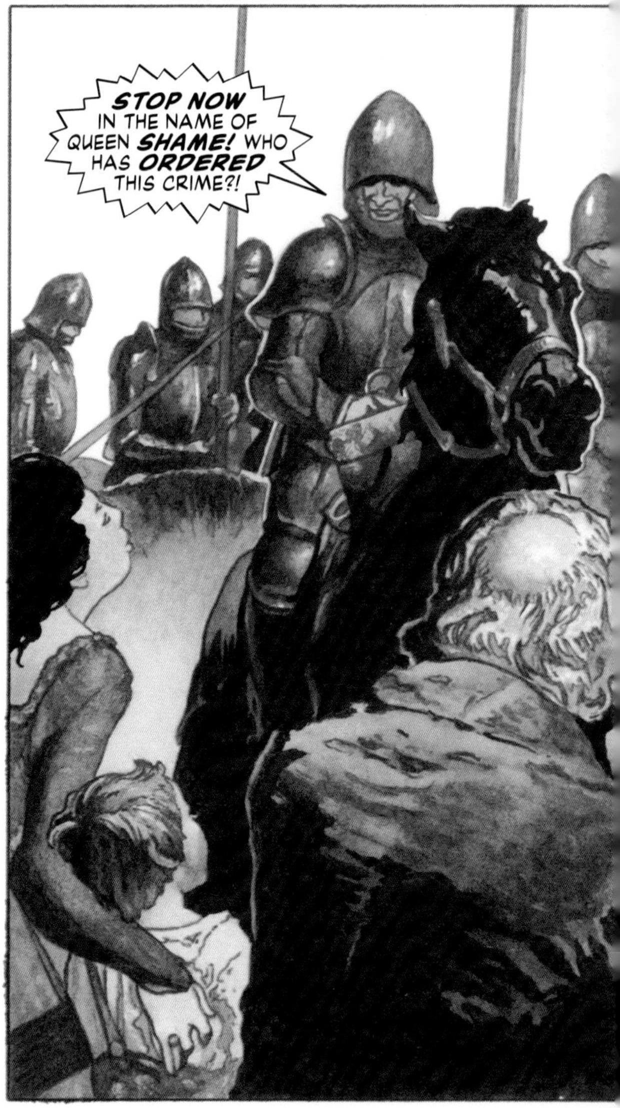
STOP NOW IN THE NAME OF QUEEN SHAME! WHO HAS ORDERED THIS CRIME?!

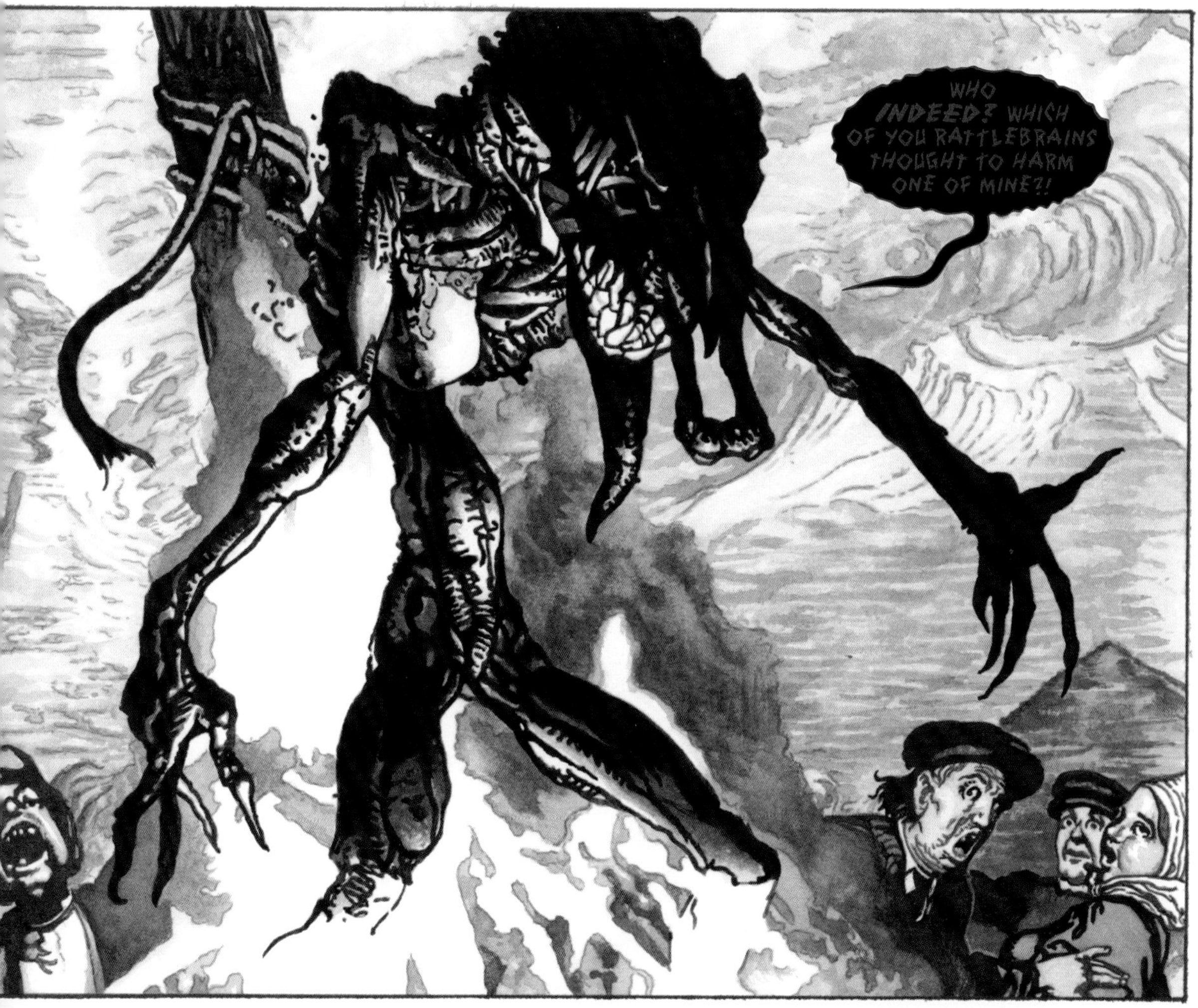
WHO INDEED? WHICH OF YOU RATTLEBRAINS THOUGHT TO HARM ONE OF MINE?!

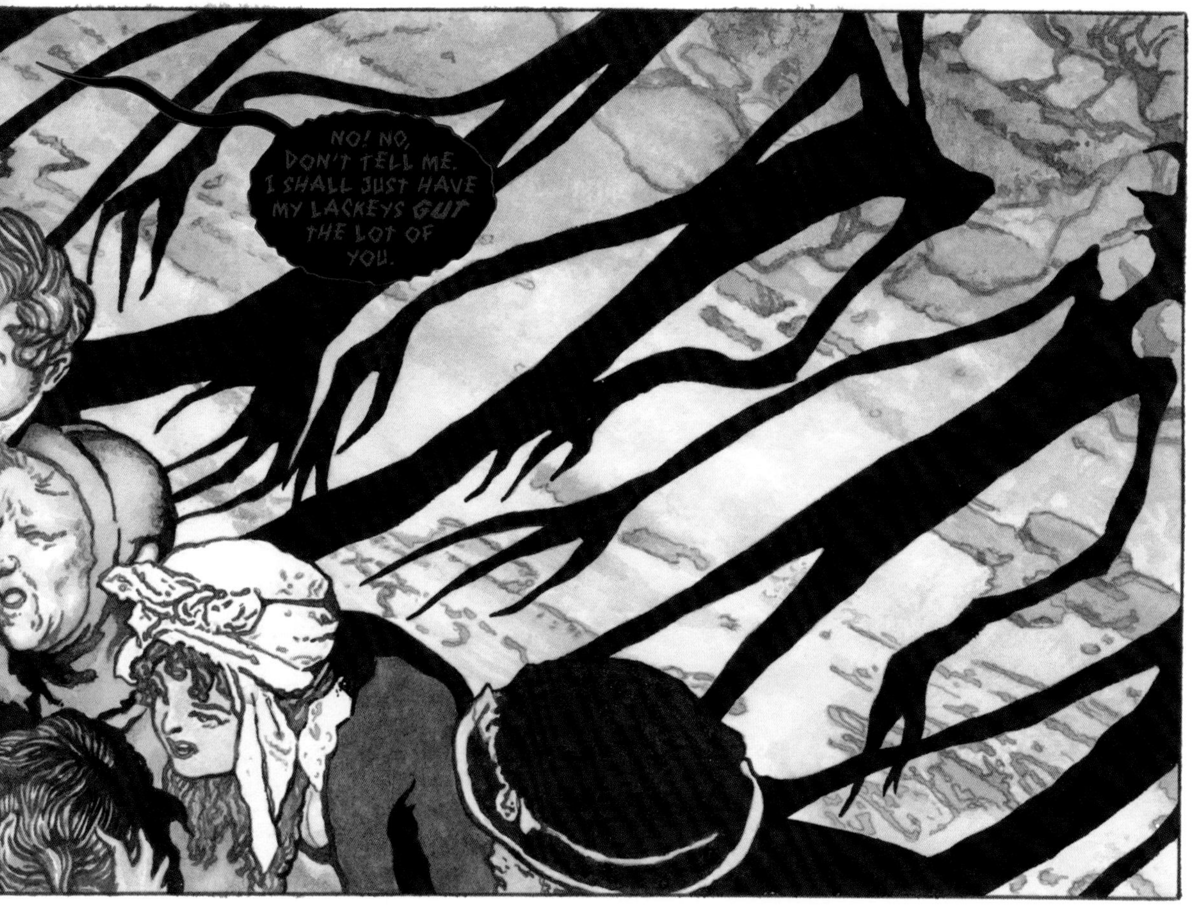
NO! NO, DON'T TELL ME. I SHALL JUST HAVE MY LACKEYS GUT THE LOT OF YOU.

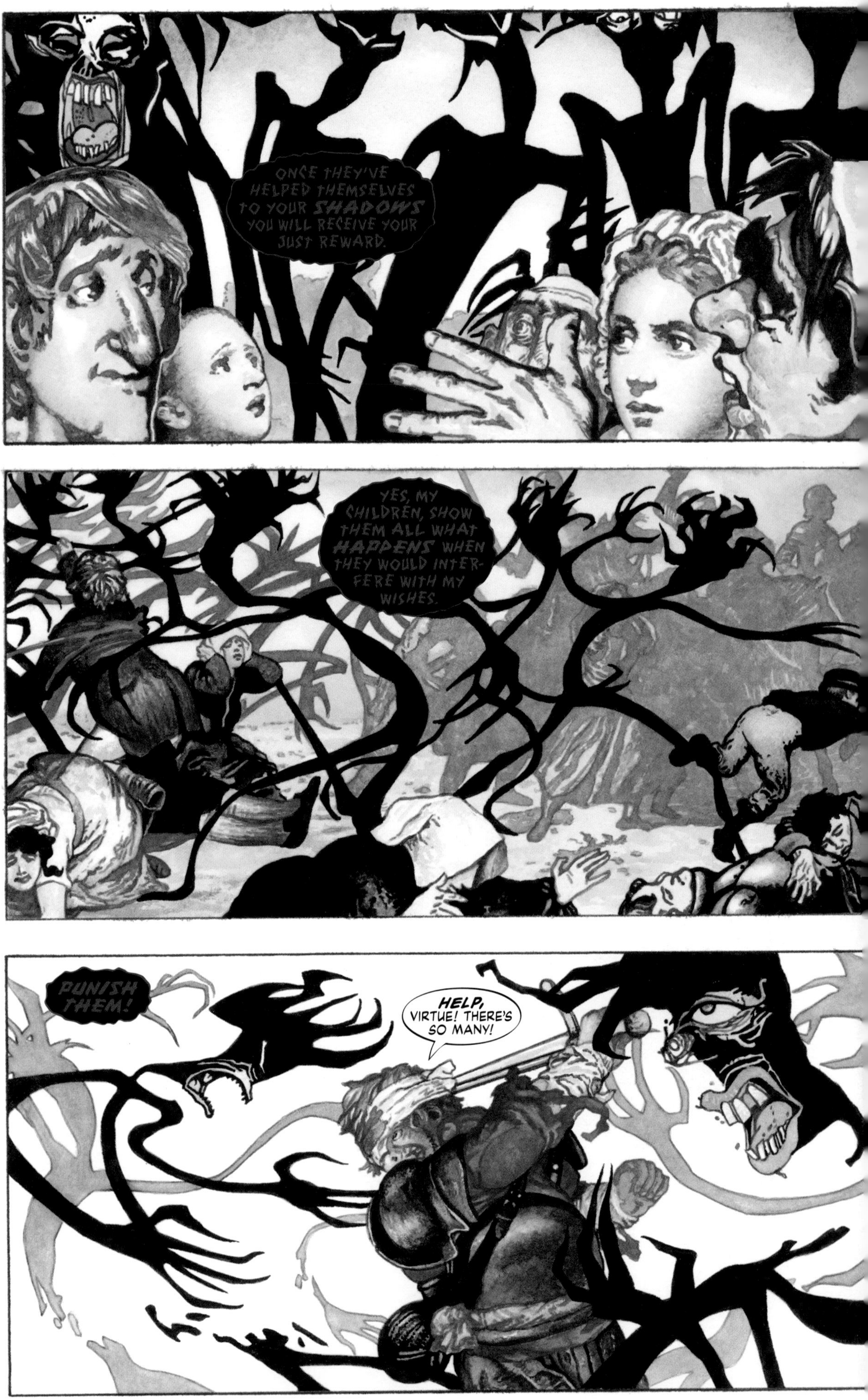
ONCE THEY'VE HELPED THEMSELVES TO YOUR *SHADOWS* YOU WILL RECEIVE YOUR JUST REWARD.
YES, MY CHILDREN, SHOW THEM ALL WHAT *HAPPENS* WHEN THEY WOULD INTERFERE WITH MY WISHES.
PUNISH THEM!
HELP, VIRTUE! THERE'S SO MANY!

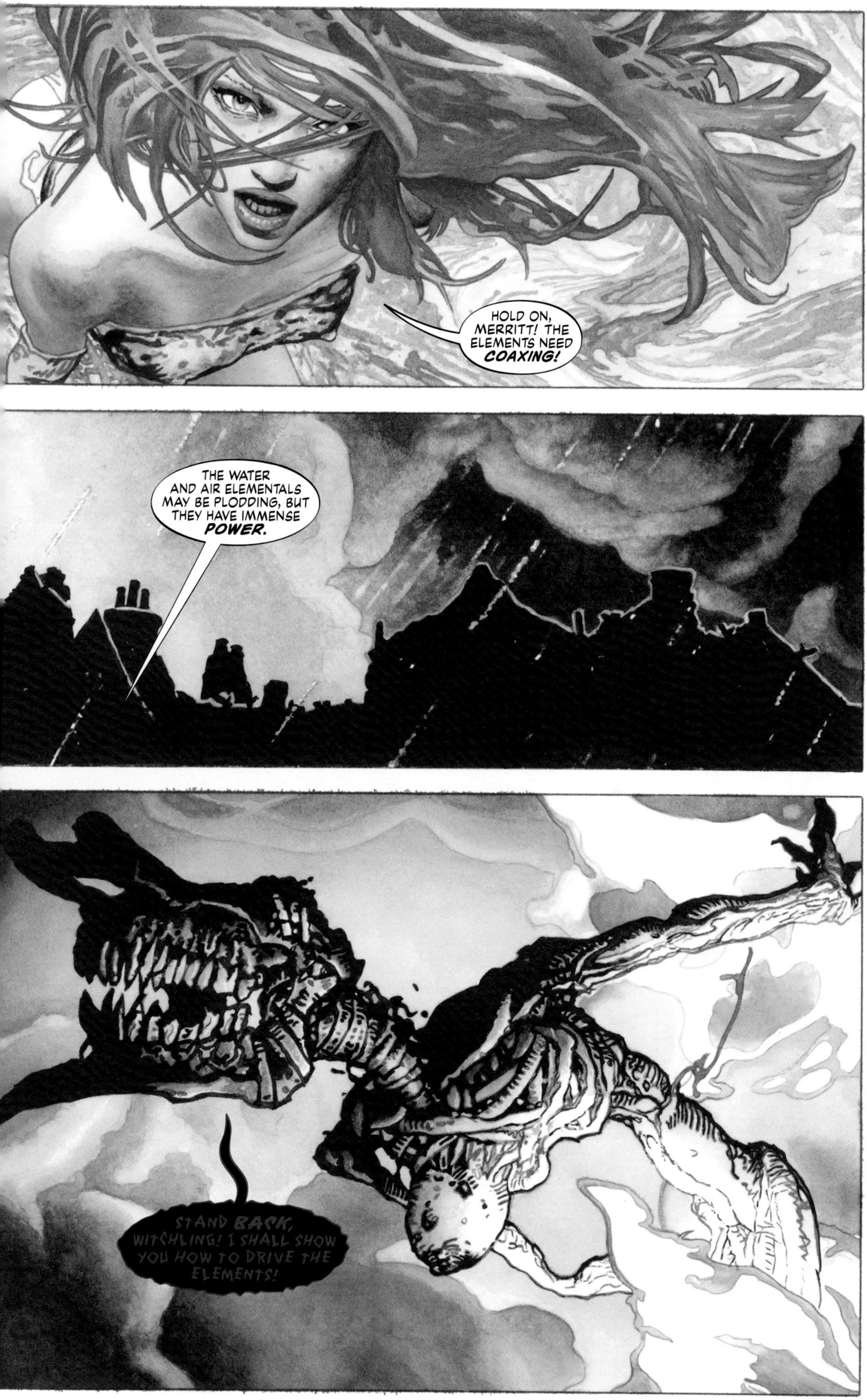
HOLD ON, MERRITT! THE ELEMENTS NEED **COAXING!**
THE WATER AND AIR ELEMENTALS MAY BE PLODDING, BUT THEY HAVE IMMENSE **POWER.**
STAND **BACK**, WITCHLING! I SHALL SHOW YOU HOW TO DRIVE THE ELEMENTS!

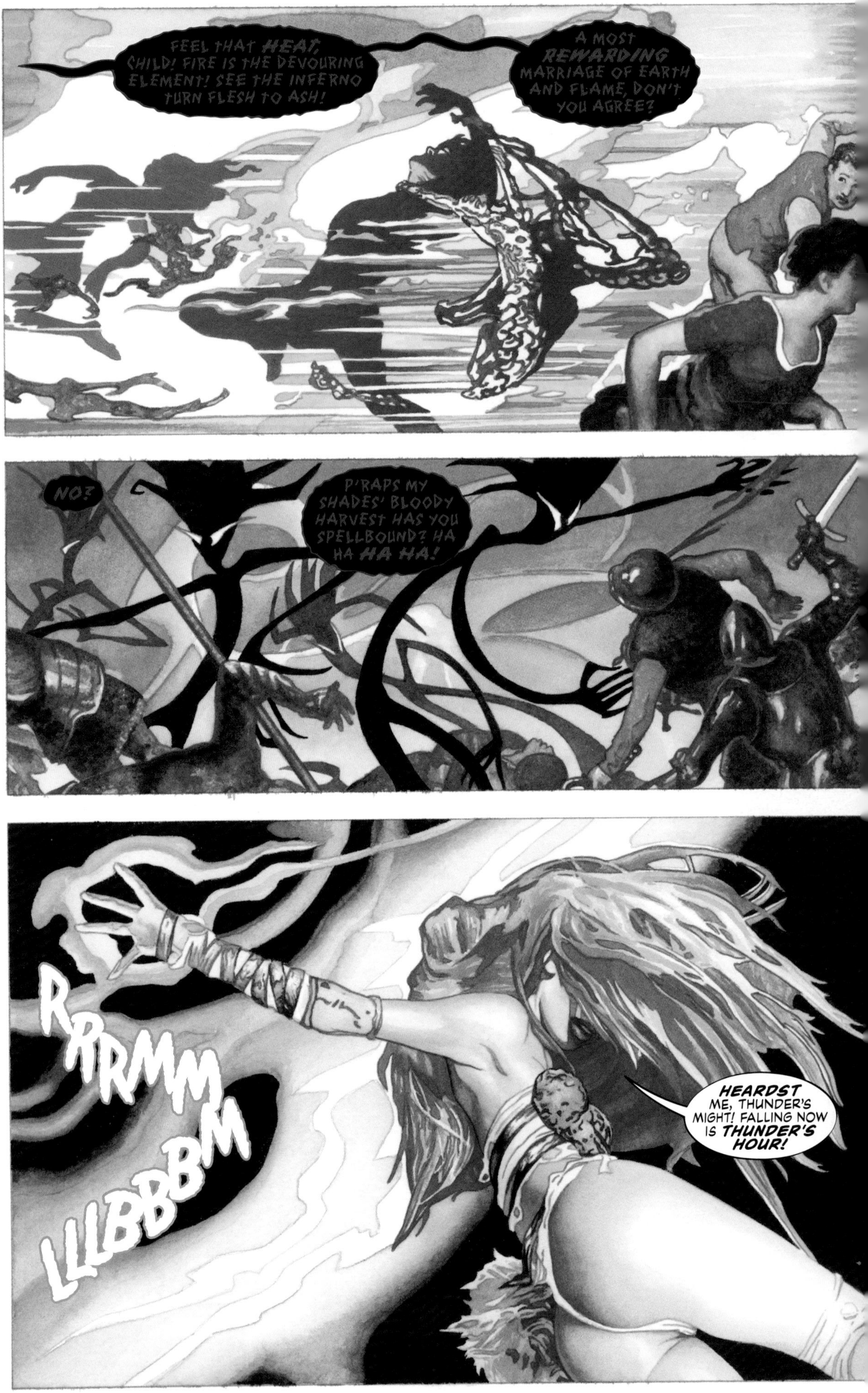
FEEL THAT HEAT, CHILD! FIRE IS THE DEVOURING ELEMENT! SEE THE INFERNO TURN FLESH TO ASH!
A MOST REWARDING MARRIAGE OF EARTH AND FLAME, DON'T YOU AGREE?
NO?
P'RAPS MY SHADES' BLOODY HARVEST HAS YOU SPELLBOUND? HA HA HA HA!
RRRMM LLLBBBM
HEARDST ME, THUNDER'S MIGHT! FALLING NOW IS THUNDER'S HOUR!

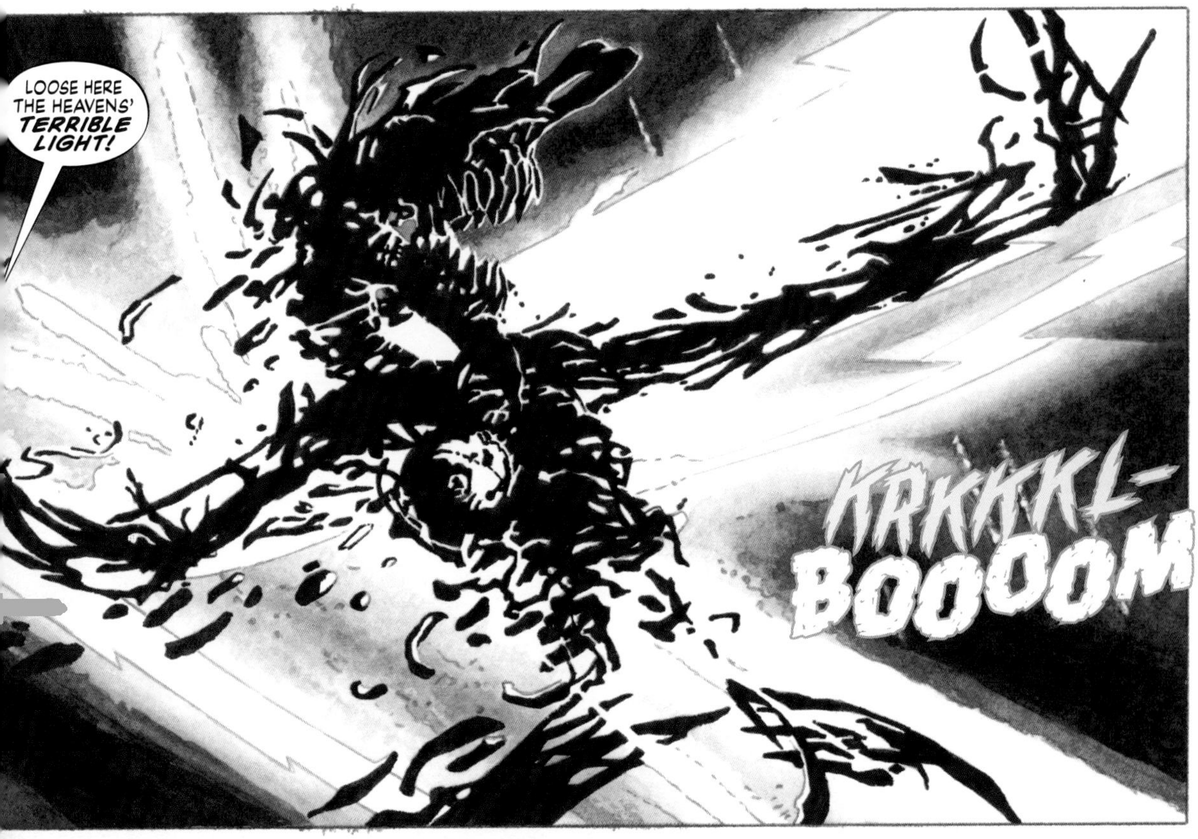
LOOSE HERE THE HEAVENS' TERRIBLE LIGHT!
KRKKKL-BOOOOM

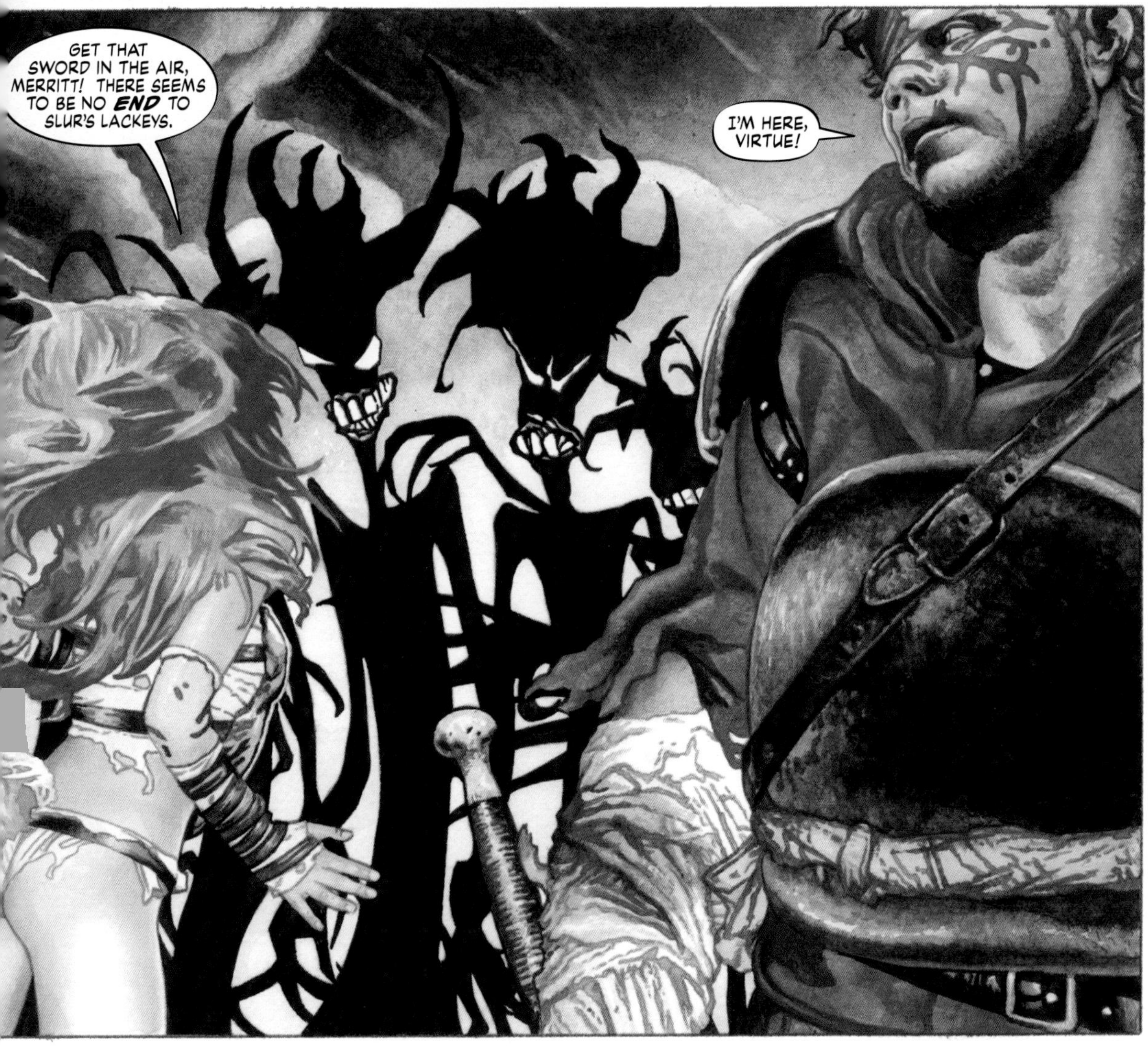
GET THAT SWORD IN THE AIR, MERRITT! THERE SEEMS TO BE NO END TO SLUR'S LACKEYS.
I'M HERE, VIRTUE!

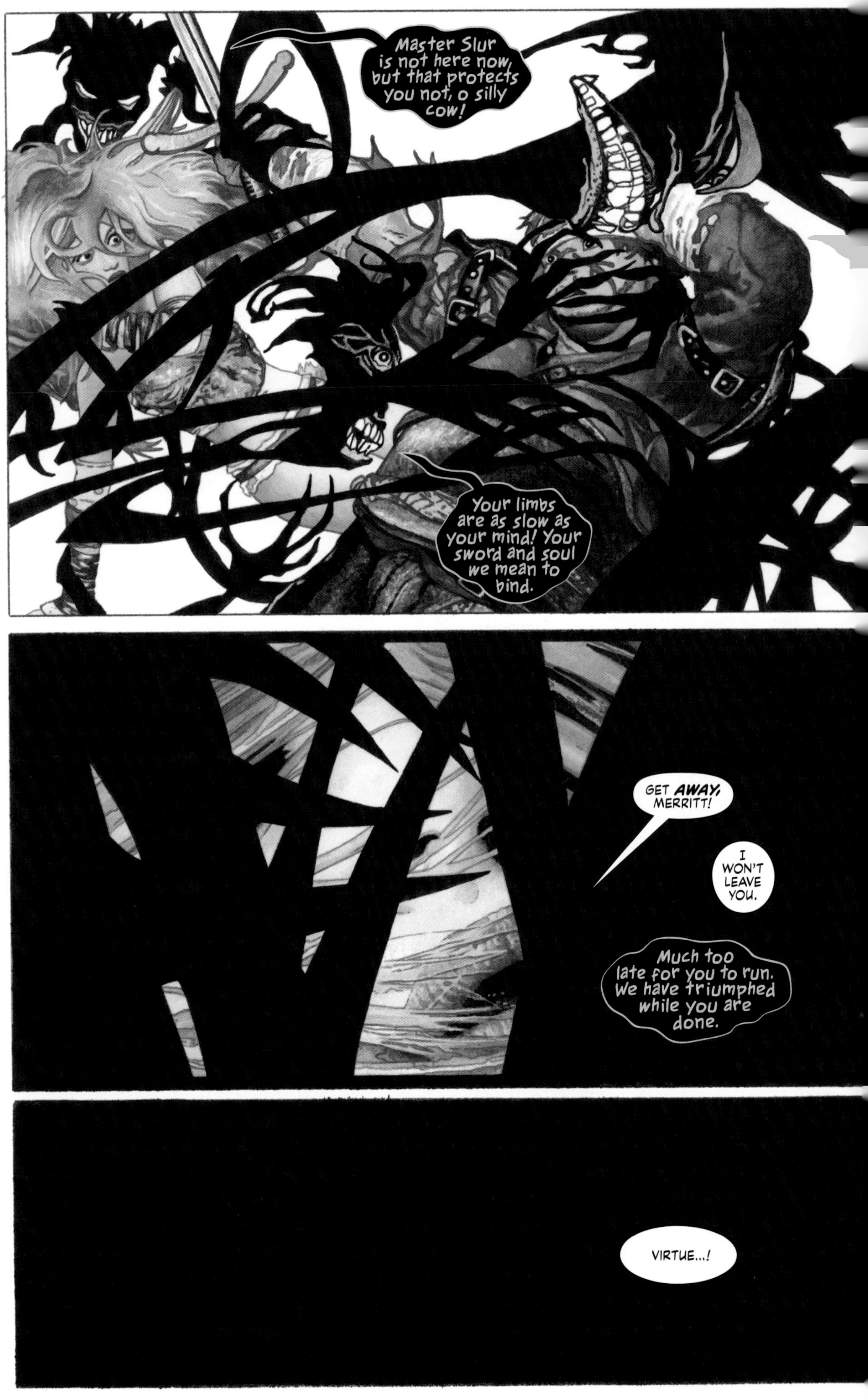
Master Slur is not here now, but that protects you not, o silly cow!
Your limbs are as slow as your mind! Your sword and soul we mean to bind.
GET AWAY, MERRITT!
I WON'T LEAVE YOU.
Much too late for you to run. We have triumphed while you are done.
VIRTUE...!

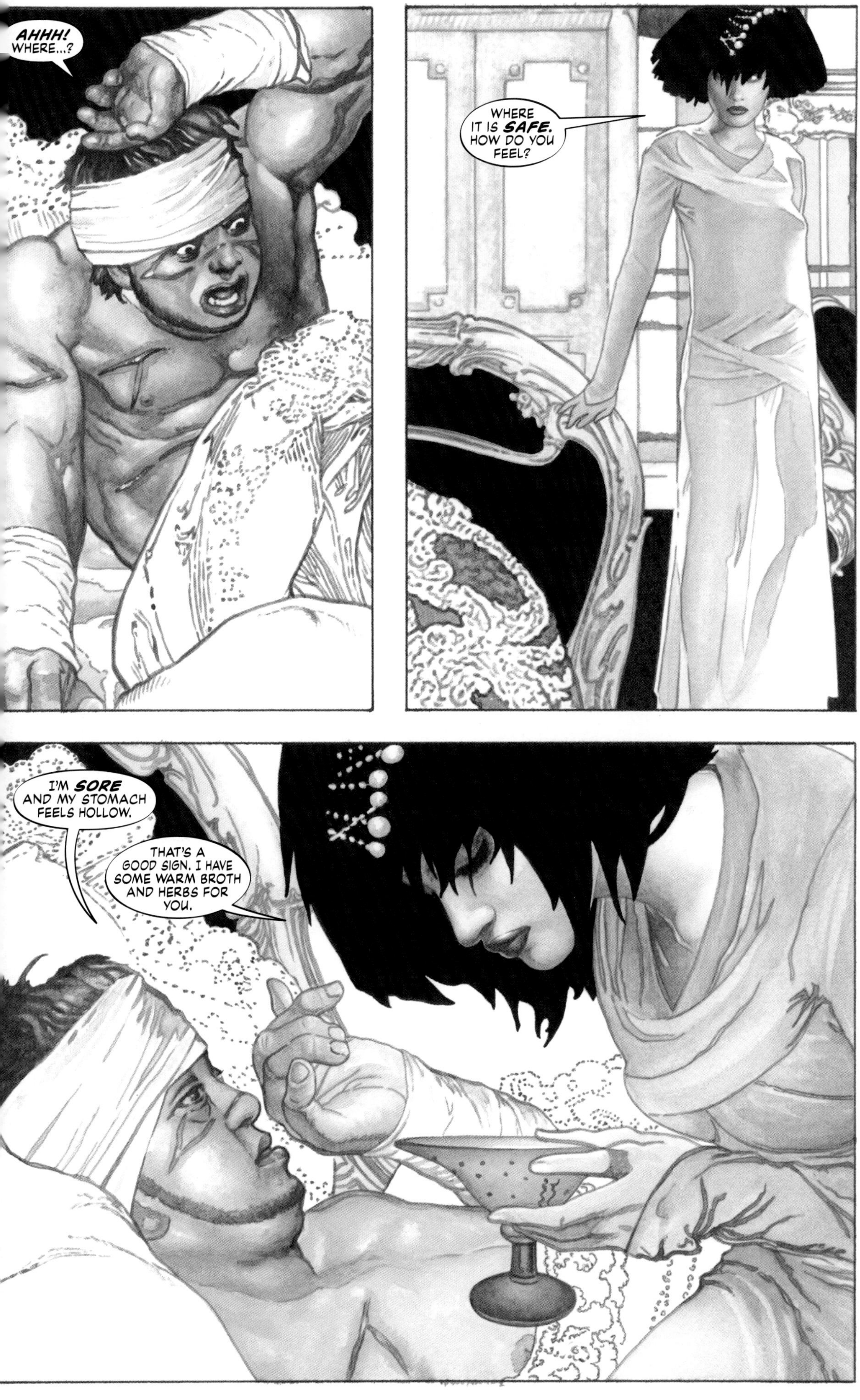
AHHH! WHERE...?
WHERE IT IS SAFE. HOW DO YOU FEEL?
I'M SORE AND MY STOMACH FEELS HOLLOW.
THAT'S A GOOD SIGN. I HAVE SOME WARM BROTH AND HERBS FOR YOU.

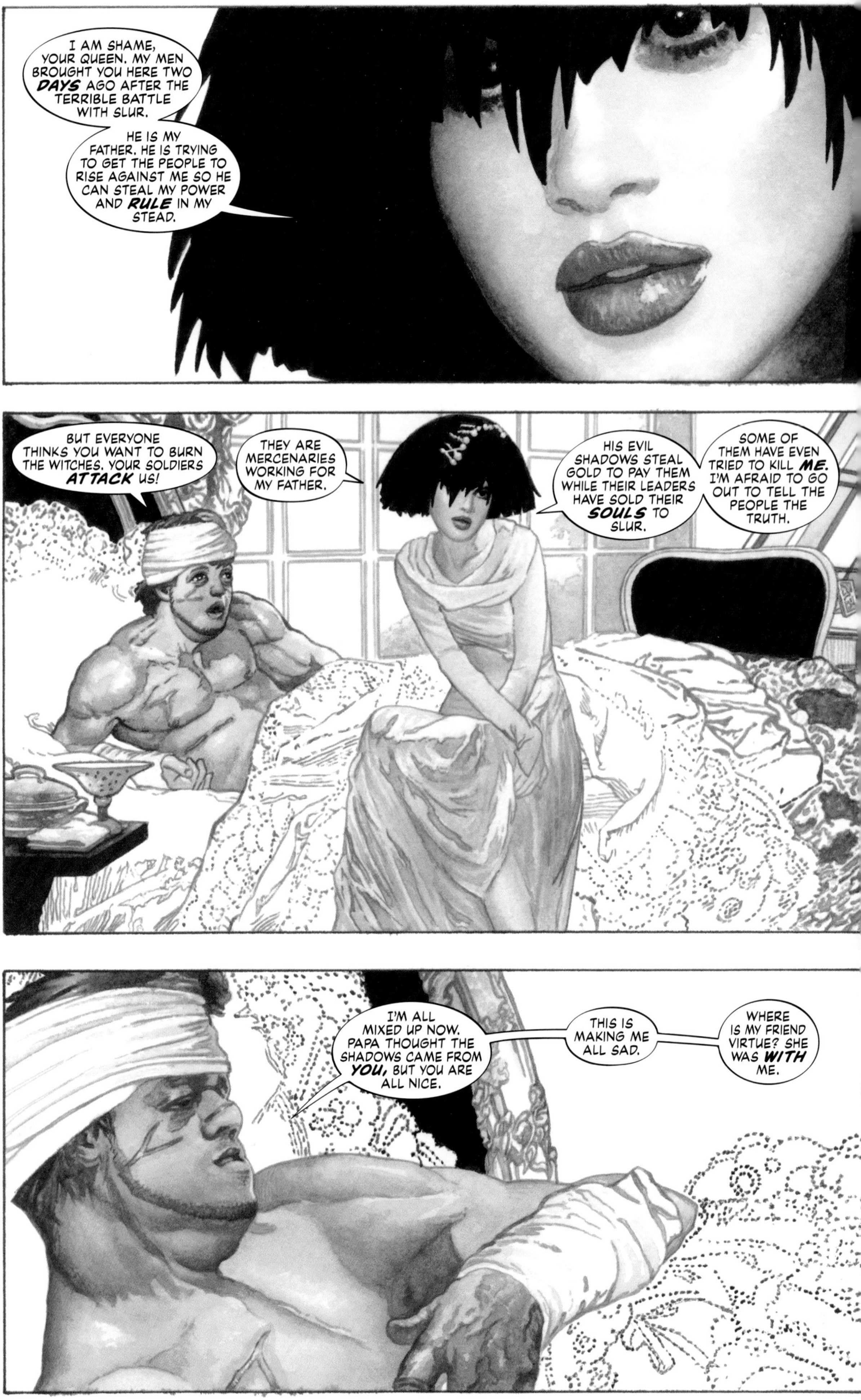
I AM SHAME, YOUR QUEEN. MY MEN BROUGHT YOU HERE TWO DAYS AGO AFTER THE TERRIBLE BATTLE WITH SLUR.
HE IS MY FATHER. HE IS TRYING TO GET THE PEOPLE TO RISE AGAINST ME SO HE CAN STEAL MY POWER AND RULE IN MY STEAD.
BUT EVERYONE THINKS YOU WANT TO BURN THE WITCHES. YOUR SOLDIERS ATTACK US!
THEY ARE MERCENARIES WORKING FOR MY FATHER.
HIS EVIL SHADOWS STEAL GOLD TO PAY THEM WHILE THEIR LEADERS HAVE SOLD THEIR SOULS TO SLUR.
SOME OF THEM HAVE EVEN TRIED TO KILL ME. I'M AFRAID TO GO OUT TO TELL THE PEOPLE THE TRUTH.
I'M ALL MIXED UP NOW. PAPA THOUGHT THE SHADOWS CAME FROM YOU, BUT YOU ARE ALL NICE.
THIS IS MAKING ME ALL SAD.
WHERE IS MY FRIEND VIRTUE? SHE WAS WITH ME.

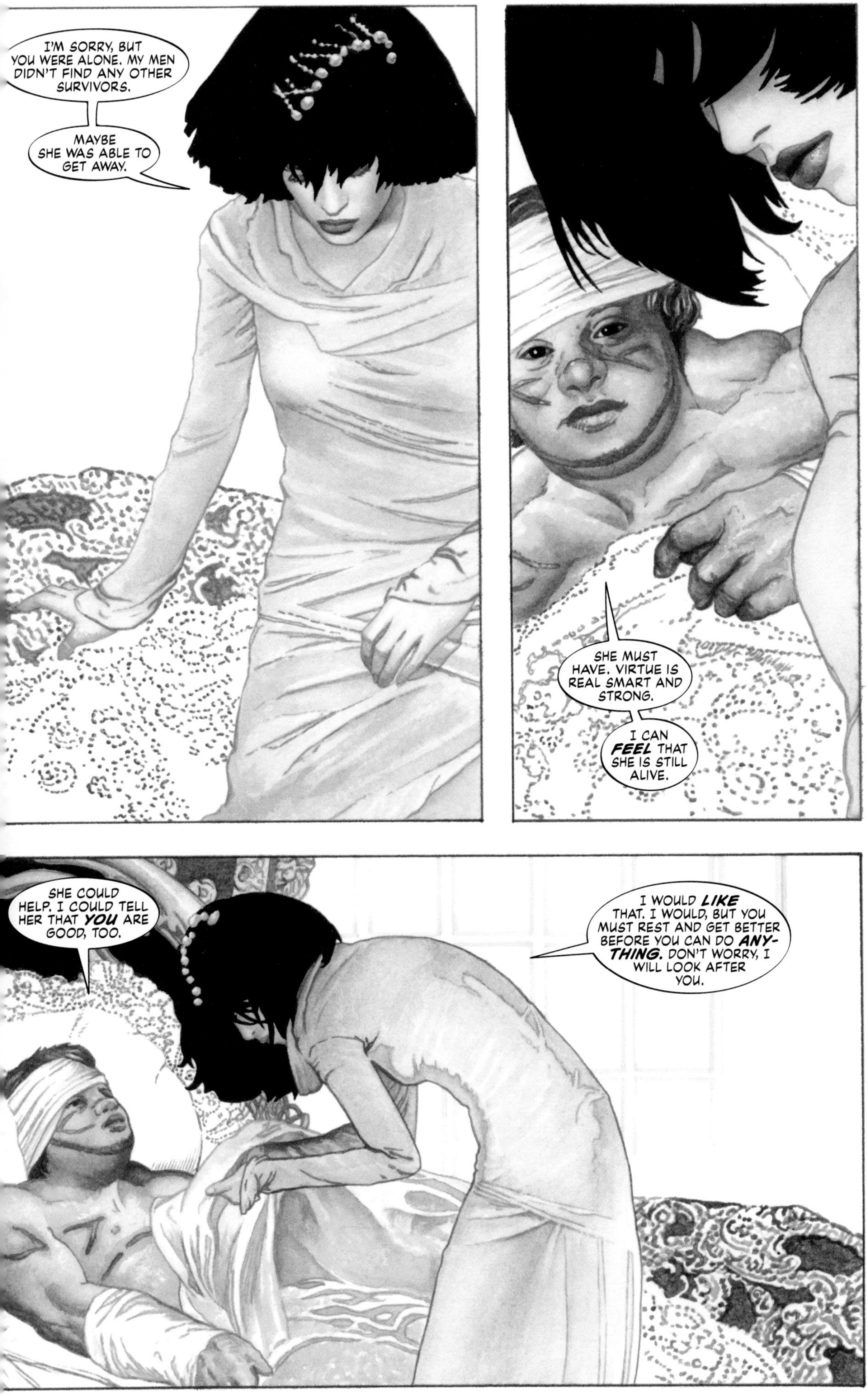
I'M SORRY, BUT YOU WERE ALONE. MY MEN DIDN'T FIND ANY OTHER SURVIVORS.
MAYBE SHE WAS ABLE TO GET AWAY.
SHE MUST HAVE. VIRTUE IS REAL SMART AND STRONG.
I CAN *FEEL* THAT SHE IS STILL ALIVE.
SHE COULD HELP. I COULD TELL HER THAT *YOU* ARE GOOD, TOO.
I WOULD *LIKE* THAT. I WOULD, BUT YOU MUST REST AND GET BETTER BEFORE YOU CAN DO *ANYTHING.* DON'T WORRY, I WILL LOOK AFTER YOU.

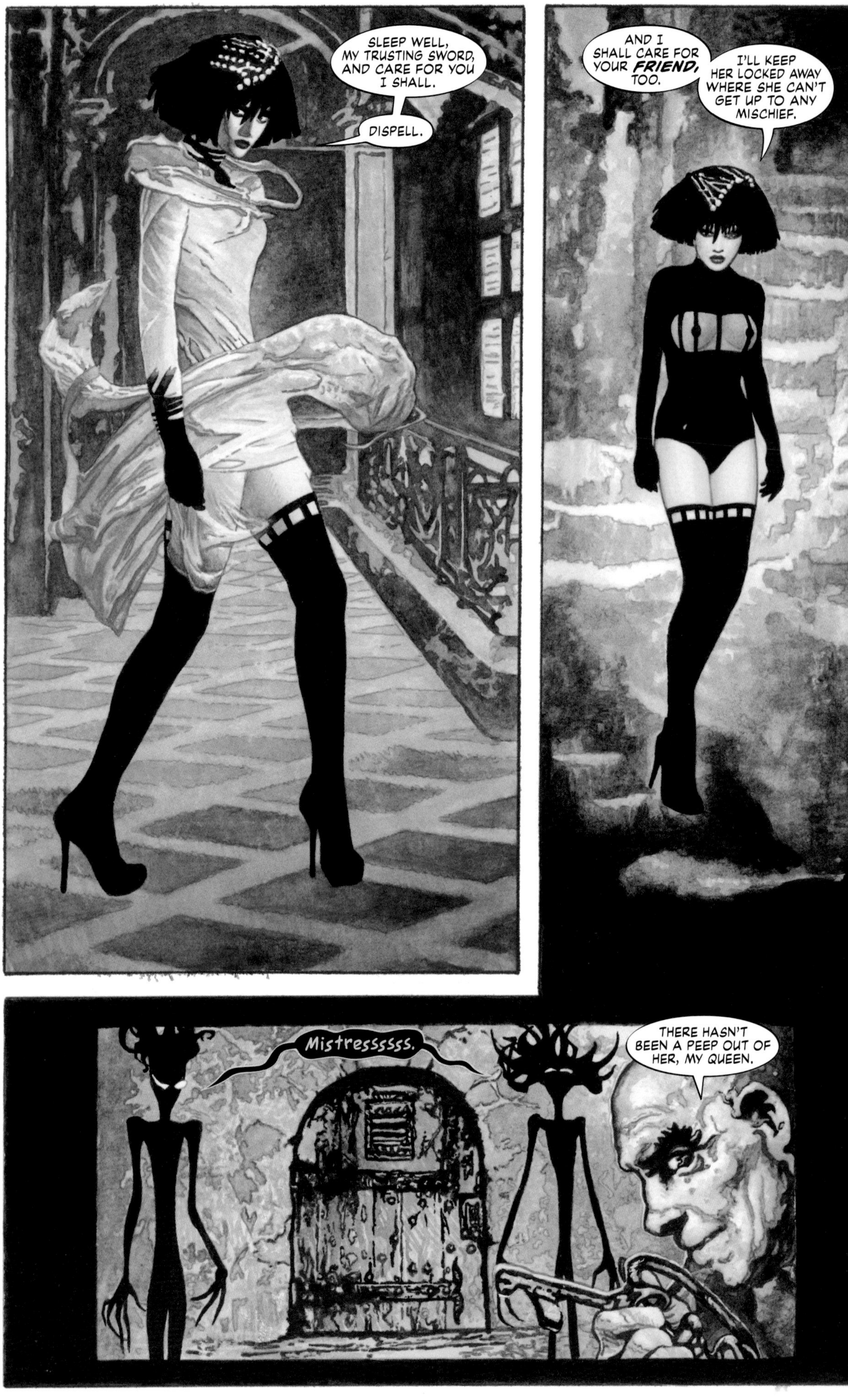

SLEEP WELL, MY TRUSTING SWORD, AND CARE FOR YOU I SHALL.
DISPELL.
AND I SHALL CARE FOR YOUR FRIEND, TOO.
I'LL KEEP HER LOCKED AWAY WHERE SHE CAN'T GET UP TO ANY MISCHIEF.
Mistresssssss.
THERE HASN'T BEEN A PEEP OUT OF HER, MY QUEEN.

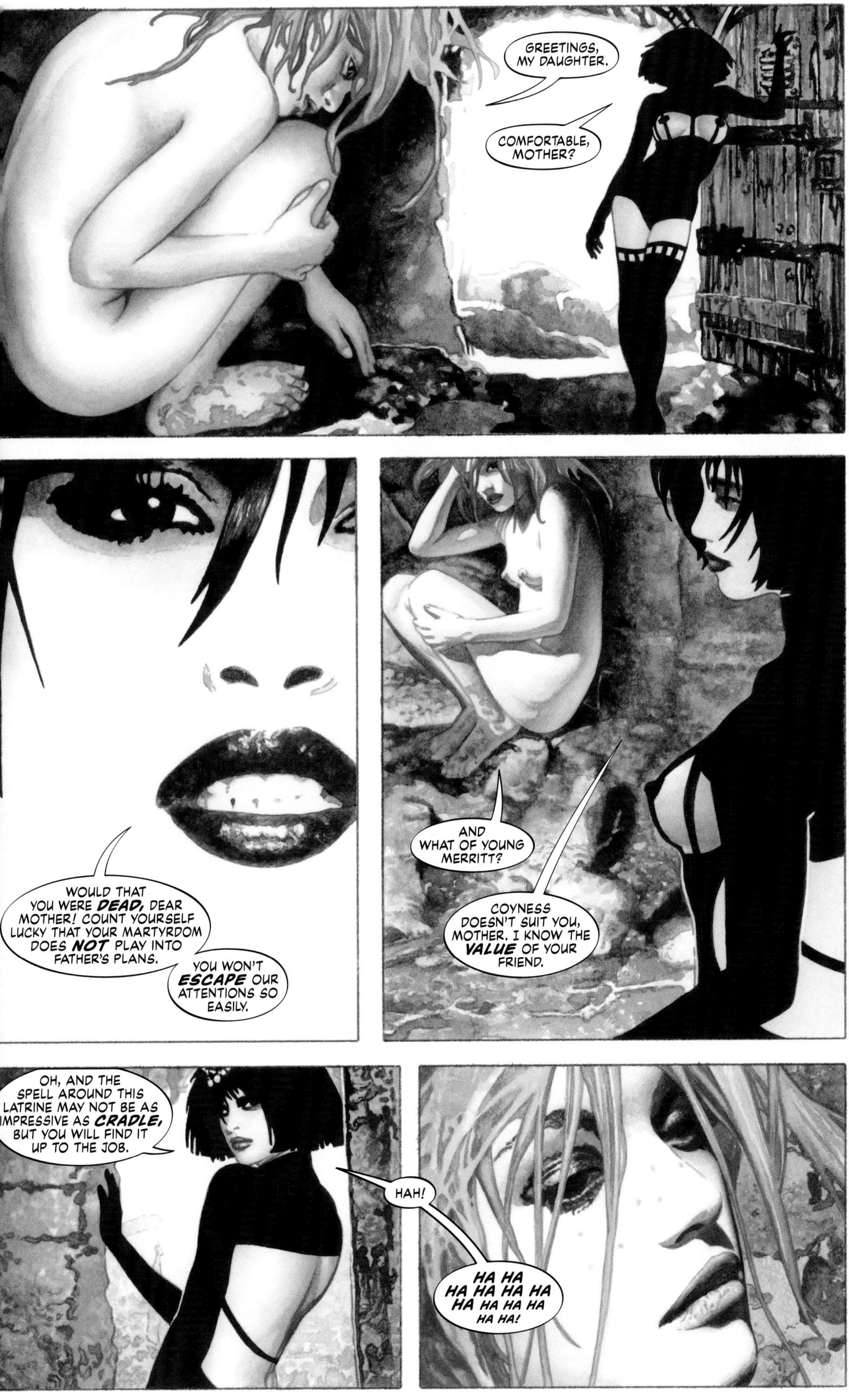

GREETINGS, MY DAUGHTER.
COMFORTABLE, MOTHER?
WOULD THAT YOU WERE **DEAD,** DEAR MOTHER! COUNT YOURSELF LUCKY THAT YOUR MARTYRDOM DOES **NOT** PLAY INTO FATHER'S PLANS.
YOU WON'T **ESCAPE** OUR ATTENTIONS SO EASILY.
AND WHAT OF YOUNG MERRITT?
COYNESS DOESN'T SUIT YOU, MOTHER. I KNOW THE **VALUE** OF YOUR FRIEND.
OH, AND THE SPELL AROUND THIS LATRINE MAY NOT BE AS IMPRESSIVE AS **CRADLE,** BUT YOU WILL FIND IT UP TO THE JOB.
HAH!
HA HA HA HA HA HA HA HA HA HA HA HA!

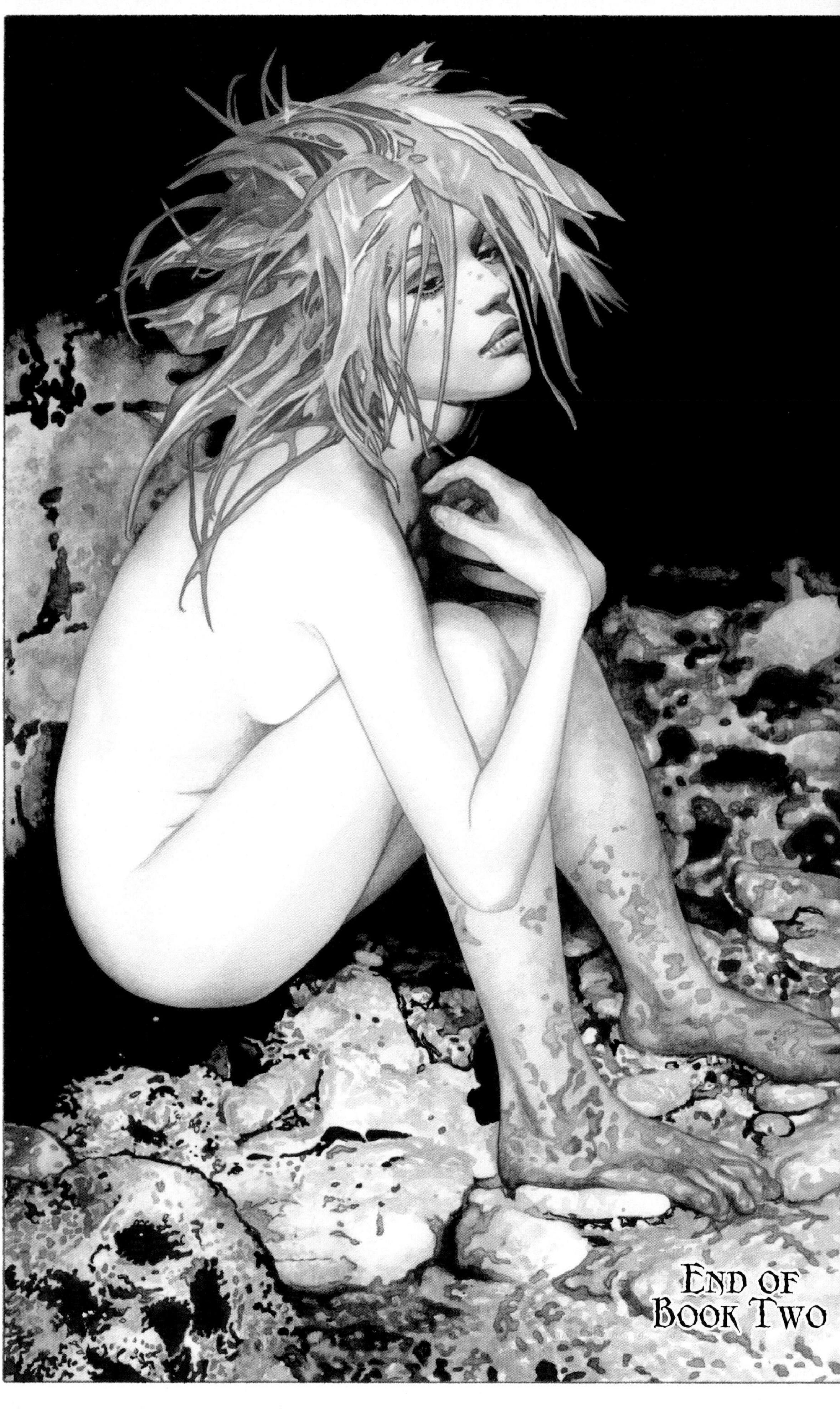
END OF
BOOK TWO

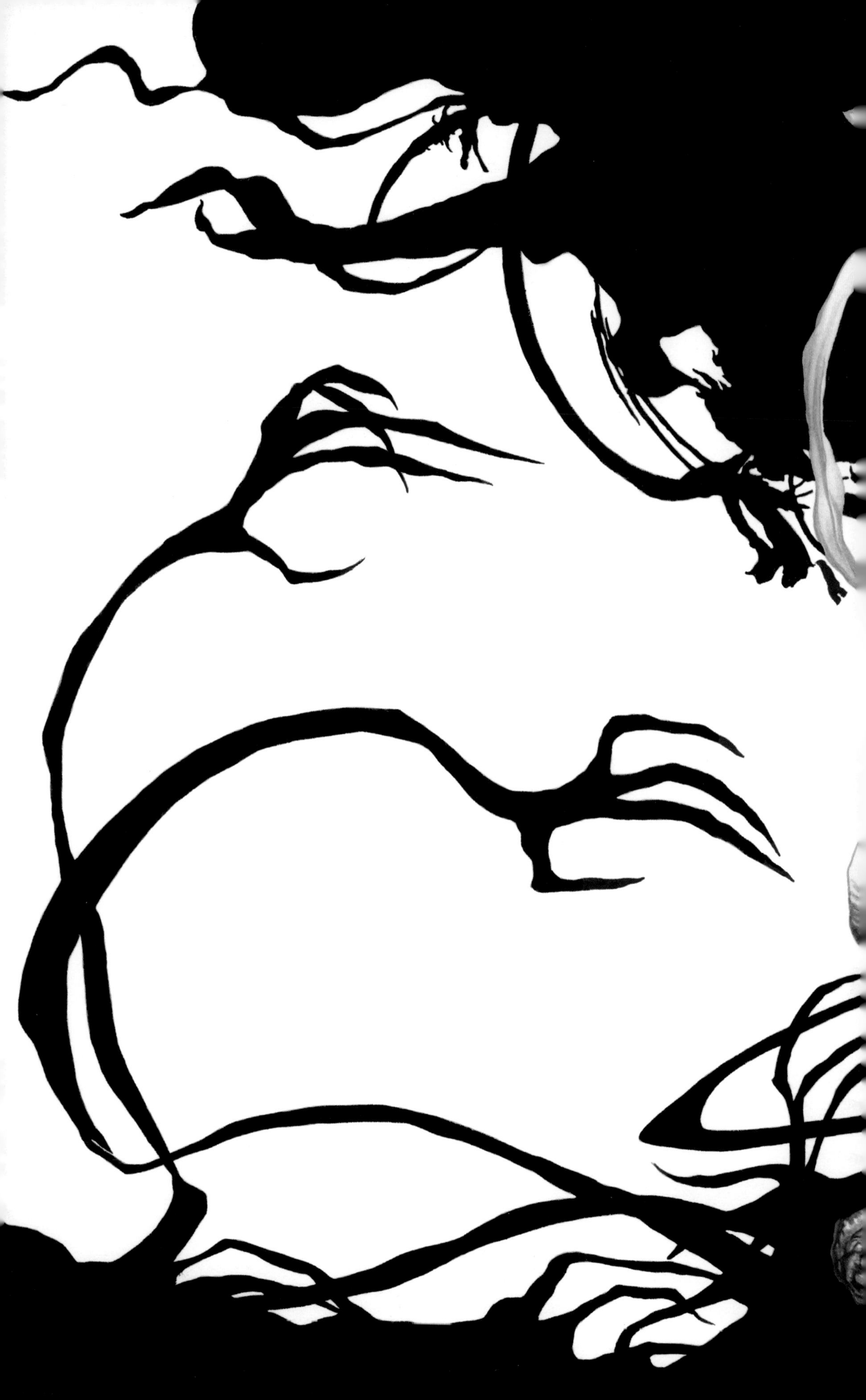

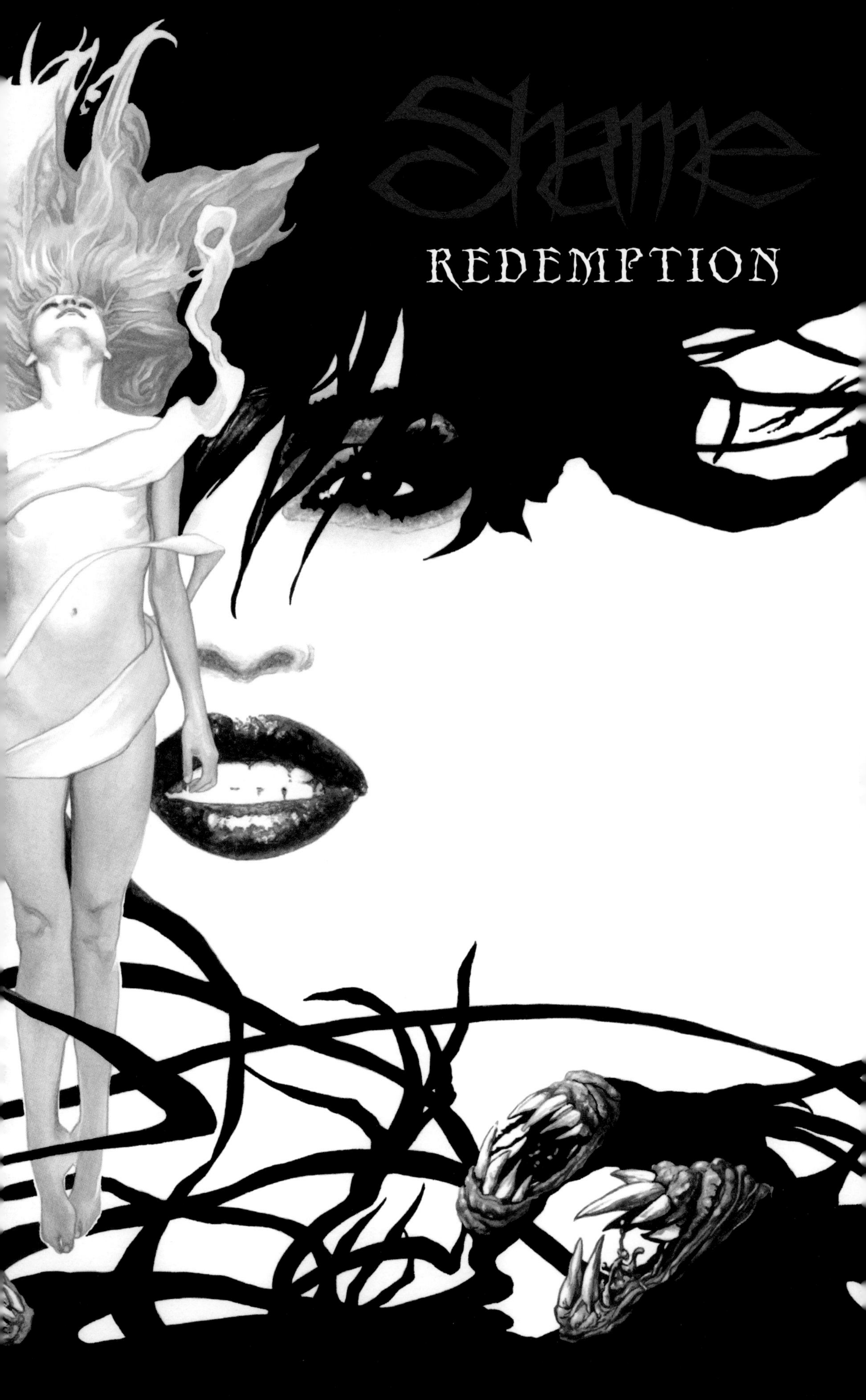
Shame
REDEMPTION

SHAME
PART THREE: REDEMPTION

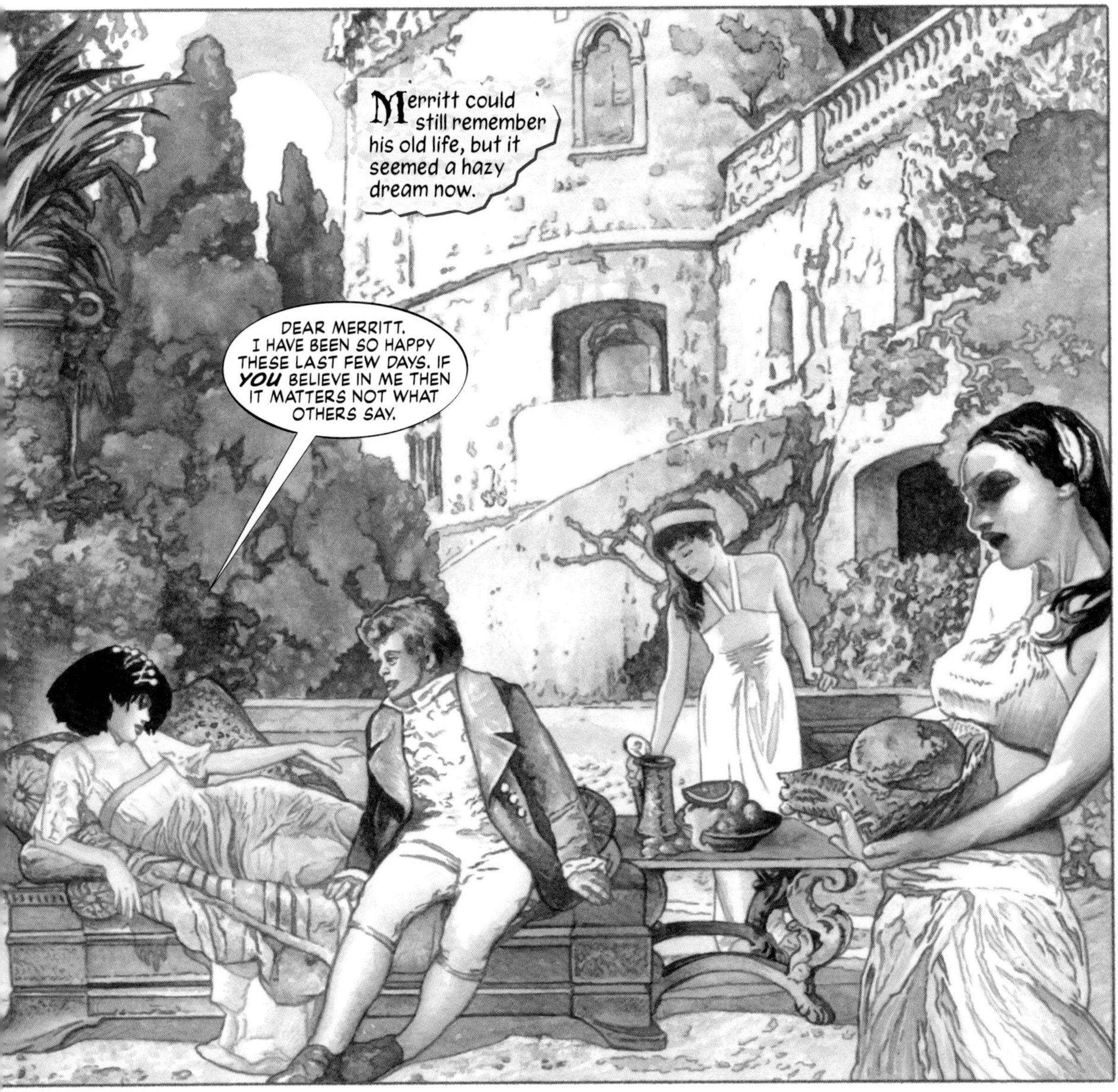
Merritt could still remember his old life, but it seemed a hazy dream now.
DEAR MERRITT. I HAVE BEEN SO HAPPY THESE LAST FEW DAYS. IF YOU BELIEVE IN ME THEN IT MATTERS NOT WHAT OTHERS SAY.

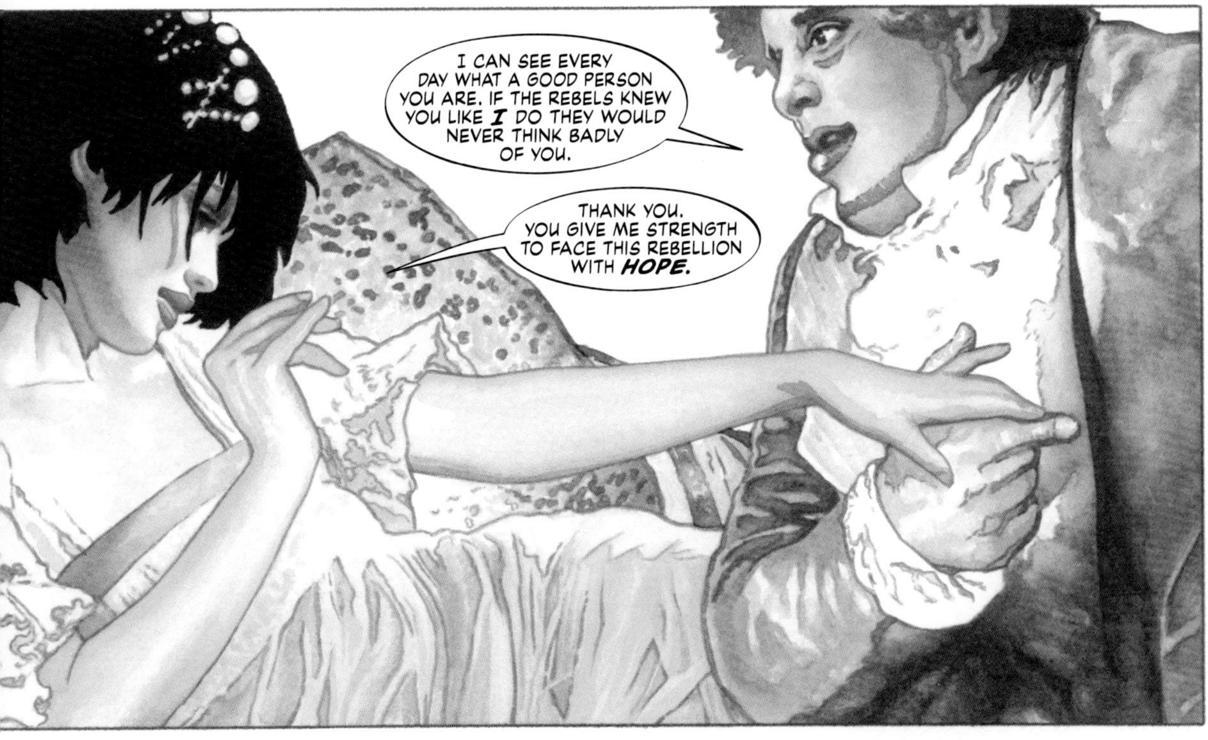
I CAN SEE EVERY DAY WHAT A GOOD PERSON YOU ARE. IF THE REBELS KNEW YOU LIKE I DO THEY WOULD NEVER THINK BADLY OF YOU.
THANK YOU. YOU GIVE ME STRENGTH TO FACE THIS REBELLION WITH HOPE.

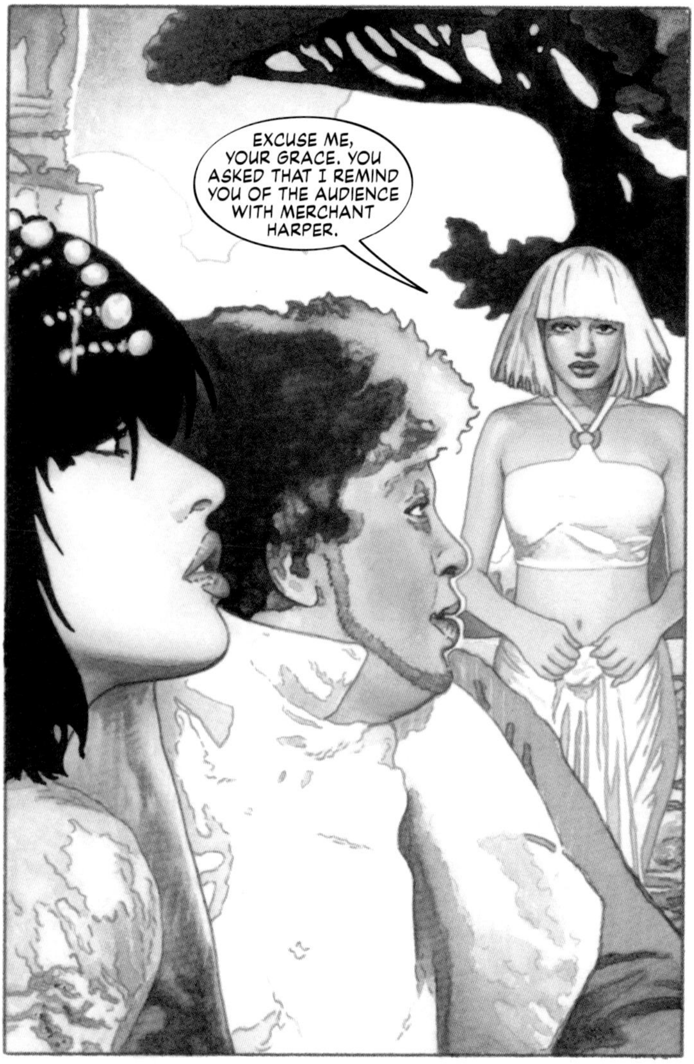
EXCUSE ME, YOUR GRACE. YOU ASKED THAT I REMIND YOU OF THE AUDIENCE WITH MERCHANT HARPER.

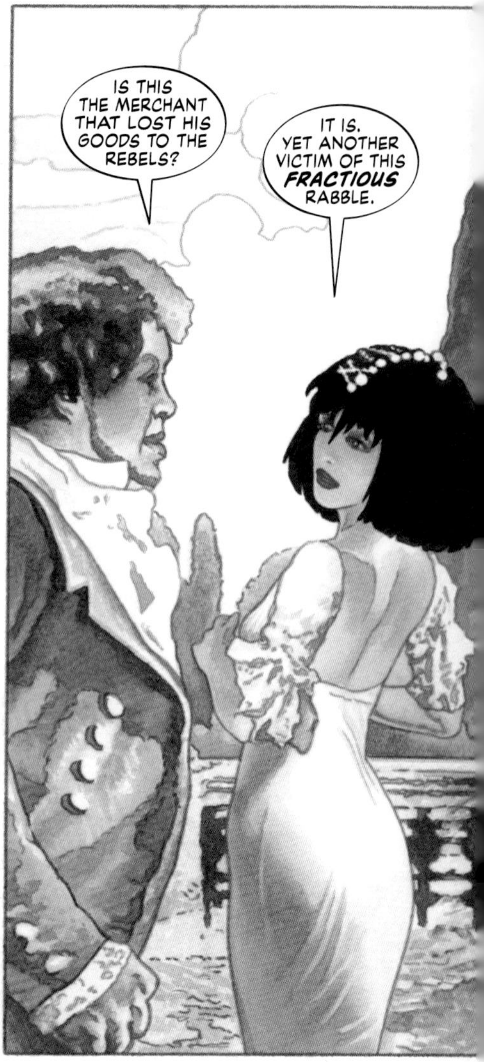
IS THIS THE MERCHANT THAT LOST HIS GOODS TO THE REBELS?
IT IS. YET ANOTHER VICTIM OF THIS *FRACTIOUS* RABBLE.

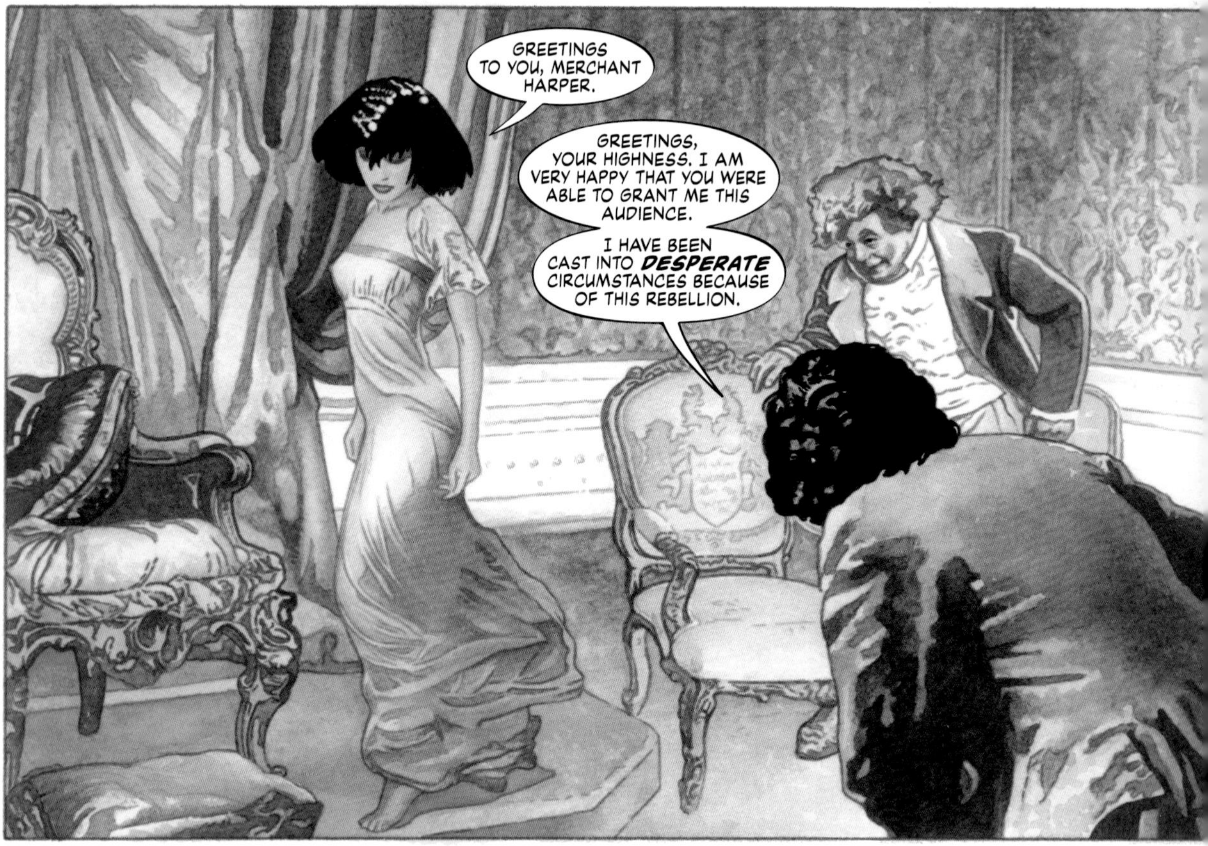
GREETINGS TO YOU, MERCHANT HARPER.
GREETINGS, YOUR HIGHNESS. I AM VERY HAPPY THAT YOU WERE ABLE TO GRANT ME THIS AUDIENCE.
I HAVE BEEN CAST INTO *DESPERATE* CIRCUMSTANCES BECAUSE OF THIS REBELLION.

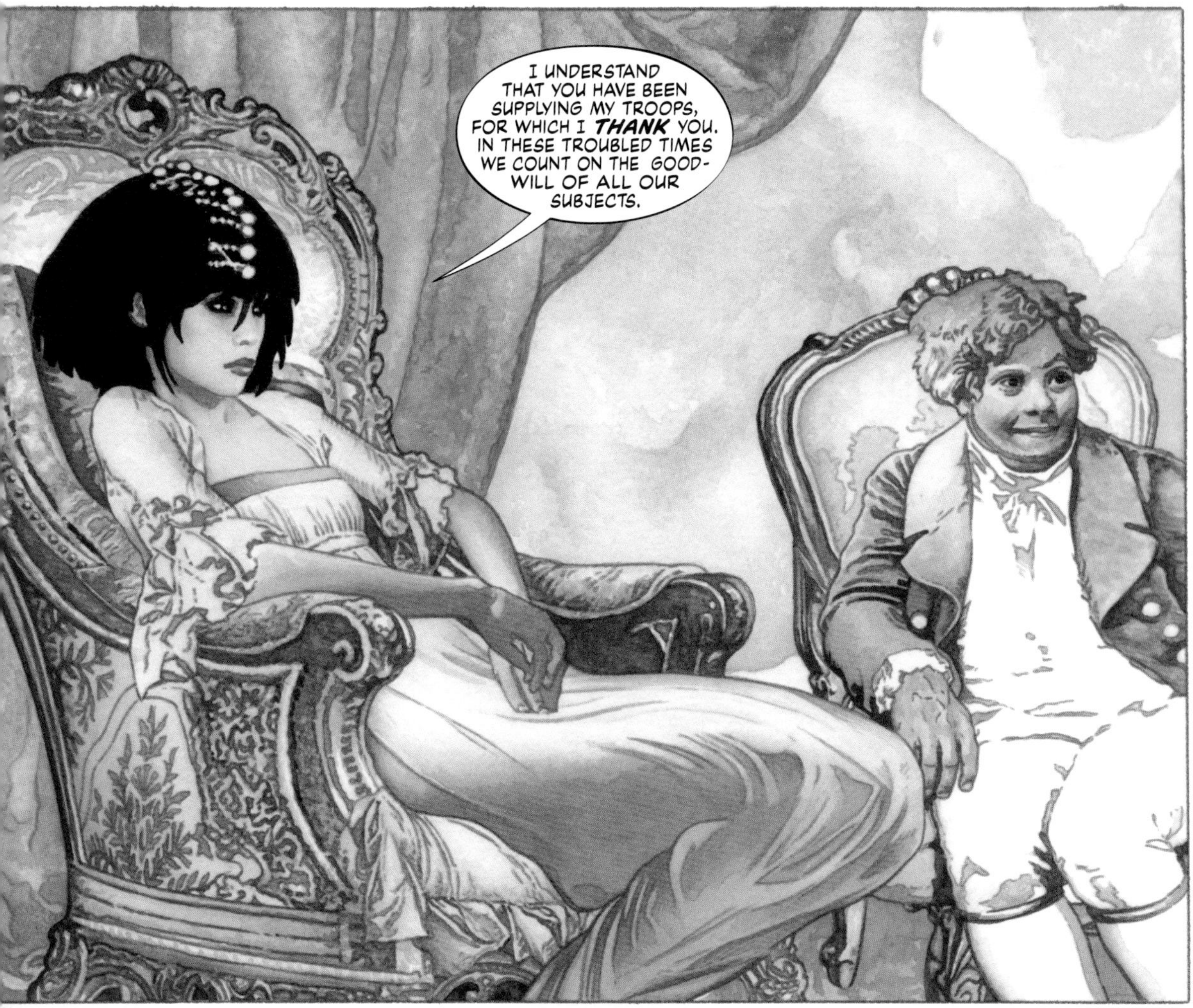
I UNDERSTAND THAT YOU HAVE BEEN SUPPLYING MY TROOPS, FOR WHICH I THANK YOU. IN THESE TROUBLED TIMES WE COUNT ON THE GOOD-WILL OF ALL OUR SUBJECTS.

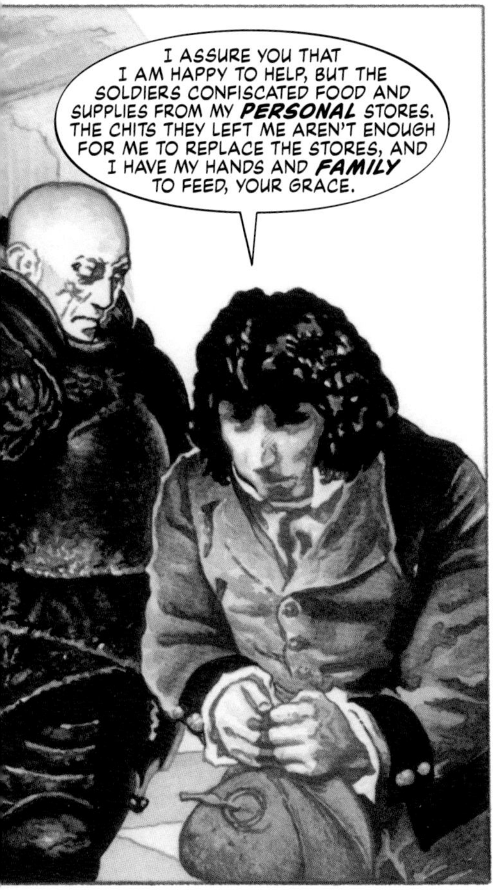
I ASSURE YOU THAT I AM HAPPY TO HELP, BUT THE SOLDIERS CONFISCATED FOOD AND SUPPLIES FROM MY PERSONAL STORES. THE CHITS THEY LEFT ME AREN'T ENOUGH FOR ME TO REPLACE THE STORES, AND I HAVE MY HANDS AND FAMILY TO FEED, YOUR GRACE.

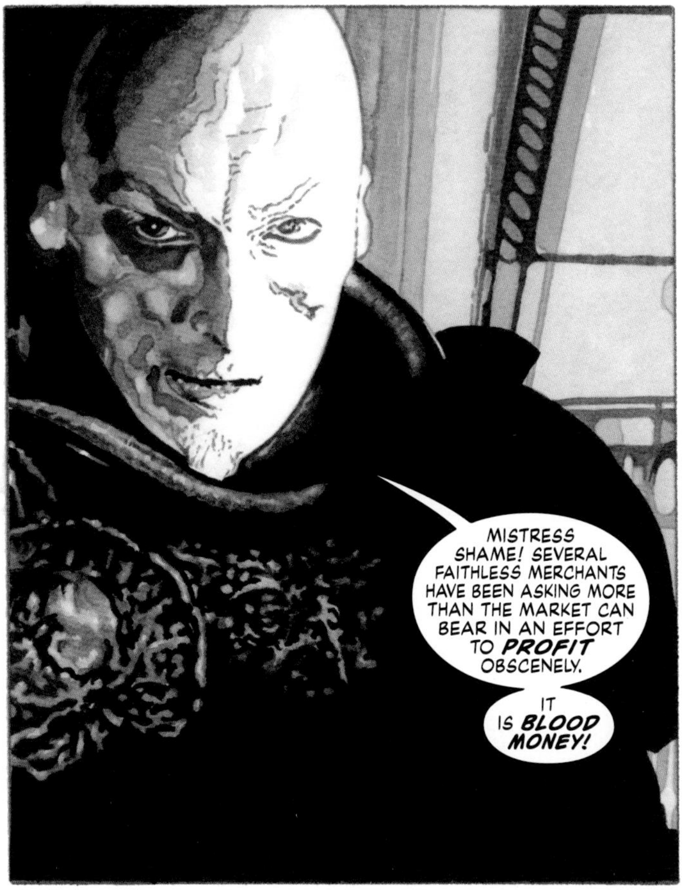
MISTRESS SHAME! SEVERAL FAITHLESS MERCHANTS HAVE BEEN ASKING MORE THAN THE MARKET CAN BEAR IN AN EFFORT TO PROFIT OBSCENELY.
IT IS BLOOD MONEY!

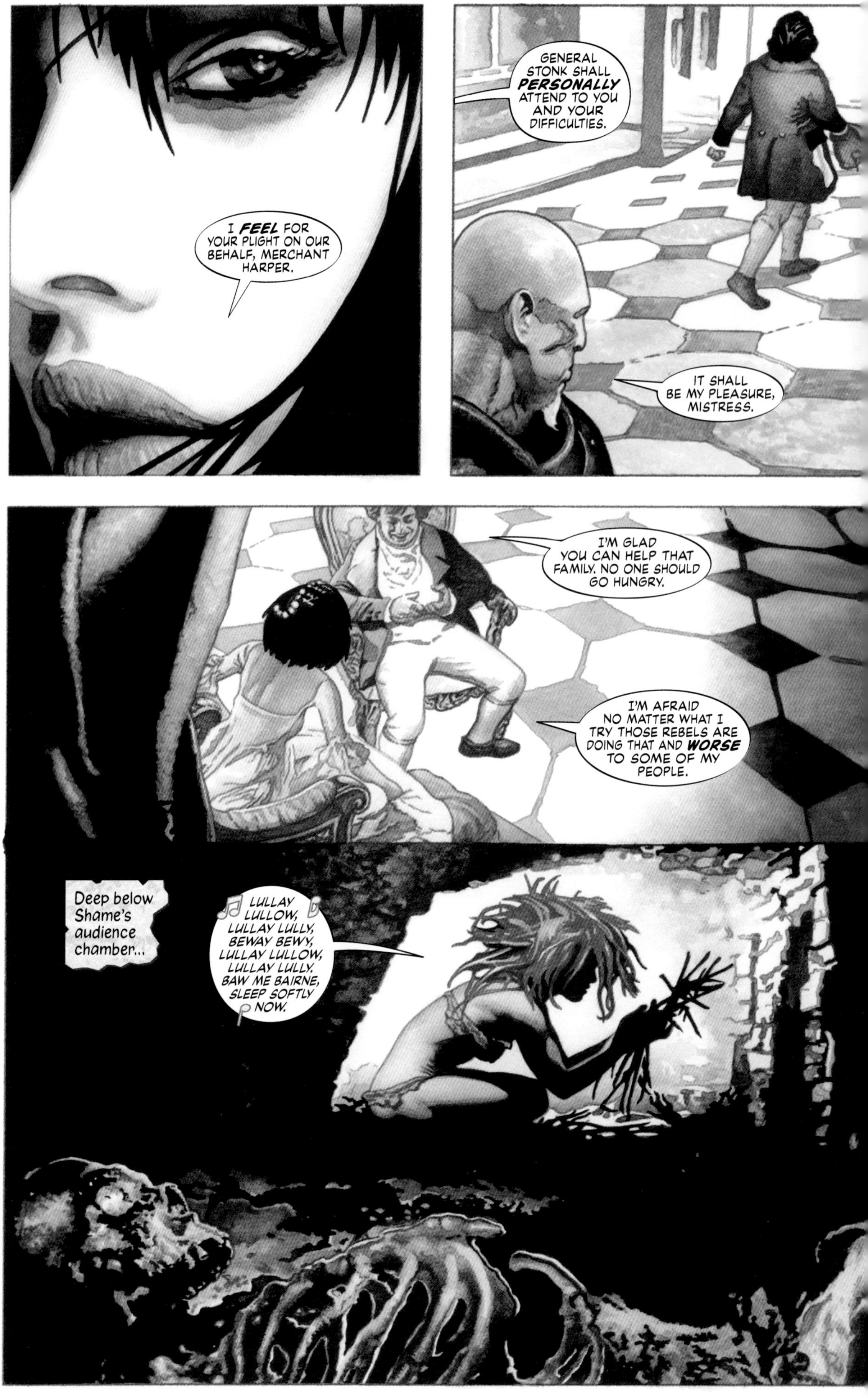
I FEEL FOR YOUR PLIGHT ON OUR BEHALF, MERCHANT HARPER.
GENERAL STONK SHALL PERSONALLY ATTEND TO YOU AND YOUR DIFFICULTIES.
IT SHALL BE MY PLEASURE, MISTRESS.
I'M GLAD YOU CAN HELP THAT FAMILY. NO ONE SHOULD GO HUNGRY.
I'M AFRAID NO MATTER WHAT I TRY THOSE REBELS ARE DOING THAT AND WORSE TO SOME OF MY PEOPLE.
Deep below Shame's audience chamber...
LULLAY LULLOW, LULLAY LULLY, BEWAY BEWY, LULLAY LULLOW, LULLAY LULLY. BAW ME BAIRNE, SLEEP SOFTLY NOW.

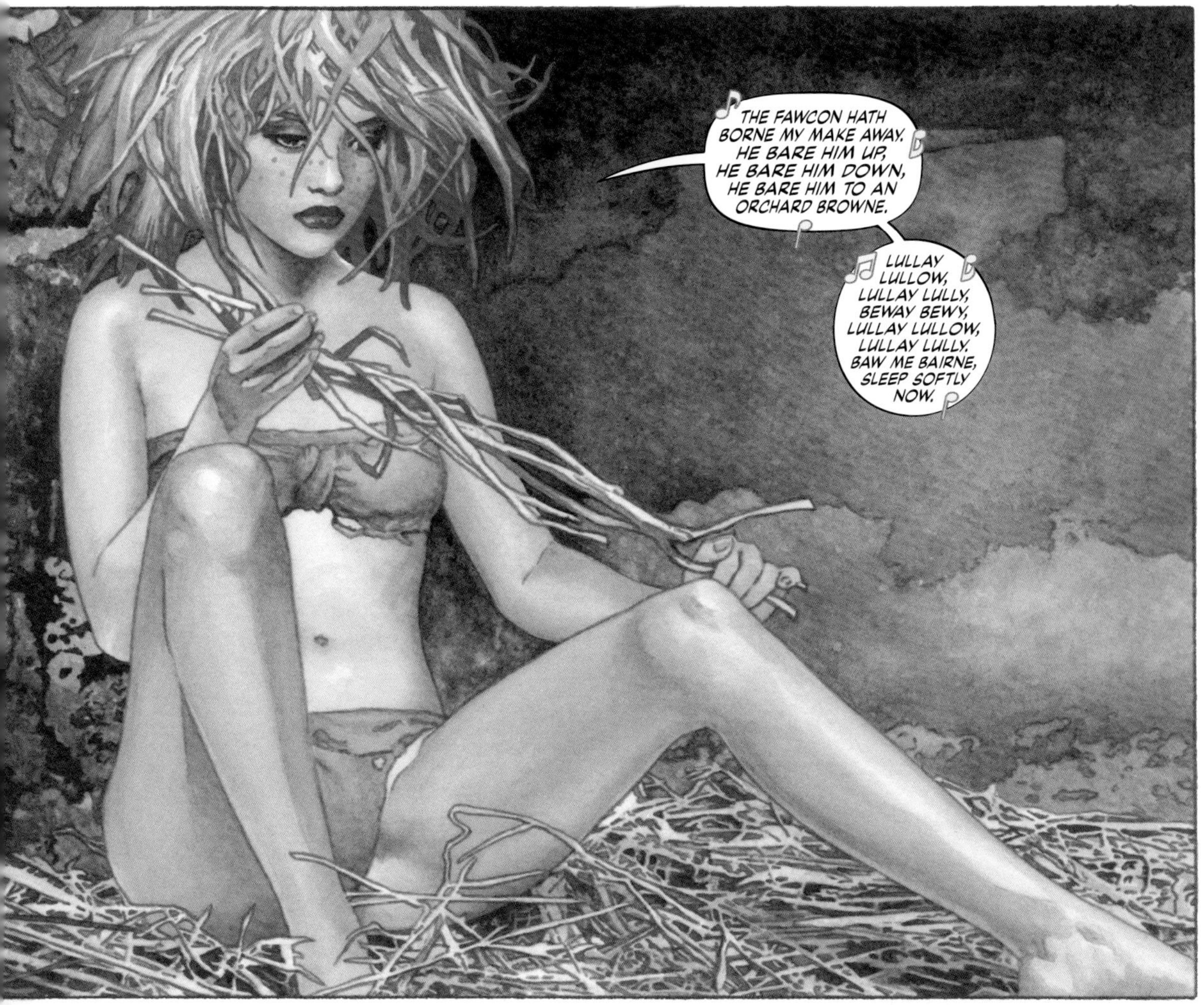
THE FAWCON HATH BORNE MY MAKE AWAY. HE BARE HIM UP, HE BARE HIM DOWN, HE BARE HIM TO AN ORCHARD BROWNE.
LULLAY LULLOW, LULLAY LULLY, BEWAY BEWY, LULLAY LULLOW, LULLAY LULLY. BAW ME BAIRNE, SLEEP SOFTLY NOW.

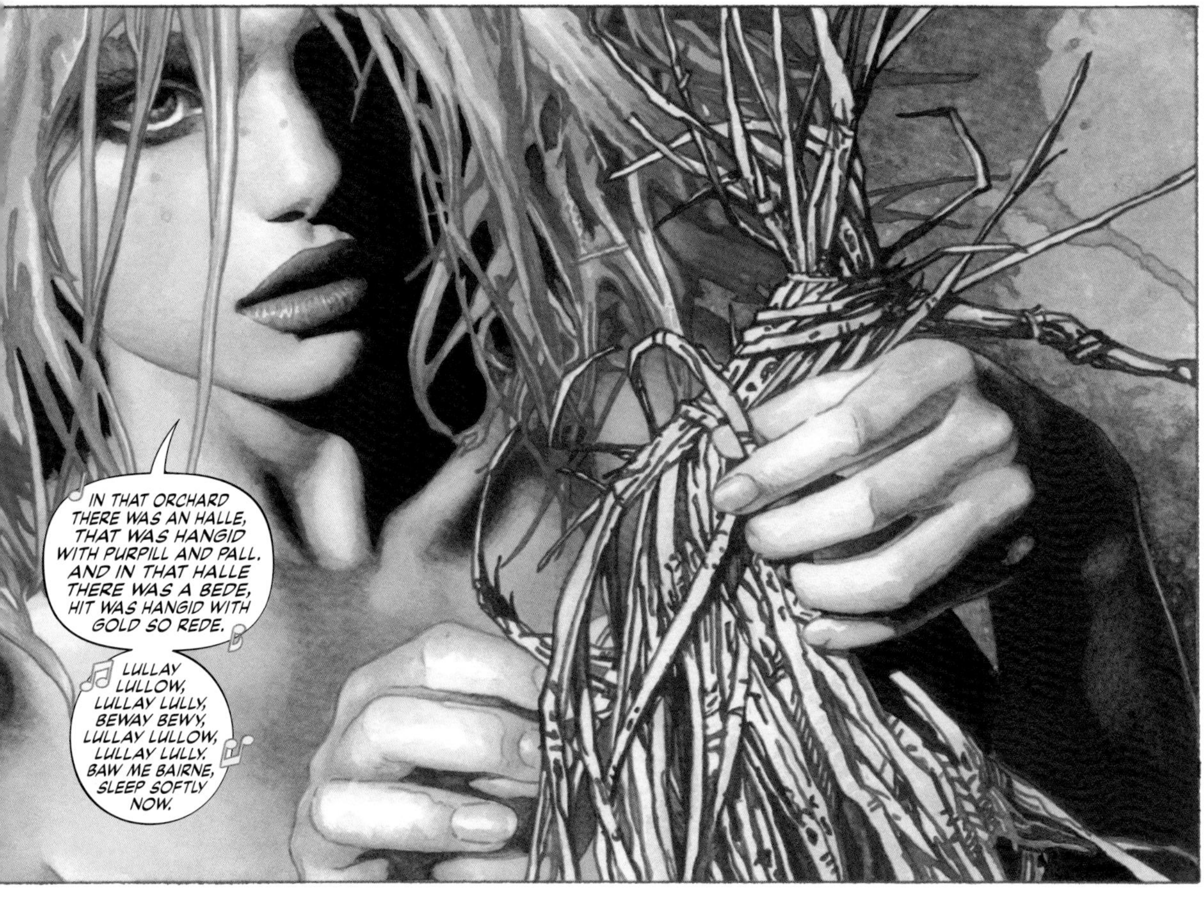
IN THAT ORCHARD THERE WAS AN HALLE, THAT WAS HANGID WITH PURPILL AND PALL. AND IN THAT HALLE THERE WAS A BEDE, HIT WAS HANGID WITH GOLD SO REDE.
LULLAY LULLOW, LULLAY LULLY, BEWAY BEWY, LULLAY LULLOW, LULLAY LULLY. BAW ME BAIRNE, SLEEP SOFTLY NOW.

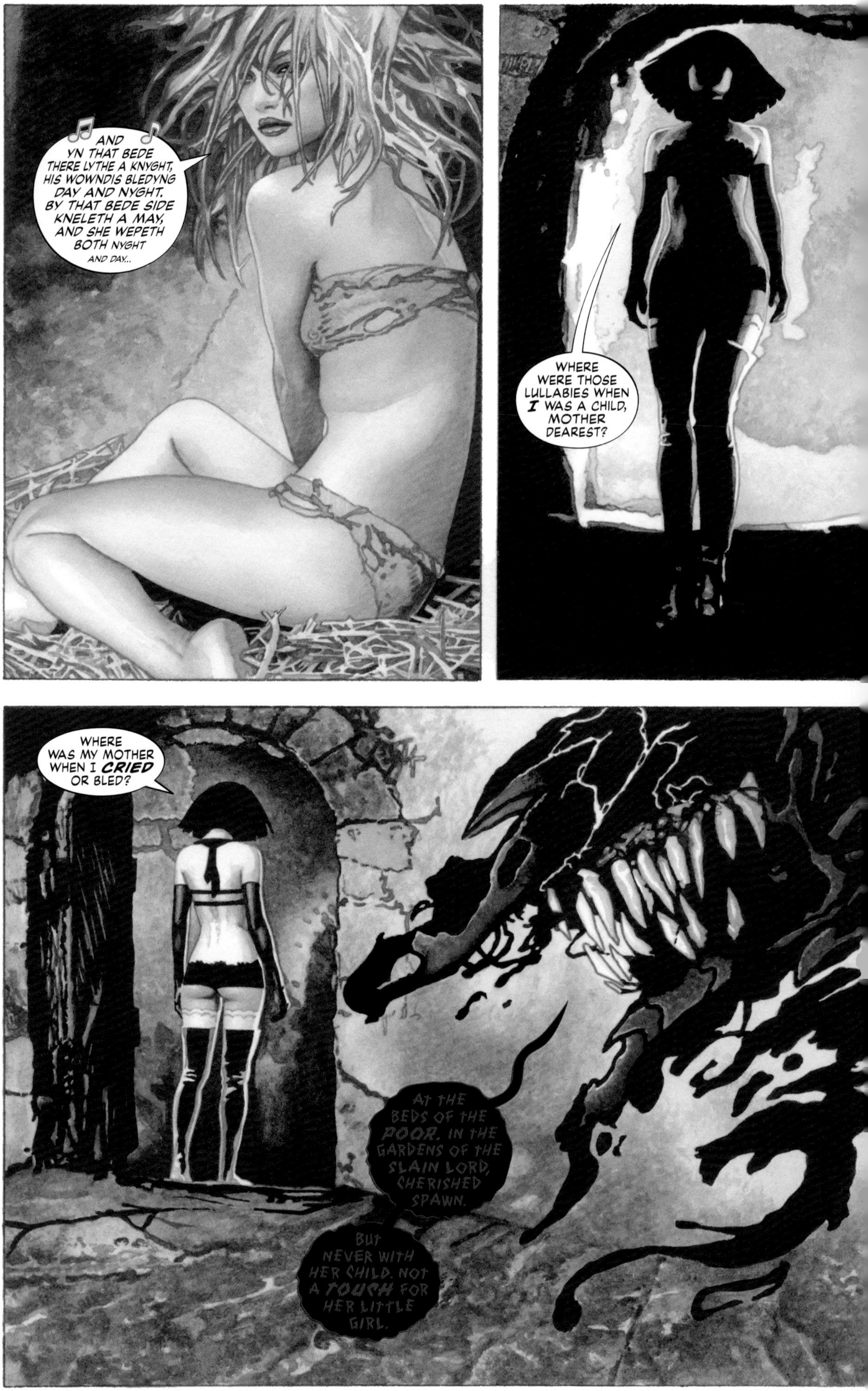
AND YN THAT BEDE THERE LYTHE A KNYGHT, HIS WOWNDIS BLEDYNG DAY AND NYGHT. BY THAT BEDE SIDE KNELETH A MAY, AND SHE WEPETH BOTH NYGHT AND DAY...
WHERE WERE THOSE LULLABIES WHEN *I* WAS A CHILD, MOTHER DEAREST?
WHERE WAS MY MOTHER WHEN I *CRIED* OR BLED?
AT THE BEDS OF THE *POOR*. IN THE GARDENS OF THE SLAIN LORD, CHERISHED SPAWN.
BUT NEVER WITH HER CHILD. NOT A *TOUCH* FOR HER LITTLE GIRL.

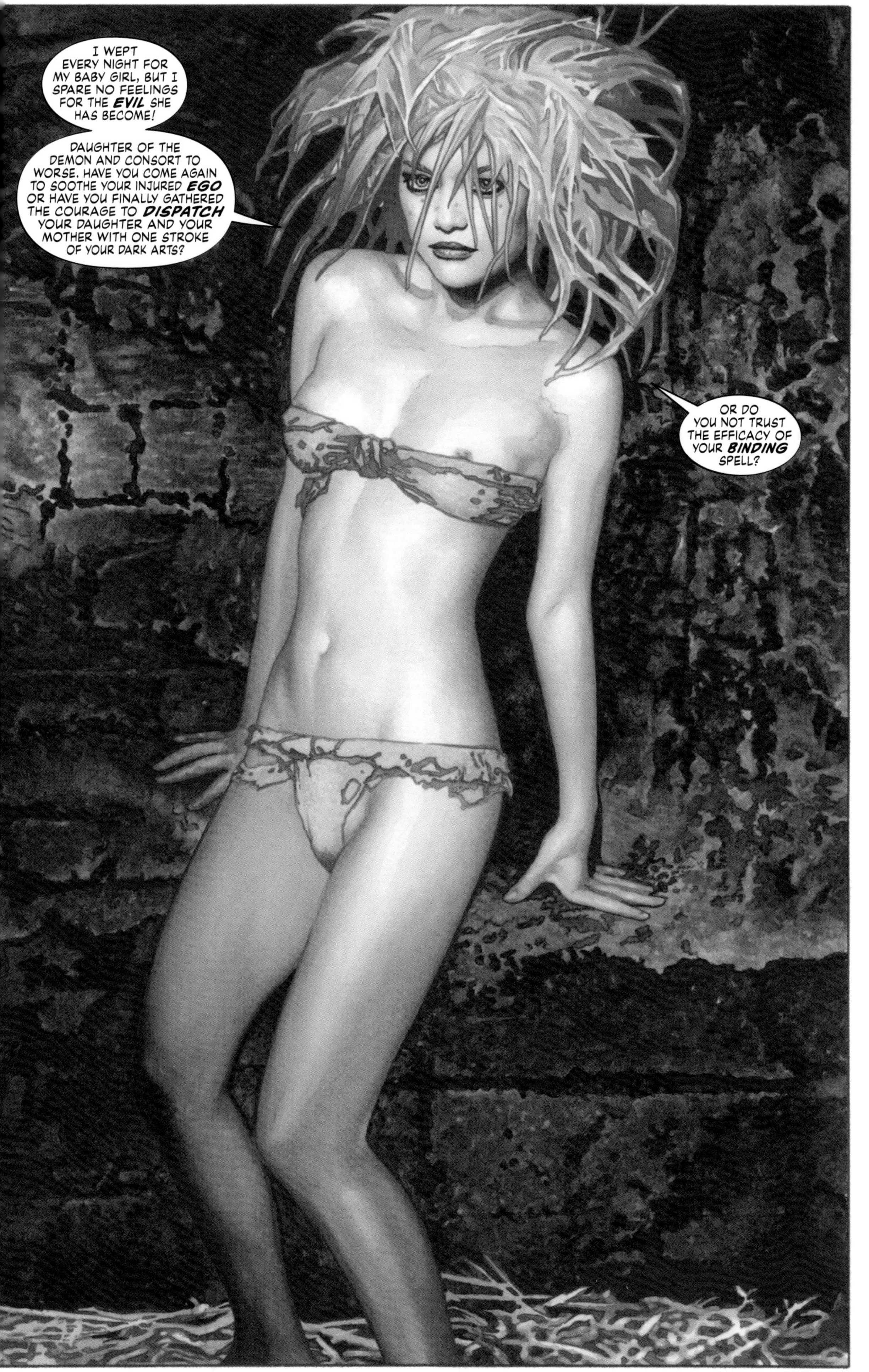
I WEPT EVERY NIGHT FOR MY BABY GIRL, BUT I SPARE NO FEELINGS FOR THE EVIL SHE HAS BECOME!
DAUGHTER OF THE DEMON AND CONSORT TO WORSE. HAVE YOU COME AGAIN TO SOOTHE YOUR INJURED EGO OR HAVE YOU FINALLY GATHERED THE COURAGE TO DISPATCH YOUR DAUGHTER AND YOUR MOTHER WITH ONE STROKE OF YOUR DARK ARTS?
OR DO YOU NOT TRUST THE EFFICACY OF YOUR BINDING SPELL?

DEAR SWEET MOTHER. WHY DO YOU THINK THAT YOU ARE EVER GETTING **OUT** OF HERE?
DO NOT THINK TO BAIT US INTO HASTY ACTIONS, MY DELECTABLE DELIGHT.
I HAVE **NO** FEAR OF MY FATE, VILE ENTITY.
BUT YOU **SHOULD**, SELF-RIGHTEOUS FOOL! YOU WILL NEVER SEE THE OUTSIDE OF THIS TOMB, AND YOUR TOMB IT SHALL **BE** UNTIL I TAKE YOUR SOUL TO FEED MY MINIONS IN HELL.

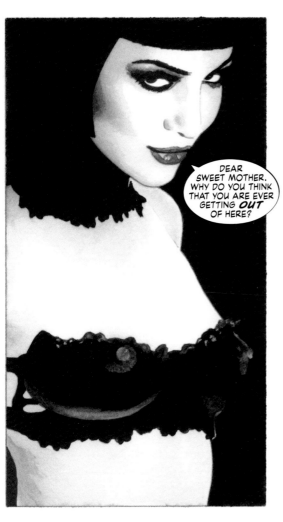

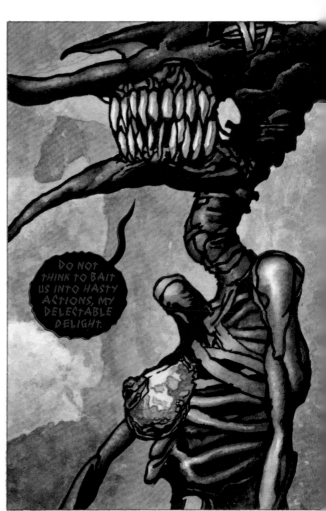

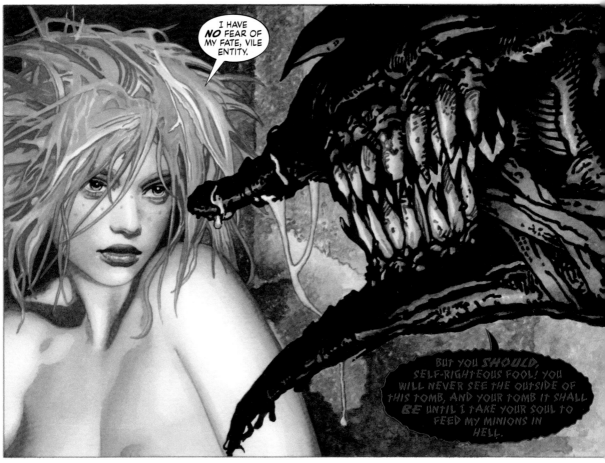

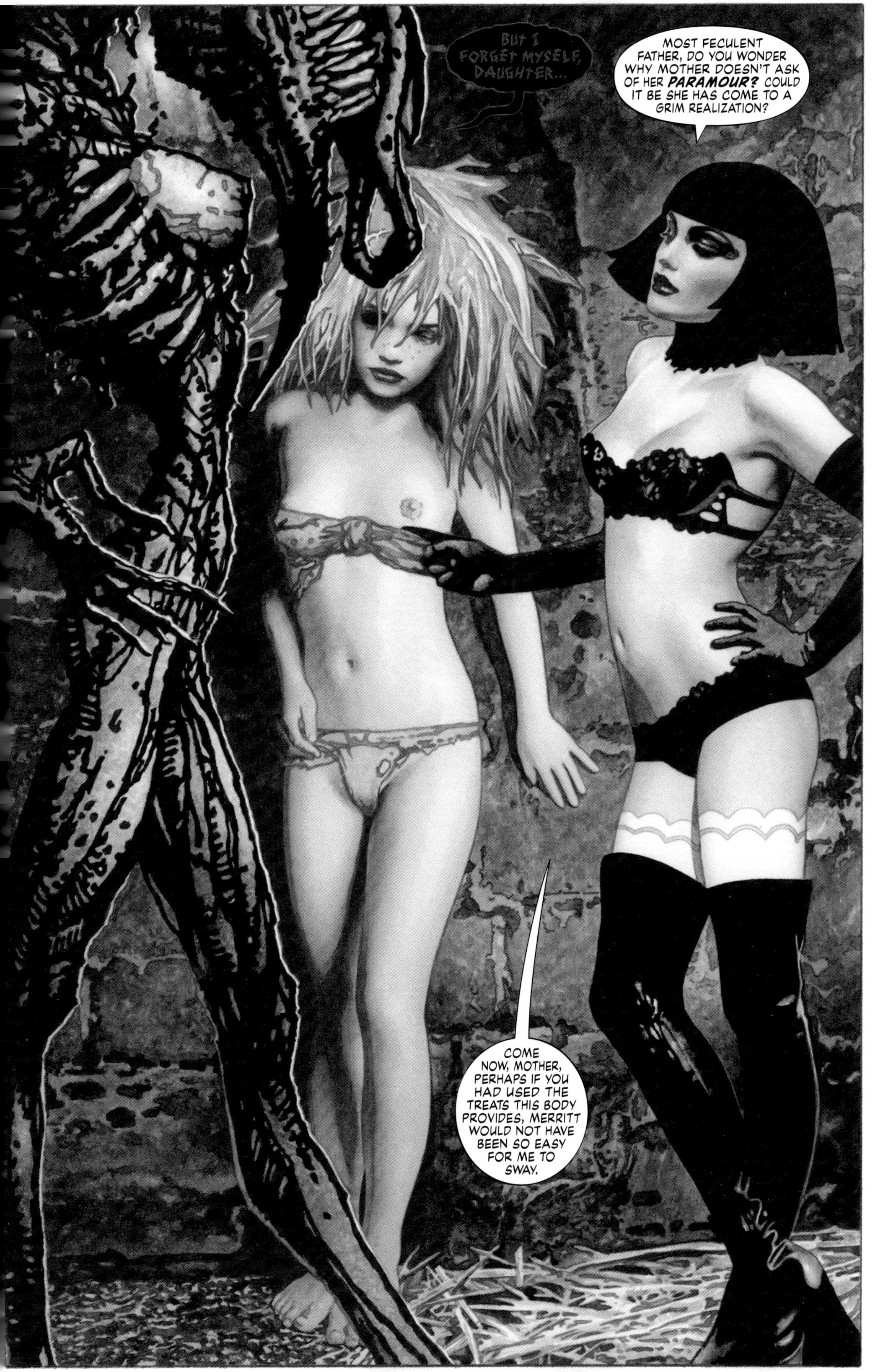
BUT I FORGET MYSELF, DAUGHTER...
MOST FECULENT FATHER, DO YOU WONDER WHY MOTHER DOESN'T ASK OF HER PARAMOUR? COULD IT BE SHE HAS COME TO A GRIM REALIZATION?
COME NOW, MOTHER, PERHAPS IF YOU HAD USED THE TREATS THIS BODY PROVIDES, MERRITT WOULD NOT HAVE BEEN SO EASY FOR ME TO SWAY.

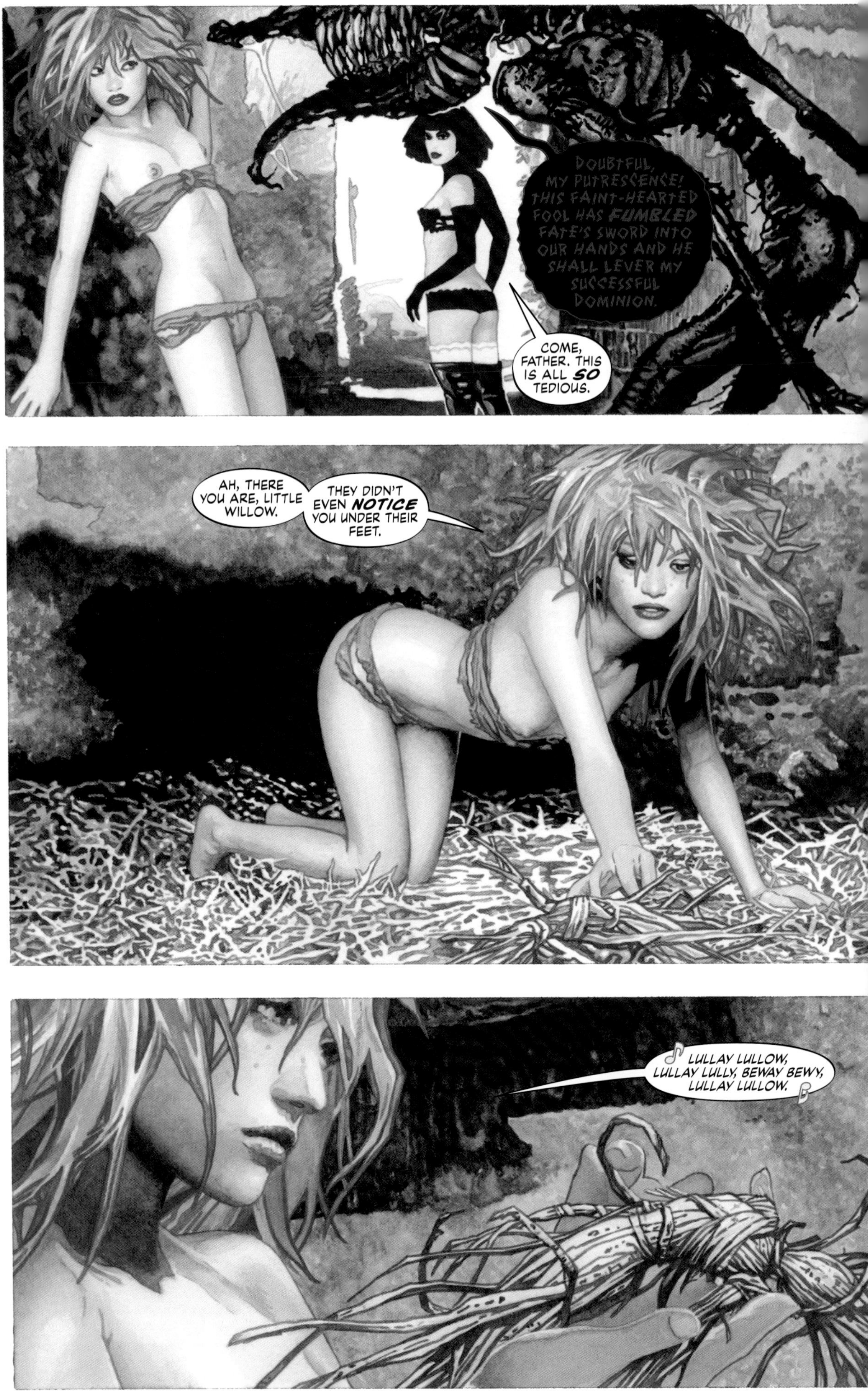
DOUBTFUL, MY PUTRESCENCE! THIS FAINT-HEARTED FOOL HAS FUMBLED FATE'S SWORD INTO OUR HANDS AND HE SHALL LEVER MY SUCCESSFUL DOMINION.
COME, FATHER. THIS IS ALL SO TEDIOUS.
AH, THERE YOU ARE, LITTLE WILLOW.
THEY DIDN'T EVEN NOTICE YOU UNDER THEIR FEET.
LULLAY LULLOW, LULLAY LULLY, BEWAY BEWY, LULLAY LULLOW.

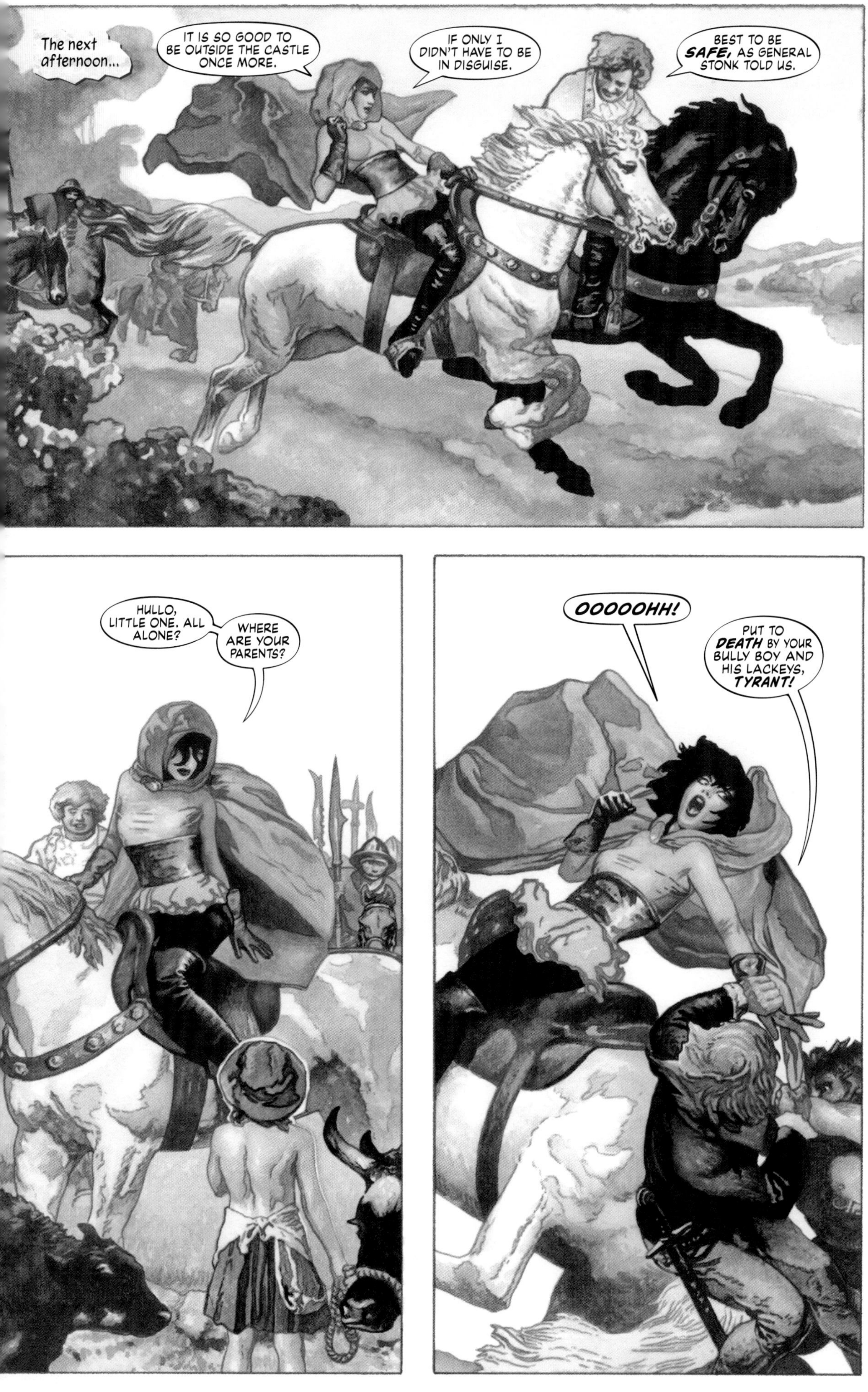

The next afternoon...
IT IS SO GOOD TO BE OUTSIDE THE CASTLE ONCE MORE.
IF ONLY I DIDN'T HAVE TO BE IN DISGUISE.
BEST TO BE SAFE, AS GENERAL STONK TOLD US.
HULLO, LITTLE ONE. ALL ALONE?
WHERE ARE YOUR PARENTS?
OOOOOHH!
PUT TO DEATH BY YOUR BULLY BOY AND HIS LACKEYS, TYRANT!

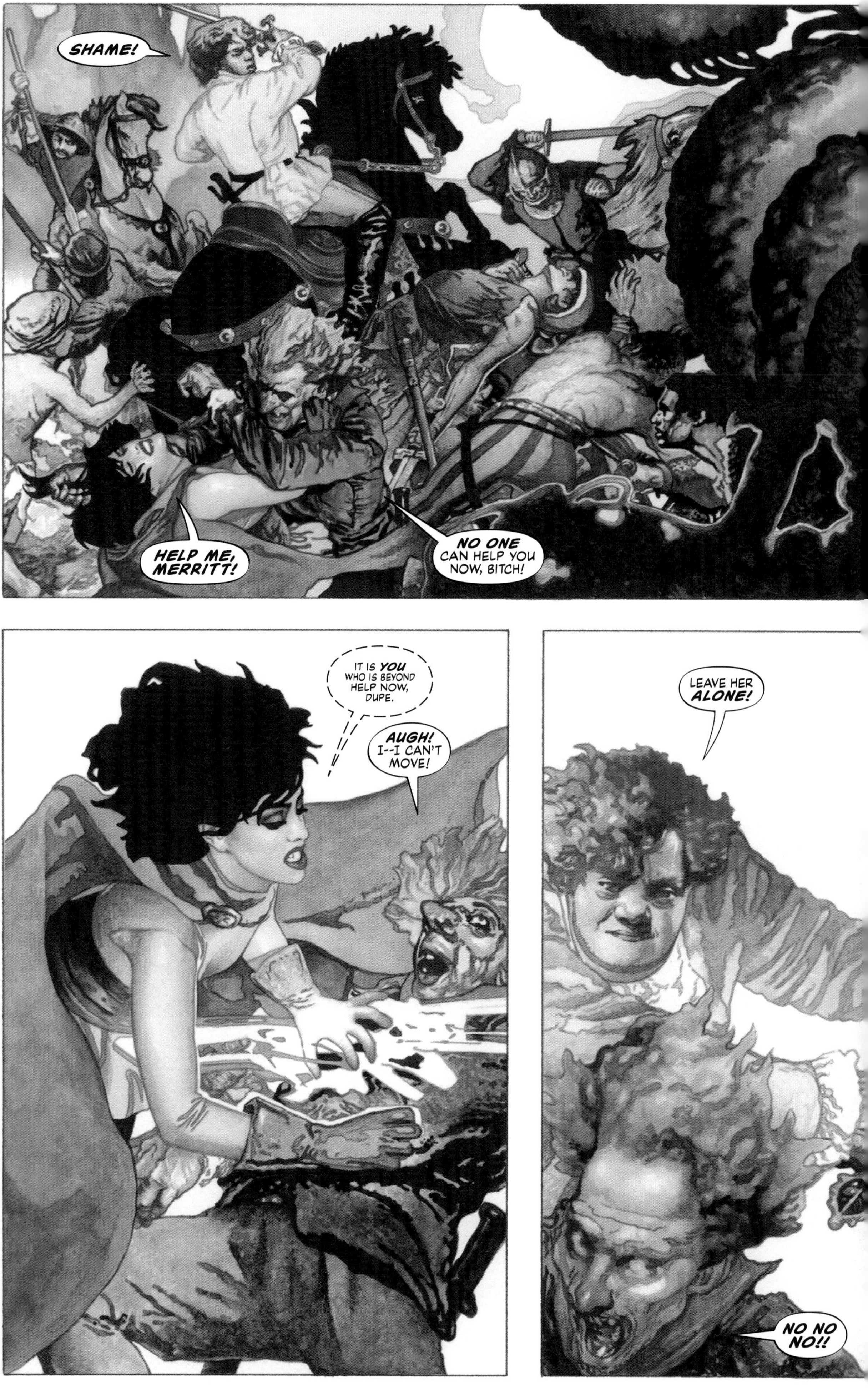
SHAME!
HELP ME, MERRITT!
NO ONE CAN HELP YOU NOW, BITCH!
IT IS YOU WHO IS BEYOND HELP NOW, DUPE.
AUGH! I--I CAN'T MOVE!
LEAVE HER ALONE!
NO NO NO!!

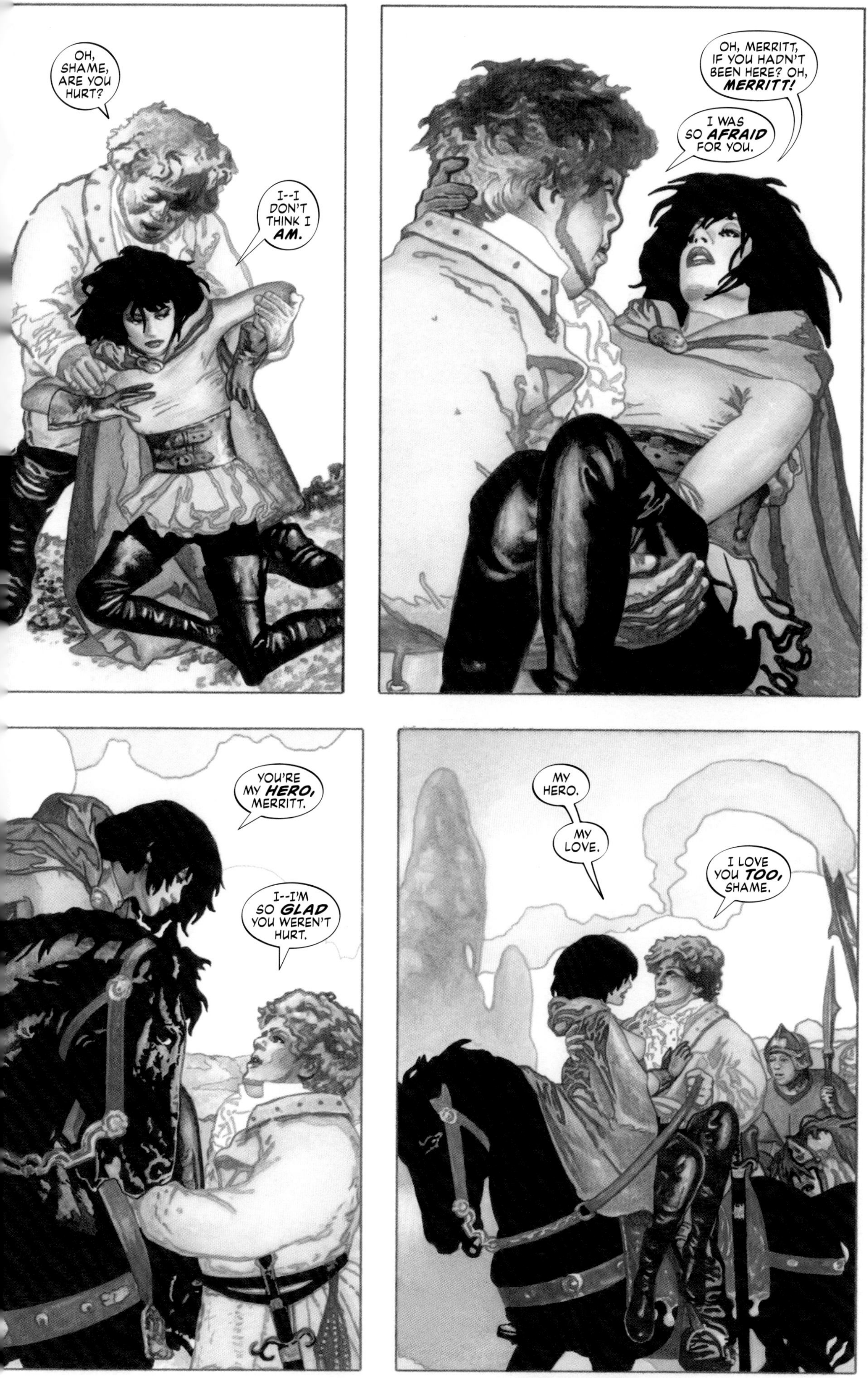
OH, SHAME, ARE YOU HURT?
I--I DON'T THINK I AM.
OH, MERRITT, IF YOU HADN'T BEEN HERE? OH, MERRITT!
I WAS SO AFRAID FOR YOU.
YOU'RE MY HERO, MERRITT.
I--I'M SO GLAD YOU WEREN'T HURT.
MY HERO.
MY LOVE.
I LOVE YOU TOO, SHAME.

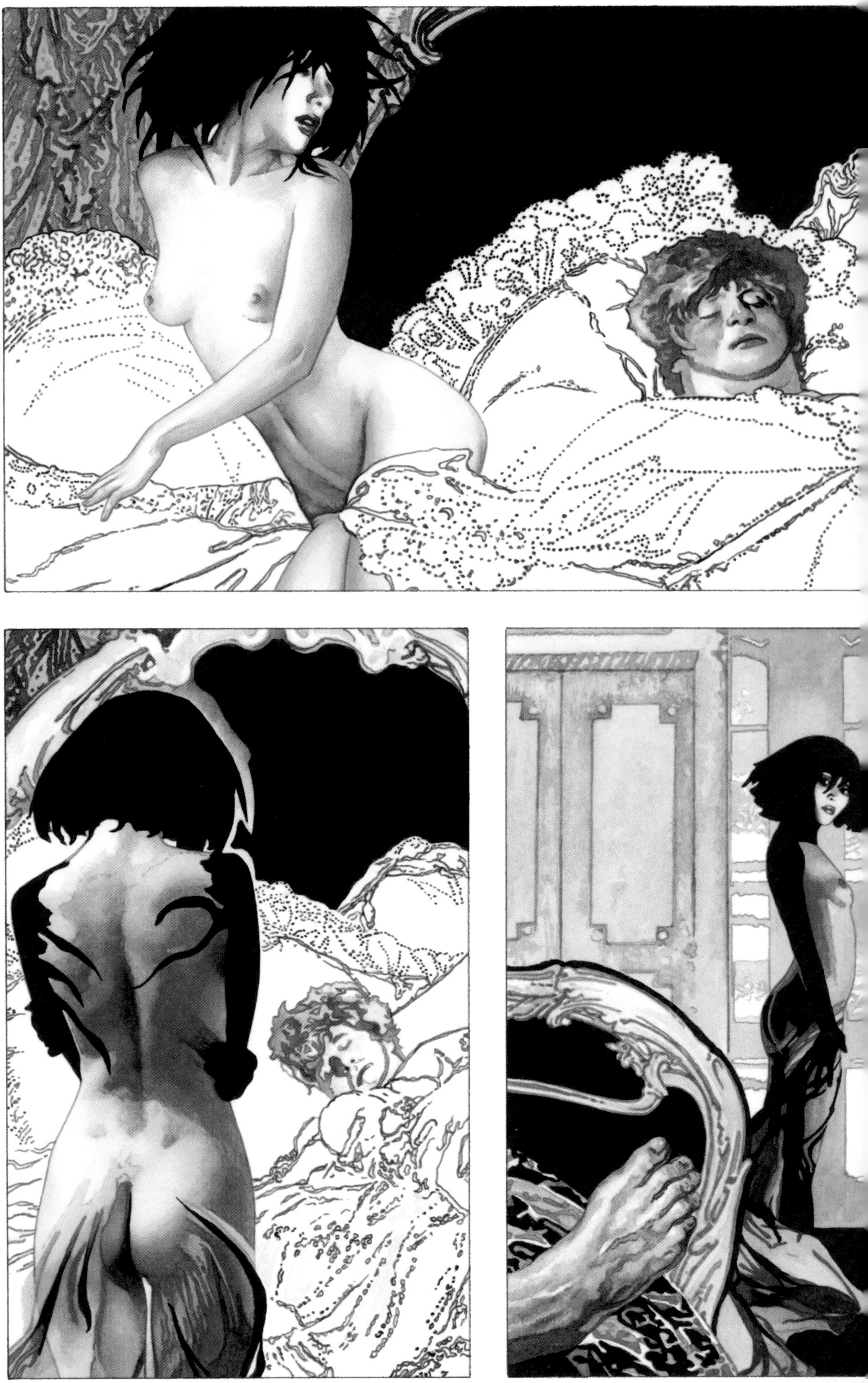

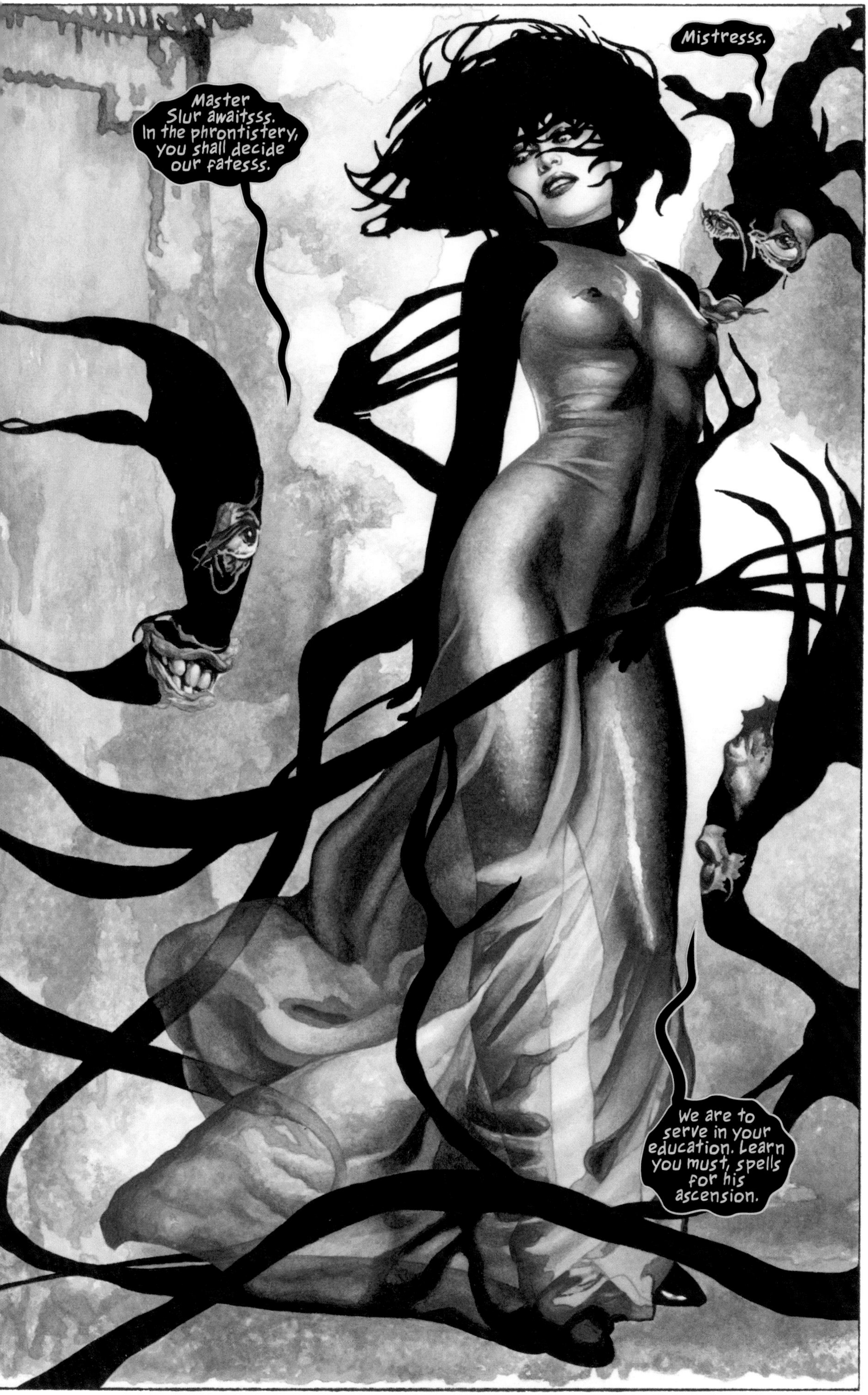
Master Slur awaitsss. In the phrontistery, you shall decide our fatesss.
Mistresss.
We are to serve in your education. Learn you must, spells for his ascension.

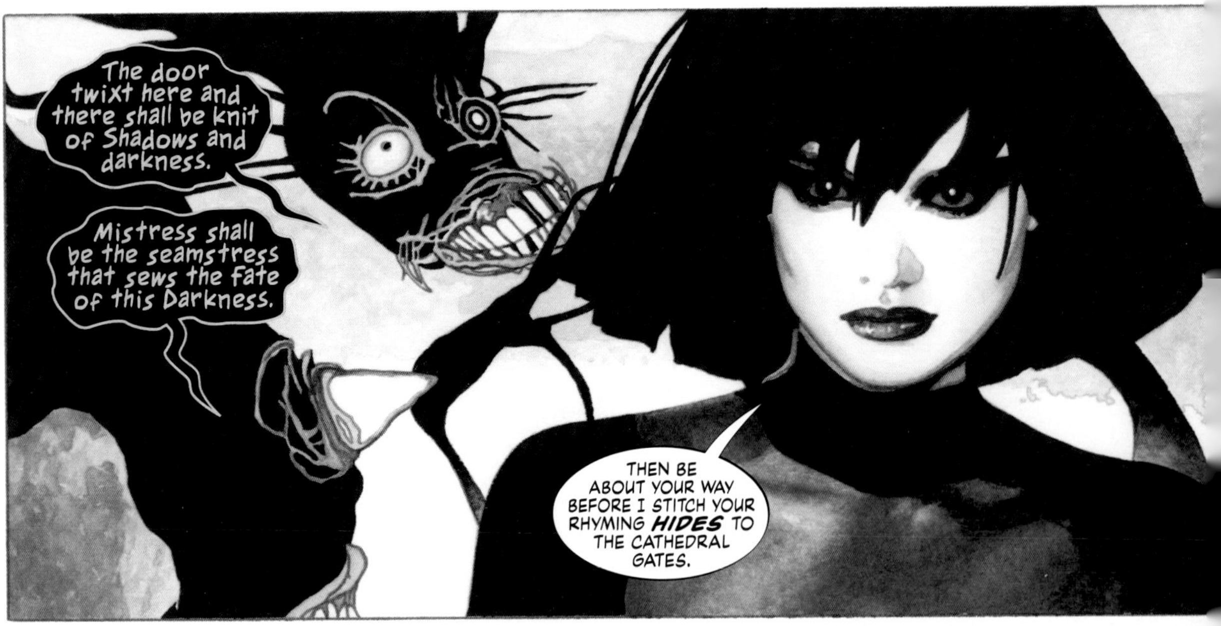
The door twixt here and there shall be knit of Shadows and darkness.
Mistress shall be the seamstress that sews the fate of this Darkness.
THEN BE ABOUT YOUR WAY BEFORE I STITCH YOUR RHYMING HIDES TO THE CATHEDRAL GATES.

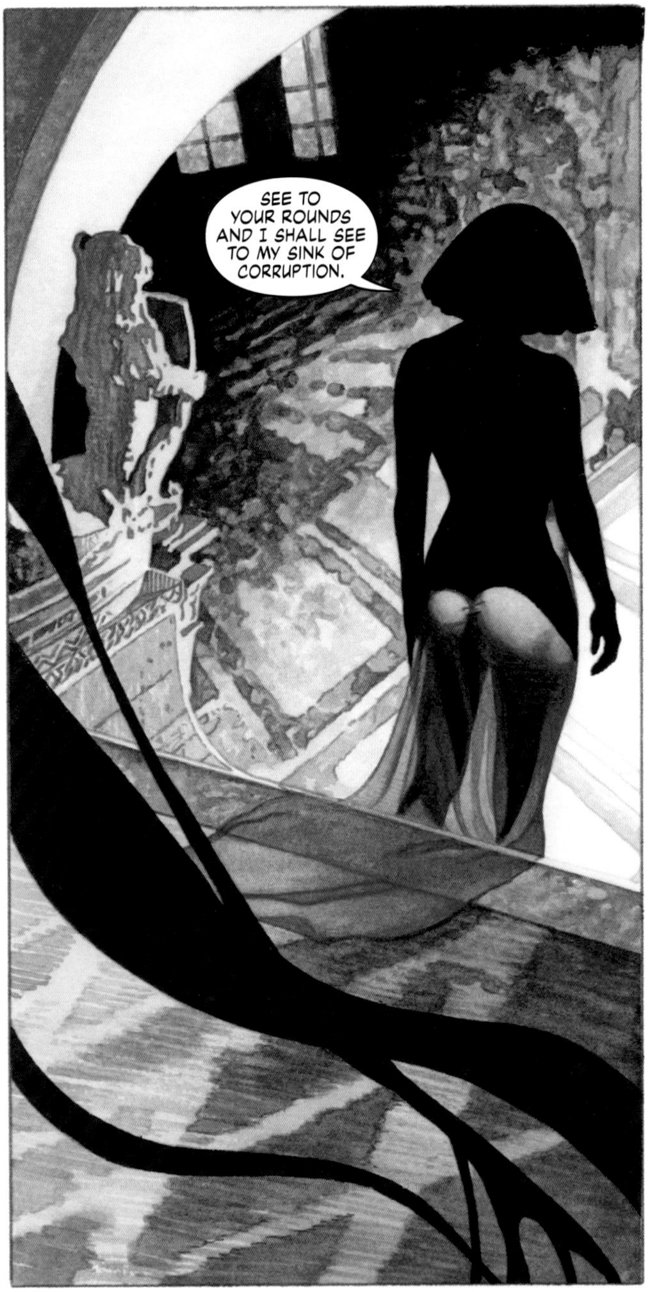
SEE TO YOUR ROUNDS AND I SHALL SEE TO MY SINK OF CORRUPTION.

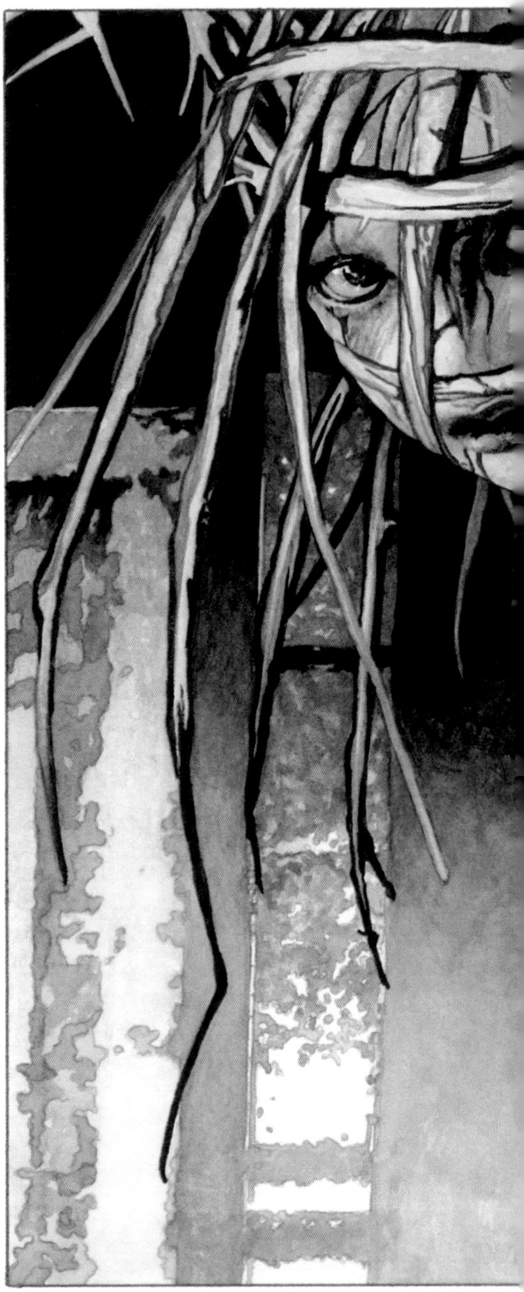

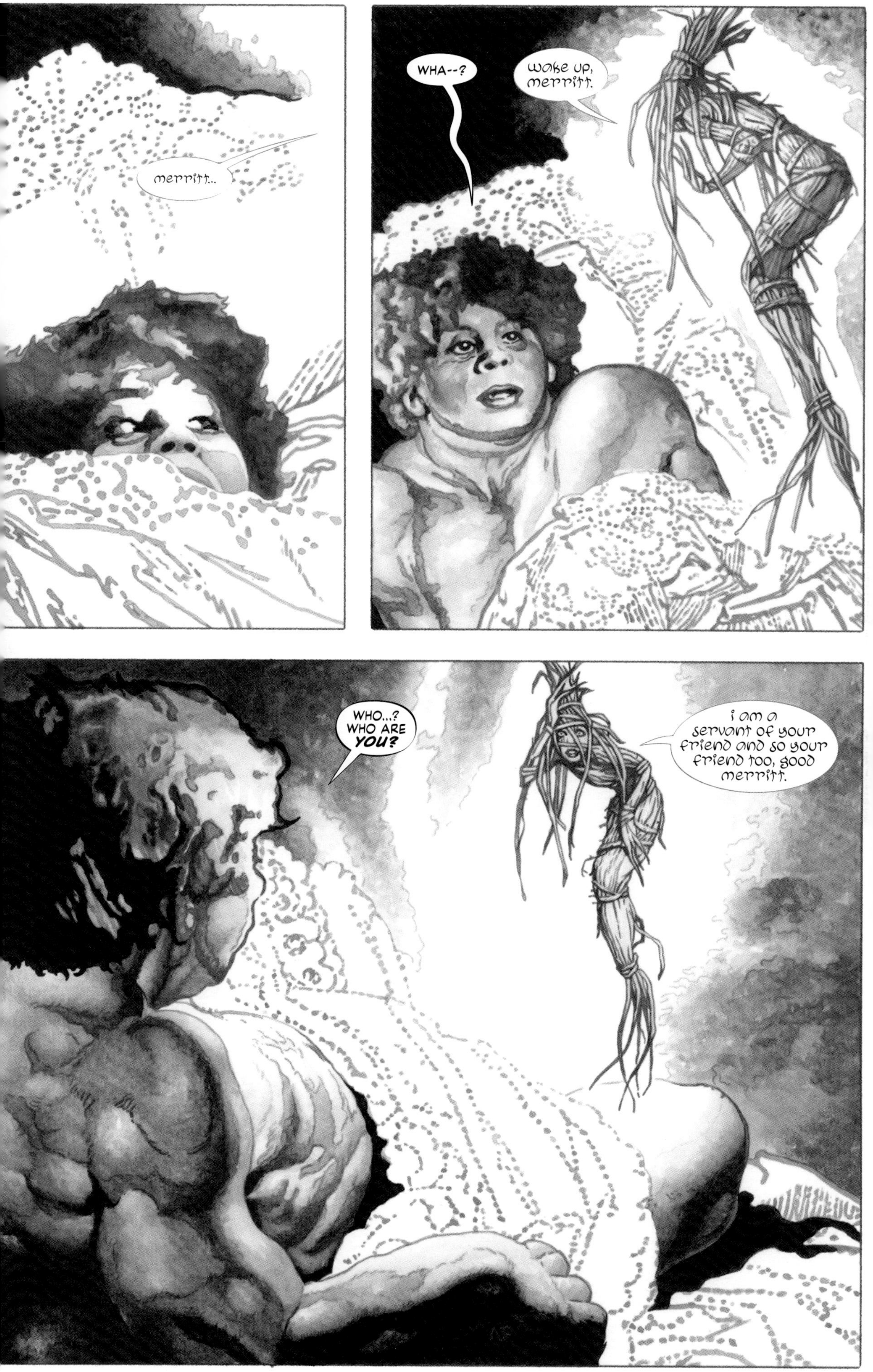
merritt..
WHA--?
wake up, merritt.
WHO...? WHO ARE YOU?
i am a servant of your friend and so your friend too, good merritt.

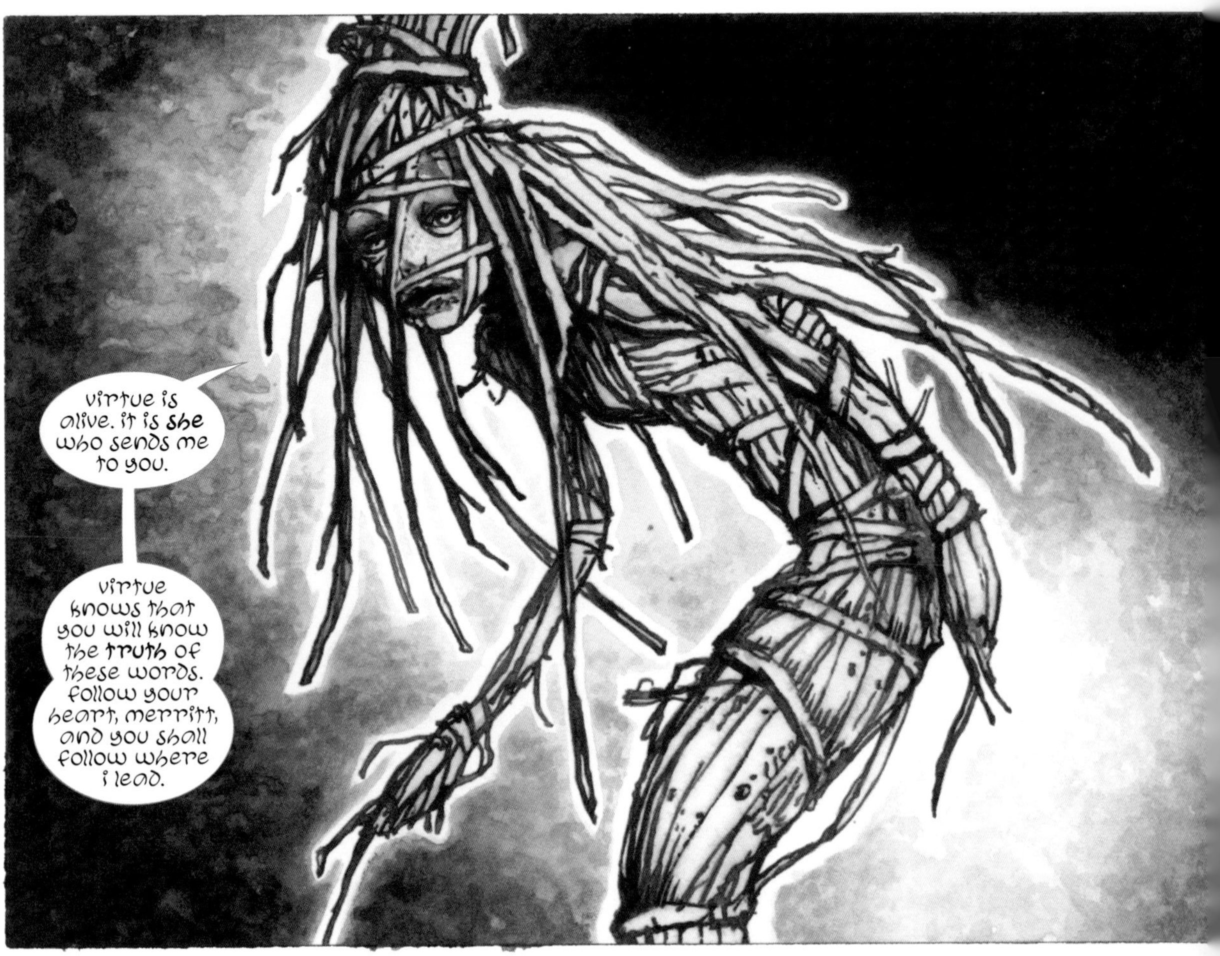
virtue is alive. it is she who sends me to you.
virtue knows that you will know the truth of these words. follow your heart, merritt, and you shall follow where i lead.

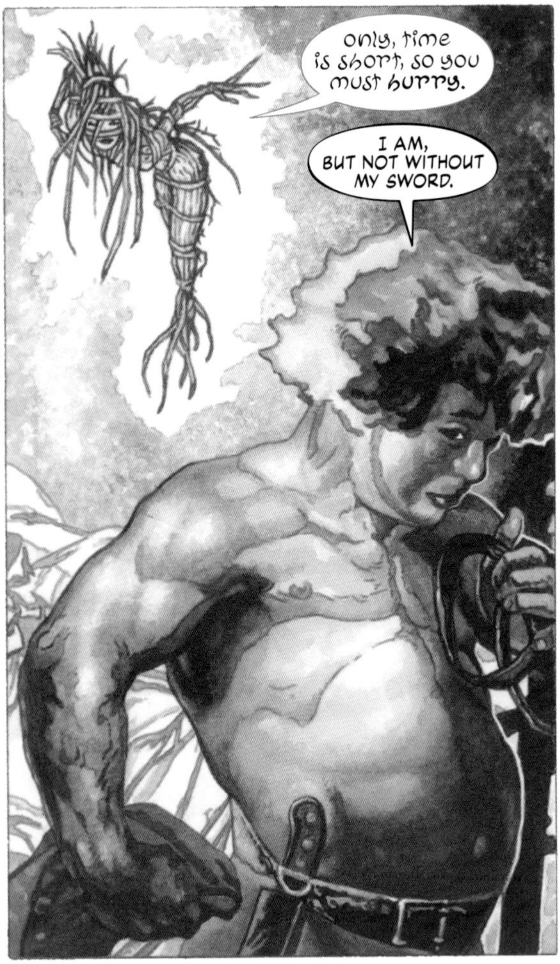
only, time is short, so you must hurry.
I AM, BUT NOT WITHOUT MY SWORD.

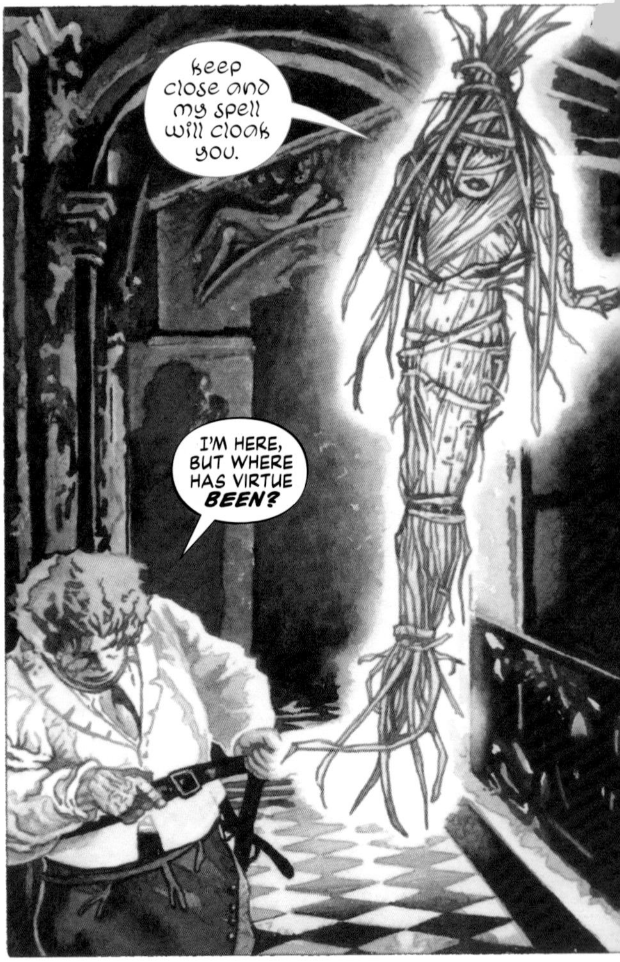
keep close and my spell will cloak you.
I'M HERE, BUT WHERE HAS VIRTUE BEEN?

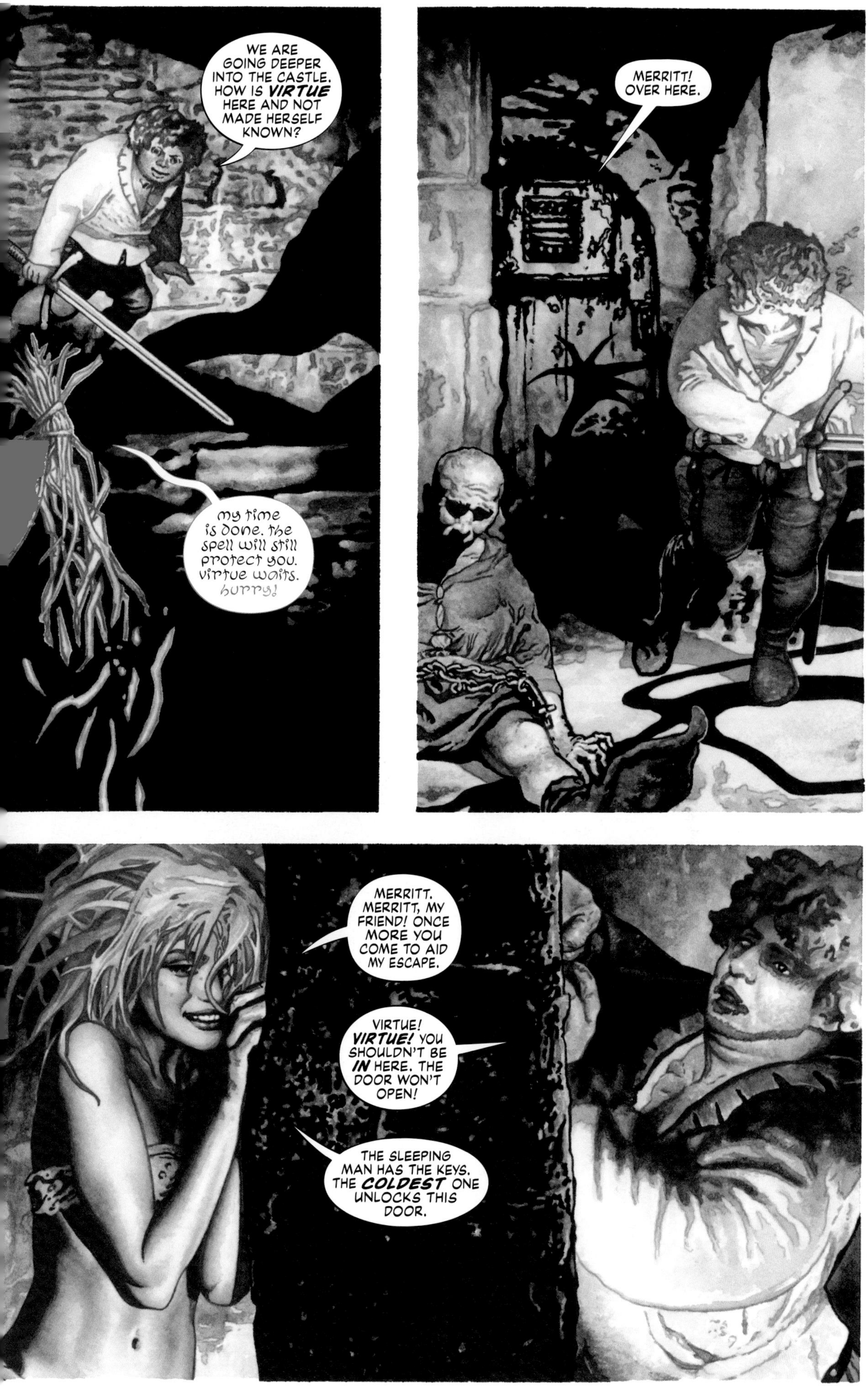
WE ARE GOING DEEPER INTO THE CASTLE. HOW IS VIRTUE HERE AND NOT MADE HERSELF KNOWN?
my time is done. the spell will still protect you. virtue waits. hurry!
MERRITT! OVER HERE.
MERRITT. MERRITT, MY FRIEND! ONCE MORE YOU COME TO AID MY ESCAPE.
VIRTUE! VIRTUE! YOU SHOULDN'T BE IN HERE. THE DOOR WON'T OPEN!
THE SLEEPING MAN HAS THE KEYS. THE COLDEST ONE UNLOCKS THIS DOOR.

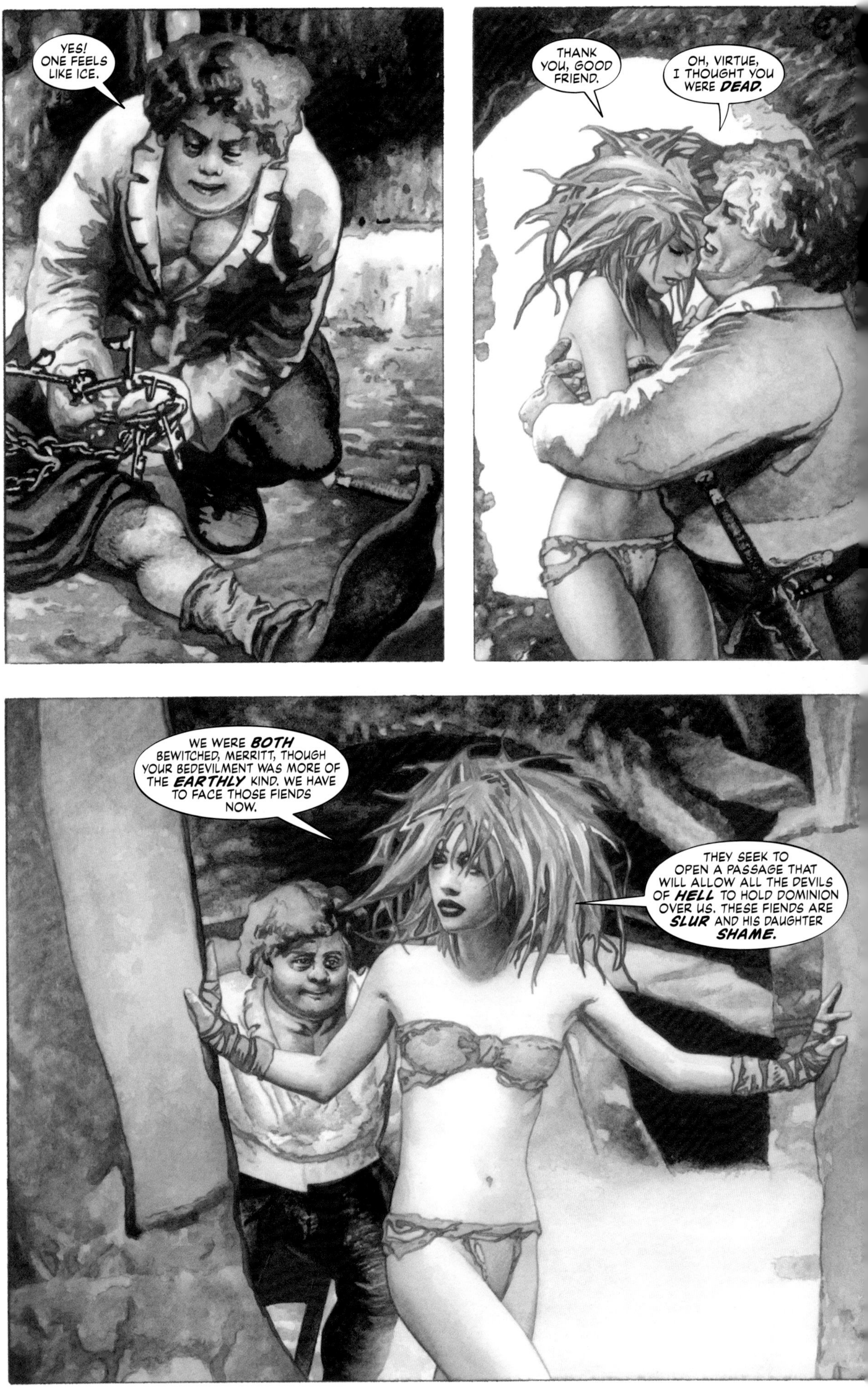
YES! ONE FEELS LIKE ICE.
THANK YOU, GOOD FRIEND.
OH, VIRTUE, I THOUGHT YOU WERE **DEAD.**
WE WERE **BOTH** BEWITCHED, MERRITT, THOUGH YOUR BEDEVILMENT WAS MORE OF THE **EARTHLY** KIND. WE HAVE TO FACE THOSE FIENDS NOW.
THEY SEEK TO OPEN A PASSAGE THAT WILL ALLOW ALL THE DEVILS OF **HELL** TO HOLD DOMINION OVER US. THESE FIENDS ARE **SLUR** AND HIS DAUGHTER **SHAME.**

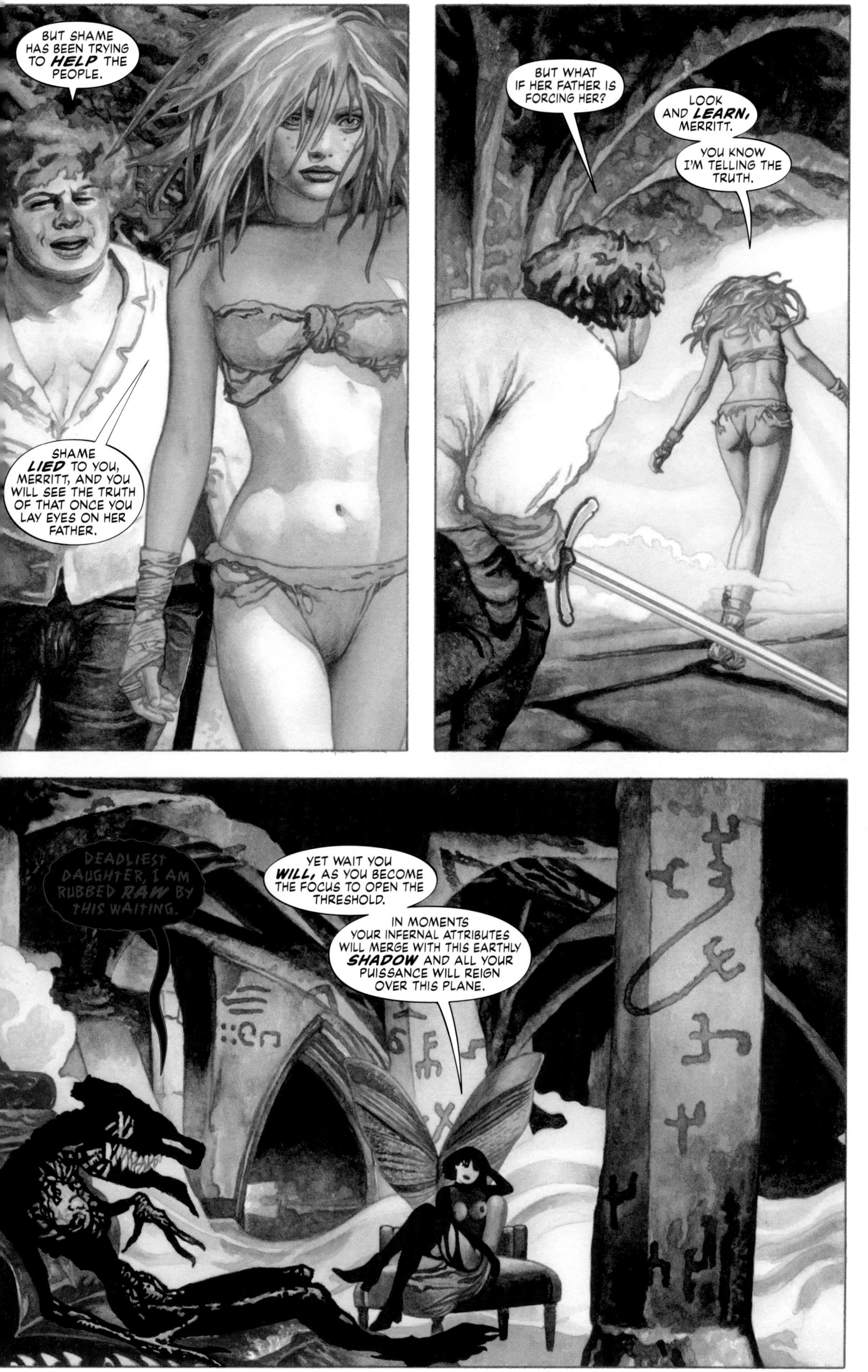

BUT SHAME HAS BEEN TRYING TO HELP THE PEOPLE.
SHAME LIED TO YOU, MERRITT, AND YOU WILL SEE THE TRUTH OF THAT ONCE YOU LAY EYES ON HER FATHER.
BUT WHAT IF HER FATHER IS FORCING HER?
LOOK AND LEARN, MERRITT.
YOU KNOW I'M TELLING THE TRUTH.
DEADLIEST DAUGHTER, I AM RUBBED RAW BY THIS WAITING.
YET WAIT YOU WILL, AS YOU BECOME THE FOCUS TO OPEN THE THRESHOLD.
IN MOMENTS YOUR INFERNAL ATTRIBUTES WILL MERGE WITH THIS EARTHLY SHADOW AND ALL YOUR PUISSANCE WILL REIGN OVER THIS PLANE.

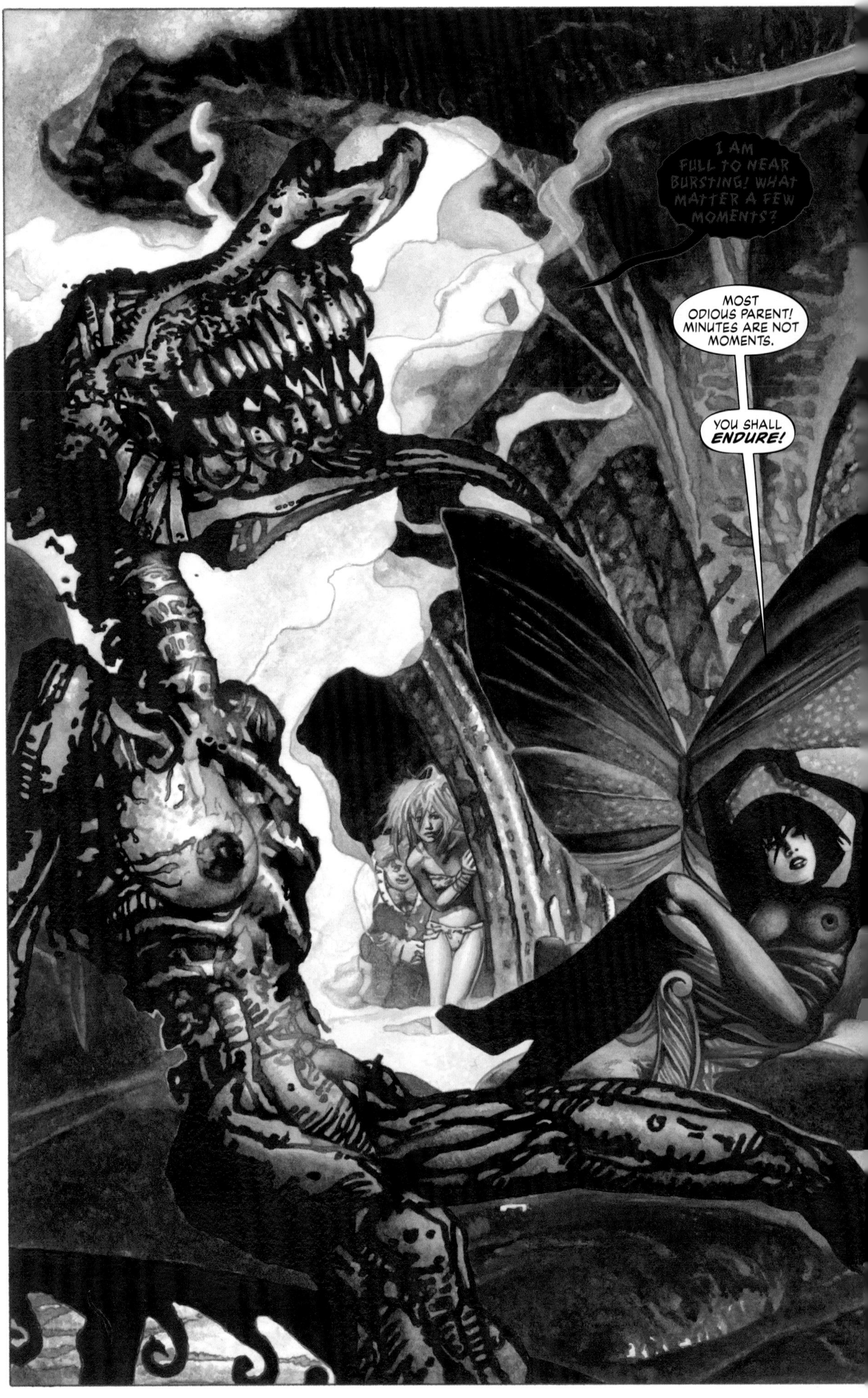
I AM FULL TO NEAR BURSTING! WHAT MATTER A FEW MOMENTS?
MOST ODIOUS PARENT! MINUTES ARE NOT MOMENTS.
YOU SHALL *ENDURE!*

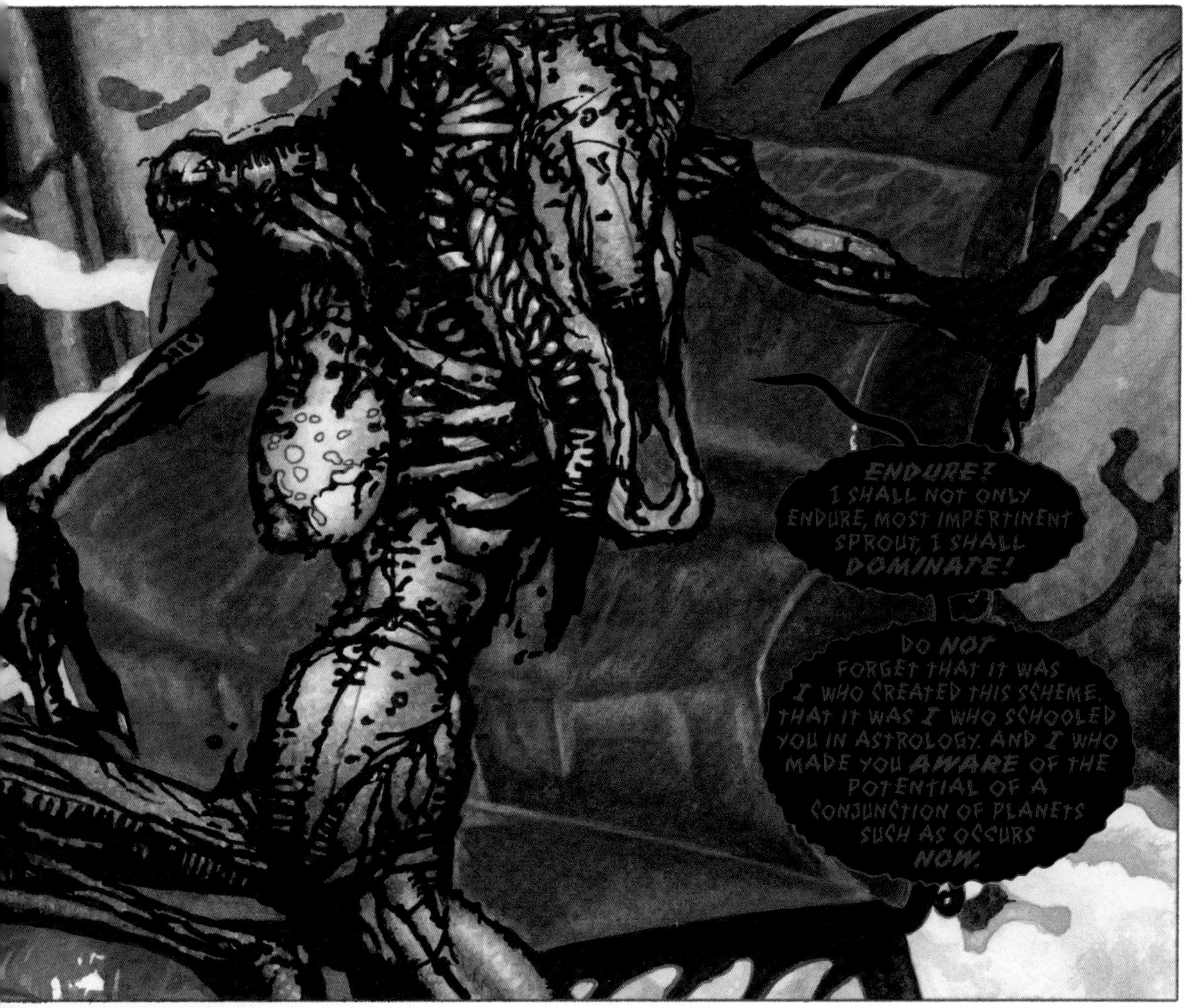
ENDURE? I SHALL NOT ONLY ENDURE, MOST IMPERTINENT SPROUT, I SHALL DOMINATE!
DO NOT FORGET THAT IT WAS I WHO CREATED THIS SCHEME. THAT IT WAS I WHO SCHOOLED YOU IN ASTROLOGY. AND I WHO MADE YOU AWARE OF THE POTENTIAL OF A CONJUNCTION OF PLANETS SUCH AS OCCURS NOW.

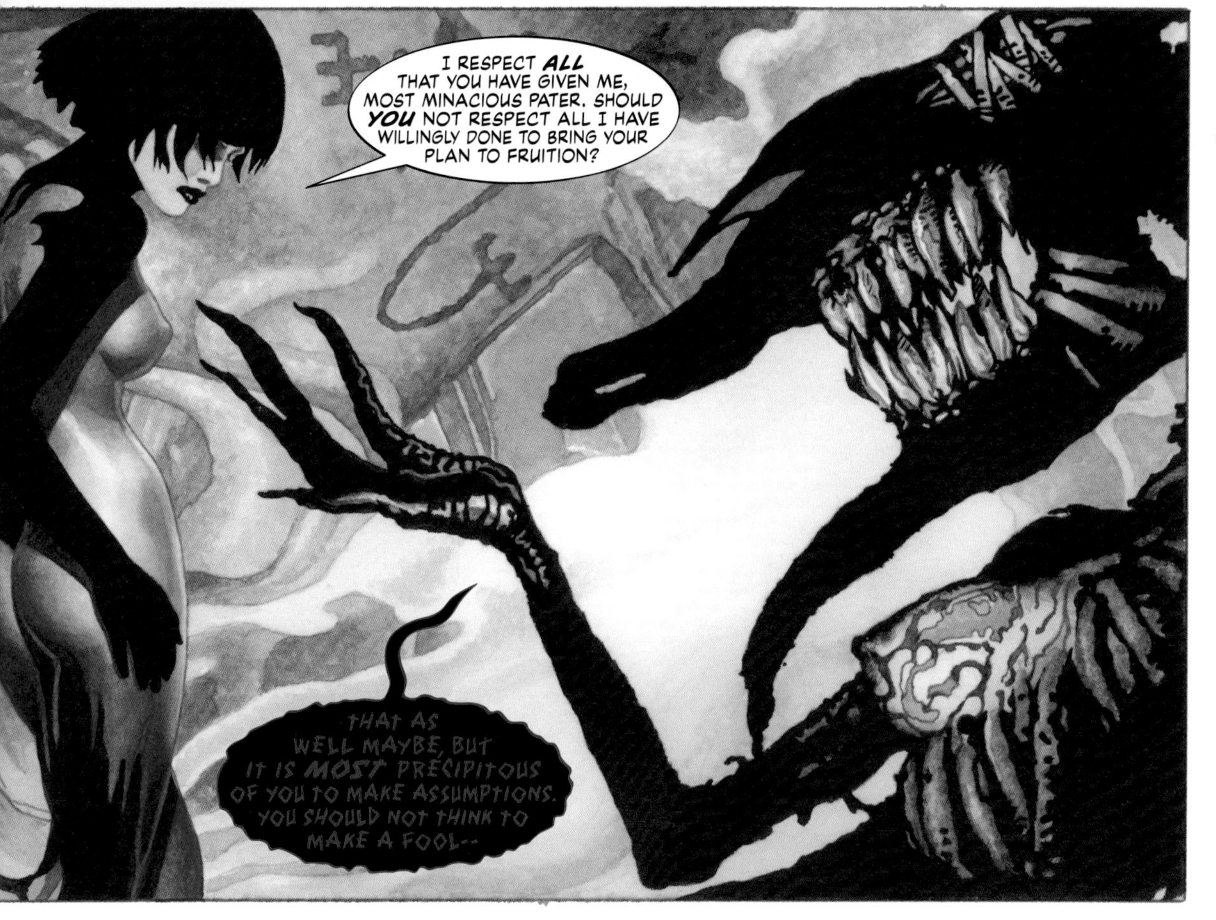
I RESPECT ALL THAT YOU HAVE GIVEN ME, MOST MINACIOUS PATER. SHOULD YOU NOT RESPECT ALL I HAVE WILLINGLY DONE TO BRING YOUR PLAN TO FRUITION?
THAT AS WELL MAYBE, BUT IT IS MOST PRECIPITOUS OF YOU TO MAKE ASSUMPTIONS. YOU SHOULD NOT THINK TO MAKE A FOOL--

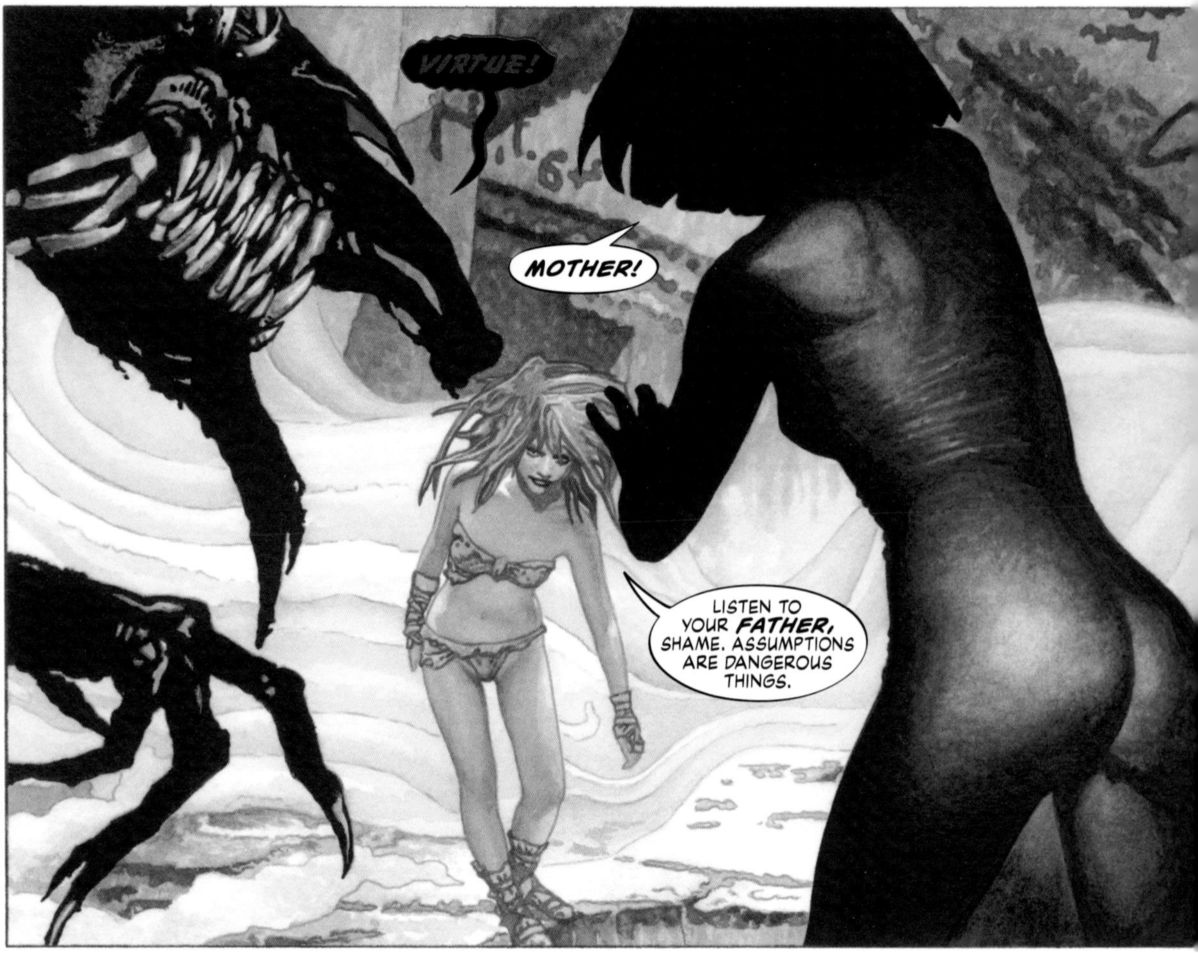
VIRTUE!
MOTHER!
LISTEN TO YOUR FATHER, SHAME. ASSUMPTIONS ARE DANGEROUS THINGS.

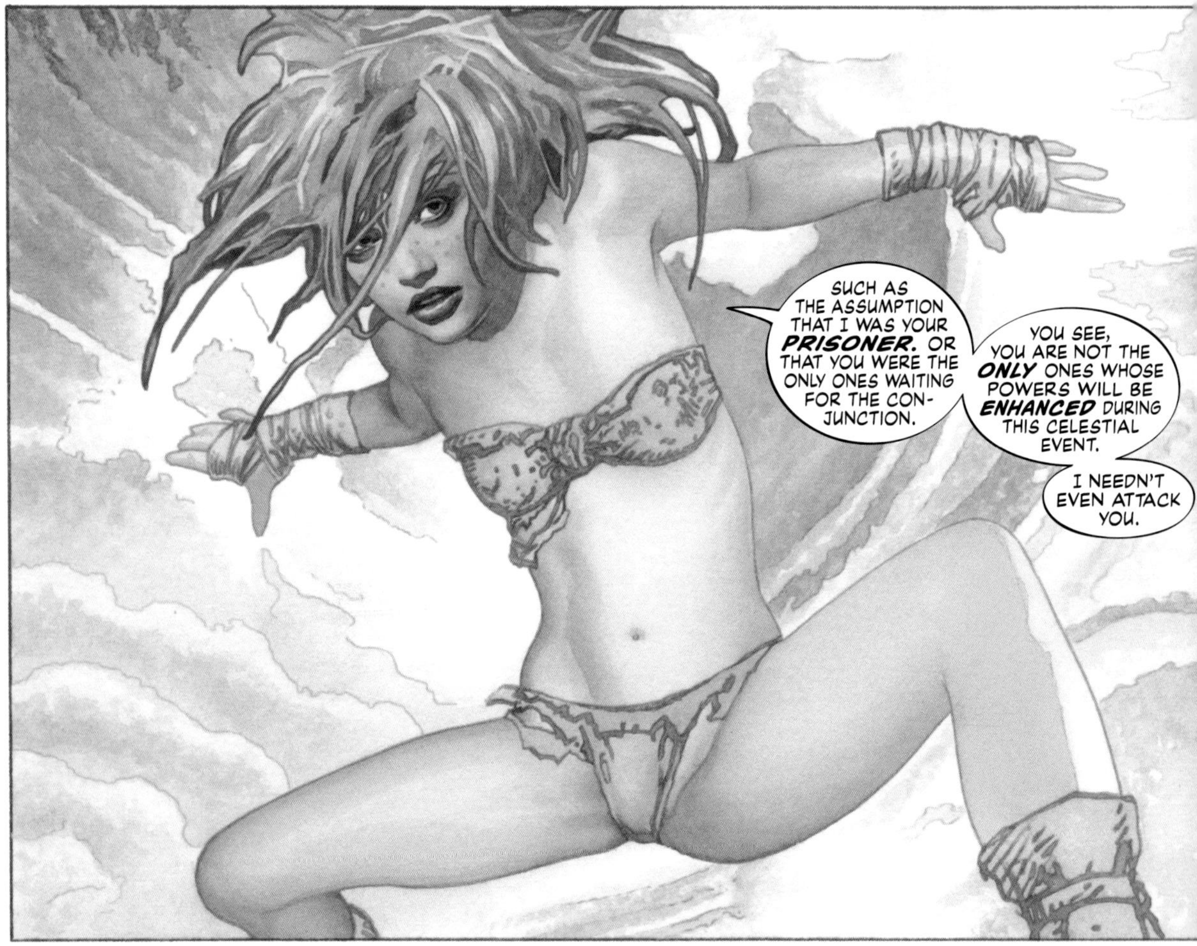
SUCH AS THE ASSUMPTION THAT I WAS YOUR PRISONER. OR THAT YOU WERE THE ONLY ONES WAITING FOR THE CON-JUNCTION.
YOU SEE, YOU ARE NOT THE ONLY ONES WHOSE POWERS WILL BE ENHANCED DURING THIS CELESTIAL EVENT.
I NEEDN'T EVEN ATTACK YOU.

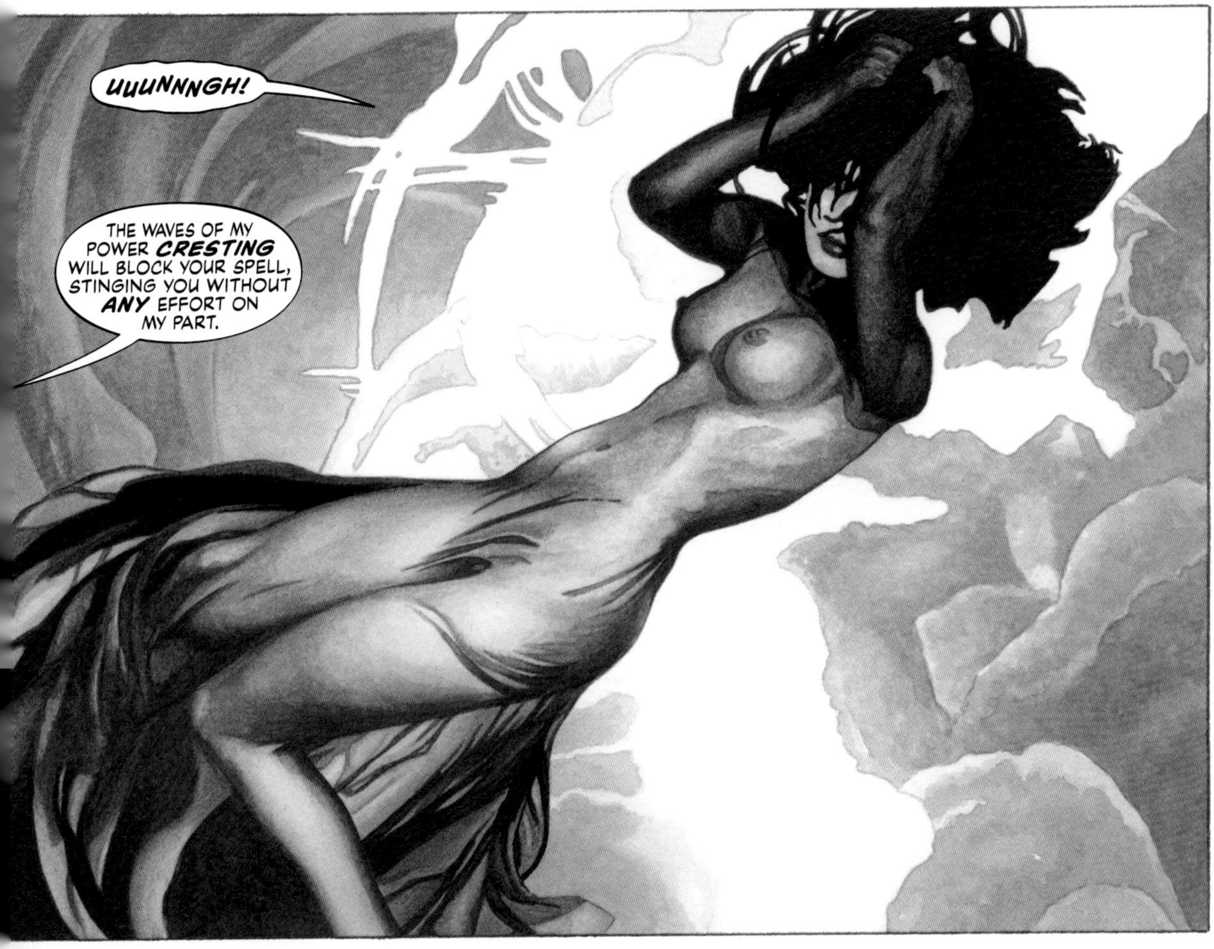
UUUNNNGH!
THE WAVES OF MY POWER CRESTING WILL BLOCK YOUR SPELL, STINGING YOU WITHOUT ANY EFFORT ON MY PART.

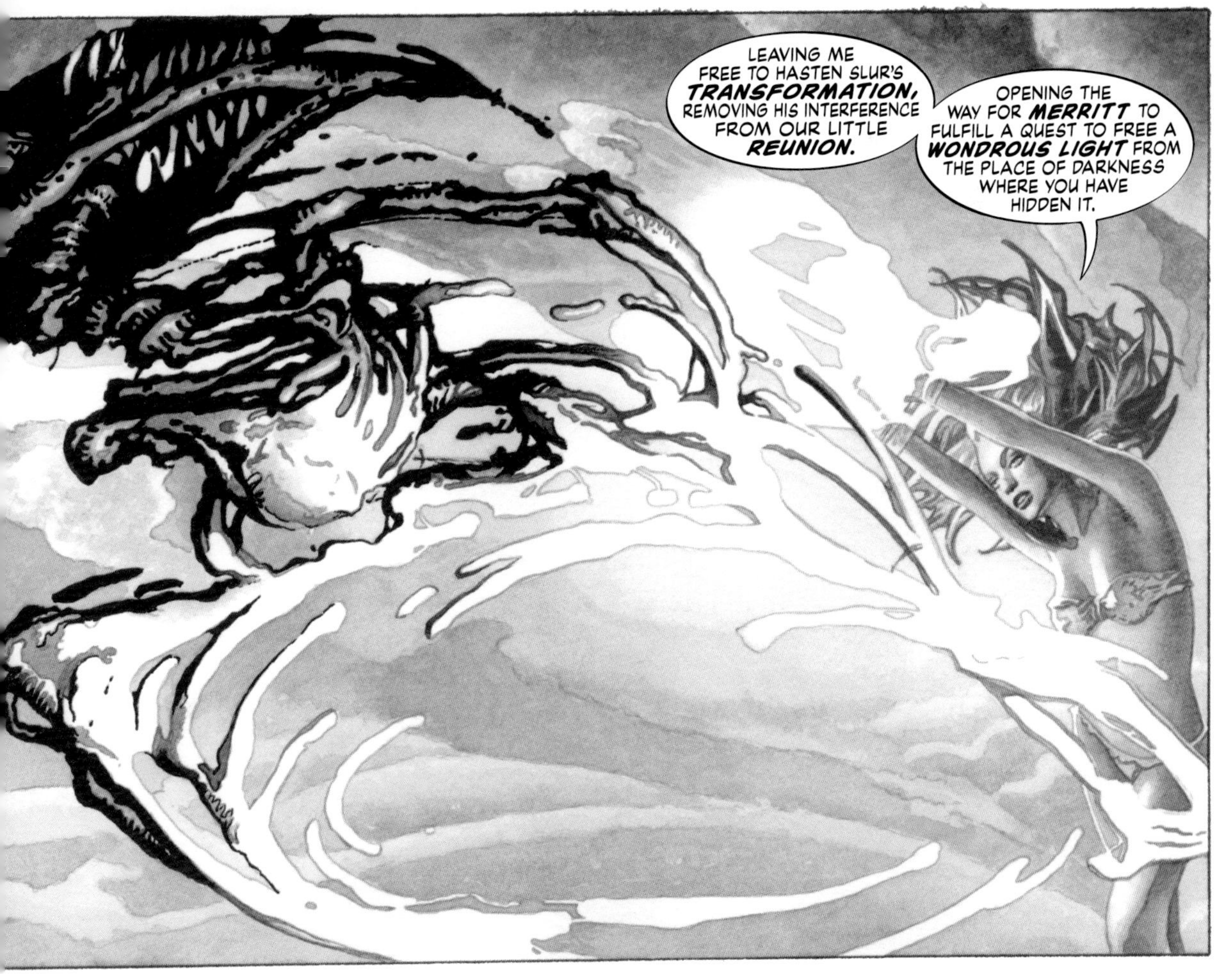
LEAVING ME FREE TO HASTEN SLUR'S TRANSFORMATION, REMOVING HIS INTERFERENCE FROM OUR LITTLE REUNION.
OPENING THE WAY FOR MERRITT TO FULFILL A QUEST TO FREE A WONDROUS LIGHT FROM THE PLACE OF DARKNESS WHERE YOU HAVE HIDDEN IT.

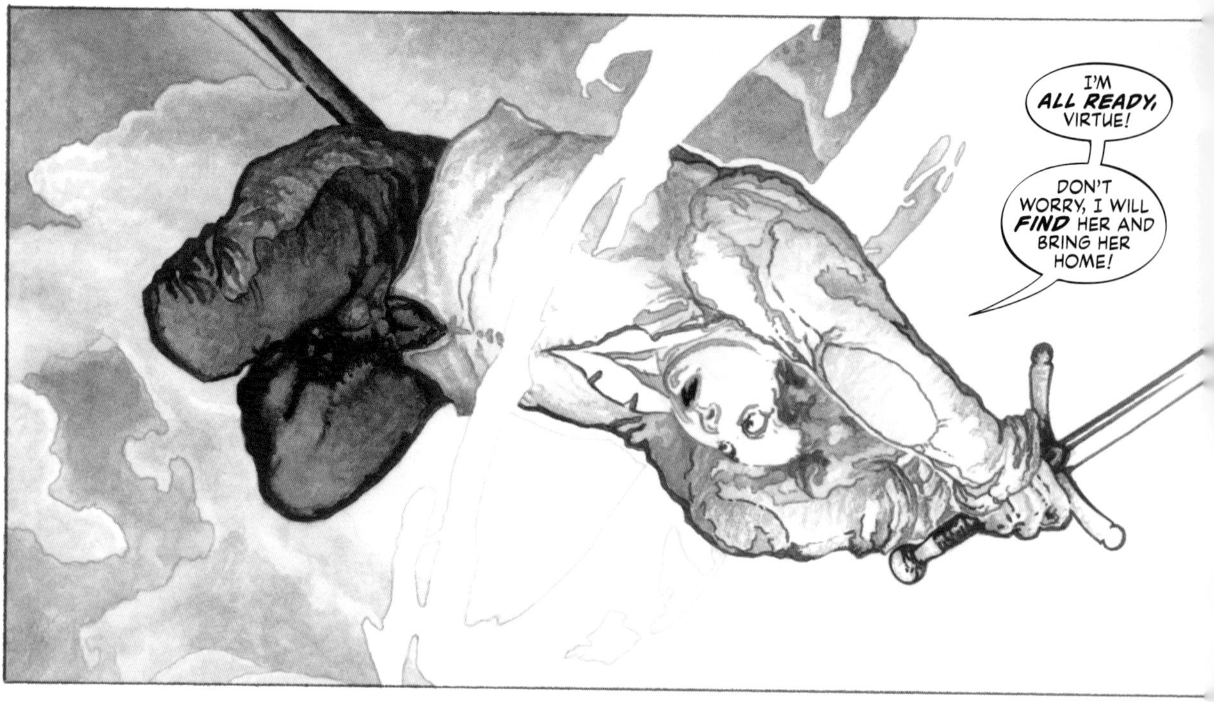
I'M **ALL READY,** VIRTUE!
DON'T WORRY, I WILL **FIND** HER AND BRING HER HOME!

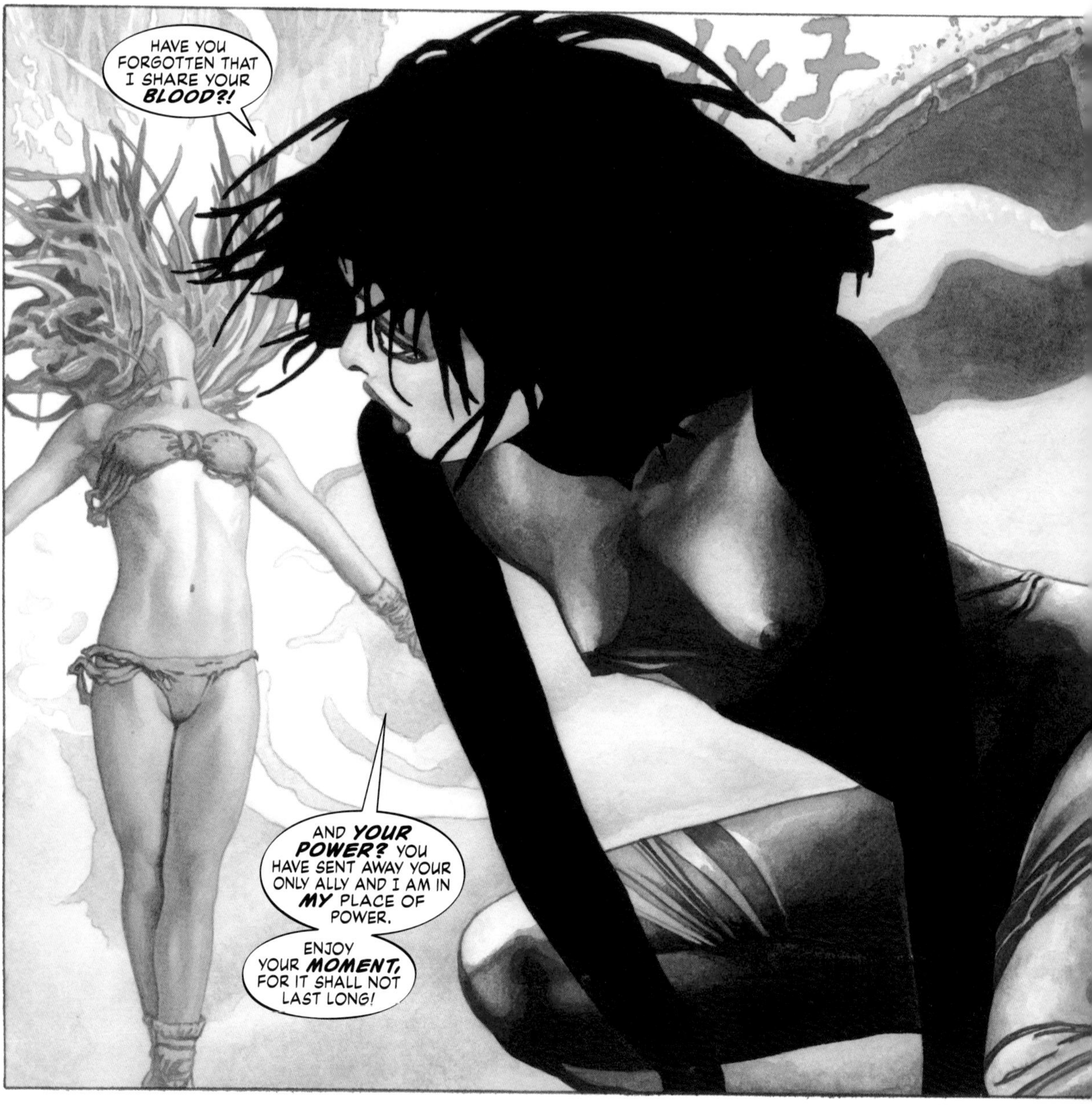
HAVE YOU FORGOTTEN THAT I SHARE YOUR **BLOOD?!**
AND **YOUR POWER?** YOU HAVE SENT AWAY YOUR ONLY ALLY AND I AM IN **MY** PLACE OF POWER.
ENJOY YOUR **MOMENT,** FOR IT SHALL NOT LAST LONG!

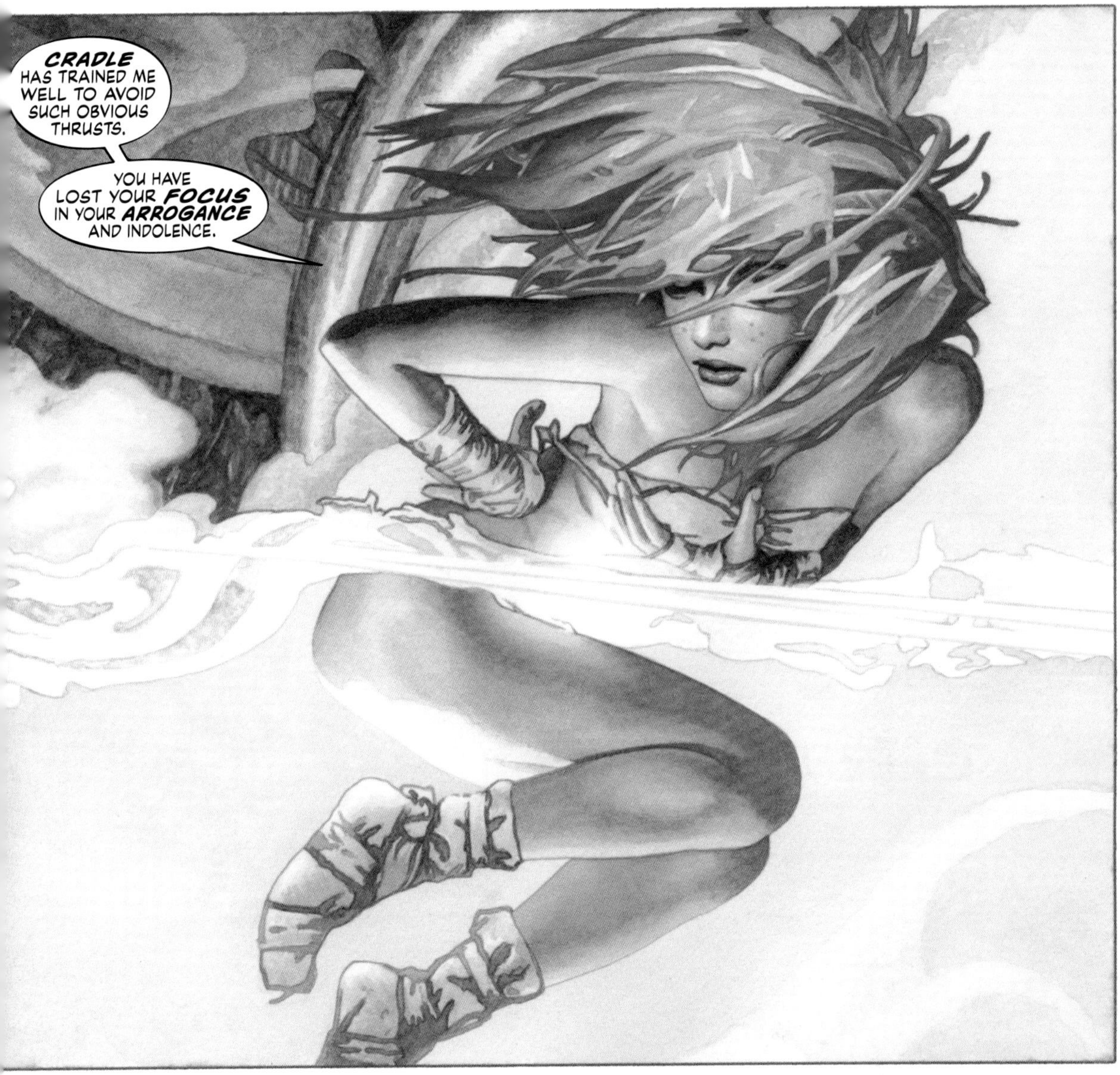
CRADLE HAS TRAINED ME WELL TO AVOID SUCH OBVIOUS THRUSTS.
YOU HAVE LOST YOUR FOCUS IN YOUR ARROGANCE AND INDOLENCE.

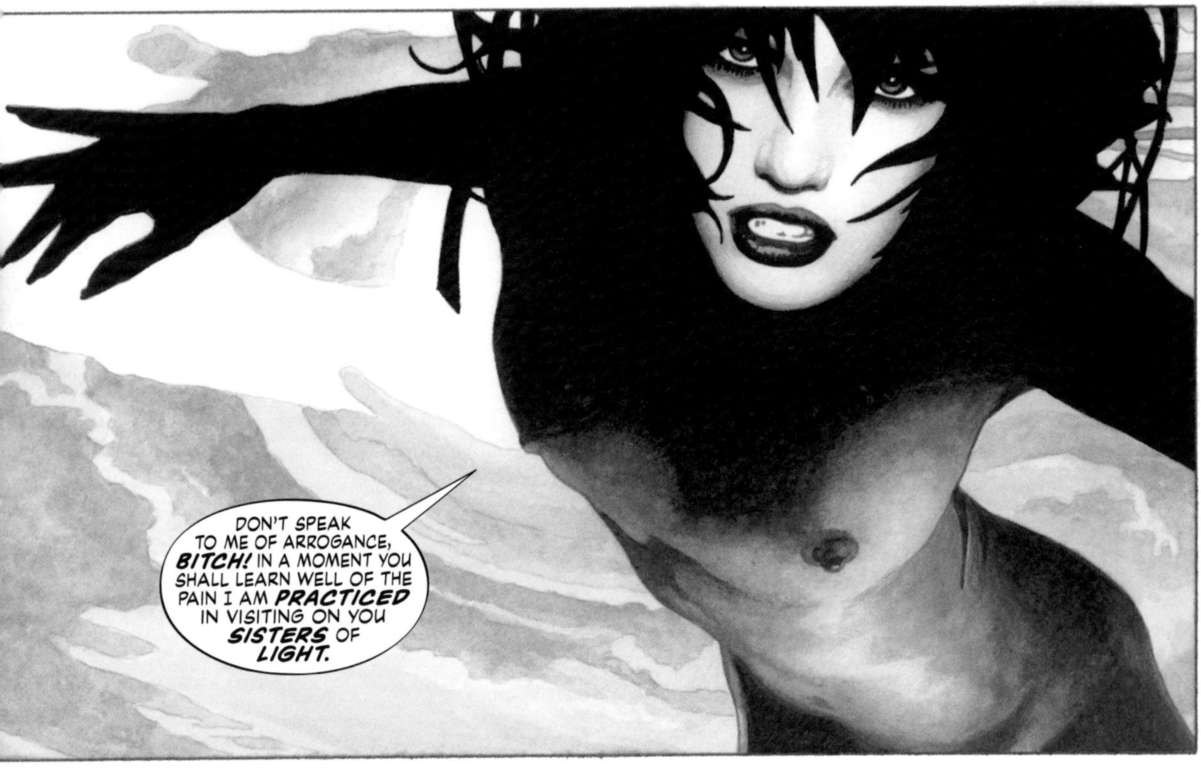
DON'T SPEAK TO ME OF ARROGANCE, BITCH! IN A MOMENT YOU SHALL LEARN WELL OF THE PAIN I AM PRACTICED IN VISITING ON YOU SISTERS OF LIGHT.

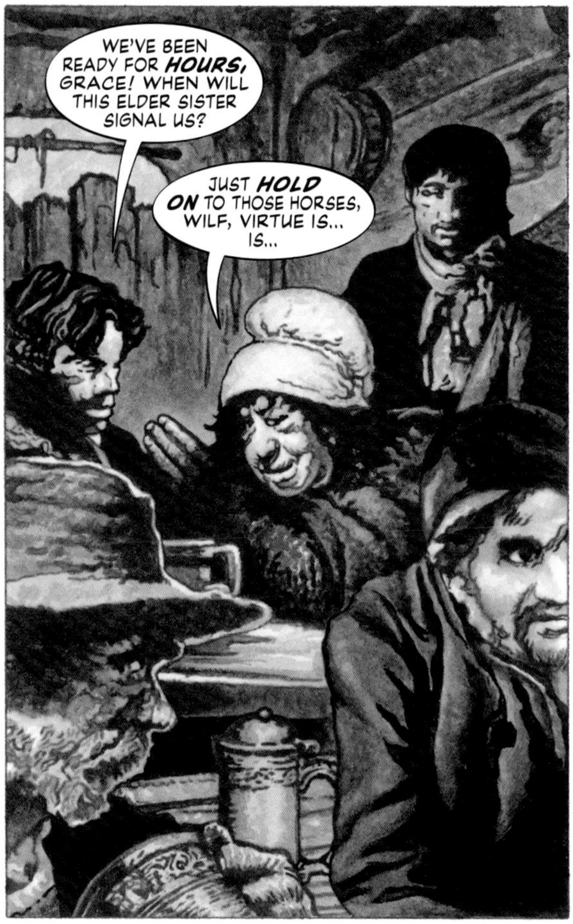
WE'VE BEEN READY FOR HOURS, GRACE! WHEN WILL THIS ELDER SISTER SIGNAL US?
JUST HOLD ON TO THOSE HORSES, WILF, VIRTUE IS... IS...

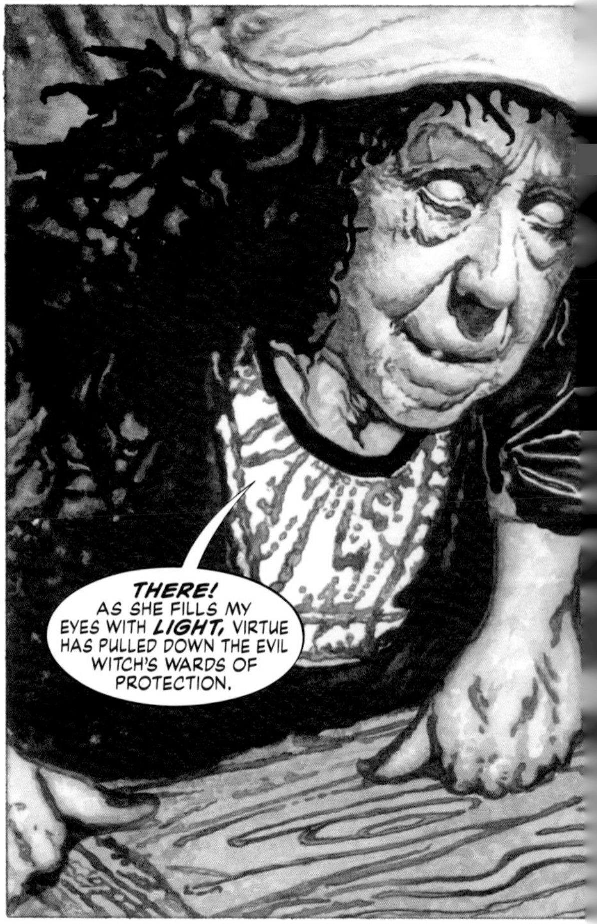
THERE! AS SHE FILLS MY EYES WITH LIGHT, VIRTUE HAS PULLED DOWN THE EVIL WITCH'S WARDS OF PROTECTION.

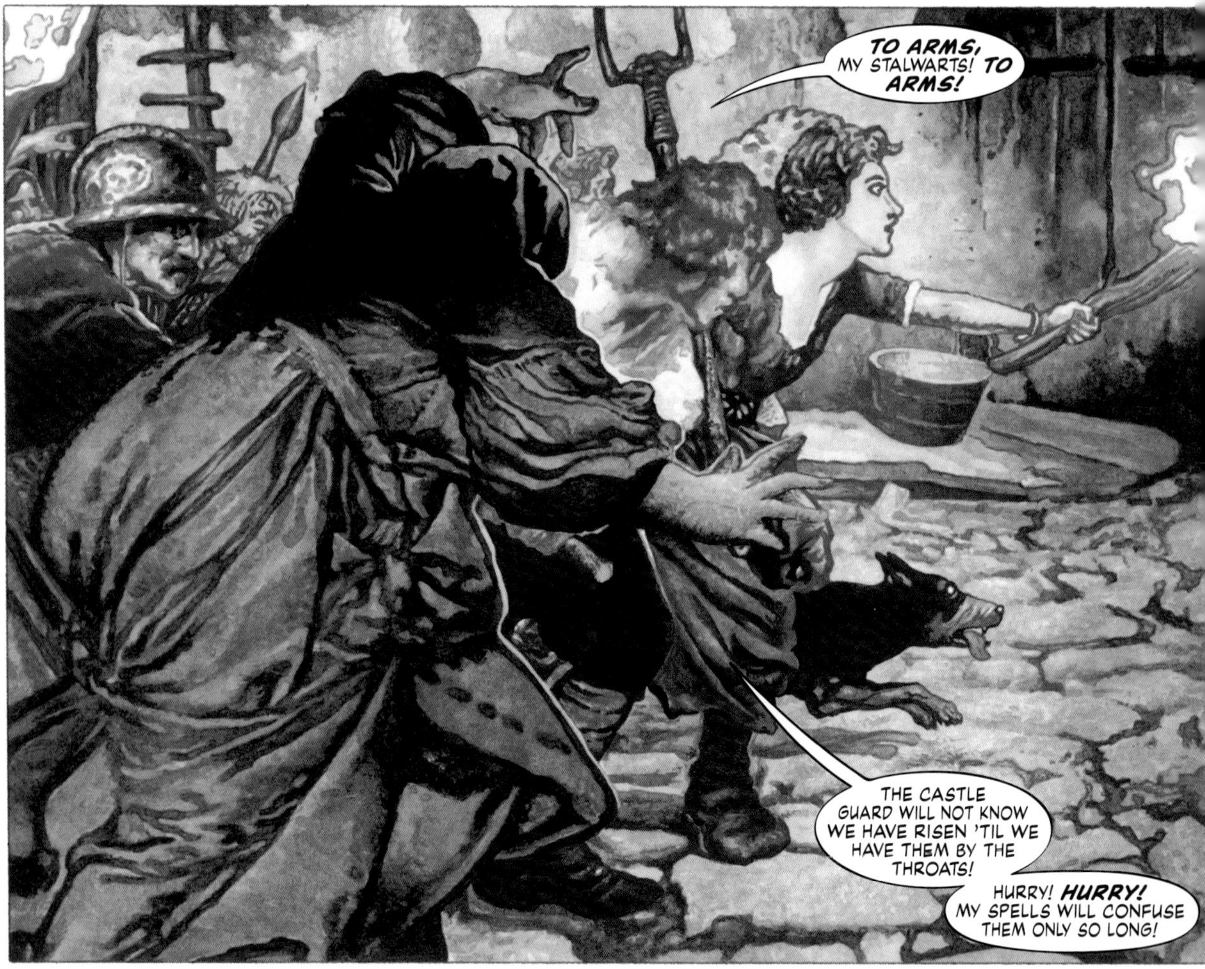
TO ARMS, MY STALWARTS! TO ARMS!
THE CASTLE GUARD WILL NOT KNOW WE HAVE RISEN 'TIL WE HAVE THEM BY THE THROATS!
HURRY! HURRY! MY SPELLS WILL CONFUSE THEM ONLY SO LONG!

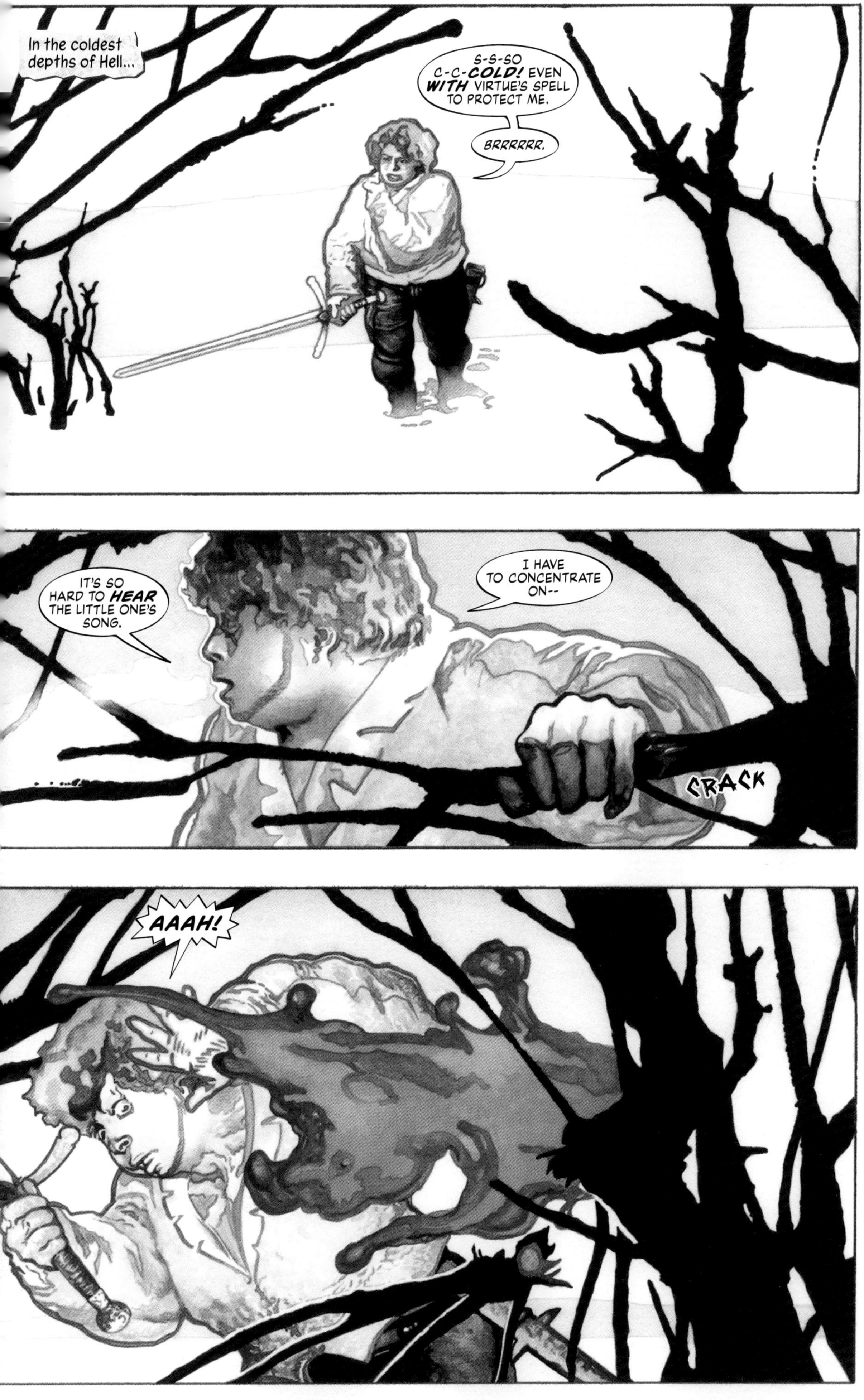

In the coldest depths of Hell...
S-S-SO C-C-COLD! EVEN WITH VIRTUE'S SPELL TO PROTECT ME.
BRRRRRR.
IT'S SO HARD TO HEAR THE LITTLE ONE'S SONG.
I HAVE TO CONCENTRATE ON--
CRACK
AAAH!

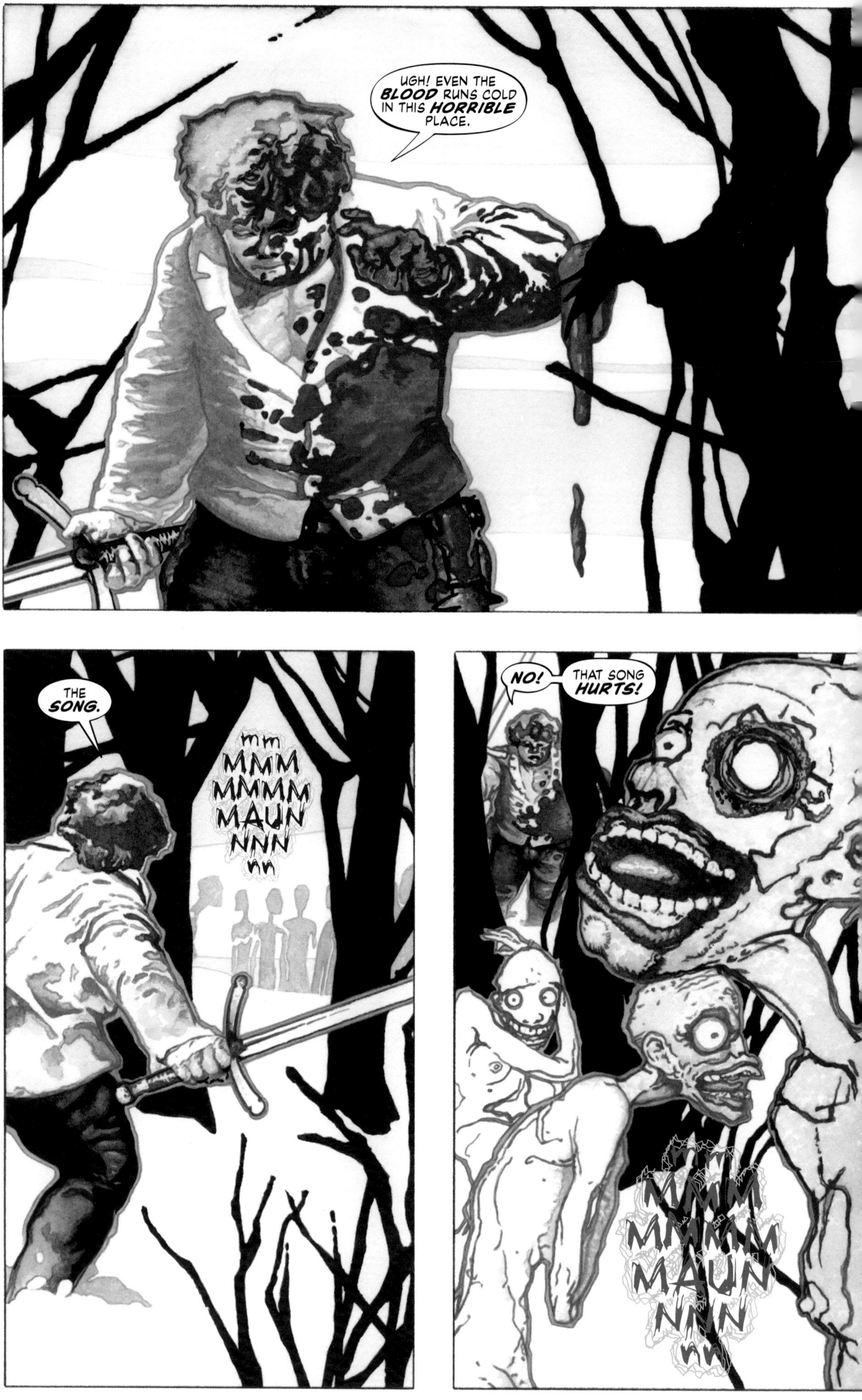
UGH! EVEN THE **BLOOD** RUNS COLD IN THIS **HORRIBLE** PLACE.
THE **SONG.**
mm MMM MMMM MAUN NNN nn
NO!
THAT SONG **HURTS!**
MMM MMMM MAUN NNN nn

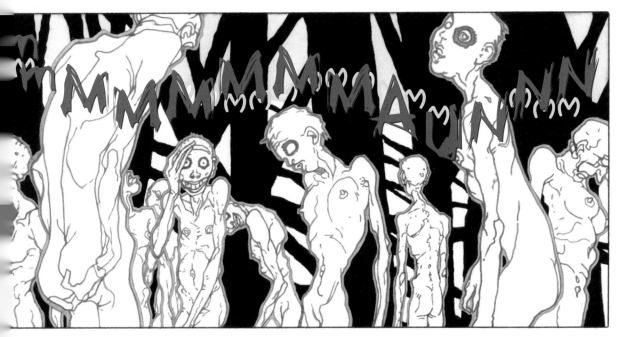

THEY ARE SO ALONE AND THEIR SONG IS SO LOUD, BUT I CAN STILL HEAR THE LITTLE ONE'S SONG.

IT'S SO SWEET.

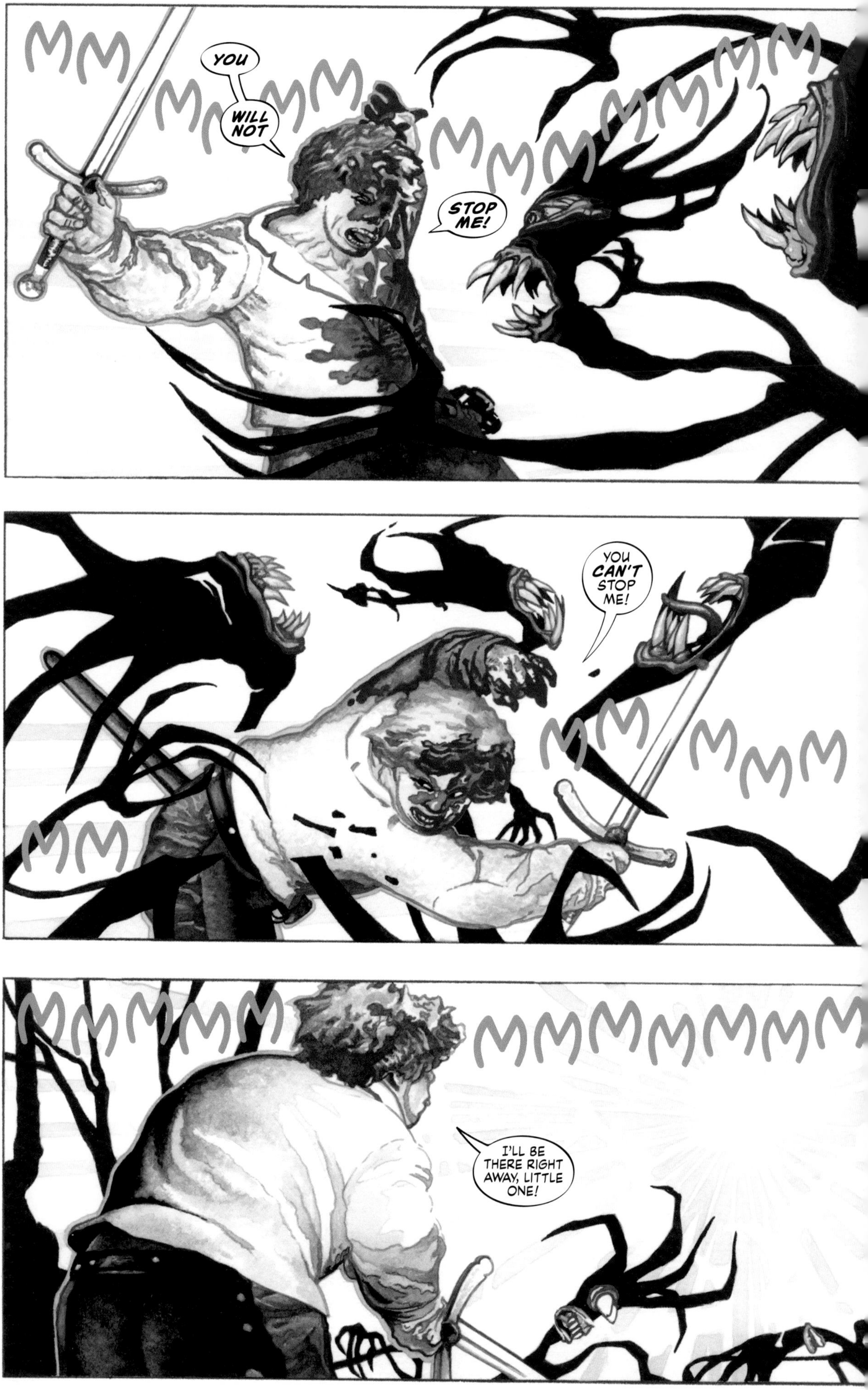
MM
MMMM
YOU
WILL NOT
MMMMMMMMMMMM
STOP ME!
YOU CAN'T STOP ME!
MM
MMMM
MM
MMMMMM
MMMMMMMMM
I'LL BE THERE RIGHT AWAY, LITTLE ONE!

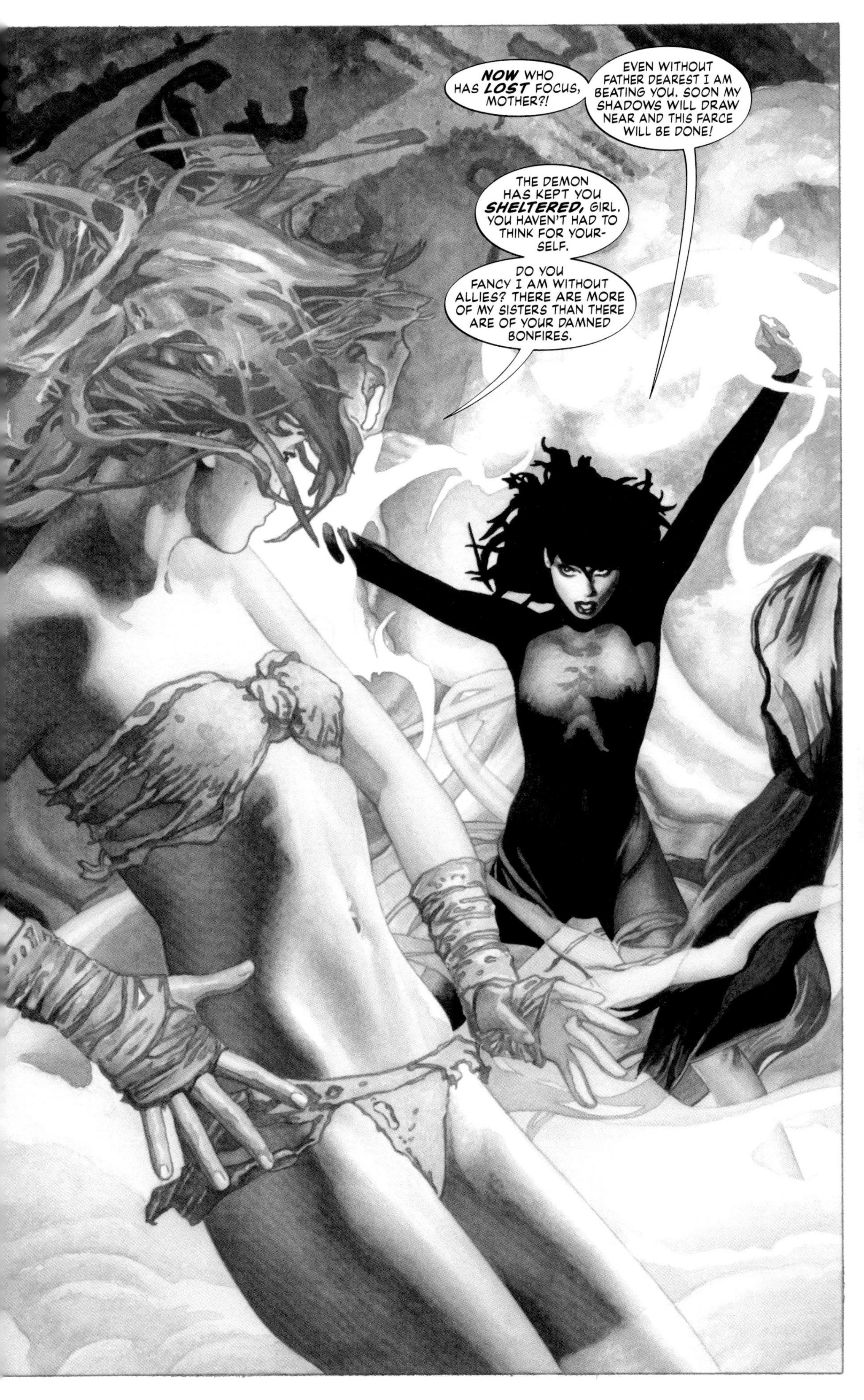
NOW WHO HAS LOST FOCUS, MOTHER?!
EVEN WITHOUT FATHER DEAREST I AM BEATING YOU. SOON MY SHADOWS WILL DRAW NEAR AND THIS FARCE WILL BE DONE!
THE DEMON HAS KEPT YOU SHELTERED, GIRL. YOU HAVEN'T HAD TO THINK FOR YOURSELF.
DO YOU FANCY I AM WITHOUT ALLIES? THERE ARE MORE OF MY SISTERS THAN THERE ARE OF YOUR DAMNED BONFIRES.

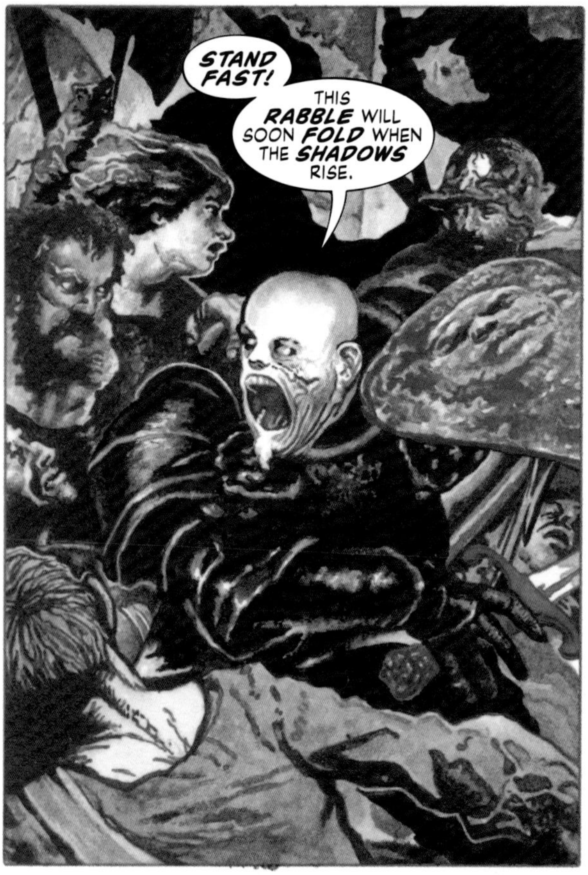
STAND FAST!
THIS RABBLE WILL SOON FOLD WHEN THE SHADOWS RISE.

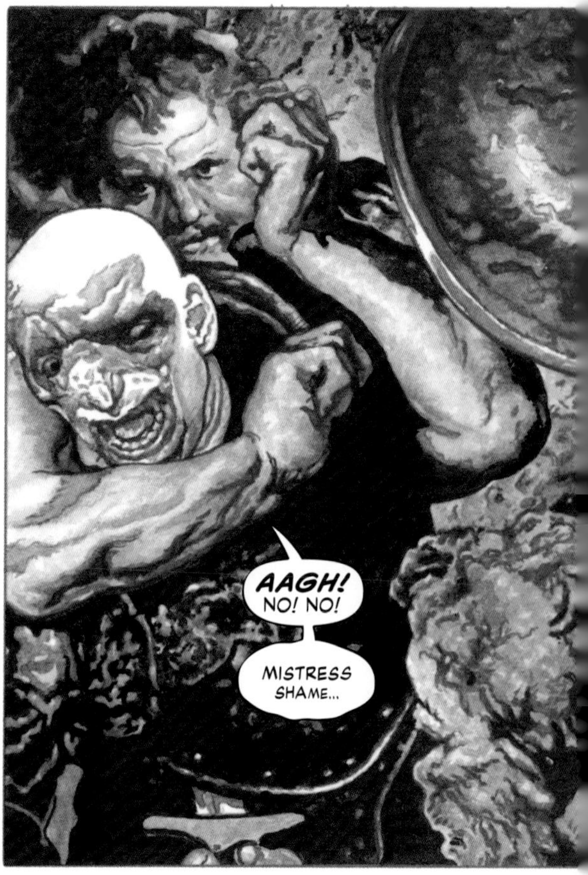
AAGH! NO! NO!
MISTRESS SHAME...

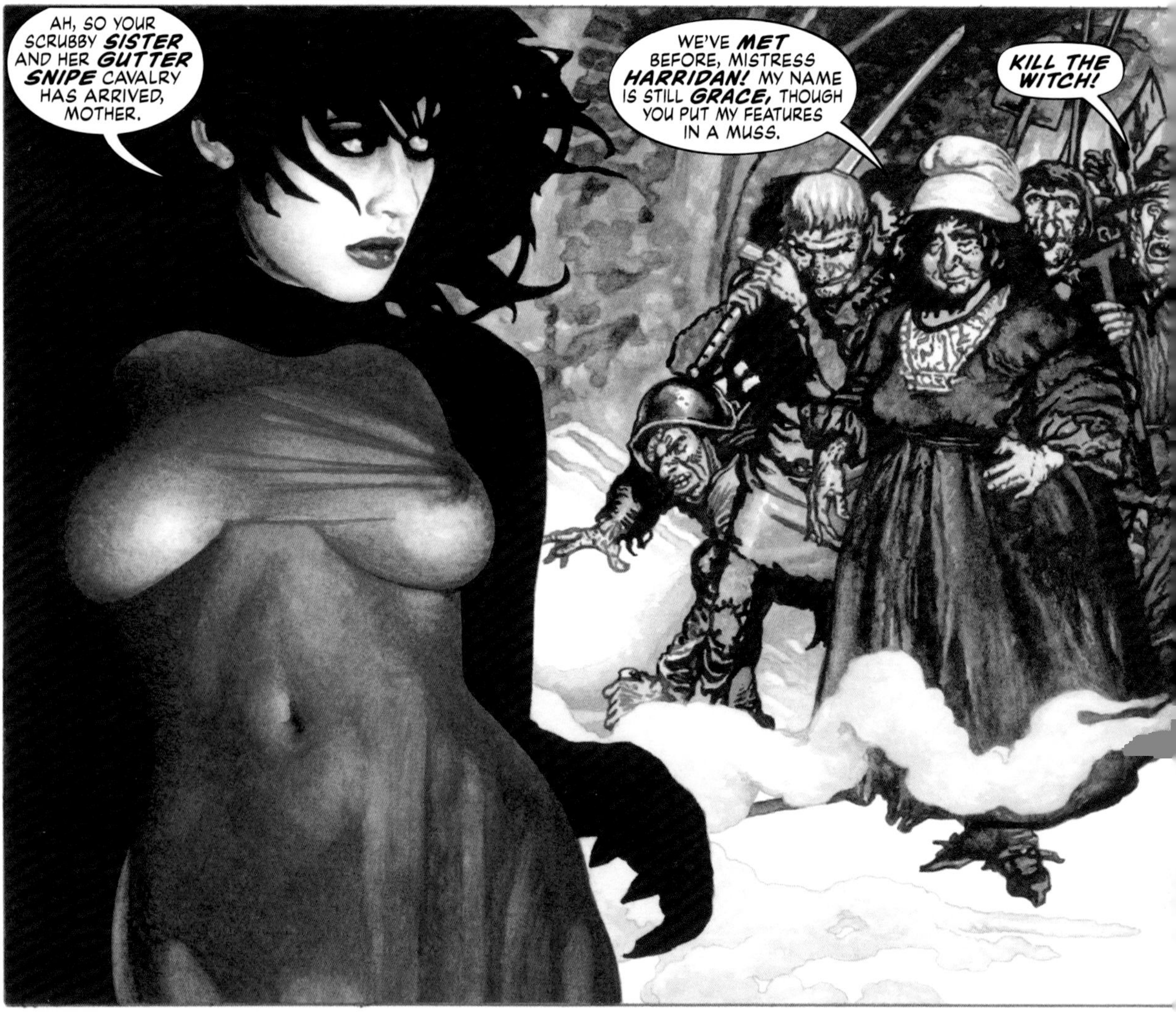
AH, SO YOUR SCRUBBY SISTER AND HER GUTTER SNIPE CAVALRY HAS ARRIVED, MOTHER.
WE'VE MET BEFORE, MISTRESS HARRIDAN! MY NAME IS STILL GRACE, THOUGH YOU PUT MY FEATURES IN A MUSS.
KILL THE WITCH!

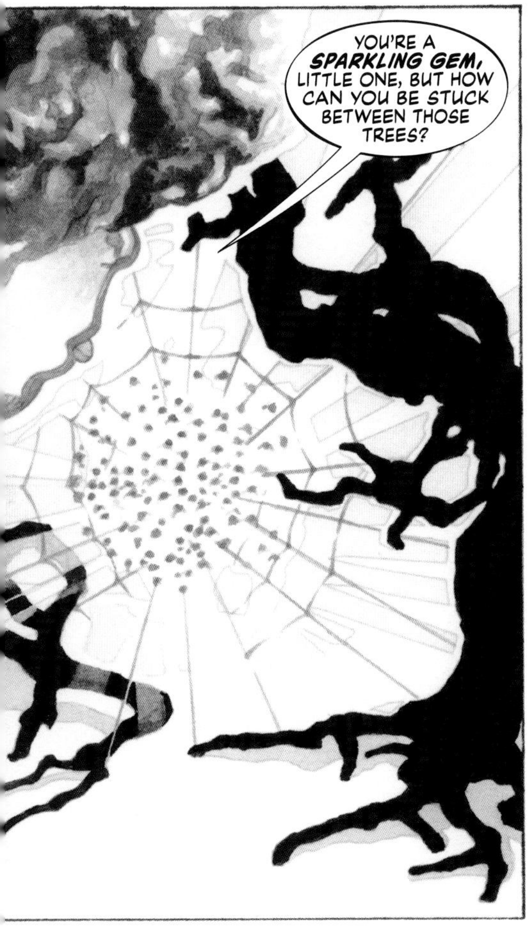
YOU'RE A SPARKLING GEM, LITTLE ONE, BUT HOW CAN YOU BE STUCK BETWEEN THOSE TREES?

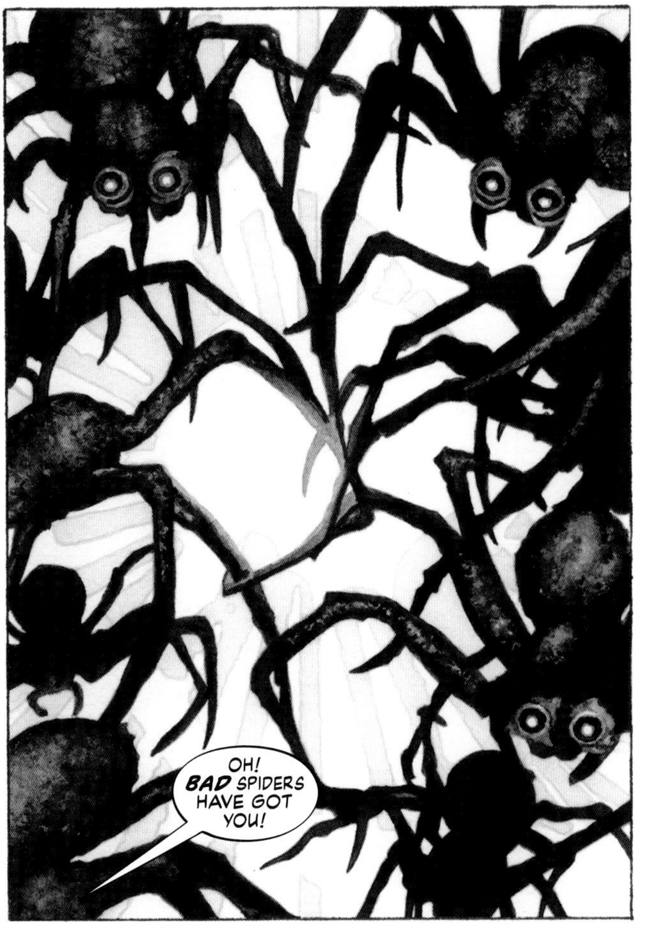
OH! BAD SPIDERS HAVE GOT YOU!

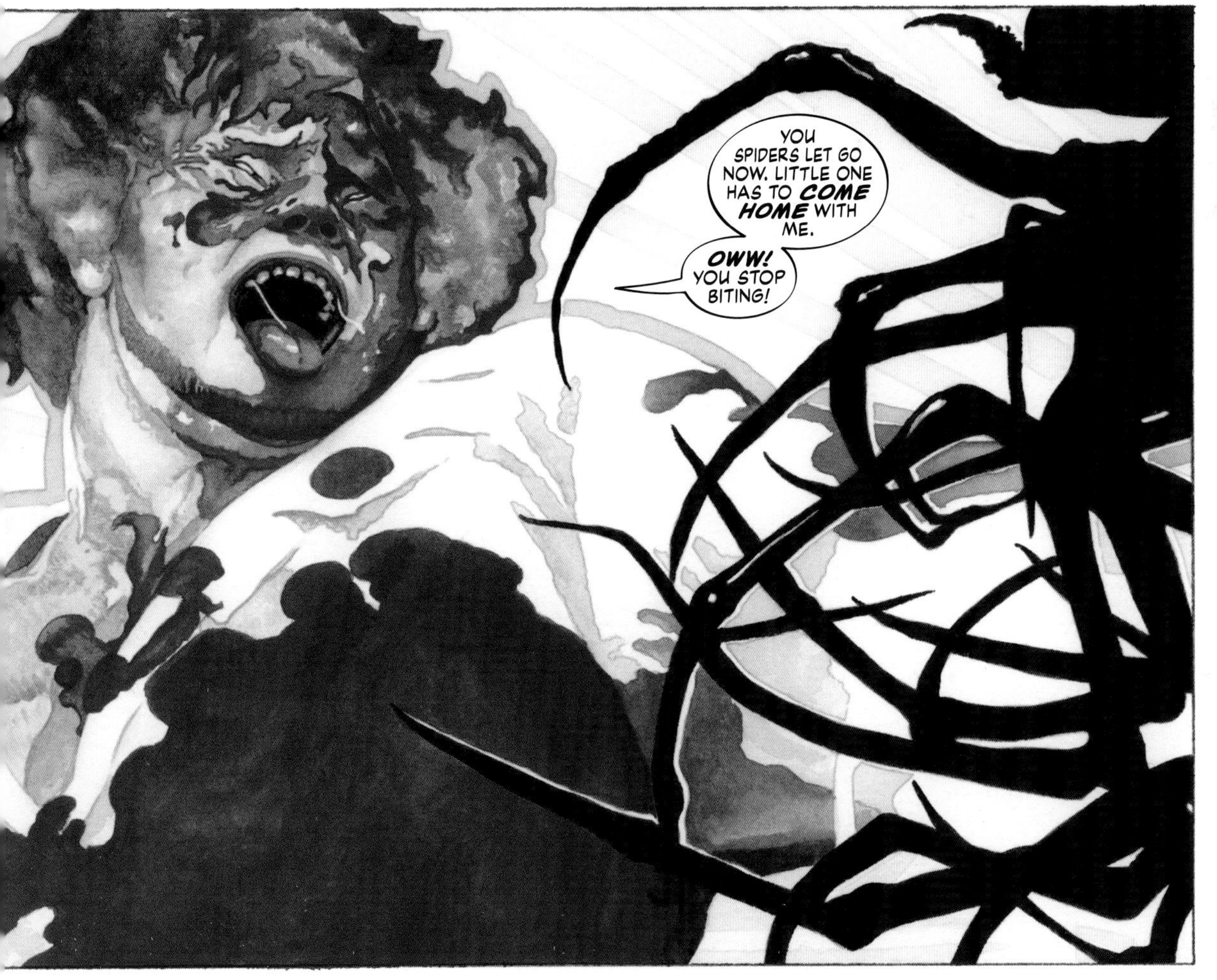
YOU SPIDERS LET GO NOW. LITTLE ONE HAS TO COME HOME WITH ME.
OWW! YOU STOP BITING!

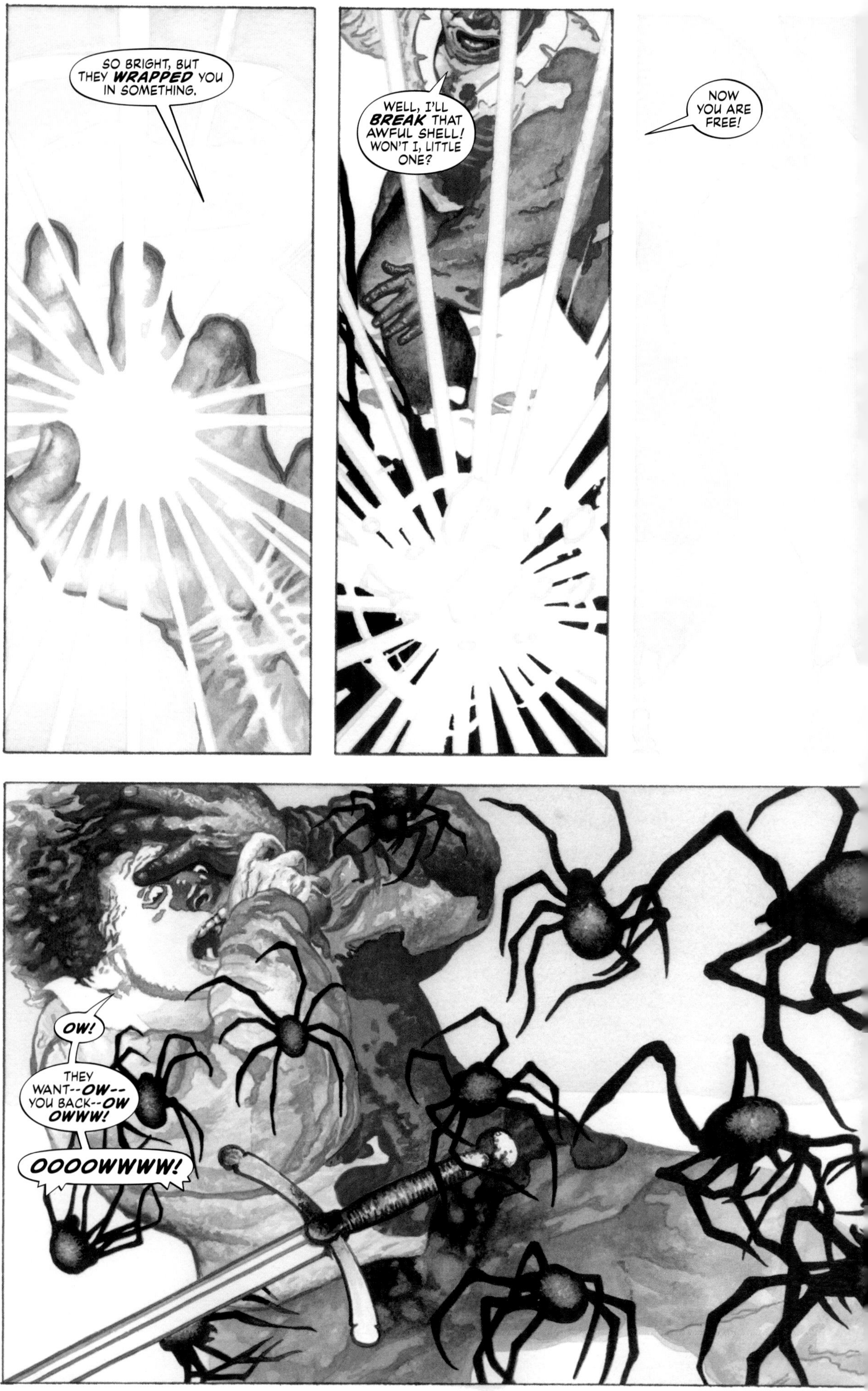
SO BRIGHT, BUT THEY WRAPPED YOU IN SOMETHING.
WELL, I'LL BREAK THAT AWFUL SHELL! WON'T I, LITTLE ONE?
NOW YOU ARE FREE!
OW!
THEY WANT--OW-- YOU BACK--OW OWWW!
OOOOWWWW!

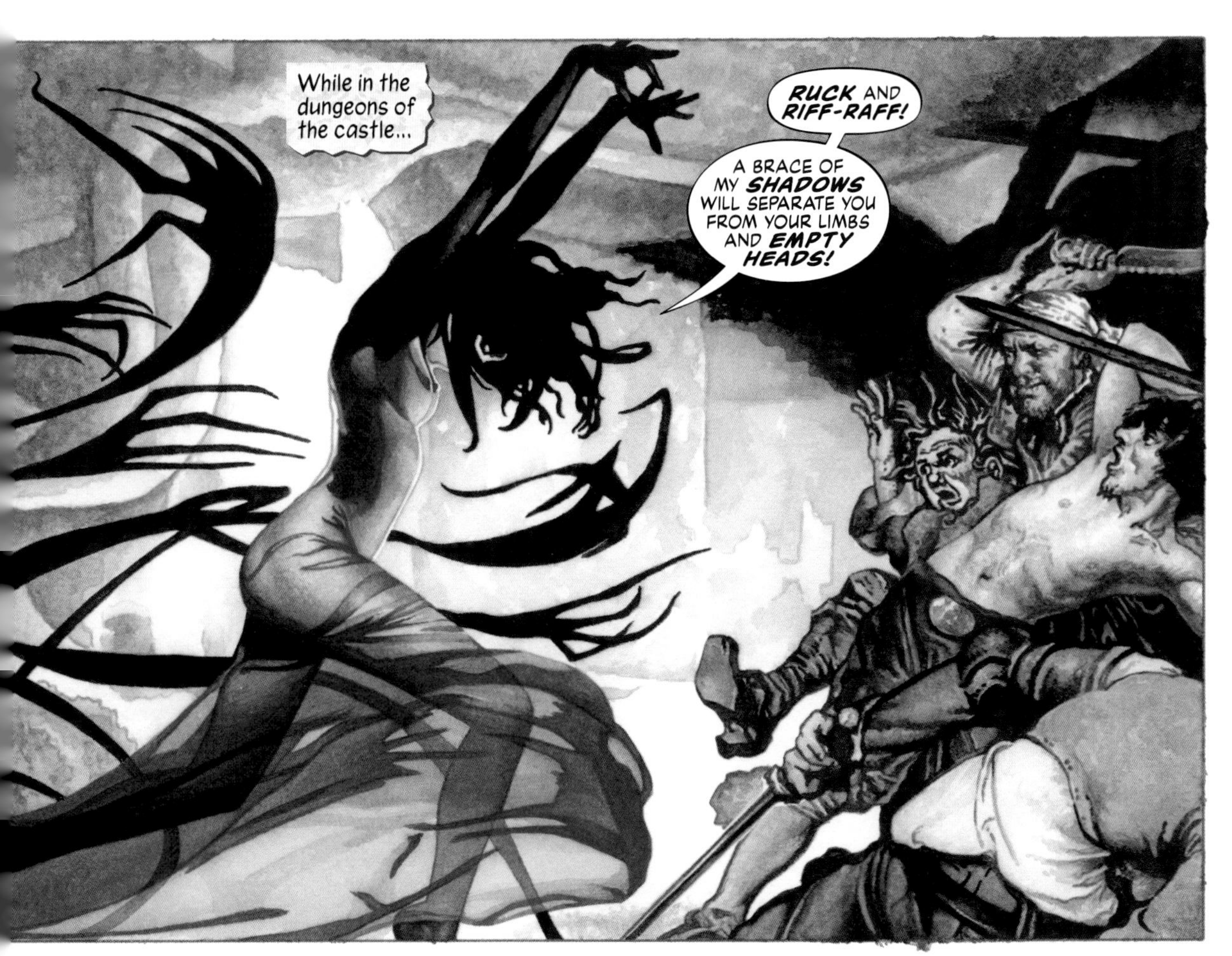
While in the dungeons of the castle...
RUCK AND RIFF-RAFF!
A BRACE OF MY SHADOWS WILL SEPARATE YOU FROM YOUR LIMBS AND EMPTY HEADS!

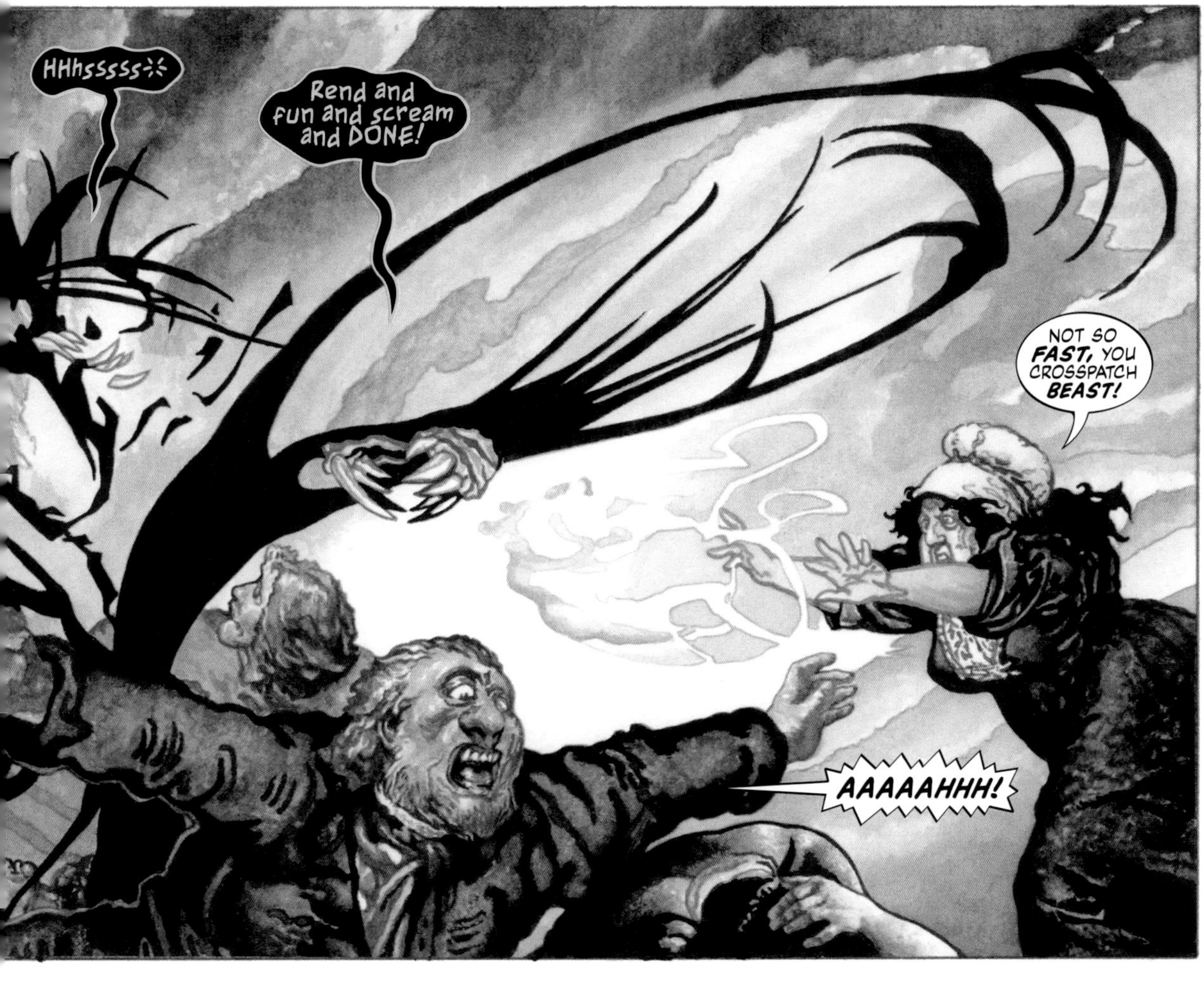
HHhsssss
Rend and fun and scream and DONE!
NOT SO FAST, YOU CROSSPATCH BEAST!
AAAAAHHH!

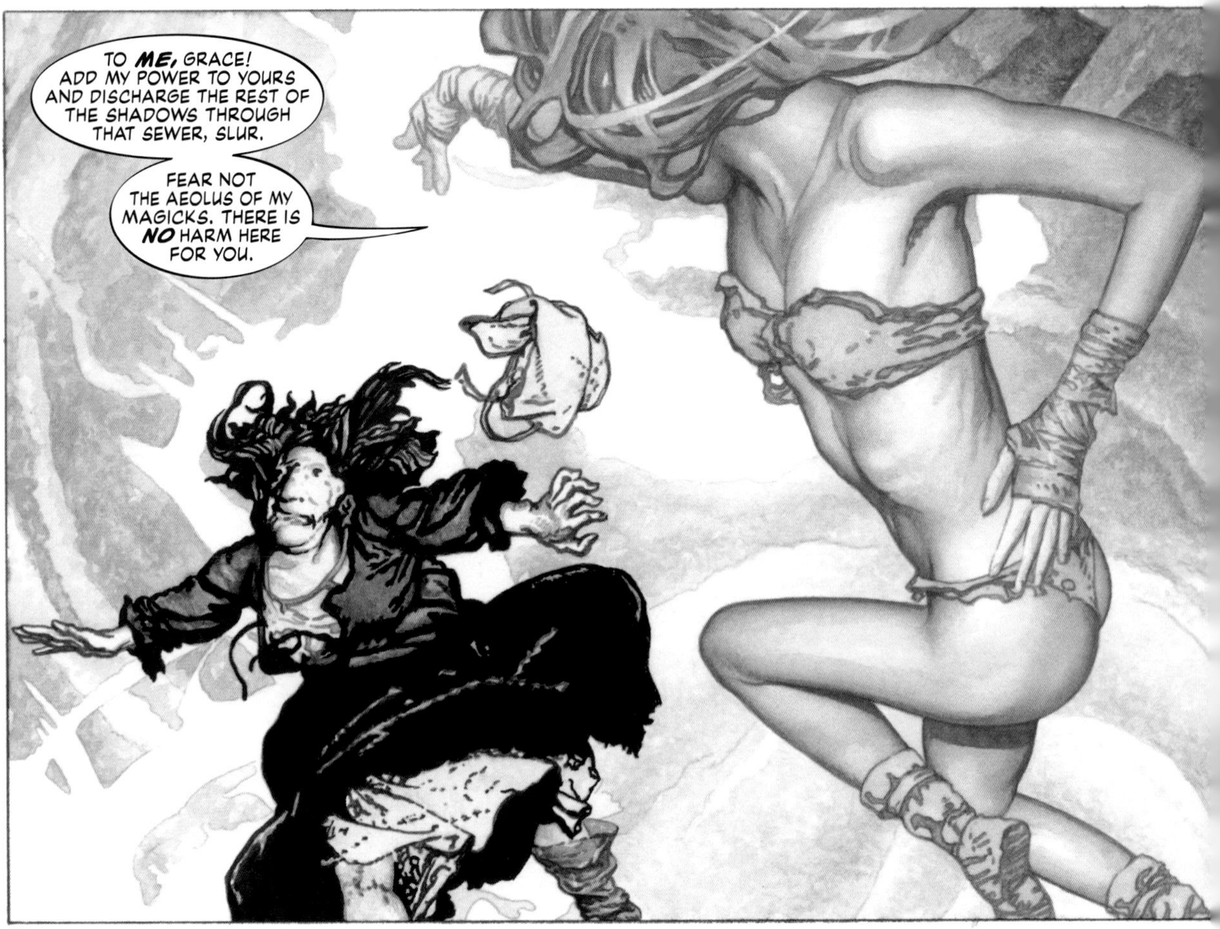
TO ME, GRACE! ADD MY POWER TO YOURS AND DISCHARGE THE REST OF THE SHADOWS THROUGH THAT SEWER, SLUR.
FEAR NOT THE AEOLUS OF MY MAGICKS. THERE IS NO HARM HERE FOR YOU.

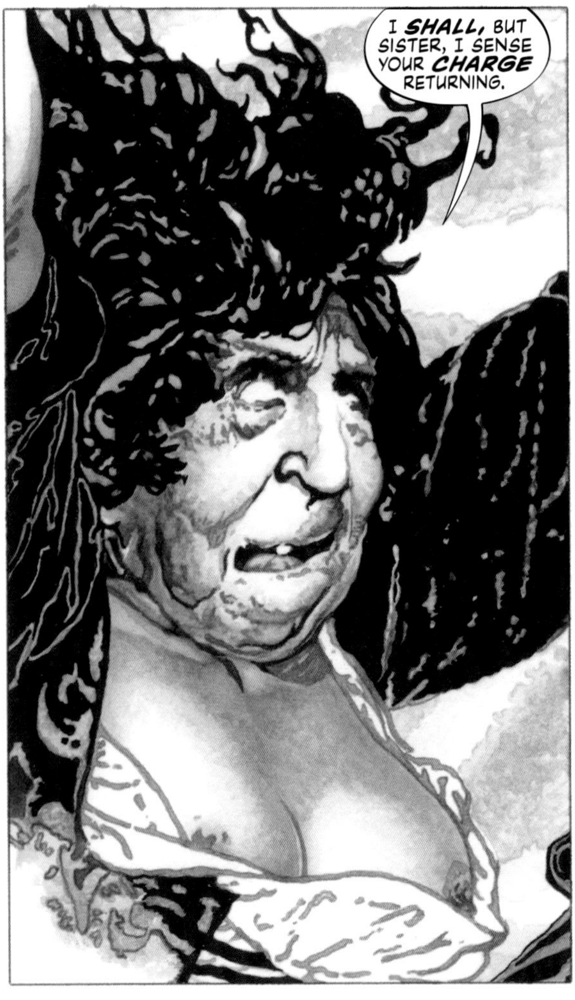
I SHALL, BUT SISTER, I SENSE YOUR CHARGE RETURNING.

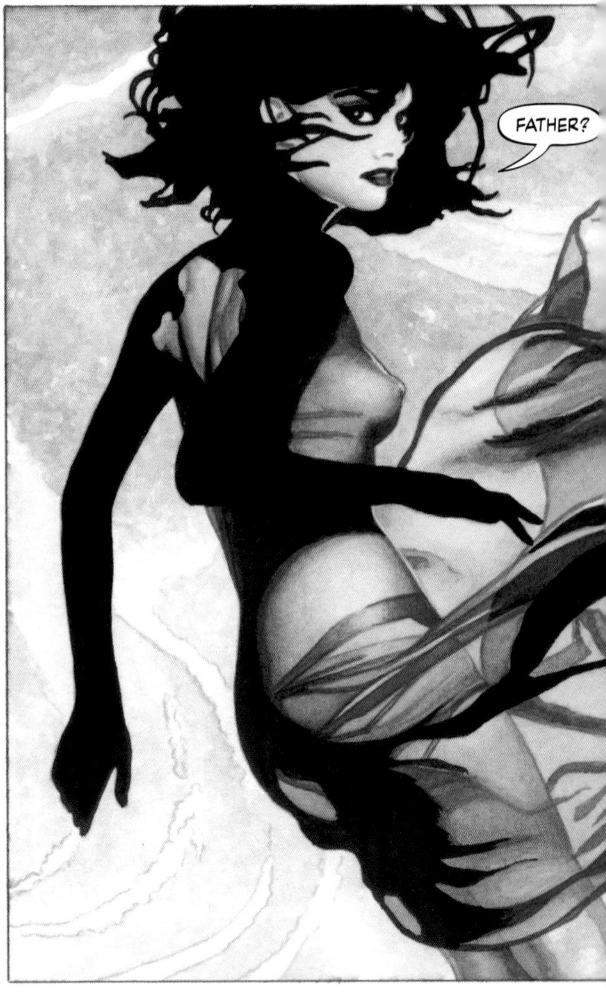
FATHER?

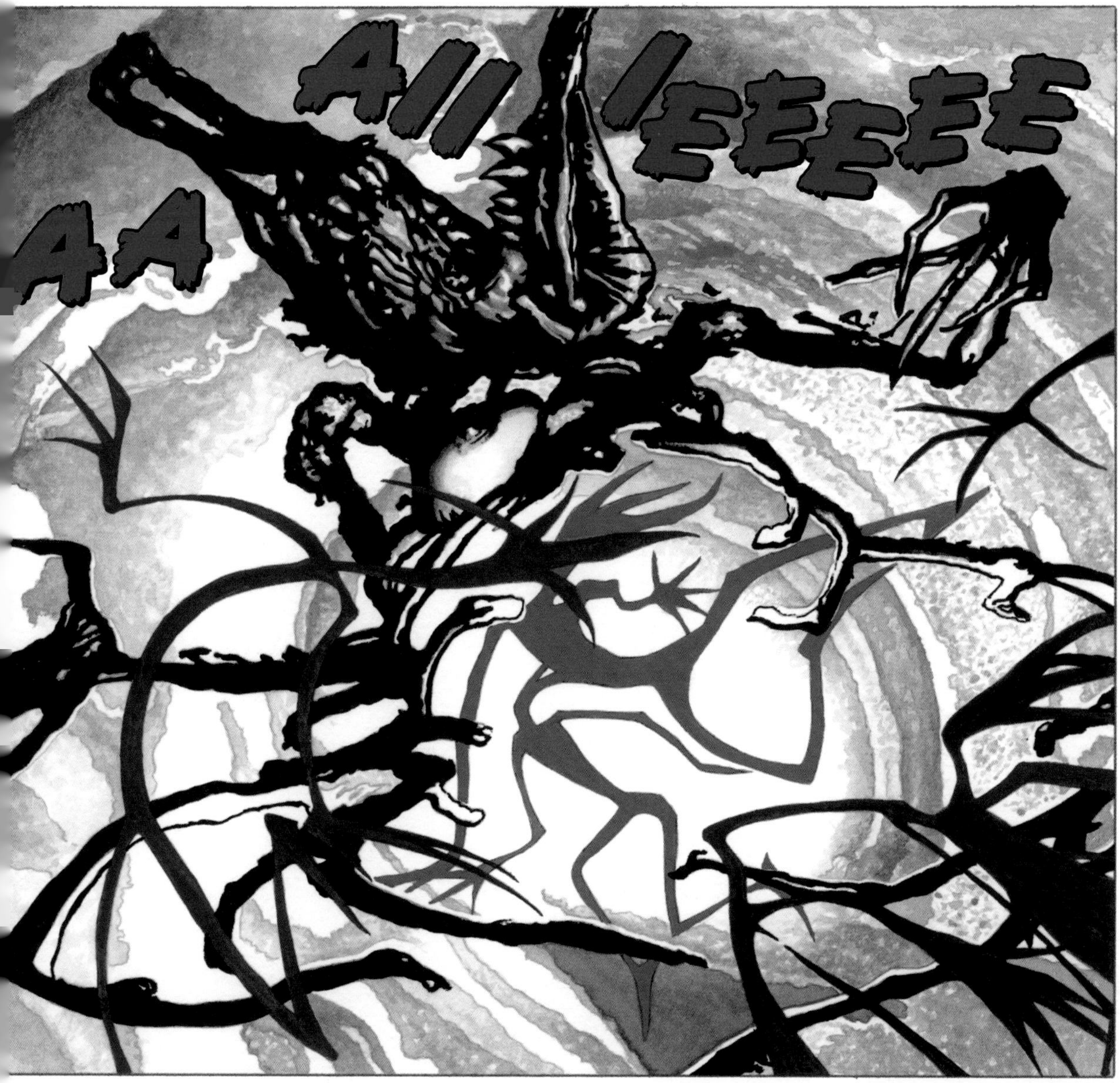
AAAIII IEEEEEE

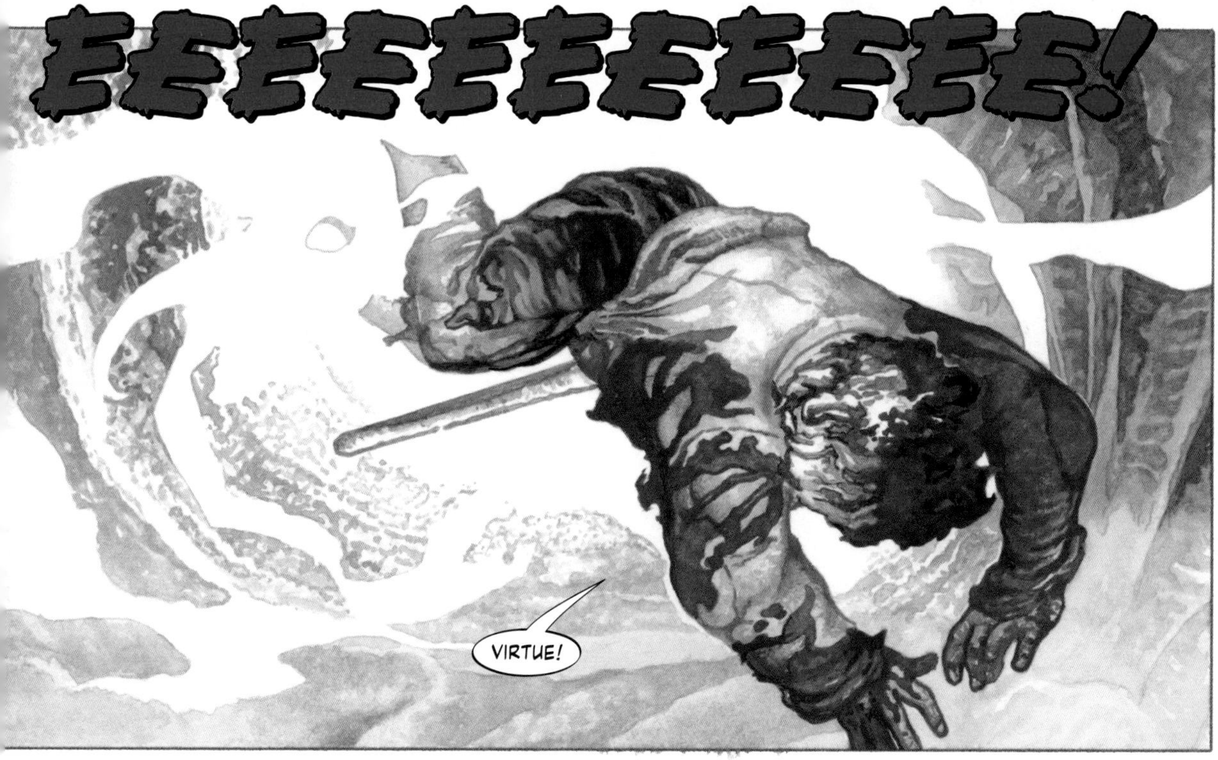
EEEEEEEEEEEE!
VIRTUE!

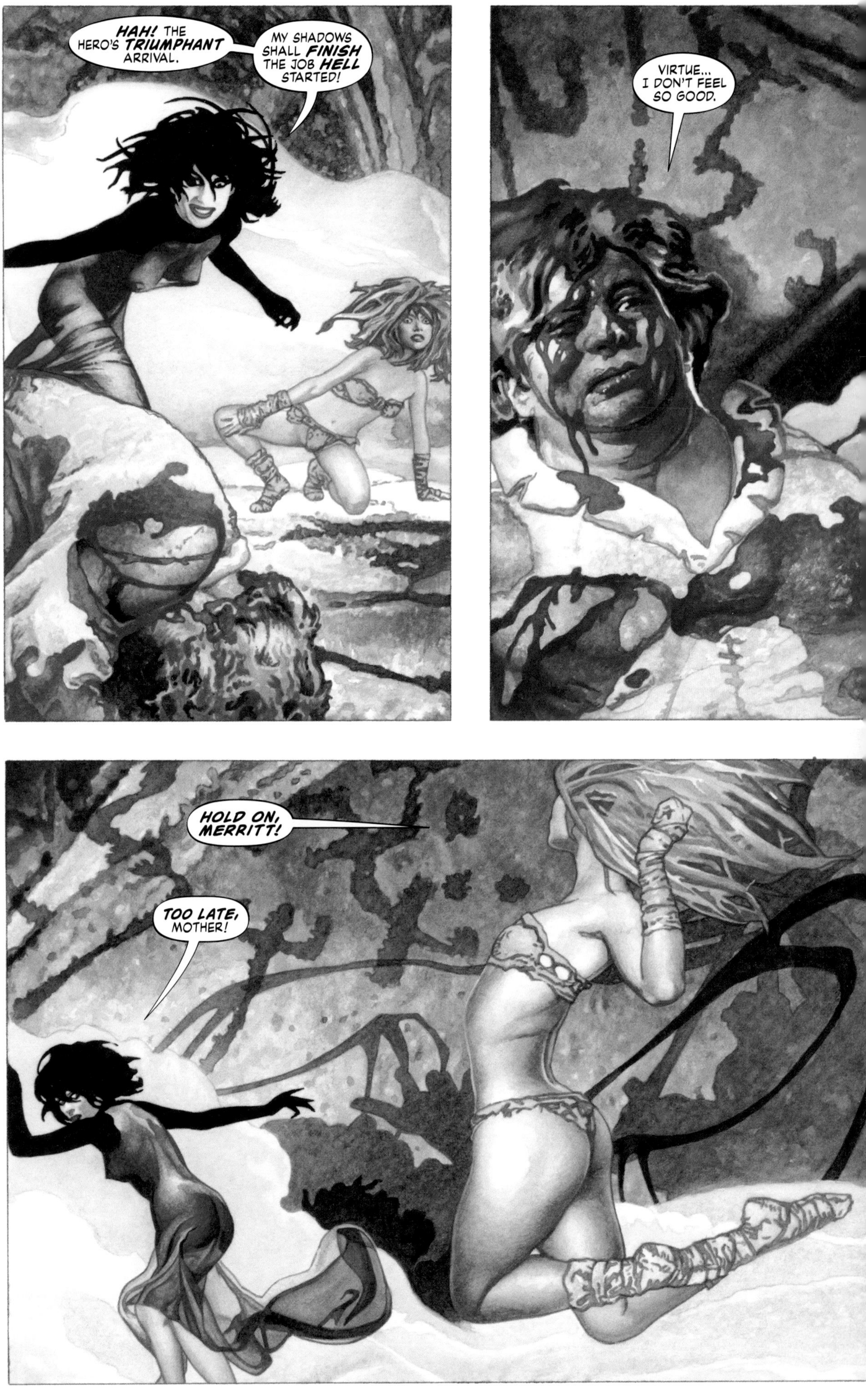
HAH! THE HERO'S TRIUMPHANT ARRIVAL.
MY SHADOWS SHALL FINISH THE JOB HELL STARTED!
VIRTUE... I DON'T FEEL SO GOOD.
HOLD ON, MERRITT!
TOO LATE, MOTHER!

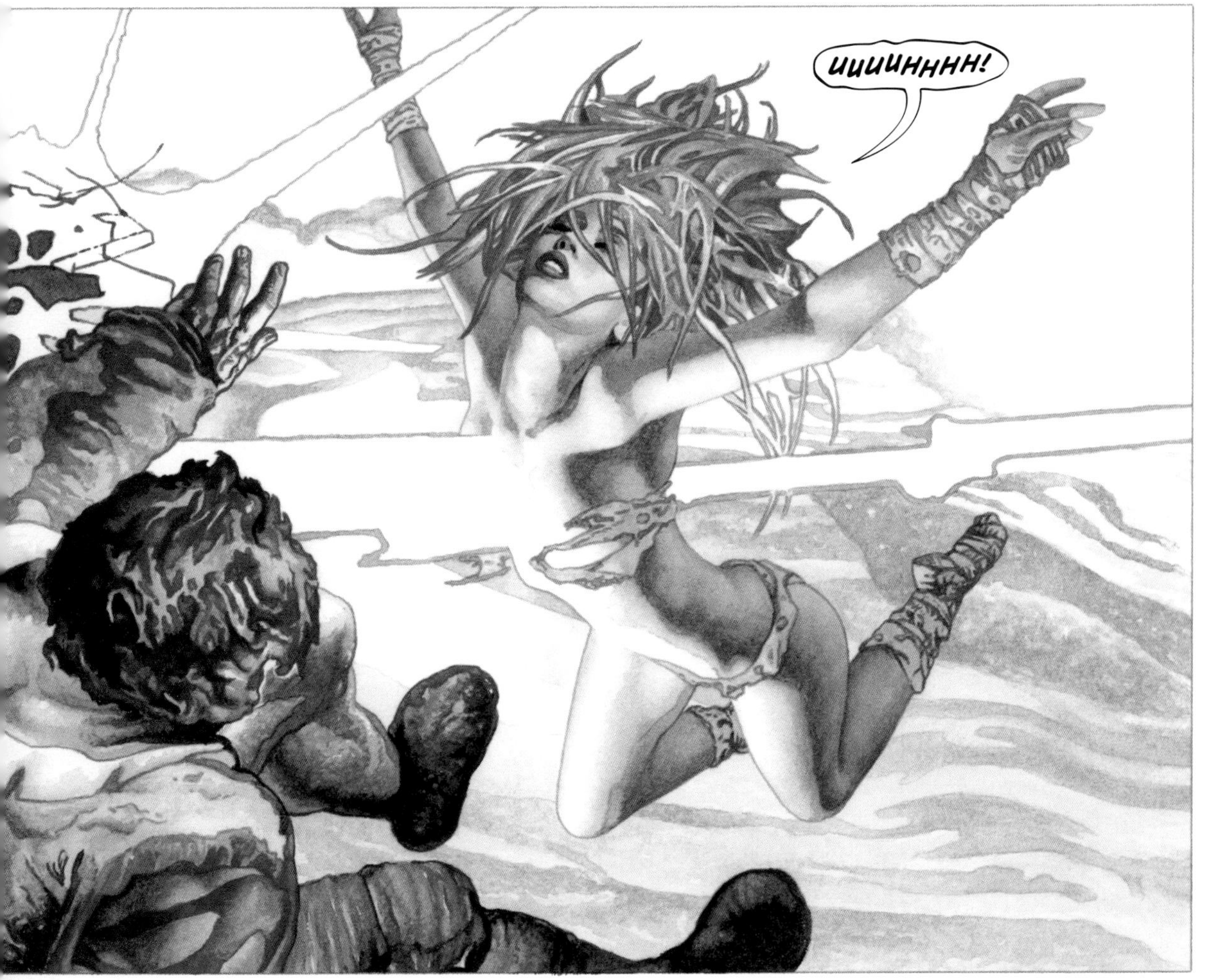
UUUUHHHH!

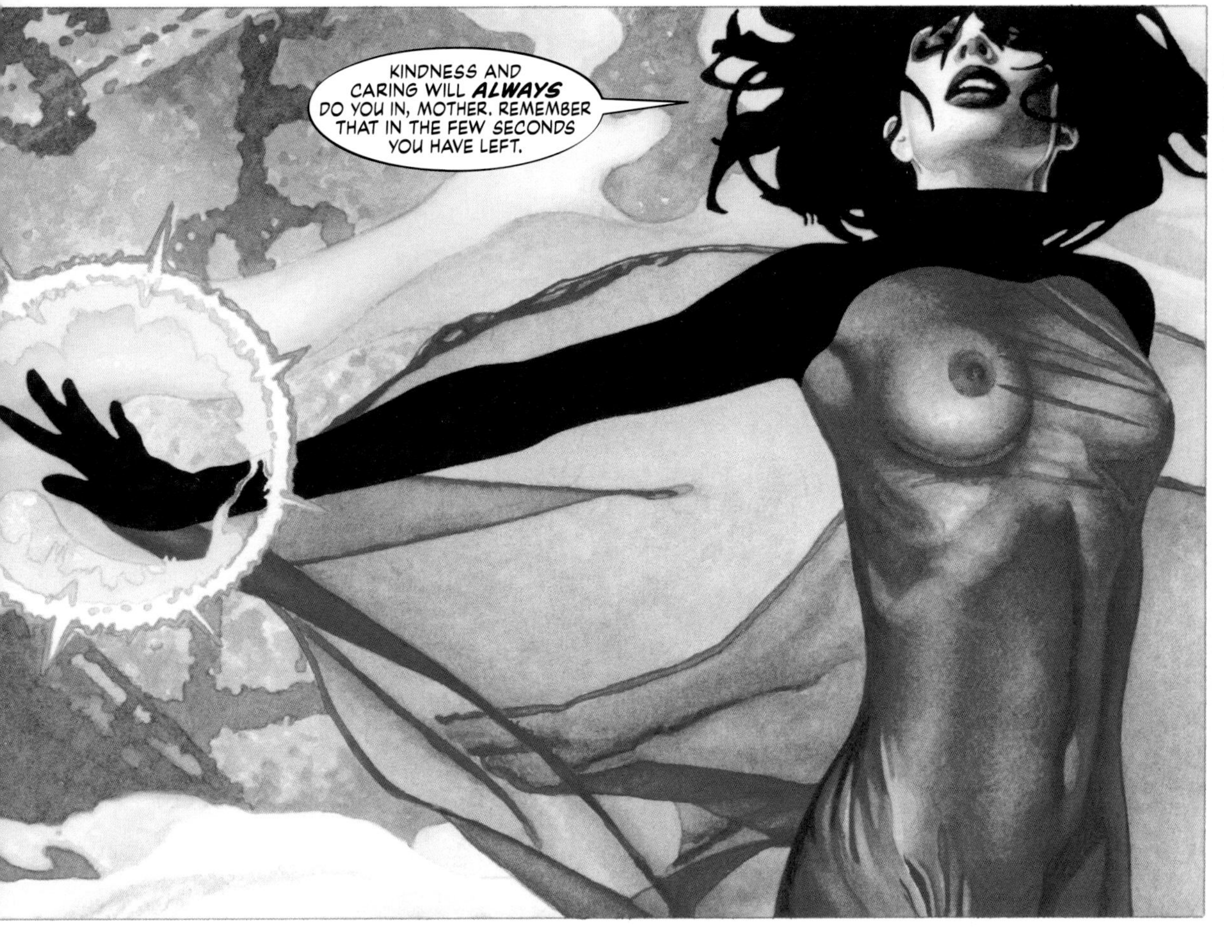
KINDNESS AND CARING WILL ALWAYS DO YOU IN, MOTHER. REMEMBER THAT IN THE FEW SECONDS YOU HAVE LEFT.

LITTLE ONE...?

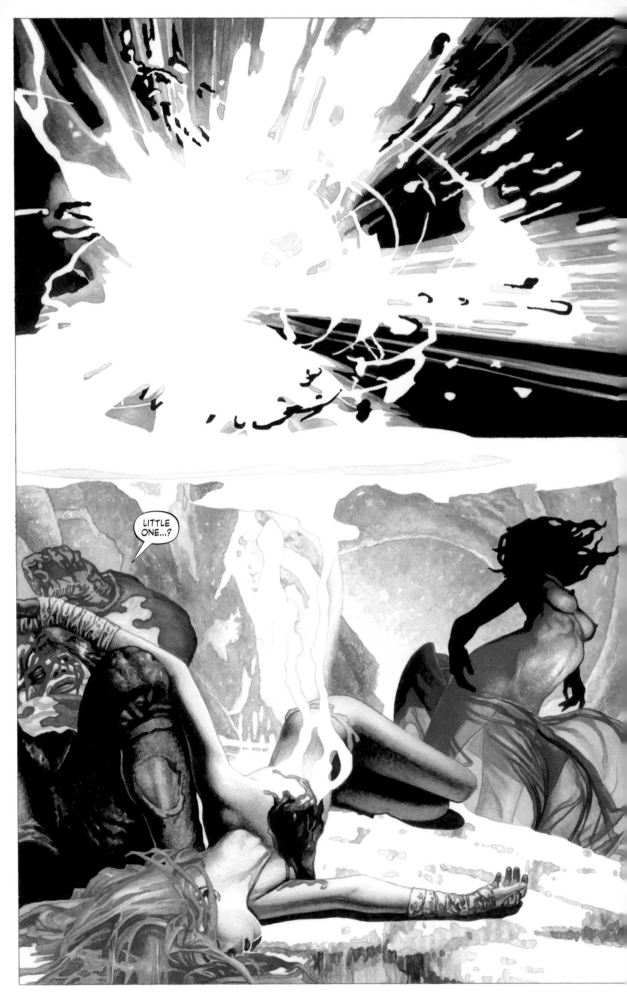

I'M SO **SORRY,** VIRTUE. SO SORRY...

YOU HAVE NOTHING TO BE SORRY FOR, MERRITT.
THINGS ARE NEARLY AS THEY *SHOULD* BE. I DIED YEARS AGO AND NOW MY SPIRIT IS FREE.
FREE?

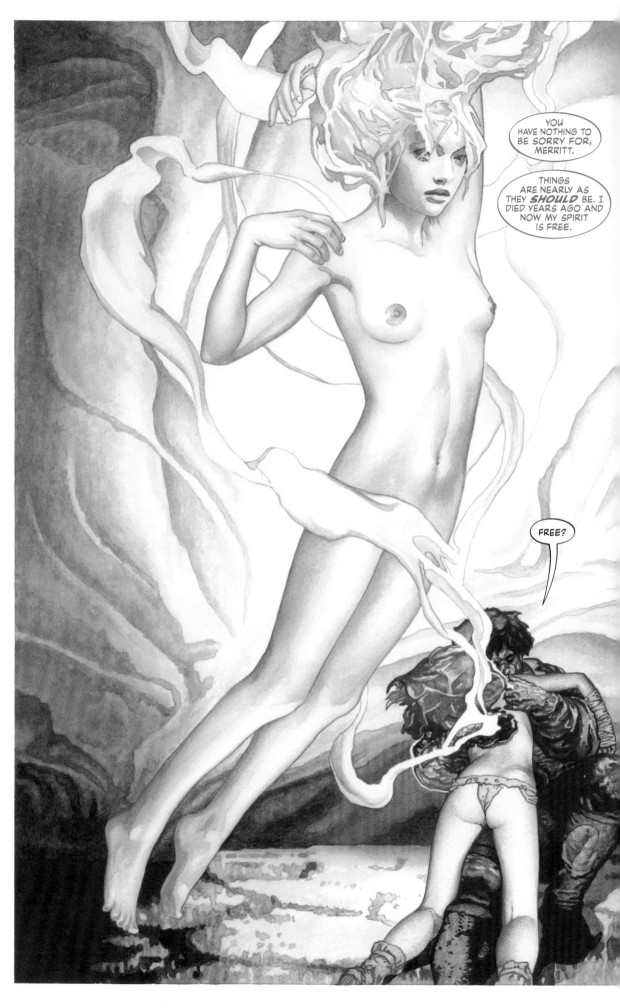

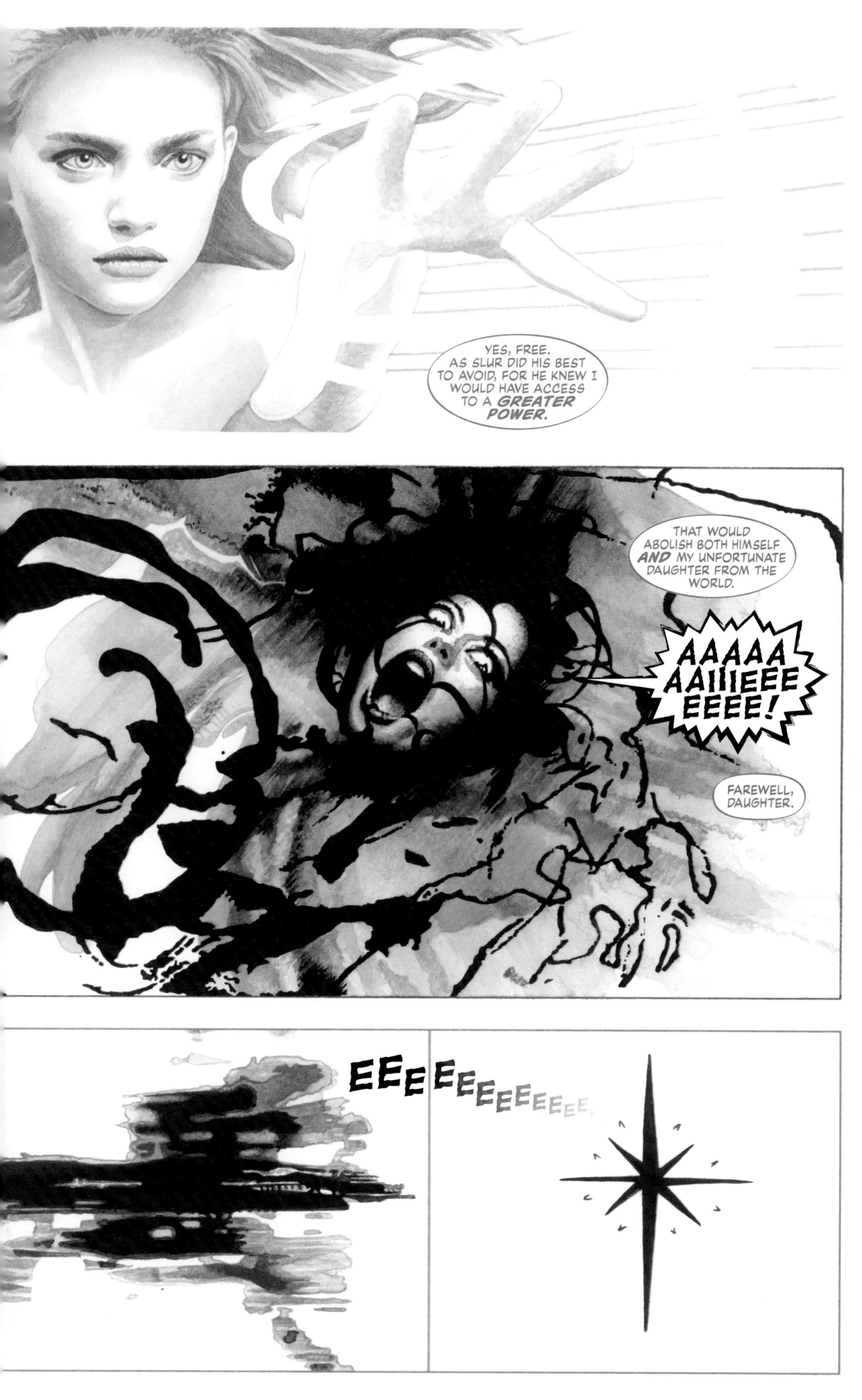
YES, FREE. AS SLUR DID HIS BEST TO AVOID, FOR HE KNEW I WOULD HAVE ACCESS TO A **GREATER POWER.**
THAT WOULD ABOLISH BOTH HIMSELF **AND** MY UNFORTUNATE DAUGHTER FROM THE WORLD.
AAAAAAAIIIIEEEEEEE!
FAREWELL, DAUGHTER.
EEEEEEEEEEEEEE

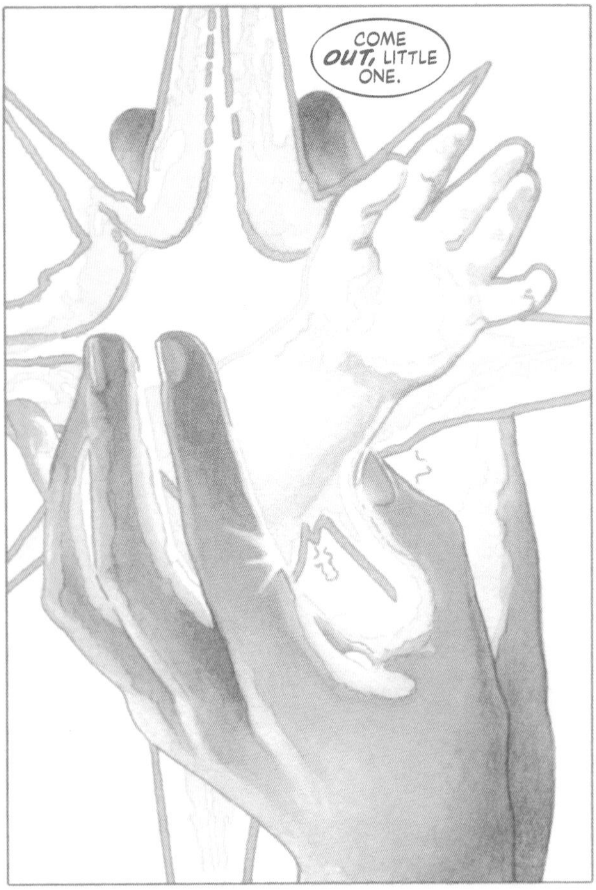
COME OUT, LITTLE ONE.

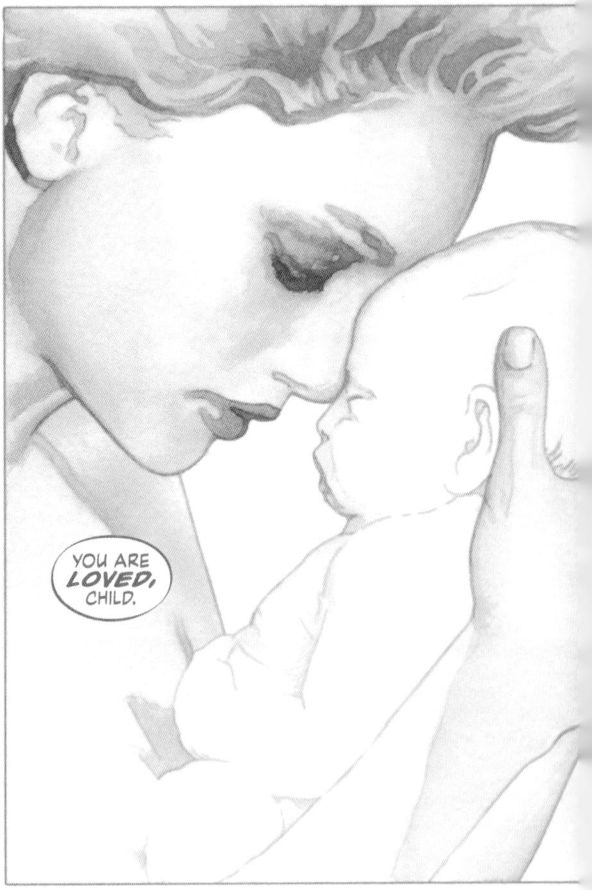
YOU ARE LOVED, CHILD.

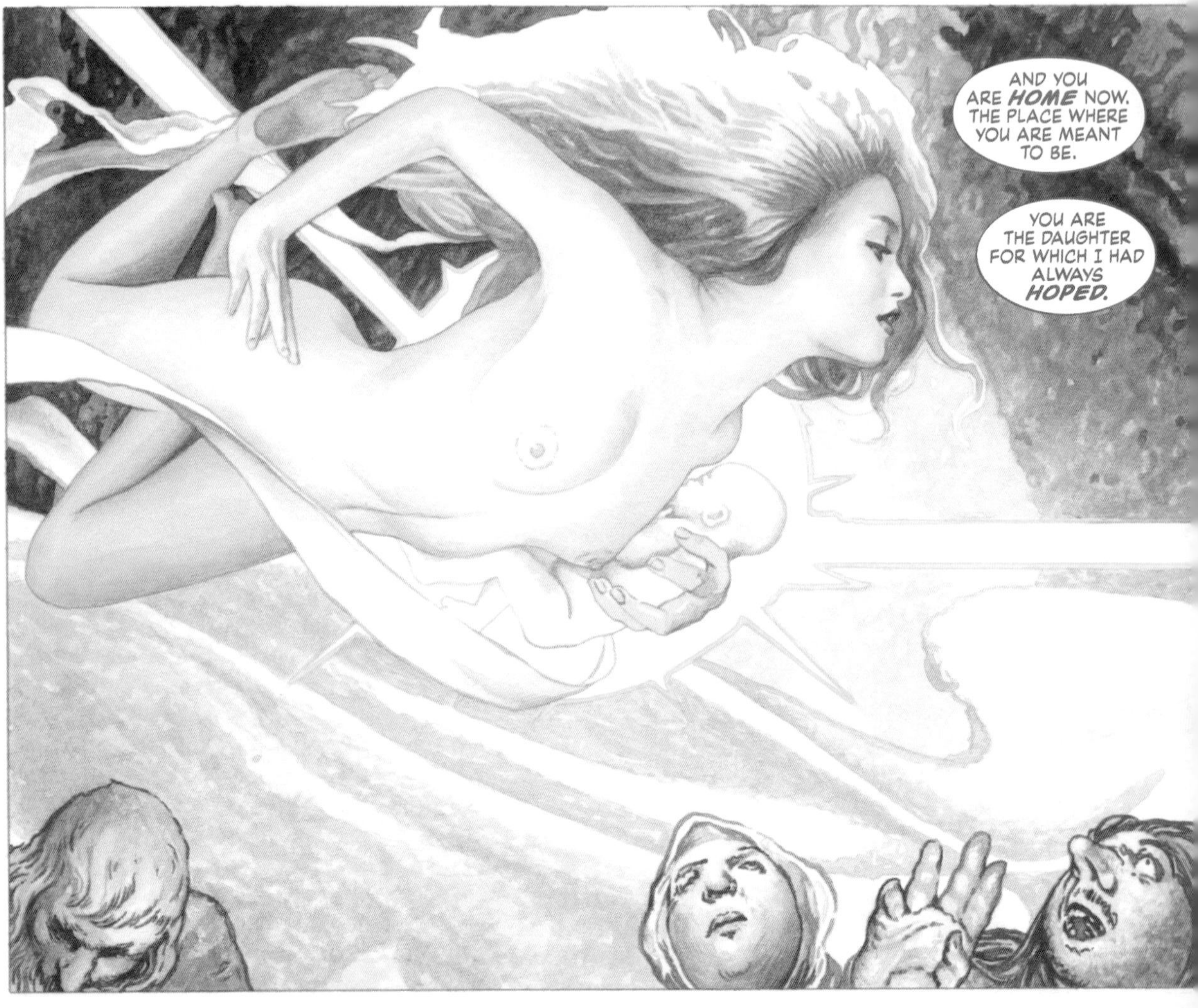
AND YOU ARE HOME NOW. THE PLACE WHERE YOU ARE MEANT TO BE.
YOU ARE THE DAUGHTER FOR WHICH I HAD ALWAYS HOPED.

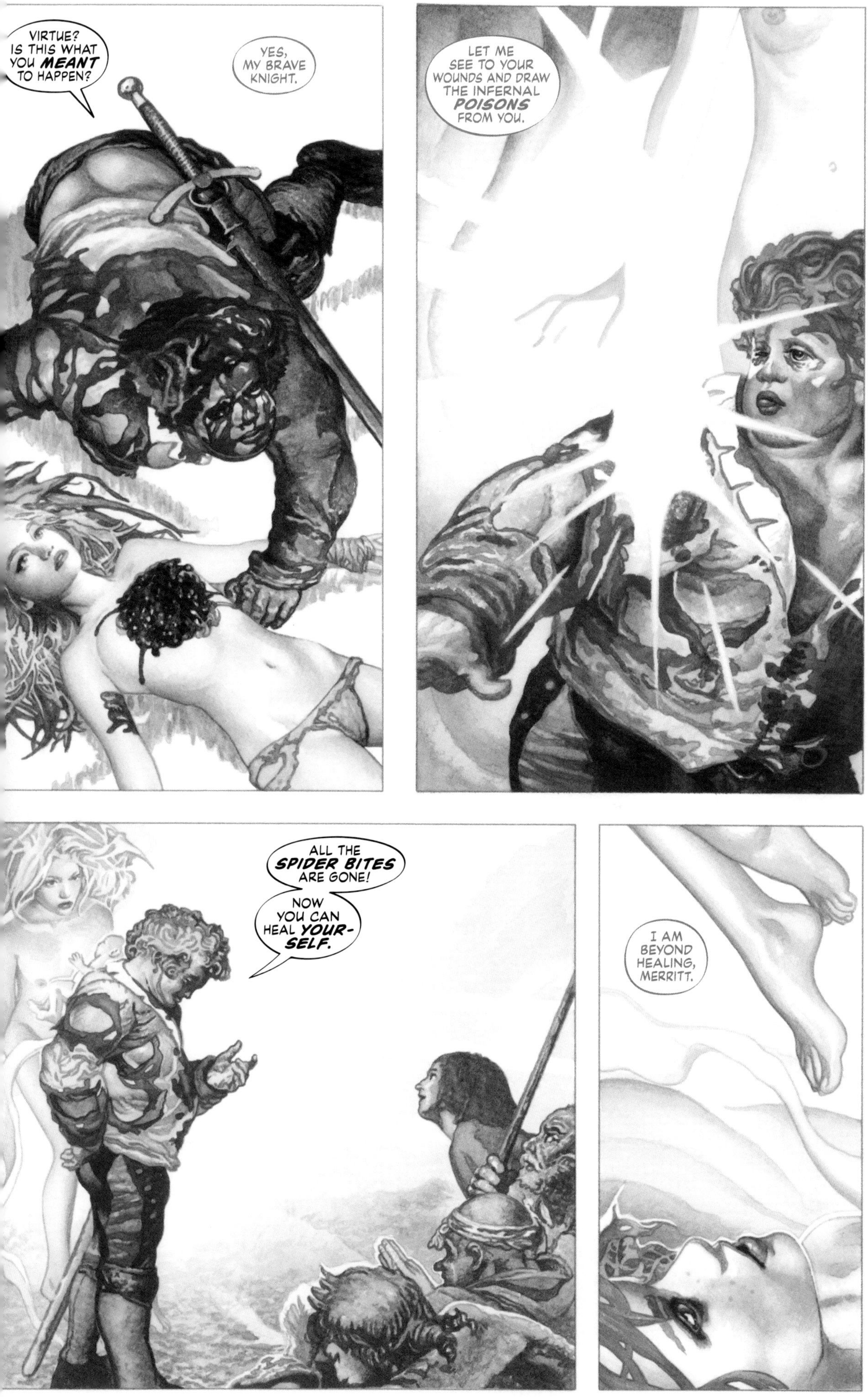
VIRTUE? IS THIS WHAT YOU **MEANT** TO HAPPEN?
YES, MY BRAVE KNIGHT.
LET ME SEE TO YOUR WOUNDS AND DRAW THE INFERNAL **POISONS** FROM YOU.
ALL THE **SPIDER BITES** ARE GONE!
NOW YOU CAN HEAL **YOUR-SELF.**
I AM BEYOND HEALING, MERRITT.

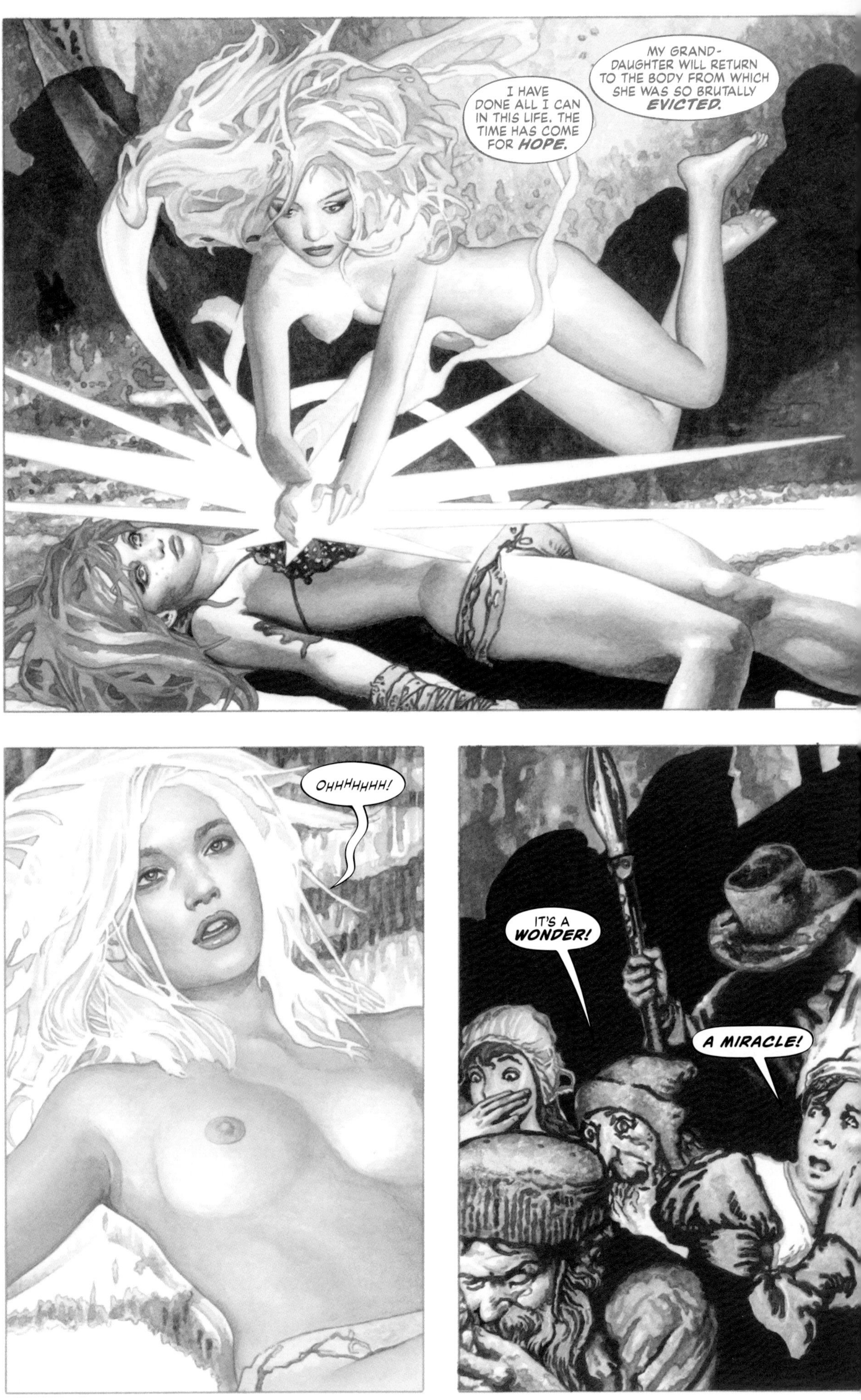
I HAVE DONE ALL I CAN IN THIS LIFE. THE TIME HAS COME FOR HOPE.
MY GRAND-DAUGHTER WILL RETURN TO THE BODY FROM WHICH SHE WAS SO BRUTALLY EVICTED.
OHHHHHHH!
IT'S A WONDER!
A MIRACLE!

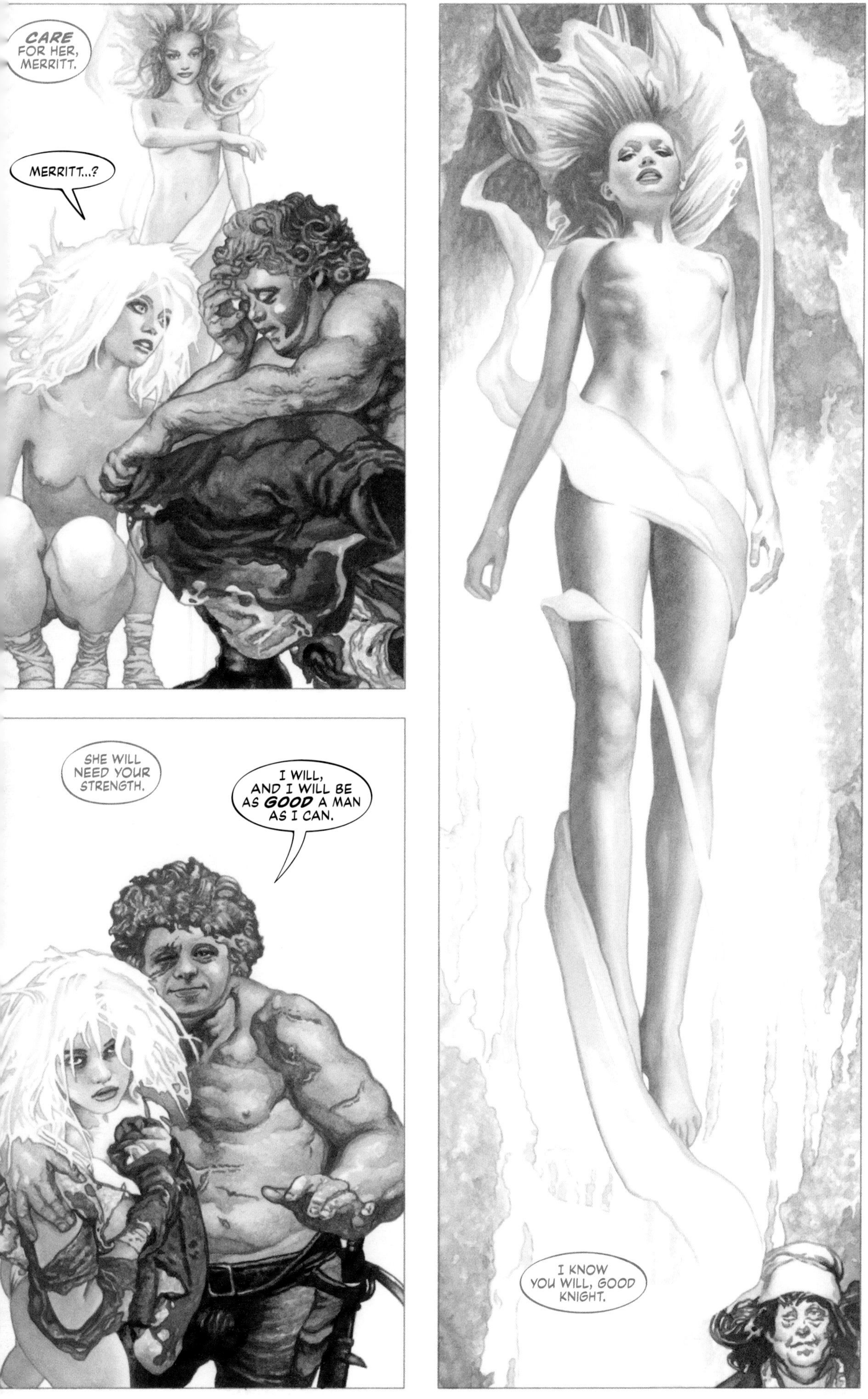
CARE FOR HER, MERRITT.
MERRITT...?
SHE WILL NEED YOUR STRENGTH.
I WILL, AND I WILL BE AS GOOD A MAN AS I CAN.
I KNOW YOU WILL, GOOD KNIGHT.

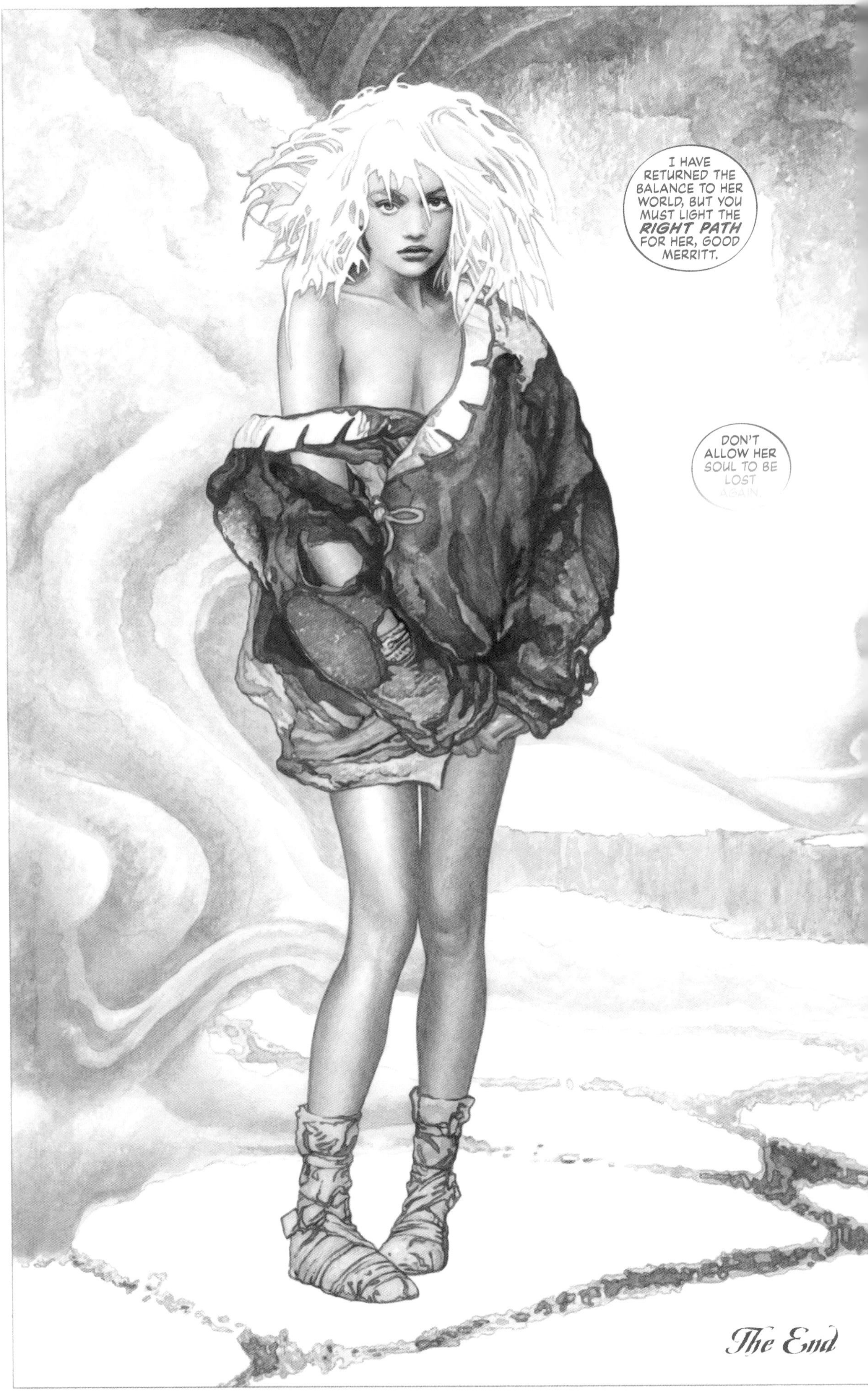
I HAVE RETURNED THE BALANCE TO HER WORLD, BUT YOU MUST LIGHT THE **RIGHT PATH** FOR HER, GOOD MERRITT.
DON'T ALLOW HER SOUL TO BE LOST AGAIN.
The End

Shame continues in 2017 with

Tales of Hope

Book 1

Turn the page for an exclusive preview.

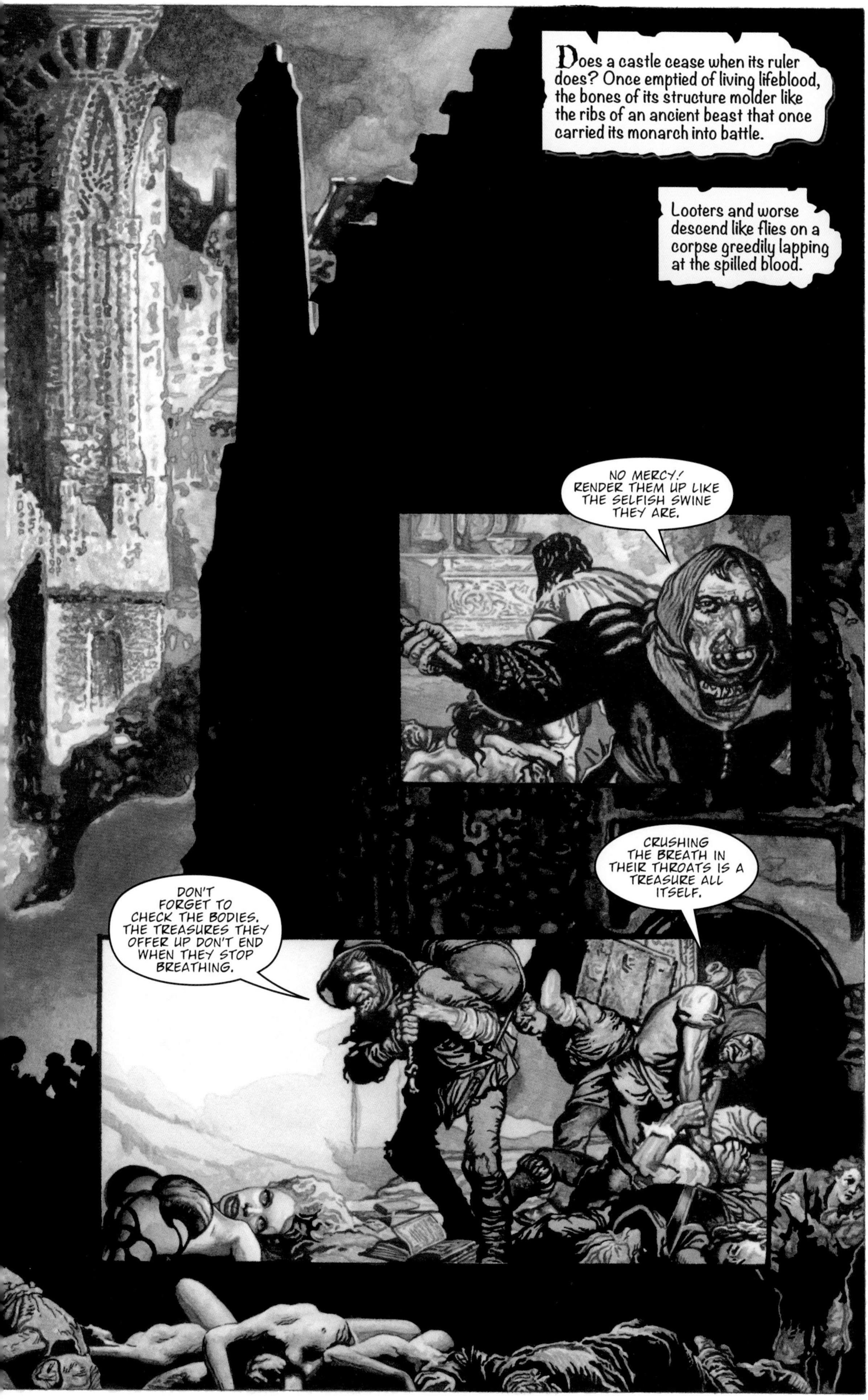
Does a castle cease when its ruler does? Once emptied of living lifeblood, the bones of its structure molder like the ribs of an ancient beast that once carried its monarch into battle.
Looters and worse descend like flies on a corpse greedily lapping at the spilled blood.
NO MERCY! RENDER THEM UP LIKE THE SELFISH SWINE THEY ARE.
DON'T FORGET TO CHECK THE BODIES. THE TREASURES THEY OFFER UP DON'T END WHEN THEY STOP BREATHING.
CRUSHING THE BREATH IN THEIR THROATS IS A TREASURE ALL ITSELF.

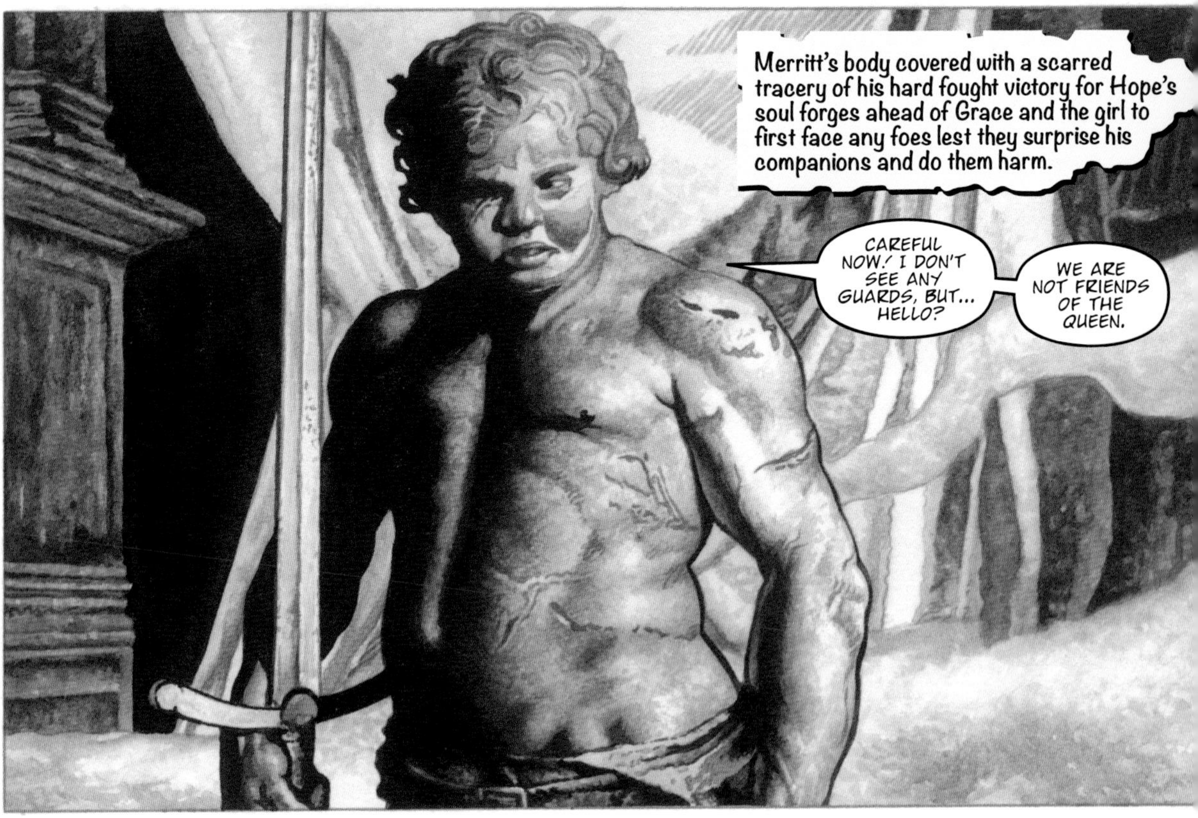
Merritt's body covered with a scarred tracery of his hard fought victory for Hope's soul forges ahead of Grace and the girl to first face any foes lest they surprise his companions and do them harm.
CAREFUL NOW! I DON'T SEE ANY GUARDS, BUT... HELLO?
WE ARE NOT FRIENDS OF THE QUEEN.

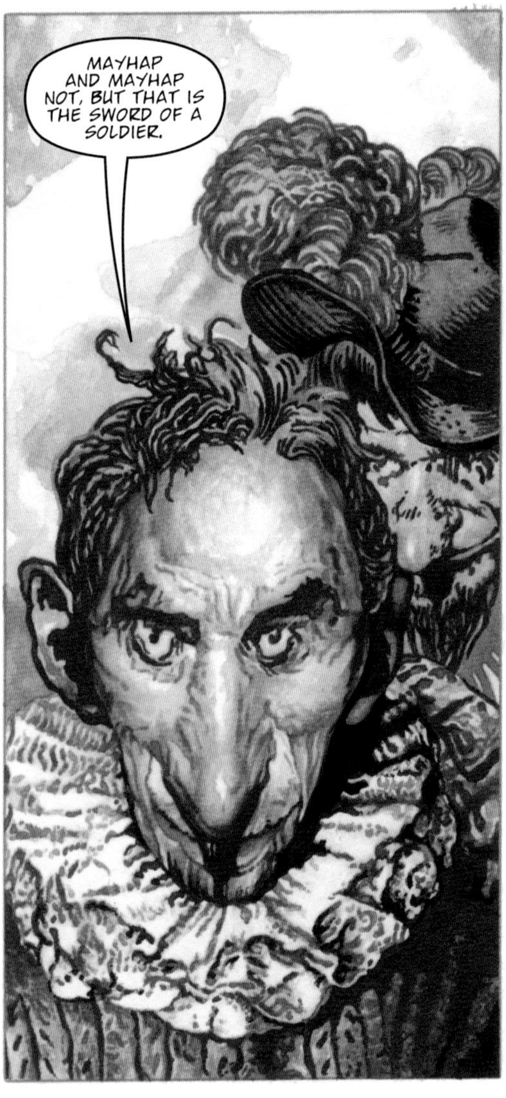
MAYHAP AND MAYHAP NOT, BUT THAT IS THE SWORD OF A SOLDIER.

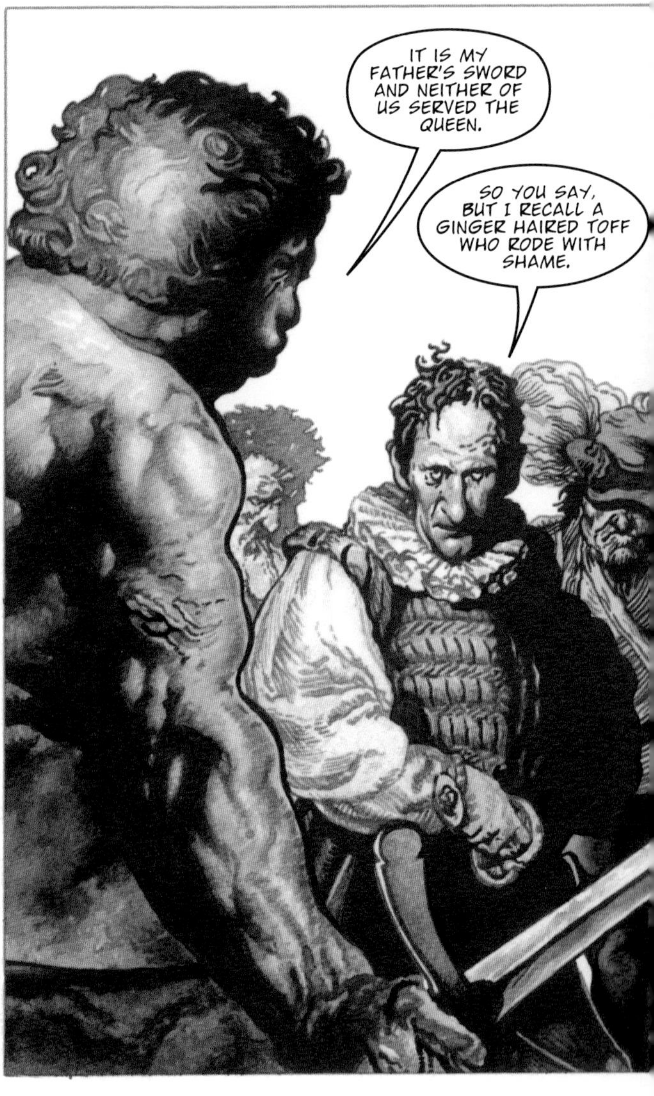
IT IS MY FATHER'S SWORD AND NEITHER OF US SERVED THE QUEEN.
SO YOU SAY, BUT I RECALL A GINGER HAIRED TOFF WHO RODE WITH SHAME.

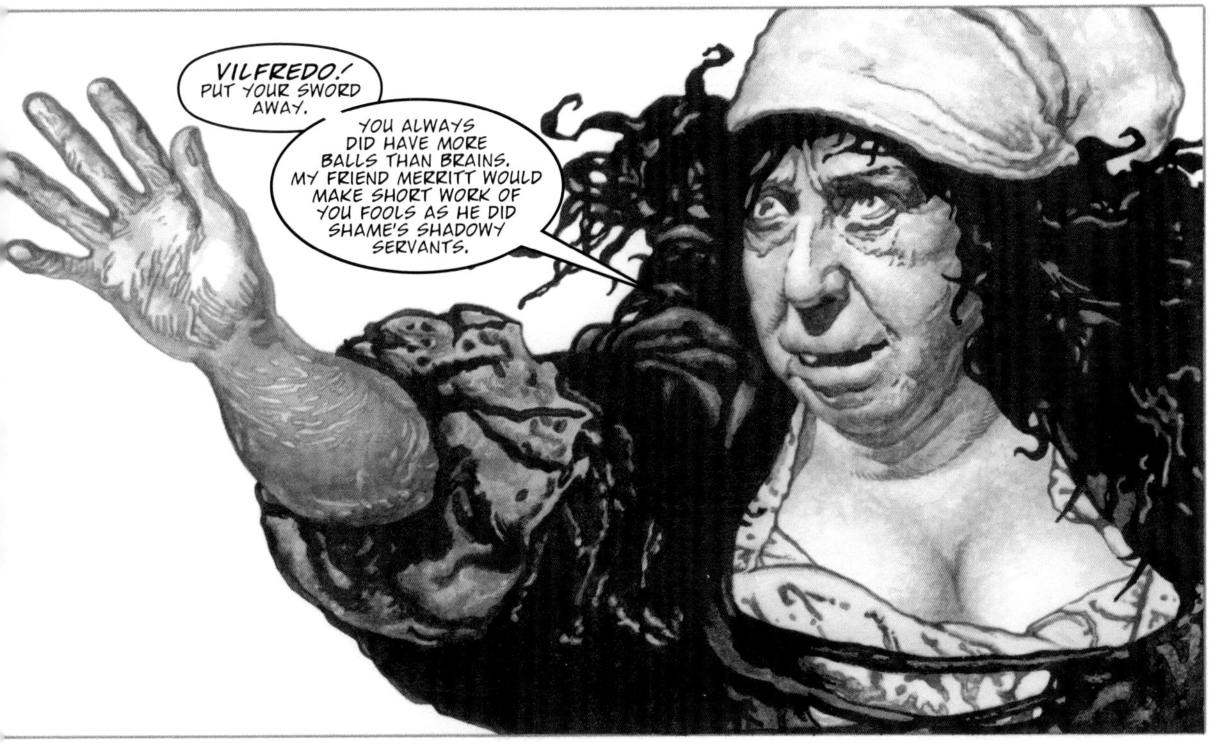
VILFREDO! PUT YOUR SWORD AWAY.
YOU ALWAYS DID HAVE MORE BALLS THAN BRAINS. MY FRIEND MERRITT WOULD MAKE SHORT WORK OF YOU FOOLS AS HE DID SHAME'S SHADOWY SERVANTS.

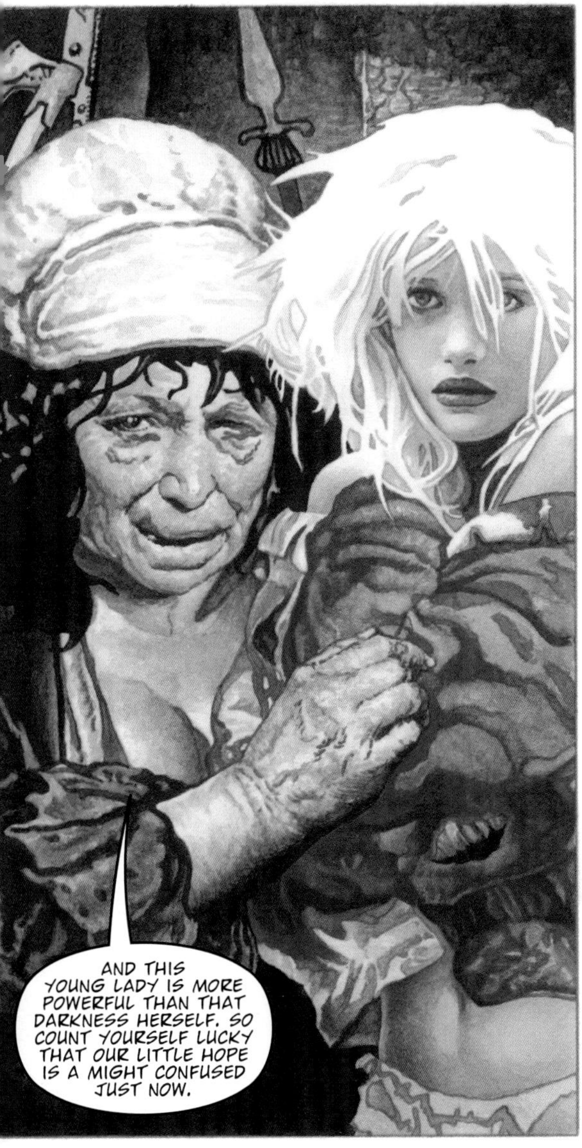
AND THIS YOUNG LADY IS MORE POWERFUL THAN THAT DARKNESS HERSELF. SO COUNT YOURSELF LUCKY THAT OUR LITTLE HOPE IS A MIGHT CONFUSED JUST NOW.

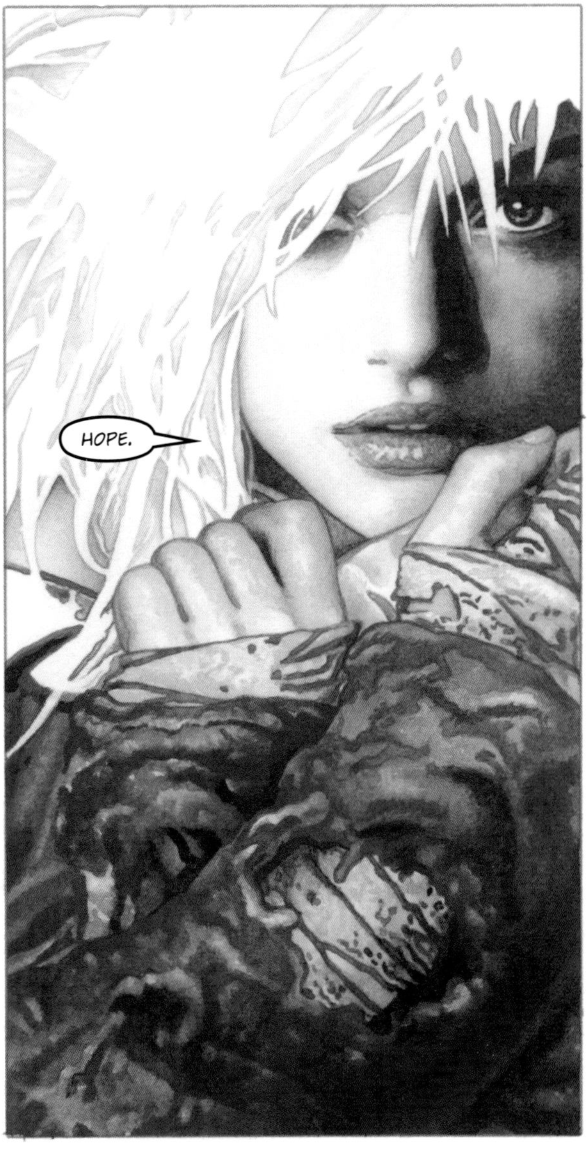
HOPE.

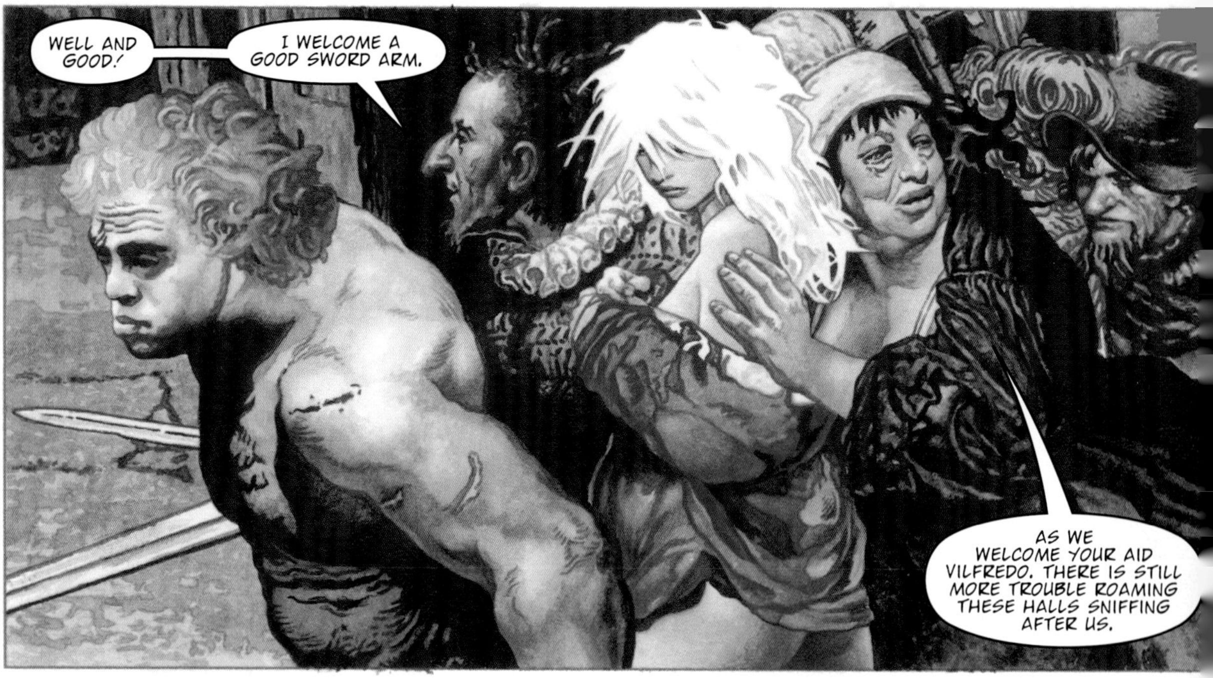
WELL AND GOOD!
I WELCOME A GOOD SWORD ARM.
AS WE WELCOME YOUR AID VILFREDO. THERE IS STILL MORE TROUBLE ROAMING THESE HALLS SNIFFING AFTER US.

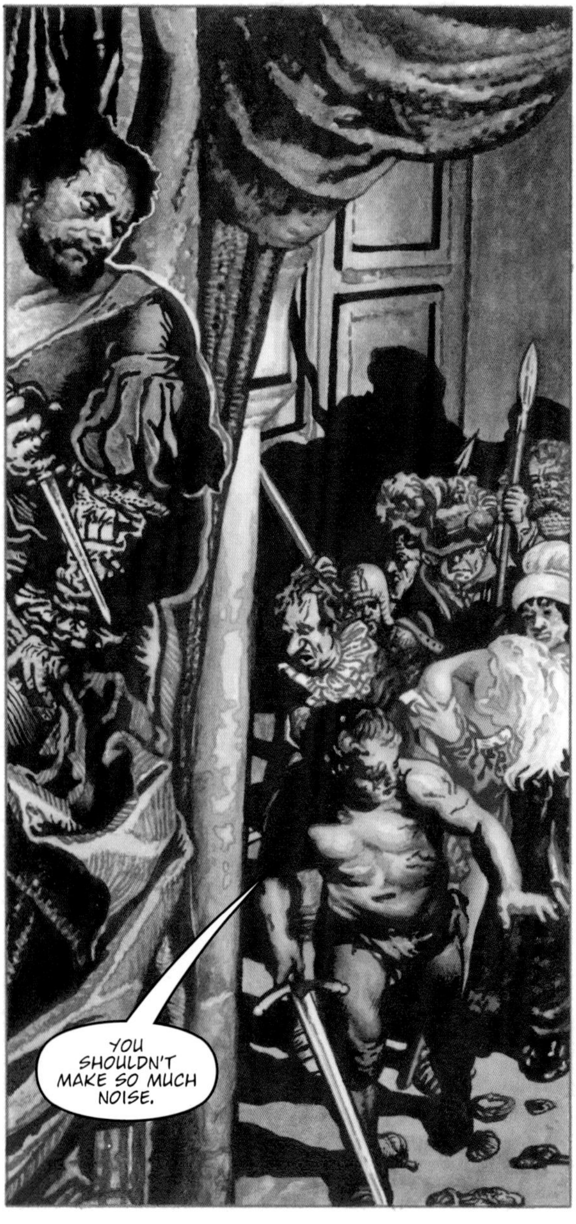
YOU SHOULDN'T MAKE SO MUCH NOISE.

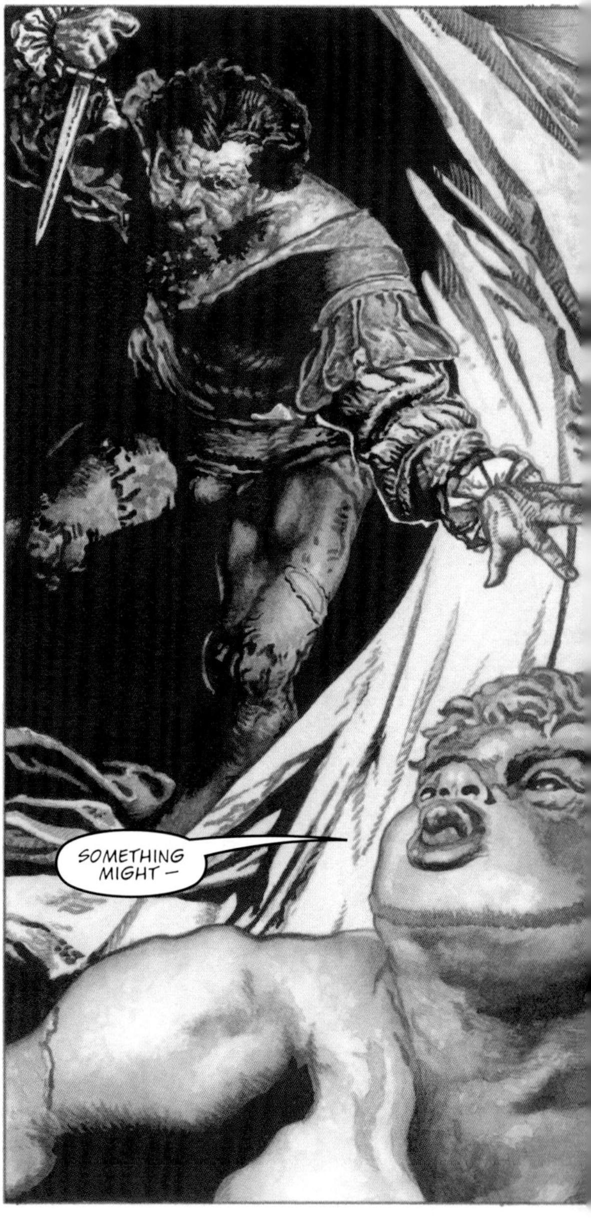
SOMETHING MIGHT —

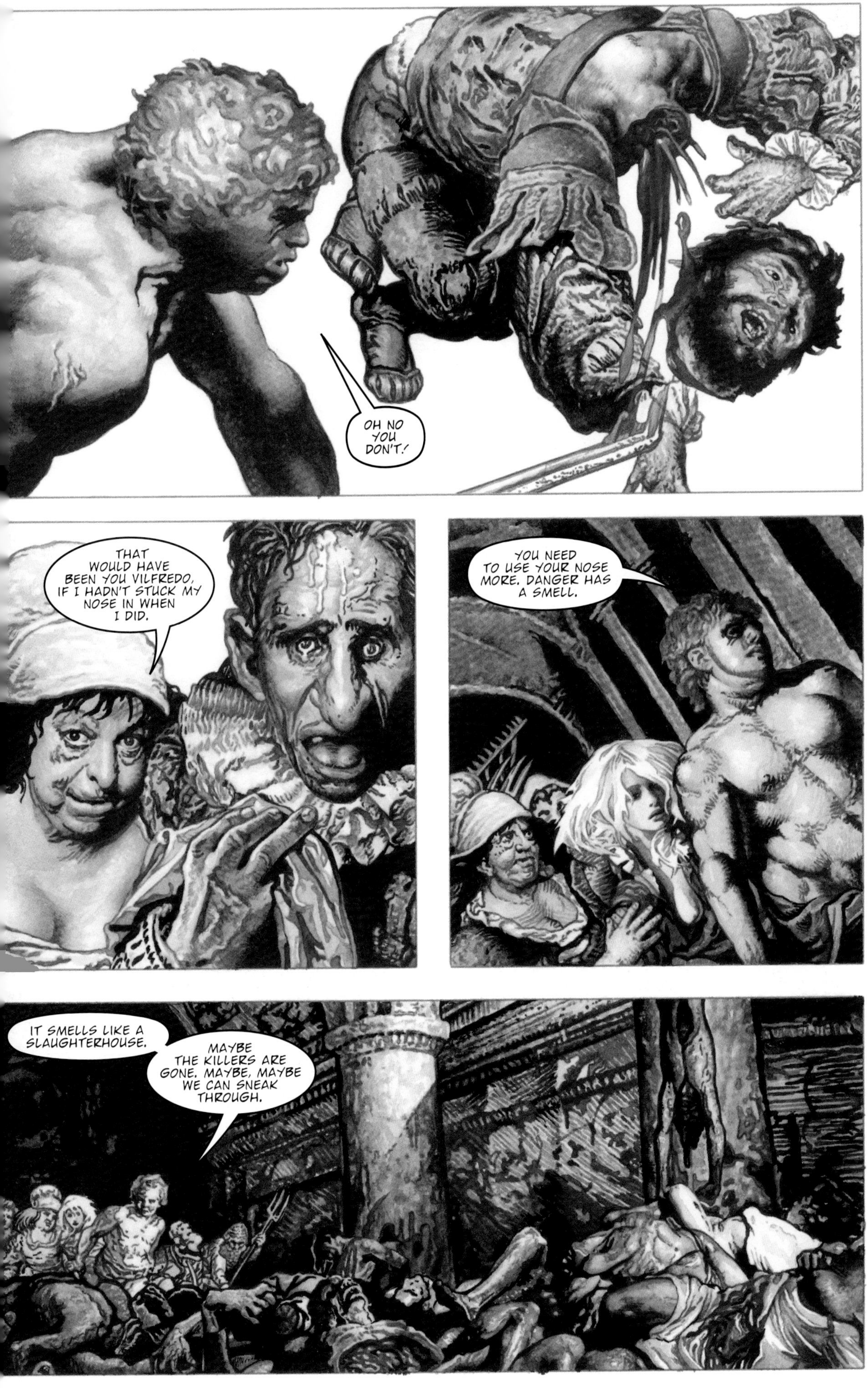
OH NO YOU DON'T!
THAT WOULD HAVE BEEN YOU VILFREDO, IF I HADN'T STUCK MY NOSE IN WHEN I DID.
YOU NEED TO USE YOUR NOSE MORE. DANGER HAS A SMELL.
IT SMELLS LIKE A SLAUGHTERHOUSE.
MAYBE THE KILLERS ARE GONE. MAYBE, MAYBE WE CAN SNEAK THROUGH.

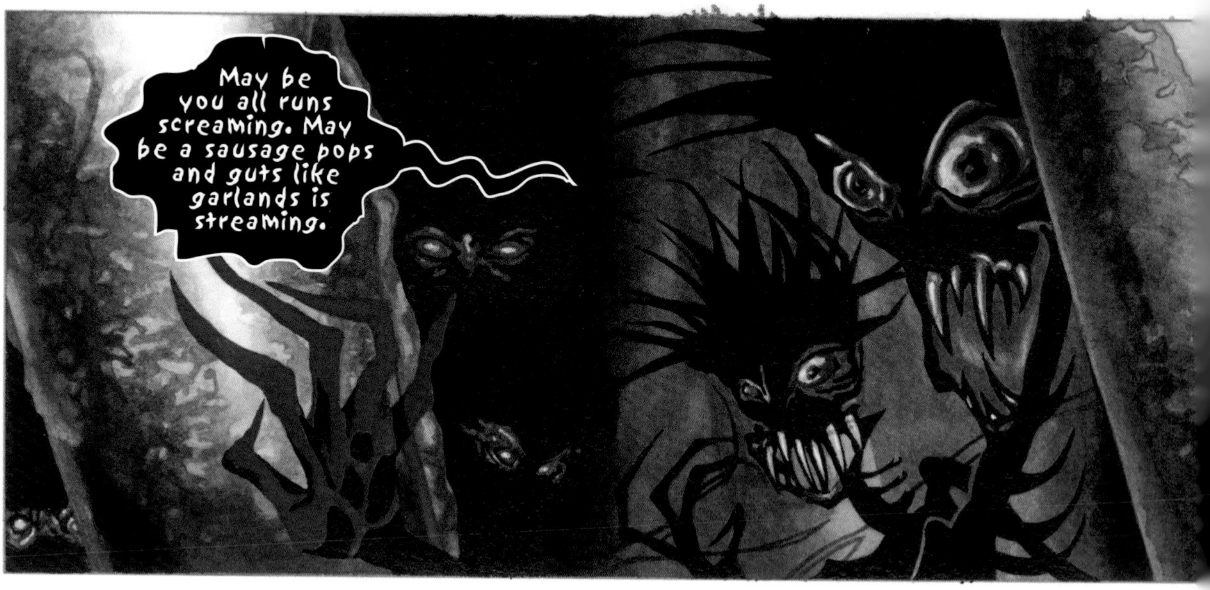
May be you all runs screaming. May be a sausage pops and guts like garlands is streaming.

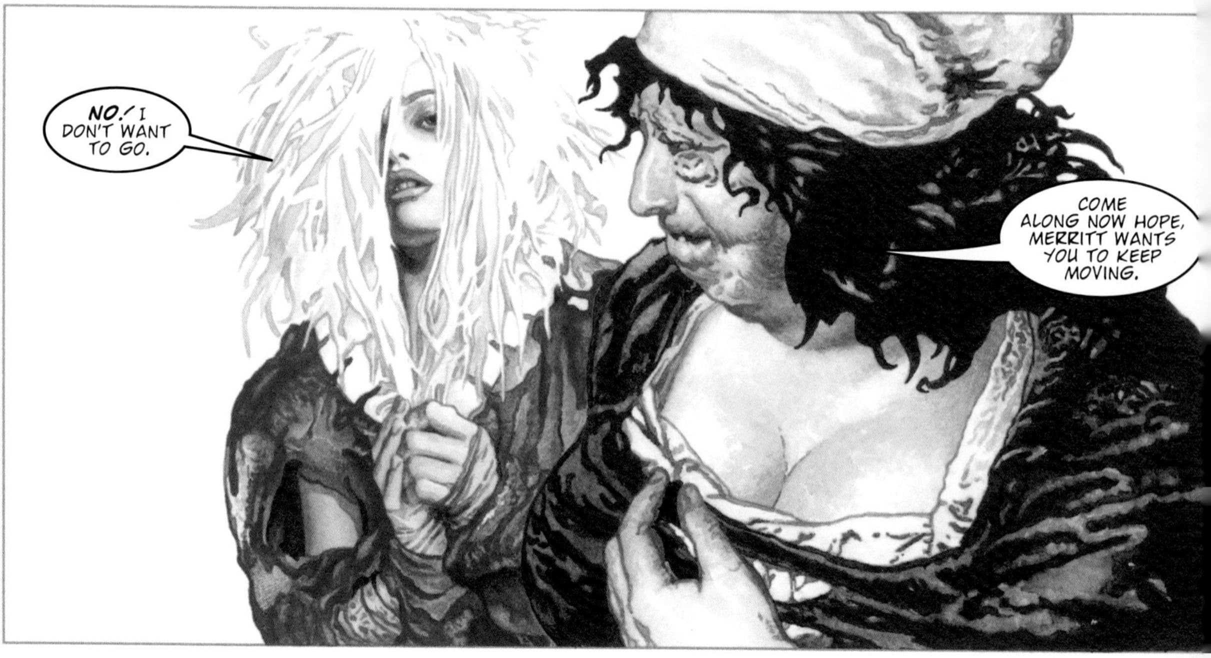
NO! I DON'T WANT TO GO.
COME ALONG NOW HOPE, MERRITT WANTS YOU TO KEEP MOVING.

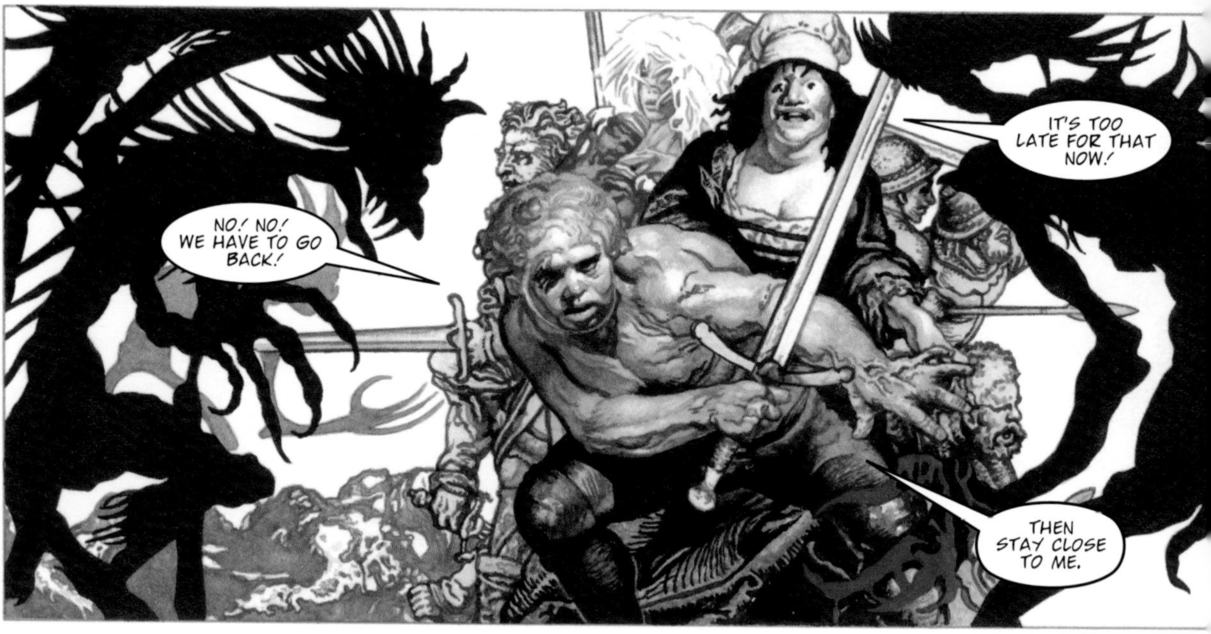
IT'S TOO LATE FOR THAT NOW!
NO! NO! WE HAVE TO GO BACK!
THEN STAY CLOSE TO ME.

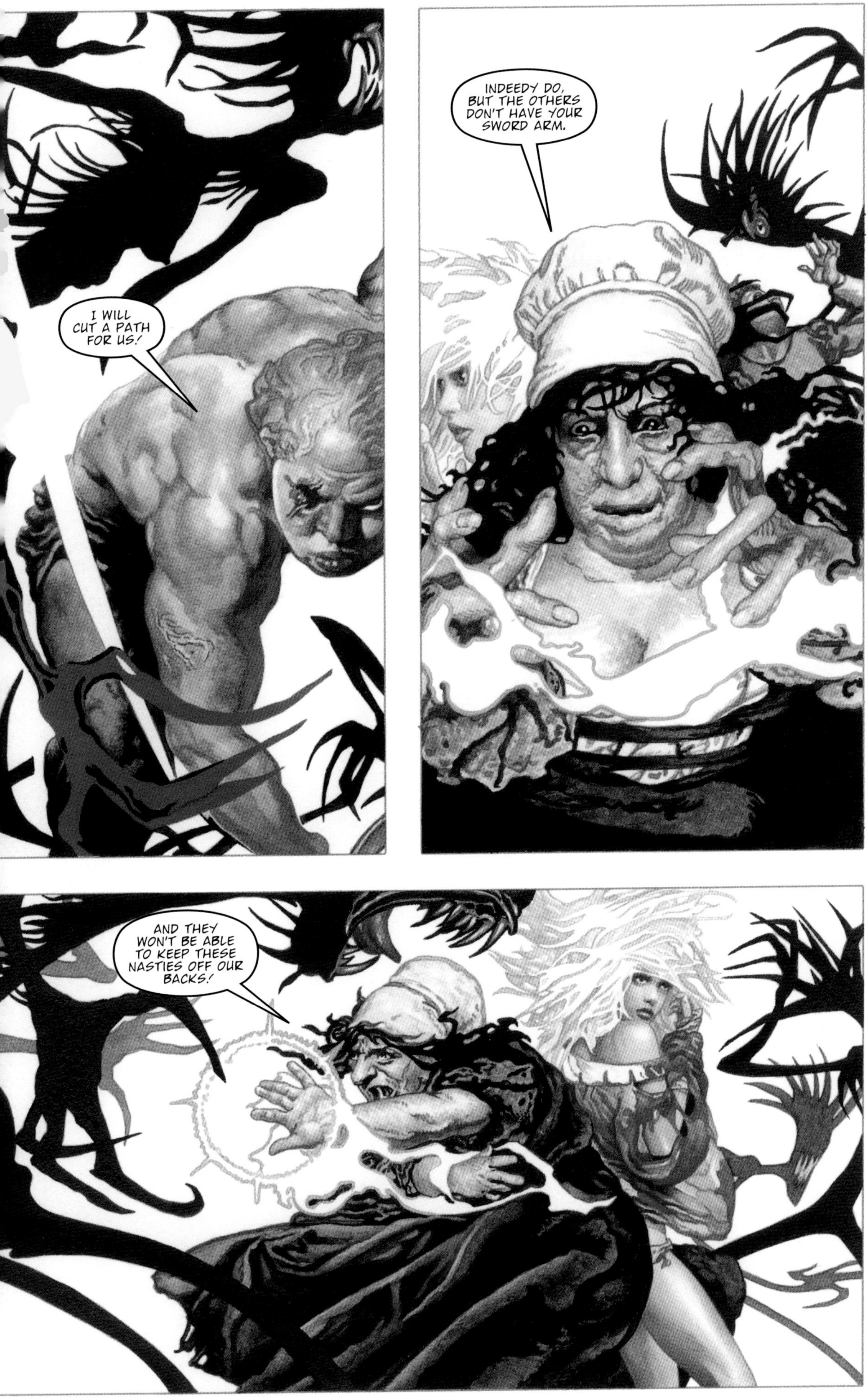
I WILL CUT A PATH FOR US!
INDEEDY DO, BUT THE OTHERS DON'T HAVE YOUR SWORD ARM.
AND THEY WON'T BE ABLE TO KEEP THESE NASTIES OFF OUR BACKS!

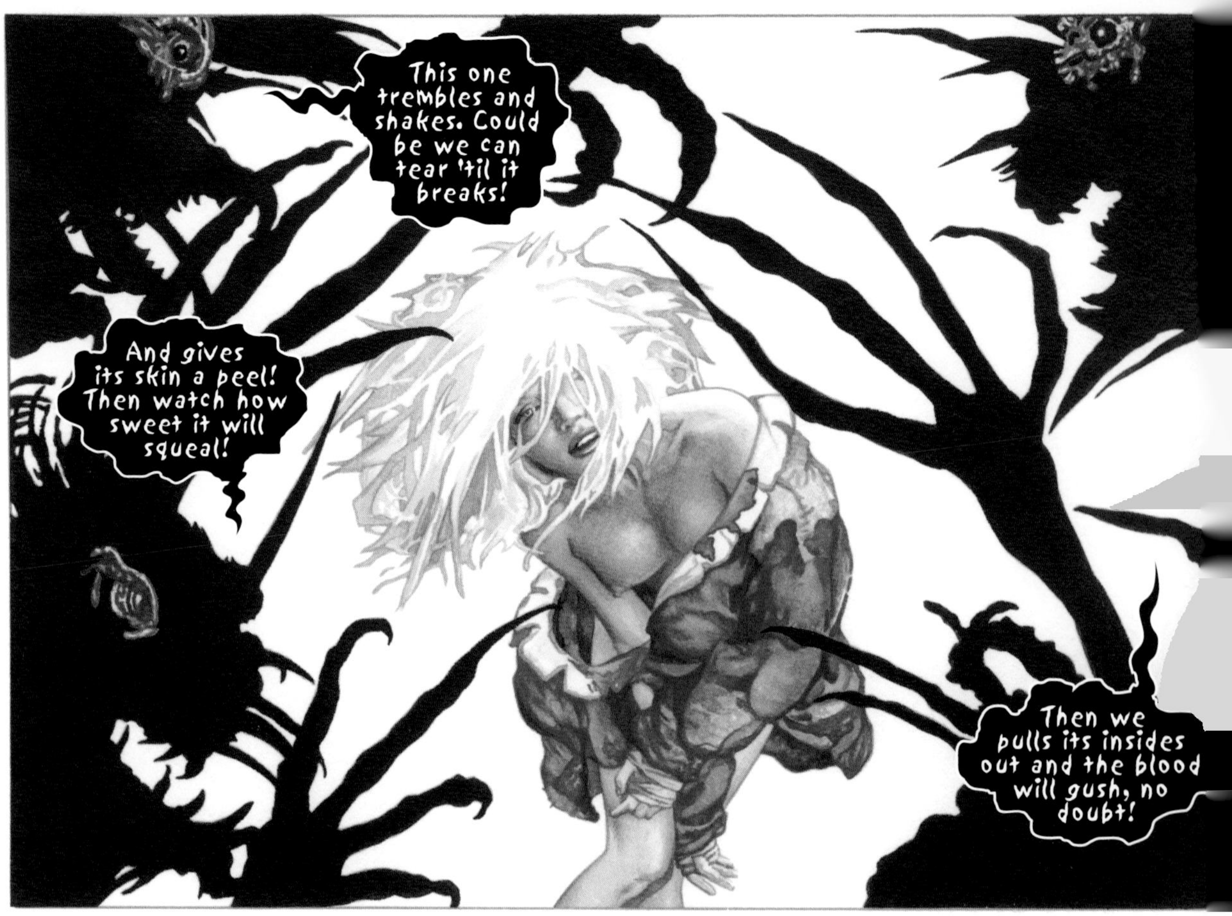
This one trembles and shakes. Could be we can tear 'til it breaks!
And gives its skin a peel! Then watch how sweet it will squeal!
Then we pulls its insides out and the blood will gush, no doubt!

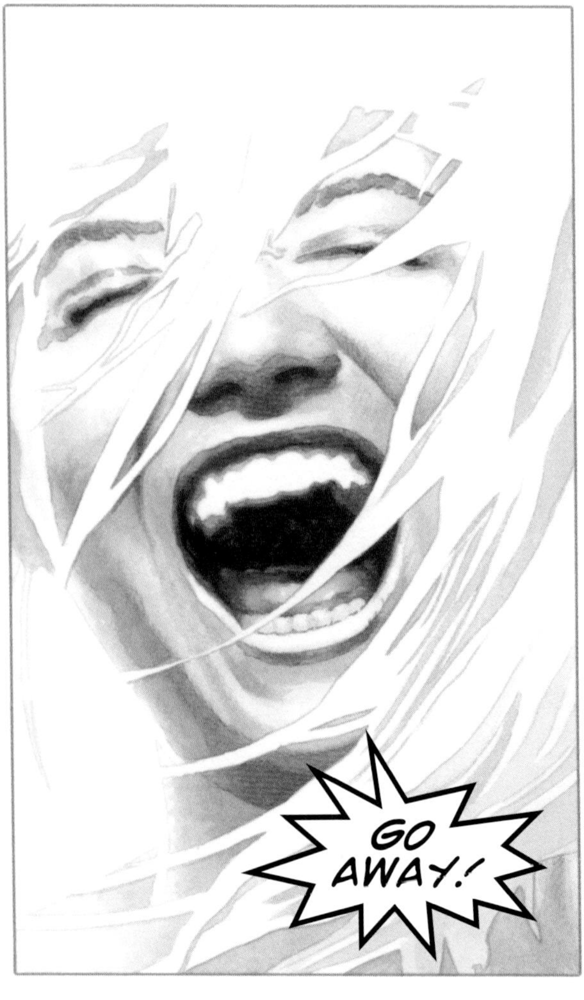
GO AWAY!

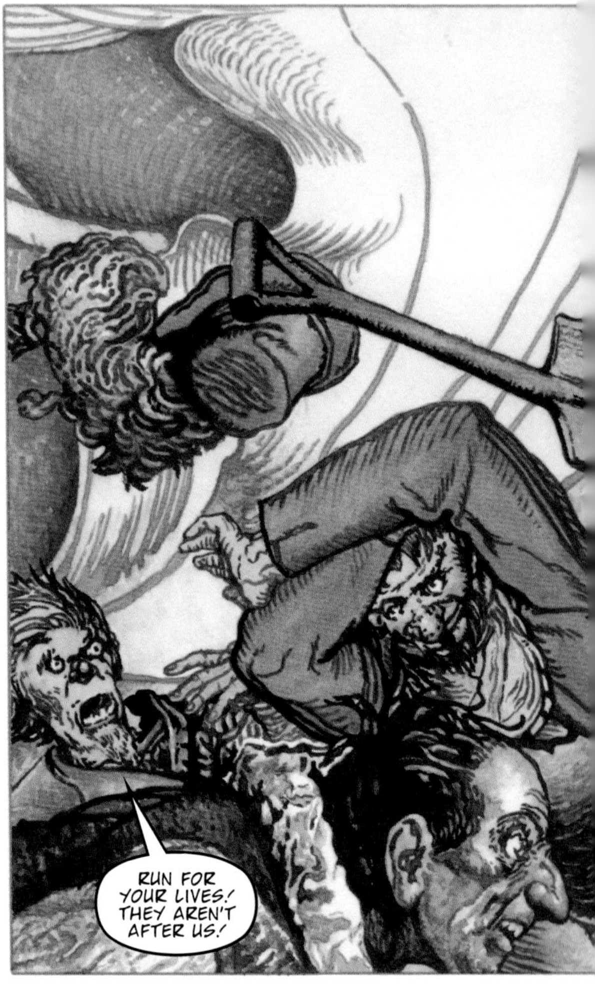
RUN FOR YOUR LIVES! THEY AREN'T AFTER US!

To be continued in

TALES OF HOPE
Book 1

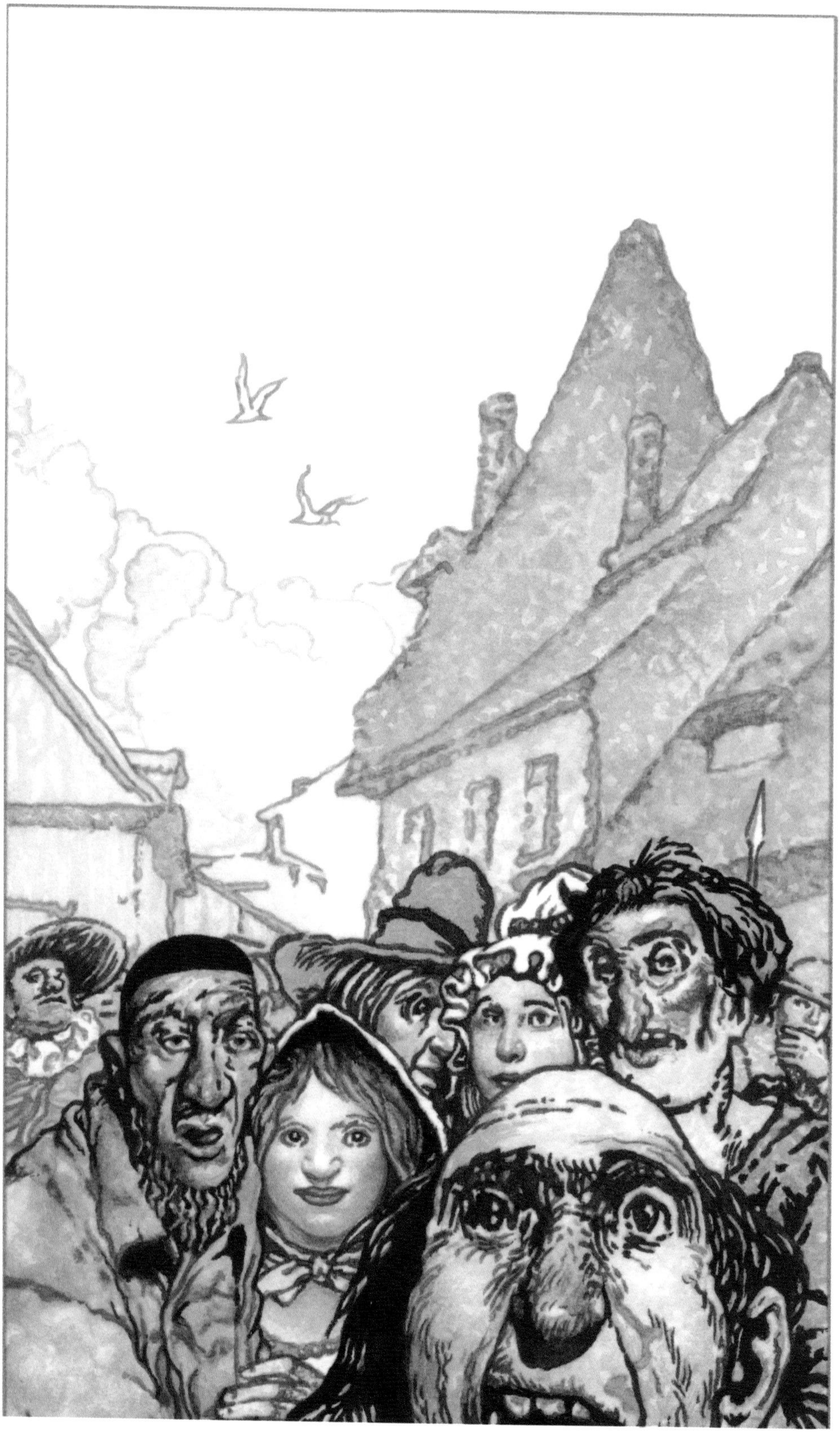

Discussing Shame

with Lovern Kindzierski, John Bolton and Alexander Finbow

Alexander Finbow:
When we published Shame: Conception, the first book in the trilogy, I recorded an interview with Lovern Kindzierski and John Bolton. It was bundled with the digital release originally.

LOVERN KINDZIERSKI ★ JOHN BOLTON
Shame
CONCEPTION
RENEGADE
ARTS ENTERTAINMENT

To mark the release of this collected edition of Shame, I spoke to the creators once more. With the three of us living thousands of miles apart - Lovern lived in Winnipeg at the time though he is now relocated to Montreal, John is in London, England - and I recorded our conversations from the Renegade Lair in the Rocky Mountains, via the magic of Skype. This interview gives a unique look into the artistic process involved in creating Shame, and a hint or two at what's coming later in the next trilogy.

John Bolton:
Can I start by saying something? It's been a book that I always wanted to work on. When Lovern first approached me with the story, I fell in love with it immediately. I had such belief in it that I did a couple of sample paintings. It was the first time I used a model, which is the girl in Conception. That's probably the first time I've ever had such strong belief that this book would happen one day.

Usually I would just get the story, do all the research and within three months have started painting. I approach everything I do like a film; the storyboards, lighting, characters and costume designs, all of it I've actually used 15 plus years since Lovern first approached me with the story. So, in a way this has been a totally unique experience for me.

Lovern Kindzierski:
I didn't know that John had sat on all of that reference for so long. It must have been tempting at times to dig into it. I hate to say this, but it was well worth the wait. Not that I ever want us to wait that long again!

AF: Looking back and comparing the original pencil approval layouts with the final art

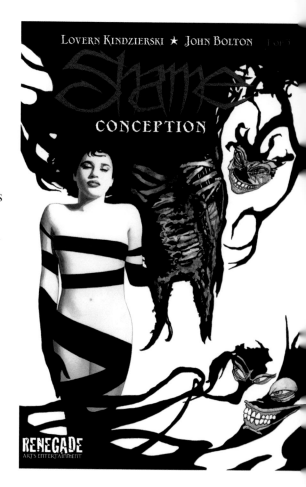

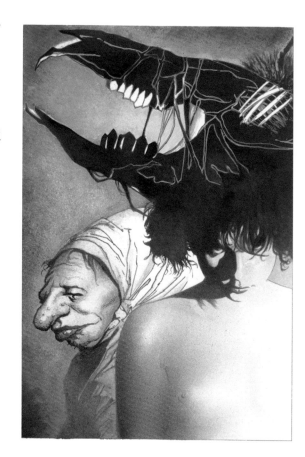

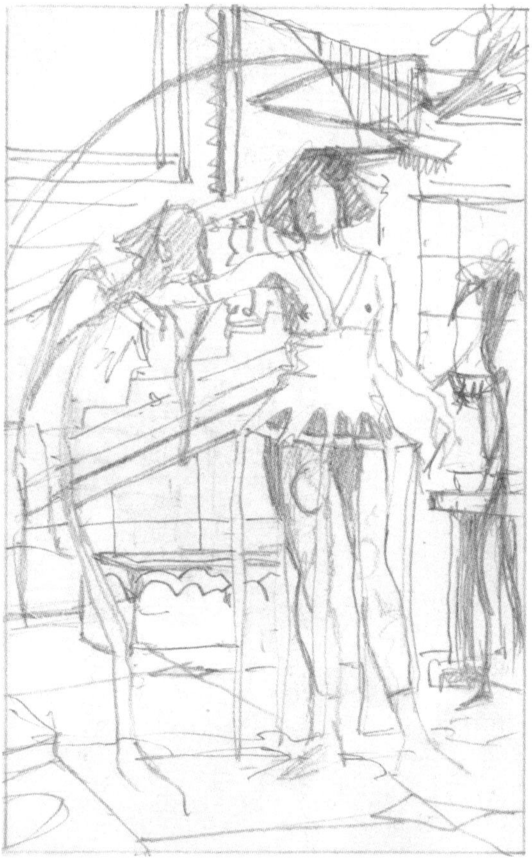

pages, in almost every single panel you can see the watercolour detail matches almost exactly what you sketched out originally. You had a very clear idea in your mind of what the story should look like from the beginning, didn't you?

JB: I never go half-heartedly once I've taken on a project. Sitting down, scribbling over the script and coming up with ideas. Then once I transfer those to the breakdown book, which is just a small A5 sketch book, those are the ideas that are kind of set in concrete. When I work in pencil, the reason why it is so detailed is I am trying to work out the colours as well, and maybe that's the difference because most comic book artists don't see the whole process through. They're on one stage or maybe two stages, but then somebody else comes in.

AF: Think back to when Renegade came onboard, you finally get the green light on the book and we're 100% committed to publishing Shame, from an artistic point of view what was your next step?

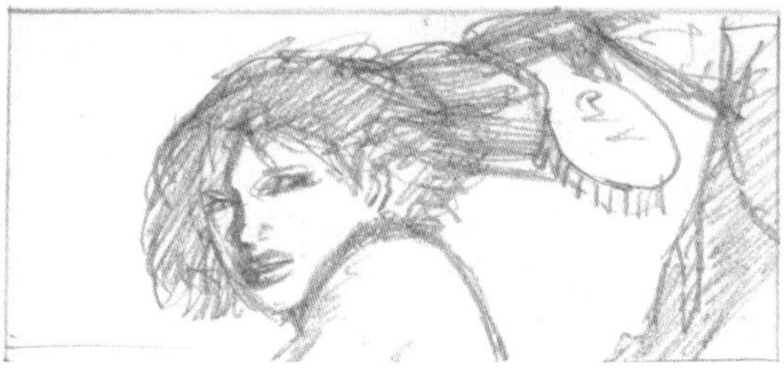

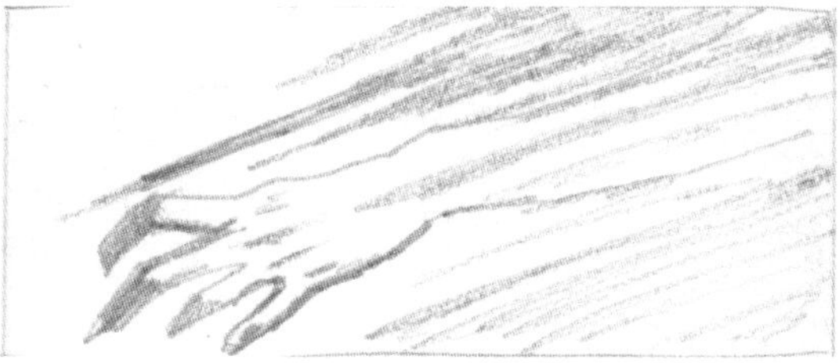

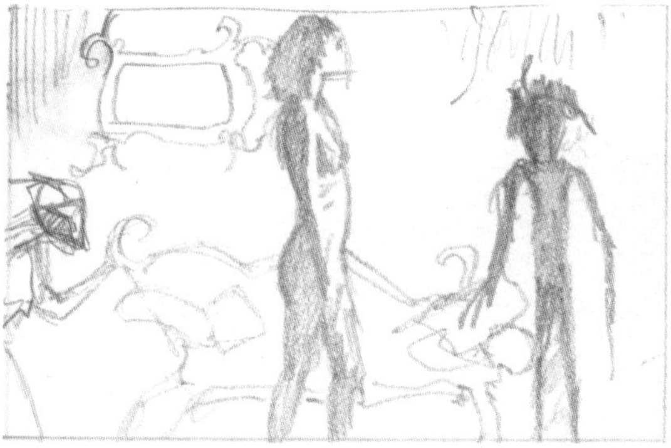

JB: I decided to go back to an older technique, watercolour, but I hadn't used it for a good five years and it's a notoriously difficult medium to work in because you can't make a mistake. The most important thing for me then was to get the right paper to paint on.

AF: Knowing that watercolour is especially challenging and time-consuming, why was it important for you to work in this medium on the Shame trilogy?

JB: What I like about watercolour is that sometimes the technique can be really obvious and you do it for a reason, for an effect. You can't get that with anything else, where you allow the watercolour to bleed into another colour or not. I could create both the subtlety and the graphic approach that I wanted.

LK: I like the bit in Conception where she's

by the pond and you've really done a lot of wet on wet texture. The paper is really inviting of it and caught all the subtleties you had. I also love how you've really captured how the light is going through the light washes and actually bouncing off the paper. It just adds another level of brilliance.

AF: John, you mentioned that you've made the colour choices before you even start painting. Can you expand on that for us?

JB: When I start painting I have a colour theme for each chapter, which may only be one or two pages. I think colours are so important to create moods. Looking at Conception now, you try to come up with a rosy looking beginning, using those soft warm colours that convey happiness and security. When Slur appears, the colour begins to drain out of the pages. Then we're back in the sunlight with the dryads and Shame playing ball.

LK: I really like your use of white as a colour.

JB: It's taken me a long time to understand that white is actually a colour. You create a much airier use of space when you start dropping colour out and just leave it white.

AF: It's very effective, and your frame composition works so well.

JB: In Conception, where they are playing ball, I cut one of the dryad's eyes off completely in the third frame to create a sense of height. There is this approach I take in the use of frames, that I will use wide angle frames to slow things down and small thin frames to speed things up.

AF: Changing tack here, what time period that relates to our own history do you see the books set in?

JB: I wanted to have a foothold in reality and I was thinking of 1895 Paris, or the way Cedric Gibbons would art direct Dickens. It

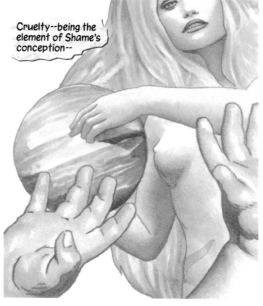

Cruelty--being the element of Shame's conception--

doesn't really have a precise place in time, it's plundered from different times, a bit like the movie Delicatessen. It's presumably set in the future and at the same time everything is 100 years old. You still have this combination of elements and you use whatever you think makes it work.

LK: I tried to make all of this very scary, like the idea of children losing their shadows to demons, but John has kept the magic rolling along in this surreal world so that we just move along with them.

JB: I thought the Shadows were a brilliant creation Lovern, they were quite difficult too. I didn't want them to be flat but at the same time they, if you pardon the pun, had to have some kind of body to them. It's completely surreal having mouths and eyes and fluffy hairstyles on these Shadows.

LK: The first time I talked about Slur, I said I was thinking of something bloated, and then you came back with your ideas and I instantly forgot about the bloated thing. It was important to me that he had sewn his eyes shut and that he was hermaphroditic. I love the idea that he had removed one of the breasts and it all just fit with him being the demon on ignorance, so I bow to your correct design decisions.

JB: I think Slur was an interesting challenge. I always see tall, skinny things as kind of a menace because they tower over something, whereas if someone is fatter you feel that you can just run away from them, you know they're not going to catch up!

LK: Well, we have ample opportunity for a variety of shapes and forms in this third book.

AF: Conception is sexy in a classical, sedate way whereas Pursuit becomes much more intense. Can you talk us through how you approached the reincarnated Virtue?

JB: I think Virtue is sexy. One has to try and convey the fact that she's on her own, she's not inhibited. It's too restricting to have her running around naked, but for all intents and purposes that's probably what she would do. I needed something very striking about her so I gave her red hair in disarray.

LK: I think the second book moves it into a more mature level with the characters, where the sexuality now becomes a real element of all of their stories.

JB: There was an innocence in the first book that we no longer have because Virtue still retains knowledge of who she was. While she looks completely different, she's still the same person with the maturity and the knowledge that she acquired to reach that age.

I wanted to make reference to the last page of Pursuit, the second book. I was trying to make her vulnerable by chopping her hair off a bit and leaving her naked, and somehow the impact is even greater because you didn't include any dialogue or captions.

LK: If I'd said anything it would have just undercut the image. What I write goes to you, and then you enlarge it and make it real. I'm then scripting after and if what you've done is so complete there's really nothing for me to say. I think I'm smart enough to know to get out of the way when I should!

JB: When I left her naked at the end of the second book, I realised I had to do something in the third book. That I couldn't really have her running around naked and so that's why I included that skeleton with a few rags on in the foreground on page three. We all know that she couldn't nip off to the shops! I suppose that's what makes graphic novels more interesting, the fact that when you first get one you read through it because you love the story and perhaps just take in the pictures as a secondary thing, and then you've got that option to go back and just pick out details.

AF: We have a lot more nudity in the third book. What was the thinking behind the more revealing costumes and scenes?

LK: Shame enhances her intimidation with her nakedness. She wears those revealing gowns that eroticise her nudity, whereas Virtue is trying to cover herself up with these little tatters. When Shame exposes her mother in front of the demon, whom she knows her mother despises and reviles, it is a humiliation, another way to twist the knife.

JB: With this you're not tied to the laws of respectability. Shame is that powerful, that strong and that independent. She can do whatever she wants. To present herself in front of Slur, her father, I just thought that it's saying that she doesn't care, that these are my weapons and I use them.

LK: One of Shame's greatest weapons is her beauty, so she's going to use everything at her disposal to make herself the most desirable woman.

AF: Let us go back to the start of Redemption, and your thinking of the artistic process for the final book in the trilogy.

JB: When we start the third book, Merritt's been seduced, advised and dressed by Shame, so he looks more of a popinjay than he did in the previous book. As he becomes more Merritt-like once more, and this seems a bit clichéd, but we have him becoming the white knight protecting Virtue.

When we enter into hell, thanks to Lovern with the idea of the barren landscape, I decided to take a more graphic approach and just have solid black and white shapes without any real detail. I like that contradiction of realistic characters and cut out shapes for the background as it gives it more space and makes the page look less complicated. I think if I have any problems with my own work it is that there's a lot of detail. I try to reduce it as much as possible.

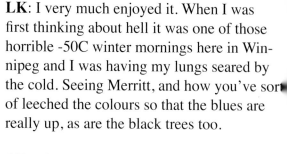

LK: I very much enjoyed it. When I was first thinking about hell it was one of those horrible -50C winter mornings here in Winnipeg and I was having my lungs seared by the cold. Seeing Merritt, and how you've sort of leeched the colours so that the blues are really up, as are the black trees too.

AF: Did you both approach Redemption in the same way you did the first two books, given that this is the third time you've delved into the world?

JB: No, because the story's so different. I think the approach has to be different because the requirements are different. It all comes out of the story.

LK: For me, the third book grows from the first two so it sets the direction. Granted there's a lot possible in this world but still, there are limits.

JB: I remember when we first talked about Shame all those years ago. We were both inspired; we were both using Mervyn Peake as a reference and Gormenghast.

LK: This world is more encompassing. I'd like to think that I've opened that door in the story. So much of what happens in the first book is because Virtue's personality controls the spell that makes Cradle, and in the second book it's Shame's personality that controls it, and in the next series nobody controls it…

JB: I find that exciting. That even in principle you're drawing similar characters to what you've seen in the previous books, but now they've developed and Virtue has to deal with all of them.

LK: You're making it so much more exciting. The way you've moved Merritt from how we see him in the second book to the way he appears at the beginning of the third…and people looking at him at the end of the third book won't recognize him from any of his

other appearances.

JB: Ultimately what we have is something that I'm incredibly happy about and I can honestly say this is the best work I've ever produced. Not because it's current, I know prior to this it would have been Menz Insana and maybe Marada, but now I understand how to really use watercolours, and I feel as though I'm going from strength to strength as an artist and storyteller.

LK: When the next trilogy comes out I hope the readers realise we're building on strengths, the story's getting richer and we're trying to do more all the time. I don't think anyone will ever see this story honed in. It's fun to pose that question "so you think you know Cradle, think again."

AF: The cat is well and truly out of the bag regarding a second Shame series, so let's turn our attentions to the next trilogy, without giving away too much of the plot.

LK: While Shame has been trying to take over the world, we haven't seen what has been happening elsewhere. They say that energy never goes away it just changes form, so there's a lot of mystical energies there. Things like Cradle were given life and then everybody just left. What happens to that great, grand dome when Merritt took Virtue away, and what was it exactly? If there was a world where Shame lived, who else is there like that? I'm just answering and building on those questions. The power's starting to leak out and grow, so I think that people will be very aware that it's a bad place and it's getting bigger.

JB: I'll treat the next trilogy with as much enthusiasm and excitement as I have with the previous three books. Even though it's an enormous chunk out of my life every day, it's still a joy to work on.

AF: Lovern, John, your passion for Shame is evident when we read the books. It truly is a fascinating project and I have thoroughly enjoyed working with you as your editor. I cannot wait to be a part of and publish the second series. Gentlemen, thank you for your insights. **Tales of Hope** will be available in 2017.

From the imagination of Lovern Kindzierski and John Bolton

September 2009, as I drove over Calgary's Bow river, Lovern called and pitched Shame to me for the first time. I was intrigued by the quick pitch and Lovern followed up with the outline for the series. Along with John's involvement, it was enough to persuade me to sign on to publish the book. This is the original outline Lovern sent over to me.

The world of Shame is one of dark enchantments, of captivating beauty, and enormous ugliness. It is a world that resembles our Medieval earth but this appearance is only superficial. In Shame's domain all of our myths and folklore are a reality. Elves, fairies, goblins, bogeymen, and all manner of fey spirits populate this place.

The main characters who appear in the story are: Shame, the beautiful and malignant daughter of Virtue; Virtue, the kind, righteous old woman whose one selfish moment brought the curse of her daughter upon her; Slur: the Shadow of Ignorance who is Shame's father.

Virtue, has the purest of souls. She is ancient and the most powerful white sorceress of her age. Virtue had lived her life for the benefit of the poor and sick of the world. She had loved and cared for many children but never one of her own. She had bestowed her healing gifts upon many. Surely she deserved a gift of her Creator? So she had prayed that she would have a little girl of her own.

However it was not bright Good which shone upon her wish, but a dark Evil which fell upon it, for this wish was a selfish one. Slur, the Shadow of Ignorance, saw his opportunity and appealed to the Great Darkness to grant Virtue her wish. She would have a child, a daughter, as dark as Virtue was light.

As soon as Virtue felt the child quickening in her, she consulted her divinations and learned that her daughter would be a most beautiful woman and the most wicked person the world had ever seen. Virtue could not suffer such evil to be loosed upon the world. However, being good, she herself could not harm this helpless being growing inside of her. Virtue raised her white magic and sought out a special place for her daughter. A place where her daughter would be safe from the world and the world would be safe from her Shame.

Virtue got herself to a great dark forest and, with the aid of her magic, made way to the heart of the black swamp at its centre. And it was there that she made a magical cottage naming it Cradle. It was in this haven of mystery that Shame was born. As quickly after the birth as Virtue could manage, she bound the sprites and forest spirits to care for the child, and turned her back on the babe. As Virtue left the swamp, she cast a spell of mystery and misdirection about the whole area. No one could find a way to Shame, nor could Shame escape the tiny world her mother had created for her.

Shame flourished in her comfortable prison home, and as she did, her dark power grew

John's original Shame concept sketch and the final, painted art.

within her. As this darkness grew, so too did her awareness. Shadow emissaries whispered to her of her birthright. And the more she learned from them the greater her darkness became. But she was unable to escape Cradle, and with each unsuccessful attempt she grew to hate her mother more. It was in this rage that she called deeper, darker Shadows around her, no longer content to wait for their visits. And in the midst of this summoned Darkness, Shame found the darkest of Shadows: Slur. Then, together, they drew their plans.

At Shame's command the Shadows lay with Shame, leaving her with child. Over the next several months Shame was hard at work preparing for the next step of her plan with Slur. At the beginning of the ninth month of her pregnancy, Shame opened the Gates of Hell and blasted the soul of her unborn child to the deepest pits of that dark domain. Shame carried the soulless thing in her until the time came for the next step in her plans of vengeance.

Finally the night of the birth arrived. Shame called upon Slur and reminded it of her gift and their bargain. At the great infernal thing's command Virtue's soul was removed before her death, she did not attain Heaven and could not access the Divine power to destroy Slur.

With the death of Virtue's body and the transplanting of her soul, the bonds of power that held her magicks to the forest and the swamp were broken. Before the spell dissolved completely Shame seized control of it and bound the spell to her will. She used her magic to rededicate the spirits and Cradle to imprisoning the child that was once Virtue. Then, as her mother before her did, Shame abandoned her newborn and left the forest, sealing the babe in a living prison. Then Shame went out to see the world...

Let's take a more detailed look at the process of creating the physical Shame books from the intangible thoughts conjured by Lovern and John's imaginations, using pages 30 and 31 from Shame Pursuit.

First, Lovern breaks down the story into pages, writing up the key action and descriptions John will need for each page of the book (see box on the right).

Next, John will draw pencil thumbnails for each page (see box below and opposite page) which he sends to Lovern and Alexander. At this point we make sure the storytelling is clear and whether any plot point needs more panels or pages.

Once approved, John then paints each page as a separate watercolour painting (see box below right, and opposite page). The amount of work that John puts into every page is stunning and produces incredible artwork.

Lovern then scripts the dialogue and captions for each page (see box opposite, bottom left)

allowing Todd Klein to create the letter layer which is combined with high resolution scans of the artwork at the Renegade studio using inDesign to create the final print document (see box opposite page, bottom left).

29) Merritt is in a frozen Hell, but he is protected by Virtue's power. He wonders through a landscape of trees that are covered with frost and ice. Their trunks are black where the frost hasn't covered them. When Merritt brakes a branch as he passes through the forest the tree shrieks and blood gouts from the broken end of the branch, spattering the snow with a red rain.

30) After a while he comes to an opening in the horrific woods. The area is filled with tortured souls milling aimlessly about in a moaning crowd.

31) Merritt makes his way through blind tormented souls toward a single light glowing in the darkness of the Underworld. When he finally makes his way to the source of the light he is confronted by demonic Shadow creatures.

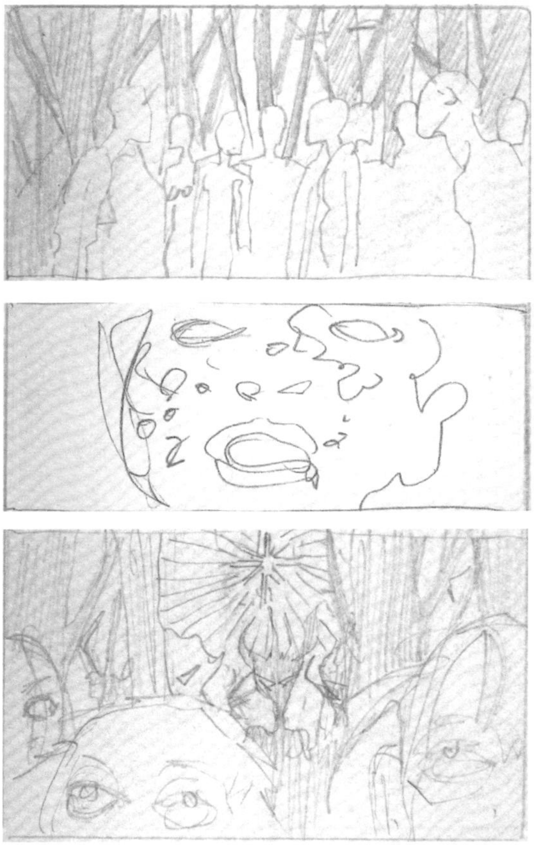

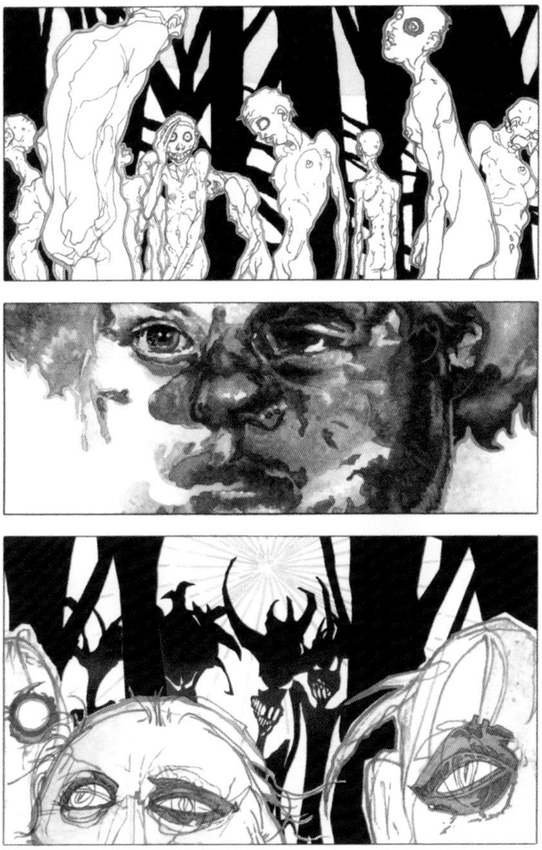

PAGE THIRTY-ONE - Merritt makes his way through blind tormented souls toward a single light glowing in the darkness of the Underworld. When he finally makes his way to the source of the light he is confronted by demonic Shadow creatures.

PANEL ONE
SFX - (The letters of the little one's song should be ghosted to grey, but still show behind or underneath the damned song. Perhaps even woven around it?) MMMMMMMMMM-MAUNNNNN

PANEL TWO
Merritt 1 - They are so alone and their song is so loud, but I can still hear the little one song.

Merritt 2 - It is so sweet.

PANEL THREE
SFX - mmmmmmmmmmmmmmmmmm

Merritt 3 - oh

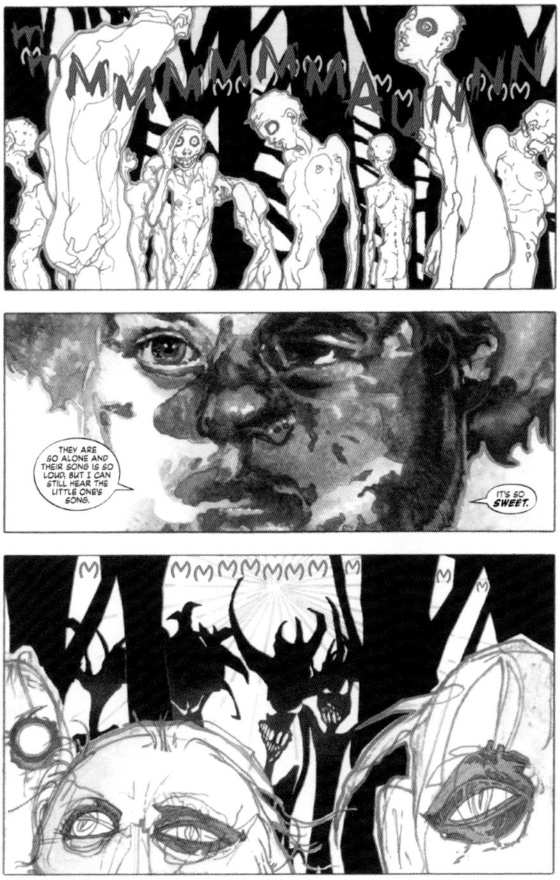
THEY ARE SO ALONE AND THEIR SONG IS SO LOUD, BUT I CAN STILL HEAR THE LITTLE ONE'S SONG.
IT'S SO SWEET.

John sometimes draws preliminary art to figure out character designs or body poses, as this prelim shows that was used for a panel featuring Shame from Redemption page 40.

Bottom of this page is the thumbnail sketch for the very first page of Tales of Hope, accompanied by the final art page.

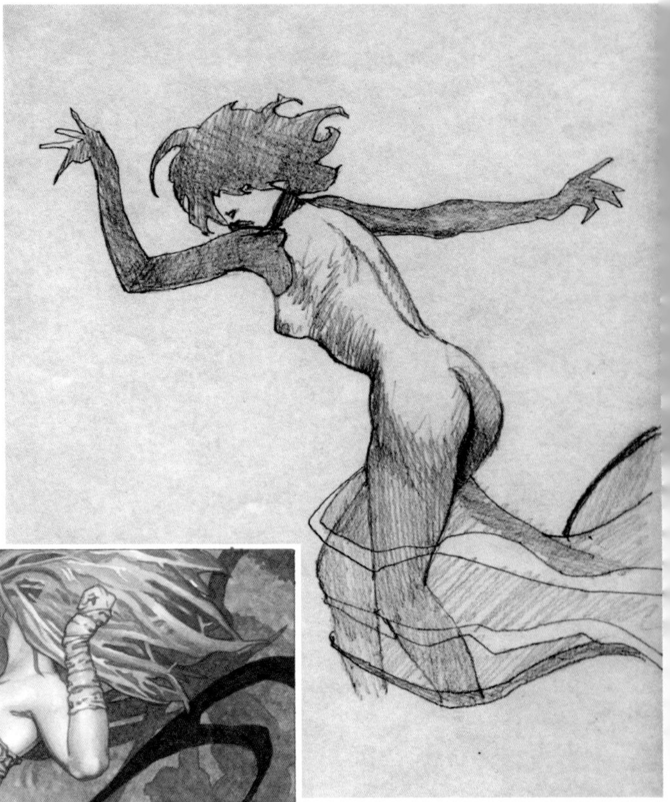

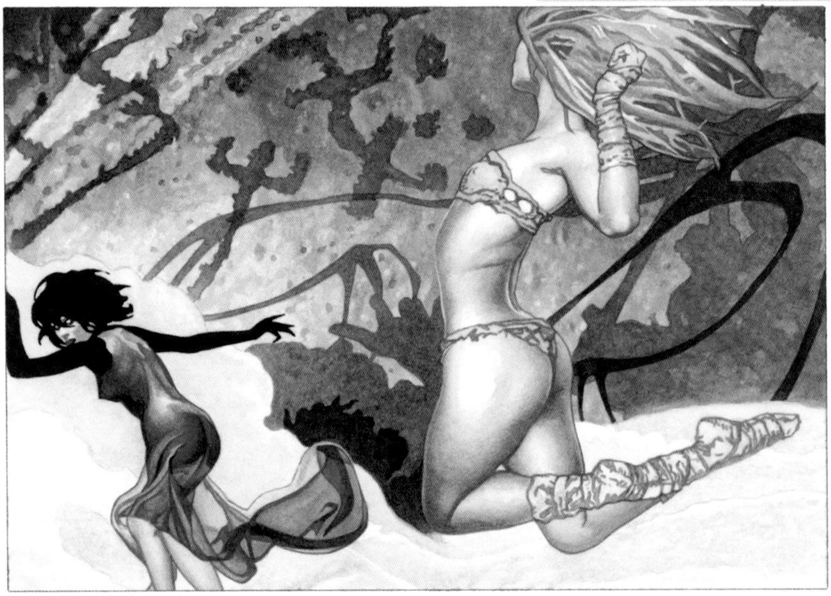

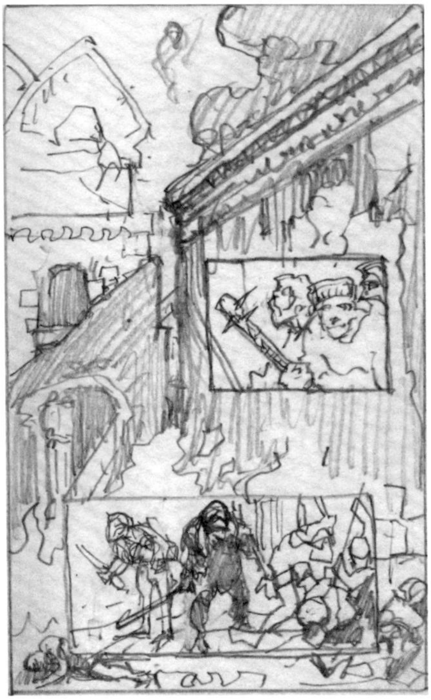

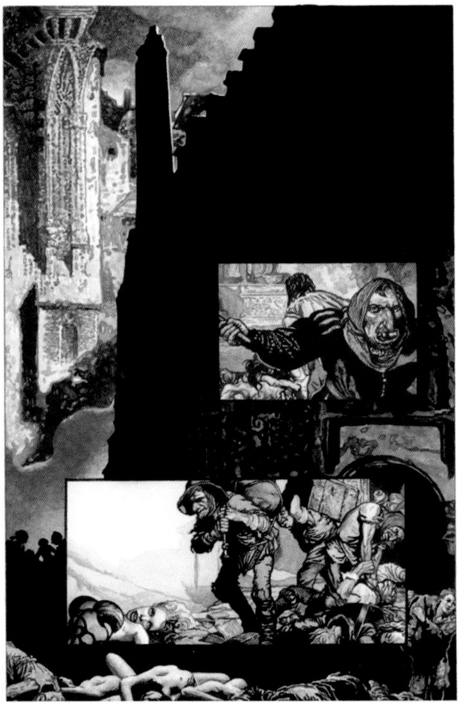

Virtue conjured a willow the wisp who was vital to her escape from Shame's second prison. Here's the preliminary piece and the final art for Redemption page 18. **Bottom** of the page is the thumbnail layout and final art for Shame's evocative dress design from Redemption page 15.

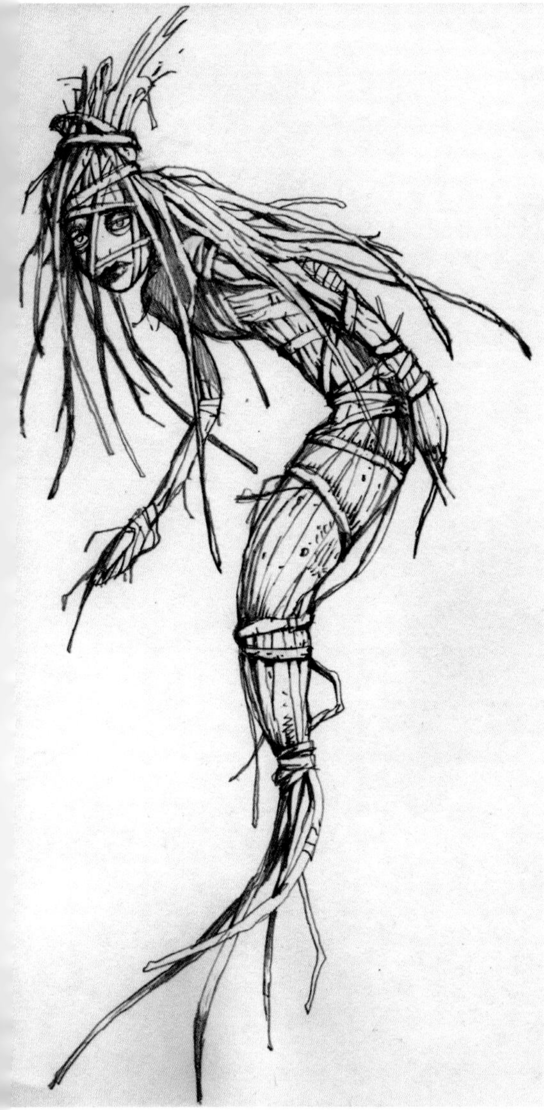

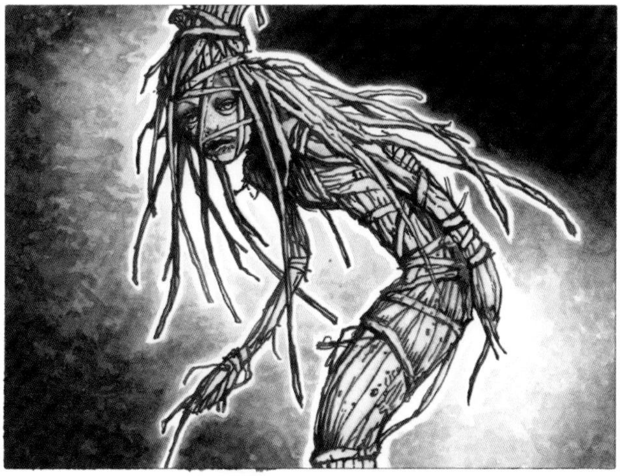

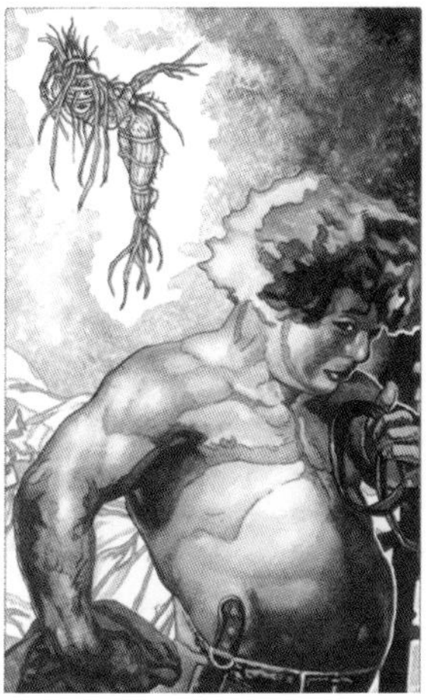

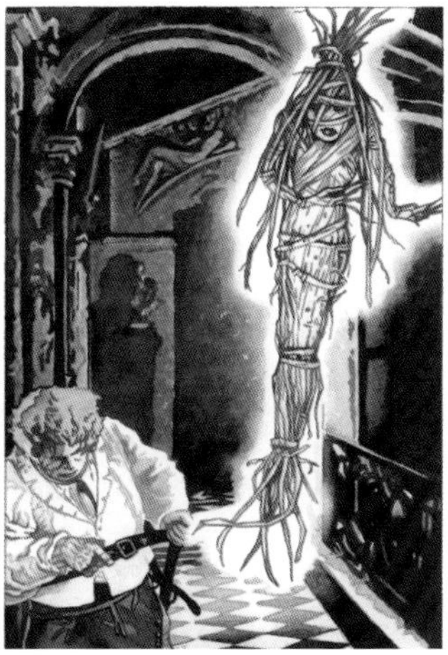

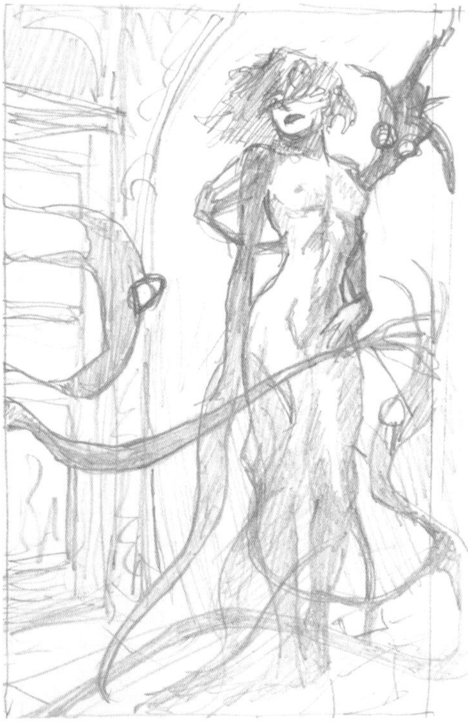

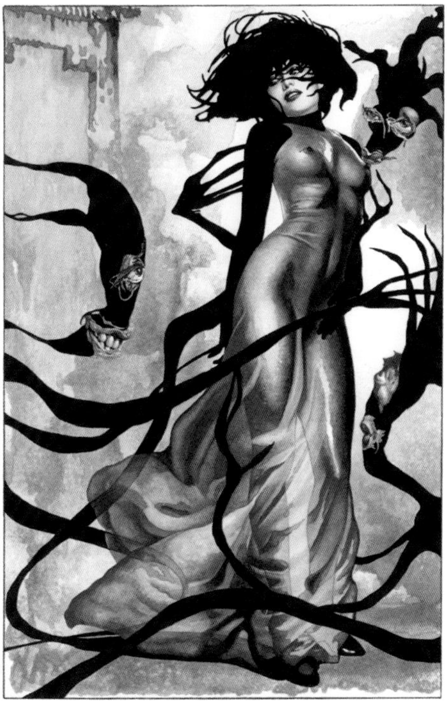

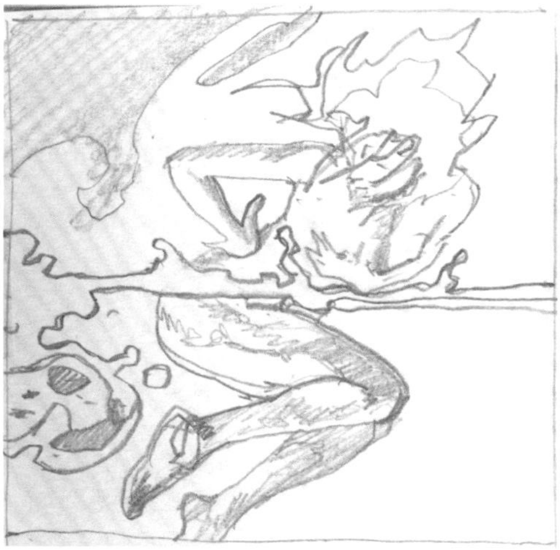

For Redemption page 27 panel 1, John sketched out Virtue as she avoids a deadly blast of power from Shame.

The first box shows John's initial thumbnail page breakdown.

The second box is the pencil preliminary sketch of Virtue.

The third box shows the final painted panel.

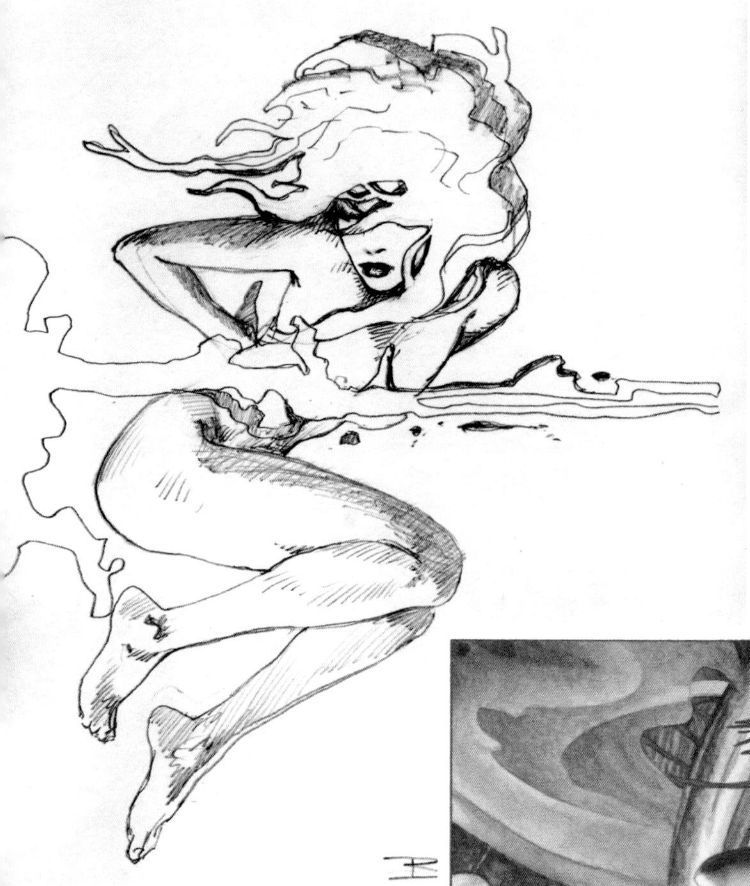

Opposite page are John's prelims and final art for panels from Pursuit page 30 and Redemption page 21.

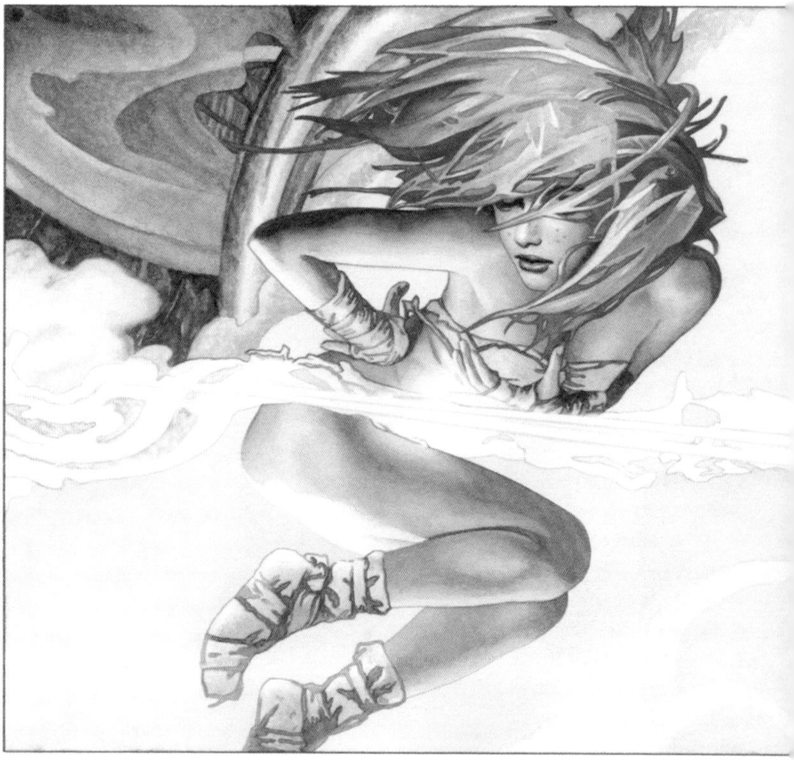

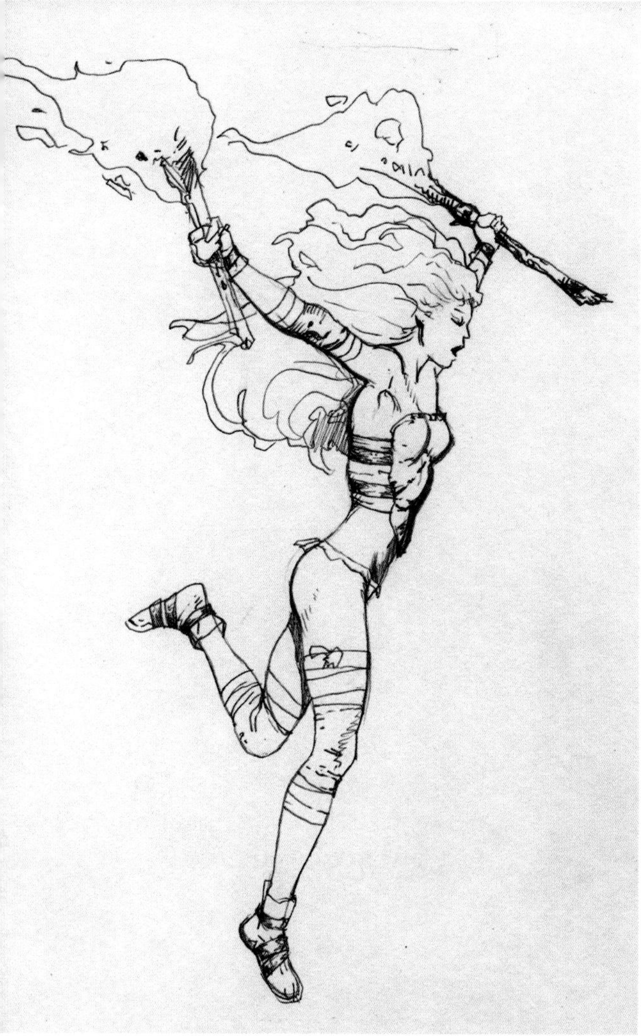
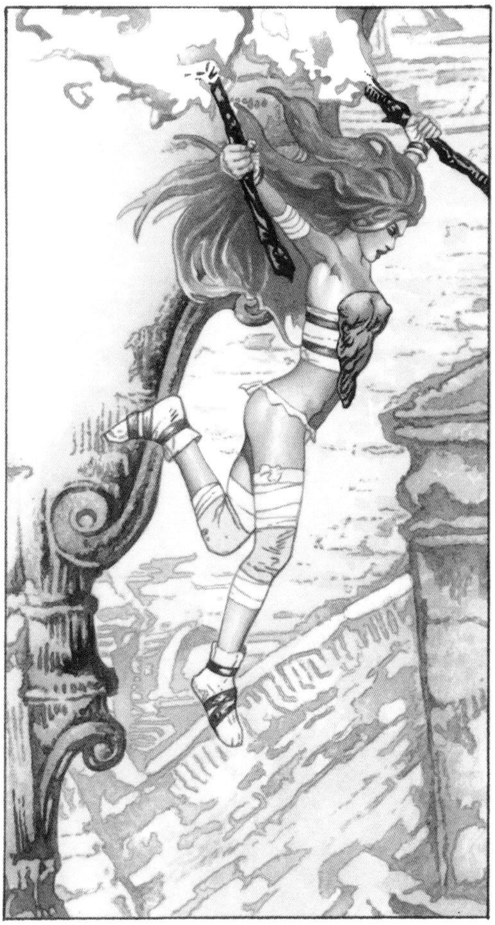
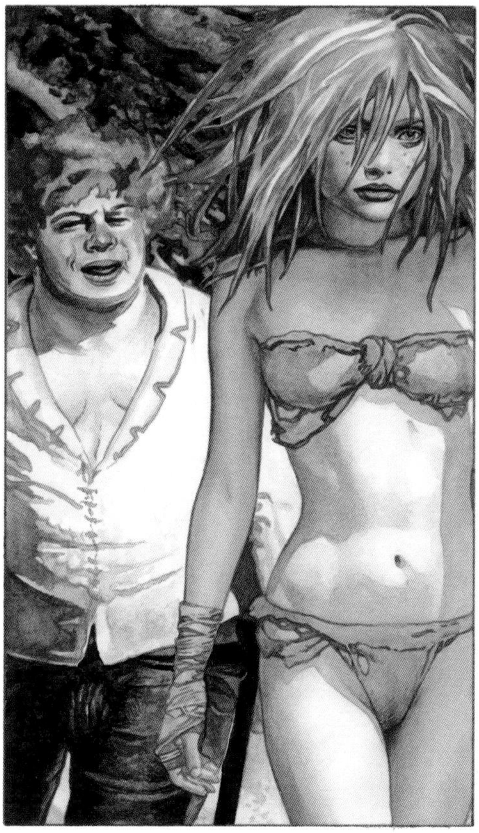
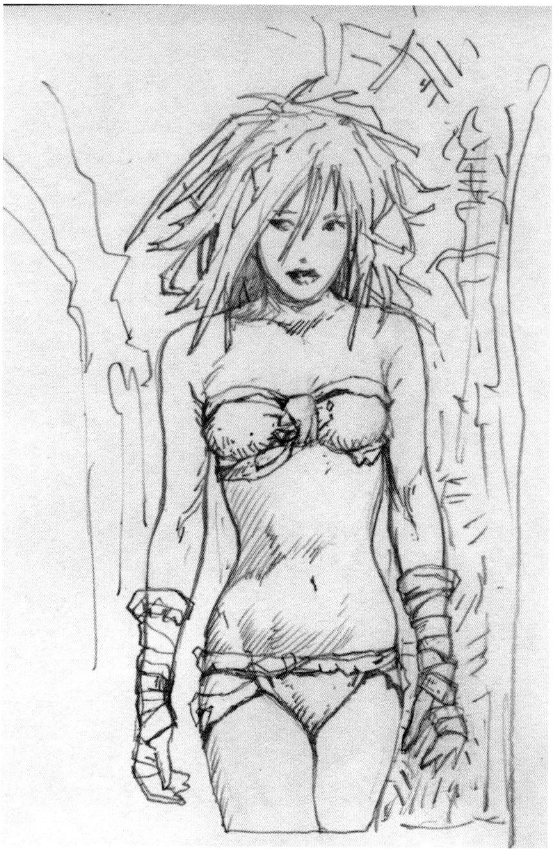

SLUR - The design for Shame's father is as disturbing as it is different, truly a creature of nightmares. John has drawn detailed preliminary sketches of the demon of ignorance many times. Here is a selection, including the thumbnail layouts and final art from Conception page 28, prelims and final art from Pursuit pages 43, 45 and 51.

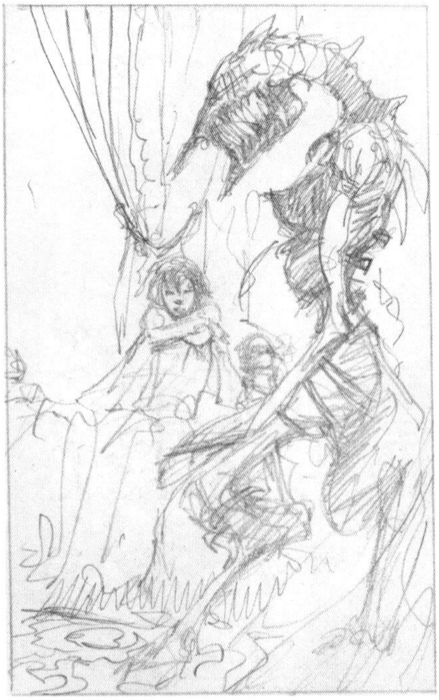

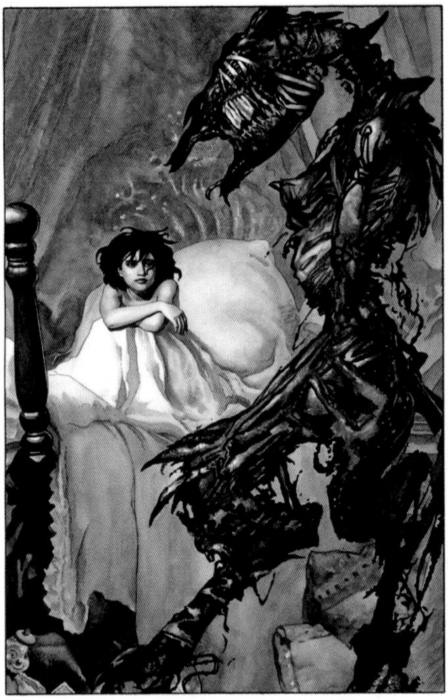

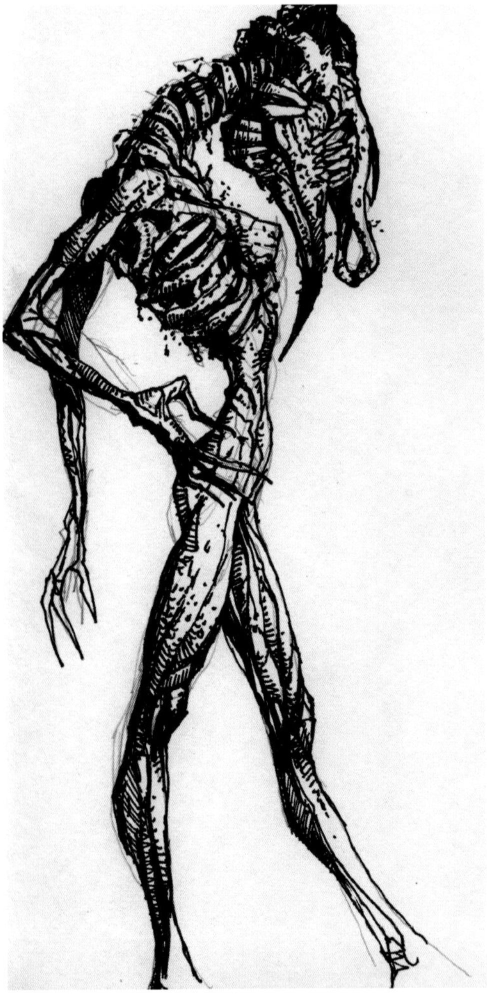

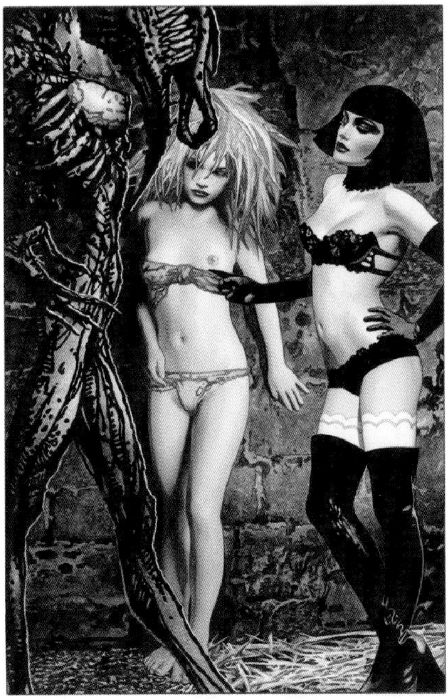

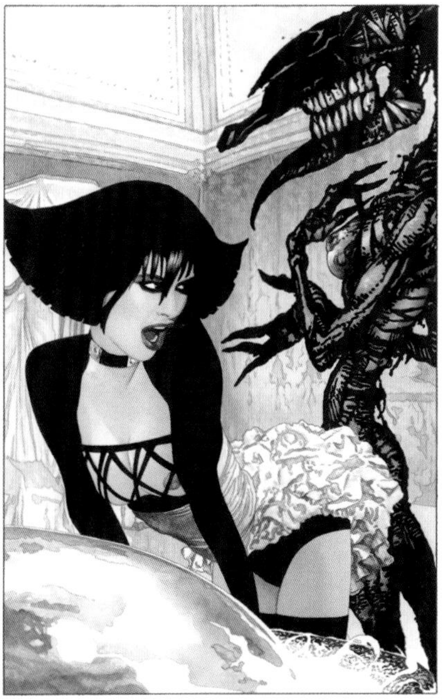

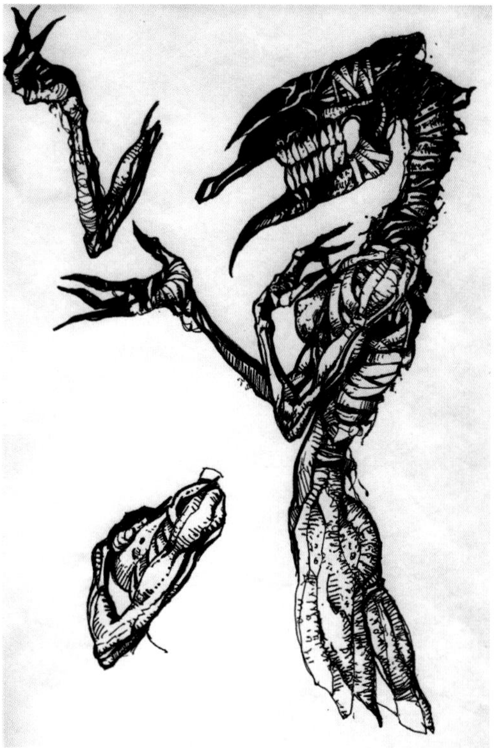

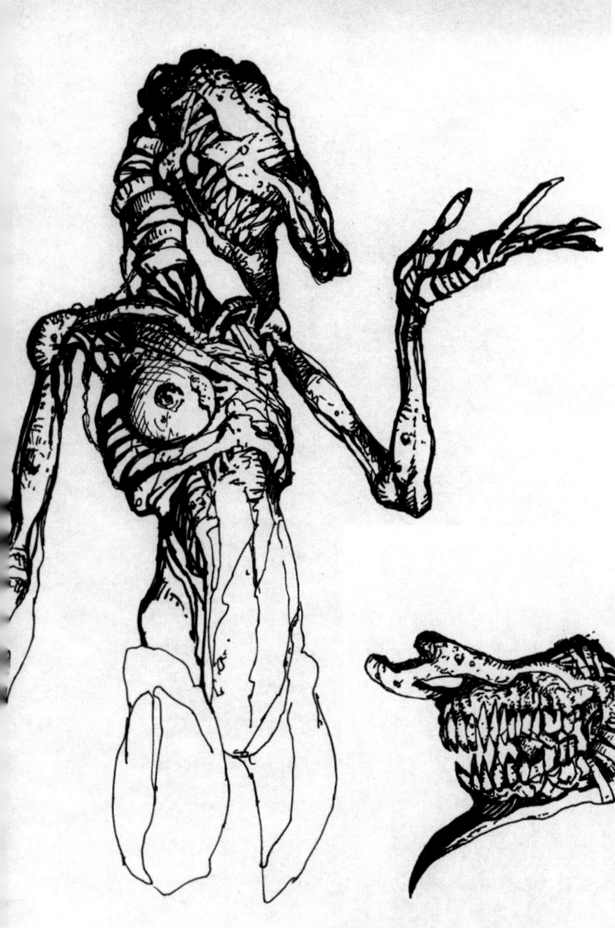

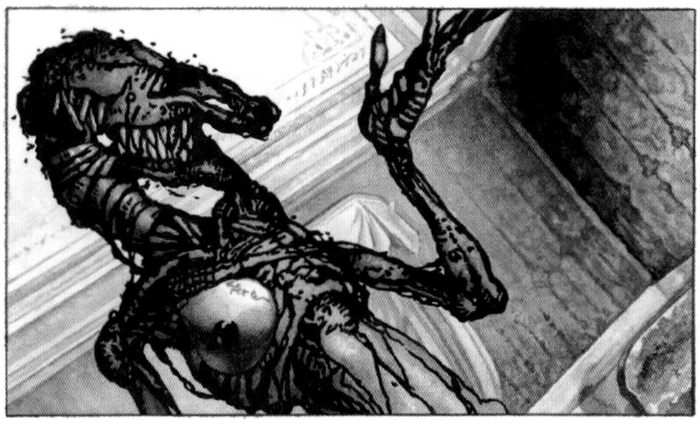

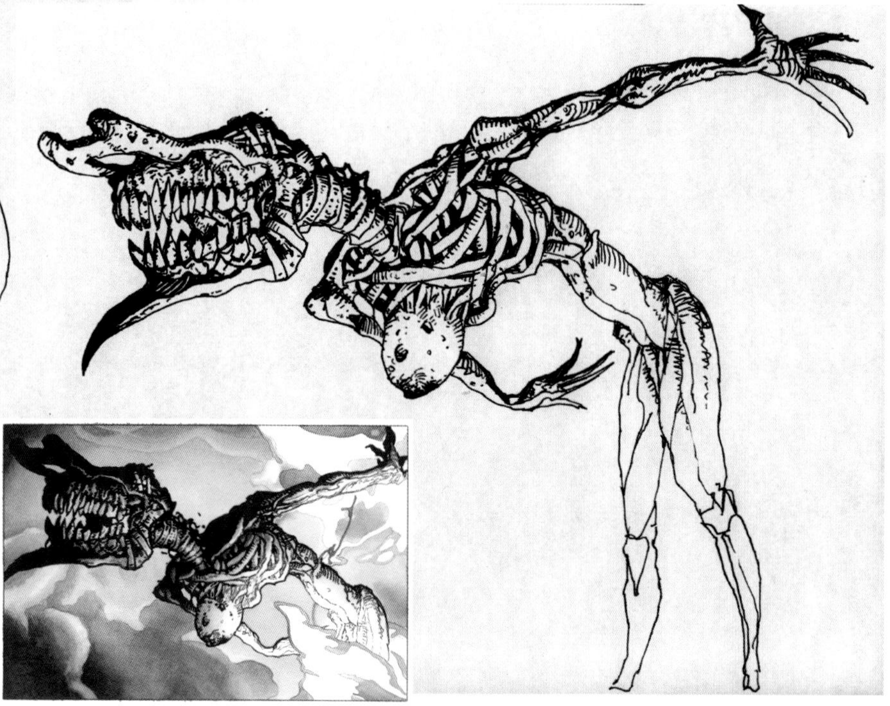

Creator Biographies

Lovern Kindzierski

Lovern Kindzierski is a writer and colour artist who lives in Montreal, Canada. He has written the series Agents of Law for Dark Horse Comics and Lunatik for Marvel. Perhaps his best known work until now was on the ongoing Tarzan series for Dark Horse, which earned him a nomination for Best Writer at the Harvey Awards. Lovern also wrote The Victorian series for Penny Farthing Press, as well as a series of stories in the tradition of the Arabian Nights for Heavy Metal magazine. These stories have been collected in an album, "Demon Wind". As well as writing the Shame trilogy for Renegade, Lovern is currently penning a new supernatural comic book series entitled Necromantic, with David Ross and Chris Chuckry on art duties, as well as the recently released, ground breaking graphic novel Underworld, illustrated by GMB Chomichuk.

John Bolton

Based in London, England, and described by director Robert Rodriguez as a "God" for his art in Peter Straub's The Green Woman, John was seven when he first encountered a paint brush. It was love at first sight, offering him an output to visualize and create what he saw in his mind and put it to paper. Thus began a life-long ambition of creativity, with influences acquired from a wide variety of sources, but all connected by one underlying theme, the interesting and bizarre. Bolton's innovative approach to sequential art has seen him rise to the very top of the current crop of artists working in comics. He digs deep into his imagination to come up with something never seen before. His painting displays a thorough understanding of each medium and subject he chooses to tackle. His inspiration comes not from outside influences,but from the story he is illustrating, the style stems from the content and emotion of a particular story. John has collaborated with a host of prestigious writers including Chris Claremont, Mike Carey, Neil Gaiman, Clive Barker and Mark Verheiden. As well as filmmakers Sam Raimi, Jonathan Glazer, and Robert Zemeckis. The Shame trilogy marks John's first work for Renegade, and the foundations have been laid for a long and successful relationship.

Todd Klein

Todd Klein's comics career began in 1977 when he was hired to work in the DC Comics production department. During 10 years on staff there, Todd tried many kinds of freelance work including writing (TALES OF THE GREEN LANTERN CORPS, THE OMEGA MEN), inking and coloring, but found lettering suited him best, and developed a freelance career as letterer and logo designer.

Todd learned from and was inspired by the work of Gaspar Saladino, John Workman, John Costanza, Tom Orzechowski, and other letterers then working in comics. After leaving staff in 1987, Todd continued to work mainly for DC, but also for Marvel, Dark Horse, Disney, Gladstone, Image and many other companies, doing lettering and logo designs. Through the years he's lettered over 65,000 comics pages and covers and designed over 00 logos. Todd has been presented with 16 Eisner Awards for Best Lettering, as well as Harvey Awards and other honors. Current projects include SANDMAN with Neil Gaiman and J.H. Williams III, MIRACLEMAN with Gaiman and Mark Buckingham, STARSTRUCK with Elaine Lee and Michael Wm. Kaluta, THE LEAGUE OF EXTRAORDINARY GENTLEMEN with Alan Moore and Kevin O'Neill, and many other projects for DC Comics. You can learn more at his website kleinletters.com.

Alexander Finbow

As Publisher and editor in chief, Alexander oversees the business development at Renegade as well as producing the Doug Bradley's Spinechillers audiobook series. He is the writer behind the Shades of Grey comic books and the graphic novel Blood Light with artist Al Davison.

The double award winning The Loxleys and the War of 1812 is the biggest project he has undertaken, combining a best-selling graphic novel, interactive app, animated movie, prose adaptation, school play, and teachers resource pack. You should read it.

Alexander began his career working in the movie industry and has worked as an actor, writer, director and producer. He directed the movie 24 Hours In London which became a cult hit around the world, before going on to work with producers in the UK and the US. After leaving London for the Candian Rocky Mountains, Alexander established Renegade to be a safe haven for passionate and committed storytellers whether those stories needed to be told as comics, movies or audiobooks.

Further reading from Renegade Arts Entertainment

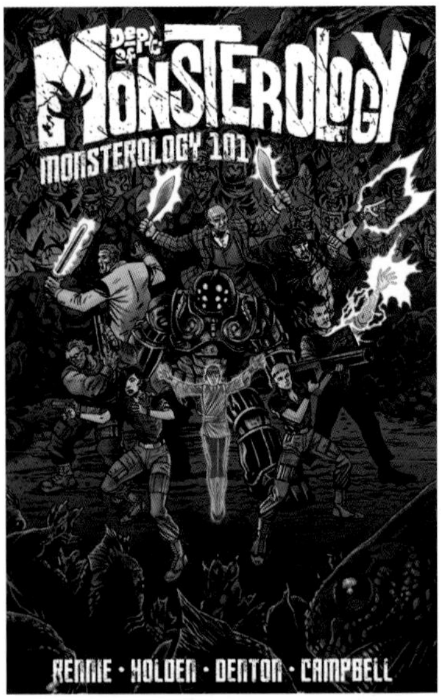
Dept. of
Monsterology
Monsterology 101
Rennie · Holden · Denton · Campbell

Dept. of Monsterology: Monsterology 101
Writer: Gordon Rennie
Art: PJ Holden
ISBN: 9780992150846

'Really, really good fun.'
- Zoe Kirk-Robinson, webcomics.com

Officially, it's the Department of Cryptozoology, Mythological Studies, Parapsychology and Fortean Phenomena. But to the rest of the students and staff at the Dunsany College, baffled by the cloak of secrecy that surrounds the Department and its affairs, it has another, more dismissive, name: the Department of Monsterology. Their brief: to investigate the dark and unexplored corners of our world - the places we've forgotten, lost or believe to be mythical. And to study those things that may still be lurking there.

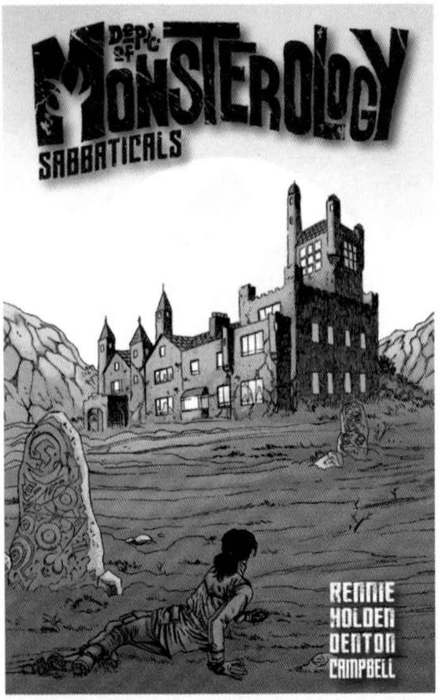
Dept. of
Monsterology
Sabbaticals
Rennie
Holden
Denton
Campbell

Dept. of Monsterology: Sabbaticals
Writer: Gordon Rennie
Art: PJ Holden
ISBN: 9781987825015

'I'm simply enjoying the hell out of it.'
- Joe Gordon, Forbidden Planet

Gordon Rennie, PJ Holden, Steven Denton and Jim Campbell return to campus with the next instalment of cryptozoological adventure. Sabbaticals picks up after the events of Monsterology 101, with several team members pursuing their own agendas following their near miss with apocalyptic catastrophe in China and the South Pacific.

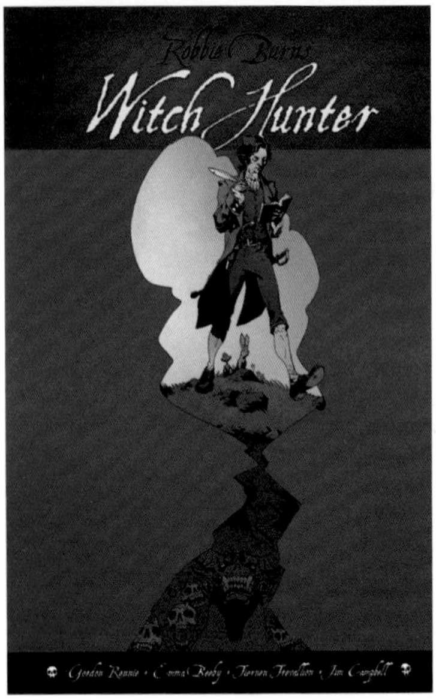
Robbie Burns
Witch Hunter

Robbie Burns: Witch Hunter
Writers: Emma Beeby, Gordon Rennie
Art: Tiernen Trevallion
ISBN: 9780992150853

'Scotland's famous son as he's never been seen before.'
- Rob Alexander, Rocky Mountain Outlook

Robbie Burns is one of the most well known and celebrated poets worldwide. However, little is ever written about the man's sideline career as one of Scotland's most renowned Witch Hunters.

The story asks what if the events of the narrative poem Tam o' Shanter, Burns' most famous work, were actually based on something that happened to Burns himself...

Underworld
Writer: Lovern Kindzierski
Art: GMB Chomichuk
ISBN: 9781987825022

'A fantastic, mystical escapade.'
- Win Wiacek, comicsreview.co.uk

Winnipeg star creators Lovern Kindzierski and GMB Chomichuk's masterful retelling of Homer's Odyssey is set on the streets of their home city as disgraced politician Hector Ashton attempts to reclaim his sanity and his family, as a crooked police detective seeks to end his life to keep control of Winnipeg's drug trade.

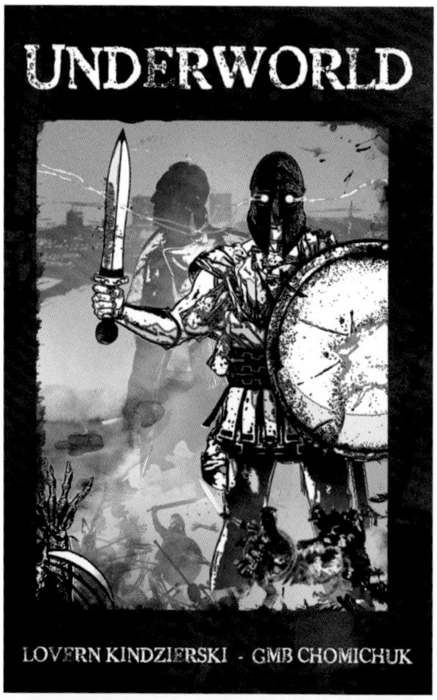
UNDERWORLD
LOVERN KINDZIERSKI - GMB CHOMICHUK

Channel Evil
Writer: Alan Grant
Art: Shane Oakley, D'Israeli
ISBN: 9780986820045

'Genuinely entertaining, thrilling and fun.'
- Richard Burton, Forbidden Planet

Channel Evil is Alan Grant's imagination unleashed without compromise. Sleazy chat show host, Jez Manson, has to decide if the apocalypse is too high a price to pay in return for personal fame and fortune.

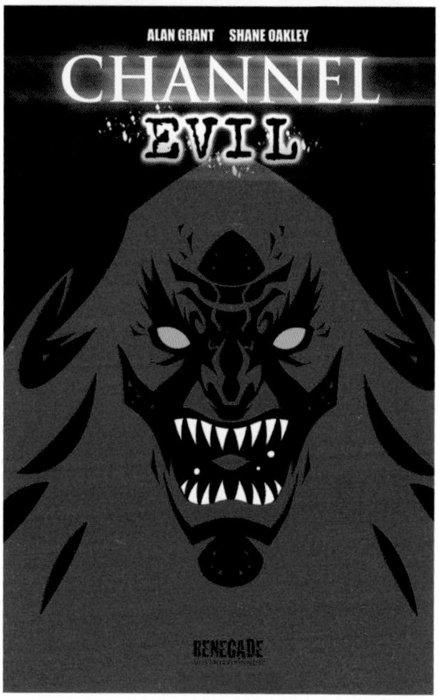
ALAN GRANT SHANE OAKLEY
CHANNEL
EVIL
RENEGADE

Frank
Writer and art: Ben Rankel

On April 29th, 1903, 82 million tonnes of rock slid down Turtle Mountain, obliterating part of the town of Frank, Alberta.

But what happened the day before the mountain fell?

Frank is a crime story that brings one of Canada's worst natural disasters to the forefront while exploring themes of loss, love, and moving on.

Coming 2017

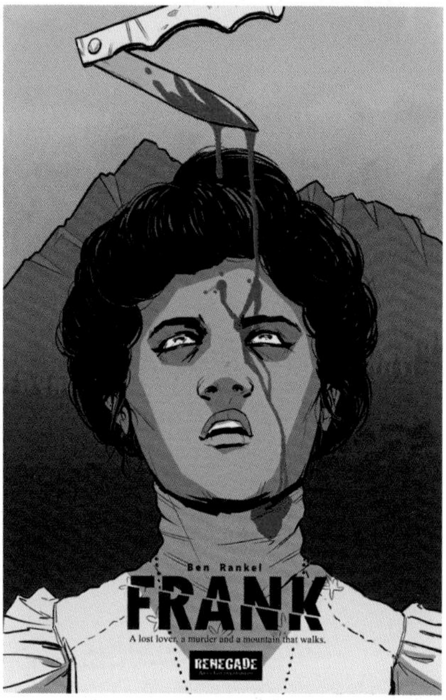
Ben Rankel
FRANK
A lost lover, a murder and a mountain that walks.
RENEGADE